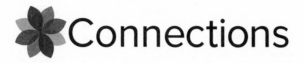Connections

Editorial Board

Year A, Volume 1
Advent through Epiphany

Connections

A Lectionary Commentary for Preaching and Worship

Joel B. Green
Thomas G. Long
Luke A. Powery
Cynthia L. Rigby
Carolyn J. Sharp
General Editors

WESTMINSTER
JOHN KNOX PRESS
LOUISVILLE · KENTUCKY

© 2019 Westminster John Knox Press

First edition
Published by Westminster John Knox Press
Louisville, Kentucky

19 20 21 22 23 24 25 26 27 28—10 9 8 7 6 5 4 3 2 1

Unless otherwise indicated, Scripture quotations are from the New Revised Standard Version of the Bible, copyright © 1989 by the Division of Christian Education of the National Council of the Churches of Christ in the U.S.A., and are used by permission. Scripture quotations marked CEB are from the Common English Bible, © 2011 Common English Bible, and are used by permission. Scripture quotations marked JPS are from *The TANAKH: The New JPS Translation according to the Traditional Hebrew Text*. Copyright 1985 by the Jewish Publication Society. Used by permission. Scripture quotations marked NIV are from *The Holy Bible, New International Version*. Copyright © 1973, 1978, 1984, 2011 by Biblica, Inc.* Used by permission. All rights reserved worldwide. Scripture quotations marked NJB are from *The New Jerusalem Bible*, copyright © 1985 by Darton, Longman & Todd, Ltd., and Doubleday, a division of Bantam Doubleday Dell Publishing Group, Inc. Reprinted by permission of the publisher(s). Scripture quotations marked RSV are from the Revised Standard Version of the Bible, copyright © 1946, 1952, 1971, and 1973 by the Division of Christian Education of the National Council of the Churches of Christ in the U.S.A., and are used by permission.

Excerpts from "Love Calls Us to the Things of This World" and "A Christmas Hymn" from *Collected Poems 1943–2004* by Richard Wilbur. Copyright © 2004 by Richard Wilbur. Reprinted by permission of Houghton Mifflin Harcourt Publishing Company. All rights reserved. Excerpts from Pope Francis, "Solemnity of the Nativity of the Lord," © Libreria Editrice Vaticana. Reprinted by permission.

Book and cover design by Allison Taylor

The Library of Congress has cataloged an earlier volume as follows:
Names: Long, Thomas G., 1946- editor.
Title: Connections : a lectionary commentary for preaching and worship / Joel
    B. Green, Thomas G. Long, Luke A. Powery, Cynthia L. Rigby, Carolyn J. Sharp, general
    editors.
Description: Louisville, Kentucky : Westminster John Knox Press, 2018- |
    Includes index. |
Identifiers: LCCN 2018006372 (print) | LCCN 2018012579 (ebook) | ISBN
    9781611648874 (ebk.) | ISBN 9780664262433 (volume 1 : hbk. : alk. paper)
Subjects: LCSH: Lectionary preaching. | Bible—Meditations. | Common
    lectionary (1992) | Lectionaries.
Classification: LCC BV4235.L43 (ebook) | LCC BV4235.L43 C66 2018 (print) |
    DDC 251/.6—dc23
LC record available at https://lccn.loc.gov/2018006372

Connections: Year A, Volume 1
ISBN: 9780664262372 (hardback)
ISBN: 9780664264796 (paperback)
ISBN: 9781611649666 (ebook)

PRINTED IN THE UNITED STATES OF AMERICA

♾ The paper used in this publication meets the minimum requirements of the American National Standard
    for Information Sciences—Permanence of Paper for Printed Library Materials, ANSI Z39.48-1992.

Contents

Sidebars

Publisher's Note

"The preaching of the Word of God is the Word of God," says the Second Helvetic Confession. While that might sound like an exalted estimation of the homiletical task, it comes with an implicit warning: "A lot is riding on this business of preaching. Get it right!"

Believing that much does indeed depend on the church's proclamation, we offer Connections: A Lectionary Commentary for Preaching and Worship. Connections embodies two complementary convictions about the study of Scripture in preparation for preaching and worship. First, to best understand an individual passage of Scripture, we should put it in conversation with the rest of the Bible. Second, since all truth is God's truth, we should bring as many "lenses" as possible to the study of Scripture, drawn from as many sources as we can find. Our prayer is that this unique combination of approaches will illumine your study and preparation, facilitating the weekly task of bringing the Word of God to the people of God.

We at Westminster John Knox Press want to thank the superb editorial team that came together to make Connections possible. At the heart of that team are our general editors: Joel B. Green, Thomas G. Long, Luke A. Powery, Cynthia L. Rigby, and Carolyn J. Sharp. These gifted scholars and preachers have poured countless hours into brainstorming, planning, reading, editing, and supporting the project. Their passion for authentic preaching and transformative worship shows up on every page. They pushed the writers and their fellow editors, they pushed us at the press, and most especially they pushed themselves to focus always on what you, the users of this resource, genuinely need. We are grateful to Kimberley Bracken Long for her innovative vision of what commentary on the Psalm readings could accomplish, and for recruiting a talented group of liturgists and preachers to implement that vision. Bo Adams has shown creativity and insight in exploring an array of sources to provide the sidebars that accompany each worship day's commentaries. At the forefront of the work have been the members of our editorial board, who helped us identify writers, assign passages, and most especially carefully edit each commentary. They have cheerfully allowed the project to intrude on their schedules in order to make possible this contribution to the life of the church. Most especially we thank our writers, drawn from a broad diversity of backgrounds, vocations, and perspectives. The distinctive character of our commentaries required much from our writers. Their passion for the preaching ministry of the church proved them worthy of the challenge.

A project of this size does not come together without the work of excellent support staff. Above all we are indebted to project manager Joan Murchison. Joan's fingerprints are all over the book you hold in your hands; her gentle, yet unconquerable, persistence always kept it moving forward in good shape and on time. Pamela Jarvis skillfully compiled the volume, arranging the hundreds of separate commentaries and Scriptures into a cohesive whole.

Finally, our sincere thanks to the administration, faculty, and staff of Austin Presbyterian Theological Seminary, our institutional partner in producing Connections. President Theodore J. Wardlaw and Dean David H. Jensen have been steadfast friends of the project, enthusiastically agreeing to our partnership, carefully overseeing their faculty and staff's work on it, graciously hosting our meetings, and enthusiastically using their platform to promote Connections among their students, alumni, and friends.

It is with much joy that we commend Connections to you, our readers. May God use this resource to deepen and enrich your ministry of preaching and worship.

WESTMINSTER JOHN KNOX PRESS

Introducing Connections

Connections is a resource designed to help preachers generate sermons that are theologically deeper, liturgically richer, and culturally more pertinent. Based on the Revised Common Lectionary (RCL), which has wide ecumenical use, the hundreds of essays on the full array of biblical passages in the three-year cycle can be used effectively by preachers who follow the RCL, by those who follow other lectionaries, and by nonlectionary preachers alike.

The essential idea of Connections is that biblical texts display their power most fully when they are allowed to interact with a number of contexts, that is, when many connections are made between a biblical text and realities outside that text. Like the two poles of a battery, when the pole of the biblical text is connected to a different pole (another aspect of Scripture or a dimension of life outside Scripture), creative sparks fly and energy surges from pole to pole.

Two major interpretive essays, called Commentary 1 and Commentary 2, address every scriptural reading in the RCL. Commentary 1 explores preaching connections between a lectionary reading and other texts and themes within Scripture, and Commentary 2 makes preaching connections between the lectionary texts and themes in the larger culture outside of Scripture. These essays have been written by pastors, biblical scholars, theologians, and others, all of whom have a commitment to lively biblical preaching.

The writers of Commentary 1 surveyed five possible connections for their texts: the immediate literary context (the passages right around the text), the larger literary context (for example, the cycle of David stories or the passion narrative), the thematic context (such as other feeding stories, other parables, or other passages on the theme of hope), the lectionary context (the other readings for the day in the RCL), and the canonical context (other places in the whole of the Bible that display harmony, or perhaps tension, with the text at hand).

The writers of Commentary 2 surveyed six possible connections for their texts: the liturgical context (such as Advent or Easter), the ecclesial context (the life and mission of the church), the social and ethical context (justice and social responsibility), the cultural context (such as art, music, and literature), the larger expanse of human knowledge (such as science, history, and psychology), and the personal context (the life and faith of individuals).

In each essay, the writers selected from this array of possible connections, emphasizing those connections they saw as most promising for preaching. It is important to note that, even though Commentary 1 makes connections inside the Bible and Commentary 2 makes connections outside the Bible, this does not represent a division between "what the text *meant* in biblical times versus what the text *means* now." *Every* connection made with the text, whether that connection is made within the Bible or out in the larger culture, is seen as generative for preaching, and each author provokes the imagination of the preacher to see in these connections preaching possibilities for today. Connections is not a substitute for traditional scriptural commentaries, concordances, Bible dictionaries, and other interpretive tools. Rather, Connections begins with solid biblical scholarship, then goes on to focus on the act of preaching and on the ultimate goal of allowing the biblical text to come alive in the sermon.

Connections addresses every biblical text in the RCL, and it takes seriously the architecture of the RCL. During the seasons of the Christian year (Advent through Epiphany and Lent through Pentecost), the RCL provides three readings and a psalm for each Sunday and feast day: (1) a first reading, usually from the Old Testament; (2) a psalm, chosen to respond to the first reading; (3) a second reading, usually from one of the New Testament epistles; and (4) a Gospel reading. The first and second readings are chosen as complements to the Gospel reading for the day.

During the time between Pentecost and Advent, however, the RCL includes an additional first reading for every Sunday. There is the usual complementary reading, chosen in relation to the Gospel reading, but there is also a "semicontinuous" reading. These semicontinuous readings move through the books of the Old Testament more or less continuously in narrative sequence, offering the stories of the patriarchs (Year A), the kings of Israel (Year B), and the prophets (Year C). Connections covers both the complementary and the semicontinuous readings.

The architects of the RCL understand the psalms and canticles to be prayers, and they selected the psalms for each Sunday and feast as prayerful responses to the first reading for the day. Thus, the Connections essays on the psalms are different from the other essays, and they have two goals, one homiletical and the other liturgical. First, they comment on ways the psalm might offer insight into preaching the first reading. Second, they describe how the tone and content of the psalm or canticle might inform the day's worship, suggesting ways the psalm or canticle may be read, sung, or prayed.

Preachers will find in Connections many ideas and approaches to sustain lively and provocative preaching for years to come. But beyond the deep reservoir of preaching connections found in these pages, preachers will also find here a habit of mind, a way of thinking about biblical preaching. Being guided by the essays in Connections to see many connections between biblical texts and their various contexts, preachers will be stimulated to make other connections for themselves. Connections is an abundant collection of creative preaching ideas, and it is also a spur to continued creativity.

JOEL B. GREEN
THOMAS G. LONG
LUKE A. POWERY
CYNTHIA L. RIGBY
CAROLYN J. SHARP
General Editors

Introducing the Revised Common Lectionary

To derive the greatest benefit from Connections, it will help to understand the structure and purpose of the Revised Common Lectionary (RCL), around which this resource is built. The RCL is a three-year guide to Scripture readings for the Christian Sunday gathering for worship. "Lectionary" simply means a selection of texts for reading and preaching. The RCL is an adaptation of the Roman Lectionary (of 1969, slightly revised in 1981), which itself was a reworking of the medieval Western-church one-year cycle of readings. The RCL resulted from six years of consultations that included representatives from nineteen churches or denominational agencies. Every preacher uses a lectionary—whether it comes from a specific denomination or is the preacher's own choice—but the RCL is unique in that it positions the preacher's homiletical work within a web of specific, ongoing connections.

The RCL has its roots in Jewish lectionary systems and early Christian ways of reading texts to illumine the biblical meaning of a feast day or time in the church calendar. Among our earliest lectionaries are the lists of readings for Holy Week and Easter in fourth-century Jerusalem.

One of the RCL's central connections is intertextuality; multiple texts are listed for each day. This lectionary's way of reading Scripture is based on Scripture's own pattern: texts interpreting texts. In the RCL, every Sunday of the year and each special or festival day is assigned a group of texts, normally three readings and a psalm. For most of the year, the first reading is an Old Testament text, followed by a psalm, a reading from one of the epistles, and a reading from one of the Gospel accounts.

The RCL's three-year cycle centers Year A in Matthew, Year B in Mark, and Year C in Luke. It is less clear how the Gospel according to John fits in, but when preachers learn about the RCL's arrangement of the Gospels, it makes sense. John gets a place of privilege because John's Gospel account, with its high Christology, is assigned for the great feasts. Texts from John's account are also assigned for Lent, Sundays of Easter, and summer Sundays. The second-century bishop Irenaeus's insistence on four Gospels is evident in this lectionary system: John and the Synoptics are in conversation with each other. However, because the RCL pattern contains variations, an extended introduction to the RCL can help the preacher learn the reasons for texts being set next to other texts.

The Gospel reading governs each day's selections. Even though the ancient order of reading texts in the Sunday gathering positions the Gospel reading last, the preacher should know that the RCL receives the Gospel reading as the hermeneutical key.

At certain times in the calendar year, the connections between the texts are less obvious. The RCL offers two tracks for readings in the time after Pentecost (Ordinary Time/standard Sundays): the complementary and the semicontinuous. Complementary texts relate to the church year and its seasons; semicontinuous emphasis is on preaching through a biblical book. Both approaches are historic ways of choosing texts for Sunday. This commentary series includes both the complementary and the semicontinuous readings.

In the complementary track, the Old Testament reading provides an intentional tension, a deeper understanding, or a background reference for another text of the day. The Psalm is the congregation's response to the first reading, following its themes. The Epistle functions as the horizon of the church: we learn about the faith and struggles of early Christian communities. The Gospel tells us where we are in the church's time and is enlivened, as are all the texts, by these intertextual interactions. Because the semicontinuous track prioritizes the narratives of specific books, the intertextual connections are not as apparent. Connections still exist, however. Year A pairs Matthew's account with Old Testament readings from the first five books; Year B pairs Mark's account with stories of anointed kings; Year C pairs Luke's account with the prophetic books.

Historically, lectionaries came into being because they were the church's beloved texts, like the scriptural canon. Choices had to be made regarding readings in the assembly, given the limit of fifty-two Sundays and a handful of festival days. The RCL presupposes that everyone (preachers and congregants) can read these texts—even along with the daily RCL readings that are paired with the Sunday readings.

Another central connection found in the RCL is the connection between texts and church seasons or the church's year. The complementary texts make these connections most clear. The intention of the RCL is that the texts of each Sunday or feast day bring biblical meaning to where we are in time. The texts at Christmas announce the incarnation. Texts in Lent renew us to follow Christ, and texts for the fifty days of Easter proclaim God's power over death and sin and our new life in Christ. The entire church's year is a hermeneutical key for using the RCL.

Let it be clear that the connection to the church year is a connection for present-tense proclamation. We read, not to recall history, but to know how those events are true for us today. Now is the time of the Spirit of the risen Christ; now we beseech God in the face of sin and death; now we live baptized into Jesus' life and ministry. To read texts in time does not mean we remind ourselves of Jesus' biography for half of the year and then the mission of the church for the other half. Rather, we follow each Gospel's narrative order to be brought again to the meaning of Jesus' death and resurrection and his risen presence in our midst. The RCL positions the texts as our lens on our life and the life of the world in our time: who we are in Christ now, for the sake of the world.

The RCL intends to be a way of reading texts to bring us again to faith, for these texts to be how we see our lives and our gospel witness in the world. Through these connections, the preacher can find faithful, relevant ways to preach year after year.

JENNIFER L. LORD
Connections Editorial Board Member

Connections

First Sunday of Advent

Isaiah 2:1–5

Psalm 122

Romans 13:11–14

Matthew 24:36–44

Isaiah 2:1–5

¹The word that Isaiah son of Amoz saw concerning Judah and Jerusalem.

²In days to come
   the mountain of the LORD's house
shall be established as the highest of the mountains,
   and shall be raised above the hills;
all the nations shall stream to it.
   ³Many peoples shall come and say,
"Come, let us go up to the mountain of the LORD,
   to the house of the God of Jacob;
that he may teach us his ways
   and that we may walk in his paths."
For out of Zion shall go forth instruction,
   and the word of the LORD from Jerusalem.
⁴He shall judge between the nations,
   and shall arbitrate for many peoples;
they shall beat their swords into plowshares,
   and their spears into pruning hooks;
nation shall not lift up sword against nation,
   neither shall they learn war any more.

⁵O house of Jacob,
   come, let us walk
   in the light of the LORD!

Commentary 1: Connecting the Reading with Scripture

Some people think that there are two beginnings to the book of Isaiah. After all, Isaiah 1 begins with "The vision of Isaiah son of Amoz . . . ," and Isaiah 2 begins with "The word that Isaiah son of Amoz saw . . ." It seems as if the final redactor of the book of Isaiah forgot to block and delete—and we are left with two beginnings.

Another approach would be to concede these strikingly similar opening verses to chapter 1 and chapter 2 and then to wonder why. The contrast between the two chapters is strong. Reflected in Isaiah 1 is a scene of unbroken doom and gloom. The judgment of God against Judah for wickedness and injustice is described

in excruciating detail. Cities are laid bare, vineyards uprooted, princes dethroned—all as a result of God's wrath. The end of chapter 1 is smoky, dark, and wretched. Chapter 2 begins again. It is a fresh start with a decidedly fresh message. Now, the house of the Lord sits on the highest mountain. All the nations of the world flow upward toward that house, and the word of the Lord flows down and blesses the nations.

Rather than being the result of carelessness of a final editor, these two adjacent prophetic words deliver a strong rhetorical wallop that demonstrates editorial skill and intent. Against the backdrop of chapter 1, a chapter of ominous shadows, chapter 2:1–5 describes the universal reach of God's gracious actions. The juxtaposition of these two "beginnings" of the book of Isaiah is not the only literary device that emphasizes God's divine purposes. In addition, there is considerable *movement* in this text: the mountain will be raised up; people go upward; God's word extends downward; the nations will beat their swords and spears into agricultural tools. The interesting images of "going up" and "going forth" suggest that the nations are drawn to the house of the Lord and that God's blessings cascade down to all nations. The images suggest flow and abundance. There is no one who can hide from the word of God that goes forth. It extends to all the earth.

God's action and intention as revealed in this text challenge some of our contemporary assumptions in interesting ways. In our time, when cultural particularity and context are highly valued, this text insists that Israel's God exerts divine authority over all nations and levels their distinctions. This may strike some of us as old-fashioned. After all, this text does not seem to take seriously particularities that are so important to us, but Isaiah is not burdened with our categories. Instead, he declares God's salvation for all nations as they stream up to the mountain of the Lord. The emphasis on all nations flowing up the mountain, as if they are being drawn by the sheer magnetism of God's divine purposes, is not necessarily a denial of cultural integrity. It is, instead, a claim on the cosmic reach of God's word.

This Advent text contains some of the most famous words of Isaiah. The images of "swords into plowshares" and "spears into pruning hooks" and "neither shall they learn war any more" are embedded in Christian imagination and piety. These images have found their way into both Christian hymnody and antiwar folk songs. They stir the hopes and longings of people exhausted by the senselessness of war and violence. Songs like "Down by the Riverside" contain lyrics that evoke Isaiah 2:4, "Gonna lay down my sword and shield, down by the riverside, and I ain't gonna study war no more."

The meaning of this text for Advent preaching reaches far beyond the longings for disarmament and universal peace, as deep and profound as those longings are. This text sits in juxtaposition on the First Sunday in Advent with Romans 13 and Matthew 24. The Romans 13:11–14 text sounds notes of urgency, "For salvation is nearer to us now than when we became believers; the night is far gone, the day is near." The Matthew 24:36–44 text warns that the timing of the Lord's return is inexplicable and famously forecasts eschatological surprises, "Then two will be in the field; one will be taken and one will be left." When read in concert with these other lectionary texts for the day, the Isaiah 2 text reveals God's character and intent for restoration.

The primary meaning of the text as revealing the determined gracious intent of God for all nations means that it is not a text of future prediction. Often congregations continue to assume that Old Testament prophecy is a window into the future. The scope of this text is much wider. This text is a breathtaking restatement of God's ongoing promises to Abraham and Sarah, Isaac and Rebecca, Jacob and Rachel. God promises that God will bless the people to be a blessing to the nations and that God will protect the people of Israel for the sake of God's own mission. Christians understand that this promise is extended to them through Jesus Christ. For them, too, God will bless the church to be a blessing to all people, and God will be faithful to the church for the sake of God's own mission. For many congregations and denominations that are declining in numbers, this is a genuine word of comfort and hope. God is not done with us yet.

Advent hope is not a yearly exercise of playing pretend. Instead, Advent hope is fully aware of what was, what is, and what is to come. Theologian Ted Smith once said,

> For when we are willing to say that we have lived in latter days, indeed, that we live in them now . . . when we are willing to say that God met Israel, kept covenant, in both the First and Second Temples, even if they were ultimately destroyed . . . when we are willing to say that the Word became flesh and dwelt among us, even if we ultimately killed that Word . . . when we are willing to say that Christmas has already come, really come, to this world in

which we live now . . . then *our hope begins to deepen.* . . . Our hope becomes . . . something other than wishful fulfillment. It is for a God whose love for us only deepens in our rejection of that love. . . . It is for a Prince of Peace who reigns even in the midst of war and rumors of war.[1]

The promise of Isaiah 2:1–4, a text set immediately after a description of vast destruction, expands our understanding of hope. Two prominent Protestant thinkers of the last century identified the deep paradox of Advent hope. Peter Gomes once preached an Advent sermon entitled "Humbug and Hope"[2] that questioned shallow understandings of Advent hope. Superficial jollity in a world of suffering and pain is not Advent hope. Joseph Sittler said that honesty compels us to admit that the track record of humanity is very grim, and there is no excuse for chirpy hopefulness. He also admitted that he regularly plants trees. Against all evidence to the contrary, Christians hope.

LEANNE VAN DYK

Commentary 2: Connecting the Reading with the World

When the typical worshiper settles in this Sunday, there will most likely be familiar sights and sounds: wreath, candles, the color purple, "O Come, O Come, Emmanuel." It must be Advent. Advent is more than the transition from Thanksgiving to Christmas. Advent is more than the beginning of the church liturgical year. Advent is John the Baptist and preparing the way. Cue the sermons on the difference between waiting and preparing. Advent is also an affirmation of living the in-between of the already and the not-yet. Indeed, Christ has come in the child Jesus, and the church again cries out for Jesus to quickly come again. Do not forget the Advent proclamation of the light of Christ shining still amid the world's darkness. Advent is a season boldly to lean into God's future unafraid. The themes of Advent are as familiar as the liturgical decorations and the congregational song. Advent is a kind of comfort food for those who gather for worship, especially those for whom the church feels like home this time of year.

The word of the Lord through the prophet Isaiah, then, can be understood as a steady refrain in the season that proclaims and affirms God's promise. Isaiah's portrayal of the divine hope strikes familiar notes in the believer's ear about the days to come. He tells of nations streaming to the mountain of the Lord and a peace that transforms the world. Isaiah's vision is less an opening trumpet blast and more like a constant, rhythmic note sounded over and over again to God's people: swords into plowshares, spears into pruning hooks, learning war no more. The preacher has to allow Isaiah to keep playing—not just because it is Advent, but because the kingdom seems so distant, the darkness so intense, the world so far removed from what the prophet describes. Tell us again, Isaiah, about the days to come!

Conversations between pastors and church members (or even strangers) seem weightier these days. Not long ago a member of my congregation that I rarely see in worship stopped me in the grocery store. "So what are you saying to people these days who worry about the state of the world? Thousands of years and we are still fighting and killing each other. It never gets any better!" He went on to tell me he was getting old and the worry was not for him but for his grandchildren. "Is a little peace too much to ask?" he said with sadness and a dismissive wave of his hand as he walked away. He was asking me about what Isaiah calls "the days to come." Our encounter in the milk aisle was less an inquiry about my preaching and more a missed opportunity on my part to offer pastoral care.

Most preachers these days are having those conversations and being asked about the bigger life pictures of strife and what has come to be called "the current climate" of bitterness and

1. Ted Smith, "Later Days, Isaiah 2:1–5." http://Day1.org/5368–later_days.
2. Preached December 4, 2005, at Harvard Memorial Church; https://soundcloud.com/harvard/peter-j-gomes-humbug-and-hope.

divide. A genuine existential angst about the world is being shared with pastor after pastor. An older member, who lives alone, wants a little comfort after reading the morning news. The young parent is looking for a bit of grounding and more than a little care and companionship along the way. A college student is asking for some assurance in the next season of life.

It is a question for Advent. It is much less an inquiry about the calendar and much more a yearning to hear of God's promise. This Advent question about "the days to come" strikes close to the heart for the followers of Jesus. It is that restless spirit that can be answered only by our hope in God. It is a longing that can be soothed only by the comfort of our future in God. The Advent plea comes with a desire for God to teach us again of God's ways. That once again God would lead us in God's path. When the hearers of the Word are overwhelmed by a fretfulness that does not go away, those who rise to preach the gospel of Jesus Christ have the responsibility and the privilege of proclaiming the Word of the Lord from the prophet and giving witness to that voice that is endless.

Years ago on a visit to a mountain cabin far into the woods and away from the busyness of life, one of our children announced at bedtime that it was so dark inside that cabin that he thought it was actually darker with his eyes open than with them shut. A successful search for a night-light or two offered a solution. The child was right. The cabin was really too dark. The wise observation, though, applies in all of life. There are moments when it feels darker with one's eyes opened.

When the nations totter, hatred is on the rise, and peace cannot be found, days can be uncomfortably frightening and overwhelmingly dark for people of all ages. Such a vivid darkness also comes in broken relationships, in conversations with doctors about a diagnosis, in caring for a dying parent. There are other kinds of darknesses in life, and it is so dark at times that it can feel as if you cannot see your hand in front of your face. A mother whose young adult child faces a heartbreak that cannot be fixed experiences a worry that causes many sleepless nights. A person who is rapidly losing independence due to dementia must look into a darkness of helplessness that is beyond description. Any sixth-grader who is convinced that absolutely everyone in the third-period class hates them can so easily slip into the shadow of despair. In every congregation on an Advent Sunday, there is darkness haunting the lives of at least some of those who gather.

Yes: wreath, candles, the color purple, "O Come, O Come, Emmanuel." It must be Advent. For worship planners and preachers Advent comes every year. Advent just will not quit. It keeps coming and coming. That is not a bad thing. It can be part of the Advent proclamation. It is as if God's promise spoken through the word of the prophet has a life of its own. In every season of a person's life, the Advent message can break through, but the Advent promise is bigger than that. In a culture that is so strikingly antithetical to the gospel of Jesus Christ, the light of God's grace still offers a flicker of hope that can guide the way. From the most personal to the most global, the prophet's Advent word can bring light. In all the days that come, whatever days that come, the Advent proclamation of God's promise plays on.

Together, the people of God will still be walking. Those who know themselves to be the body of Christ will be walking in the light of the Lord. Taking their cue from Isaiah and the rest of the Hebrew prophets, they will be reassuring one another and telling the world of the comfort of God's grace. The followers of Jesus will be yearning to hear and proclaim the assurance of God's mercy. They will be crying out again to know of the hope of God's promise. While basking again in God's presence, they are still, and will always be, crying out for more peace. Basking in the light of God's presence and crying out for more peace. It must be Advent.

DAVID A. DAVIS

Psalm 122

¹I was glad when they said to me,
　　"Let us go to the house of the LORD!"
²Our feet are standing
　　within your gates, O Jerusalem.

³Jerusalem—built as a city
　　that is bound firmly together.
⁴To it the tribes go up,
　　the tribes of the LORD,
as was decreed for Israel,
　　to give thanks to the name of the LORD.
⁵For there the thrones for judgment were set up,
　　the thrones of the house of David.

⁶Pray for the peace of Jerusalem:
　　"May they prosper who love you.
⁷Peace be within your walls,
　　and security within your towers."
⁸For the sake of my relatives and friends
　　I will say, "Peace be within you."
⁹For the sake of the house of the LORD our God,
　　I will seek your good.

Connecting the Psalm with Scripture and Worship

The word *shalom* provides a drumbeat through this psalm, where it is translated as "peace." The word *shalom* is also included in the Hebrew name of God's city, Jerusalem, which means "foundation of peace." In Hebrew, the sound of peace is echoed as the name Jerusalem is read. Isaiah's vision of peace involves people journeying to the mountain of the Lord's house, where they will learn God's ways that they may "walk in his paths" (Isa. 2:3). God's way is a journey of and toward peace.

The sound of peace is not merely the absence of conflict but also the presence of justice, prosperity, and goodness. *Shalom* is also reflected in Isaiah 2, where the prophet proclaims that God shall judge between the nations, and the people will convert their swords into plowshares and their spears into pruning hooks, tools of

abundance and provision. Shalom means we do not have to study war anymore.

Our course of study will not be war, but peace. God's path leads us out into the world, as bearers of what we have learned, so we may teach others of God's peace. "For out of Zion shall go forth instruction, and the word of the LORD from Jerusalem" (v. 3). The Gospel text of the day instructs hearers to "keep awake therefore" (Matt. 24:42), which reinforces the active nature of our preparation, our instruction, and our work as we walk God's paths. These texts call us to see our faith not as the destination, but as an involved and continued journey, where we are always learning, always transforming our violent ways into instruments of peace, abundance, and provision.

Isaiah invites people to "walk in the light of the LORD" (v. 5), which picks up themes in the

New Testament passages assigned for the day. Paul instructs people to "lay aside the works of darkness and put on the armor of light" (Rom. 13:12). Matthew does not mention light, but the instruction to "keep awake" suggests the dangers of darkness, when thieves break in to steal. Advent occurs during the darkness of winter in North America. It is a dark and difficult season for many people. How can we invite people to "walk in the light of the Lord" through the darkness of a season?

Psalm 122 describes Jerusalem as a city that is "bound firmly together" (Ps. 122:3). To the psalmist, perhaps the reference is more about the soundness of physical construction, the strength of walls and fortifications. For us, the psalm offers an image of our connectedness, of being deeply built together, one to another; it may be the image of hope in a fractured world that speaks of peace more than the reminder of military fortifications. How is God binding us together for peace? How are we connected and united across divisions?

As pilgrims, seeking God's shalom, God's peace, we find our common purpose with one another. We are not just journeying on the same road; we belong together. The salvation of the world is a call for "all the nations" of the world to stream to God's mountain (Isa. 2:2). Isaiah's prophecy also calls us to common purpose, across divisions. All nations will stream to God's mountain, where the things that divide us will not be stronger than the call to learn God's ways and walk in God's paths.

Advent, then, begins with a psalm for pilgrims, journeying to God's city of Jerusalem. Not only does it echo the imagery of Isaiah 2, where all nations shall stream to the mountain of the Lord's house; it reminds us too of our own journey, our pilgrimage, through Advent. For what is it we are "preparing the way"? What is preparing to begin, to arrive, in our lives through Advent? The root of the word "advent" is the same root found in "adventure." Is Advent something we are excited to experience or something we need to "get through" as we survive the holiday season? These passages help us invite people into a journey that leads us through a season of peace toward the mystery of the nativity.

Our Advent journey is not without a destination. We do not wander in the wilderness with no goal. The mountain of the Lord (Isa. 2) and the house of the Lord (Ps. 122) give us imagery for our destination, as does a stable in Bethlehem. There is also a destination of time, a completion of time, the time for which we are keeping awake, when swords are transformed into plowshares and God's peace can be heard over the sound of God's people, rejoicing.

On this First Sunday of Advent, God might call us to worship through the words of Psalm 122.

Reader 1: I was glad when they said to me, "Let us go to the house of the Lord!"

Reader 2: May there be peace within our walls.

Reader 1: We gather in prayer for the well-being of our community.

Reader 2: May there be peace within our neighborhoods, beyond these walls.

Reader 1: We gather in hope for the flourishing of the city.

Reader 2: May there be peace within our nation that builds bridges of hope across walls of division.

MARCI AULD GLASS

Romans 13:11–14

[11]Besides this, you know what time it is, how it is now the moment for you to wake from sleep. For salvation is nearer to us now than when we became believers; [12]the night is far gone, the day is near. Let us then lay aside the works of darkness and put on the armor of light; [13]let us live honorably as in the day, not in reveling and drunkenness, not in debauchery and licentiousness, not in quarreling and jealousy. [14]Instead, put on the Lord Jesus Christ, and make no provision for the flesh, to gratify its desires.

Commentary 1: Connecting the Reading with Scripture

While Romans is often viewed as presenting the essence of Paul's theology for all time and people, it is important to remember that it was a letter written in his particular historical situation. In writing Romans, Paul interacted with the followers of Christ in the church in Rome, the capital city of the Roman Empire. Despite the plight of humanity, Jews and Gentiles alike, Paul argues God's righteousness is manifested in the gospel—God's saving power through Jesus Christ's faithful obedience (1:16–17). This good news is available for all who believe in Christ regardless of their different human conditions such as ancestry, status, and gender (Gal. 3:28).

After addressing God's impartial saving grace through Jesus Christ in Romans 1–11, Paul provides more practical exhortations in chapters 12–16. Paul begins this latter section with the general appeal that the Roman Christians should present their bodies as living sacrifices. Paul then highlights that the holy place is not limited to the temple, but is where the believers' embodied worship takes place in everyday life (Rom. 12:1). This spiritual worship is communal. Paul indicates, bracketing this entire exhortation section with the same imperative (12:16; 15:5): "live in harmony with one another," or, differently rendered, "be like-minded toward one another."

This teaching is neither an abstract principle nor a simple community ethics. Instead, if one considers the situation of the house churches in Rome, living in harmony in the community is the way they should respond to the outside world. The Christians in Rome, particularly Jewish Christians who returned after Emperor Claudius's expulsion of Jews in 49 CE, faced pressure and intimidation in the imperial capital city. This is the context in which Paul warns that the Christians should overcome evil with good (12:17, 21) and be obedient to the governing authorities (13:1–7).

Paul's emphasis on peace with the hostile society and obedience to the human authorities is closely linked, by the concept of indebtedness, to the following advice on loving one another (13:8–10). Paul recommends them to pay to all what is owed (*opheilē*), whether it is taxes or honor to the authorities (13:7). Yet he continues to argue that they ought not to owe (*opheileis*) anyone anything, except to love one another (13:8). This means, then, that Christians do not owe anything to the governing authorities in principle, but should pay them what is required. Living in harmony and loving one another are acts of resisting the Roman economic system of debt-bondage.

Paul invites the audience to a deeper perception of why they should maintain such a proactive way of life under adverse social conditions: "Besides this, you know what time it is" (v. 11). This "time" is not clock time but *kairos*, the right or critical moment for action. The time is "now." Paul uses "now" and "time" together to indicate "present time" elsewhere in Romans. This "now time" is not only the time to demonstrate that

God is just and also justifies the one who believes in Christ (3:21, 26; cf. 11:5), but is also the time of sufferings that awaits "the glory about to be revealed to us" (8:18). In this strong anticipation, Paul can say that "our" salvation is nearer now than before (13:11).

This approach to our collective salvation is better understood with the metaphors of day/ night and light/darkness. This dualistic language describes the contrast between this age and the age to come. While the death and resurrection of Christ manifest the dawn of the new age, or the "incursion of the future age into the old age" in J. Christiaan Beker's terms, the believers live in the overlap of the two ages until Christ's return.[1] This passing age persists with the bondage of sin and death as well as the lust of the flesh (13:14; 8:1–11). Paul demonstrates, however, that the night is almost over and the day is near (13:12a). In 1 Thessalonians 5:5–10, where Paul employs the same dualistic metaphors, he says, "we belong to the day" (1 Thess. 5:8).

Though it is still dark outside, those who live as if it is the day are awake, sober, and "put[ting] on the armor of light" (Rom. 13:12b). This way of living honorably is further defined in contrast with the vices listed as the works of darkness in 13:13 (see also Gal. 5:19–21). However, putting on the armor of light does not entail merely engaging ethical behaviors that the believers should choose; it also describes believers' ontological status as those who put on Jesus Christ (Rom. 13:14; Gal. 3:27–28). In the new age, humanity is renewed into Christlike people.

The same word "armor" is used to mean "instrument" in Romans 6:12–13: "Therefore, do not let sin exercise dominion in your mortal bodies, to make you obey their passions. No longer present your members to sin as *instruments* of wickedness, but present yourselves to God . . . as *instruments* of righteousness" (cf. 12:1). The power of sin and death has not been totally defeated, but believers putting on Jesus Christ are free from their death-dealing power. Many people sense that the night is darkest just before dawn. Romans 13:13 indicates that the day has not fully come: "live [walk] honorably as in the

day." One sees the day dawning, not necessarily knowing the exact time of sunrise, and puts on the armor of light that shines in darkness.

In times of uncertainty, especially regarding Christ's coming and the end of the age (Matt. 24:3), what is needed is watchful living. Matthew is the only one among the Gospel writers who uses the Greek noun *parousia* for Christ's second "coming" (also "appearance" or "presence"). Recognizing the critical time of now does not involve knowing the day and hour of his coming (Matt. 24:36). Rather, unpredictability about the day of Christ's *parousia* leads the Christians to keep awake (Matt. 24:42; 25:13), as Paul calls attention to the critical time for the Roman Christians to "wake from sleep" (Rom. 13:11). Staying awake requires believers to discern the dawn of the age and to prepare for the work of the day in their ordinary lives.

"The house of the Lord" on Mount Zion stands for the presence or coming of God in both lectionary readings of Psalm 122 and Isaiah 2:1–5. Psalm 122 expresses longing for the peace of Jerusalem. When the songs of ascent (Pss. 120–134) were recited, however, the audience heard Psalms 120 and 121, which illustrate the situations of alienation, attack, and war. Isaiah envisions the establishment of God's reign in the dark moment of history when Judah was corrupted in the sight of God and under the upcoming threat of Assyria. Looking for the peaceful "days to come" when weapons will be transformed into farming instruments, Isaiah exhorts, "Let us walk in the light of the Lord" (Isa. 2:2, 5).

Jesus came into the world filled with violence, suffering, and death, but his first coming gave the world the ultimate hope of salvation. Anticipating Christ's second coming, Paul says, our "salvation is nearer" (Rom. 13:11). As he envisions the advent of salvation more than ever, he highlights living in harmony with one another and loving one another. Staying awake or living in the divine light in the end times is not an individual or sectarian practice of spirituality. What is the life context in which today's Christians await the coming of Christ? Waiting is not passive but active resistance to darkness.

---

1. J. Christiaan Beker, *The Triumph of God: The Essence of Paul's Thought* (Minneapolis: Fortress Press, 1990), 28.

When it is darkest, hope shines. In times of suffering, people hold together in love. Thus there is a strong connection between eschatological hope and love.

JIN YOUNG CHOI

Commentary 2: Connecting the Reading with the World

For many of us, our first exposure to Christian eschatology was not altogether pleasant. The idea that Christ was coming again to sweep believers into heaven and bring history to an end was not, in my young mind, good news. I was very much enjoying life as it was in the present: the nurturing love of my parents and family, the bright sun on a summer afternoon, the sweet taste of an apple, the incredible burst of an autumn color on the Allegheny Mountains that surrounded our town, and an abundance of snow to shovel and play with in winter. There was also baseball—the one constant and adhesive that held time together between the end of the season at a World Series, the anticipation of spring training, and then, finally, opening day. Early on I experienced the tension between the promise of future times and the goodness of the present time, between waiting in anticipation and loving life in the world now. This tension remains.

It is not possible to avoid the persistent and pervasive scriptural focus on the future. Both the Hebrew Scriptures (e.g., Isa. 2:1–5) and the Gospels (e.g., Matt. 24:36–44) look forward to God's promised day of fulfillment. The apostle Paul clearly assumed that the last days and the return of Christ were imminent. To the Christians in the early church in Rome, he urges alertness and invokes the images of darkness and light, night and day. He envisions the mysterious dawn, slowly pushing back the darkness, and a new day with all its promise and potential emerging. "Stay awake! Be alert! Full attention!" Paul insists. "Do not miss it when it happens and, by the way, live in light of its nearness: honorably, soberly, honestly, justly, peaceably." That is good advice at any time and in any circumstance, particularly as the season of Advent begins.

Yet, Paul's timetable was wrong. The early church lived with a clear and urgent sense that Christ would return in the immediate future. In a threatening environment full of very real danger, the idea that the end times were near was good news, because it meant God was about to make everything right again. The first major adjustment the Christian church had to make was to deal with the reality that Christ had not returned and that, therefore, a strategy for long-term survival was necessary. The challenge for the early church was to retain Paul's urgent sense of imminent fulfillment while at the same time facing the reality of living indefinitely in the real world.

That challenge is ours as well. We are still living in the in-between time. The kingdom of God came into history in Jesus Christ, but we still wait for its final fulfillment.

Unhappily, the sense of the nearness of the end times can be a distraction from the task of living faithfully in the world. It can be and has been exploited. The *Left Behind* series of sixteen novels, regaling readers with the drama of a final, bloody end of history, has sold a phenomenal sixty-five million books. *The Apocalyptic* is a popular movie that has also inspired instances of human tragedy, as believers become convinced that the world's end is immediately ahead, leading many to sell all their belongings and wait in unfulfilled expectation.

Bedrock Christian faith trusts that history has a final goal. For in Jesus Christ, God has entered human history to point humanity toward ultimate reconciliation and redemption. Also, God is constantly present in human history—nudging, urging, pushing, prodding, and leading us toward the promised end. Unlike modern purveyors of eschatological nonsense, Paul urges the community to settle in and live responsibly and honorably, avoiding excessive behavior and getting along with one another. He exhorts them to live life as thoroughly as Jesus lived it, instructing them to "put on the Lord Jesus Christ" as if it were a new suit of clothing.

Among the influential books in theological education and academia is Jürgen Moltmann's *Theology of Hope.* Its primary objective was to rescue eschatology from fringe fanatics and charlatans and place it at the center of Christian discourse. Moltmann laments the fact that eschatology has become for so many of us today "a loosely attached appendix that wandered off into obscure irrelevance."[2] He argues that relegating eschatology to the end times robs it of its significance both for the church and for individual believers in the present.

Moltmann reminds readers that "Christianity is eschatology, is hope, is forward looking and forward moving and therefore revolutionary in transforming the present" (21). Scripture promises that God gives newness, fulfillment, and hope. In it we are told that God is always before us, out in front of us, bidding us to a new and hopeful future.

People who trust the God of the future will never be complacent about the present. Again, as Moltmann states, "faith, when it develops into hope, causes not rest but unrest, not patience but impatience. It does not calm the unquiet heart but is itself the unquiet heart in us. Those who hope in Christ can no longer put up with reality as it is, but begin to suffer under it, to contradict it" (21).

Instead of patiently waiting to be transported from this world into heaven, faithful people are impatient for justice, fairness, equality, and peace in this world. Because history is moving toward God's goal of the reconciliation of all things, the church is a "constant disturbance in human society . . . the source of continued new impulses toward the realization of righteousness, freedom, and humanity here, in the light of the future that is to come" (22). Hopeful people are troublemakers in the world, and the hope that is in them is the source of vitality, energy, courage, and life itself.

Viktor Frankl, an Austrian neurologist and psychiatrist caught up in World War II, was a survivor of Nazi death camps. After the war he reflected on his experience. In two important books, *Man's Search for Meaning* and *The Unconscious God,* Frankl concludes that the prisoners who survived were those who somehow did not sink into despair but lived with hope. Hope turned out to be a life-giving source. "Only those who were oriented toward the future, toward a goal in the future, toward a meaning to fulfill in the future were likely to survive."[3]

There is a freedom that accompanies trust and confidence that in Jesus Christ ultimate issues have been resolved: that whatever chaos, suffering, and cruelty are happening in the world at the moment, history's final outcome remains safely in God's hands. That freedom allows believers to live thoroughly in the now, awake and alert to the presence of God. As Cynthia Rigby writes: "God's presence allows us to enjoy our experiences on this earth by reminding us that these moments are not all there is. . . . The eternal future, as it breaks into the present, frees us from worrying. . . . Advent is a fine time to remember that the One who is coming is already here, freeing us to be fully present to this very day."[4]

JOHN M. BUCHANAN

---

2. Jürgen Moltmann, *Theology of Hope: On the Ground and Implications of a Christian Eschatology* (New York: Harper & Row, 1967), 15. The next three quotes are from Moltmann, with page source in parentheses.

3. Viktor Frankl, *The Unconscious God: Psychiatry and Theology* (New York: Simon & Schuster, 1975), 139.

4. Cynthia Rigby, "Meandering Hope," *Presbyterian Outlook* 199 (2017): 46.

Matthew 24:36–44

36"But about that day and hour no one knows, neither the angels of heaven, nor the Son, but only the Father. 37For as the days of Noah were, so will be the coming of the Son of Man. 38For as in those days before the flood they were eating and drinking, marrying and giving in marriage, until the day Noah entered the ark, 39and they knew nothing until the flood came and swept them all away, so too will be the coming of the Son of Man. 40Then two will be in the field; one will be taken and one will be left. 41Two women will be grinding meal together; one will be taken and one will be left. 42Keep awake therefore, for you do not know on what day your Lord is coming. 43But understand this: if the owner of the house had known in what part of the night the thief was coming, he would have stayed awake and would not have let his house be broken into. 44Therefore you also must be ready, for the Son of Man is coming at an unexpected hour."

Commentary 1: Connecting the Reading with Scripture

Many in the early church were preoccupied with the question of when exactly Jesus might return. There were speculations about the exact time and manner of Jesus' second coming (*parousia*). Not surprisingly, there were predictions about when exactly Jesus would return and where he might appear (Matt. 24:26–28), resulting in excessive anxiety about the delay in Jesus' return. Such a preoccupation, or a critique of it, is evident in Paul's First Epistle to the Thessalonians as well as in this lectionary reading, Matthew 24:36–44. In this text, the Matthean Jesus cautions his disciples against allowing themselves to be misled by anyone who might offer false guidance about this major, life-changing event in the early church. A basic but essential clarification here is that, although the words themselves are attributed to Jesus, the concerns and the perspectives expressed in the text reflect the historical context of the Matthean community in late first century.

In the preceding section (24:30–35), Jesus offers the assurance, at least for the elect, that the Son of Man will indeed return. He insists that he will return before that generation passes away, and even gives some clues that will precede and signify arrival of the expected event. However, as the text implies, his audience might still be asking for information about the exact time of his return. They are right to ask how long they will have to wait for an event that has already consumed much of their energy and attention. The Matthean Jesus employs two analogies to address that question, the Noah flood story and the thief who comes during the late night. These two analogies represent two extreme and dangerous attitudes of Matthean community vis-à-vis this climactic and life-changing event.

In the story of flood, the issue is the occurrence of the unexpected and unforeseen event that cost the lives of countless humans and living creatures. People were so focused on their earthly concerns—eating, drinking, marrying and giving in marriage—that they were caught entirely off guard by the flood. The Noah story also highlights people's preoccupation with their own concerns and sense of normalcy in a manner that made them oblivious to and distant from the ways of the Divine. Their main concern was the earthly dimension (human-to-human) rather than the vertical relationship between God and human. Their all-consuming emphasis on their earthly existence and all its attendant issues made them wicked in the eyes of God.

Matthew then addresses the question of the time of Jesus' second coming by employing an analogy that Paul also employs in First

Obey with the Best Heart We Have

Year passes after year silently; Christ's coming is never nearer than it was. O that, as He comes nearer earth, we may approach nearer heaven! O my brethren, pray Him to give you the heart to seek Him in sincerity. Pray Him to make you in earnest. You have one work only, to bear your cross after Him. Resolve in His strength to do so. Resolve to be no longer beguiled by "shadows of religion," by words, or by disputings, or by notions, or by high professions, or by excuses, or by the world's promises or threats. Pray Him to give you what Scripture calls "an honest and good heart," or "a perfect heart," and, without waiting, begin at once to obey Him with the best heart you have. Any obedience is better than none,—any profession which is disjoined from obedience, is a mere pretense and deceit. Any religion which does not bring you nearer to God is of the world. You have to seek His face; obedience is the only way of seeking Him. All your duties are obediences. If you are to believe the truths He has revealed, to regulate yourselves by His precepts, to be frequent in His ordinances, to adhere to His Church and people, why is it, except because *He* has bid you? And to do what He bids is to obey Him, and to obey Him is to approach Him. Every act of obedience is an approach,—an approach to Him who is not far off, though He seems so, but close behind this visible screen of things which hides Him from us. He is behind this material framework; earth and sky are but a veil going between Him and us; the day will come when He will rend that veil, and show Himself to us. And then, according as we have waited for Him, will He recompense us. If we have forgotten Him, He will not know us; but "blessed are those servants whom the Lord, when He cometh, shall find watching. . . . He shall gird Himself, and make them sit down to meat, and will come forth and serve them, And if He shall come in the second watch, or come in the third watch, and find them so, blessed are those servants." May this be the portion of every one of us! It is hard to attain it; but it is woeful to fail. Life is short; death is certain; and the world to come is everlasting.

John Henry Newman, "Watching," in *Selections adapted to the Seasons of the Ecclesiastical Year from the Parochial and Plain Sermons of John Henry Newman* (London: Longmans, Green & Co., 1900), 36–37.

Thessalonians, of the thief who comes late at night. This analogy heightens the need for believers to be aware and watchful, as well as addressing the folly of trying to predict the exact timing of Jesus' earthly return. Since it is impossible to predict at what point in the late night the thief might come, the owner of the house must focus on being thoroughly prepared for the event, irrespective of when he might arrive. More importantly, he must devote his energies to safeguarding the house against a possible intrusion. An excessive focus on the time of the event is not only futile; it can also undermine a believer's ability to do the necessary preparatory work.

Jesus seems to suggest that his return is both certain and yet unpredictable. Therefore, an excessive focus on when the Son of Man will return entirely misses the point, as it will have the effect of shifting one's attention and energies away from the present into the future. Such an attitude would be the exact opposite of how

people responded in Noah's time, in that they were primarily concerned with their present earthly relationships.

Given the difficulty of predicting the time of Jesus' return, the goal for the Matthean community was to be sufficiently prepared for it, so that the exact time of the eschatological event became irrelevant. No believer can know when Jesus will return to earth. Yet believers must be vigilant and remain in a state of preparation for such a grand event. Although the second coming of Jesus is a future event, believers' energies should be directed toward being ready for the event. In other words, the process of preparing for Jesus' return, rather than predicting its occurrence, remains the primary goal for every Christian.

What does this process of preparing for *parousia* entail? Matthew's explicit and consistent highlighting of Jesus' engagement with sociopolitical realities of his own time suggests that the evangelist wants his readers to engage similar issues of his own time. The social ethic of feeding the hungry, clothing the naked, and siding with the marginalized is a recurrent theme in Jesus' ministry throughout the Gospel. The metaphor of thief at night indicates the need for a deeper and more sustained commitment to that social ethic on the part of believers. Any precise knowledge of the time of the thief's arrival would allow the owner of the house to prevent an intrusion without necessarily addressing any structural deficiencies that render the house vulnerable to an intrusion.

On the contrary, lack of such precise knowledge would require the owner continually to be on guard and to reinforce the house. Similarly, unpredictability about the time of the *parousia* becomes a positive factor as it has the effect of motivating believers to be constantly committed to a life that is consistent with the values and ethos of the gospel. The Matthean Jesus seems to suggest that, precisely because it is impossible to make accurate predictions about the time of the *parousia*, the best approach for believers is continually to lead faithful lives. Believers need to make good deeds and commitment to horizontal relations with fellow humans the ongoing focus of their lives, rather than a seasonal or momentary exercise. An ethic of communal responsibility and commitment to the welfare of others becomes an identity marker, rather than a phase that one goes through at Jesus' return. Seen this way, the text links the expectation of Jesus' return to certain moral and ethical

expectations and shifts the goal of Christian living from eschatology to ethics.

The subsequent section, the parable in Matthew 24:45–47, is about using believers' time and talents to enrich others rather than looking out for oneself. The preparedness of believers is judged by how they work for the benefit of others in the community rather than focusing solely on a future prize and, in the process, losing their souls. Believers are judged not so much by how well they are prepared to enter heaven but by how much they have been attending to the concerns of others in the community. Along those lines, discipleship is not an event or a phase but a constant state of being prepared and committed to fellow humans.

In the story of Noah, people were overly focused on attending to their own matters, but people in Matthew's community, as in many other early Christian communities, were primarily interested in the eschatological event rather than attending to the needs of others. Common to both contexts, however, is the tendency for humans to look out for their own interests rather than be attentive to the needs of others. The lectionary text seems to call for a balance between the two, the here and now and the eschatological. In addition, it offers assurance and certainty about the *parousia* but provides no specificity about the time. The believers are encouraged to dwell in that tensive space between certainty and specificity, but such a space can engender true discipleship as it encourages them to be at their best.

RAJ NADELLA

Commentary 2: Connecting the Reading with the World

In this passage, we are told we cannot know the time of an event but warned to be prepared for it anyway! The only solution to such a conundrum, of course, is to always be prepared, and therefore it is not that we are to do something out of the normal. Our "being prepared" is supposed to become the new normal! What is called for in this passage, therefore, is nothing less than an alternative lifestyle: living in Advent.

The biblical literature that deals with the anticipation of significant changes in the world is "apocalyptic," based on the Greek term for "revelation" or "something uncovered." The New Testament draws upon the images we are familiar with, not only from the Hebrew Scriptures but even more from the apocalyptic writings of Jewish writers before (and after) Jesus' time. Typical of this genre are bizarre visions combined with a profound expectation of a coming change in circumstances. Here in Matthew the issue is less the strange symbolism, and more the urgency and unexpectedness of Jesus' return to complete what he started in his first appearance.[1]

Three times in this passage, reference is made to what we do "know"—but more importantly to what we do not know (vv. 36, 42, and 43, from *oida*), and another two times about what we do or do not "perceive" (from *ginōskō*, vv. 39 and 43). In this passage, "no one knows" the time (rendering this as "hour" is a bit of a euphemism; the Greek suggests simply a short measure of time, even a "moment," cf. Gen. 18:14, "set time"; or Sir. 11:27, rendered in NJB as "a moment's adversity"; and significantly Daniel 11:35, given its similar apocalyptic context: "appointed time"; cf. Mark 13:32). The images used in the passage involve unexpected events while living a regular life.

What does being unprepared mean? It is interesting that the flood story is used here to refer to "eating and drinking," as well as to engaging in marriage arrangements. Excessive eating and drinking are associated with the wealthy and oppressive elite in the prophets. Isaiah condemns those whose attitude is not repentance, but rather a refusal to change, to literally go down as defiant gluttons: ". . . eat and drink, for tomorrow we die" (Isa. 22:12–14). Amos bitterly condemns those who engage in what we might call the "lifestyle of the rich and famous" (Amos 6:4–6); Micah bitterly denounces false prophets who say what they are paid (and fed!) to say (Mic. 3:5).

The issue is not merely "eating and drinking" (Jesus, you will recall, describes himself this way [Matt. 11:18–19]; ironically, Jesus is recognized as the risen Lord only when he eats, in Luke 24:30–31), but rather being uncaring in gluttonous overconsumption and focusing only on the things of this world. The point here is that "preparation" or "watchfulness" has nothing to do with obsessing over numbers, signs, and meanings. Rather, it has to do with living in the

expectation that the teachings and example of Jesus are the norm! To "fear judgment" is surely another way of trying to live the right way. Luke puts a stronger edge on this thought in Luke 17:33 ("Those who try to make their life secure will lose it, but those who lose their life will keep it") and then lists a slightly different version of two being together and one being taken. In Matthew, two are in the field, while Luke adds: "on that night there will be two in one bed; one will be taken and the other left" (Matthew refers to sowing "in the field" also in chap. 13). Luke further adds another example to the Noah story mentioned in Matthew: "Likewise, just as it was in the days of Lot: they were eating and drinking, buying and selling, planting and building" (Luke 17:28).

Finally, verse 43 refers to the owner of a house and a thief. These references make considerably more sense when seen in the light of the presumably older version in Mark:

> "It is like a man going on a journey, when he leaves home and puts his slaves in charge, each with his work, and commands the doorkeeper to be on the watch. Therefore, keep awake—for you do not know when the master of the house will come, in the evening, or at midnight, or at cockcrow, or at dawn, or else he may find you asleep when he comes suddenly. And what I say to you I say to all: Keep awake." (Mark 13:34–37)

In this context, then, it is important to note the phrase that appears in the verse just before our passage; Jesus refers to his words not "passing away" (from *parerchomai*, v. 35; cf. Ps. 148:6). This same term for "pass away" appears in Daniel, referring both to imperial decrees (especially from Persian rulers, Dan. 6:12, cf. Esth. 8:8) that are thought to be permanent, but then contrasted with the power of God whose "decrees" and authority truly are eternal (so Dan. 7:14). A similar thought is expressed in that New Testament prophetic work, James, referring to the self-inflated rich folks who

---

1. Dale C. Allison. "Matthew," in *The Oxford Bible Commentary*, ed. John Barton and John Muddiman (Oxford: Oxford University Press, 2001), 878.

imagine themselves powerful, but who will "pass away" "like a flower in the field" (Jas. 1:10). In short, the same contrast between the things of this world and the things of God is a biblical theme connected to apocalyptic discussions and social criticism.

It seems to be an especially human trait to be obsessive about what we really want to know, but simply do not (at least not yet). Is that why we love Agatha Christie's Miss Marple and Monsieur Poirot and especially Conan Doyle's Holmes (in all his modern versions in film and television)? Scientists also thrive on mysteries, which drive their work. In religious faith, if anything, we are even more obsessive about what we would like to know! While apocalyptic themes do not occupy major portions of the biblical text, the significance of apocalyptic fervor in troubled times is almost a cliché. Furthermore, however, the sheer persistence of speculation about the end and the relish with which some Christians speak of "end times" are both surely testaments to our capacity to endure difficulty by holding on to some kind of hope—especially a hope for change—and at the same time our incapacity to live without a sure knowledge of what is coming. Interpretations of Christianity that emphasize the imminence of the "end of time" are especially popular among the disenfranchised—affirming Marx's critique of religion as an "opiate" to numb people against their suffering. Yet his famous criticism also reveals a crucial tin ear when it comes to understanding how this perspective can itself be an expression of revolutionary "advent" fervor.

Apocalyptic interests in future changes often go hand in hand with a clear critique of the present. In his fascinating work about the early twentieth century, for example, James R. Green argues that socialist movements in parts of the United States (e.g., Texas, Oklahoma, Kansas, and Arkansas) are hardly ever associated with political radicalism today. Green notes the frequency with which apocalyptic-minded Pentecostal movements fed directly into socialist activism![2] Christian concern for the future need not be hopelessly otherworldly. Matthew calls on us to live in the world precisely because we are in the advent of Christ!

DANIEL L. SMITH-CHRISTOPHER

---

2. See James R Green, *Grass-Roots Socialism* (Baton Rouge: Louisiana State University Press, 1978).

Second Sunday of Advent

Isaiah 11:1–10
Psalm 72:1–7, 18–19

Romans 15:4–13
Matthew 3:1–12

Isaiah 11:1–10

¹A shoot shall come out from the stump of Jesse,
 and a branch shall grow out of his roots.
²The spirit of the LORD shall rest on him,
 the spirit of wisdom and understanding,
 the spirit of counsel and might,
 the spirit of knowledge and the fear of the LORD.
³His delight shall be in the fear of the LORD.

He shall not judge by what his eyes see,
 or decide by what his ears hear;
⁴but with righteousness he shall judge the poor,
 and decide with equity for the meek of the earth;
he shall strike the earth with the rod of his mouth,
 and with the breath of his lips he shall kill the wicked.
⁵Righteousness shall be the belt around his waist,
 and faithfulness the belt around his loins.

⁶The wolf shall live with the lamb,
 the leopard shall lie down with the kid,
the calf and the lion and the fatling together,
 and a little child shall lead them.
⁷The cow and the bear shall graze,
 their young shall lie down together;
 and the lion shall eat straw like the ox.
⁸The nursing child shall play over the hole of the asp,
 and the weaned child shall put its hand on the adder's den.
⁹They will not hurt or destroy
 on all my holy mountain;
for the earth will be full of the knowledge of the LORD
 as the waters cover the sea.

¹⁰On that day the root of Jesse shall stand as a signal to the peoples; the nations shall inquire of him, and his dwelling shall be glorious.

Commentary 1: Connecting the Reading with Scripture

A friend reports to me that whenever he reads Isaiah 11:1–10, he weeps. His eschatological longing is so deep that the motifs of the peaceable kingdom in this familiar text move him to his core. These images of the lion and the lamb, the child and the snake, the wild bear and the domesticated cow, have profoundly moved others as well. Nineteenth-century American painter Edward Hicks created more than a hundred depictions of this text; more than sixty survive. John Buchanan notices that Hicks portrays the animals looking straight at the viewer with wide-eyed wonder. "Peace is startling. You don't see it often, maybe ever. In the middle of the picture is a child, a little girl or boy, with eyes also wide open as if startled by this unlikely reality."[1]

The peaceable kingdom portrays unlimited inbreaking of the kingdom of God and harmony between humans and animals. These are clearly images that reflect an expansive hope for justice, good order, and the well-being of the weakest and most vulnerable members of society. Children will not be hurt. Those vulnerable ones will be protected. Transformations and reversals abound.

This text was written by representatives of a people facing impending doom by Assyrian conquerors coming from the north. Situated most likely in the eighth century BCE, the authors used words that evoke hope and longing for a Davidic king who would rescue the threatened people. This stirring text of hope, however, was set in a thematic structure that begins with words of devastation in 10:33–34: "Look, the Sovereign, the LORD of hosts, will lop the boughs with terrifying power; the tallest trees will be cut down, and the lofty will be brought low. He will hack down the thickets of the forest with an ax, and Lebanon with its majestic trees will fall."

The hope and promise of Isaiah 11:1–10 cannot be understood apart from what precedes it in chapter 10. The Lord judges all the nations. The destruction referenced by these verses includes Judah and the surrounding nations who put their trust in invading armies and political alliances. Yet even in these grim images of punishment and wrath, a hint of promise sounds: the prophet says there will be a "remnant" who "will lean on the LORD" (10:20–21). Both the promise of a remnant and the scorched-earth judgment of the Lord are the thematic precursors of the Isaiah 11 text. Isaiah, here and always, is a prophet of both cleansing judgment and gracious restoration. The metronome of Isaiah

ticks back and forth between these two motifs of judgment and hope.

The lectionary text is identified as Isaiah 11:1–10, although the boundaries of the text are likely verses 1–9; verse 10 is a later addition. Nevertheless, the inclusion of verse 10 gives the text a reference to Jesse both at the beginning and the end. There is some exegetical debate about these two references. Verse 1 refers to a tender shoot coming from "the stump of Jesse" and verse 10 refers to "the root of Jesse." Many commentators conclude that these are rough equivalents. Some see interpretive movement between the two terms. One commentator suggests that the first reference, "stump of Jesse," indicates a Davidic king who will serve as a deliverer empowered and commissioned by God and that the second reference, "root of Jesse," indicates the restored postexilic community.[2] It is unlikely that such an exegetical debate would be fruitful in the context of a sermon, but the possibility of a progression in meaning from Davidic ruler to restored community is intriguing.

The bookends of this text, then, refer to some God-appointed person or community. The middle of the text is an extended elaboration of the results of empowered action by the spirit of the Lord. The repeated parallel phrases in verse 2 establish with growing intensity the agency of God, through the spirit of the Lord. It is God who acts with intent to restore and renew. The ruler is a means, an instrument of God's initiative. The action of the spirit of the Lord does not make the ruler a mere pawn; genuine work is accomplished by the ruler. Indeed, the ruler is busy; the ruler judges, decides, and metes out reward and punishment (vv. 3b–5), but it is the spirit of the Lord that animates and empowers the ruler.

It is also the spirit of the Lord that endows the ruler with an impressive list of capacities and qualities. Wisdom, understanding, counsel, might, knowledge, and the fear of the Lord will all qualify the ruler. The list of qualities of the leader (v. 2) and the resulting actions

---

1. John Buchanan, "Preaching the Advent Texts: Hope, Peace, Courage," *Journal for Preachers* 34, no. 1 (2010): 10.

2. Jacob Stromberg, "'The Root of Jesse' in Isaiah 11:10: Postexilic Judah, or Postexilic Davidic King?," *Journal of Biblical Literature* 127, no. 4 (2008): 657.

of the leader (vv. 3–5) are both expansive and particular. The scope of this God-appointed leader is broad and ambitious as well as attentive and perceptive. The leader pays attention to the meek and the poor; this requires a level of care and patience that reflects the care and patience of God toward all of God's creatures. The leader is effective in the work of righteousness (*tsedeq*) because God's righteousness has equipped him. In Isaiah 11, as throughout all of Isaiah, the author and initiator of restoration is God.

Close regard of several phrases or words add to the texture of this text. The first verse refers to a shoot that emerges from a dead stump. A tender shoot is frail hope for new life. This evocative phrase reminds the reader of a similar image from Isaiah 42:3, referring to the Suffering Servant: "A bruised reed he will not break, and a dimly burning wick he will not quench." The images of frail shoot, a broken blade of grass, and a barely smoldering candle wick are all precarious signs of life. This image from Isaiah 11:1 demonstrates how much God can do with so little. Another word that bears a closer look is the word "signal" in 11:10. Other close English equivalents are "banner" and "sign" and "standard." The Hebrew word is *nes*; it has connotations of declaration and announcement.

The root of Jesse, whether this is the messianic leader or the restored community, broadcasts the knowledge of the Lord to all nations. This proclamation is comprehensive and universal; it goes out to all peoples.

The relationship of Isaiah 11:1–10 with the other lectionary texts for the Second Sunday of Advent can be identified in a number of ways. One thematic link is that of divine gracious initiative. Psalm 72:18 restates the theme of Isaiah 11:1–10 by saying, "Blessed be the LORD, the God of Israel, who alone does wondrous things." Another thematic link is that of harmony and peace, versions of the peaceable kingdom. Romans 15 is an extended benediction of Paul, urging the believing community to take up patterns of harmony and hospitality. Romans 15:12 quotes the Isaiah text, drawing explicit connection between the "root of Jesse" and our "joy and peace in believing" (Rom. 15:13). One more thematic link is the longing and expectation of God's Messiah. In the Matthew 3 text, John the Baptist comes crashing into the Second Sunday of Advent, with blazing heat and intensity. Although very different in tone, the messages of Isaiah 11 and Matthew 3 both look forward with expectation for the inbreaking of the kingdom of God.

LEANNE VAN DYK

Commentary 2: Connecting the Reading with the World

When it comes to Advent and biblical texts, it may not get any more familiar than this. "A shoot shall come out from the stump of Jesse, and a branch shall grow out of his roots." The spirit of the Lord rests on him through discerning wisdom, strong counsel, and knowledge that drips with the fear of the Lord. Delight in the worship of God! The poor are judged with righteousness. Fairness shall abide with the meek. Upon the earth, evil and wickedness will be brought to ruin by his word and breath. Word and Spirit along with righteousness and faithfulness will surround him. Young animals will curl up together. Cows and bears will graze in the same place. Even the lion will eat straw. The nursing child will play with venomous snakes.

There will be no hurt or destruction in God's holy mountain.

More than just an Advent text, these words of Isaiah represent the soundtrack of a lifetime of Christmas Eves. On that day the root of Jesse shall stand as a signpost for the people. All the nations will seek him out, and his dwelling place will be glorious. The evils of war, violence, and oppression shall be stomped out. The most vulnerable, whose lives are threatened by the lack of health care and poor education, shall experience the bounty of the world's resources. The poor will be lifted as God's righteousness abolishes poverty and all the hungry are fed. God's kingdom on that day will be a land full of wisdom and understanding. God's peaceable kingdom is

God's eternal dwelling place. According to Isaiah, it is more than peaceable. It is glorious.

Glorious! That is what Isaiah's audience ought to be saying as they wrap their imagination around the prophet's vision. Of course, for Isaiah and the rest of the Hebrew prophets, it was never about an audience. Prophets do not look for spectators. They do not seek to attract a crowd of bystanders motivated by a spirituality of self-interest. They are about creating, shaping, pruning, sending a kingdom people. They are calling God's people to do the work of justice and righteousness and sculpting God's people to be servants. Prophets send people to further the mission of God, working to bring about the promise of the peaceable, glorious kingdom.

Edward Hicks was the early-nineteenth-century Quaker who created the famous painting *The Peaceable Kingdom*. The painting is a memorable portrayal of the biblical scene with all the animals together in the forefront in such bright colors and with such vivid features. One finds a lamb at the feet of the lion and a child in their midst. The painting was posterized in churches and homes long before the word "posterize" made it into the urban dictionary. Hicks actually painted more than sixty different versions of the peaceable kingdom. Art historians think he probably painted more, but just over sixty exist today. One wonders if his persistence was about an artist trying to get it right or someone with a Quaker heart trying to decorate a lost world with as many visions of peace as he could.

One of the features in most (if not all) of the "peaceable kingdom" paintings is a contemporary scene to the left of the animals, sort of in the background, just beyond some body of water. Interpreters say it is most often a depiction of William Penn and associates making peace with a group of Native Americans. The stunning animal scene dominates the foreground of the painting with a depiction of the artist's nineteenth-century concept of peacemaking off to the left. Of course the twenty-first-century viewer should question the artist's understanding of true peacemaking in that scene of Native Americans and Quakers and place it within the truthful context of history.

Yet Hicks's numerous attempts at the peaceable kingdom cast a vision of the prophet's promise of shining a light on humanity's world. The artist sees around him the peacefulness of a new creation spilling into the world. The eternal hope of a glorious kingdom gives perspective to and even injects hope into a present reality always marred by the reality of human sin. Hicks offers a visual depiction of the prophet's "already and not yet." While waiting for that promised glorious kingdom to come, God's kingdom people are called to point to, work for, shout out, and claim the reign of God now. Maybe this is not a bad definition of Advent—an understanding of Advent that offers a vision of Christ's promised kingdom that sheds light on the world in real time; the peacefulness of God's new creation, which is yet to come, spilling into the here and how; the eternal hope of Christ's glorious kingdom inspiring, informing, and guiding the life of God's people in the present.

Early one morning, my wife and I were driving through Grand Teton National Park. It was not that long after we had passed through the gate that we came upon a park ranger standing smack in the middle of the road with one of those bright orange vests on. Facing us, he was rather energetically pointing to his left. I thought he was telling me to pull over, but this was a narrow road in a national park. Also, there was no berm to the road at all. So I just stopped and rolled down my window. Before I could say a word, the ranger blurted out in the loudest of voices, "You can't miss this!" He tossed his arm to the side like a referee signing first down. We turned to look in that direction. There was a moose, just off the road, taking a bath in a beaver pond. The moose was completely unruffled by the ranger's booming voice. They must have been friends. Without his clarion call we certainly would have missed it.

Sometimes the prophet's message can be communicated in the subtlety of a renowned artist's lasting work. At other times Isaiah's kingdom song comes in the complexity of the Hebrew Bible and is to be studied with the best tools of scholarship: history, theology, and language. Every now and then God's kingdom people have to stand with the prophet smack in the middle of the road, pointing and shouting, "You can't miss this!"

Some Advent seasons, a cantata just is not enough. With the help of Isaiah, the preacher can help the people of God look around at the world. The exhortation then is to stand up with Elijah and point to the eternal hope of Christ's glorious kingdom that sheds light in the world now.

However, pointing is not really enough, because prophets are not interested in spectators. Prophets are not interested in Christians who sit in the pew and say the church should stay out of politics. Prophets are not interested in self-absorbed believers who have concluded that it is really all about them and their punched ticket to eternity. Prophets call people to do justice, and to love kindness, and to walk humbly with their God (Mic. 6:8). Prophets inspire people to let justice roll down like waters and righteousness like an ever-flowing stream (Amos 5:24). Prophets tell of the Messiah, the Savior, the Son of God who stood up in the synagogue and unrolled the scroll of the prophet Isaiah to read. Prophets proclaim the Messiah and his glorious kingdom. Prophets are about pruning, shaping, sending, creating, empowering, inspiring, encouraging, and calling a kingdom people. God's kingdom people are willing to point and shout and work and serve and love.

DAVID A. DAVIS

Psalm 72:1–7, 18–19

[1]Give the king your justice, O God,
  and your righteousness to a king's son.
[2]May he judge your people with righteousness,
  and your poor with justice.
[3]May the mountains yield prosperity for the people,
  and the hills, in righteousness.
[4]May he defend the cause of the poor of the people,
  give deliverance to the needy,
  and crush the oppressor.

[5]May he live while the sun endures,
  and as long as the moon, throughout all generations.
[6]May he be like rain that falls on the mown grass,
  like showers that water the earth.
[7]In his days may righteousness flourish
  and peace abound, until the moon is no more.
. . . .
[18]Blessed be the LORD, the God of Israel,
  who alone does wondrous things.
[19]Blessed be his glorious name forever;
  may his glory fill the whole earth.
Amen and Amen.

Connecting the Psalm with Scripture and Worship

Psalm 72 is described as a psalm "Of Solomon." It is a psalm full of hyperbole and exalted description of his kingship. We hear the hope for the king to "live while the sun endures, and as long as the moon" (Ps. 72:5) and wonder if this is a messianic description, one of a king who is to come. Solomon did not, of course, endure as long as the moon. Robert Alter, in his translation of the psalms, writes, "The poem itself offers no compelling evidence for that reading. Court poetry everywhere revels in flattering hyperbole."[1]

The psalmist's description of the king is lush; he is like the rain that falls on the newly mown grass (v. 6), nourishing the earth. In his book *Seeing the Psalms: A Theology of Metaphor*,

William P. Brown writes: "The image of steady rain, moreover, targets the constancy and potency of royal rule, its benefits and its promises. The rain sets the stage for the 'flourishing' of righteousness and peace, as if the moral order were a crop to be harvested."[2]

If Solomon is the king described in this psalm, he is a king of justice and righteousness, causing the very earth to serve as benefit for his people. The mountains yield prosperity and the hills yield righteousness. "In his days may righteousness flourish and peace abound, until the moon is no more," declares the psalmist, who then offers praise to God, "who alone does wondrous things" (v. 18). The king is described as an actor on God's stage. He does the work given

---

1. Robert Alter, *The Book of Psalms: A Translation with Commentary* (New York: W. W. Norton & Co, 2007), 248.
2. Willliam P. Brown, *Seeing the Psalms: A Theology of Metaphor* (Louisville, KY: Westminster John Knox Press, 2002), 127.

to him by God (v. 1), yet the praise does not go to the king, but to the Lord. "Blessed be the LORD, the God of Israel, who alone does wondrous things" (v. 18). We are not to confuse the created with the Creator. The good works we do reflect back to God, the source of our blessings.

Psalms are often filled with evocative images communicating God's steadfast love and mercy toward God's people, images that draw us toward a vision of a heavenly kingdom that is ordered differently than our human kingdoms. These images often come from mundane, familiar objects, envisioned with unfamiliar purpose. Psalm 72 is filled with trees, branches, mountains, rain—all images that would be very familiar to people who live on the land.

Imagery from nature continues in the lection from Isaiah 11. "A shoot shall come out from the stump of Jesse, and a branch shall grow out of his roots" (Isa. 11:1). Stumps are not usually signs or images of life. Stumps remind us of what used to be there. In this case, it hearkens to rulers of the past, mainly David and Solomon. While we cannot water, prune, or nurture a dead stump to become a tree again, God can send a shoot from the stump, a branch to grow from its roots. Whether we expect to become messianic branches from kingly tree stumps or not, the image of being rooted in God's wisdom, understanding, counsel, might, and knowledge is pertinent to us all. Can our Advent journey be one of grounding?

This branch from the tree of Jesse will be a ruler like the one described in Psalm 72, girded with righteousness and faithfulness. The spirit of the Lord will rest on this branch, which makes clear that this leader is an agent of divine goodness, not the source of goodness and mercy. It is human nature, perhaps, to bestow our hopes on, and credit our successes to, human leaders. Both of these texts make

clear that even the most righteous rulers point us to the steadfast love, mercy, and justice of God. Our praise is misdirected if it does not point toward God.

Isaiah paints an image of a new creation, with a new arrangement of relationships. Wolves and lambs live together. Predatory animals change their diets and become vegetarians, grazing next to former prey. Children will safely play with snakes. God's new day is one where every person and every animal is safe. "They will not hurt or destroy on all my holy mountain," says the Lord (Isa. 11:9). The prophet and the psalmist encourage us to make our Advent journey be one of renewed commitment to creating safer communities and safer relationships as we work for God's new heaven and new earth. Used together, these texts also lend themselves to a call to worship.

Reader 1: A shoot shall come out from the stump of Jesse, and a branch shall grow out of his roots.

Reader 2: Blessed be the Lord, the God of Israel, who alone does wondrous things.

Reader 1: Holy Spirit, rest on us this day; bring us your spirit of wisdom and understanding, a spirit of counsel and might.

Reader 2: Blessed be the Lord, the God of Israel, who alone does wondrous things.

Reader 1: May we create a world where the wolf shall live with the lamb, and the leopard shall lie down with the kid.

Reader 2: Blessed be the Lord, the God of Israel, who alone does wondrous things.

Reader 1: Blessed be God's glorious name for ever; let us worship in peace, hope, and love.

MARCI AULD GLASS

Romans 15:4–13

⁴For whatever was written in former days was written for our instruction, so that by steadfastness and by the encouragement of the scriptures we might have hope. ⁵May the God of steadfastness and encouragement grant you to live in harmony with one another, in accordance with Christ Jesus, ⁶so that together you may with one voice glorify the God and Father of our Lord Jesus Christ.

⁷Welcome one another, therefore, just as Christ has welcomed you, for the glory of God. ⁸For I tell you that Christ has become a servant of the circumcised on behalf of the truth of God in order that he might confirm the promises given to the patriarchs, ⁹and in order that the Gentiles might glorify God for his mercy. As it is written,

> "Therefore I will confess you among the Gentiles,
>   and sing praises to your name";
> ¹⁰and again he says,
>   "Rejoice, O Gentiles, with his people";
> ¹¹and again,
>   "Praise the Lord, all you Gentiles,
>   and let all the peoples praise him";
> ¹²and again Isaiah says,
>   "The root of Jesse shall come,
>   the one who rises to rule the Gentiles;
> in him the Gentiles shall hope."

¹³May the God of hope fill you with all joy and peace in believing, so that you may abound in hope by the power of the Holy Spirit.

Commentary 1: Connecting the Reading with Scripture

The hope of Advent is not unwarranted. Paul finds "endurance" and the "comfort" of the Scriptures (rendered "steadfastness" and "encouragement" in the NRSV, respectively) as the basis of Christian hope (Rom. 15:4). He argues that hope that is seen is not hope; thus we are required to wait for what is not seen with patience, aided by the Spirit's intercession (8:23–25). During the time of waiting, the Spirit is the pledge of the new age that is already at work through the death and resurrection of Christ.

Although we hope for what we do not see, hope has another tangible foundation, that the teachings of the Scripture were written not only for God's people in the past but also for those in the present days. Paul argues in Romans 13:9 that the law is summed up in this commandment,

"Love your neighbor as yourself" (Mark 12:31; cf. Lev. 19:18). Just before our passage he quotes another Scripture speaking about the insults and shame King David experienced because of his zeal for God's house (presence), as well as his hope in God (Rom. 15:3; Ps. 69:9). Applying this biblical text to Christ's example, Paul now argues that the Roman Christians must follow his example in pleasing their neighbors rather than pleasing themselves (Rom. 15:2–3).

Paul's argument is consistently that the purpose of the Scriptures is to encourage Christians to love one another as they hope for their salvation. Actually, the source of the endurance and comfort is God, and that gift is for us, again, to "live in harmony with [or be like-minded toward] one another" (v. 5). This "life together" involves glorifying God in unison, which is extended to this worshiping community's practice of welcome (vv. 6–7).

Paul uses Christ's example one more time to explain how this welcoming of one another serves the glory of God. Christ, as a Jew, was born in human form and was killed by crucifixion. Christ's faithful obedience and righteousness in the sight of God resulted in the Gentiles' access to the promises that were previously given to the patriarchs of Israel like Abraham (v. 8). Paul integrates hope into the promise of the Scripture and the hope of glory through the ministry of Christ. Just as Christ's welcoming of Gentile believers led them to glorify God and abound in hope, they must welcome one another and build up their neighbors (15:2, 7–13).

Worshiping God cannot be separated from welcoming others. These are essential components of Advent hope as Christians eagerly wait for the Day of the Lord when all the nations— usually translated as the "Gentiles" in English— will worship God together. Accordingly, this concrete vision of a future inclusive community inspires believers to practice welcome. Actually, for Paul, welcoming one another is neither a trivial nor a new issue in a church in which the Gentile and Jewish Christians coexist. His exhortations of mutual acceptance bracket 14:1–15:13.

> 14:1–12 Welcome those who are weak in faith (v. 1); God has welcomed them (v. 3).
> *Christ died and lived again* (v. 9).
>
> 15:7–13 Welcome one another; Christ has welcomed you (v. 7).
> *Christ has become a servant of the circumcised* (v. 8).

Between these two passages, the same message is repeated. In 14:13–23, Paul admonishes primarily the so-called strong in faith not to judge the weak, whose faith led them to uphold Jewish traditions such as observances of dietary regulations. According to Paul, *Christ* died for the weak who might be offended by those strong enough to exercise freedom based on their faith. Even more important than strong faith is "peace and mutual upbuilding [*oikodomē*]" (14:19). Similarly, in 15:1–6, while including himself

among the strong, Paul reiterates that they must not please themselves, for Christ did not please himself. Instead, they are to please their neighbor (a singular noun, and thus indicating the weak) for the good purpose of "upbuilding [*oikodomē*]" them (15:2–3).

In practicing mutual acceptance and building up the community, the burden is more on those in the strong position to accept those in the minority position. In the same manner, Paul has associated "living in harmony [*to auto phronein*] with one another" with the lowly rather than exalting oneself over others (12:16). For Paul, it is clear that this particular practice of welcome is "in accordance of Christ" here in Romans 15:5. The Christ hymn provides the same foundation: "be of the same mind [*to auto phronēte*], having the same love, being in full accord and of one mind. . . . Let the same mind be in you that was in Christ Jesus" (Phil. 2:2, 5). Practicing the same mind and the same love as Christ displayed on the cross is not limited to the members in the community. When Paul speaks about the same mind and the same love, he starts with brotherly/sisterly love (*philadelphia*) and then extends it to the love of strangers (*philoxenia*, Rom. 12:9, 13, 16).

Yet Paul is speaking about more than communal ethics. Accepting one another in the mixed assemblies of Jews and Gentiles testifies to the hope in Christ, who will consummate the gathering of the nations. Paul is determined to describe this future hope when he quotes various Scriptures in 15:9–12 to describe the Gentiles' joining with God's people (Pss. 18:49; 117:1; 2 Sam. 22:50; and Deut. 32:43). Again, remember that it is in the Roman imperial context that Paul is quoting the Isaiah passage (Isa. 11:10): "the root of Jesse"—a Davidic Messiah will rise to rule the "nations"; in this crucified Messiah the nations shall hope (Rom. 15:12). This prophecy has been now fulfilled as God fills the Roman Christians with the same hope and the power of the Holy Spirit (v. 13).

Such a claim, though cited, is already subversive enough that Paul does not describe the full picture of Isaiah's prophetic vision of God's reign. However, he must know that on that day Christ will judge the wicked with truth and justice (most frequently translated as "righteousness" in Paul's letters), while vindicating the poor and the meek (Isa. 11:4–5). Furthermore, justice will come along with a peace and harmony that is extended to nonhuman creatures. Isaiah depicts "living in harmony with one another" in the cosmic vision of transformation of domination and violence into restoration and harmony (Isa. 11:6–9).

Psalm 72, attributed to Solomon, also depicts a similar vision of the just peace that the king of Israel is commissioned to establish by judging the oppressor and liberating "God's poor" (Ps. 72:2, 4). While our lectionary passages so far employ the images of the Davidic Messiah to describe the eschatological hope of God's reign with justice, what is also highlighted is the future glory of God (Rom. 15:9; Isa. 11:10c; Ps. 72:18–19).

The Matthew reading affirms the inclusivity of salvation, redefining the significance of

Abraham as the ancestor of all, as Paul does in Romans 4. Such a reading resists using the antagonism expressed by John the Baptist in Matthew 3:7–10 to legitimate anti-Judaism. Rather, following the prophetic tradition, John both speaks to the powers from the political and religious center and restores people in the wilderness. In this marginal space, those who do not have any privilege are freed from the bondage of sins. Above all, John prepares for the way of the Lord (Matt. 3:3).

Today's readings extend the scope of the eschatological vision, connecting the promise of the past and the hope of future glory. In our welcoming of others, the future global worshiping community is anticipated. In this welcoming, we have a foretaste of flourishing justice and abounding peace (Ps. 72:7).

JIN YOUNG CHOI

Commentary 2: Connecting the Reading with the World

"We're not frayed at the edges—we're ripped at the damn seams," the cover of *Time* announced. Nancy Gibbs introduced her editorial in the December 11, 2017, issue:

> The Pew Research Center found that across a range of issues—immigration, race, security, the environment—the partisan split is now greater than differences in age, race, gender and income. The center has all but vanished. . . . You could conclude that the U.S. is so deeply divided that our name is little more than wishful thinking.[1]

American culture has been divided before but never this bitterly since the Civil War. The preamble to our Constitution makes a huge assumption in its first three words:

> We the People of the United States, in order to form a more perfect Union, establish Justice, insure domestic Tranquility, provide for the common defence, promote the general Welfare, and secure the Blessings of Liberty to

> ourselves and our Posterity, do ordain and establish this Constitution for the United States of America.

Notice the words the authors capitalized for emphasis: "People," "Union," "Justice," "Tranquility," "Welfare," "Blessings," "Liberty," and "Posterity." It is a litany of the founders' values as well as their hopes and aspirations that the people of this new nation would be a community. Of course they themselves fell short of their own high aspirations. Many of them were slave owners, and few of them paid much attention to the displacement and sometimes extermination of the native peoples who were already here. Nevertheless, "We the People" implied a connection, a unity, a promise to attend to one another's welfare.

Writing in the first century to the early Christian church in Rome, it seems that Paul is also speaking to us: people, churches, individual Christians living in the first decades of the twenty-first century. We are profoundly divided politically, socially, economically, racially. Indeed, our divisions reach all the way down to

---

1. "How We Deserted Common Ground," *Time* 190, no. 24 (December 11, 2017): 23–27, 23.

Let Us Purify Our Spirit

If . . . those of this world celebrate the birthday of an earthly king . . . for the sake of the glory of present honor, with what solicitude ought we to celebrate the birthday of our eternal king Jesus Christ, who in return for our devotion will bestow on us not temporal but eternal glory! Nor will He give us the administration of an earthly honor, which comes to an end when someone else inherits it, but the dignity of a heavenly empire which has no end. . . . Let us seek, then, to be found before Him proven in faith, bedecked with mercy, and arrayed in virtues. And whoever loves Christ more devotedly is more shiningly intent upon the observance of His commands, so that He may really see that we believe in Him when we so shine on His feast day; and the purer He sees us the happier He is.

Before many more days, then, let us make our hearts pure, let us cleanse our consciences and purify our spirits, and, shining and without stain, let us celebrate the coming of the spotless Lord, so that the birthday of Him whose birth was known to be from a spotless virgin may be observed by spotless servants.

Maximus of Turin, "Sermon 60: To Be Given before the Birthday of the Lord," in *The Sermons of St. Maximus of Turin*, trans. Boniface Ramsey, OP, Ancient Christian Writers (New York: Newman Press, 1989), 144–46.

---

our communities, our churches, and even our families.

Paul was writing to what apparently was a number of small gatherings of believers in the capital city of the Roman Empire. Scholars surmise that these small groups, perhaps organized on the basis of race, social class, and/or geographical proximity, came together to celebrate the Lord's Supper. For these believers, this important event had caused conflict and divisiveness. So Paul stressed the essential unity believers have in Jesus Christ, a unity that transcended everything that was dividing them. In the first few verses of chapter 15, Paul especially urged the strong to put aside personal opinions and preferences and principles in order to affirm and empower the weak. He pointed to the example of Christ, who did not "please himself" but emptied himself in service to others. The surprising purpose, Paul wrote, is the "building up of the neighbor." Could it be that the apostle was looking beyond the small groups of believers to the vastness of the entire city of Rome, the Roman Empire, and the world?

In verse 4 Paul arrived at a crucial point in his message. Unity, caring for one another's welfare, being responsible to and for one another is not merely an exercise in niceness and good feelings. Its bold purpose is for the whole church to glorify God, the Father of the Lord Jesus Christ, "with one voice" (Rom. 15:6).

The unity of the young church is central to Paul's teaching. There is no walking away from one another in Christ. Of course, individuals will disagree with one another, have different opinions and convictions on a variety of issues, including religious beliefs and practices. Beginning here, with the earliest church, this essential unity is threatened by individuals insisting that their way is the only way. As for Paul, however, unity comes first. Separating from one another, for whatever reason, is not an option in the church.

In her book *When in Romans*, Beverly Gaventa observes that "being members of one another means there is a relationship from which there is no exit plan."[2] Paul's radical ecclesiology, which claims the primacy of unity and community as Christ's gift to the church, transcends our Western obsession with individualism and judges and challenges the contemporary churches, all of whom seem to reflect the profound divisions in American culture. Mainline churches have recently experienced the tragedy of disunity and separation as hundreds of congregations have voted to leave the denominations over disagreement about doctrine and church policy. If anyone is guilty of sacrificing unity in Christ on the altar of individualism, individual opinions,

---

2. Beverly Roberts Gaventa, *When in Romans* (Grand Rapids: Baker Academic, 2016), 105.

convictions, commitment, interpretations of doctrine, and Scripture, it is us.

Paul's hope for the church was that it might glorify God in one voice. Paul understood not only the power but also the evangelical imperative of unity in Christ. Perhaps Paul knew that Jesus himself, on the last night of his life, prayed for his disciples: "Holy Father, protect them in your name that you have given me, so that they may be one, as we are one. . . . As you, Father, are in me and I am in you, may they also be in us, so that the world may believe that you sent me" (John 17:11, 21). Jesus desires that something of God and God's love be reflected in the oneness and unity of the church of Jesus Christ.

What a powerful witness we would be in this divided nation, culture, and world if somehow followers of Jesus remembered the essential importance of their unity in him, if somehow they showed the world that human beings can remain together in spite of their different politics and religious convictions.

Paul had a huge, cosmic vision for the gospel. Early Christianity was a Jewish project in an overwhelmingly Gentile world. The looming issue for the early church had to do primarily with boundaries between Jews and Christians. The pressure for the church to push out into the Gentile world was enormous. Would it imply the rejection of Judaism and individual Jews? Paul thought long and hard about this and came up with a graceful and gracious metaphor. He did not envision a boundary or a wall of separation, but rather a graft onto a living vine. Israel is the vine; the church is the graft (Rom. 11:17–24). Paul knew very well that God had not rejected a chosen people, realizing that Jews continued to be loved, cared for, and sustained by God. As Christians, we are grafted onto the solid, robust, growing vine that is Judaism.

In his collection of essays *For the Sake of Heaven and Earth*, rabbi and theologian Irving Greenberg offers these words about Jewish-Christian relationships: "The group that would bring the message of redemption to the rest of the world had to grow out of the family and covenanted community of Israel. But the community was not intended to be a replacement. . . . Christianity had to start within Judaism, but it had to grow into its own autonomous existence."[3]

Paul had a magnificent vision of God's universal love poured out on the whole creation, a vision of humankind bound together in that universal, holy love. It all rests on the strong, deep, profound "root of Jesse," father of David the king, the many-times great-grandfather of Jesus.

JOHN M. BUCHANAN

3. Irving Greenberg, *For the Sake of Heaven and Earth* (Philadelphia: The Jewish Publication Society, 2004), 22.

Second Sunday of Advent

Matthew 3:1–12

¹In those days John the Baptist appeared in the wilderness of Judea, proclaiming, ²"Repent, for the kingdom of heaven has come near." ³This is the one of whom the prophet Isaiah spoke when he said,

"The voice of one crying out in the wilderness:
'Prepare the way of the Lord,
  make his paths straight.'"

⁴Now John wore clothing of camel's hair with a leather belt around his waist, and his food was locusts and wild honey. ⁵Then the people of Jerusalem and all Judea were going out to him, and all the region along the Jordan, ⁶and they were baptized by him in the river Jordan, confessing their sins.

⁷But when he saw many Pharisees and Sadducees coming for baptism, he said to them, "You brood of vipers! Who warned you to flee from the wrath to come? ⁸Bear fruit worthy of repentance. ⁹Do not presume to say to yourselves, 'We have Abraham as our ancestor'; for I tell you, God is able from these stones to raise up children to Abraham. ¹⁰Even now the ax is lying at the root of the trees; every tree therefore that does not bear good fruit is cut down and thrown into the fire.

¹¹"I baptize you with water for repentance, but one who is more powerful than I is coming after me; I am not worthy to carry his sandals. He will baptize you with the Holy Spirit and fire. ¹²His winnowing fork is in his hand, and he will clear his threshing floor and will gather his wheat into the granary; but the chaff he will burn with unquenchable fire."

Commentary 1: Connecting the Reading with Scripture

In the previous chapter, the scene of action shifted rapidly from one location to another. It started with the birth of Jesus in Bethlehem and moved to Jerusalem and then to Egypt, before finally ending in Nazareth, where Jesus and his family settled down. This chapter marks an abrupt shift in location to the Judean wilderness, where John has been preaching a baptism of repentance.

John's baptism is often described as a mark of initiation into the movement that would usher in the kingdom of heaven. The Matthean John, unlike the Markan John, does not offer a baptism that leads to forgiveness of sins. Matthew seems to be reserving that privilege exclusively for Jesus. Matthew does not yet specify what the emerging kingdom will look like. The readers will learn later that the kingdom inaugurated by

Jesus will ensure that the poor, the blind, the lame, and other marginalized groups will have a place at the table. The people who respond to John's ministry in this story are not ones at the margins of society. Instead, it is the Sadducees and the Pharisees from Judea and Jerusalem who respond to John in great numbers.

John is calling on the religious and political elite from Judea and Jerusalem to repent. The Greek word *metanoia* literally means taking on a new mind-set. It has the connotation of making an about-turn and changing course. John is suggesting that participation in the new kingdom requires a new worldview. It also requires them to turn their backs on everything in which they have been participating and from which they have been benefiting. John is inviting those in positions of power and privilege to cease their complicity in oppressive structures and to turn their backs on structures of exclusion that have become prevalent in Judea.

This pericope highlights John's role vis-à-vis Jesus. However, John is not simply preparing the way for the Lord, as verse 3 seems to suggest. He is also showing the way. He is modeling for the many, especially the Judean elite, how to become a part of the new kingdom of God that is at hand. As John has demonstrated by example, participation in the new kingdom entails a radical change in one's lifestyle. John has turned his back on the Judean society in several ways. He has established a residence in the wilderness and has adopted a new way of clothing and a radically new food diet of locusts and honey. Several commentators have observed that John's hairy mantle resembles that of prophets in the Old Testament, especially Elijah's (Zech. 13:4). Like Elijah, John is challenging the ethos and corrupt practices of political and religious leaders.

In this context John's call to the religious elite to repent becomes especially significant. Are the religious leaders taking on a new mind-set and turning their backs on their privilege and their complicity in oppression? Are they simply seeking to join the emerging kingdom so as not to be left out? John seems to assume the latter when he calls them a "brood of vipers." The religious elite have been poisonous to the society and have been undermining its health. Can they suddenly change course and be transformed? Can they take on a new mind and turn their backs on the very systems that have served them well?

John is refusing to offer them the easy absolution the Judean elite might have hoped for. In a somewhat paradoxical suggestion, he is making it clear that it is by turning around and being transformed that they can retain their status as the children of Abraham. From his perspective, acting in ways that are consistent with the new mind-set and turning their back on an old lifestyle are much more important than physically leaving Jerusalem and going into the wilderness.

Matthew's use of the Isaianic quote (Isa. 40:3) also depicts John the Baptist as one who will "make straight paths for him" (Matt. 3:3). Although this call to make his paths straight is given in the wilderness, the meaning is primarily metaphorical and pertains to a very different location.

It is aimed at people who live far from the wilderness and is intended for those living in urban areas of Judea such as Jerusalem. Accordingly, the paths that need to be straightened exist in the royal courts and the power corridors of Judea.

John is not simply calling on people to join the new kingdom. He is also inviting them to a new space that he has embraced and made home: the wilderness. Several scholars have noted that wilderness functions as a liminal space in the history of Israel. It was where the Hebrew community spent a considerable amount of time after fleeing Egypt and before entering the promised land. Later in Matthew's story, the readers will learn that Jesus will spend a formative period of forty days in the wilderness. Within the context of Matthew's Gospel, wilderness is also an alternative space, one that espouses values that are diametrically different from the civilizational values of Roman cities.

Wilderness is also depicted as a safe space. When Jesus hears about the death of John and goes into the wilderness with his disciples (Matt. 14:13; Mark 6:31–33), it becomes an act of escape from the violence Herod had unleashed against his critics. On an intertextual level, there are parallels to the Israelites fleeing Egypt and Jesus going into the wilderness to be tempted. When the crowds in Matthew learn that Jesus has withdrawn into the wilderness, they follow him by foot. One of the key aspects of this story is the idea that when people in urban areas were terrorized by the empire, they fled into the wilderness, supposedly looking for a safe space. Rome depicted its cities as citadels of civilization and took pride in them. Therefore, Matthew's suggestion, that wilderness became a place of refuge for those escaping the city's barbaric violence, would have been an explicit challenge to the empire's claims that its cities represented enlightenment and civilization.

The feeding miracles in Matthew also take place in the wilderness, away from the Judean capital (14:14–21; 15:32–39). In a context where food was scarce, and given the urban ethos of hoarding, convincing people to share their basic resources was a miracle. Matthew's audience would have known that cities in the

Roman Empire were both symbols and locales of the empire's oppressive economic practices. They played a key role in perpetuating Rome's practice of systematically moving resources from peripheries to imperial centers. Matthew 14:3–17 highlights a paradox whereby a Roman city—a seat of civilization—becomes the location of John's murder, while the wilderness becomes a place of refuge and compassion for the masses. In doing so, the Gospel affirms the wilderness that was marginal to Rome's imperial imagination but central to its worldview and ethos.

Matthew's emphasis on the location of John's ministry highlights the extent to which people's ideologies may be connected to, and influenced by, the spaces they inhabit. Those living in marginal locations like the wilderness have the capacity to be compassionate and are inclined to challenge the powers in ways that those inhabiting the center are not. What happens when those at the margins move closer to the center? Can they live in Roman cities such as Tiberias and Rome and not be influenced by their oppressive ethos and values? Will they still have the capacity to resist the empire? As the church becomes increasingly urban and moves into metropolitan spaces, will Matthew's audience espouse imperial values, or will they remain committed to challenging them?

RAJ NADELLA

Commentary 2: Connecting the Reading with the World

The standard ceremony of symbolizing God's choice of a monarch (and occasionally other officials) was anointing the person's head with olive oil. Thus the rise of the association between "the anointed one" and the "Messiah" (for references to anointing, see 1 Sam. 2:10, 35; 12:3, 5; and Ps. 2:2; for references to Messiah as the anointed one, see Isa. 45:1 and Hab. 3:13). Old Testament reflections about the future of the people of God ordered under a kind of monarchical restoration are based on three interwoven themes: (1) that the rule of the Davidic line will end with the exile (although there was clearly speculation around Zerubbabel [Zech. 1–6], it came to naught); (2) that the line of David will continue to rule in perpetuity, as God promised David (2 Sam. 7:16); and (3) that the line will be restored as a fulfillment of the promise.

It is clear, however, that notions of the restoration became complicated in the centuries after the Babylonian conquest of Jerusalem and the Judean exile, with some ideas surrounding a heavenly being descending from heaven. In Daniel 7, for example, we are told of an angelic one "like a son of man," which most likely refers to Michael the archangel. In Enoch, God sends a figure that is judge-like; chapter 48 refers to one who will be a "light to the Gentiles" (though this might be a later Christian interpolation). In Second Isaiah, God even uses a foreign ruler, Cyrus the Persian, who rather surprisingly is called a "messiah."

One idea closely associated with the coming of an anointed person leading a restoration, a messiah figure or a similar figure, is that this person would have a forerunner. The purpose of the forerunner is to announce the anointed one's imminent arrival. In Malachi 3:23–24 (NJB) (the final sentences of the Protestant Old Testament) that person is explicitly identified as Elijah: "Look, I shall send you the prophet Elijah before the great and awesome Day of Yahweh comes. He will reconcile parents to their children and children to their parents, to forestall my putting the country under the curse of destruction."

The traditions surrounding the return of Elijah grew in both Christian and Jewish writings, starting already in Sirach (48:1–11) and into the noncanonical Jewish tradition (*Targum Pseudo-Jonathan* on Exod. 6:18). In her helpful overview, Christine Joynes notes how often Elijah is mentioned in the Gospels combined with notions of his "coming" or having "appeared."[1]

---

1. Christine Joynes, "The Returned Elijah? John the Baptist's Angelic Identity in the Gospel of Mark," *Scottish Journal of Theology* 58, no. 4 (2005): 455–67, 456.

Elijah's ability to return, of course, is directly connected to his having been "taken up" to heaven without dying, according to the tradition (see 2 Kgs. 2:11; Enoch; and Gen. 5:24, which led to speculation about Enoch's capacity to return). He is thus available for return duty!

Matthew, from Mark, picks up on this tradition of early Christian interest (and probably historic relationship) to John the Baptist and his reforming movement. It is normally supposed by New Testament scholars that many of the Jewish followers of John then joined the Jesus movement.[2] The Synoptic tradition (Mark 1:3; Matt. 3:3; Luke 3:4) rather powerfully associates John/Elijah not only with the prophetic forerunner, but also rather clearly with the "new exodus" language of Isaiah 40:3, a "way in the desert" (language of "desert," "way," "path," etc.; cf. Exod. 13:18; Deut. 1:19; but esp. Ps. 107:4).[3] That John the Baptist is associated with the desert, then, is not only representative of his "fringe" and "outsider" status (again, like Elijah, who is contrasted with, say, a Nathan or Isaiah, who served close to the king and probably lived rather comfortably), but also closely connected to liberation language associated with the exodus under Moses.

Key terms here recall biblical themes of change: the wrath of God, ax to roots (Mal. 4:1), and burning fire (Isa. 33:14). We should not miss the challenge to "the establishment" represented not only in John's wilderness location (to which the people come in startling numbers: "all Judea and the whole Jordan district," my trans.) but also using the Hebrew symbolism of washing impurities (throughout Leviticus, but see especially Ps. 51:2). The wilderness represents leaving the places where power structures are firmly in place. The sociological term is liminal space—that is, an "in between" place where change is possible because, we would say informally, it is a place where "all bets are off"—a place undefined and unconquered and, more to the point, not under control. This, then, is combined with the Levitical symbol of purity—washing—as a way of

further symbolizing a rejection of the former reality ("dirty") for the new (now "clean"). The combination of the two makes this a socially and politically threatening act.

That is why John attacks representatives of the "old power structures," who clearly show up to examine how serious this threat may be. John spits an insult at them, calling them the "off-spring" of poisonous snakes ("brood of vipers" is the traditional term, but brood is less common in modern American English). The reference is probably to snakes from the genus *Echis* (itself derived from Greek, as opposed to "asp" or Egyptian cobra in Ps. 140:3), the modern viper found also today in Asia and the Middle East, which is highly poisonous.

Finally, not to be missed are two themes associated with Jesus in this powerful reading of John the Baptist's symbolic movement. First, Jesus (in contrast to John's Levitical purity symbolism) is associated with "the Holy Spirit" and "fire." The Holy Spirit is virtually always associated in the Hebrew Bible with the turbulent, raging lives of the prophets, and fire is a frequent symbol of judgment associated with the prophets (with Elijah, 1 Kgs. 18; see Amos 1:4, 7, 12, etc.; Isa. 33:14). The second theme is separations—separating good from bad—thus the references to agricultural separations of grain from stalks.

The themes of judgment suggest change. The Chilean biblical scholar Pablo Richard has written a number of works on Revelation and has noted the popularity of the book of Revelation among Latin American peasants! Whereas themes of judgment are often upsetting to North Americans, these same themes are relished by the poor. It is not difficult to determine why: judgment is upsetting only when you think the judgments will go against you, rather than in your favor! The poor clearly hope for "their day in court," whether it is a world court of human rights, or the heavenly court of God. It is important then to read these words with the appropriate joy in the hearing about coming judgment and Christ as the judge who

2. Dale Allison Jr., "Matthew," in *The Oxford Bible Commentary*, ed. John Barton and John Muddiman (Oxford: Oxford University Press, 2001), 844–86.

3. Ulrich Luz, *Matthew 1–7*, trans. Wilhelm Linss, vol. 1 (Minneapolis: Fortress Press, 1989).

will vindicate the righteous. Do we imagine that "all Judea and the whole Jordan district" were streaming into the wilderness for fear of judgment or to celebrate the coming change? Clearly the latter; Jesus represented revolutionary change. What we see is that evil prospers.

What we anticipate—what we literally live for, in Advent—is the fulfillment of the transformative justice of the kingdom, when right will be vindicated as right, and wrong clearly identified as wrong.

DANIEL L. SMITH-CHRISTOPHER

Third Sunday of Advent

Isaiah 35:1–10   James 5:7–10
Luke 1:46b–55 or Psalm 146:5–10   Matthew 11:2–11

Isaiah 35:1–10

¹The wilderness and the dry land shall be glad,
    the desert shall rejoice and blossom;
like the crocus ²it shall blossom abundantly,
    and rejoice with joy and singing.
The glory of Lebanon shall be given to it,
    the majesty of Carmel and Sharon.
They shall see the glory of the LORD,
    the majesty of our God.

³Strengthen the weak hands,
    and make firm the feeble knees.
⁴Say to those who are of a fearful heart,
    "Be strong, do not fear!
Here is your God.
    He will come with vengeance,
with terrible recompense.
    He will come and save you."

⁵Then the eyes of the blind shall be opened,
    and the ears of the deaf unstopped;
⁶then the lame shall leap like a deer,
    and the tongue of the speechless sing for joy.
For waters shall break forth in the wilderness,
    and streams in the desert;
⁷the burning sand shall become a pool,
    and the thirsty ground springs of water;
the haunt of jackals shall become a swamp,
    the grass shall become reeds and rushes.

⁸A highway shall be there,
    and it shall be called the Holy Way;
the unclean shall not travel on it,
    but it shall be for God's people;
    no traveler, not even fools, shall go astray.
⁹No lion shall be there,
    nor shall any ravenous beast come up on it;
they shall not be found there,
    but the redeemed shall walk there.
¹⁰And the ransomed of the LORD shall return,
    and come to Zion with singing;
everlasting joy shall be upon their heads;
    they shall obtain joy and gladness,
    and sorrow and sighing shall flee away.

Commentary 1: Connecting the Reading with Scripture

The historical context of First Isaiah is most likely the political crisis of impending invasion by Assyria in the eighth century BCE. Judah is scrambling for security and is under pressure by the northern kingdoms of Israel and Syria to join in a coalition to repel Assyria. Judah rebuffs that option but considers the possibility of a coalition with Egypt. At all of this political maneuvering, the book of Isaiah scoffs. Repeatedly, the futility of pinning hopes on earthly powers is exposed. The prophet foretells the wrath of God against such pointless endeavors.

A literary feature of this lectionary text is the addition of verse 10. Most likely, it does not belong in the pericope. Its later provenance is an interesting literary detail but is not a hindrance to the exegete or preacher. The fact that verse 10 is included in the Third Sunday of Advent texts suggests that verse 10 is consistent with the themes of the Advent texts as a whole.

The literary location of chapter 35 can be described in a variety of ways. A particularly vivid description is that of John Goldingay, who memorably calls the six previous chapters, 28–33, the "hey, you!" chapters.[1] The first word of each of these chapters is an attention-getting *eui* or *en*, translated in various English translations as "woe!" or "alas!" or "see!" or, as Goldingay charmingly suggests, "hey, you!" The urgency of this form of address is clear, and the accumulated weight of prophetic warning is significant.

Finally, after the "hey, you!" chapters, a new section begins in chapter 34. Chapters 34 and 35 are a two-chapter diptych set as strong contrasting parallels. Isaiah 34 announces judgment on the nations; chapter 35 promises return and redemption. The stirring promises of restoration in Isaiah 35:1–10 cannot be understood apart from the broader context of Isaiah as a whole or apart from the narrower context of this diptych. The first part of the two-chapter pair is an unrelieved and unbroken account of God's judgment and resulting destruction. The second part is a sudden reversal of restoration and healing.

The contrasts between these two chapters are certainly striking. Chapter 34 recounts God's judgment against Edom; chapter 35 promises the restoration of Zion, or Judah. The contrasts extend even to creation. Chapter 34 identifies the thorns, thistles, and nettles of judgment (34:13), and chapter 35 identifies the reeds and rushes of abundance and life (35:7). The parched and lifeless land is so severe in chapter 34 that it has turned to burning pitch and sulfur (34:9); the renewed life of the land is so abundant in chapter 35 that dried grasses have turned into reeds swaying in pools of water (35:7). The animals of chapter 34 include scavengers like jackals and buzzards (34:13 and 34:15); in contrast, the animals of chapter 35 are leaping deer by flowing waters (35:6). No road exists for those judged by God (34:10), but the Holy Way, a road for God's people, extends through the fruitful land in 35:8. The desolation of chapter 34 contains no vestige of flourishing human habitation, as all is broken and rotting and dead; but fruitful human life is promised in chapter 35, as people are healed and thriving (35:3–6).

This diptych emphasizes a profound paradox that is seen throughout the book of Isaiah. The dual insistence of the prophet can be seen concisely in 35:4b: "Here is your God. He will come with vengeance, with terrible recompense. He will come and save you." The paradox of punishment and salvation is deep in Isaiah. It is not an easy paradox to understand or resolve and stands as a perennial tension in the life of faith.

Salvation has at least three aspects in this text. First, salvation includes both people and creation. We see this in both halves of the diptych. In Isaiah 34, creation as well as nations and peoples suffer the consequences of God's wrath. In Isaiah 35, creation and God's people receive the healing and joy of God's restoration. People, nations, land, plants, and animals: all are included both in judgment and in salvation.

Second, salvation does not remain a generic and abstract concept in Isaiah 35. The texture and particularity of salvation is unpacked in

1. John Goldingay, *The Theology of the Book of Isaiah* (Downers Grove, IL: IVP Academic, 2014), 58.

the images. Strong visual and truly stunning poetic images are everywhere: blooming flowers in landscapes that had been decimated by fire and flame, flowing rivers where there once were parched sands, leaping deer full of the joy of life where once there had been scavenging animals. Salvation is minutely detailed. It is also hospitable, reaching into aspects of the world often overlooked. It includes those who have physical and emotional impairments. The blind and the deaf and the lame are included. Those who are fearful and anxious are included. Salvation takes persons and creation where they are, in situations of limit and loss, and restores them.

Third, salvation is all-encompassing, both for present and future. Patricia Tull says that the vision of Isaiah 35 is for the future, "when justice and only justice inhabits the road" and for the present, when we carry "the insistent vision of what is meant to be."[2]

Several key words in this text reveal significant theological meaning about salvation. One of the most important words in the text, in 35:9, comes from the verbal root *ga'al*, "to redeem." The participle form is *go'ēl*, the redeemed. The meaning of *go'ēl* includes the implication of a generous sharing of resources in the context of a family relationship. Goldingay says that "it is of the essence of the idea of a *go'ēl* that the person who extends these resources does so on the basis of a family relationship that the *go'ēl* and the needy person share."[3]

The primary point of this text is that Yahweh accepts this family obligation. This is a striking insight. God's restoration of a wounded and broken people does not come from a divine place of external observation or detachment. God's restoration is a gracious divine action as a family member. The homiletical and pastoral potential of this key insight is substantial and evocative.

Another important word is *naqam*, often rendered "vengeance" in English, in verse 4. The word "vengeance" has unfortunate connotations of vindictive retribution laced with strong negative emotions. A better rendering of *naqam* would be "appropriate consequence of punishment." This rendering does not solve the paradox of God's judgment and God's mercy; that paradox is deep and wide in all of Isaiah. However, it does avoid the wrongful implication of divine reprisal.

The central message of Isaiah 35:1–10, along with the other lectionary texts of the Third Sunday of Advent A, emerges as "God is with us." The epistle text, James 5:7–10, like Isaiah 35, employs agricultural imagery that conveys renewal and hope. The Gospel text, Matthew 11:2–11, reassures a doubting John the Baptist that God's restoration is at hand, and Psalm 146:5–10 describes God's healing actions. All point to the primary Advent theme of longing for the fulfillment of God's plans for the healing and restoration of heaven and earth and all that is in them.

LEANNE VAN DYK

Commentary 2: Connecting the Reading with the World

Those who rise to preach each Sunday of Advent may never have seen blind eyes opened and deaf ears unstopped. However, most pastors have seen weak hands made strong and feeble knees made firm. They have seen someone find the strength to rise one more day in the face of a great struggle. They have watched the faithful, who, when confronted with fear, lean again on the Rock of Salvation. They have talked to the

young adult who tells of the Sunday school faith that gave them a whole lot of strength when the college years were not so easy. They have sat with the widower who learned that the abundant life in Christ that flourished in forty-five years of married life could also sustain in the years of life alone.

They have been humbled over and over again by those who, with just a glimpse of the majesty

---

2. Patricia Tull, *Isaiah 1–39* (Macon, GA: Smyth & Helwys Publishing, 2010), 519.

3. Goldingay, *Theology of Isaiah*, 58.

For Whom Did the Savior Come?

In coming to the world, Christ shows preference for certain categories of men; or rather, he causes us to see that there are human conditions which in themselves constitute an advantage with respect to his announcement of salvation. Thus Christ comes as Savior where the need for salvation is greater; his mission of salvation in that case is more proximate and more operative. . . .

Christ, who came for us all, Christ, who promises the fortune of salvation to those who are unfortunate, Christ will be reached by those who wish to reach him. His salvation will not be granted without our cooperation. His salvation is not magical, it is not automatic. It is not an inevitable predestination; it is not a gift imposed on those who do not wish to receive it. The fact of God's one-sided and overwhelming compassion does not dispense us from an untrammeled and personal commitment of good will on our part or from at least a conditional receptiveness. As a matter of fact, the coming of Christ into our midst causes the vocation to our freedom and the working out of our salvation to loom as a great challenge, as a fateful choice. Bidden as we are to a supernatural destiny, we are free and we are responsible for the choice of accepting the challenge or rejecting it. The moral drama of the world and of souls becomes mighty and fearful!

Pope Paul VI, "Whom Did Christ Come to Save, and From What?," in *Homilies on Christmas and Epiphany,* trans. Michael Campo (Baltimore: Palm Publishers, 1964), 74, 78.

of God and the nudge of the Spirit, have the strong hands and the firm knees to speak for those this culture would rather silence and to give to others in ways that shatter the idolatry of selfishness. They have stood at the grave with those who grieved and listened in wonder as with broken hearts they proclaim, "Christ is risen! He is risen indeed!"

So take a chance with the Hebrew prophet in Advent and offer the gathered community a word of hope and promise. At first, Isaiah 35 seems out of place. Scholars discuss whether this vision of Zion restored belongs in Second Isaiah or Third Isaiah. That might be one kind of "out of place." Isaiah 35 also sticks out in a less scholarly sense. Isaiah's self-contained kingdom description is a chapter surrounded on both sides by judgment, destruction, and battle. The familiar refrains of the peaceable kingdom are offered with nothing but words of despair and devastation coming before and after. In the life of faith, God's kingdom promise of grace and strength may be the most compelling when it is received as hope wanes.

Perhaps the preacher could invite consideration of the jarring juxtaposition of such a beautiful vision when suffering abounds. Samuel

Barber's stunning *Adagio for Strings* is perhaps best known for the times it has been played in funerals and at various memorial services after September 11, 2001. The striking beauty of the piece rises out of the grief and heartbreak of those listening as if such art refuses to be silenced by death. Another example could be found simply in nature, when a stunningly beautiful sunrise greets those who rise to survey the damage of a storm, a fire, or an earthquake. This follows nature's torment the night before. Days of struggle and putting life back together are yet to come. Creation's beauty is, for a moment, dropped right in the middle.

However, Isaiah's descriptions of creation rejoicing and singing, and the hot sand becoming a pool of refreshment, must be more than a bit of beauty intended to offset the reality of human suffering. In her unforgettable novel *Beloved*, Toni Morrison tells of the preacher Baby Suggs, who is the spiritual matriarch of a slave community. As Morrison puts it, Baby Suggs is an "uncalled, unrobed, unanointed" preacher who has nothing left to give after a lifetime of slavery but her heart.[4] Fairly early in the novel, there is a remembering of how the slave community would come out to hear Baby Suggs preach on a

4. Toni Morrison, *Beloved* (New York: Alfred A. Knopf, 1987), 87, later quotation page number in parentheses.

summer night from a flat rock in "The Clearing." The remembered sermon is about loving yourself, loving your flesh, loving your heart, and understanding yourself not as the slave owner sees you but as God created you. When she could say no more, the author tells, Baby Suggs stands up and starts to dance what "the rest of her heart had to say," as the gathered congregation opens their mouths and offers the song.

Morrison describes the music as "long notes held until the four-part harmony was perfect." Morrison's theological framing of the community gathered in "The Clearing" to listen and sing is gripping. About Baby Suggs's preaching, Morrison writes, "She told them that the only grace they could have was the grace they could imagine" (88).

Serving as both preacher and prophet to her community, Baby Suggs nurtures the sacred imagination of God's people when brokenness, oppression, and suffering threaten to tear away at the collective sense of what it means to be created in the image of God. With an appeal to the imagination and the promise of grace, she is a prophet of hope. Similar to Baby Suggs, Isaiah offers a message of hope for a community surrounded by despair. Here in chapter 35, the prophet once again lifts up the vision of God's triumphant kingdom. Of course, the image comes surrounded by devastation and war. For the sacred imagination of God's people requires spark and encouragement when suffering is all around. More than offering a contrast to human suffering or giving a slice of beauty to those in despair, Isaiah seeks to implant deep within God's people the yearning for a kingdom of righteousness.

When reading and preaching Isaiah 35 in Advent, the promise of the incarnation should not be missed. Put another way, the powerful and familiar images of the coming kingdom can easily overshadow the promise of Emmanuel and the affirmation of God's presence. The assurance comes in Isaiah's words to those who are afraid: "Here is your God. God will come with vengeance, with terrible recompense. God will come and save you" (Isa. 35:4). God's passion is on display in the intent to rescue; God's judgment is directed at all that threatens the coming kingdom. Here is your God. God will come and save you. It is the language of incarnation.

Perhaps the word of a prophet is to be experienced like a work of art. For one does not always experience a song or a poem in a linear, start-to-finish kind of way. That is not always how a poem means. An Advent reading of Isaiah 35 may best begin in the middle at verse 4 with "Here is your God!" The promise of an everlasting joy, where sorrow flees away, stands forever. Visions of the glory of the Lord and a highway to heaven for God's people shall seed the faithfuls' imaginations of the eternal. Grieving hearts, reminded once again of their loss as the nights grow longer, yearn to know of God's presence now. The young adult struggling to find a vocation and direction after several attempts to launch afresh comes to hear of God's promise today and tomorrow. It is an Advent word from Isaiah. For right in the middle of Isaiah's soaring promise of a victorious kingdom, he stops to whisper to those who are lost and hurting now that God is here now. God with us. God for us, now.

If the congregation is hearing Isaiah 35 in only one direction, if the church is reading from start to finish, then it would seem that Isaiah's vision of the Holy Way is a vision of the eternal highway of a future heaven yet to come. In Advent, why not invite the congregation to experience the prophet's word for the here and now, rather than just a promise for what is to come. Amid all of life's complexity, hear the prophet whisper the good news of God's promise of God with us. "Here is your God."

DAVID A. DAVIS

Third Sunday of Advent

Psalm 146:5–10

[5]Happy are those whose help is the God of Jacob,
　　whose hope is in the LORD their God,
[6]who made heaven and earth,
　　the sea, and all that is in them;
who keeps faith forever;
　　[7]who executes justice for the oppressed;
　　who gives food to the hungry.

The LORD sets the prisoners free;
　　[8]the LORD opens the eyes of the blind.
The LORD lifts up those who are bowed down;
　　the LORD loves the righteous.
[9]The LORD watches over the strangers;
　　he upholds the orphan and the widow,
　　but the way of the wicked he brings to ruin.

[10]The LORD will reign forever,
　　your God, O Zion, for all generations.
Praise the LORD!

Luke 1:46b–55

[46b]"My soul magnifies the Lord,
　　[47]and my spirit rejoices in God my Savior,
[48]for he has looked with favor on the lowliness of his servant.
　　Surely, from now on all generations will call me blessed;
[49]for the Mighty One has done great things for me,
　　and holy is his name.
[50]His mercy is for those who fear him
　　from generation to generation.
[51]He has shown strength with his arm;
　　he has scattered the proud in the thoughts of their hearts.
[52]He has brought down the powerful from their thrones,
　　and lifted up the lowly;
[53]he has filled the hungry with good things,
　　and sent the rich away empty.
[54]He has helped his servant Israel,
　　in remembrance of his mercy,
[55]according to the promise he made to our ancestors,
　　to Abraham and to his descendants forever."

Connecting the Psalm with Scripture and Worship

On the Third Sunday of Advent, *Gaudete* (Rejoice) Sunday, three different passages give voice to our rejoicing. Mary's glorious Magnificat in Luke's Gospel often receives our focus in worship, and it is full of joy. The few verses of Psalm 146 included in the lectionary provide a corroborating voice of rejoicing and of hope for a world where the hungry are fed, the prisoners are released, the blind can see, and justice is served. This psalm well supports a liturgical celebration built around the Magnificat. Isaiah 35 also adds imagery of deserts rejoicing and the wilderness being glad, also reflecting a reversal of injustice and suffering.

"Magnificat" is the first word we would hear, if we were to hear Mary's song in Latin. Her soul *magnifies* the Lord, and her spirit rejoices in God, her savior (Luke 1:46–47). Her song is not a halfhearted praise; this is more than "my soul thanks the Lord and I trust that he'll get me through this mess and things will turn out okay." Her song is much bigger. It shows that she, correctly, connects the details of her life to God's bigger plan for the world. If God can use a teenaged girl from a backwater town, then surely God will fill the hungry with good things and send the rich away hungry. Surely God will bring down the mighty and lift up the lowly. Mary's song becomes not a prophecy or prediction, but a description of reality. She does not even bother to use future tense. She does not sing "God will . . ." She sings, "God has . . ."

For Mary, the angel's annunciation of her role in Jesus' birth does not erase the challenges she still may face as an unmarried, pregnant teenager. Joy is not the absence of struggle or conflict. Joy comes in the connection to a greater story, to hope for more than can be seen at the present moment. Joy comes from the fulfillment of promises God made to our ancestors (v. 55).

"Happy are those whose help is the God of Jacob." What is announced in Psalm 146:5 is brought to fruition in the life of Mary. In verse 9 God brings the way of the wicked "to ruin."

The Hebrew verb עָוַת (*avath*) means "to be bent or crooked." It evokes the consistent refrain in biblical imagery of God's preference for straight, level paths, as opposed to the crooked paths on which the wicked travel. While the translation "the way of the wicked he brings to ruin" is correct, it loses the connection to righteous people walking God's straight paths, down clear and straight roads prepared in the wilderness. In the Gospel reading for the day, Jesus will say of John the Baptist, "See, I am sending my messenger ahead of you, who will prepare your way before you" (Matt. 11:10).

Themes of good, straight paths are also lifted up in today's reading from Isaiah 35:8: "A highway shall be there, and it shall be called the Holy Way; the unclean shall not travel on it, but it shall be for God's people; no traveler, not even fools, shall go astray." To those of a fearful heart, Isaiah says, "Be strong, do not fear! Here is your God" (Isa. 35:4) and offers them visions of water breaking forth in the desert, where burning sand becomes a pool (v. 7). He also echoes a vision of the blind receiving vision and hearing for the deaf. The promise is for "everlasting joy" to be on their heads, and "sorrow and sighing" to pass away (v. 10).

The NRSV translates verse 9 of the psalm as "strangers." The Hebrew word, גֵּר (*ger*), means "sojourner" or "resident alien." While "stranger" is an appropriate translation, it loses the connection to other sojourners in Scripture, such as Abraham, who was sent by God to be a sojourner in a foreign land. Sojourners, along with orphans and widows, in biblical literature are emblematic of vulnerable people. God's preference for the sojourners, the orphans, the widows is lifted up in the canticle of Mary. God "has brought down the powerful from their thrones, and lifted up the lowly" (Luke 1:52).

Glory to God[1] includes lovely hymns that give us songs to sing Mary's Magnificat. "My Soul Cries Out with a Joyful Shout (Canticle of the Turning)" by Rory Cooney (#100) and "My Soul Gives Glory to My God" by Miriam Therese

---

1. *Glory to God* (Louisville, KY: Westminster John Knox Press, 2013).

Winter (#99) both offer opportunities to use hymns as liturgy. "Could the world be about to turn?" is a question that is asked in "Canticle of the Turning" and that easily lends itself to a call to worship (see below) or a call to confession. "Sing Out, My Soul," a Taizé setting of the Magnificat (#646), could be sung as a prayer response, or during communion. Isaac Watts's paraphrase of Psalm 146, "I'll Praise My Maker," is set to OLD 113TH (#806). While not an Advent hymn, "Light Dawns on a Weary World" (#79) by Mary Louise Bringle captures well the joy of these texts: "We shall go out in joy."

A Sunday of rejoicing is a good prescription for people overwhelmed by the news of the world, stressed by the crush of Christmas preparations, or feeling no reason at all to rejoice. These lectionary texts for the Third Sunday of Advent all lift up the depth of rejoicing that is deeper than feelings of fleeting happiness, emotions that may be nice in the moment, but are not grounded in deeper theological concepts of justice, healing, vision, and provision. The word translated "happy" in Psalm 146:5a, "Happy are those whose help is the God of Jacob," is אַשְׁרֵי (from *esher*) and can also be translated "blessed."

People in the pews feeling overwhelmed, or in the midst of grief and loss, might find their hope renewed through a service emphasizing joy as blessedness, rather than happiness. If we preach God's vision of justice for the oppressed where the hungry are filled, perhaps people will find a straight path down which to journey through Advent toward the deep joy of Christmas.

Call to Worship (adapted from Psalm 146 and Luke 1)

Reader 1: Blessed are those whose help is the God of Jacob. Blessed are those whose hope is in the Lord their God, who made heaven and earth.

Reader 2: Our souls magnify the Lord, and our spirits rejoice in God our Savior, for God has looked with favor on us, humble servants of the Most High.

Reader 1: God is faithful forever and executes justice for the oppressed, gives food to the hungry. Could the world be about to turn?

Reader 2: God has brought down the powerful from their thrones, and lifted up the lowly; God has filled the hungry with good things, and sent the rich away empty. Could the world be about to turn?

Reader 1: The Lord watches over the strangers; God upholds the orphan and the widow. The Lord makes crooked the way of the wicked. Could the world be about to turn?

Reader 2: The Mighty One has done great things for us, and holy is God's name. God's mercy is for those who fear him from generation to generation.

Reader 1: May our souls cry out with a joyful shout as we worship this day.

MARCI AULD GLASS

James 5:7–10

> [7]Be patient, therefore, beloved, until the coming of the Lord. The farmer waits for the precious crop from the earth, being patient with it until it receives the early and the late rains. [8]You also must be patient. Strengthen your hearts, for the coming of the Lord is near. [9]Beloved, do not grumble against one another, so that you may not be judged. See, the Judge is standing at the doors! [10]As an example of suffering and patience, beloved, take the prophets who spoke in the name of the Lord.

Commentary 1: Connecting the Reading with Scripture

James emphasizes that his fellow Christians must "be patient," using the same imperative verb in verses 7 and 8. In both cases the phrase "the coming [*parousia*] of the Lord" follows. The meaning of being patient is further illustrated by the image of the farmer waiting for the precious crop from the earth (Jas. 5:7b). Only until the earth receives the early rain for plowing and planting seeds and the late rain for swelling and ripening the grain can he anticipate the harvest. Some may question if the Lord is too slow in coming. However, verse 8 clarifies that Christ's second coming is near (cf. Mark 1:15; Matt. 4:17).

Since the coming of the Lord is near, Christians must also strengthen their hearts. Paul relates Christ's strengthening of the believers' hearts to the judgment at his coming (1 Thess. 3:13). Yet James speaks more about judging one another in the community than the final judgment. In the situation of prevailing injustice, some believers doubt God's justice, instead grumbling against one another (Jas. 1:6–7; 5:9). So, judging others demonstrates a lack of patience. According to James, if one judges another, he judges the law. If he judges the law, he is not the doer of the law but a judge (4:11–12).

Who is the judge? "See, the Judge is standing at the doors" (5:9b). Be patient. Trust in God's justice, for "anger does not produce" God's justice (*dikaiosynē*, rendered "righteousness" in the NRSV 1:20). While the imagery of the judge standing at the doors highlights the nearness of

the *parousia*, James is concerned primarily with the present trials that the Christians face. He describes such trials as "suffering and patience" and gives two examples, the prophets and Job, who suffered afflictions but showed their endurance (5:10–11).

The themes of our passage are repeated from chapter 1. When one considers any trials (*peirasmoi*) nothing but joy, the testing of faith produces endurance (1:2–3). Anyone who endures temptation (*peirasmos*) is blessed and will receive the crown of life promised by God (1:12; 5:11). James's concern is not to explain the causes of suffering (theodicy), but to encourage the Christians to endure suffering. God does not test anyone because God is full of compassion and tender mercy (1:13–14; 5:11).

If the Letter of James was written around 60–70 CE, when the First Jewish-Roman War occurred (66–73 CE), it may reflect the suffering and disruption experienced by both Jews and Christians. Whether "the twelve tribes in the Dispersion [*diaspora*]" as the addressee (1:1) is literal or symbolic, the displacement of a religious minority group in the Roman Empire must cause suffering and "trials of any kind" (1:2). This may be the social context in which James urges the audience to care for the lowly and the humble (1:9; 4:6); orphans and widows (1:27); the poor and the oppressed (2:2–6); the naked and the hungry (2:15); the unpaid laborers and harvesters (5:4); and the suffering and the sick among them (5:13–14).

Many biblical passages portray God's righteousness in terms of retributive justice represented by violent punishment of the wicked at the Day of the Lord. James also describes that the coming of the Lord will bring condemnation and destruction, particularly to the rich who oppress the poor: "weep and wail for the miseries that are coming to you" (5:1). Judgment has already begun to besiege the rich. Notwithstanding, there are double-minded wealthy Christians in the assemblies, as well (1:9–10; 2:1–13; 4:1–10). Warning against the assemblies that show partiality and favoritism toward the rich, James admonishes them to fulfill the royal law: "love your neighbor as yourself." If they show no mercy, judgment will be without mercy. From this argument James draws the conclusion that "mercy triumphs over judgment" (2:8–13).

It is noteworthy that both those who endure the trials and the poor are promised recipients of God's love and rewards (1:12; 2:5). Does God show partiality? James highlights God's preferential option for the poor and the humble and the reversal of the present order (1:9–10; 4:6, 10). Trusting in God's justice in times of trial, those who practice mercy bear the fruit of endurance (patience) through the testing of faith—the faith "brought to completion by the works" (2:22; cf. Gal. 5:22). The fruit of justice is sown in peace by (or for) those who make peace (3:18).

The Christians are the first fruits of God's creatures (1:18). As his view of restorative justice includes creation, it is not accidental that James likes to use the imagery of heaven, earth, rain, and fruits, along with other aspects of the natural world (5:7, 12, 17–18; cf. 1:9–11). Despite being persecuted, "the just" (*dikaios*) patiently and fervently pray for the rain that will bring fruits on earth, as the prophet Elijah did (5:7, 16–18). Enduring hope for Christ's coming is doing justice and making peace on earth in the present time.

In our other lectionary readings, a couple of the same points can be made. First, the enduring hope of the coming of the Lord survives in times of trials and suffering. Second, such hope envisions the reversal of world order and the liberation of the oppressed. Last, the coming of Christ will bring the restoration of creation.

The wilderness, dry land, desert, burning sand, and thirsty ground are not where flowers blossom or places from which water springs (Isa. 35:1, 7). Yet the glory (presence) of the Lord will manifest in the wilderness, so God's people should strengthen their fearful hearts (Isa. 35:4). While God's salvation shall include judgment and recompense, the more prominent imagery is restoration of all creation: the healing of the blind, the deaf, the lame, and the speechless (vv. 5–6); the water bringing the barren desert back to life (v. 7); and the rebuilding of God's people in peace (vv. 8–10).

For the Virgin Mary, her conception was a trial, but in the presence of God (Luke 1:28) she is blessed not only by showing endurance but also with the grace granted to the lowly (Luke 1:39, 48; Jas. 4:6; 5:11). Extraordinarily, Christ's coming has been embodied in Mary so that she perceives and experiences the eschatological reversal in her. The powerful will be brought down, but the lowly will be lifted up. Whereas the hungry will be filled, the rich will be sent away empty. Reversal and restoration are proleptically fulfilled in her body, and her womb becomes the sign of hope for all the fruits on earth: "Blessed is the fruit of your womb" (Luke 1:42). The blessing was given by Elizabeth, and the child in her previously barren womb leaped for joy (v. 44).

The child who leaped for joy for the coming of Christ is John the Baptist. Just like Jesus, John in Matthew appears to proclaim in the wilderness that the kingdom of heaven has come near (Matt. 3:2). Now in prison, he waits not only for trial but also for the coming of Christ (Matt. 11:3). According to Jesus, heaven's reign has dawned in his healing all of the wounds and brokenness of Israel (v. 5). John himself is the one standing on the margins, and now as a captive, but the reversal occurs when Jesus blesses him: "among those born of women no one has arisen greater than John the Baptist" (v. 11a). Blessed is the fruit of the womb. If the least in heaven's reign is greater than John, a fruit of justice sown in peace (v. 11b), Advent is full of hope.

JIN YOUNG CHOI

Commentary 2: Connecting the Reading with the World

As the culture begins the year-end celebration with bright lights, intense colors, and jolly music, the mood in the church turns sober. In contrast to the greens and reds festooning department stores, the church brings out its somber purple. In marked contrast to "Jingle Bells," "Winter Wonderland," and "Chestnuts Roasting on an Open Fire," the lyrics of Advent hymns are stately: "Let all mortal flesh keep silence, and with fear and trembling stand . . ." and "O come, O come, Emmanuel, and ransom captive Israel, that mourns in lonely exile here . . ."

The contrasts of Advent reflect the paradoxical polarities of Christian faith: strength in weakness, power in self-emptying, winning in losing, receiving in giving, living in dying, the almightiness in a manger, resurrection in crucifixion. The polarities happen in each verse of the beloved hymn "O Come, O Come Emmanuel": "Disperse the gloomy clouds of night, and death's dark shadows put to flight. Rejoice! Rejoice!"

Advent is a reminder that waiting is a major biblical theme and, at the same time, an evocative description of the human condition, elegantly expressed in Samuel Beckett's *Waiting for Godot*. In this classic drama, two characters, Vladimir and Estragon, wait for Godot, who never comes. The experience of waiting—to grow up, graduate, get a job, make money, have a family, and even find happiness—is universally human. It is also eloquently represented in every child's waiting for Christmas morning, as well as in the familiar annual complaint in the church about singing morose hymns and waiting to sing the familiar carols while the culture outside is in full celebration mode. Pastors hear it every year on the Sundays of Advent: "Why can't we sing our favorite carols, 'Joy to the World!' and 'Hark! The Herald Angels Sing,' instead of those gloomy Advent hymns?"

The Third Sunday of Advent is known as *Gaudete* or Rejoice Sunday. The candle on the Advent wreath this Sunday is a lively pink, a reminder that while we are waiting in darkness impatiently, redemption is on the way. The reading from the Letter of James has always been something of a puzzle. Martin Luther famously called James an "epistle of straw" because of its apparent emphasis on works instead of the grace that Luther believed was the central message of the gospel. Modern scholarship suggests that the community to which the letter was written was beset by prejudice, oppression, and persecution. The surrounding culture found the members of this community too different to tolerate because of their beliefs and practices. Imperial Rome began to suspect that, because they affirmed the lordship of Jesus Christ, they must be disloyal to the emperor.

The writer of James counsels patience, but it is a nuanced patience. It is not a stoic acceptance of whatever was happening but anticipatory—an "until the coming of the Lord" sort of patience. Current reality is not the permanent, final state of affairs. The Lord is coming! The reference to a farmer's waiting is nuanced as well. Anyone who knows anything about farming knows that farmers do more than sit around and wait for rain. Farmers continue to work hard toward the ultimate goal of a robust crop. So it is an active waiting, preparing while waiting for the coming day of promised fulfillment.

Our fast moving, frenetic lifestyle, which is pervasive throughout modern American culture, almost demands impatience. Urban traffic, gridlock on the freeway at rush hour, long security lines at the airport all strain whatever patience we have. Impatient stress is so pronounced that medical research keeps warning us about the negative effects of stress on our health, and spiritual directors have to teach us the discipline of deep breathing to protect both health and sanity.

We have also witnessed how patient waiting can and sometimes must evolve into impatience. Leading clergy in Birmingham, Alabama, in April 1963 urged Martin Luther King Jr. and the Southern Christian Leadership Council to be patient in the struggle against racial segregation and for equal justice. King's response to his fellow clergy, "Letter from Birmingham Jail," is now a classic in the literature of protest and liberation. He expressed his respect for his fellow clergy, but wrote, "'Wait' almost always has meant 'Never.'" He said African Americans had been waiting a long time and had waited enough and quoted one of our distinguished jurists who said, "Justice delayed is justice denied." Progress, King noted, takes not only time but also "tireless effort of people of good will."[1]

The reference in the James text to prophets as an example of suffering patience is so peculiar and paradoxical that one wonders if the author is employing sarcasm, a tongue-in-cheek, insider joke. Anyone familiar with Hebrew Scripture, and the community James was certainly addressing, knew that prophets are not patient. The prophets bore suffering, to be sure, but Amos and Jeremiah were anything but patient.

The situation around the community that James was addressing was such that nuanced patience was undoubtedly a survival tactic. The enormous power of the cultural, social, and political structures that were oppressing and persecuting was so overwhelming that expressions of impatience would have been futile if not outright dangerous. In this instance, patience was sound, practical advice.

One who practiced a faithful patience was Dietrich Bonhoeffer, a victim of profound oppression and persecution. After resisting the Nazi regime in his preaching, writing, leading, and teaching at an underground theological seminary, Bonhoeffer's patience gave way to his profound conviction that "when Christ calls a man, he bids him come and die."[2] Arrested by Nazi authorities for his participation in the resistance and an attempt to assassinate Adolf Hitler, Bonhoeffer (as King did a generation later) left a priceless legacy in letters written from a prison cell.

On December 17, 1943, he wrote to his parents from Tegel Prison:

> For a Christian there is nothing particularly difficult about Christmas in a prison cell. I dare say it will have more meaning and will be observed with greater sincerity here in this prison than in places where all that survives of the feast is the name. . . . Christ was born in a stable because there was no room for him in the inn—these are the things that a prisoner can understand better than anyone else. For him the Christmas story is glad tidings in a very real sense. And that faith gives him a part in the communion of saints, a fellowship transcending the bounds of time and space and reducing the moments of confinement here to insignificance.[3]

Bonhoeffer's Christmas in a prison cell is a reminder that Christians live and wait in hope for promised deliverance, redemption, and salvation, sometimes patiently and sometimes in faithful impatience.

The writer interrupts his exhortation to be patient with a peculiar admonition: "Beloved, do not grumble against one another" (Jas. 5:9a). Apparently there were divisive issues within the community that erupted in personal complaints and attacks. Once again, Scripture reminds us that the way believers regard and relate to one another has evangelical implications. Arguing, quarreling, and name calling, Christians discredit the gospel they espouse. Nothing does more damage to the mission of the church, in the twenty-first century as well as the first, than our shameful disunity.

JOHN M. BUCHANAN

---

1. Martin Luther King Jr., "Letter from a Birmingham Jail," *Christian Century*, June 12, 1963, 767, 770.
2. Dietrich Bonhoeffer, *The Cost of Discipleship* (London: Macmillan Co., 1937), 79.
3. Dietrich Bonhoeffer, *Letters and Papers from Prison* (New York: Macmillan Co., 1953), 77–78.

Matthew 11:2–11

²When John heard in prison what the Messiah was doing, he sent word by his disciples ³and said to him, "Are you the one who is to come, or are we to wait for another?" ⁴Jesus answered them, "Go and tell John what you hear and see: ⁵the blind receive their sight, the lame walk, the lepers are cleansed, the deaf hear, the dead are raised, and the poor have good news brought to them. ⁶And blessed is anyone who takes no offense at me."

⁷As they went away, Jesus began to speak to the crowds about John: "What did you go out into the wilderness to look at? A reed shaken by the wind? ⁸What then did you go out to see? Someone dressed in soft robes? Look, those who wear soft robes are in royal palaces. ⁹What then did you go out to see? A prophet? Yes, I tell you, and more than a prophet. ¹⁰This is the one about whom it is written,

'See, I am sending my messenger ahead of you,
who will prepare your way before you.'

¹¹Truly I tell you, among those born of women no one has arisen greater than John the Baptist; yet the least in the kingdom of heaven is greater than he."

Commentary 1: Connecting the Reading with Scripture

John the Baptist, one of Jesus' earliest supporters, had given an enthusiastic endorsement of Jesus' future ministry and messianic identity at the time of baptism (Matt. 3:11–14). He now appears to have turned ambivalent about his ministry. Since Matthew has already informed his readers that John had heard about the "deeds of the Messiah" (11:2, my trans.), the readers are left wondering why John had sent his disciples to Jesus seeking confirmation of his messianic identity. Perhaps the nature of Jesus' ministry, as well as the manner in which it had been unfolding, did not match John's expectations. It is in this context that Jesus' words "Blessed is anyone who does not stumble on account of me" (11:6, my trans.) become significant.

John's ambivalence possibly suggests that the kind of reports he had received about Jesus did not convince him sufficiently that he was indeed the awaited Messiah. We learn that people have given John reports of Jesus' ministry, but we are not privy to the exact content of what he had heard. Did they, John's disciples, accurately and fully represent what Jesus had been doing as part of his ministry? Was there a disconnect between

Jesus' actual deeds and people's interpretation of them? Jesus' response to John's question sheds some light on these questions.

Jesus instructs John's disciples to "go and tell John what you hear and see" (v. 5). It is worth noting that two of the miracles Jesus highlights as signifying his ministry are about seeing and hearing. The blind receive sight, and the deaf hear. The same two verbs, "hear" and "see," occur in Jesus' commandment to John's disciples. Jesus' ministry has been primarily about enabling people to see and hear the things they could not see or hear. Yet some people—John's disciples included—could not perceive his true messianic nature. Perhaps, they did not fully and accurately report what they heard and saw. John's question at the beginning of the story pertains to Jesus' messianic identity. Jesus turns it into a question about his audience and about their ability, or lack thereof, to properly hear and see him and respond to the acts of God they have witnessed.

On a metaphorical level, Jesus' ministry has been about enabling people to sense the reality around them in entirely new ways and to respond to it prophetically. Similarly, all of the miracles performed by Jesus—the blind seeing, the deaf hearing, the lame walking, lepers being cleansed, and the dead being raised—were subversive socially, culturally, and politically. More specifically, cleansing people of leprosy would have had the effect of restoring outcasts into the society, and dead being raised indicated a revival in the community. All these deeds testify to the messianic nature of Jesus' mission. However, as Jesus implies in 11:5, those who had witnessed them did not testify sufficiently to his ministry.

Jesus also highlights a disconnect between the nature of John's ministry on the one hand and people's expectations of him on the other. He begins by contrasting John the Baptist with the religious and political elite. In chapter 3, Matthew had implicitly critiqued the lifestyle of religious leaders and the political elite by highlighting that John embraced an alternative lifestyle, as evidenced in his clothing, food, and location. In this story, the Matthean Jesus is more explicitly contrasting the lifestyle of the elite with that of John. Furthermore, by talking about a reed swayed by the wind, Jesus is likely referring to Herod Antipas, who had imprinted the symbol of the reed on certain Roman coins. Jesus is, with these words, juxtaposing Herod with John the Baptist (vv. 7–8). This juxtaposition offers a critique of the elite, but it also informs Jesus' audience that joining the movement John had initiated entails significant changes to one's lifestyle, ethos, and worldview. It is a call to people to alter their expectations of John's ministry and of themselves. Jesus also seems to be highlighting the strength and courage John had demonstrated in the face of persecution and unjust structures.

There are several intertextual allusions in this text. References to the attire of John and the elite (v. 8) conjure up for the readers memories of prophet Elijah (1 Kgs. 22). John dresses in a manner that is very similar to Elijah. Elijah challenges kings who are dressed in soft robes like those mentioned here. In 1 Kings 22 and 2 Kings 1, those royal figures dressed in fine attire incur the wrath of Yahweh by turning to foreign gods such as Baal-zebub, the god of Ekron, in times of crisis. In Matthew, the religious and political elite anger the prophet because of their lifestyle, which was sustained at the expense of

people at the margins. Both Elijah and John have challenged people associated with centers of power and have paid a heavy price for it.

By calling attention to John's ministry, specifically the subversive nature of his mission, Jesus is also predicting the direction his own ministry will take. In other words, he is positioning himself as the successor to John and as the inheritor of his movement. In fact, when Jesus hears about John's death, he goes to the very wilderness where John had ministered prior to his imprisonment. A large crowd follows him into the wilderness (Matt. 14:13–14). Along those lines, John's question "Are you the one to come?" is not just about Jesus' messianic role and identity. Within the context of this text, which highlights John's imprisonment and foreshadows his death at the hands of Herod Antipas, the question is also about whether Jesus will continue the mission John had initiated.

The phrase "the one to come" recalls Matthew 3:11, where Jesus is introduced as the one who comes after John. The Greek word *opisō* has the connotation of following someone in their footsteps. It refers to someone who will continue what the other has done. John is asking Jesus for the assurance that Jesus will indeed continue the mission he, John, had initiated. Now that John is in prison and possibly looking at the end of his mission, such an assurance becomes especially significant.

The question of continuity becomes clearer in the subsequent section, where Jesus draws parallels between John's mission and his own future ministry. Jesus also suggests at one point that, in the end, his own fate will resemble that of John. Matthew informs his readers later that John was executed by Herod Antipas (14:6–11). Similarly, Jesus will also face death at the hands of political and religious leaders for the subversive work he carries out.

This pericope is certainly about the parallels between John's ministry and Jesus' own mission. Both Jesus and John have been engaged in extraordinary ministry and called people's attention to unjust political and social structures, leading to confrontation with people in power. Seen in that light, this text is about having the ability and willingness to perceive things in new ways. More importantly, it is about having the courage to speak and report what one sees. Truth, in whatever form it occurs, has the capacity to bring about change and transformation in society, but truth depends on reliable messengers to be passed on from one location to another and from one generation to the next. The question for modern audiences is not whether John's disciples were reliable messengers but whether we are willing to be such courageous messengers, even when doing so might entail a heavy cost.

RAJ NADELLA

Commentary 2: Connecting the Reading with the World

Immediately preceding this passage, in verse 1, we have one of the phrases that is traditionally seen by modern Matthean scholars as a sign of a change in literary sections of Matthew: "after he finished" (NRSV "Now when Jesus had finished," 7:28; 11:1; 13:53; 19:1; 26:1), of which there are traditionally five (perhaps as a way to model a kind of Matthean Pentateuch). Thus we have shifted to the proposed Book Two of this Gospel, often called the "Missionary Discourse" because of an emphasis on traveling to spread the word.[1] So perhaps we are to understand this particular passage as a clarification of who and what, precisely, we are spreading the word about when questions arise! This lends a certain weight to what follows as the "opening words" of a major section.

In this passage, "the one who is to come" is equated with "the Messiah." John clearly hopes that he has been correct in his ideas about the Nazarene. When it comes to "the one"/"Messiah," the corresponding action is wait. John and the people have been waiting. The earliest Christians also waited for the coming change (see 2 Pet. 3:13: "But, in accordance with his promise, we wait for new heavens and a new earth, where righteousness is at home"). Note that the word "wait" in Matthew 11 (from *prosdokaō*) is not the more common term that appears in the frequent calls in Hebrew literature, especially in the Psalms, to "wait upon the Lord," which uses *hypomenō* (cf. Isa. 40:31; Mic. 7:7). Clearly, what is described here is not a pious patience.

It is crucial to take careful note of the evidence of the kingdom of God, according to Jesus. He does not merely say, "I'm here. That's all the proof you need!" For the evidence of the kingdom is justice and change—change for the blind, the lame, the poor, and even the dead. We see for whom the change is occurring: those who suffer. As in all times, it is the poor and disenfranchised whose oppressive living conditions, lack of care, and hard labor cause them to suffer the lion's share of disease and premature death. In many Western societies, the poor have to exist on fast food and processed packaged sugar, both of which are slowly destroying their health. In Jesus' famous synagogue homily in Luke 4 (where Jesus reads from Isaiah's promises in Isa. 61), Jesus uses the prophetic passage to announce his own mission of liberation—a liberation that will burst nationalist boundaries and include the suffering of all peoples.

So, what are we waiting for? In this passage, a certain impatience is discernible in Jesus. He honors John, but there is a certain edge to his gentle needling of those listening to him, stating perhaps, "What are you waiting for?"

In this passage, Jesus asks the crowds about their curiosity in regard to John: did they expect to see a "reed shaken in the wind"? The reed (*kalamos*) occurs in the LXX on a few occasions simply as the plant that grows by water (Ps. 68:30). Hence, many commentaries suggest that Jesus was asking, in so many words, "Did you go to see something so commonplace as the reeds by the Jordan?"[2] However, the very same phrase (with perhaps a pleasant euphonic cadence, *kalamon . . . anemou*) appears in 3 Maccabees 2:22 in reference to God's punishing of Ptolemy IV: "He shook him on this side and that as a reed is shaken by the wind, so that he

1. Dale C. Allison, "Matthew," in J. Barton and J. Muddiman, eds., *The Oxford Bible Commentary* (Oxford: Oxford University Press, 2001), 858.

2. Ulrich Luz, *Matthew 8–20*, Hermeneia (Minneapolis: Fortress Press, 2001), 138.

lay helpless on the ground and, besides being paralyzed in his limbs, was unable even to speak, since he was smitten by a righteous judgment."

The earliest proposed dates for 3 Maccabees (second century BCE) and even the latest proposed dates (30–40 CE) would still predate the Gospels. If it might therefore be supposed that a "reed shaken by the wind" alludes to the powerlessness of a person in the face of superior might (in this case, God's might over an oppressive ruler!), then is it possible that a combination of this use with a near reference to royalty and wealth—that is, those who wear "soft robes" in "palaces"—would suggest a rather strong political commentary from Jesus?

Is Jesus thus asking whether people were hoping that John, like Elijah before him, would enact some kind of direct punishment on the wealthy and powerful (certainly well within common prophetic themes)? Did they think that if John were really someone impressive, he would have been a leader in "soft clothing" (Luke 7:25 has "fine" clothing)? This would mean Jesus is saying, in effect, "You are looking in the wrong place for that kind of people."

Either way, Jesus follows this up by talking about how important John actually is. In the context of a political commentary, this would make some interesting sense. If John were expected to be powerful, perhaps to lead some kind of revolt or even miraculously to enact some kind of demonstration of God's power, as with Elijah, then Jesus' response is quite striking, for as important as John is, "you" are at least as important as he is! In the Old Testament, the term for "least" (*mikroteros*, constructed from *mikros*, "small") appears in Gideon's description of himself as the least or smallest in his family (Judg. 6:15) and Benjamin as the "youngest" or "smallest" of the remaining brothers (Gen. 42:32).

What Jesus thus seems to be saying is that his revolution is neither a violent revolution of vengeful violence (which would allow you to watch someone ending up as powerless as a reed shaken in the wind when confronted with God's mighty power) nor an uprising of a powerful few. By telling the common people that "they" are as important, indeed just as powerful, as John is "in kingdom terms," Jesus is making a profoundly Gandhi-like call on "the masses." Such a reading would perhaps seem exaggerated, were it not for the passages that immediately follow our section: "From the days of John the Baptist until now the kingdom of heaven has suffered violence, and the violent take it by force. For all the prophets and the law prophesied until John came; and if you are willing to accept it, he is Elijah who is to come. Let anyone with ears listen!" (Matt. 11:12–15).

Gil Scott-Heron, in reference to black liberation movements in the 1960s and 1970s, wrote a poem (and then song) titled "The Revolution Will Not Be Televised." One way of reading this often-quoted line is that social change is not something we can simply watch with little participation, like the evening news. It is not proffered by celebrities (political or media) on our behalf. It would be hard to think of a better modern "interpretation" of our passage here, where Jesus chides the masses who flock to see John, hoping that they will come to see something—something that will be done for them. As great as John was, you are all even greater in terms of the kingdom of God! The Advent will not be televised! It will be lived out in the prophetic witness of the people of God through which oppressive power structures are resisted and reversed.

DANIEL L. SMITH-CHRISTOPHER

Fourth Sunday of Advent

Isaiah 7:10–16
Psalm 80:1–7, 17–19

Romans 1:1–7
Matthew 1:18–25

Isaiah 7:10–16

[10]Again the LORD spoke to Ahaz, saying, [11]Ask a sign of the LORD your God; let it be deep as Sheol or high as heaven. [12]But Ahaz said, I will not ask, and I will not put the LORD to the test. [13]Then Isaiah said: "Hear then, O house of David! Is it too little for you to weary mortals, that you weary my God also? [14]Therefore the Lord himself will give you a sign. Look, the young woman is with child and shall bear a son, and shall name him Immanuel. [15]He shall eat curds and honey by the time he knows how to refuse the evil and choose the good. [16]For before the child knows how to refuse the evil and choose the good, the land before whose two kings you are in dread will be deserted."

Commentary 1: Connecting the Reading with Scripture

Isaiah 7–8 was originally an account of the prophet's advice to Ahaz, king of Judah, in light of the Syro-Ephraimite War of 734–733 BCE (see 2 Kgs. 16:1–20 and contrast 2 Chr. 28). In our text, Ahaz is sometimes referred to as "the house of David." Syria is variously referred to as "Aram," "Damascus" (the capital), and "Rezin" (the king). The northern kingdom is "Ephraim," "Israel," "Samaria" (the capital), and "Pekah" or "the son of Remaliah" (the king). A bit like a Russian novel, the passage requires keeping these references in mind in order to keep the characters straight.

The crisis occurred when the Assyrians, ruled by Tiglath-pileser III, began to move west from Mesopotamia toward Syria and Israel. The leaders of those two countries appealed to Ahaz of Judah to join with them in resisting the Assyrian threat, but Ahaz refused. Rezin and Pekah then threatened to engineer a coup and put someone called "the son of Tabeel" on the throne of Judah, obviously assuming that he would cooperate in their coalition.[1]

For the prophet, the issue is whether to trust the faithfulness of God's covenant promises to the Davidic dynasty or to choose instead to make a pragmatic decision to submit to Assyria (the choice that Ahaz in fact made, 2 Kgs. 16:7–9). In his efforts to persuade Ahaz to trust God, Isaiah assures the king that the coalition will not succeed, being led by mere humans, who cannot stand against God (Isa. 7:7–9). Then the Lord, through the prophet, invites Ahaz to ask for a sign of God's faithfulness, but Ahaz refuses with a hypocritically pious claim that he "will not put the LORD to the test" (v. 12). This is the context for the sign that Ahaz receives anyway: the sign of Immanuel, which means "God with us" (vv. 10–16).

The notice that God or the Lord "was/will be with" a person or group signals throughout the Old Testament that, despite threatening circumstances, the presence of God brings assurance and the faithfulness of God will bring deliverance. This is said of Ishmael (Gen. 21:20), Joseph (Gen. 39:2, 3, 21, 23), Joshua (Josh. 3:7; 6:27), the tribe of Judah (Judg. 1:19), "the house of Ephraim" (Judg. 1:22), the judges (Judg. 2:18), Samuel (1 Sam. 3:19), David (1 Sam. 18:12, 14, 28; 2 Sam. 5:10; 1 Chr. 11:9), the early reign of Solomon (2 Chr. 1:1), Asa (2 Chr. 15:9), Jehoshaphat (2 Chr. 17:3), Hezekiah

---

1. Peter D. Miscall, *Isaiah*, 2nd ed. (Sheffield: Sheffield Phoenix Press, 2003), 47.

(2 Kgs. 18:7), God's people (Isa. 41:10; 45:14), and Daniel (Dan. 4:8; 5:11). In fact, it is the explicit notice that "the Lord was with" Hezekiah (2 Kgs. 18:7) that reinforces the claim of some scholars that Hezekiah is the one whose birth is predicted in Isaiah 7:14.

However, scholarship on Isaiah has not determined with certainty who the "young woman"[2] in 7:14 was in Isaiah's historical context and, therefore, who the promised child was supposed to be, whether Ahaz's son Hezekiah (the consensus) or someone else. In its present form, the book of Isaiah does not require a solution to this question. Constructed probably in the sixth century BCE from oracles and historical accounts handed down and preserved through the exile, Isaiah as it now stands is a testimony to the faithfulness of the covenant-keeping God, as well as a call to trust that ever-present God in the midst of the horrific destruction of dearly held hopes and dreams for the future. God provided righteous leadership for God's people in the person of Hezekiah and promises God's own presence through threatening times.

However, even a righteous leader does not guarantee the political future of God's people as they prefer to imagine it. The covenant with the descendants of David, apparently unconditional in 2 Samuel 7:12–16, is qualified in 1 Chronicles 28:4–8. The line of David will continue "if [Solomon and his descendants] continue resolute in keeping [God's] commandments and ordinances." By the time of the final construction of Isaiah as we have it today, it had become clear that because of the failure of people and kings to remain faithful, God has chosen to work through "the great empires of Assyria, Babylon, and Persia."[3] God has kept the promise of Immanuel, never abandoning the people even in their idolatry, but has not spared them the humiliation of defeat and subjugation by imperial powers that do not acknowledge the Lord.

The prophet warns Ahaz that although the Syro-Ephraimite coalition against Judah will fail, Assyria will sweep over Judah, shaving it like a razor (Isa. 7:20), leaving it a wasteland of briars and thorns (7:23–25) and overwhelmed as in a flood (8:5–8). This will happen even though God is with Judah (8:8, 10b), but the devastation will not last forever, because a remnant will be preserved (7:3). Although Hezekiah will renounce his father's treaty with Assyria (2 Kgs. 18:7), and Jerusalem will not be taken (2 Kgs. 19:32–37), all of Judah except for Jerusalem will be devastated, and Hezekiah will eventually be forced to strip the temple of its treasures to pay tribute to Assyria (2 Kgs. 18:13–16).

The theme of judgment and redemption in our passage pervades the whole of Isaiah in its present form, aligning it with the Deuteronomic history and the other prophetic books. The order of the readings for the Fourth Sunday of Advent moves from Isaiah to Psalm 80, a communal lament of the defeated and humiliated people of God, who cry out for deliverance. If only God's face would shine on them (Ps. 80:3, 7, 19), they would be saved. In Psalm 80:17 the people call for God's hand to be upon "the one at your right hand, the one whom you made strong for yourself." Whatever the original reference, in the context of the other readings for this Sunday, the Christian congregation is invited to hear a call for God to send the promised deliverer whose appearance will not only restore the people's fortunes, but will also enable their obedience (v. 18: "Then we will never turn back from you; give us life, and we will call on your name").

When the author of Matthew's Gospel cites Isaiah 7:14 to alert his audience that God is once again raising up a ruler from the line of David (Matt. 1:1–17) to deliver God's people, he is appealing to them to trust in the God who has always been faithful, even in the midst of sin and judgment. At last the Savior has arrived, just as the prophet had promised and the people had cried out for. This new deliverer represents not only God's presence, but also God's solution for the problem that had led to conquest and exile in the first place: "You are to name him Jesus, for he will save his people from their sins."

---

2. The Hebrew word that the NRSV translates "young woman" has a more general meaning than another word in Hebrew that precisely means "virgin." See Joseph Blenkinsopp, *Isaiah 1–39*, Anchor Bible 19 (New York: Doubleday, 2000), 233, or any other commentary on Isaiah.

3. Miscall, *Isaiah*, 24.

Jesus' commission to preach to the Gentiles at the end of Matthew (28:18–20) is then taken up by the apostle Paul, who writes to the Roman Christians that he has been sent "to bring about the obedience of faith among all the Gentiles for the sake of his name, including yourselves who are called to belong to Jesus Christ." Jesus' Davidic descent (Rom. 1:3) and the prophetic promise of Scripture (v. 2) complete the resonance with the other readings.

SHARYN DOWD

Commentary 2: Connecting the Reading with the World

What exactly is the nature of God's offer of a sign to King Ahaz? When God says to make it as "deep as Sheol or high as heaven" (Isa. 7:11), what does that mean? Is this a willingness to enter into a meaningful dialogue on the part of God, or is this something more akin to a genie dispensing wishes to the one who has rubbed a magic lamp? Whatever we may think, Isaiah's account is not a whimsical story about wish fulfillment. This is a call for faithfulness in the face of crisis and a declaration of God's willingness to act on behalf of God's people.

Considering the various dynamics at play in this moment in history, the threats faced by Judah, the shifting alliances at work in the world, Ahaz might have asked for a glimpse of the future, some sense of potential well-being, a theophany like what Isaiah himself experienced in the temple in Jerusalem. Frankly, these are exactly the sort of things that we ourselves might ask of God if we were offered a sign. What will our world look like in the next decade? Is there some reassurance for us that life will be filled with possibility and prosperity? Can you show the divine face, O Lord, or let us hear your voice in such a way that your presence will become real, tangible, of relevance for our lives?

Imagine the meeting of a long-range-planning task force interrupted suddenly by God's offer of a sign. How would a typical group of church members respond? What sign would they request? More participants in worship? An expanding outreach budget? A more active youth group? An end to strife within the congregation? Is this the shape our requested sign might take? Is this really what it means to be the people of God when the world is faced with crisis? So many questions! This is God talking. If our heads do not spin with the possibilities, we are not paying attention.

In the Second Helvetic Confession, written in 1561 by Swiss reformer Heinrich Bullinger, there is a reminder of what it means to be God's people at work in the world. In a paragraph from chapter 27 titled "Of the Catholic and Holy Church of God, and of the One Only Head of the Church," Bullinger cites John 10:5, 27: "My sheep hear my voice and I know them and they follow me. . . . They do not know the voice of strangers."[4] Years ago, on a church-related camping trip, I and some friends found ourselves in a large open field by a river. On the far side of the field was a flock of sheep. When the sheep became aware of our presence, they began to gather around us, expectant and curious. Being one never to pass up a funny situation, I began to address the sheep the way a politician might address a rally, hamming it up for my friends. Within seconds the sheep began to turn and walk away, first one or two at a time, and then in larger groups until they were all gone. The joke was on me! But here was a literal demonstration of the sheep not knowing the voice of a stranger.

Indeed, the church finds its truest purpose when it hears and responds to the word of God in Jesus Christ, "the One Only Head of the Church." So when we read God's offer of a sign to Ahaz, we should take it as no small matter. Those fully attuned to God's voice and God's will heed God's message. If God offers a choice, the people of God are most faithful

---

4. *The Constitution of the Presbyterian Church (U.S.A.)*, Part I, *Book of Confessions* (Louisville, KY: Office of the General Assembly, Presbyterian Church (U.S.A.), 2014), 112.

when they acknowledge the offer and seek to be enabled by it.

Note that the Lord has set *two* choices before Ahaz. The implicit one is to trust in God and the divine promise of salvation. The implied one is to trust in human wisdom and human aspirations, while ignoring God altogether. The choice that Ahaz makes reveals the king's mindset. Ahaz has chosen typical human understanding, what we would call a pragmatic or practical way by which to evaluate his circumstances and those of the nation he rules. Ahaz knows that to accept God's offer of a sign at this moment will set limits on his ability to act independently and will draw him into God's plan and God's desired outcome, which the king himself does not appear willing to follow. Where God offers the divine will, Ahaz would rather invest in strategies and diplomacy to solve his problems.

Ahaz gives his reply: "I will not ask, and I will not put the LORD to the test" (v. 12). In doing so, the king displays amazing disingenuousness. While God was willing to engage Ahaz honestly, the king has offered up a weak excuse that is as dishonest as it is lacking in faithfulness. In act 3, scene 2 of *Romeo and Juliet*, Juliet's nurse speaks of Romeo in harsh terms: "There's no trust, no faith, no honesty in men. All perjured, all forsworn, all naught, all dissemblers."[5] The nurse might have been speaking of Ahaz, who in his response does not fool the prophet. Isaiah, as God's witness, sees that the king has "no faith, no honesty," and is in fact a perjurer and dissembler.

Isaiah's retort to Ahaz begins with a clear recognition of what the king is doing. The king is not fooling anyone. Now, far from giving the king a clear and unmistakable sign, God, through the prophet, speaks in ambiguous terms about a young woman, a baby, and an unspecified time in which the will of God is to be accomplished. What woman? What child? There is no way to be sure. Only hindsight based on events centuries later allows us to know.

The church deals with what may appear to the rest of the world as divine ambiguity in much of its life and work. As a human institution called into being by God, the church reaches its greatest clarity when it adheres to the will of its Creator through faithful engagement and active discernment, living in openness to what it believes God to be calling it to do, even at the risk of losing social prominence or cultural relevance. When the church veers off in a direction of its own choosing, when it puts even survival ahead of God's will, the path becomes murky.

Advent offers the church an opportunity to reflect on this course of direction. even as we prepare for the coming of God's reign in its fullness. The choice before us is far more profound than whether to use purple or blue candles in the Advent wreath. It is the challenge to welcome God's implicit offer of guidance and grace, while consciously turning from the desire to dictate our own future with programs and strategies designed to lead us to what the world might call success. During Advent preachers can help their congregations to discern which choices to make and to recommit themselves to the salvation God is offering.

JAMES D. FREEMAN

---

5. William Shakespeare, *Romeo and Juliet* (New York: Penguin Putnam, 2000), 74.

Fourth Sunday of Advent

Psalm 80:1–7, 17–19

¹Give ear, O Shepherd of Israel,
    you who lead Joseph like a flock!
You who are enthroned upon the cherubim, shine forth
²   before Ephraim and Benjamin and Manasseh.
Stir up your might,
    and come to save us!

³Restore us, O God;
    let your face shine, that we may be saved.

⁴O LORD God of hosts,
    how long will you be angry with your people's prayers?
⁵You have fed them with the bread of tears,
    and given them tears to drink in full measure.
⁶You make us the scorn of our neighbors;
    our enemies laugh among themselves.

⁷Restore us, O God of hosts;
    let your face shine, that we may be saved.
. . . .
¹⁷But let your hand be upon the one at your right hand,
    the one whom you made strong for yourself.
¹⁸Then we will never turn back from you;
    give us life, and we will call on your name.

¹⁹Restore us, O LORD God of hosts;
    let your face shine, that we may be saved.

Connecting the Psalm with Scripture and Worship

From accounts both biblical (2 Kgs. 16; 2 Chr. 28) and historical, Ahaz was not a good king. "Father of Hezekiah" might be his best appellation. Rather than calling on God for deliverance from his enemies, Ahaz called on the Assyrians. The ruler Tiglath-pileser delivered Ahaz from his enemies, and then delivered him from autonomy over his own kingdom. Ahaz also gave homage to Tiglath-pileser and the Assyrian gods, incorporating Assyrian religious practices into the temple rituals in Jerusalem.

Isaiah records a time when God instructed Ahaz to ask God for a sign. Ahaz responds to God by saying he will not put the Lord to the test. In his reply we hear echoes of Deuteronomy 6:16: "Do not put the LORD your God to the test, as you tested him at Massah." Jesus remembered the same direction when he was tempted by the devil in Luke 4. Knowing what we know of Ahaz, it seems less that he was trying to be a faithful follower, obeying the commandments of Scripture, and more that he was using Scripture as a shield, afraid, or at least unsure, of what a sign from the Lord his God might be or require of him.

We have encountered people who hide behind the words of Scripture, pretending piety, refusing to engage what God is doing in their midst.

Ahaz is also not the only one of us to rely on military might, or the tangible powers and riches of this world, rather than rely on the power of God. If God were to say to us, "Ask a sign of the LORD your God; let it be deep as Sheol or high as heaven," would we have the courage to ask?

Isaiah is not impressed with Ahaz's hiding behind Deuteronomy. He tells him to stop wearying God the way he wearies mortals. "Therefore the Lord himself will give you a sign. Look, the young woman is with child and shall bear a son, and shall name him Immanuel" (7:14).

Is that a sign that Ahaz would have recognized? If he was impressed with Assyria's power, gods, and rulers, would he have noticed a young woman with a baby? Is it a sign that we would recognize, were it to happen today? A young woman having a baby—when is that something we notice as a sign from God? Historically, young women having children are pretty far removed from the halls of power, or from economic security and independence, and tend to be subject to the whims of the men in their lives or the societies in which they live.

During Advent, God asks us to ask God for a sign. Do we have the courage to ask? Do we recognize God's signs as they appear, or do we look past the young woman, pregnant with child, as we scan the crowds for someone big and impressive?

The psalmist is willing to ask for a sign. In faith, he cries out for God to "Stir up your might, and come to save us! Restore us, O God; let your face shine, that we may be saved" (Ps. 80:2–3).

These are people who have lived on a diet of tears (v. 5), loss, and sadness. When we rely on our own wiles, or on our powerful neighbor in Assyria, we end up hungry for restoration. The psalmist voices the people's cry for God's might to save them, restore them. They have lived through darkness. They cry out for God's face to shine on them.

In the darkest part of the year, we gather and proclaim: "The people who walked in darkness have seen a great light; those who lived in a land of deep darkness—on them light has shined" (Isa. 9:2).

Where is the good news for people in darkness during this Advent season? As God's face shines, are they able to see hope for restoration?

As God's face shines, will they see how the birth of a child to a young woman can be a sign of God's faithfulness and power?

God's face shining is a subtle kind of light. It is not a spotlight, strongly beaming so brightly that everyone is blinded. Perhaps it is a light that reflects gently onto us, giving us a chance for our eyes to adjust, as things come into focus more clearly. We can navigate an entire journey in the dark, as long as we have enough light to see the path right in front of us.

If God chose to shine light by being born in a stable to a young woman, maybe we need to reconsider how we see the darkness and light. Maybe we need to worry less about banishing all of the darkness, which can seem an endless task. Maybe all we are called to do is reflect God's light that shines on us, and trust it is enough.

The inbreaking of God's light to the world did not, and does not, mean that people do not still experience darkness in their lives. Plenty of people around the world relate to the psalmist's words: "You have fed them with the bread of tears, and given them tears to drink in full measure" (v. 5). Advent hope rests in the promise that in the darkness, we will see the light. As God's face shines on us, the shadows recede, and we have clearer vision to understand how a young woman with child might actually save the world. God responded to the darkness in a stable in Bethlehem. A child born for us. A son, given unto us. God's face shines on us. We are restored.

Call to Worship (adapted from Psalm 80 and Isaiah 9)

Reader 1: Give ear, O Shepherd of Israel, you who lead Joseph like a flock!

Reader 2: Give us hope in the darkness that we might see the light.

Reader 1: Restore us, O God, let your face shine, that we may be saved.

Reader 2: Give us hope in the darkness that we might see the light. Stir up your might, and come to save us!

Reader 1: The people who walked in darkness have seen a great light; those who lived in a land of deep darkness—on them light has shined.

Reader 2: Let us worship God in joy and praise.

MARCI AULD GLASS

Romans 1:1–7

¹Paul, a servant of Jesus Christ, called to be an apostle, set apart for the gospel of God, ²which he promised beforehand through his prophets in the holy scriptures, ³the gospel concerning his Son, who was descended from David according to the flesh ⁴and was declared to be Son of God with power according to the spirit of holiness by resurrection from the dead, Jesus Christ our Lord, ⁵through whom we have received grace and apostleship to bring about the obedience of faith among all the Gentiles for the sake of his name, ⁶including yourselves who are called to belong to Jesus Christ,

⁷To all God's beloved in Rome, who are called to be saints:
Grace to you and peace from God our Father and the Lord Jesus Christ.

Commentary 1: Connecting the Reading with Scripture

Paul begins every letter with a standard opening greeting. The opening of Romans, however, is the fullest expression of Paul's "gospel" *in nuce*. After the apostle offers his view of his position in Christ (as Christ's "slave," *doulos*), he links the gospel to the prophets of old (1:2); he connects Jesus Christ to David (1:3); he announces the resurrection. This greeting provides the basic *confession* of the gospel: a messianic Lord and a resurrection by means of the Spirit, which expresses God's power and claim over God's Son.

When compared to the Apostles' Creed, we find absent references to Jesus' crucifixion, the virgin birth, and Christ's ascension. It is not Paul's intent, however, to provide a straightforward confession for the early church, although the words move in that direction. Rather, he relates God's gospel of Christ with his own specific mission, which he describes here—and which bookends this letter later—as "the obedience of faith among all the Gentiles" (1:5; 16:25–26). Significantly, this confession has ethnic consequences.

Following the opening greeting, Paul provides a typical "thanksgiving," even while he acknowledges the great respect others have for the faith of Roman Christians (1:8). Then, he returns to a discussion on the meaning of the gospel. According to the letter, the gospel is for the ethnic other: "to the Jew first and also to the Greek" (1:16). As a result, this decentralizes

the ethnic makeup of small house-church communities, even within the heart of the Roman Empire at a church not established by the apostle. In Rome, many different people groups gathered together, some by force (through war), others by choice (through business). Here, in this regional space, was a local Christian community that was struggling with its diversity. Since the beginning of Christianity, the gospel has called for a breakdown of ethnic, cultural, economic, gender, and class divides that often become the rationale for developing communities. The gospel beckons us to investigate the logic of the world's divisions and to probe deeply into our religious associations.

Paul provides insight into the cultural and religious conflict of this ethnically divided community (cf. 14:1–15:6): "Some believe in eating anything, while the weak eat only vegetables" (14:2); "Some judge one day to be better than another, while others judge all days to be alike" (14:5). To be sure, the conflict was not as ethnically divided as these differences regarding food selection and special days implied. Some Jewish Christians, Paul included, self-identified with the "strong" (15:1). It is not clear whether Paul ate everything set before him or was simply (more likely) untroubled by those (Gentiles) who did. On the other hand, I imagine there were Gentile Christians who upheld the tradition of Torah as an essential practice for maintaining unity within the community. Most importantly, for the well-being of the community, Paul directs his guidance to the strong, as those who must be willing to "build up the neighbor" (15:1–2).

God's gospel, as Paul calls it, is central to Paul's mission and a central motif in the opening chapters of this letter as well. It is the "message" about God's Son (1:9) and God's plan for saving humanity (1:16), Jews and Gentiles (1:16–17; cf. 16:25–27). For Paul, it also includes God's judgment of humankind, through Jesus Christ (2:16). Even though Paul is eager to proclaim the gospel (1:15), he desires to do so in places where the message has not yet been preached (15:20), which further explains his plans to go farther west to Spain (15:24). He does not envision Christian mission as an act of competition but, rather, communal responsibility.

The term "gospel" (*euangelion*) does *not* occur again until 10:16, at which point Paul exegetes Isaiah 52–53 and the prophet's use of the language of "gospel" (see below). Paul's gospel depicts Israel as "enemies" of the Gentiles (Rom. 11:28), which allows for the inclusion of the non-Jewish population into Pauline communities. Gentile inclusion is the crux of the matter for the apostle, as one who was focused on the "offering of the Gentiles" (15:16). The final usage in the letter, 16:25, again spells out the gospel in a nutshell and provides a bookend to the opening use of the term "gospel" at 1:3.

Moreover, Paul is a "slave" (*doulos*) to this gospel, Christ's slave to be exact (1:1). In imperial Rome, the presence of slaves was ubiquitous. So it was, in some ways, apropos to self-identify as one enslaved to the will of a deity, one who had no honorable status on one's own. (In light of the history of the United States, in particular the Atlantic slave trade, it is more troubling for contemporary Christians to identify in this way, as if value can be found in this nomenclature. Even the metaphorical use of it remains problematic in the highly racialized context of the US.) In Jewish tradition, this self-identification places Paul in good stead, along with Jewish heroes of the faith, Abraham (Gen. 26:24), Moses (Exod. 14:31; 2 Chr. 24:9; Rev. 15:3), and David (2 Sam. 7:5, 8).

Paul's Letter to the Romans went to the heart of the empire. Language in these opening verses—e.g., Messiah, gospel, King David's heir, resurrection—has consequences for those living under the policies and ethos of an empire. Even the apparent quietist attitude promoted in chapter 13 cannot downplay so easily the challenges of believing in another empire, God's kingdom, while living in an earthly one: "For the kingdom of God is not food and drink but righteousness and peace and joy in the Holy Spirit" (14:17). Christ is the only true "master" (*kyrios*; 1:4), not Rome (or the US).

Finally, Paul points to an engagement with Scripture, especially Isaiah—"which he promised beforehand through his prophets in the holy scriptures" (1:2). In chapter 10, Paul will utilize words from Second Isaiah in order to grapple with his own context (10:14–17). Part of Paul's attraction to this book is Isaiah's use of the verbal form for "proclaiming the gospel," *euangelizō* (at Isa. 52:7), a term that is central to the Letter to the Romans and the opening of the gospel letter: "How beautiful are the feet of those who bring good news!" (Rom. 10:15; cf. Isa. 52:7).

Other lectionary readings highlight the sign of Immanuel ("God with us"), a child who is born to symbolize God's presence among God's people, as a way to remind people of God's protection (Isa. 7:10–16) and God's restoration (Matt. 1:18–25). Paul's recognition of the coming incarnated God—"declared to be Son of God"—includes expectation of service from all who follow this one. Christ is God's gift, a gift that we must anticipate, receive, and share.

During the season of Advent, a season in which we wait and hope for God's coming into the world in human flesh, Paul's gospel for the ethnic other ("Gentile") reminds us that this gospel message is a message on behalf of the "other," who also will recognize this Savior through nothing more than the "obedience of faith." The contemporary challenge is whether our faith communities are prepared for the influx of the ethnic other (or economic or sexual other), who may not, symbolically, eat the same foods or hold to the same traditions that we have come to cherish. Will we allow God's gospel to visit us one more time this Advent season?

EMERSON B. POWERY

Commentary 2: Connecting the Reading with the World

Let's be honest. By the Fourth Sunday of Advent, most Christian churches are deep into the elaborate preparations of Christmas. If this reading were to come to us in the midst of Ordinary Time, followed by a close reading of Romans week after week, we would preach it very differently. As it is, we get Paul's greeting without the content of his long and complex message to the Romans. We get a beginning without a middle or end. We start a letter just as we are finishing a quiet season and preparing for a loud one.

That said, there is never a bad time to reintroduce Paul. The modern church's experience of preparing for Christmas begs for Paul's passion and expertise. Whether it is the remnants of old-time church families, visiting family members of church regulars, curious neighbors, or people who seek the comfort of familiar stories and music on one holy night each year, the church speaks to a wider range of listeners on Christmas than on possibly any other day. Speaking to wide ranges of new listeners is Paul's specialty.

From the very opening of Paul's greeting, he models a broad message that takes into account the diverse cultural and religious contexts of his audience. He speaks boldly to both Jewish and Gentile Christians, as well as to people who may not yet number themselves among the followers of Jesus. When Paul says, "all God's beloved in Rome, who are called to be saints," he really does mean everyone. The introduction to Romans provides an opportunity to turn away from the more inward-looking and anxiety-producing aesthetic preparations of the season and look outward toward our neighbors, "all God's beloved . . . who are called to be saints."

One of the hallmarks of Paul's writing and of reports of his preaching is his use of others' cultural and religious vocabulary to tell the story of the gospel. Even in this introduction, he weaves together both Jewish and Gentile-friendly religious vocabulary. His reference to the spirit of holiness declaring Jesus to be Son of God may even have referred to more political Roman ways of describing the divine authority of the emperor. The Letter to the Romans, of course, goes on to make a complex case for the gospel as fulfillment of hopes and promises that both Jewish and Gentile followers of Christ bring from their respective cultural and religious heritages.

As we prepare with our congregations to receive Christmas visitors, this reading offers a chance to invite congregational reflection on the context of the people who may not regularly grace our pews or chairs. The preacher might introduce anecdotal or demographic information about who is around in the neighborhood. Who are our neighbors, God's beloved among us? What is their vocabulary? What are the longings of their hearts that we might have a chance to meet with accessible words, gestures, music, and offerings of beauty this Christmas?

Paul spends time on many things in his letters, but rarely on cultural conversion. He is adamant that Gentiles can be adopted into the church without first becoming Jews. He allows for significant variation in dietary practices and other outward signs of holiness and religious observance. The message is what is important. Paul communicates the gospel by entering into others' mind-sets and experiences, rather than by critiquing or seeking to change them. He reserves his critiques—which can be harsh—for practices within the churches that erect stumbling blocks to the widest possible dissemination of the gospel. As we meet our neighbors, churches often stumble over others' failure to appreciate and adopt church culture. We ask, "What do you *mean*, 'spiritual but not religious'?" We point out contradictions and thin spots in our neighbors' cultural vocabulary when we could be finding ways to speak about the gospel in the language that would be most compelling to those outside our doors.

Paul's Letter to the Romans is his magnum opus, his most ambitious attempt to communicate the gospel that burns so urgently in his heart. The preacher might approach this text through the lens of communications, reflecting on the letter-writing traditions of Paul's time and ours. While long handwritten letters are certainly out of style for most modern listeners, we live in a time of flourishing public communications. Anyone with an urgent message to broadcast has multiple choices for dissemination. A congregation might be invited to imagine Paul as a prolific blogger or tweeter. What might his message look like broken into 140-character pieces? How might he have attracted the thousands of followers that he so clearly craved? What were the other voices and communication techniques that Paul was responding to? What did the first-century "Twitterverse" look like?

The preacher can easily make the case that Paul was a prolific user of the cutting-edge communications technology of his time, even to the point of sending this ambitious and probably unsolicited letter to the church in Rome, a city he may never have even visited at the time of its writing. He was also clearly an avid consumer of alternative perspectives, weaving in responses to others' claims as he made his own.

Paul's insistence in communicating the gospel calls to mind another insistent, visionary communicator, recently memorialized in the wildly popular musical *Hamilton*. Many listeners will be familiar with the musical itself. Those who are not will almost certainly have heard enough to be puzzled by how anyone could have imagined Alexander Hamilton out of the history books and into a rap musical. Both fans and the puzzled can be engaged in reflecting on how Paul cuts a similarly odd and fascinating figure. Paul too "writes like he is running out of time." He articulates a whole new theology that disquiets Jews and Gentiles alike. He makes even his allies nervous. He is an outsider—a self-proclaimed apostle whose authorization is disputed by more established figures in the

The Fulfillment of His Coming

It is strange that the Gospel read at the beginning of the time of preparation for Christmas is that of the end of the whole history of the world. Yet that is not really surprising. For what is afoot in a small beginning is best recognized by the magnitude of its end. What was really meant and actually happened by the coming, the advent, of the redeemer is best gathered from that completion of his coming which we rather misleadingly call the second coming. For in reality it is the fulfillment of his one coming which is still in progress at the present time.

For that reason, however, our church Advent is not a mere looking back to something past but is the human being's entrance by faith, hope, and love into the process which began when God himself entered the history of his world and made it his own. As a result, that history is inexorably moving toward the day which today's Gospel places prophetically before our eyes. From the picture of the fulfillment we are to gather what in reality is already happening in the depth of our life and our reality, though unobtrusively and quietly and therefore in a way which in our sinful blindness we may overlook. God has started on his way.

Karl Rahner, *Everyday Faith*, trans. W. J. O'Hara (New York: Herder & Herder, 1968), 11–13.

fledgling church. He desperately wants to be "in the room where it happens." Of course, in the Roman Empire, where else could that room be but in Rome?

Paul can be an unpopular figure in the modern church, often dismissed by feminist and egalitarian Christians as hopelessly conservative and outdated. I have come to love Paul in much the way that Lin-Manuel Miranda came to love Alexander Hamilton. His very obnoxiousness and insistent long-windedness indicate a level of passionate sincerity. He cannot and will not let go of the vitality of the gospel and his place in its proclamation. His willingness to lay his own insecurity out in writing, with sometimes embarrassing levels of self-disclosure, speaks to his genuine faith that God uses our weaknesses just as well as our strengths. The preacher may want to point out that even in this rather brief introductory reading, Paul uses an impossibly long sentence to communicate the whole of the gospel in one fell swoop. It would take a seasoned performer to manage that unwieldy sentence in a single breath. Imagining Paul's claims set to modern musical beats—even as one side of a rap battle—is really not terribly difficult.

In keeping with the themes of Advent waiting and expectation, the preacher might pay special attention to the greeting at the end of this reading: "Grace to you and peace." Paul speaks carefully when he speaks on behalf of God, but he is not shy in articulating God's desire for those whom God loves. As an apostolic community, sent out to carry and to be good news to the world, how do we communicate in word and deed the depth of God's grace and the peace that grace can sow among us?

ANNA OLSON

Matthew 1:18–25

18Now the birth of Jesus the Messiah took place in this way. When his mother Mary had been engaged to Joseph, but before they lived together, she was found to be with child from the Holy Spirit. 19Her husband Joseph, being a righteous man and unwilling to expose her to public disgrace, planned to dismiss her quietly. 20But just when he had resolved to do this, an angel of the Lord appeared to him in a dream and said, "Joseph, son of David, do not be afraid to take Mary as your wife, for the child conceived in her is from the Holy Spirit. 21She will bear a son, and you are to name him Jesus, for he will save his people from their sins." 22All this took place to fulfill what had been spoken by the Lord through the prophet:

23"Look, the virgin shall conceive and bear a son,
  and they shall name him Emmanuel,"

which means, "God is with us." 24When Joseph awoke from sleep, he did as the angel of the Lord commanded him; he took her as his wife, 25but had no marital relations with her until she had borne a son; and he named him Jesus.

Commentary 1: Connecting the Reading with Scripture

The Gospel reading for the Fourth Sunday of Advent in Year A begins the biography of Jesus by an unknown author. That is, the author is not named at any point in the text; later identification of the author as Matthew, the tax collector and disciple, is speculation. The use of the name Matthew in this commentary refers to the text, not its author. Because those for whom the Gospel was written would have experienced it by hearing it read aloud, they are referred to here as the audience or the auditors.

Coming immediately before our focal passage, Matthew 1:1–17 is a genealogy of Jesus traced through Joseph, the husband of his mother Mary. It is Joseph who provides the link to David that is essential to Matthew's definition of "Messiah" (anointed one/Christ, christos), but the author is committed to the tradition, shared by the Gospel of Luke, that Jesus was miraculously conceived by the Holy Spirit and was not Joseph's biological offspring. Matthew 1:18–25 explains why Joseph went ahead with the arranged marriage after Mary

"was found to be with child" and justifies calling Jesus a descendant of David by pointing out that, by naming him, Joseph acknowledges the child as legally his.[1]

Joseph makes the decision not to cancel the marriage (not yet consummated) because of instructions he receives in a dream (1:20–21). This dream is one of five in Matthew's birth narrative: in 2:12 the magi are warned in a dream not to report to Herod; in 2:13 Joseph is warned in a dream to take Jesus and Mary out of Bethlehem to escape Herod's slaughter of the male children of Bethlehem; in 2:19 Joseph is informed about Herod's death; in 2:22 Joseph is sent to Galilee by a dream, which explains how Jesus ends up being associated with Nazareth, which has not been mentioned in the story so far.

The name assigned to the baby by "an angel of the Lord" is "Jesus," the equivalent of the OT Joshua ("YHWH saves"). Matthew makes the salvation brought by YHWH through Jesus specific: "for he will save his people from their sins"

---

1. Charles H. Talbert, *Matthew* (Grand Rapids: Baker Academic, 2010), 33. Luke also traces Jesus' genealogy through Joseph. Mary's genealogy does not appear in the New Testament.

(1:21). Matthew's audience of Jewish believers in Jesus' messiahship might have heard in the name of Mary's son not only an echo of the successor to Moses, but also a more recent echo of Joshua the son of Jehozadak, the first high priest after the return from exile, who mediated forgiveness of sins for his people. Only Matthew, according to some textual traditions, mentions that Jesus was also the name of the "notorious prisoner" that Pilate released at the demand of the Jerusalem crowd (27:16). We are not told in Matthew why Jesus Barabbas was "notorious/well known" (*episēmon*), but those familiar with the tradition that he was a violent revolutionary may have seen a contrast with Jesus the true "Son of the Father" (*bar+abba*).

By quoting LXX Isaiah 7:14, the Gospel writer establishes the theme of Jesus' biography in the first of ten "fulfillment" quotations that occur throughout the Gospel: "All this took place to fulfill what had been spoken by the Lord through the prophet: 'Look, the virgin shall conceive and bear a son, and they shall name him Emmanuel,' which means, 'God is with us'" (1:22–23). The final words of Jesus in this Gospel are addressed to his disciples: "And remember, *I am with you* always, to the end of the age" (28:20b). If Jesus' *mission* in Matthew can be said to be saving his people from their sins, then the *significance* of his birth, life, death, and resurrection must be said to be the promise that whatever appearance may suggest, God is not absent from the world but present among God's people.

Matthew explicitly extends the repeated promise of God's presence from the OT to the community of Jesus-followers made up of both Jews and Gentiles (the nations [*ethnē*] to whom the disciples are sent in 28:19). The presence of the risen Christ, identified by 1:23 with the presence of God, enables the obedience of the community of Jesus-followers, but it does not guarantee their immunity from suffering and persecution (10:16–31; 25:31–46).[2]

Despite later church traditions that associate Jesus' miraculous conception with his death as a perfect sacrifice for sin, it is unlikely that the original audience would have interpreted the message of Matthew 1:18–25 in this way. Certainly those who knew the writings attributed to Isaiah would not have seen Isaiah 7:14 as predicting something that would happen in the first century BCE. In the ancient Mediterranean world a life that was extraordinary in its power and benefaction would have required explanation. The explanation frequently turned to by biographers was that the person must have had a divine father whose action (sometimes sexual, but sometimes not) was the cause of the pregnancy in a human mother. The author of Matthew follows the Septuagint in translating Isaiah's "young woman" as "virgin," and goes on to specify that Mary's pregnancy was a miracle "from the Holy Spirit" (1:20).

Both Matthew and Luke adhere to the tradition that the Holy Spirit was the cause of Mary's pregnancy and that Joseph was Jesus' legal, but not biological, father. But the Matthean audience, not yet taught by Christian tradition to regard human procreation as the source of alienation from God, would have heard the announcement of Jesus' divine parentage as an explanation for his life of wisdom, healing, exorcism, and obedience to God. Further, the miraculous conception of Jesus could have served as a counterargument to an adoptionist Christology that would have attributed Jesus' status as exalted Son of God to his own virtue and obedience. "Not so," Matthew's audience would have concluded. Jesus' life of power and obedience were the result of God's prior initiative at his conception.

The link between Jesus and the line of David is found in all four Gospels (though Mark is ambivalent about it). The earliest NT passage to make the claim that Jesus is descended from David is today's epistle reading, the salutation section of Romans. In these few lines Paul collects the christological titles that are also important to Matthew: descendant of David, Son of God, and Christ/Messiah. The baby who signifies the presence of God in Isaiah 7:14 is explicitly linked with the "house of David" in

---

2. Talbert, *Matthew*, 20–24. See the Connections comments on the reading from Isaiah 7 for this Sunday for more on the promise of God's presence in the Old Testament. For the argument that "the least of these" in 25:31–46 are those sent to make disciples in 28:18–20, see Talbert, *Matthew*, 276, and the other scholars cited there.

7:13 as well. That the Savior of God's people would be a Davidic ruler can be traced to 2 Samuel 7:16, where the prophet Nathan delivers God's promise to David: "Your house and your kingdom shall be made sure forever before me; your throne shall be established forever."

The Davidic ruler as a son of God and the one anointed/chosen by God to rule appears in the royal coronation theme of Psalm 2, alluded to in reference to Jesus in Matthew 3:17, 17:5, Acts 13:33, and Hebrews 1:5, 5:5.[3]

SHARYN DOWD

Commentary 2: Connecting the Reading with the World

Joseph is center stage on Advent 4.

In a way, his centrality feels mildly annoying. After all, we have finally come to a Gospel reading that seems to anticipate Christmas. Advent's earlier Gospel readings focused more on eschatological expectation: injunctions to keep awake; depictions of the coming of the Son of Man; John the Baptist calling us to repent, and warning of axes at the roots of trees. Finally, on the Fourth Sunday of Advent, we turn our attention to that other mode of Advent expectation: anticipating not the second coming, but the birth of baby Jesus. You might think, therefore, we would get a nice Marian tale—but not this year. One can be forgiven for feeling slightly irked that this year's Advent lectionary sequence relegates Mary to an optional-instead-of-the-psalm response to Isaiah.

Here he is: Joseph, who, in this annunciation of sorts, joins Abraham and Zechariah in receiving angelic information about impending fatherhood,[4] Joseph, who joins Luke's Mary in agreeing to do something difficult and strange.

Joseph is central to Advent 4, but he is a peripheral figure in the grand sweep of the Christian tradition. Relative to Mary and the apostles, we do not sing much about him. We rarely see him in art (and when Joseph does appear in a painting, he is rarely alone; he is typically accompanied by Mary and/or Jesus). Compared to his wife, Joseph has been the object of much less cultic devotion.

Like the rest of the church, I do not think of Joseph very often, but I thought of him a few months ago when binge watching the BBC show *Call the Midwife*. The third episode of season one depicted an expectant father who was over the moon about his wife's pregnancy—and who did not bat an eye when the newborn's skin color made clear that the child had, in fact, been conceived in an adulterous liaison. The TV husband took one look at the baby, pronounced him the most beautiful child ever, and took him into his heart and his family without missing a beat. This was, in its way, a secularized picture of Joseph; in fact, the TV husband was behaving with even more extravagant generosity than Joseph, because the TV husband did not have reason to believe that his adoptive fathering was key to the salvation of the world.

There is something transfixing about those situations in which a faithful spouse takes into his or her life a child conceived in adultery. Of course, the parallel is not perfect—the Gospels stress that Mary exactly had *not* committed adultery, but Jesus was, indeed, another father's child, and Joseph could have spurned Mary and her son (the possibility of that spurning is part of what gives today's reading its narrative tension and energy). When we encounter similarly complex family formation in our own communities, we are captivated by the hint of scandal, and bowled over by the maturity and openheartedness of the adoptive parent: "I am amazed that so-and-so was able to take that other woman's child into her life! I certainly could never do that!"—but so-and-so did.[5] So did Joseph.

---

3. Walter Brueggemann and William H. Bellinger Jr., *Psalms* (New York: Cambridge University Press, 2014), 35.

4. NB: it is Luke, rather than Matthew, that refers to Joseph as Jesus' father.

5. For a moving and theologically rich contemporary account see, Rhonda Mawhood Lee, "How I Learned to Love and Raise the Child from My Husband's Affair," *America: The Jesuit Review*, https://www.americamagazine.org/faith/2017/01/11/how-i-learned-love-and-raise-child-my-husbands-affair.

Few of us will find ourselves in the situation of Joseph or the husband from *Call the Midwife*—although, in every community, we have opportunities to welcome and help women who are pregnant in unexpected or atypical situations. The church that hosts the baby shower for the pregnant fifteen-year-old, who needs diapers and onesies every bit as much as the pregnant thirty-two-year-old, is acting in imitation of Joseph and so is the church that takes a public stand against the shackling of incarcerated women in labor.

At a subtler but perhaps more unsettling level, the Joseph story poses a fundamental ethical challenge that goes beyond the specifics of welcoming mothers: the challenge to exceed our culture's norms of standard-issue ethical behavior, and pursue a course of action that is excessively good, excessively generous. Joseph was poised to behave ethically. Because he wanted to protect Mary's reputation, he planned to "dismiss [Mary] quietly." This was a respectful and upright thing to do—but he was called by God to do something even more "righteous." He was called by God to an abundantly righteous act that required violating his culture's mores. He was called by God to go beyond his society's script for righteousness—in a way that risked bringing shame upon himself.

Joseph thus asks us to consider whether we have the opportunity to become more like him. Are our congregations embracing the culturally appropriate good deed (raising money at Christmastime to provide gifts for the children of incarcerated mothers, say), but not yet undertaking the bolder, riskier, more excessively good deed (welcoming a mother just released from prison into the congregation, into the ranks of Sunday school teachers, into our lunch bunch and church supper club)?

If Joseph models an ethics of excessive goodness for us, he also models spiritual receptivity.

Intriguingly, Joseph hears from God through his dreams. The Gospel of Matthew takes pains to show him receiving a word from God in a dream *four times*: in the Advent 4 text and thrice in Matthew 2, where Joseph's dreams contain various instructions about keeping Jesus safe.

In our day, of course, there is no consensus about the status of dreams, and those of us who receive insights into our desires and fears through our dreams may think those insights come not externally, from God, but from our own deepest self. Of course, if our deepest self is the image and likeness of God that we are, then who is talking, really, in the stories told to us by our dreams? The depths of December, when many are moving more quietly than we moved in May or September, can be a wonderful time to sit with Joseph and be a bit more attentive to the vehicles—dreams or otherwise—with which God is calling to us. Of course, that attention is risky: if we listen for God, we might actually hear from God. Who among us is as willing as Joseph to receive a word that fundamentally alters the course of our life?[6]

Joseph is not the only character in this reading. As Joseph is often accompanied by Jesus and Mary in art, so he is accompanied by them here. The Advent 4 reading concludes by turning our attention to the theme of incarnation, declaring that the child in question is not only Jesus, but also Emmanuel, God with us. The Joseph story in Matthew 1 and 2 shows, fundamentally, one person's response to God come among us, and as the church reaches the culmination of Advent, the Joseph story offers each of us the chance to think anew about how we respond to Emmanuel, the God who is with us: in the words of Scripture just proclaimed, in the Eucharist some churches will celebrate after the sermon, and in the incarnation we soon will celebrate.

LAUREN F. WINNER

---

6. On dreams in Matthew as a tool with which God directs "human action . . . often changing the natural direction initially undertaken by people," see Robert Gnuse, "Dream Genre in the Matthean Infancy Narratives," *Novum Testamentum* 32, no. 2 (1990): 119.

Christmas Eve/Nativity of the Lord, Proper I

Isaiah 9:2–7   Titus 2:11–14
Psalm 96   Luke 2:1–14 (15–20)

Isaiah 9:2–7

²The people who walked in darkness
      have seen a great light;
those who lived in a land of deep darkness—
      on them light has shined.
³You have multiplied the nation,
      you have increased its joy;
they rejoice before you
      as with joy at the harvest,
      as people exult when dividing plunder.
⁴For the yoke of their burden,
      and the bar across their shoulders,
      the rod of their oppressor,
      you have broken as on the day of Midian.
⁵For all the boots of the tramping warriors
      and all the garments rolled in blood
      shall be burned as fuel for the fire.
⁶For a child has been born for us,
      a son given to us;
authority rests upon his shoulders;
      and he is named
Wonderful Counselor, Mighty God,
      Everlasting Father, Prince of Peace.
⁷His authority shall grow continually,
      and there shall be endless peace
for the throne of David and his kingdom.
      He will establish and uphold it
with justice and with righteousness
      from this time onward and forevermore.
The zeal of the LORD of hosts will do this.

Commentary 1: Connecting the Reading with Scripture

The lectionary readings for Christmas Eve and Christmas Day (The Nativity of the Lord) are the same every year. Isaiah 9:2–7 is the Old Testament reading for one of three choices available to the liturgist.

Our passage follows an account of Isaiah's critique of the faithless response of Ahaz of Judah to a military threat from the combined armies of Syria (Aram) and Israel after Ahaz's refusal to join them in opposing the imperial advance of Assyria. The first verse of chapter 9 provides a transition between the judgment oracles against the people of Judah and the promise of a righteous ruler from the line of David in 9:2–7, but in 9:8–10:4 the prophet returns to oracles of condemnation of Israel's idolatry and social injustice and descriptions of the consequences of these offenses against God. There are four of these, each ending with, "For all this [God's] anger has not turned away; his hand is stretched out still" (Isa. 9:8–12, 13–17, 18–21, and 10:1–4).

Assyria, through "the rod of [God's] anger" (10:5), will come under its own judgment. This will happen once God's hand is withdrawn from punishing Israel and Judah, when "a remnant will return" (10:21). In Isaiah 11–12 the prophet imagines an eschatological future in which the Creator has restored the original peace and harmony of Eden. This includes the reuniting of Israel and Judah (11:11–16), which in its original context may have been intended as a promise for the historical future. When that reunion failed to happen, the promise was transformed into an eschatological hope.

The darkness surrounding 9:2–7 is briefly lifted by "a great light" (9:2). Light and clear sight are contrasted in Isaiah with darkness and blindness, a theme found throughout the Old Testament (Deut. 28:29; Job 5:14; Isa. 29:18; 42:7; 42:16; Mic. 3:6). Our passage is quoted in Matthew 4:16, and the Gospel reading for Proper I (Luke 2:1–14 [15–20]) uses the theme as well; the shepherds "keeping watch over their flock by night" (Luke 2:8) are suddenly overwhelmed by God's glory that "shone around them" (Luke 2:9).

Isaiah 9:3–5 celebrates the deliverance of Israel and Judah from oppression "as on the day of Midian." Although Moses had found refuge with "the priest of Midian" (Exod. 2–4) when he fled from Egypt after killing an Egyptian overseer, for the most part Midian was portrayed as the enemy of the Israelites (Num. 22, 31; Judg. 6–9; Hab. 3:7). The reference in Isaiah 9:4 and 10:26 is to Gideon's defeat of the Midianites with a force so small that the victory could be attributed only to God (Judg. 7:2–7). The message to Isaiah's audience during the Syro-Ephraimite crisis, during the exile, and during the struggles of the postexilic period is that just as God had promised Gideon, "I will be with you, and you shall strike down the Midianites" (Judg. 6:16), God will be with God's people again and again to deliver them from oppression (Isa. 7:14; 8:8 [Immanuel], 41:10; 45:14).

The choice by the author of Gideon's defeat of the Midianites as part of the promise of deliverance from oppression evokes the memory of Gideon's request for a sign from God, that his attack on Midian will be successful (Judg. 6:36). Having received one sign, Gideon asks for and receives another (Judg. 6:39–40).[1] Here is a sharp contrast with Ahaz, who was invited to ask for a sign that God would protect Judah but refused to do so with the hypocritically pious remark, "I will not ask, and I will not put the LORD to the test" (Isa. 7:12).

The biblical witness is ambivalent about "testing" God. The passage most familiar to a Christian audience will probably be Jesus' quotation of Deuteronomy 6:16 in both Matthew's and Luke's account of the temptation story: "Do not put the Lord your God to the test" (Matt. 4:7; Luke 4:12; see Sir. 18:23). However, in Malachi 3:10, God's people who are reluctant to believe that they can afford to comply with the teaching of Torah about tithing are told, "Bring the full tithe into the storehouse, so that there may be food in my house, and thus put me to the test, says the LORD of hosts; see if I will not open the windows of heaven for you and pour down for you an overflowing blessing."

There is not room here for an extended discussion of this issue, but it is enough to say that when Gideon asks for a sign, he has already demonstrated his readiness to obey God's direction by summoning the other Israelites to war against the oppressor. Ahaz, on the other hand, refuses to ask for a sign because he wants no further confirmation of what God wants him to do, since he has already decided to disobey. The son of Ahaz, Hezekiah, does not hesitate to ask for a sign indicating whether he will recover from an illness, and God does not hesitate to give the requested sign (2 Kgs. 20:1–11). Before they can ask, the shepherds in today's Gospel reading are given a sign by which they can recognize the truth of the angel's message: "This will be a sign for you: you will find a child wrapped in bands of cloth and lying in a manger" (Luke 2:12).

---

1. This story is familiar enough in some parts of the Christian subculture that people have been heard to say, "I'm putting out a fleece," when they are in a difficult discernment situation.

The Patience of God

"The people who walked in darkness have seen a great light; those who dwelt in a land of deep darkness, on them has light shined" (*Is* 9:1). "An angel of the Lord appeared to [the shepherds] and the glory of the Lord shone around them" (*Lk* 2:9). This is how the liturgy of this holy Christmas night presents to us the birth of the Savior: as the light which pierces and dispels the deepest darkness. The presence of the Lord in the midst of his people cancels the sorrow of defeat and the misery of slavery, and ushers in joy and happiness.

We too, in this blessed night, have come to the house of God. We have passed through the darkness which envelops the earth, guided by the flame of faith which illuminates our steps, and enlivened by the hope of finding the "great light." By opening our hearts, we also can contemplate the miracle of that child-sun who, arising from on high, illuminates the horizon.

The origin of the darkness which envelops the world is lost in the night of the ages. Let us think back to that dark moment when the first crime of humanity was committed, when the hand of Cain, blinded by envy, killed his brother Abel (cf. *Gen* 4:8). As a result, the unfolding of the centuries has been marked by violence, wars, hatred and oppression. . . .

Through the course of history, the light that shatters the darkness reveals to us that God is Father and that his patient fidelity is stronger than darkness and corruption. This is the message of Christmas night. God does not know outbursts of anger or impatience; he is always there, like the father in the parable of the prodigal son, waiting to catch from afar a glimpse of the lost son as he returns; and every day, with patience. The patience of God.

Isaiah's prophecy announces the rising of a great light which breaks through the night. This light is born in Bethlehem and is welcomed by the loving arms of Mary, by the love of Joseph, by the wonder of the shepherds. When the angels announced the birth of the Redeemer to the shepherds, they did so with these words: "This will be a sign for you: you will find a baby wrapped in swaddling clothes and lying in a manger" (*Lk* 2:12). The "sign" is in fact the humility of God, the humility of God taken to the extreme; it is the love with which, that night, he assumed our frailty, our suffering, our anxieties, our desires and our limitations. The message that everyone was expecting, that everyone was searching for in the depths of their souls, was none other than the tenderness of God: God who looks upon us with eyes full of love, who accepts our poverty, God who is in love with our smallness. . . .

Dear brothers and sisters, on this holy night we contemplate the Nativity scene: there "the people who walked in darkness have seen a great light" (*Is* 9:1). People who were unassuming, people open to receiving the gift of God, were the ones who saw this light. This light was not seen, however, by the arrogant, the proud, by those who made laws according to their own personal measures, who were closed off to others. Let us look to the crib and pray, asking the Blessed Mother: "O Mary, show us Jesus!"

Pope Francis, "Solemnity of the Nativity of the Lord," Vatican website, December 24, 2014, http://w2.vatican.va/content/francesco /en/homilies/2014/documents/papa-francesco_20141224_omelia-natale.html.

There is also in the recollection of the story of Gideon a warning about reliance on human leaders, even those chosen by God. Gideon has no sooner defeated the Midianites than he creates an "ephod" from the gold taken as booty "and all Israel prostituted themselves to it." The people return, after Gideon's death, to idolatry, "making Baal-berith their god" (Judg. 8:24–35). Although Gideon had refused to be proclaimed king, his unworthy son Abimelech sought and obtained the kingship, leading to division and bloodshed (Judg. 9). If, as many scholars contend, the child promised in Isaiah 7:14, whose birth is announced in Isaiah 9:6, was Hezekiah, son of Ahaz, the celebration of 9:6–7 proved to be premature. Hezekiah, for all his zeal against Assyria and the Assyrian gods, is ultimately forced to pay tribute to the Assyrians (2 Kgs. 18:13–16). Then, like Gideon, Hezekiah is succeeded by a son who, in the evaluation of the Deuteronomists, did things "more wicked than" all his predecessors. Peter Miscall points out that in Isaiah 6:1 and 66:1 "the throne belongs to the divine king" and not to any human ruler.[2]

It is this stark reality that moves the final editor of the Isaianic oracles to shift into an eschatological mode in 9:6–7, thus guaranteeing the place of Isaiah 9:2–7 in the lectionary for Christmas Eve. After his resurrection the followers of Jesus saw in him the fulfillment of the promise of a Davidic ruler who would bring light to the world's darkness, and peace, justice, and righteousness for a humanity that had waited, and still waits, in darkness for deliverance.

The just kingship of God is also celebrated by the psalm for Christmas Eve (Ps. 96:10–13) and the epistle (Titus 2:11–14) extols the positive effects "in the present age" on the behavior of those who "wait for the blessed hope" of ultimate salvation.

SHARYN DOWD

Commentary 2: Connecting the Reading with the World

For many worshipers, Christmas Eve will feel as much like the end of a weeklong ordeal as it will the cusp of a new liturgical season. In recent years, the weeks before Christmas have become an ever-expanding secular period full of stress and strain for Christians and non-Christians alike. It comes complete with an overindulgence of food, shopping, and social obligations (which is how some may even consider traditional candlelight or family-oriented worship services). By the time we gather to sing "It Came upon a Midnight Clear," that great light of which Isaiah speaks in verse 2 may be more reminiscent in some minds of garishly decorated homes and shopping centers than of a welcome word of hope and comfort from God.

In 1995, the *New York Times* reported that an annual Christmas display erected at a private residence in Little Rock, Arkansas, that had once included 3.2 million individual lights and caused hours-long traffic jams had been reduced to a mere 12,000 lights. This came only after the United States Supreme Court declined to address a lower court's ruling that the display was a nuisance and not an act of free speech.[3] Having once unhappily witnessed the display in its full glory, I can attest that the image was almost literally burned into my consciousness. Is this the sort of thing that comes to the minds of our congregants when Isaiah speaks of a light in the darkness?

Of course, it should not be. Isaiah instead makes a connection between the light in the darkness and a sense of joy that will surround the people. Hence, one of the challenges that confronts preachers on Christmas Eve comes in helping listeners lay claim to the joy of which the prophet speaks. Unfortunately this particular passage might seem to be of little help. Urban listeners may have no idea what it means to rejoice at the harvest, and one can only hope that none are accustomed to dividing plunder. The images of broken rods and vanquished oppressors may be slightly more relevant in light of the ongoing social upheaval around the world, but they along with references to the boots of warriors and the burning of bloodstained garments are not likely to generate much in the way of joy in a typical worship setting.

Times change; specific images become unfathomable. In 1916 Carl Sandburg published his poem "Happiness" as a part of his collection entitled *Chicago Poems*. (There are significant ways in which joy and happiness differ, but in this context there is a helpful overlap.)

> I asked the professors who teach the meaning
> of life to tell me what is happiness.
> And I went to famous executives who boss
> the work of thousands of men.
> They all shook their heads and gave me a
> smile as though I was trying to fool
> with them.

---

2. Peter Miscall, *Isaiah*, 2nd ed. (Sheffield: Sheffield Phoenix Press, 2003), 54.
3. "A Wealth of Christmas Lights Dims in Little Rock," *New York Times,* December 18, 1995.

And then one Sunday afternoon I wandered
out along the Desplaines river
And I saw a crowd of Hungarians under the
trees with their women and children
and a keg of beer and an accordion.[4]

For Isaiah's original audience, experiences such as completing the harvest or dividing the spoils of war were apt as illustrations, but that does not mean these images are timeless. Carl Sandburg too offers a problematic definition of joy/happiness as he speaks of a particular nationality of men surrounded by "their women and children." At best, Sandburg shows that the ordinary activities of life can cause such emotion. Joy may be difficult to explain, but it is this sense of well-being or contentedness that brightens our living. When I think of joy, I remember how I felt when I first began to ride a bicycle. Perhaps it is with such personal experiences that we find the truest understanding of joy.

In the film *Harry Potter and the Prisoner of Azkaban*, based on the book by J. K. Rowling, Harry, a young wizard, must draw on a memory that gives him great joy. He needs it in order to master a new and very difficult magic spell. Initially Harry recalls his first experience flying on a broomstick, but that is not nearly joyous enough. What does provide him with the necessary emotion is a mental image of his deceased parents interacting with him when he is still a child. He is not even sure that it is an actual recollection, but it is this experience that gives him the feeling of joy he needs in order to master the spell.

When it comes to identifying joy then, one person's divided plunder may be another's afternoon by the Des Plaines River and yet another's knowledge that he or she has been loved. Isaiah gives us the chance to explore what joy means for us—a very worthwhile conversation. In the end, though, the prophet brings us back to the one source of joy-out-of-light, the one aspect of God's salvific work that resonates above all others. Perhaps it too was intended as a metaphor, but in time it has become a truth we are invited to celebrate during all seasons of our lives. "For a child has been born for us," writes the prophet, "a son given to us" (Isa. 9:6). The reason we gather for services on Christmas Eve (and at any other time) is that this child is God in human form. What can be said about God in this situation?

Along with the potential for garishness that plagues the Advent season, the worshipers who gather on Christmas Eve will also have been bombarded by the commercialism that emerges at this time of year. Advertising slogans, product endorsements, reasons why one item is a "must buy" and why some toy is the "it" plaything for the year: all of these and more will have been popping up on computer screens and smartphones and interrupting our TV programs since early October. Some of these pronouncements may even be true as far as it goes. However, nothing that the world can offer by way of consumerism or can be found on a store shelf or ordered from a catalog or shipped from an online retailer, can match the nature of the child whom Isaiah announces: "And he is named Wonderful Counselor, Mighty God, Everlasting Father, Prince of Peace" (v. 6).

In a world where superlatives are essential if one's message is to be heard amid a fog of language, these phrases may seem like no more than a typical ad campaign, yet what they offer is nothing short of subversive. Referring as they do to God, these descriptive terms tell us that there is a singular factor at work, a source of authority beyond whatever we can fathom or the world can offer.

Look at the first three modifiers: "Wonderful," "Mighty," "Everlasting." We normally attach such terms to more human endeavors like sports or the accumulation of wealth. We engage in discussions as to who might be the greatest athlete of a generation. Isaiah draws our attention to God whose work plays out in our world in a way that transcends the superlatives to which we are accustomed. God is doing something worth noting and worth struggling to define, especially in the face of an over-lit, overly commercial landscape.

JAMES D. FREEMAN

---

4. Carl Sandburg, "Happiness," in *Chicago Poems* (New York: Henry Holt & Co., 1916), 20.

Psalm 96

[1]O sing to the LORD a new song;
  sing to the LORD, all the earth.
[2]Sing to the LORD, bless his name;
  tell of his salvation from day to day.
[3]Declare his glory among the nations,
  his marvelous works among all the peoples.
[4]For great is the LORD, and greatly to be praised;
  he is to be revered above all gods.
[5]For all the gods of the peoples are idols,
  but the LORD made the heavens.
[6]Honor and majesty are before him;
  strength and beauty are in his sanctuary.

[7]Ascribe to the LORD, O families of the peoples,
  ascribe to the LORD glory and strength.
[8]Ascribe to the LORD the glory due his name;
  bring an offering, and come into his courts.
[9]Worship the LORD in holy splendor;
  tremble before him, all the earth.

[10]Say among the nations, "The LORD is king!
  The world is firmly established; it shall never be moved.
  He will judge the peoples with equity."
[11]Let the heavens be glad, and let the earth rejoice;
  let the sea roar, and all that fills it;
    [12]let the field exult, and everything in it.
Then shall all the trees of the forest sing for joy
    [13]before the LORD; for he is coming,
  for he is coming to judge the earth.
He will judge the world with righteousness,
  and the peoples with his truth.

Connecting the Psalm with Scripture and Worship

Psalm 96 is an enthronement psalm, a song of gladness, deep joy, and in many ways, a song of relief from pain and deep woundedness. One can feel the exuberance in each verse of the psalmist's phrasing. God has seen the people's pain, heard their cries, and responded with care. God has righted the world and corrected what was unjust. The psalm is divided thematically into two parts. Part one begins with the praising of God's work among creation as well as a description of God's attributes, and part two expounds on the revelatory nature of God's justice and judgment.

Witnessing God's Majesty and Power. The psalmist is calling all of creation, including humankind, to witness to who God is and what God has done. This means actively engaging nations, peoples, communities, and even families in the retelling of who God is and what God has done for those God loves. The psalm is a call to stand at attention, to notice the shift in the world, and ultimately to give credit where credit is due—and embody a spirit of defiance against the histories of injustice in the world.[1] Psalm 96 echoes the sentiments of Isaiah 9:2–7, which begins with the people who have been submerged in darkness witnessing a great light. In Isaiah as with the psalm, the writer actively names the ways God has brought light again into the world.

God's Power as Equity. Though we might not feel excited about the judgment of humanity, the psalmist rejoices at the coming judgment of God. This is a joy that can emerge only from those who have been wronged, hurt, and downtrodden. This joy is not about the total destruction of one's enemies, for God "will judge the peoples with equity" (Ps. 96:10). God is different from the human judges encountered by this writer. The psalmist declares the tremendous power and majesty of God in the first half of the psalm, yet also shows the intentional restraint present in God's actions. Though God may be all-powerful, God delivers judgment, not with an overreaching arm of destruction, but with ultimate fairness and righteousness.

Therefore, the psalmist describes the mutuality of the joy experienced by all creation, nations, and people in response to this equitable God, who models a permanent spirit of restoration of relationships between nations, people, God's creation, and God. The psalmist describes the world as "firmly established" and immovable. With God's arrival come a new system, culture, and way of life. As in Isaiah 9, the tools and methods of oppression and pain—the yoke, the rod, the boot, and bloody garments—are destroyed, never to be re-created.

There is a feeling of "at last!" in the psalmist's tone when describing the arrival of God's justice among the nations, between people, and in the neighborhood. God has heard and answered a deep communal and collective yearning. As in the earlier part of this psalm, we hear resonances with Isaiah 9, particularly verses 3 and 4. One gets the undeniable sense that when God arrives with justice and judgment, there is no going back to the former oppressions or the time of captivity to pain. Oppressors and those whom they have oppressed are reconciled to one another and are beholden to a different way of relationality and life. Instead, there is a permanent sense of rejoicing and jubilance that cannot help but be externalized by those who bear witness to the cosmic shift toward good that the prophet and the psalmist both describe.

Preaching the Text. Psalm 96 describes a world that has been reconciled to itself and to its Creator. There is neither pain from oppression nor fear of God's judgment. As worshipers celebrate the birth of Jesus Christ, they sing praise, for God has ushered in the eternal reign of justice. The psalm announces that God's power restores what has been broken, and God's truth reveals that all people are beloved. Through the power and might of God, our biases, distrust, and hatreds—all of which we weaponize against one another—are ultimately torn away to reveal our deep connectedness and belonging to one another. The new song that God's people sing tells of a joy that comes only when God has judged all the people with equity, imbued the world with righteousness, and established endless peace. Even though we still wait for that reign to be complete, we can sing with joy because we have confidence in the promises of the God who has sent a Savior.

CHRISTINE J. HONG

---

1. J. Clinton McCann Jr., "Psalms," in *New Interpreter's Bible* (Nashville: Abingdon Press, 1996), 4:1067.

Titus 2:11–14

¹¹For the grace of God has appeared, bringing salvation to all, ¹²training us to renounce impiety and worldly passions, and in the present age to live lives that are self-controlled, upright, and godly, ¹³while we wait for the blessed hope and the manifestation of the glory of our great God and Savior, Jesus Christ. ¹⁴He it is who gave himself for us that he might redeem us from all iniquity and purify for himself a people of his own who are zealous for good deeds.

Commentary 1: Connecting the Reading with Scripture

Children heighten our sense of the gift at Christmas time. Their anticipation symbolizes a type of human desire for the unexpected. Even those who may not be around children during this festival season often recall memories of their own childhood longings. In the season of Advent, we would do well to reclaim some of that childlike expectancy. It might well help us appreciate the renewal of God's greatest gift to the world— God's grace in the giving of God's Son. This gift draws us closer to the Divine so that we might become agents of kind actions in the world. The lectionary selection from Titus focuses our attention on the appearance of God's grace—God's gift—and reminds us to heighten our attention to its appearance once again.

The preacher should not ignore the challenges the Pastor (probably one of Paul's followers writing in his name) poses to the contemporary post-Enlightenment, postindustrial world. It is easier to focus on the lectionary selection only (2:11–14) and ignore the immediate context of these joyful verses, incorporated in the lectionary context as part of a celebratory season. The literary context, however, is not a season of celebration for the pastor but, rather, one of order, orderliness, and stability. We should also remember it was a society that in many ways was unlike our own.

Before 2:11–14, the Pastor encourages an arrangement, not uncommon to the Roman households of the day, a structure that indicated (on the surface) that all was well and orderly within the empire. This was the Roman way. For the Pastor, it was also the ecclesial way: "for if someone does not know how to manage his own household, how can he take care of God's church?" (1 Tim. 3:5). So, instructions are given to the elderly ("old men," Titus 2:2; and "old women," 2:2–5), with three times as much advice for the female Christian population. There are directions also for the "young men" (2:6–8), though none are given directly to "young women," who should be taught by older women and (apparently) not by the male teacher. Finally, there are directives for "slaves" (2:9–10), as the house churches intersected with regular household activities and structures.

Unlike his Christian proslavery counterparts, the Pastor omits any religious reminder of the "heavenly Master" as a way to curb the behavior of Christian masters: "Stop threatening them, for you know that both of you have the same Master in heaven, and with him there is no partiality" (Eph. 6:9; cf. Col. 4:1). Leonard Black, who escaped slavery from the Southern states in 1837, recognized this dilemma: "Should we not remember them that are in bondage as bound with them? Say not only slaves be obedient to your masters according to the flesh, but also say, masters, render unto your servants that which is right and if that principle were carried out, slavery would be abolished."[1] Black may have been overly hopeful that sermons to that effect

---

1. Leonard Black, *The Life and Sufferings of Leonard Black, a Fugitive from Slavery, Written by Himself* (New Bedford: Benjamin Lindsey, 1847), 54.

would have assisted in the downfall of the peculiar institution in the United States, but Titus has no such warning to masters. Neither did the Pastor encourage enslaved believers to pursue their freedom if the opportunity presented itself (as suggested in some manuscripts of 1 Cor. 7:21). Rather, the enslaved believer's commitment to his or her master would, according to the Pastor, benefit the gospel: "so that in everything they may be an ornament to the doctrine of God our Savior" (Titus 2:10). This cultural definition of God's "gospel" is difficult to appreciate in the modern world. It does, however, force this interpreter to reflect on our own cultural trappings and the way we may associate them with the gospel as well.

Into this "orderly" world, the passage proclaims the appearance of God's "grace" (*charis*) that includes an expectation of the coming "blessed hope" (2:13). It is this longing for the reappearance that makes the passage appropriate for the Christmas season. An emphasis on God's salvation coming to "all people" causes a rereading of the immediate context. Perhaps one can read the previous instructions to males *and females*, to old *and young*, and to the enslaved as somehow "inclusive" of all. This act of God's grace leads to redemption, which in turn leads to developing agents of meaningful actions (2:14). (Of course, in a context in which human bondage is considered a crime, we would define those righteous actions differently than the Pastor did.) The season of eager waiting is also a season of activity, not just the kind that participates in the commercialization of Christmas but the kind of activity that requires God's followers to imagine the arrival of God's grace as an opportunity for doing something good on behalf of someone who is unable to return the favor.

The alternative lectionary readings emphasize the significance of this appearance. The prophet longs for the visitation of a "child" who will maintain long-lasting peace and "righteousness" in Israel (Isa. 9:6–7). The psalm broadens this longing beyond human desire to exclaim how all of nature longs for the day of the Lord's appearance, when God will rule with "equity." Destruction and warfare do as much damage to the earth as to its population, so the psalmist cries outs, "all the trees of the forest sing for joy before the Lord; for he is coming" (Ps. 96:12–13). The Gospel reports Jesus' birth as a sign of God's favor and fulfillment of the claims of the traditions of Scripture. Like nature, the shepherds also rejoice at God's gift to the world (Luke 2:1–20). More than the other passages, the epistle lays bare the implications of this coming gift for humankind. God's grace touches human character, expects tangible human change, and grants followers strength to pursue matters of a "godly" nature (Titus 2:11–14).

Equally surprising to the appearance of this gift of God, this "grace," is its ongoing "teaching" activity (*paideuō*, 2:12). The NRSV's "training us" emphasizes the disciplining nature of this term, which the Greek meaning may also carry. Other translations prefer its educational quality (CEB, NIV, KJV) and recall the value of a gift that keeps on giving. As a teacher, "grace" discourages certain characteristics—"impiety and worldly passions" (NRSV)—while encouraging others: "to live lives that are self-controlled, upright, and godly" (2:12).

Grace still has much to teach Christians. Recognition of God (*eusebōs/eusebeia*) is a starting point. That is, to act "godly" (or, to act as if God matters) is the opposite of "impiety" (NRSV's translation of *asebeia*). Beginning here, grace encourages its followers to avoid the passions of the world. The capitalistic ventures that dominate present-day realities should come under careful scrutiny of grace-followers. Indeed, more as a product of his own age, the Pastor suggests that grace encourages a type of "self-control" that may avoid passions altogether. Certainly, grace's disciples would pursue proper passions, those that bring benefit to others in meaningful and bodily ways.

The disruptive presence of grace may attract our attention this Christmas season. In the midst of the orderliness of the season—lighting of candles, decorations of sacred spaces, colorful bulletins—may the appearance of God's grace manifest itself as something new, something uncommon, something (even) disorderly to remind us of the divine rupture into our everyday, orderly, human-centered lives, so that we might once again recall the reason for the season "zealous for good deeds" (2:14).

EMERSON B. POWERY

Commentary 2: Connecting the Reading with the World

Titus shows up in the Revised Common Lectionary only on Christmas. This passage is traditionally read Christmas Eve, while Titus 3:4–7 is one of the choices for Christmas Day.

Titus is troubling to the modern reader. Its tightly organized hierarchical household, which the epistle proposes as a model for the church, is predicated on the dominance of masters over slaves and the subordinate position of women. Titus, along with 1 and 2 Timothy, expresses concern for the reputation of the early Christian communities, advocating an acceptance of existing mores of respectability. These Pastoral Epistles were important texts used to support slavery in the United States and remain the source of proof texts that undermine women's full participation in the church and equal standing in family life. A critical reading suggests that these second-century epistles must be understood as part of a larger dialogue or controversy, in which alternative manifestations of early Christian community upended hierarchical relationships in the name of the gospel. All in all, a reading from Titus begs for a larger contextual discussion of the Pastoral Epistles and their household codes. However, the liturgical timing at Christmas imposes not insignificant constraints. A few options present themselves to the preacher, ranging from engaging closely with only the limited text at hand to more contextualized and potentially controversial approaches.

In most congregations, the expectation for the Christmas Eve sermon will include at the very least an explicit tie to the nativity story. The Advent waiting has culminated in the birth of the Christ child; the church is bathed in soft light and draped in greenery: the people want the magic of Christmas. This particular bit of Titus, separated from its larger context, offers several images that fit well with an invitation to delve deeply into the meaning of the nativity. There is salvation for all, the manifestation of God's glory, the self-giving of Christ, and even a reference back to Advent's time of waiting "for the blessed hope." Each of these images offers the preacher an opportunity to connect Christmas to the larger gospel story, including explicit reference to the cross and the resurrection. Given

that many congregations will have a number of Christmas visitors whose exposure to the Christian story may be limited, the larger connections will add substance and significance to the well-known Christmas story. The preacher has the opportunity to invite listeners through the doorway of Christmas into the larger fullness of Christian life.

Titus's references to "impiety and worldly passions" may invite some preachers to address the rampant materialism of Christmas in our consumer culture. Many Christians arrive at the Christmas services exhausted by the material demands of Christmas, worn out from shopping and decorating, worried about debts incurred or family members' hopes disappointed. Even in church, the attention of many congregational leaders may veer away from the central Christian story and work of welcome in favor of demanding perfection in décor and music. Titus's prim emphasis on "self-controlled, upright, and godly" lives may come as good news to those who have struggled to live up to the images of Christmas imposed by advertisers and secular expectations, or even church obsessions with "proper" preparation for Christmas.

Whether or not the home is beautifully decorated, the tree stocked with gifts, a perfect meal under preparation, the harmonious family gathered in love and joy, Christmas Eve in church is a time when anyone who approaches the altar in faith can find room at the Christmas table. Christ is born for the lonely, the broke, the disorganized, and the conflicted, just as for those who better fit society's measures. The invitation to live a life of faith is one that is open to all and one that the preacher can hold up in contrast to the often unattainable ideals of secular Christmas. Even if the choir hits the occasional sour note or someone's idea of beautiful clashes with someone else's in the congregation, Christmas comes in all its power when we open up the Bible once more.

The adventurous preacher with a congregation open to social-justice messages may find in Titus an opportunity to engage boldly with the issues of the day. Opening the door on the church's long history of debate and contention about the relationship between Christian community and secular norms in relation to social hierarchy offers an exciting angle on the disruptive potential of the nativity. After all, Mary has just proclaimed during Advent that God "has brought down the powerful from their thrones, and lifted up the lowly; [God] has filled the hungry with good things, and sent the rich away empty." The competing claims of hierarchy and egalitarianism on the authority of the gospel echo the pressing controversies of our time.

For a congregation that will tolerate Christmas Eve references to #BlackLivesMatter and #MeToo, Titus offers a clear point of entry. The unexpected arrival of the Messiah in the form of a baby from a poor family, born in a manger to unmarried parents, speaks directly to the ways that the gospel story consistently deviates from claims of respectability and prioritization of social stability. The questions of whose lives matter and whose stories hold sway are both ancient and modern. The question of respectability versus radical faith is very much a live one in a church that is rapidly losing political and social sway. A preacher who takes this direction has the opportunity to explore the qualities of a faithful church that stands with and among those who live at the margins of power and wealth.

Not every congregation will pivot well from a hard-nosed consideration of racism and sexual abuse to the traditional candlelight singing of "Silent Night." For the preacher who is considering taking a risk in this direction, this might be an important time to gather a trusted group of parishioners who represent a variety of perspectives and can offer some honest feedback before the big night.

Preaching on Christmas Eve demands attention to the diversity of faith journeys present within the gathered congregation. While it is certainly important on Christmas to speak with attention to those who may not often hear Christian preaching, it is equally important to attend to the needs of the dedicated people of faith who have committed to living by "every word that comes from the mouth of God." For those who are in church regularly, Christmas represents a different sort of highlight—a milestone in the repeating cycle of the church year, an opportunity to approach the familiar project of Christian life and growth from a new angle.

While I personally as a preacher would offer a disclaimer about my discomfort with Titus's conclusions about the qualities that comprise a godly life, the questions Titus raises are worth considering. How do we shape our households and churches according to God's precepts? How might we commit to lives as people who are "zealous for good deeds"? Specifically, given the Christmas context, how do we live as Christmas people and Christmas communities? Christians may be more accustomed to being asked about how their lives reflect the sacrifice of the cross or the glory of Easter. The devoted Christian will also benefit from self-inquiry focused on the nativity. For those in the congregation already further along in their Christian formation, the preacher may offer spiritual direction as to the implications of God's gift and the Christ child's vulnerability in shaping Christian life and bearing witness to the good news.

ANNA OLSON

Luke 2:1–14 (15–20)

[1]In those days a decree went out from Emperor Augustus that all the world should be registered. [2]This was the first registration and was taken while Quirinius was governor of Syria. [3]All went to their own towns to be registered. [4]Joseph also went from the town of Nazareth in Galilee to Judea, to the city of David called Bethlehem, because he was descended from the house and family of David. [5]He went to be registered with Mary, to whom he was engaged and who was expecting a child. [6]While they were there, the time came for her to deliver her child. [7]And she gave birth to her firstborn son and wrapped him in bands of cloth, and laid him in a manger, because there was no place for them in the inn.

[8]In that region there were shepherds living in the fields, keeping watch over their flock by night. [9]Then an angel of the Lord stood before them, and the glory of the Lord shone around them, and they were terrified. [10]But the angel said to them, "Do not be afraid; for see—I am bringing you good news of great joy for all the people: [11]to you is born this day in the city of David a Savior, who is the Messiah, the Lord. [12]This will be a sign for you: you will find a child wrapped in bands of cloth and lying in a manger." [13]And suddenly there was with the angel a multitude of the heavenly host, praising God and saying,

[14]"Glory to God in the highest heaven,
  and on earth peace among those whom he favors!"

[15]When the angels had left them and gone into heaven, the shepherds said to one another, "Let us go now to Bethlehem and see this thing that has taken place, which the Lord has made known to us." [16]So they went with haste and found Mary and Joseph, and the child lying in the manger. [17]When they saw this, they made known what had been told them about this child; [18]and all who heard it were amazed at what the shepherds told them. [19]But Mary treasured all these words and pondered them in her heart. [20]The shepherds returned, glorifying and praising God for all they had heard and seen, as it had been told them.

Commentary 1: Connecting the Reading with Scripture

Luke's narrative in chapter 2 locates the story of Jesus' birth within a larger context: the Roman Empire, and specifically Emperor Caesar Augustus (63 BCE–14 CE). The emperor's edict of a census for the inhabited world brings Mary and Joseph to Bethlehem. This registration is not benign: by means of a census the emperor identifies taxable subjects who can also be soldiers. At the same time, those who receive news of the birth of Jesus from Gabriel and its saving message for all people are itinerant, poor, homeless, shepherds—not the elite of cities like Rome. Thus good news is anchored in joyous songs

of the Savior's birth sung by angels connecting earth and heaven. These echoes will continue in the songs of Mary, Zechariah, Simeon, and even the lost song of Anna. Perhaps the shepherd songs brought to the manger by terrified nomads bring the significance of the birth home to Mary.

For us to grasp the wider perspective of what Luke is doing, we need to recall that the birth narratives of John and Jesus in Luke 1–2 are composed after the Gospel narrative of Jesus' adult ministry, death, and resurrection. They therefore reflect the Gospel's emphases in that narrative, particularly God's preference for the poor, the voiceless, and the wounded, as well as God's inclination to reverse human values that favor the rich and the powerful. The project Luke brought about under the patronage of Theophilus (Luke 1:1–4) is indeed for the elite, yet it is the poor and the outcasts who grasp its significance and on whom God's favor rests while the rich "go away empty."

We need also remember that Luke's Gospel is part of a two-volume work: Luke–Acts. The gospel that in Luke is announced by the angels to the shepherds—somewhere near Bethlehem and in the darkest night—will, by the end of Acts, be announced by Paul "openly and unhindered" in the heart of the Roman Empire. Luke's accommodation to the Roman Empire must be tempered by our knowledge that Jesus was crucified by the Roman elite. Finally, the atmosphere Luke 1–2 conveys, through the language he uses, evokes the narrative worlds of Hebrew Scriptures, in which, for example, barren women like Sarah and Hannah become pregnant through God's agency, despite male skepticism and disbelief.

The phrase "Now it happened . . ." in 2:1 will be repeated in 2:6 as an echo of the language of 1:5 and 8, originating from the narrative language patterns of the Septuagint, the Greek translation of Hebrew Scriptures made in the second century BCE.

The phrase "all the inhabited world," also in 2:1, indicates Luke's reductionist worldview since the "inhabited world" (Greek, *oikoumenē*) is greater than the Roman Empire circumscribing Luke–Acts. The preacher would do well to reflect on the consequences of the text's orientation toward Rome. Christianity in fact expanded in the first century CE eastwards into Armenia and Syria, and to the south into ancient Nubia, Ethiopia, and sub-Saharan Africa. Torah-observant Jewish followers of Jesus were not, as the Acts of the Apostles would have us believe, a tiny minority swept aside by the rising tide of Gentile Christianity led by Stephen and then by the apostles Peter and Paul as they broke from Judaism. No, indeed; in Antioch, Edessa, and Syria, Jewish Christian followers of Jesus continued, not as a heretical minority, but flourishing openly as

radical prophets. Luke overlooks this historical reality. We need to mind Luke's gaps.

We find in Luke 2:2 the name Quirinius, the man who was governor in Syria in 6–7 CE. Luke seems to describe the time shortly after Herod's death, which he connects to the census for taxation under Quirinius in 6 CE. This occurred after the removal by Rome of Herod's son Archelaus and was followed by a return to Roman rule. The birth of Jesus under the rule of Herod the Great, which ended in 4 BCE, as described in Matthew, cannot have taken place under the census. By connecting the birth of Jesus to the time when Caesar Augustus was emperor, Luke declares not only the political significance of these events but that they are verifiable. Into a Roman world in which the emperor exercises absolute power, is adored in temples, and is shown on coins to be savior and benefactor, comes an unknown Jewish baby declared by angels and received by nomadic shepherds as Savior and Lord.

In Luke 2:7, the "inn" was a gated enclosure with a central courtyard for the animals; it was encircled by covered rooms without doors, permitting animals to be seen. The regular, closed rooms ordinarily stood at the back. If all the inn rooms are occupied by people there for the official census, and there is "no room for them" (Mary and Joseph), then with his parents in the middle open space, Jesus is born among farm animals and placed in their feeding trough. That space is at the center of the inn rather than away in a separate building behind it, as a traditional interpretation of the story indicates. The Greek word *phatnē* ("manger" or "feeding trough") has a strange and wonderful resonance with Luke's descriptions of Jesus' commensality or table fellowship with every human class and condition, together with lengthy accounts of symposia among Jesus and strangers, and instructions for dining practices (Luke 5:29; 7:36–49; 11:37; 14; 16:21; 17:7; 22; 24:30; cf. Acts 2:42, 46). Reclining or sitting at table, we see Jesus with outcasts and sinners, breaking bread together as a sign of egalitarian community and in anticipation of the messianic banquet in the age to come.

Since the shepherds are keeping guard at night over their flocks, the terrifying appearance of the glory of God creates an extraordinary image of light breaking through a dark, cold night, well before the invention of electricity (Luke 2:9). Commentators note the apposite messianic texts. For example, in Isaiah 9:2, "The people who walked in darkness have seen a great light; those who lived in a land of deep darkness—on them light has shined."

We should note that the light of divine glory shines not around the manger but around singing—celestial, articulate angels seen and heard through human fear and terror for the third time in Luke's birth narratives. In each of these cases, angelic words and song praise the actions of God in specific human lives, bringing about the possibility of earthly change: the lowly are exalted; prophetic voices are heard. God's glory shines forth in the world, not in a private space or designated holy places like the Jerusalem temple or local synagogues, but in the open, boundless, dark fields at night.

The "joy" in Luke 2:10 is already an aspect of Luke's account of the celebration of the birth and the in utero activity of John the Baptist (Luke 1:14, 44). It is emphasized here, since Luke's contrast of the births of John and Jesus in Luke 1–2 is done to show Jesus' birth in a broader light. God's activity in events around human births at the beginning and end of the Gospel is attested by angels (24:4), realized in the concomitant peace amongst people (24:36) and perceived with great joy (24:52). Creating an inclusio as an ending for his Gospel is more than a stylistic technique employed by Luke. It is, as many commentators note, a fitting human appropriation of the birth of the Son, and his rebirth in the resurrection.

DEIRDRE J. GOOD

Commentary 2: Connecting the Reading with the World

The commonplaces about preaching Christmas Eve are all true: it is one of the hardest sermons of the year, because pastors feel pressure to live up to the glorious excesses of the service (poinsettias, congregants decked out in finery) and because we want to charm and impress those people who attend church only once a year (people who, especially if you serve in a small church, may register in the preacher's mind as "potential members"). The Christmas Eve sermon is hard because the emotional landscape of the event is tricky to read. We know from countless studies that Christmas is a time when depression skyrockets—because people who are alone, people who are grieving, people who are estranged from family feel their lives do not match the Christmas-jolly script.[1] Yet preaching toward that blue note (as I disastrously did, my very first Christmas Eve sermon) can be a misstep: blue though people feel, the mood of the Christmas Eve service, after all that caroling and eggnog, is usually pretty festive.[2]

Indeed, the liturgical context puts the preacher in a frustrating position: Luke 2 opens many windows that are theologically, pastorally, and politically important, but the Christmas Eve service might not feel like the right time to climb through any of them. For example, one might wish to preach toward the details Luke 2:6–7 omits and depict the birth of Jesus with more granularity—highlighting the vulnerability of an infant.

One might wish to vivify the dangers of being born in a barn and consider how the circumstances of Jesus' birth connect him in special ways to, say, babies born in refugee camps. One might wish to ponder the question, Could Jesus have died in childbirth? One might wish to complicate the ancient church teaching that Mary labored without pain ("It came about, when [Mary and Joseph] were alone, that Mary then looked with her eyes and saw a small infant and was astonished" is how the pseudepigraphical *Ascension of Isaiah* makes the point).

---

1. See, e.g., Jordana Mansbacher, "Holiday Depression Is Real," *Pediatrics for Parents* 28, no. 5/6 (2012): 22–23.
2. An excellent articulation of many of the challenges of the Christmas Eve sermon may be found in David Lose, "Christmas Eve/Day C: Keep It Simple," http://www.davidlose.net/2015/12/christmas-eveday-c-keep-it-simple/.

Every December, I decide to describe both Mary and Jesus releasing oxytocin, which got Mary's contractions moving; I decide to describe Jesus' head pushing Mary's cervix open. Then I lose my nerve. Climbing through the window that Luke 2:6–7 just barely nudges open would be a decidedly incarnational thing to do—and yet, in many of our contexts, it might jar with the larger liturgical and pastoral requirements of the Christmas Eve service.[3] This is a question for the preacher's discernment: Is it pastorally responsive and theologically sound, or is it playing it safe, to determine that on Christmas Eve, we need and want to hear the familiar Christmas story, and we need and want to hear the most basic theological gloss that story invites, which is also a commonplace: *God came from heaven and took on our human form because God loves us*?

That is a commonplace, but perhaps not an idea easy to grasp, because two thousand years after the incarnation, many of us are accustomed to thinking of God exactly as loving us from afar—loving us but not seeming urgently inclined to be bodily near us. Luke 2 offers a chance to sketch the choreography of love: when you love someone, you want to be near her. Thus the incarnation: the God who loves does not want to loll about on Mount Olympus, far away, loving us but communicating only via occasional theophanies and text messages. The God who loves wants to be near the creatures God loves.

When we consider human relationships, the idea becomes less abstract; human relationships abundantly illustrate that *love engenders a desire for nearness*—embodied nearness. Sex, of course, is one illustration. Another illustration can be found precisely in the many visitors who make the Christmas Eve service atypical. The reason our churches have visitors at Christmas is that people have traveled to be with family, and they have done so because when you love someone, you want to do more than phone that person and say, "Merry Christmas"—you want to be with him in the flesh. The presence of all those stress-inducing visitors, then, is one way the Christmas Eve service connects to the deep theme of Christmas (lovers want to get bodily near the beloved) and to the reading from Luke 2 (just as the shepherds have traveled to be near the object of their love, so our congregants' grown kids and grandkids have traveled to be near their beloved family members).

The presence of visitors is not the only feature of the Christmas Eve service that connects with the Gospel reading. Some favorite Christmas carols—the very songs we sing when processing into church—reprise Luke's account. The lyrics of "O Come, All Ye Faithful," for example, are directly responsive to Luke 2. In its reprisal of Luke 2, the hymn depicts the choreography of Christians' life with God. After establishing, in stanzas 1 and 2, that God "abhors not the Virgin's womb" and came to earth in the form of a baby, most of the song is actually about the way that people (and angels) respond to God's arrival: God draws near and, empowered by God's love, we come to God. Thus, in the third stanza of "O Come, All Ye Faithful" (and in Luke 2:15–16), the shepherds, summoned to the cradle of Jesus, leave their flocks and "draw nigh to gaze." It is no good for the shepherds to stay home and ruminate about the birth of Jesus. The shepherds are supposed to go; and we are supposed to go ("we too will thither," says the song), which is why our congregants left their cozy homes and interrupted family dinners or postponed final wrapping and "thithered" to church. (If your Christmas Eve sermon includes the Eucharist, there is an additional way in which participants in the Christmas Eve service imitate the characters in Luke 2: when we go to the altar we are—like the shepherds, and like Mary and Joseph—gathering around the flesh of Christ.)

In many other sermons, we preach about the places we go after the worship service ends—the places of brokenness and suffering to which, inspired by the example of Jesus and empowered by the Holy Spirit, we are called. The Christmas Eve sermon on Luke 2 gives us

---

3. For various imaginings of and engagements with the details Luke 2:6–7 did not record, see Elizabeth Gandolfo, "A Truly Human Incarnation: Recovering a Place for Nativity in Contemporary Christology," *Theology Today* 70, no. 4 (2014): 382–93; Jennifer A. Glancy, *Corporal Knowledge: Early Christian Bodies* (New York: Oxford University Press, 2010), 81–136; and Lauren F. Winner, *Wearing God: Clothing, Laughter, Fire, and Other Overlooked Ways of Meeting God* (San Francisco: HarperOne, 2015), 158–62.

an opportunity—by attending to the actions of the shepherds, and the actions of our auditors who came to church—to underline instead the Christian call to draw near to the God who in the incarnation drew near to us. Of course, all our worldly sojourns can be a drawing near to God, too—but only because they have been made so by a God who came to the world, for the sake of Love.

LAUREN F. WINNER

Christmas Day/Nativity of the Lord, Proper II

Isaiah 62:6–12
Psalm 97

Titus 3:4–7
Luke 2:(1–7) 8–20

Isaiah 62:6–12

⁶Upon your walls, O Jerusalem,
    I have posted sentinels;
all day and all night
    they shall never be silent.
You who remind the LORD,
    take no rest,
⁷and give him no rest
    until he establishes Jerusalem
    and makes it renowned throughout the earth.
⁸The LORD has sworn by his right hand
    and by his mighty arm:
I will not again give your grain
    to be food for your enemies,
and foreigners shall not drink the wine
    for which you have labored;
⁹but those who garner it shall eat it
    and praise the LORD,
and those who gather it shall drink it
    in my holy courts.

¹⁰Go through, go through the gates,
    prepare the way for the people;
build up, build up the highway,
    clear it of stones,
    lift up an ensign over the peoples.
¹¹The LORD has proclaimed
    to the end of the earth:
Say to daughter Zion,
    "See, your salvation comes;
his reward is with him,
    and his recompense before him."
¹²They shall be called, "The Holy People,
    The Redeemed of the LORD";
and you shall be called, "Sought Out,
    A City Not Forsaken."

Commentary 1: Connecting the Reading with Scripture

Isaiah 62 reaffirms themes found throughout Isaiah. Past, present, and future are telescoped together as the prophet calls the people to reflect, celebrate, and claim the divine promises. Using architectural imagery, Isaiah celebrates the restoration of Jerusalem and the temple and, more expansively, represents the people themselves as a rebuilt city in which God dwells. The city has walls, gates, and highways, and in it the people praise God.

In today's lection the architectural imagery begins with the city's walls, upon which are posted sentinels (*shomerim*). The sentinels do not stand silent guard. They are there to prompt both the people and YHWH, speaking the divine promises ceaselessly even as those promises are being fulfilled. Some believe God has predestined future outcomes and therefore intercession is futile; trusting in God's goodness, we should simply praise God. Others believe frequent, fervent intercessory prayer somehow compels the Deity to do our bidding. The ancient Israelites held thankful praise to God comfortably together with continually reminding God of divine promises yet to be fulfilled (cf. Pss. 89, 119). For the prophet's community, urging God to remember was not a denial of God's goodness or of God's expansive knowledge.

Isaiah 62:7–9 likely represents a summary of the sentinels' message: these are among the promises God has made to Israel throughout history. YHWH swears by the divine self as ultimate authority and wielder of power. Raising the right hand to swear an oath is still familiar to us through courtroom practice and the act of taking public office. In Deuteronomy, God's paradigmatic act of delivering Israel from slavery in Egypt is frequently described as having been by means of the "mighty hand and outstretched arm" (Deut. 4:34; 5:15; 7:19; 11:2; 26:8); similar language appears throughout the Hebrew Bible, especially in Exodus, the Psalms, and Jeremiah, where God's "outstretched arm" is also an image of divine power in creation (Jer. 27:5; 32:17). For God to swear by the divine right hand and mighty arm is for God to swear by the power of the One who created the universe itself.

The threat that others will eat and drink the produce of one's own labors is one of the most common and chilling in the Hebrew Bible. The promise that one will enjoy one's own harvest is one of the Hebrew Bible's most powerful images of peace and plenty. Deuteronomy 28 is an extended treatise on the relations among obedience, disobedience, and blessing. Obedience

to divine commandments will result in blessings and prosperity, including "the fruit of your womb, the fruit of your ground, and the fruit of your livestock, both the increase of your cattle and the issue of your flock" (Deut. 28:4). Disobedience would mean, "You shall become engaged to a woman, but another man shall lie with her. You shall build a house, but not live in it. You shall plant a vineyard, but not enjoy its fruit" (28:30). Similar threats appear in Amos 5:11 and Micah 6:15.

The prophets' audience was people who were intimately familiar with the struggle to raise crops against the threats of poor harvest and pests, and who also knew that even good harvests could be taken from them by burdensome taxation or outright conquest. While in postindustrial contexts today, fewer laborers are directly involved in producing the food that sustains them, many know the frustration of working hard for inadequate wages. Those whose income is sufficient (and who, indeed, may profit from the labor of others) need to remember that God is the champion of the downtrodden.

Interestingly, our Isaiah 62 passage does not leave the people simply consuming their food and drink in the isolation of their own homes. The overarching architectural imagery of the text reasserts itself exactly at this point, placing the people in God's holy courts to consume their bounty as they praise YHWH. Christians reading this passage will likely hear eucharistic overtones in the imagery of consuming grain and wine in the divine presence. In any case, the celebration of God's generosity and protection is not an act to be performed in isolation. We praise God as a community by eating and drinking together—which also implies that our labor should not be narrowly self-serving. The fruit of the people's efforts is for themselves and not "enemies" or "foreigners"; but at the same time it is to be consumed as a community, shared rather than hoarded.

From the vision of the divine courts, the camera lens draws back to depict the procession into the rebuilt city. Because time is telescoped, the addressees are at once the worshiping congregation entering the city and the workers who have preceded them, making it possible for the procession to enter. The many commands image a flurry of activity making the parade possible: Go through! Prepare the way! Build up the highway! Clear it of stones! Lift an ensign! Once all these are done, the procession can begin.

The call to "prepare the way for the people" resonates for us with multiple echoes. It appears in Isaiah's familiar "A voice cries out: 'In the wilderness prepare the way of the LORD, make straight in the desert a highway for our God'" (Isa. 40:3), and in the Synoptic Gospels' citations of Isaiah: "This is the one of whom the prophet Isaiah spoke when he said, 'The voice of one crying out in the wilderness: "Prepare the way of the Lord, make his paths straight"'" (Matt. 3:3; cf. Mark 1:2–3; Luke 3:4). Some of us may even read these words and hear music, whether the tenor soloist in Handel's *Messiah* or Stephen Schwartz's "Prepare Ye (the Way of the Lord)" from *Godspell.*

The passage concludes with a proclamation of YHWH directed to the entire world (62:11–12). All people are called to be witnesses to the divine favor granted to Jerusalem. "Daughter Zion" is a frequent biblical term signifying the deep connection between YHWH and the people, heightening both the pathos of the people's rebellion and downfall (see esp. Isa. 1:8; Jer. 4:31, 6:23; Lam. 2; Mic. 1:13) and the joy of deliverance (see Ps. 9:14; cf. the bridal imagery in Isa. 62:1–5). The message from the world's people seems to point to the procession of verse 10, telling Zion to "Look!" or "Behold!" the advent of salvation. Notably, the first *hinneh* ("behold!") is translated "See" in the NRSV; there is a second, untranslated *hinneh* before the phrase "his reward is with him," intensifying the drama of the prophetic call to behold.

The final statement of the divine proclamation turns to renaming (actually, returns to renaming; see vv. 2–4), another theme closely connected to divine favor in Scripture, for example, in the stories of Abram renamed Abraham (Gen. 17) and Jacob renamed Israel (Gen. 32). Other prophetic texts also speak of the renaming of Jerusalem: "At that time Jerusalem shall be called the throne of YHWH" (Jer. 3:17); "And this is the name by which it will be called: 'YHWH is our righteousness'" (Jer. 33:16); "And the name of the city from that time on shall be, The LORD is There" (Ezek. 48:35).

The desire to be called by a name that specifies the relationship between God and people is not only an ancient one. Modern congregations sometimes seek a name change to pinpoint their contemporary mission. In this passage, it is important to note that the city is named not by its inhabitants, but by God. Indeed, all the action of this rebuilding passage, even the procession of its people, stems from God's initiative and mighty act. In response, the people gather in the holy courts and praise the LORD.

SANDRA HACK POLASKI

Commentary 2: Connecting the Reading with the World

Our cultural observation of Christmas presumes that it is the culmination of something: the fulfillment of the expectations of Advent, when presents long hidden are opened and wishes long held are fulfilled. The festival of lessons and carols is now behind the exhausted choir, and the bleary-eyed preacher at last has a chance to recover from the Christmas Eve midnight service. We have arrived at the destination toward which we have been headed for a month, a year, a lifetime, an eternity. Jesus is born. The king has come.

How strange, then, that on Christmas Day the lectionary has us read Isaiah's declaration that we are still to be watching, that "sentinels" are posted on the walls, that we are to "remind the LORD" and "give him no rest until he establishes Jerusalem and makes it renowned throughout the earth." It is worth recalling that while the arrival of Christmas Day signals the end of Advent, it is the beginning of Christmastide, the first step in the journey toward Easter. Christmas marks not just the arrival we were anticipating but, just as significantly, the point of departure for other destinations. To preach on Christmas Day is not, therefore, to nestle into warm feelings of accomplishment. It is to renew the watch for fulfillment of all that Advent has promised and God has not yet delivered.

Contemporary Christians read Isaiah's words aware that Jerusalem is no less the center of controversy in our day than in the prophet's. Jerusalem remains divided, claimed by competing powers and the scene of regular bloodshed. The preacher need not look further than the daily news for examples of the discrepancy between Isaiah's vision of the "established" city "renowned throughout the earth" and the political powder keg it currently represents. Equally ironic, perhaps, is Isaiah's promise that the produce of the land will be the food not of foreigners, but of those who dwell in it.

Surely any reading of the situation in present-day Israel-Palestine causes the preacher to wonder whether such a promise is true for *all* the inhabitants of the land. The dissonances between prophetic vision and present reality point the preacher back to the call to watchfulness, and to the need for a persistent hopeful nagging at God to make good on these promises. The eschatological promise of Advent is not realized in the manger. Now is not the time to relax.

Isaiah employs the image of the monarch returning victorious from battle (Isa. 62:10–11); he summons those within reach of his voice to "go through the gates" and "prepare the way," to "lift up an ensign over the peoples." The one who comes is the king who brings "salvation" and "recompense," an eschatological setting-to-rights what has gone historically wrong. How does that look in the twenty-first-century American congregation?

The imagery of monarchy is problematic. It reminds us of oppressive systems of economic, racial, and gender-based privilege. It has always carried a mixed value at best; Samuel offered a stern warning to the people of Israel when they cried out for a king (1 Sam. 8), and the Samuel–Kings tradition as a whole is far more critical of monarchy's failings than appreciative of its rewards. In our own time, when elitism born of wealth or class and preserved through access to and retention of political power can replicate the injustices of monarchies, what word should

the preacher say in celebration of the coming eschatological king?

One approach is to warn of its dangers. William Butler Yeats's famous poem "The Second Coming" powerfully accomplishes this mission with its apocalyptic darkness and monstrous images, culminating in the question, "And what rough beast, its hour come round at last/ Slouches towards Bethlehem to be born?"[1] Yeats, writing in 1919 immediately after World War I, echoed western Europe's horror at what monarchy had wrought: entangling alliances of kinship and economics that had brought Europe to the brink of destruction. For Yeats, nothing good happens in the birth of kings.

The core testimony of Christian faith is that the reign of Christ is a dominion of an altogether different sort, a realm of reversed expectations and rekindled hope. The long arc of the gospel teaches that the rule of Christ is not a monarchical monstrosity but a revival of the human spirit, that the hopes of this day are not fulfilled by the exercise of power but through its repudiation, and that nothing—no power or force—will prevent this kingdom's coming, precisely because it is not a kingdom of power and force. He calls the faithful to "build up the highway, clear it of stones" in preparation for the announcement that "your salvation comes."

Richard Wilbur's simple poem "A Christmas Hymn" recasts the image of the coming of the eschatological king by using Jesus' words in Luke 19:40 that "the stones would shout out." Each stanza of Wilbur's poem rehearses a part of the Gospel narrative, featuring the recurring refrain that "every stone shall cry." The poem's final stanza echoes not only the silence of the empty tomb but the hope of Mary's Magnificat (Luke 1:46–55):

> But now, as at the ending,
> the low is lifted high…
> The stars shall bend their voices,
> and every stone shall cry.
> And every stone shall cry
> in praises of the child
> by whose descent among us
> the worlds are reconciled. [2]

---

1. W. B. Yeats, "The Second Coming," in *The Collected Poems of W. B. Yeats* (New York: Macmillan, 1989).

2. Richard Wilbur, "A Christmas Hymn," in *The Poems of Richard Wilbur* (New York: Harcourt Brace & World, 1963), 56–57.

Isaiah seals the promise of reversal in the granting of new names to Jerusalem and its people: "Holy People," "The Redeemed of the LORD," and "Sought Out, A City Not Forsaken." The prophet knows the tremendous psychological and spiritual power in the granting of a new name; names can reshape identities and redirect life and mission.

In his 1997 film *The Apostle*, actor Robert Duvall portrays a Pentecostal preacher, Eulis F. "Sonny" Dewey, pastor of a large suburban white congregation. At the beginning of the film, Sonny is forced out of his pulpit by his wife, Jessie, and her lover, Horace. In a fit of rage, Sonny kills Horace, then flees the scene in shame and fear. Coming to a river, Sonny abandons his car, throws away his wallet and identification, and plunges into the water in an act that mimics his baptism. Upon emerging, he takes on a new identity—Apostle E. F.—and begins a ministry in a small rural African American congregation willing to take him in despite his shady past. He is instrumental in growing the congregation and in convincing a local man to repent of his racism. Eventually, however, E. F. is discovered and surrenders peaceably to police. In the film's final scene, he is preaching to the chain gang to which he has been sentenced.

Isaiah's promise of a new name for Jerusalem and its people, one that does not deny but also does not remain bound by its past, is another reminder that the dawn of Christmas Day is not the end, but rather the beginning, of the narrative of the life of faith. In this time of relational upheaval, when the networks in which we live—networks of race, gender, socioeconomics, and politics—are under renegotiation, this text awakens us from a complacency born of comfort with the past. However strong the temptation to rest from the liturgical and emotional exertions of Advent and Christmas Eve, both prophet and day impel us forward toward a new year, a new identity, and a new hope.

PAUL K. HOOKER

Psalm 97

¹The LORD is king! Let the earth rejoice;
    let the many coastlands be glad!
²Clouds and thick darkness are all around him;
    righteousness and justice are the foundation of his throne.
³Fire goes before him,
    and consumes his adversaries on every side.
⁴His lightnings light up the world;
    the earth sees and trembles.
⁵The mountains melt like wax before the LORD,
    before the Lord of all the earth.

⁶The heavens proclaim his righteousness;
    and all the peoples behold his glory.
⁷All worshipers of images are put to shame,
    those who make their boast in worthless idols;
    all gods bow down before him.
⁸Zion hears and is glad,
    and the towns of Judah rejoice,
    because of your judgments, O God.
⁹For you, O LORD, are most high over all the earth;
    you are exalted far above all gods.

¹⁰The LORD loves those who hate evil;
    he guards the lives of his faithful;
    he rescues them from the hand of the wicked.
¹¹Light dawns for the righteous,
    and joy for the upright in heart.
¹²Rejoice in the LORD, O you righteous,
    and give thanks to his holy name!

Connecting the Psalm with Scripture and Worship

How might it feel to live in such a powerless state that you need an advocate who overcompensates for your state of disempowerment? Psalm 97 is an enthronement psalm that describes such an advocate. God arrives on the scene, not at all subtly, with absolute purpose and in a display of undeniable power, a power that automatically demands a response from those who witness it. This fierce, protective nature toward the vulnerable echoes the description in Isaiah 62, where God shows stalwart faithfulness to those who have sustained their faith, particularly in the face of despair and injustice.

God's Power Displayed. Psalm 97 begins with a description of God's incredible power. The psalmist declares that God is king, then names the attributes upon which God's sovereignty is based, righteousness and justice (Ps. 97:1–2). God's appearance in Psalm 97 is "the cosmic reality that God has entered the process of the world in a decisive way that changes

O Birth Pleasing and Welcome

"The voice of gladness hath resounded in our land, the voice of exultation and salvation in the tents of sinners. A good word has been heard, a consoling word, a speech full of joyfulness, a rumour worthy of all acceptance. Sing praise, O ye mountains, and all ye trees of the woods. Clap your hands before the face of the Lord, because He cometh. Hear, O ye heavens, and give ear, O earth! Be amazed, and let every creature give praise; but thou beyond others, O man!"

Jesus Christ, the Son of God, is born in Bethlehem of Juda.

What heart so stony as not to be softened at these words? What soul is not melted at this voice of her Beloved? What announcement could be sweeter? what intelligence more enrapturing? Was its like ever heard before? or when did the world ever receive such tidings?

Jesus Christ, the Son of God, is born in Bethlehem of Juda.

O short word, telling of the Eternal Word abbreviated for us! O word full of heavenly delights! The heart is oppressed by its mellifluous sweetness, and longs to pour forth its redundant riches, but words refuse their service. So overpowering is the music of this short speech that it loses melody if one iota is changed.

Jesus Christ, the Son of God, is born in Bethlehem of Juda.

O Nativity of spotless sanctity! O birth honourable for the world, birth pleasing and welcome to men, because of the magnificence of the benefit it bestows; birth incomprehensible to the angels, by reason of the depth and sacredness of the mystery! In all its circumstances it is wonderful because of its singular excellence and novelty. Its precedent has not been known, nor has its like ever followed. O birth alone without sorrow, alone without shame, free from corruption, not unlocking, but consecrating the temple of the Virgin's womb! O Nativity above nature, yet for the sake of nature! Surpassing it by the excellence of the miracle, repairing it by the virtue of the mystery! Who shall declare this generation? The angel announces it. Almighty Power overshadows it. The Spirit of the Most High comes upon it. The Virgin believes. By faith she conceives. The Virgin brings forth. The Virgin remains a virgin. Who is not filled with astonishment? The Son of the Most High is born. The Son, begotten of God before all ages, is Incarnate! The Word is become an infant! Who can sufficiently admire? . . .

Jesus Christ, the Son of God, is born in Bethlehem of Juda.

Bernard of Clairvaux, "On the Joy His Birth Should Inspire," in *Sermons of St. Bernard on Advent and Christmas: Including the Famous Treatise on the Incarnation Called "Missus Est,"* trans. St. Mary's Convent in York (London: R. & T. Washbourne Ltd., 1909), 75–77.

---

everything toward life."[1] In the psalm, the very presence of this God who is righteous and just consumes those who would align themselves against God (v. 3). The appearance of a righteous and just sovereign also sheds light on the existing evil and corruption thriving on the earth. This description of a God who destroys those opposed to a life of righteousness and justice mirrors the description of God in Isaiah. God remains sovereign and does not rest from righting the wrongs of the world. Instead, God's very appearance sets into motion the coming of justice, as the Lord promises to rescue those who have been oppressed by the forces of evil. This sets the stage for the collective response of all

creation; all peoples and even other gods erupt in joyful worship of the God who establishes a realm of righteousness on earth.

A Joyful Response. As in Psalm 96, in Psalm 97 God's arrival and presence provokes an immediate and joyful response. Only those who have been opposed to all things good experience fear. Even the mountains, those ancient and holy places, "melt like wax" (v. 5) at the display of God's power; even they cannot withstand God's dominion. When God appears, those who claimed to hold power—including other gods and earthly rulers—shrink before the righteous sovereign. Judah bears witness to

---

1. J. Clinton McCann Jr., "Psalms," in *New Interpreter's Bible* (Nashville: Abingdon Press, 1996), 4:1070.

God's setting the world right and responds with deep gladness. The prophet Isaiah describes this turning of the world as God's own determination to no longer see God's people suffer under oppression. God's commitment to justice does more than elicit joy from the people of God; it empowers them to further the way for God's justice to be proclaimed and shared with the wider world. This empowerment gives birth to a deep and sustaining hope for change.

An Interpersonal God. The person of God in Psalm 97, as in Isaiah 62, is not only an overwhelming and conquering God. God also possesses a commitment to people's lives, to their lived experiences of pain, and calls them by name out of despair and oppression (Isa. 62:12). In Psalm 97, the people know the holy name of God; in Isaiah 62, God calls out to them by their own names: "The Holy People," "The Redeemed of the LORD," and "Sought Out, A City Not Forsaken."

The people of God are not named and called by their own attributes, or even by the measure of their suffering, but by the attributes that God bestows upon them by claiming them as God's own people. Not only does God diminish those who work against righteousness and justice; God sees those who have lived faithfully against all odds. God sees the hope they have sustained through hardship and pain, acknowledges them as God's own, rescues them from those who would seek to destroy them, and protects them from all evil (Ps. 97:10).

Preaching the Text. The preacher might draw on Psalm 97 to highlight the dynamic juxtaposition of God's overarching sovereignty and majesty with God's tenacious seeking out of personal connection and relationship, particularly with those who have suffered under the evils of oppression and injustice. This God of power is also a God of tenderness. This is a God of ultimate justice but also a God who seeks to know and be known by God's own people, to wipe their tears, and to empower them to proclaim the turning of the world toward righteousness, justice, and peace. Such a juxtaposition is seen in the Christ child, the infant Messiah, who in his very person is both divine power and human vulnerability. On Christmas Eve, we welcome such an extraordinary gift with awe and deep joy.

CHRISTINE J. HONG

Titus 3:4–7

[4]But when the goodness and loving kindness of God our Savior appeared, [5]he saved us, not because of any works of righteousness that we had done, but according to his mercy, through the water of rebirth and renewal by the Holy Spirit. [6]This Spirit he poured out on us richly through Jesus Christ our Savior, [7]so that, having been justified by his grace, we might become heirs according to the hope of eternal life.

Commentary 1: Connecting the Reading with Scripture

On Christmas Day we celebrate the coming of a Prince of Peace. At the same time, we struggle with conflict in our relationships, congregations, and denominations. Christian communities are also divided over what posture to adopt toward the broader culture. Should we confront a way of life we see as impure or unjust? Should we, rather, be more accommodating in our efforts to live in peace with our neighbors? Titus offers a resource for preachers interested in considering how the incarnation might tangibly impact our interactions with culture and with one another.

Although not in uniform agreement, modern scholarship largely affirms the Pastoral Epistles' non-Pauline authorship. One significant reason for this opinion is the presence of much vocabulary not seen in letters written by Paul. Furthermore, this vocabulary is composed of words used by Christians of the second century, suggesting a later date for the Pastoral Epistles.[1] In addition, the Pastorals are much more concerned with issues of the later church and, in contrast to the undisputed letters of Paul, they are not concerned over preparation for the second coming. The people addressed in the Pastorals, like us, are living in a time in between the "comings" of Jesus. The life of Christ is a historical happening, and the second coming is not viewed as imminent. They envision a church that needs to settle down, make long-term plans, and negotiate the boundaries between church and culture.

Reflecting these concerns, the author of Titus takes up issues of right teaching, primarily defined in terms of moral purity, and seeks to establish ecclesial leadership tasked with maintaining these standards. This concern is expressed through the household codes—instructions to older men (Titus 2:2), older women (2:3), younger women (2:4–5), younger men (2:6), and slaves (2:9–10)—and also when the author urges the community to devote themselves to good deeds (2:14; 3:8). We also see this concern for purity negatively expressed in the slander of the surrounding culture (e.g., 1:12), and in the impurities he sees creeping into the church community in the form of false teaching and bad behavior (3:9–11). Church leaders are instructed to establish boundaries between church and culture, and to weed out unhealthy values that have made their way into the church community.

Purity, however, whether in doctrine, morality, or ethics, is a value often held in tension with the value of peace. My own denomination, the Presbyterian Church (U.S.A.), places this tension in the form of a question to candidates for ordination: "Do you promise to further the peace, unity, and purity of the church?"[2] It is understood that those who desire to further purity must also somehow find a way to seek peace and unity with those who do not share their convictions about the purity God requires of us.

---

1. Bart D. Ehrman, *The New Testament: A Historical Introduction to the Early Christian Writings*, 2nd ed. (New York: Oxford University Press, 2000), 357.
2. *The Constitution of the Presbyterian Church (U.S.A.), Part II, Book of Order* (Louisville, KY: Office of the General Assembly, Presbyterian Church (U.S.A.), 2015), W-4.0404g.

Within the church, differing convictions can result in conflicts in styles of worship or even over the menu for the annual church brunch. Within denominations, differing ethics place the church in the headlines of major newspapers as we struggle with issues of conscience. Outside of the church, Christians find themselves with differing perspectives as to how to engage with politics or to what degree a Christian should participate in a morally questionable culture or economic markets. If each person pursues their own conscience without regard for peace and unity, conflict can destroy the community. Those seeking to live their faith with integrity will quickly encounter the tension between the value of purity and the value of peace and unity.

Unsurprisingly, then, the author of Titus finds he needs to help his community live in peace, even as they strive to attain the purity he urges. So, after two chapters of urging purity, fretting about the impurities in the culture outside the church, and worrying that these influences are creeping into the church, the author begins to urge them to do their best to get along with everyone. He instructs them "to speak evil of no one, to avoid quarreling, to be gentle, and to show every courtesy to everyone" (3:2).

The author has just cited a Cretan authority who described his compatriots as "liars, vicious brutes, [and] lazy gluttons" (1:12). So how will the author now persuade his audience to treat Cretans with kindness? The author uses Pauline theology, finding a unifying factor among all people, the pure and the impure: all require and find a savior in Jesus Christ: "For we ourselves were once foolish, disobedient, led astray, slaves to various passions and pleasures, passing our days in malice and envy, despicable, hating one another" (3:3). So we can find our motivation for kindness as we see ourselves in those whose behavior we find sinful. Paul communicates similar theology in Romans as he urges Gentiles and Jews to find commonality, "since all have sinned and fall short of the glory of God" (Rom. 3:23). Our common humanity and need, expressed here as our sinfulness, brings us together, creating community, restraining any prideful sense of superiority.

Perhaps most compelling on Christmas Day, the author draws our attention to the incarnation. The author considers the state in which these Christians were previously and then recalls to them how Jesus "appeared" in their lives and how this appearance changed them (Titus 3:4). Before Christ appeared, they were "foolish, disobedient, led astray, slaves to various passions and pleasures, passing our days in malice and envy, despicable, hating one another" (v. 3). This language is almost as harsh as the language the author uses to describe the culture. Apparently, the members of the Christian community were once no different than those whose behavior the author has condemned so harshly. Yet Christ appeared to them, and they were changed.

Moreover, they experienced Christ's appearing as sheer grace. Note the emphasis upon God's initiative in the text. God is the actor throughout the passage. The people simply receive the gift of God's appearance. It is God who appears (v. 4), God who saved them (v. 5), God who "poured out" the Spirit on them (v. 6), God who justified them by grace and gave them "the hope of eternal life" (v. 7). The author also emphasizes they had no part in earning God's appearance, specifying that this event occurred "not because of any works of righteousness that we had done" (v. 5). This community may have been far away from the historical event of Christ's appearing, and they were no longer living in expectation of an imminent second coming. Nonetheless they experienced the reality of Jesus' appearing, and it transformed them.

Titus brings the preacher an opportunity to help her congregation experience Christmas not as a historical memory, but as the grace of Christ's living appearance in our own lives. Christ appeared for the people of this epistle. This appearance was experienced as a grace that enabled them to seek peace with a culture they perceived to be entirely opposed to their values. Christ also appears to us and changes us, freeing us from undue pride as we approach those with whom we are in conflict. The grace of Christ's appearance erases the false boundaries we create among people whom God loves. On Christmas, we celebrate the Prince of Peace who appears among and to us today.

PATRICIA J. CALAHAN

Commentary 2: Connecting the Reading with the World

The New Testament lesson for Christmas Day relates one of Scripture's most remarkable confessions of faith. It provides the congregation with a succinct grammar of Paul's interpretation of salvation's history. Strikingly, Paul begins by personifying God as "goodness" (*chrēstotēs*) and "kindness" (*philanthrōpia*, lit. "love for humans"); this is the apostle's epitome of "God our Savior," which should concentrate our attention as we celebrate the Messiah's birth on Christmas. Advent's month-long retelling of biblical stories that plot the actions of a promise-keeping God prepares a congregation for the exuberant announcement on Christmas Day that God's promise of salvation is now realized in Christ. His birth is confessed as an act of God's goodness and kindness.

In particular, Paul's unusual use of *philanthrōpia*, found only here in the Pauline letters, alerts the congregation to the principal effect of salvation's arrival in Christ. While the noun "goodness" envisages God's empathy toward a helpless people, God's "philanthropy" stretches down to a needy people to deal decisively with humanity's root problem. Through Christ, God our Savior has delivered all people from the deadening effects of sin.

In my Methodist congregation, whenever this claim is made in worship on Christmas Day voices shout out "Hallelujah!" and handbells clang across the sanctuary. We sing with gusto Charles Wesley's great Christmas hymn as our collective witness to this day's essential grammar of faith:

> Mild he lays His glory by,
> Born that we no more may die;
> Born to raise us from the earth,
> Born to give us second birth.[3]

Paul's expression of God's grace as philanthropic activity requires elaboration, especially for our day, when much is made by social media of the civic activism of philanthropists who personally finance solutions to problems that threaten our future. In a polarized world characterized by distrust and division, their generous gifts sound a contrary tone. Pundits debate the who, where, why, and how of these gifts; none, however, disputes their importance for the common good.

Neurologists suggest this kind of generosity is cued by brains hardwired to reward ourselves for acts of kindness toward others. Gift-giving is something we do to survive and thrive. Perhaps for this reason the drumbeat of appeals for charitable gifts reaches its greatest intensity during Christmas season. Whether out of guilt or goodwill, most of us feel pressure to upgrade our giving in response to these appeals. We often engage in considerable hand-wringing to find the right gift to shape beneficial relationships with important others, or to project the right public image to those we seek to impress. In all these senses, gift-giving at Christmas becomes the cultural version of works righteousness—a *philanthrōpia* we should find deeply ironic.

A recent Pew poll found that while 90 percent of Americans celebrate Christmas, only 55 percent regard it as a religious holiday, and still fewer are inclined to think theologically with Paul about how divine philanthropy secures our salvation from sin and death. Christmas has been overwhelmed by the materialism and secularism that shape much American life. Many celebrate the season by creating neighborhood rituals and public gestures that reflect our cultural diversity, the resulting intermingling of holiday traditions creating a phenomenon independent of religious beliefs. Some sing Christmas carols because they are familiar and recall fond memories with family and friends. Still others weaponize Christmas to wage a culture war in support of conservative politics; the freedom to say "Merry Christmas" to our neighbors or in public school classrooms has become an icon of religious freedom. The result is the end of Christmas as the church's moment to remember the beliefs at the heart of Paul's confession.

---

3. Stanza 3 of "Hark! The Herald Angels Sing," #240 in *The United Methodist Hymnal* (Nashville: Abingdon, 1989). Words by Charles Wesley, 1739; alt. by George Whitefield, 1753, and others.

Preaching on Christmas Day affords the opportunity to reassert the indispensable theological claims Paul sets out in this lesson, especially the peculiar nature of God's grace-filled way of philanthropy. Toward this end, we do well to focus on the prior contrast between vices (3:3) and virtues (3:1–2) that frames Paul's confession of salvation's history. This contrast between vice and virtue frames his implied contrast, developed in his other letters (esp. Romans), between our failed attempts to earn God's salvation by "righteous works" (v. 5a) and the triumph of God's mercy through Christ and in the Spirit (vv. 5b–7).

This contrast lies at the heart of Paul's gospel and provides commentary on the Messiah's birth. Here, the conflict between human works and divine mercy is made even more emphatic in the Greek text by placing the main verbal idea, "God saved us," *after* the contrast is asserted (rather than before it, as in most translations). Often in Paul's letters the phrase "because of works" explains why the biblical Torah is an ineffective means of acquiring God's grace. Of course, in making this point Paul is responding to one of the great controversies of his mission to non-Jews: sinners are initiated into their life with God by trusting in the results of Jesus' messianic death alone, rather than in the rites and rituals prescribed by mainstream Judaism.

Here, however, the meaning of the phrase is much broader and intends to subvert *any* human activity, no matter how righteous and pleasing to God. God's saving grace breaks into our lives because of Jesus, not because of our good deeds. Clearly, Paul does not disregard good works; in fact, he underscores their importance (3:1–2). Nevertheless, Paul rejects works as a precondition for initiation into life with God. The way to salvation has already been paved by the appearance of Christ alone, and we now experience salvation in the realm of his Spirit alone.

The connection of the catchphrase "in the Holy Spirit" (v. 5), and the believer's "washing, regeneration, renewal"—words that elsewhere in Paul's letters refer to spiritual formation—presents an opportunity, during the Christmas season, to link Christ's advent with the Pentecostal advent of the Holy Spirit.[4] Although it is difficult to discern logical relationships or fine distinctions among these properties of the Spirit's work in transforming the believer's life, the pairing of "regeneration and renewal" envisions the result of the Spirit's "washing" (or baptism).

Regeneration refers to the Spirit's initial work in mediating God's salvation-creating grace, whereby the believer experiences life in brand-new ways. Renewal is similar in meaning, although in Pauline thought the idea is associated with transforming the way we think (so Rom. 12:2; Col. 3:10). Renewal is not only conceptually knowing better God's will for our moral practices. Renewal is embodying in public places—as "living sacrifices" to God (Rom. 12:1)—what we come to know as the gospel truth. In Acts the emphasis is slightly different: the Spirit's baptism (or "filling") is more prophetic and tied to the community's empowerment to witness publicly by word and deed to the risen One. At stake for Paul is the Spirit's role in a congregation's moral and spiritual transformation, from a life of vice to one of virtue (Titus 3:1–3; Gal 5:16–26). Christmas Day worship, then, also cues this Spirit-filled meaning of regeneration and renewal, which seems to envisage a maturing process in distinct stages by which the covenant-keeping community comes to imitate the wondrous goodness and kindness of God manifest in the Messiah's birth.

ROBERT W. WALL

4. Robert W. Wall, "Salvation's Bath by the Spirit: A Study of Titus 3:5b–6 in Its Canonical Setting," in *The Spirit and Christ in the New Testament and Christian Theology*, ed. I. Howard Marshall, Volker Rabens, and Cornelis Bennema (Grand Rapids: Eerdmans, 2012), 198–212.

Luke 2:(1–7) 8–20

[1]In those days a decree went out from Emperor Augustus that all the world should be registered. [2]This was the first registration and was taken while Quirinius was governor of Syria. [3]All went to their own towns to be registered. [4]Joseph also went from the town of Nazareth in Galilee to Judea, to the city of David called Bethlehem, because he was descended from the house and family of David. [5]He went to be registered with Mary, to whom he was engaged and who was expecting a child. [6]While they were there, the time came for her to deliver her child. [7]And she gave birth to her firstborn son and wrapped him in bands of cloth, and laid him in a manger, because there was no place for them in the inn.

[8]In that region there were shepherds living in the fields, keeping watch over their flock by night. [9]Then an angel of the Lord stood before them, and the glory of the Lord shone around them, and they were terrified. [10]But the angel said to them, "Do not be afraid; for see—I am bringing you good news of great joy for all the people: [11]to you is born this day in the city of David a Savior, who is the Messiah, the Lord. [12]This will be a sign for you: you will find a child wrapped in bands of cloth and lying in a manger." [13]And suddenly there was with the angel a multitude of the heavenly host, praising God and saying,

[14]"Glory to God in the highest heaven,
	and on earth peace among those whom he favors!"

[15]When the angels had left them and gone into heaven, the shepherds said to one another, "Let us go now to Bethlehem and see this thing that has taken place, which the Lord has made known to us." [16]So they went with haste and found Mary and Joseph, and the child lying in the manger. [17]When they saw this, they made known what had been told them about this child; [18]and all who heard it were amazed at what the shepherds told them. [19]But Mary treasured all these words and pondered them in her heart. [20]The shepherds returned, glorifying and praising God for all they had heard and seen, as it had been told them.

Commentary 1: Connecting Reading with Scripture

Christmas Day's Gospel reading opens with a decree from Emperor Augustus that has compelled Joseph and Mary to travel to Bethlehem to register (Luke 2:1–5). The registration was meant to ensure that each family would give due tribute to Rome. Tributes, in the form of crops, supplied food to the Roman military and to Roman cities.[1] The Jewish people were familiar with tributes, for they had lived through subjugation under the Assyrian and Babylonian Empires. The lection from Isaiah, written in the postexilic period, speaks directly to this experience when God promises, "I will not again give your grain to be food for your enemies . . . but those who garner it shall eat it" (Isa. 62:8–9). It expresses the community's deep longing for enduring liberation from foreign powers.

The rest of Isaiah presses the hope that God will reconstitute Israel under God's power: "For I am about to create new heavens and a new

---

1. Richard A. Horsley, *Jesus and Empire: The Kingdom of God and the New World Disorder* (Minneapolis: Augsburg Fortress, 2003), 30–34.

earth. . . . I am about to create Jerusalem as a joy" (65:17–18). This longing for liberation and renewal reverberates through the centuries; it takes on distinctive meaning in Jesus and is echoed in the words of the angel to Mary: "He will reign over the house of Jacob forever, and of his kingdom there will be no end" (Luke 1:33). All of God's people are still waiting for new heavens and new earth. The lection provides insight into the character of waiting in hopeful expectation.

Colonizing empires such as Rome and Babylon not only seized land and crops; they also violated the cultural self-understanding of those they subjugated. The Babylonian Empire destroyed the Jerusalem temple in 586 BCE and deported its priests and rulers, destroying core symbols of Jewish identity. In Isaiah, God heals this ruptured identity, calling the people "My Delight Is in Her" and "The Holy People, The Redeemed of the LORD" (Isa. 62:4, 12). Instead of "Forsaken," they are "Sought Out" (v. 12). God speaks a counternarrative to rebuild the people from within as they begin to rebuild Jerusalem from without.

A similar pattern, seen in Luke 2, illustrates the power inherent in God's refashioning of identity. Elites in Rome looked down upon people living in Judea and Galilee. The orator Cicero once said that Judeans, among others, were "born to be slaves."[2] In the eyes of power, Mary, Joseph, and Jesus were "born to be slaves." So, too, were the shepherds. God says otherwise. To the shepherds, God's angel says, "to *you* is born this day in the city of David a Savior" (Luke 2:11). The counternarrative: born not slaves but beloved of God, those for whom a Savior is given.

This counternarrative was embodied completely by Mary, and it changed her. Mary was a woman living under the power of Rome, defined by her relationship to Joseph as "the betrothed to him one" (2:5, my trans.). Yet Mary is the one God choses. Mary gives birth to Jesus. Mary treasures the shepherds' words in her heart. Mary receives Simeon's prophesy about Jesus (2:34–35) and admonishes Jesus at

the temple (2:48). Mary has voice and power, all drawn from her intimate connection with God. In Luke 1:48, Mary declares in her song, "Surely, from now on all generations will call me blessed." Surely they do.

Mary is transformed, but even she waits for fulfillment of her vision: "He has brought down the powerful from their thrones, and lifted up the lowly; he has filled the hungry with good things, and sent the rich away empty" (1:52–53). Hers is a story of transformation and hope in the midst of waiting. God refashions her identity, and it changes how she moves through the world. The church can participate in this work today by transforming destructive narratives that rupture people's identities. Proclaiming life-giving, God-loving counternarratives can transform us and change how we move through the world, even amid ongoing suffering and injustice.

The metaphor of giving birth is instructive about our waiting on God's promise of new heavens and earth. In Luke, the Greek root for "giving birth" is *tiktō*. Its usage elsewhere shows the importance of *tiktō* for understanding God's remaking of the world. In the Gospel of John, Jesus foretells his death and resurrection to his disciples, saying, "Very truly, I tell you, you will weep and mourn, but the world will rejoice; you will have pain, but your pain will turn into joy" (John 16:20). He then likens what is coming to a woman giving birth (*tiktē*) experiencing pain and anguish until the child is born (v. 21). One can imagine Mary at the foot of the cross experiencing a second labor as her son, Jesus, dies, and then rises three days later.

Transformation requires a gestational period often accompanied by pain. This is not a justification of suffering. It simply acknowledges that waiting in hope and struggling in pain are noticeable rhythms in the life of the people of God living in a world not yet fully made new. Suffering does not mean forsakenness.

The metaphor of birth is used again in Revelation 12:2, where a woman is "crying out in birth pangs, in the agony of giving birth" (*tekein*). In 12:4 a great dragon, symbolizing Satan, tries to

---

2. Cicero, *Epistulae ad Quintum Fratrem* 1.1.19; Cicero, *De Provinciis Consularibus* 10; cited in David Nystrom, "We Have No King but Caesar: Roman Imperial Ideology and the Imperial Cult," in *Jesus Is Lord, Caesar Is Not: Evaluating Empire in New Testament Studies*, ed. Scot McKnight and Joseph B. Modica (Downers Grove, IL: InterVarsity, 2013), 25.

devour her child as it is being born. That child is the same Messiah announced in Luke 2:11. Here, the period of giving birth occupies the space between the new and the old; it is a space of primal pain and danger. There is a tangible threat to hope. The Savior is not yet born; the battle is not yet won and may seem unwinnable from this side of time. That is true of life in this world. Sometimes it feels as if the darkness is winning. The Scriptures know this reality and urge us never to lose hope. Revelation goes on to describe a battle of cosmic proportions between God, Satan, and all the angels, where God vanquishes the enemy and fulfills the promise of new heavens and earth.

While pain and suffering are part of the Christmas story, the primary focus of Luke 2 is the joy that is possible amid suffering. In Luke 2:10 the angel declares "good news of great joy for all the people." The word Luke uses for joy is *charan*, the same word John uses in 16:22 when Jesus tells the disciples, "Your hearts will rejoice, and no one will take your joy from you." Joy is possible in the midst of things unfulfilled because God does not wait to refashion God's people in power and love. As the faith and life of Mary illustrate, joy springs from an intimate connection with God already growing and taking shape within. There is joy in trusting that even though the darkness is great, "Light dawns for the righteous, and joy for the upright in heart" (Ps. 97:11). After the pain of labor, we will see the face of God. Heavens and earth will be reborn, life will be a joy, and of God's loving Day there will be no end.

ERICA KNISELY

Commentary 2: Connecting the Reading with the World

Adi Nes is an Israeli artist known for his photography. His most famous work is a version of Leonardo da Vinci's *The Last Supper*, a photo in which young Israeli soldiers, members of the Israeli Defense Forces (IDF), are substituted for Jesus and his disciples.[3] In Nes's piece, the men are in uniform and are in various stages of conversation or isolation. Some soldiers demonstrate fellowship, sitting close in intimate, quiet conversation, hands over one another's shoulders. One lights a cigarette for a companion; another pours his comrade a drink; one kneels to listen in on two peers. One stands by himself, watching his fellows; another, in the center, is caught up in reverie. These men have gathered for their last supper before going into battle, but the photo disrupts established notions of masculinity and warfare, and provides a startling new point of comparison for thinking about Leonardo's painting and the Last Supper.

Like the soldiers in Nes's photograph, the narrative of shepherds receiving the news of Jesus' birth in the Gospel of Luke disrupts our perspectives. The shepherds form their own community of fellowship; they are also persons on the fringes, who in spite of, or maybe because of, their position are able to receive and be transformed by the angel's message.

Much like the shepherds, Adi Nes lives on the margins of his community. Nes belongs to his community. Yet, as the child of Iranian émigrés and as a gay man, he perceives that he is not quite aligned with what some hold to be normative Israeli culture.[4] Nes relates that when he became an IDF soldier—a requirement for Jewish Israeli citizens—he felt he was integrated into his society; yet, because of some aspects of his identity, he also continued to be an outsider. What does it mean to be part of something, yet set apart? What is the value of seeing something not only from the insider perspective but also from the position of an outsider? Nes's photography explores these questions, providing a perspective that is fresh and challenging.

The shepherds in the Gospel of Luke are literally on the fringes of their community, living in

---

3. The 1999 photographic work, "Untitled (The Last Supper Before Going Out to Battle)," measures 90 × 148 inches. Adi Nes created it for a series entitled *Soldiers, Boys, and Biblical Stories.*

4. James Estrin and David Furst, "Underpinnings of Greek Tragedy in Israel," *New York Times/Lens*, July 17, 2012.

fields and working throughout the night. They are not part of the centralized community that hustles and bustles throughout the daytime; they are in many ways their own community, though they still exist within the boundaries of the larger community. Through their story we are provided with a viewpoint that deserves consideration. It is a perspective that, like Nes's photography, causes us to pause and reconsider our established notions of how the world works.

We might expect that news of Jesus' birth, which Luke proclaims brings the Son of God into the world, would be delivered to the powerful, to those who, having more resources than shepherds, would be able to proclaim the message far and wide. It seems counterintuitive to think such significant news, news about the birth of a royal and political figure destined to change the world, would be given to people without much standing or significance, a marginalized group living under the authority of the Roman Empire.

Some biblical scholars assert that shepherds were lowly people, not well respected, perhaps even people of ill repute or thieves. This could be the way Luke viewed shepherds. Given Luke's themes of status reversal, where the lowly are exalted and the exalted are made low, it might make sense in this Gospel, which seeks to disrupt the status quo, that the shepherds receive the good news about the birth of Jesus. This Gospel is full of the unexpected, relating stories like the one about Lazarus and the rich man, who find themselves in reversed positions in the afterlife. If disruption of status norms is a gospel norm, then the shepherds are indeed the appropriate recipients of the message in this narrative.

Other scholars take a different view, noting that the idea of the shepherd as caretaker is found throughout the Old Testament. For instance, in Psalm 23 the metaphor of shepherd is used to convey something about the very nature of God. Moses provides another positive example of the role of shepherd. In Exodus, Moses leads his community out of slavery in Egypt, but before that, he works for his father-in-law as a shepherd. So there is precedent for viewing the shepherds in Luke as persons of lowly station

who are marginal to the central community, but also as trustworthy and honored recipients of the news of Jesus' birth.

Whether the shepherds are viewed primarily as lowly figures, or are held in high regard for their vigilance over their flocks, in Luke they are among the first to know God is doing something new in the world. Because of their ambiguous social location (being part of the larger community but also separate from it), they might easily be overlooked, Nevertheless, their response to the angelic announcement merits our attention. The shepherds offer us both an insider perspective and a perspective from the margins.

The idea that we gain something of value by attempting to understand Scripture from a variety of vantage points is not new. Various writers and theologians have expressed such ideas. For example, Dietrich Bonhoeffer, the German theologian and pastor executed by the Nazis near the end of World War II because of his participation in a plot to overthrow Hitler, coined the phrase "the view from below." The view from this position helps us pay attention to the voices of the marginalized and calls us to work toward achieving social justice in our communities.

Theologian Sallie McFague takes such thinking to a personal level. In *Life Abundant* she notes that for much of our society the ideal, hegemonic human being is a young, white, heterosexual male. Anyplace where we as individuals fail to fit this ideal is our "wild space," the space where we are most creative and imaginative and can, from a place of self-reflection and introspection, be transformed and transformative.[5]

The shepherds in Luke are transformed characters. As part of the community, insiders, they are recipients of good news they are able to comprehend: the promised Messiah has arrived. Because they are also outsiders, viewing things from below or from the margins, they see and believe what the powerful may be slow to recognize: a baby in a manger is the Messiah. They also return to their place, to their sheep.

Dietrich Bonhoeffer returned to his home in Germany from the safety of the United States because he believed he was called to transform his country from within. Similarly, Adi Nes at

5. See Sallie McFague, *Life Abundant: Rethinking Theology and Economy for a Planet in Peril* (Minneapolis: Augsburg Fortress, 2001), 47–50.

one point contemplated leaving Israel but did not. He decided he had to be part of Israel, given that the country and its people are the source of his artistic expression.

What connections might we make in the communities within which we remain embedded? Are we as receptive as the shepherds were to the angelic message they received? What wild spaces in our lives provide opportunities for transformation, for transformative work for others? Finally, how carefully do we listen to those on the margins, those with less opportunity to share their good news, but simultaneously those who may be in a privileged position for hearing gospel truths?

SALLY SMITH HOLT

Christmas Day/Nativity of the Lord, Proper III

Isaiah 52:7–10
Psalm 98

Hebrews 1:1–4 (5–12)
John 1:1–14

Isaiah 52:7–10

⁷How beautiful upon the mountains
>   are the feet of the messenger who announces peace,
> who brings good news,
>   who announces salvation,
>   who says to Zion, "Your God reigns."
> ⁸Listen! Your sentinels lift up their voices,
>   together they sing for joy;
> for in plain sight they see
>   the return of the LORD to Zion.
> ⁹Break forth together into singing,
>   you ruins of Jerusalem;
> for the LORD has comforted his people,
>   he has redeemed Jerusalem.
> ¹⁰The LORD has bared his holy arm
>   before the eyes of all the nations;
> and all the ends of the earth shall see
>   the salvation of our God.

Commentary 1: Connecting the Reading with Scripture

My husband and I once found ourselves alone, much longer than anticipated, in a hospital waiting room on Mother's Day morning, while our three-year-old underwent a bit of "routine" surgery. There was no more beautiful sound in the world that morning than that of the surgeon's footsteps coming down the hall; even before he spoke to us, we were confident that the procedure was complete and our daughter was on the way to recovery.

This is the sense in which the messenger of Isaiah 52:7 is said to have "beautiful" feet. By placing us not at the scene of divine triumph, but at the moment when news of God's reign is delivered, the story collapses into one overwhelmingly joyous moment. We imagine people waiting for a message to arrive, straining their ears for distant footsteps, desperately eager to hear the news but at the same time dreading the possibility that the tidings might not

be good. The herald finally comes: peace, good news, happiness, salvation—all are rolled up together in the dynamic pronouncement: "Your God reigns."

Our passage, situated just before the fourth of Isaiah's Servant Songs, comes at a climactic point in Deutero-Isaiah (Isa. 40–55), and is part of the Zion poem of Isaiah 52:1–12. The historical setting of chapters 1–39 shifts markedly in chapter 40 to a setting that is clearly the Babylonian exile, describing the relationship of the people to God during this difficult time, and imagining life beyond exile. Beginning with the familiar passage "Comfort, O comfort my people, says your God" (Isa. 40:1), Deutero-Isaiah expresses God's continuing love and care for the people, and promises that they will once again worship YHWH in Jerusalem/Zion.

The Zion poem comes near the end of this section of Isaiah and recapitulates and summarizes many of Deutero-Isaiah's themes. At this climactic point, the poem's various voices interact in what might be described as a symphony of praise to God. Indeed, it is fitting that this text has frequently been set to music, because the poetry loses something of its power in translation and exposition and might better be conveyed as a piece of music. Imagine a contrapuntal polyphony, in which each voice part has its own coherent melody, and harmony is created by the ways the parts relate to one another.

I imagine the first verse of our passage, the first theme in this textual symphony, as a bold, stirring melody, a celebration that sweeps up both message and messenger. Paul makes the connection between proclaimer and proclamation in citing this text (also frequently set to music):

> But how are they to call on one in whom they have not believed? And how are they to believe in one of whom they have never heard? And how are they to hear without someone to proclaim him? And how are they to proclaim him unless they are sent? As it is written, "How beautiful are the feet of those who bring good news!" (Rom. 10:14–15)

It may be difficult to discern whether preachers are tempted more to discount their role as messengers of the gospel or egotistically to overplay it. Are we embarrassed when our feet are called "beautiful"? Do we instead exploit the opportunity and ask for expensive shoes? In any case, focusing as this verse does on the moment of proclamation reminds professional proclaimers and laypeople alike that we can and should find joy and satisfaction in transmitting faithfully the message with which we have been entrusted.

If the theme of verse 7 is a melodic solo, then verse 8 introduces a small ensemble, singing in counterpoint to that melody. The idea of sentinels posted on the destroyed walls of Jerusalem is present foolishness but, more significantly, also signals future hope. Sentinels have no business being on walls that are not there; there is nothing for them to look out for, no one for them to warn of coming danger, no way for them to defend from invasion if an enemy is approaching. Yet there they are. As it turns out, there

is in fact something for them to see: "in plain sight . . . the return of YHWH to Zion." Joyful hearing (of the messenger, Isa. 52:7) becomes joyful seeing, and joyful seeing becomes joyful singing.

There is yet another musical line to add to the text's symphony. The ruins themselves—which ought to be silent and, well, destroyed—now add their chorus to the composition! If Handel's *Messiah* is playing in your head, you have just come to the "Hallelujah Chorus." If you are hearing Beethoven's Ninth Symphony, these are the first strains of "Ode to Joy." The ruins' message is that the imperative of the beginning of Deutero-Isaiah has been realized: "Comfort, O comfort my people" (40:1) is now, "YHWH has comforted his people." YHWH is the Redeemer, and the people are redeemed—a frequent theme in Deutero-Isaiah (see especially 52:3, in which the people "shall be redeemed without money").

In addition to "redeemed," other thematic words from Deutero-Isaiah tie the various voices in this composition together. Note the frequency and variety of the key terms: "peace," "good news," "salvation," "reigns" (v. 7); "joy," "return" (v. 8); "comforted," "redeemed" (v. 9); "holy," "salvation" (v. 10). The melodic voices are varied, but the central theme is clear: what God has promised, God has begun to do and will continue to do. Even though the city is yet in ruins, the message is good news.

Finally, we find clearly proclaimed a core theme that Deutero-Isaiah shares with the whole of Isaiah: God's salvation of Jerusalem has the attention of the whole world. Isaiah's emphasis on the universal nature of God's reign, beginning in Jerusalem and extending through the entire earth, is not unique to this prophetic book, but the theme appears more prominently in Isaiah than anywhere else in the Hebrew Bible. In Isaiah 2, nations stream to Jerusalem for instruction and judgment, resulting in universal peace and prosperity in which "they shall beat their swords into plowshares, and their spears into pruning hooks; nation shall not lift up sword against nation, neither shall they learn war any more" (2:4). Isaiah 25 offers the vision of the mountain on which "YHWH of hosts will make for all peoples a feast of rich food, a feast of well-aged wines," and "will swallow up death forever" (25:6, 8). There is the promise of a Servant who "will bring forth justice to the nations" (42:1), a Servant who is "a light to the nations, that my salvation may reach to the end of the earth" (49:6). There is also God's promise to foreigners that "my house shall be called a house of prayer for all peoples" (56:7). The extension of divine favor to all the peoples of the world, then, is a common Isaianic theme.

The passage's final emphasis on the universality of divine salvation is one appropriate place for Christian interpreters to connect Isaiah's proclamation with the story of Christmas. In the birth of the holy child, Christians profess that God, out of love for the whole world, has fulfilled the promises recorded in Isaiah, "and all the ends of the earth shall see the salvation of our God."

SANDRA HACK POLASKI

Commentary 2: Connecting the Reading with the World

It is almost like Christmas morning, this joyful, exuberant text. Only a few verses earlier the prophet is urging Jerusalem, the holy city, "Awake, awake, put on your strength. . . . Shake yourself. . . . rise up!" Isaiah seems almost like a child urging her parents to rouse from sleep and come downstairs to the Christmas tree, surrounded by gifts, to see what those gloriously wrapped presents might contain. Excitement is in the air, anticipation now about to be gratified. She can hardly contain herself. This text is, to extend the metaphor, what she sees from the top of the stairs.

As in Isaiah 62:6–12, the prophet here draws on the image of the returning king, victorious in battle, having accomplished the deliverance of the people from an enemy. Our text shows us not the victory itself, but only the rumor of it: messengers sent ahead of the vanquishing army to announce the good news of deliverance and peace, the arrival of the king, sentinels on the parapets who "break forth together into singing" the praises of the Lord who "has bared his holy arm before the eyes of all the nations."

At the risk of sounding a discordant note, the preacher on Christmas Day does well to temper enthusiasm, especially when proclaiming the news triumphant. The coming of Isaiah's envisioned king is as yet only announced; it is not realized. The promised deliverance is not yet fulfilled, at least from the prophet's perspective. What the text celebrates is the "beautiful feet" of those advance messengers who bring good news

of a coming salvation, not the arrival of the salvation itself. However inevitable the king's coming, he still has some ground to cover before he reaches the city gates. This is the situation every believer faces on Christmas morning: Christ has come, but the world still seems committed to its same old hurtful ways.

This is a moment for revisiting the ancient Christian theological tension between a realized and a future eschatology. Is the kingdom here, or yet to come? Do the birth, life, death, and resurrection of the Messiah mean that rulers are now deprived of their ultimate power, or is that messianic victory still ahead of us? The answer, of course, is yes. The world is still the world; the powers are still the powers. Yet the testimony of Scripture is that there is a direct line from the manger to the cross to the tomb to the mountaintop in Galilee to the final consummation of the hope of salvation. The Christian liturgical cycle has it right: the hope of Advent, birthed at Christmas, grows through the ordinariness of things, until at year's end it blooms as Christ the King, and then returns to hope again. David Jensen has put it well: "Jesus proclaims the kingdom as something yet to come, but he also embodies it in acts of healing, blessing, and table fellowship. As Christians yearn for Christ to come again, we do not simply stare into the far-off distant future, *we remember the future* as we recall the person of Jesus Christ, who represents the coming of the kingdom."[1]

---

1. David H. Jensen, *Living Hope: The Future and Christian Faith* (Louisville, KY: Westminster John Knox Press, 2010), 26, emphasis added.

The notes of Handel's *Messiah* linger in the air around this text. Handel's musical setting of verse 7 is subtle. It is set in G minor, so that the celebration of the "beautiful feet" is strangely muted by the vaguely mournful tone of the minor key. The soaring soprano line adorns the beauty of the message of coming salvation, but not without restraint. Handel could have chosen to set the announcement of salvation, the bringing of "glad tidings of good things," in a more triumphant, expansive major key, lending a sense of finality and satisfaction to the message. Instead he darkens the news of salvation with musical yearning for something as yet unrevealed, still searched for.

Handel's librettist, Charles Jennens, contributes to this theme by placing it not in Part I, following the birth of Jesus, but near the end of Part II, after Christ's passion, death, resurrection, and ascension, in a section on the proclamation of the church. The soprano aria on this text precedes an extended treatment of Psalm 2 (begun in the bass with the aria "Why do the nations rage?") dealing with the rejection of the gospel by the world. Only after the gospel is proclaimed and rejected does the tenor foretell that God "will break them with a rod of iron" (Ps. 2:9) and the great Hallelujah sounds to close the earthly vision and open the way to history's culmination in the divine kingdom. Like the prophet, Handel and Jennens place this text in a median position, announcing a salvation that, though present, is still emerging against resistance.

It may fairly be said of this text that for us who have become accustomed to seeing only the drudgery of daily life, it lifts our eyes to see that something else is possible, and—with the right tilt of will—even visible in our midst. What we celebrate at Christmas is the good news borne by messengers upon the mountains (dare one say angels?) that there is—within, behind, and below the world of the grit and grime—another world of justice and peace. Part of the task of preaching on Christmas Day is to speak that world into being, to be one of those whose beautiful feet are visible upon the mountain, one of the sentinels who see from the parapets what those of us on the ground cannot: the return of the Lord to Zion.

The American poet Richard Wilbur knew something of this task. Wilbur had a way of taking mundane realities and making them luminous. In his 1956 poem "Love Calls Us to the Things of This World," he describes a man waking in the early morning to the sound of a clothesline being pulled through a pulley, laden with drying laundry. As his soul "hangs for a moment, bodiless and simple / as false dawn," he is aware that "the morning air is all awash with angels":

> Some are in bed-sheets, some are in blouses,
> Some are in smocks: but truly there they are.

For a moment, the man wishes the angelic vision would remain unchanged, that "there be nothing on earth but laundry," but he knows that the moment is only that: a moment. If it is to remain, it must be merged with the struggle of the present, awaiting a fulfillment yet unrealized. And so,

> Bring them down from their ruddy gallows;
> Let there be clean linen for the backs of
>   thieves;
> Let lovers go fresh and sweet to be undone,
> And the heaviest nuns walk in a pure floating
> Of dark habits,
> keeping their difficult balance.[2]

That, it would seem, is the task of preaching on Christmas Day: to keep the difficult balance between hope and hopelessness, between grime and glory, between the already and the not yet. Preaching on Christmas Day is the announcement from the top of the stairs that the tree is surrounded with presents yet unopened, that the future is a region yet unexplored. Preaching on Christmas Day is that sound outside the window, early in the morning, that awakens us to the cries of sentinels, calls us to raise our eyes to see the beautiful feet upon the mountains, and gives us the courage to trust that, whether we can see them or not, there are angels in the laundry.

PAUL K. HOOKER

---

2. Richard Wilbur, "Love Calls Us to the Things of This World," in *The Poems of Richard Wilbur* (New York: Harcourt, Brace & World, 1963), 63–64.

Psalm 98

¹O sing to the LORD a new song,
 for he has done marvelous things.
His right hand and his holy arm
 have gotten him victory.
²The LORD has made known his victory;
 he has revealed his vindication in the sight of the nations.
³He has remembered his steadfast love and faithfulness
 to the house of Israel.
All the ends of the earth have seen
 the victory of our God.

⁴Make a joyful noise to the LORD, all the earth;
 break forth into joyous song and sing praises.
⁵Sing praises to the LORD with the lyre,
 with the lyre and the sound of melody.
⁶With trumpets and the sound of the horn
 make a joyful noise before the King, the LORD.

⁷Let the sea roar, and all that fills it;
 the world and those who live in it.
⁸Let the floods clap their hands;
 let the hills sing together for joy
⁹at the presence of the LORD, for he is coming
 to judge the earth.
He will judge the world with righteousness,
 and the peoples with equity.

Connecting the Psalm with Scripture and Worship

Psalm 98 is an enthronement psalm, as are the other two psalms appointed for Christmas, Psalms 96 and 97. This psalm celebrates and honors the arrival of an all-powerful God who intentionally engages the world and humankind with purposeful justice and equity. God is one who undoubtedly governs and rules but, unlike human rulers, does so with the ultimate motivation of seeing goodness flourish in the world for all of creation. The basis of God's work of equity and justice in the world is God's faithfulness to, and love for, creation.[1]

God is not a Creator who abandons creation after setting it in motion. God does not govern at a distance. Instead, God actively seeks engagement with the world, its ecosystem, and its people, in order to see it thrive and produce good. In Psalm 98, God arrives in power and majesty but is still a Creator God who is deeply relational and personal in God's overwhelming love. As in Isaiah 52, when the world recognizes and receives this sovereign judge, it cannot help but shout for joy.

1. J. Clinton McCann Jr., "Psalms," in *New Interpreter's Bible* (Nashville: Abingdon Press, 1996), 4:1072.

The Judge Par Excellence. In this psalm, the psalmist sings in an eschatological key. The deep hope and yearning of the world for righteousness and justice have culminated in this moment of God's arrival. The psalm begins with the psalmist's proclamation of God's ultimate victory and triumph over injustice in the world. God arrives, not covertly or in secret, but visibly and with authority. God makes known what God has done and is continually doing. There is no secrecy here, only complete transparency and clarity.

The worst type of judge would be one who works without clarity or transparency. How could judges or rulers who do not listen to the people before them garner trust or loyalty? The psalmist describes God in just the opposite terms. This God is undeniably concerned with the visibility of God's love and faithfulness, which then gives birth to God's just and equitable reign. There is no need to fear this God, who chooses to act and govern visibly and faithfully.

Proclamation of God's Creation. In Psalm 98, the psalmist calls all of creation to declare God's power and justice and to sing with joy and praise. The psalm reflects a feeling of being so consumed with the totality of God's arrival and the overturning of the world's injustice that one cannot help but proclaim it with gladness. God's very presence in the world—this intentional and incarnational appearance of divine justice—elicits a joyful response not only from God's people, but from all of creation as well.

It is not enough that only humankind expresses their deep joy, but all of the earth must do so as well—the sea and all its creatures, the world and all who live in it. The joy is so overflowing that floods break out in applause and hills burst out in song. In this way, Psalm 98 echoes the exuberant joy expressed in Isaiah 52:7–10. In Isaiah, even sentinels, those that are called to watch and guard against enemies, are called outside of their designated roles to join the chorus of singing in celebration and proclamation. There is no longer any need for people to guard and watch for enemies, for God has arrived. In Isaiah, even the lonely ruins of Jerusalem, which evoke feelings of destruction, despair, and hopelessness, are called upon to sing a song of triumph at God's arrival, effectively changing their very nature. Even the ruins of the Holy City are redeemed and reclaimed in this collectively joyous moment.

Preaching the Text. The thunderous hope of Psalm 98 and its resonances with Isaiah 52 may inform worship and preaching on Christmas. In Psalm 98, God is a judge of tremendous power that emanates from everlasting love. Those who claim God's equitable sovereignty have no cause to fear such a God. How might we respond when we bear witness to this powerful expression of love? How might we be in relationship to this God who is faithful? How might we also be in relationship with the rest of creation, which also rejoices at the arrival of the Creator? Are we prepared to receive not only God's presence among us, but also the new order of righteousness and justice permeating the world, a reign of justice that might even overturn and convict us of our own privilege and power? In Psalm 98, the flourishing of our shared world begins with God's proactive presence. As we mark the arrival of the Christ child, we join all of creation in bearing witness in exuberant celebration, making a joyful noise unto the Lord.

CHRISTINE J. HONG

Hebrews 1:1–4 (5–12)

¹Long ago God spoke to our ancestors in many and various ways by the prophets, ²but in these last days he has spoken to us by a Son, whom he appointed heir of all things, through whom he also created the worlds. ³He is the reflection of God's glory and the exact imprint of God's very being, and he sustains all things by his powerful word. When he had made purification for sins, he sat down at the right hand of the Majesty on high, ⁴having become as much superior to angels as the name he has inherited is more excellent than theirs.
⁵For to which of the angels did God ever say,

"You are my Son;
today I have begotten you"?

Or again,

"I will be his Father,
and he will be my Son"?

⁶And again, when he brings the firstborn into the world, he says,

"Let all God's angels worship him."

⁷Of the angels he says,

"He makes his angels winds,
and his servants flames of fire."

⁸But of the Son he says,

"Your throne, O God, is forever and ever,
and the righteous scepter is the scepter of your kingdom.
⁹You have loved righteousness and hated wickedness;
therefore God, your God, has anointed you
with the oil of gladness beyond your companions."

¹⁰And,

"In the beginning, Lord, you founded the earth,
and the heavens are the work of your hands;
¹¹they will perish, but you remain;
they will all wear out like clothing;
¹²like a cloak you will roll them up,
and like clothing they will be changed.
But you are the same,
and your years will never end."

Commentary 1: Connecting the Reading with Scripture

This epistle reading for Christmas Day provides a connection to themes in today's Gospel text, John 1:1–14. The theme of Jesus as a manifestation of God's Word, the role of Jesus in the creation of the universe, and the high Christology identifying Jesus as God, stand out in both texts. However, the Hebrews reading provides the preacher with a unique opportunity to connect high Christology to humanity.

The author of Hebrews is unknown, and the date of writing is uncertain, with a probable date between 60 and 100 CE.[1] The circumstances of the audience are more easily determined. This is a Christian community, likely made up of both Jews and Gentiles. They are facing persecution for their Christian faith, with prison and torture noted in 13:3 and suffering and public abuse noted in 10:32–33. As noted early in the work (Heb. 2:1; 3:12–15), the author is concerned the community will falter or even abandon their faith. They appear to be tempted to leave faith in Jesus and take up Judaism.

The genre of the work is unique, framed as a public teaching or sermon in the opening, but ending as a letter. The purpose of the work is framed by the author as a "word of exhortation" (13:22). The writing as a whole is polemic, establishing Christianity as both superior to and consistent with Judaism, represented as the fulfillment of the law and foreshadowed in Jewish teaching.

The larger text of the day (1:5–12) begins a defense of Christianity, establishing Jesus' superiority to angels. This text may inspire preaching possibilities, spurring believers to reflect on the mystery of angels worshiping Christ as a catalyst for deepening their own lived praise to God's glory (v. 6), or perhaps proclaiming the enduring truth of Christ as bedrock for those who feel unsettled by life's uncertainties. The shorter reading (vv. 1–4) is the prologue of the letter, a concise affirmation of the faith, presented more as a common confession of faith than the argument that follows. This reading presents many parallels with the Gospel reading and incarnational themes perhaps more useful to preaching on Christmas Day.

The high Christology of this text is notable and fairly unique in the New Testament. Its closest theological relationships are in the first chapter of the Gospel of John and in the confession of faith found in Colossians 1:15–20. Jesus is represented as preexisting, creating the universe. He is confessed in a priestly role, making "purification for sins," and in a royal role, sitting "at the right hand of the Majesty on high" (Heb. 1:3). Notably, these opening verses of Hebrews not only present Jesus as God's Son (v. 2), but nearly identify Jesus as God (v. 3).

We rarely see Jesus so closely identified as God elsewhere in the New Testament. Rather, the Synoptic Gospels more frequently call Jesus God's Son, as seen in Jesus' baptism (Matt. 3:17; Mark 1:11; Luke 3:22), and Jesus frequently calls himself, "Son of Man" (Matt. 8:20; Mark 2:28; Luke 22:69). These titles represent more of a relationship to God and to humanity than a clear identification of Jesus as God. By contrast, language in Hebrews confesses Jesus and God in a way that is much closer to sharing an identity.

However, while Hebrews offers this high Christology, the work also portrays a strikingly human Jesus. For example, the author describes Jesus going to the cross not with calm purpose but with very human pleas to God and "loud cries and tears" (Heb. 5:7). This Jesus also "learned obedience through his suffering" (5:8), displaying a man who perhaps is not perfect, but needs to learn and grow as the rest of us do. In our text Jesus is, remarkably, described as the "reflection"—or as the Revised English Bible translates, "radiance"—"of God's glory and the exact imprint of God's very being" (1:3). The same words that identify Jesus as God also portray the very body of the human Jesus as both a reflection and a physical copy of God.

A human Jesus offers the opportunity for a close relationship with one who experiences their struggles with pain and suffering and discovers the need to grow when facing hard circumstances. Specifically, this suffering, struggling Jesus, who is so closely identified with both God and humanity, provides the community with a companion in the persecution they are facing. Perhaps their faith could be a source of strength for their lives rather than only a source of hardship as they struggle with the antagonisms of society. Today's preacher might extrapolate further, noting the issues of a particular people or congregation and lifting up Jesus

---

1. Cynthia Briggs Kittredge, "The Letter to the Hebrews," in *The New Oxford Annotated Bible, New Revised Standard Version with the Apocrypha*, 4th ed. (New York: Oxford University Press, 2010), 2103.

as a source of both divine and human comfort and strength in the face of their troubles. One could decide to cling to their faith, rather than running from their faith or, perhaps more subtly in our congregations, ignoring or doubting their faith in the face of suffering.

In addition to offering strength and comfort in the midst of adversity, as the "exact imprint of God's very being," Jesus offers an affirmation of humanity. This human body of Jesus, so closely identified with God, looks like our own. In the context of the ancient world, a context in which there was far less hope for treating illness and physical pain than we have today, human bodies were a sign of frailty. This teaching also stands in contrast to theologies, prevalent both in the first-century context and in ours, that saw the physical world and the flesh in particular as the source of sin and evil. In contemporary contexts and social media, body images elevated by advertising and film, or social contexts that emphasize a particular vision of beauty, often cause us to consider ourselves less valuable. This text in Hebrews offers a more positive view of our bodies, however frail or imperfect we may feel them to be, as sharing the same form as Jesus, whose body is the "imprint of God's very being" (1:3).

In a similar way, the portrayal of Jesus as the "reflection" or "radiance" of God's glory (1:3) may empower Christians in their role as ones who show the face of God to the world. Their human walk of life, their struggles, their very bodies, can be a manifest witness, radiating God's glory. This can be true even if they find themselves walking into their struggles with "loud cries and tears" and pleading with God for better circumstances. This can be true even as they doubt and falter in their faith. This can be true even as they find themselves imperfect and needing to learn and grow as they find their way forward.

The Gospel reading of the day is more familiar and may be the one congregations expect to hear on Christmas Day. The use of Hebrews alone or as a companion text, however, offers an opportunity to give flesh to the Word that "became flesh" in a tangible way, providing a companion in our hardship, an affirmation of our very bodies as being in the image of God, and encouragement in our role as Christian people to show God's face even in the midst of our own struggles. The incarnation gains a present reality as the high Christology of Hebrews finds its location in a human body like our own.

PATRICIA J. CALAHAN

Commentary 2: Connecting the Reading with the World

Christ is introduced differently in Hebrews than in the Gospel narratives of his birth. Popular imaginings of Christmas, shaped by the joyful lyrics of carols inspired by the Gospels and the artistic representations of Gospel nativity narratives, concentrate our attention upon Christ's humanity. The liturgical gestures of our weekly Sunday worship, when we remember and apply the teachings of Jesus, his exemplary life, and his bodily death and resurrection, humanize him as well. He comes near to us as we rehearse the Gospel's Christmas story with our mouths and ponder it in our hearts.

The arresting acoustics of the prefatory sentence (Heb. 1:1–3), which we also read on Christmas Day, sound a way of thinking about

Jesus different from that of the Gospels. Here is perhaps Scripture's most profound articulation of his deity: this infant Jesus is none other than God's exalted Son. Christmas is the season when the church considers this extraordinary claim that Jesus of Nazareth, whose humanity we rather too easily embrace, is the Son of God, celebrated by the angels as creation's reigning Lord (vv. 4–13). Clarifying and explaining the significance of this radical dissimilarity is the preacher's daunting challenge in proclaiming the implications of today's lesson from Hebrews.

Preachers can drill down on this opening sentence, which provides sufficient theological content for any Christmas Day! Observe, first, the astounding claim that Israel's God, disclosed in the gospels of the prophets, speaks a revelatory word to us again today through a Son. His identity as "heir of all things" is bracketed by images of the created order (1:2c and 3b). God not only "created the worlds" through him—the odd plural "worlds" suggests the totality of creation. This totality of "all things," seen and unseen, is providentially "sustained by his powerful word." That is, the Son, made incarnate in Jesus, shapes the meaning and destiny of human existence.

Patricia Ranft has argued that no doctrine of Christian faith is more catalytic than the incarnation. The doctrine of incarnation led architects of modern Western culture to forge what Charles Taylor calls a "Western social imaginary."[2] In particular, medieval reflections on the idea of a reconciling incarnation made of opposites—the divine with human nature, the heavenly transcendent made immanent and accessible, the savior dwelling with sinners—framed a new way of thinking about various cultural forms. According to Ranft, belief in the Son's incarnation cued the church's best thinkers to imagine an economy that exchanged goods so that all may prosper, a public square where diverse people met together to settle issues of common concern, and a political order with transcendent commitments that avoid the exclusive concerns of the self-interested powerful and privileged. In this sense, the vocation of Jesus' disciples is to maintain a public square checked-and-balanced by his revelation of an orderly creation.

Not only are natural and social worlds constructed and maintained through the Son, but God is embodied in the Son: Jesus of Nazareth is "the exact imprint [*charactēr*] of God's very being" (1:3). There is not another phrase like this in Scripture. The Greek noun translated "very being" is *hypostasis*, which became the centerpiece of the decisive debate over Jesus Christ's nature during the fourth century. Harold Attridge's translation of this noun as "fundamental reality" is especially compelling.[3] Scripture's witness to the incarnate Word is the essential metric by which every claim of truth

is measured; Jesus supplies us with the definitive resource by which we may know and love God more completely. The church does well to remember this in these skeptical days: God's kingdom inaugurated by Jesus is the real world.

For all its theological heft, Hebrews is written as a pastoral "word of exhortation" (13:22). These opening claims about God's exalted Son may seem abstract to a contemporary audience, but they remain the pivot point of our daily discipleship. For example, God's incarnation reminds us that our Christian identity essentially involves embodied, public devotion. Consider, for instance, today's widespread and divisive battle over sexuality. At the very least, the church should reject any ethic that divides body from soul and our sexual practices from our deeply held beliefs (and emotions) about Scripture-shaped relationships.

A Christlike sexuality is not about what adjective we use in distinguishing a sanctified marriage from a secular one. Nor is our sexuality a matter of civil rights. It concerns this "fundamental reality." The incarnation—the act of the Son "imprinting" God's love and loyalty in his various human activities—should insinuate itself into every discussion of sex. Debates among Christians about sexual identity, if detached from sexual practice, are unhelpful and unwinnable. More constructive is the incarnational model in which the daily practice of our sexuality cultivates and secures intimate, covenant-keeping relationships with one other.

Finally, we are ourselves among "all things" created and sustained by the Son. In a world in which secularism grows increasingly narcissistic, and human problems are given over to economic or political solutions, Hebrews makes the stunning claim that the world's future depends upon its spiritual cleansing, not upon a more effective government or more productive economy. The divine Son became a priest for us and "made purification for sins" to reconcile people to God (Heb. 2:9–18; 7:1–10:18). What becomes clear as this letter's word of exhortation unfolds is that Christ's atoning death does more

2. See Patricia Ranft, *How the Doctrine of Incarnation Shaped Western Culture* (Lanham, MD: Lexington Books, 2012); Charles Taylor, *Modern Social Imaginaries* (Durham, NC: Duke University Press, 2004).

3. Harold W. Attridge, *Hebrews*, Hermeneia (Minneapolis: Fortress Press, 1989), 44.

than purify sinners; it also sanctifies a purified people, setting them apart in a cultural wilderness to give bold witness to God's victory over sin in the world.

Jesus' priestly sacrifice for our salvation required his *human* body. Moreover, his atoning death presumes his unbending fellowship with and for us all. The word of exhortation repeated in our reading from Hebrews sharpens our focus here. According to Hebrews, to deny the importance of the manner of Christ's priestly self-sacrifice is to reject not only its purifying effect in relation to God, but also its social implication. Believers are purified and enabled to practice holiness in their relations with all others, from spouses to strangers (see Heb. 13:1–4). The expectation of following the lead of the divine One who "made purification for sins" centers us on his faithfulness to God, fidelity that required his suffering and self-sacrifice.

Christmas Day celebrates such a self-emptying and its corresponding discipleship:

the Son of God sacrificed his divine prerogatives to become one with us in order to save us all from sin, both structural and personal. The word of exhortation preachers should seek to sound, especially on this day, should include a renewed call for a congregational ministry of reconciliation that shares in his fellowship. Such a calling should resist any promise of human flourishing that hits the delete button on self-sacrifice or suffering; it should also resist joining in a march that protests social injustice without a deep commitment to Christ.[4] The hard work that purifies such evils finds its true source in a community's deep commitment to following the lead of Christ, whose suffering and self-sacrificial love make us whole. This is the work of Christian discipleship, and it must begin within the congregational life of brothers and sisters who are unconditionally committed to one another's growth in grace and love toward our neighbors.

ROBERT W. WALL

---

4. See Luke Timothy Johnson, *Hebrews*, New Testament Library (Louisville, KY: Westminster John Knox Press, 2006), 56–60.

John 1:1–14

¹In the beginning was the Word, and the Word was with God, and the Word was God. ²He was in the beginning with God. ³All things came into being through him, and without him not one thing came into being. What has come into being ⁴in him was life, and the life was the light of all people. ⁵The light shines in the darkness, and the darkness did not overcome it.

⁶There was a man sent from God, whose name was John. ⁷He came as a witness to testify to the light, so that all might believe through him. ⁸He himself was not the light, but he came to testify to the light. ⁹The true light, which enlightens everyone, was coming into the world.

¹⁰He was in the world, and the world came into being through him; yet the world did not know him. ¹¹He came to what was his own, and his own people did not accept him. ¹²But to all who received him, who believed in his name, he gave power to become children of God, ¹³who were born, not of blood or of the will of the flesh or of the will of man, but of God.

¹⁴And the Word became flesh and lived among us, and we have seen his glory, the glory as of a father's only son, full of grace and truth.

Commentary 1: Connecting the Reading with Scripture

"In the beginning" echoes for John the familiar opening of Genesis, linking the story of Jesus to the story of Israel's God. "In the beginning was the Word" (John 1:1) not only makes Jesus part of the biblical story; it also makes a claim upon the Greco-Roman world into which this Gospel was written. John is making truth claims about Jesus that find a place in both worlds: the world of the Hebrew Bible and the Greco-Roman world where Christian faith spread.

When does the gospel of Jesus Christ begin? For Mark, it begins with Jesus' baptism by John in the Jordan. Matthew offers a genealogy for Jesus that explicitly connects Jesus with Israel, tracing Jesus back to Abraham. Luke, a Gentile, traces his genealogy back to Adam, suggesting Jesus is Savior for the whole human family. John goes back further still, to the dawn of creation: "In the beginning was the Word." The Word, or Logos, a Greek term that emphasized the meaning a word holds, became a dramatic and imaginative way of speaking about Jesus. So this term, Logos, had one set of meanings for the Greco-Roman world and another set of meanings for Jewish readers. Biblical texts are dense, thick with meaning, and often multivalent. They hold different meanings for different readers. This is part of what we mean when we say that the Bible is a living word.

This multivalence is vitally meaningful in the prologue to John's Gospel. For the Greco-Roman world, to call Jesus the Logos, the Word, was to suggest that Jesus embodied the very mind of God. Jesus as the Word suggested Jesus was the wisdom or the divine reason at the heart of all things. For Jews, the claim that Jesus Christ was the Word, or Logos, suggested a different set of connections and assumptions. Through God's Word the heavens and the earth were created. This would have led Jewish readers back to Genesis, where, "In the beginning, God created the heavens and the earth" (Gen. 1:1).

All good Christian theology is faithful to the biblical story and closely connects the doctrines of creation and of redemption. John is doing just this and doing it brilliantly and imaginatively. To speak of Jesus Christ as the Word is, first, to claim the generative power of the Creator through Christ: "He was in the beginning with God. All things came into being through

109

The Place Where God Was Homeless

There fared a mother driven forth
Out of an inn to roam;
In the place where she was homeless
All men are at home.
The crazy stable close at hand,
With shaking timber and shifting sand,
Grew a stronger thing to abide and stand
Than the square stones of Rome.

For men are homesick in their homes,
And strangers under the sun,
And they lay their heads in a foreign land
Whenever the day is done.
Here we have battle and blazing eyes,
And chance and honor and high
    surprise,
But our homes are under miraculous
    skies
Where the yule tale was begun.

A Child in a foul stable,
Where the beasts feed and foam,
Only where He was homeless
Are you and I at home;

We have hands that fashion and heads
    that know,
But our hearts we lost—how long ago!
In a place no chart nor ship can show
Under the sky's dome.

This world is wild as an old wives' tale,
And strange the plain things are,
The earth is enough and the air is enough
For our wonder and our war;
But our rest is as far as the fire-drake swings
And our peace is put in impossible things
Where clashed and thundered unthinkable
    wings
Round an incredible star.

To an open house in the evening
Home shall men come,
To an older place than Eden
And a taller town than Rome.
To the end of the way of the wandering star,
To the things that cannot be and that are,
To the place where God was homeless
And all men are at home.

G. K. Chesterton, "The House of Christmas," in *The Home of Verse*, vol. 1, ed. Burton Egbert Stevenson (New York: Henry Holt & Co., 1912), 213–14.

---

him, and without him not one thing came into being" (John 1:2–3). John also links Jesus Christ as the Word to the activity and identity of Israel's God as redeemer.

God's work of creation and redemption are one and the same activity, brought together in Jesus Christ, the Logos of God. How fitting that John moves from this breathtaking claim about Jesus to the affirmation, "What has come into being in him was life, and the life was the light of all people" (v. 4)! In John's Gospel, Jesus Christ is light, love, and life. All these claims are sounded by John in the prologue and reiterated throughout the book. In John 14:6, Jesus says, "I am the way, and the truth, and the life." In 8:12, Jesus proclaims, "I am the light of the world. Whoever follows me will never walk in darkness but will have the light of life." In 13:34–35, Jesus states, "I give you a new commandment, that you love one another. Just as I have loved you, you also should love one another. By this

everyone will know that you are my disciples, if you have love for one another."

While we can safely assume John had no inkling how the church would work out its Christology over the centuries, it is hard to conceive of a doctrine of a triune God coming to life without the claims John makes in his prologue. These verses also aided an increasingly diverse Greco-Roman world to embrace Christian faith. New ways of speaking open up new ways of seeing and interpreting reality. In this sense, John's novel ways of speaking of Jesus as the Word, or Logos, helped give birth to a whole world of new thinking about Christianity.

The Gospel moves from ethereal, philosophical identification of Jesus as the very Word of God and concretely anchors this Word in contemporary human history by reference to John the Baptist: "There was a man sent from God, whose name was John" (1:6). John the Baptist plays a vital role in establishing Jesus as Israel's

Messiah. Josephus, the noted historian of the Jewish people, speaks of John the Baptist more extensively than he speaks of Jesus. All the Gospel writers make reference to the Baptist and to John's baptism of Jesus. John goes to great lengths to emphasize both the importance and the relative unimportance of John the Baptist: "He came as a witness to testify to the light, so that all might believe through him. He himself was not the light, but he came to testify to the light" (vv. 7–8). Later in this same chapter, the Baptist will say, "I am not worthy to untie the thong of his sandal" (v. 27), adding, "After me comes a man who ranks ahead of me because he was before me" (v. 30). In John's Gospel, John the Baptist is clearly subordinate to Jesus Christ, the Word. John even locates Jesus "before me" in time, a conclusion we would not draw from any other Gospel narrative.

John wants his readers to be clear about the scope and horizon of the light that the Word came to shed: "The true light, which enlightens everyone, was coming into the world" (v. 9). John knows Jesus came as the Logos in order to save and bless the world, but in these early verses we learn Jesus' relationship with the world will be difficult and complicated: "He was in the world, and the world came into being through him; yet the world did not know him. He came to what was his own, and his own people did not accept him" (vv. 10–11). John speaks of the world as the place God loved and sent Jesus to save, but also as a hostile, even deadly place. Remembering the history of Christian anti-Semitism, note well that John is himself a Jew, writing to an early Christian community made up of both Jews and Gentiles. So it would be mistaken to read into John's veiled criticism of some fellow Jews and some Gentiles any sort of general condemnation of any one people.

John wants Jew and Greek alike to believe in Jesus as the Word. "But to all who received him, who believed in his name, he gave power to become children of God" (v. 12). The whole of John's Gospel is aimed at sharing this good news. All of this comes to fruition for John in the central claim of the Gospel that follows: "And the Word became flesh and lived among us . . . full of grace and truth" (v. 14). Jesus Christ is the Word of God incarnate. The Presbyterian Church (U.S.A.)'s Confession of 1967 echoes Karl Barth: "The one sufficient revelation of God is Jesus Christ, the Word of God incarnate."[1] This is why we celebrate Christmas as the birth of God into the world.

TODD B. JONES

Commentary 2: Connecting the Reading with the World

The opening chapter of the Gospel of John is considered one of the most beautiful and profound, but also one of the most difficult, passages in the New Testament. It has the potential to leave readers exasperated and confused. Today's lection traces the Word or Logos as eternal and transcendent, and then moves to the Word becoming part of this world, taking on flesh. It unfolds a tension, a paradox that pushes us to make connections as we seek understanding.

The idea of incarnation is familiar for Christians. At the same time, the idea of God taking human form stretches the limits of our imaginations. The history of the church illuminates the struggle early Christians faced as they worked to formulate an orthodox understanding of incarnation. Before the councils of Nicaea (325) and Constantinople (381) settled on *homoousion* in the Nicene Creed, for instance, some espoused the docetic claim that only Jesus' spirit was divine, that is, that the divine spirit had taken on only the appearance of being human. There was also the very different Arian view, explicitly rejected at Nicaea, that Jesus Christ was not an eternal being at all, but a creature created in time when the Word "became flesh" (John 1:14). While today we

---

1. *The Constitution of the Presbyterian Church (U.S.A.)*, Part I, *Book of Confessions* (Louisville, KY: Office of the General Assembly, Presbyterian Church (U.S.A.), 2014), 291.

may readily accept the Nicene doctrine of the incarnation—Jesus Christ is "Light of Light, very God of very God, . . . of one substance with [*homoousion*] the Father"—Christians still ponder and study what it means to make such claims about Jesus Christ.

Recently I overheard two small children discussing the story of Jesus at Christmastime, and the challenge of thinking clearly about incarnation was made starkly apparent. The older sister explained to her younger brother that the same Jesus who died on the cross at Eastertime was also born to Mary, and that this Jesus is the Son of God. The younger child, frustrated and disbelieving, responded, "That's just ridiculous!" The child's comment illustrates the difficulty the church faces trying to examine the mystery of Christ as fully God and fully human, transcendent and immanent. How do we make sense of a God beyond this world, yet as close to us as our own breath? Clearly, complicated issues are raised when we consider the doctrine of the incarnation.

Contemplating how God relates to the world is not limited to Christian conversation. Philo (ca. 25 BCE–50 CE), a Jewish philosopher living in Alexandria and heavily influenced by Hellenistic thought, believed in a God not limited by place or space and absent of human attributes and emotions.[2] Philo's God is totally transcendent and not corporeal. For Philo, the Logos is the intermediary between God and the world, inferior to God and yet a reflection of God in the world. The Logos is the universal substance, an instrument of God utilized in the formation of the world.

The Christian understanding of the Word or Logos in the Gospel of John is distinct from Philo's view. For Christians, John equates the Logos with Jesus, and points to the Trinitarian belief that God is one and yet relational (triune) at the same time. These verses also demonstrate the Christian view that God is both transcendent and immanent. No contradiction in human logic deters the author of John from confessing the divinity of the human Jesus Christ: Jesus as Logos is eternal spirit and wholly other and *at the same time* was flesh in the first century in Galilee, absolutely corporeal.

Terrence Malick's 2011 film *The Tree of Life* explores how God is removed and yet also present, eternally unbound and also fully human flesh. The film tells the story of a family marked by tragedy. In one pivotal scene, the parents learn about the death of one of their sons. The scene is so painful and intimate that the viewer feels a need to look away out of respect; at the same time, the universal reality being portrayed is so compelling one cannot look away. Interwoven with these intimate scenes are expansive sequences that depict changes on a vast scale: we see the big bang at the beginning of the cosmos, the formation of earth, and the emergence of life.

In a blog post about the film, Robert Barron, a Catholic priest and theologian, describes a visually captivating scene of hot lava flowing into cold, crashing waves. This vision of grand natural processes starkly contrasts with another, where the audience is brought face to face with the grief on the face of the father. Barron sees a theological message. Both nature and grace are grounded in God. God is responsible for the creation of the cosmos, and at the same time, thoroughly involved in human affairs.[3]

This interplay between the cosmic and the intimate in *The Tree of Life* is not unlike today's lection from the Gospel of John. The passage starts with the phrase "in the beginning," which immediately calls to mind the seven days of creation narrated in Genesis 1. The reader learns that the Word is coeternal with God and responsible for creation. This makes a clear connection to Genesis 1, where God forms the world by speaking, and God's transcendence and control over nature are affirmed as order is shaped from chaos. The Word also becomes flesh, thus becoming part of the world.

This portion of the text compels us also to consider the Adam and Eve creation narrative in Genesis 2. The contrast between the two creation accounts may be a bit disconcerting, because

2. Frederick Copleston, *A History of Philosophy*, vol. I: *Greece and Rome from the Pre-Socratics to Plotinus* (New York: Doubleday, 1946, repr. 1993).

3. Robert Barron, "Tree of Life Glorifies God," *The Seeker* (blog), *Chicago Tribune*, May 25, 2011, https://newsblogs.chicagotribune.com/religion_theseeker/2011/05/tree-of-life-is-film-about-god.html.

instead of creating by speaking, as in Genesis 1, in Genesis 2 God forms creatures from the ground and breathes life into them. Then we might realize that what seems disconcerting should be taken as enlightening, for the distinct portrayals of God as either grandly or intimately creating are in perfect accord with the contrast between transcendent and immanent, between far and near, at the heart of today's lection. God creating out of dust and walking in the garden is God intimately involved in the world; in John, God is the Word made flesh and living among us. Taken together, the two creation narratives communicate the nature of God with us, and their witness is remarkably consistent with the prologue to the Gospel of John.

It may seem difficult to hold in one vision the tension present in the Gospel writer's description of the Word as both beyond and yet with us, the light shining in the darkness that cannot be overcome. There is a form of faith that does not stumble over the limitations of human logic. Such faith acknowledges mystery and celebrates complementary principles. For instance, there is no understanding of transcendence without an understanding of immanence. There is no comprehension of light without an experience of darkness.[4] We do not appreciate acceptance if we have never felt rejection. The evangelist who authored John explores such ideas with the reader and uses powerful words like "glory," "grace," and "truth" in order to describe what is revealed in the paradox of the Word become flesh. John is proclaiming the possibility of inhabiting a harmonious and holy space when we live into this mystery. Through the wonder and gift of the incarnation, we are invited to experience the glory, grace, and truth of this space.

SALLY SMITH HOLT

---

4. Kristin Johnston Largen, *Finding God among Our Neighbors: An Interfaith Systematic Theology*, vol. 2 (Minneapolis: Fortress Press, 2013).

First Sunday after Christmas Day

Isaiah 63:7–9

Psalm 148

Hebrews 2:10–18

Matthew 2:13–23

Isaiah 63:7–9

⁷I will recount the gracious deeds of the LORD,
   the praiseworthy acts of the LORD,
because of all that the LORD has done for us,
   and the great favor to the house of Israel
that he has shown them according to his mercy,
   according to the abundance of his steadfast love.
⁸For he said, "Surely they are my people,
   children who will not deal falsely";
and he became their savior
   ⁹in all their distress.
It was no messenger or angel
   but his presence that saved them;
in his love and in his pity he redeemed them;
   he lifted them up and carried them all the days of old.

Commentary 1: Connecting the Reading with Scripture

Isaiah 63:7–9 begins an extended communal lament that extends to 64:12. This context is important in interpreting this soaring proclamation of "grace" in action emanating from the eternal well of God's "favor" and "mercy" (Isa. 63:7). If a reader stops at verse 9, the mood seems to be one of unabashed optimism, but even a cursory reading of the next twenty-two verses reveals that our lection actually introduces a lament. This prophecy was shared sometime between the Babylonian conquest of Jerusalem in 586 BCE and the rebuilding of the temple seventy-one years later. The heartfelt sadness of this pericope reveals the emotional vertigo of a people in exile. Like Psalm 44, a psalm of lament, Isaiah 63:7–64:12 begins by recounting God's more active engagement with God's people "in the days of old" (Ps. 44:1). This is genuine praise, but it also serves a practical agenda. When the prophet asserts, "I will recount . . . the praiseworthy acts of the LORD," he is making an appeal. He is attempting to goad his Lord into action.

The preceding verses of chapter 63 accentuate this image of God as a bold and decisive actor. Verses 1–6 provides the poignant—yet repellent—picture of YHWH as a warrior who returns from battle with robes stained with the blood of his enemies, enemies who have been crushed in the wine press of divine wrath (vv. 3, 6). Part of the message seems to be that God will take matters into God's own hands. Crushing grapes in a wine press is a communal activity, but God performs this task as a solitary work. Verses 1–6 represent a deep longing for a proactive Lord who will set things right by any means necessary.

If Isaiah 63 were set to music, the melody would be the redemptive presence of God. Yet there would also be a strong countermelody, a lament that the same God who is present often seems absent. We witness the fierce warrior melt into a parent who provides maternal care of equal intensity: "In his love and in his pity he redeemed them; he lifted them up and carried them." Perhaps this refers to the ancient practice (ferocious to modern ears) of swaddling. Newborns were rubbed with salt and oil and then wrapped tightly with bands of cloth. This protected the infant at a time when much of daily life was spent outdoors, exposed to every change of weather. Swaddling also made it possible for a mother to pick up and move with her child on her hip quickly in the event of some sudden danger.

To be "lifted and carried" was a symbol of security in a dangerous world. When God was assigned the role of lifter and carrier, it was even more a sign—a maternal sign both intimately caring and fiercely protective—of divine engagement. Yet, countermelody remains. By the time we reach verse 15, God has seemingly stepped away. No longer on the front lines of battle, no longer associated with imagery of tender child care, God is portrayed as distant, even aloof, withholding "your zeal and your might . . . your heart and your compassion" (63:15). All this leads to the crescendo of a desperate plea: "O that you would tear open the heavens and come down!" (64:1).

Both melody and countermelody resound throughout Third Isaiah. The message is one of redemptive presence (57:19; 58:9, 11; 59:1; 60:2, 19; 62:4; 64:8; 65:24). Yet the atmosphere of the larger literary context is one of disenchantment. In Third Isaiah, the temple has been restored, yet right worship and righteous living remain out of reach. The people of God are dividing into competing factions that all display a propensity for idolatrous practice and unrighteous life (56:10; 57:13; 59:3; 65:5; 66:3–4). As a result, God seems far away. "We grope like the blind along a wall" (59:10), the prophet laments; believers are suffering the experience of divine abandonment: "You have hidden your face from us, and have delivered us into the hand of our iniquity" (64:7).

To read our lection in context, it must be remembered that the very next word is "but." After our beautiful portrait of divine mercy comes the stark reality of human rebellion: "But they . . . grieved his holy spirit; therefore he became their enemy" (63:10). Chapters 56–66 were written during a time of intense disappointment; in 63:10–19 the prophet suggests that the Babylonian exile was punishment for Judah's sin. The prophet then moves to strengthen faith by rekindling hope in the promise of immediate redemption.

The countermelody of God's aloof disfavor is just that, a mere "counter." It is overridden by hope as the extended lament draws to a close: "Yet, O LORD, you are our Father; we are the clay, and you are our potter" (64:8). We find evidence of this in our lection. In verses 8–9, the prophet alludes to God's own guiding hand during the exodus. Following yet another act of disobedience, God decides to withdraw from the stage of history. God will send an intermediary, a proxy to lead God's people. Ultimately God is persuaded by Moses to remain fully engaged. God himself goes before the people (Exod. 33). "It was no messenger . . . but his presence that saved them" (Isa. 63:9). This is preceded by the even more remarkable statement: "he became their savior" (63:8).

This glorious theme runs like a red thread through the lectionary texts for the First Sunday after Christmas, pointing toward the saving acts of the second person of the Trinity. Isaiah 63:8 proclaims that out of the abundance of divine mercy, God "became their savior in all their distress." Matthew 2:13–23—presenting the Holy Family as refugees from Herod's wrath—implies that as God becomes our Savior through Christ, a terrible cost is exacted. The point is sharpened in Hebrews 2:10: "It is fitting that God . . . should make the pioneer of their salvation perfect through suffering." It ultimately places our lection in canonical context.

We are immediately brought back to the lection for Christmas Day (John 1:1–14) and a Trinitarian conception of incarnation. Our eyes are glued to the primary point: "And the Word became flesh and lived among us [with] the glory of . . . a father's only son, full of grace and truth" (v. 14). Returning to today's lection, we now see clearly that redemption is God's own deeply personal work that graciously includes us, despite our propensity to fall well short both in worship and in life. Thus, when our lection is placed in its broadest (canonical) context, we see that it is ultimately not as a ferocious warrior (Isa. 63:1–6) that God encounters us, but rather as the fiercely protective mother risking herself for her young (v. 9).

What remains is a central practical question: How does the preacher proclaim such shocking intimacy in the work of redemption? To stay true to Third Isaiah, how does she accomplish this without resorting to what Dietrich Bonhoeffer described as "cheap grace"? Perhaps the only homiletical way forward is to emphasize that while redemption is God's work, it is accomplished only through relationship.

We have a part to play, a countermelody in tune with God's melody. Grace is complemented by gratitude, redemption by right worship and right living. On the Sunday after Christmas, we renew our calling to faithful obedience. We respond to redemption through Christ not simply by claiming a status for ourselves but by actively engaging in God's work of redemption for ourselves, our community, and our world. Like Isaiah, we find ourselves "sent" by the very God who risked everything by sending the spotless Son into our mottled world.

MARK RALLS

Commentary 2: Connecting the Reading with the World

Today's lection, similar to a psalm, extols and enumerates God's gracious deeds for Israel: God's compassion and kindness; the merciful attention God has shown to chosen people; and, most importantly, God's redemption of the community from distress (Isa. 63:7–9). Intimate images elucidate and personalize the significance of God's salvation. Israel is pictured as a weakened, afflicted person supported and carried by God, who is imagined as ever loyal and supportive (v. 9).

Such images inspire like action. How can we imitate God by supporting those who are sick, distressed, or weak? This support may entail substantial gestures: volunteering at food kitchens, providing financial support to nonprofit organizations, offering pastoral care. However, as this passage shows, help need not be offered on a grand scale. The prophet also praises God for constant love, goodness, compassion, kindness, and loyalty, and so we also exhibit God's goodness with small gestures of love and care. Just lending someone a friendly ear, sharing a meal, or taking a few moments to express appreciation can display and emulate the divine love the prophet celebrates. We may not have to look far for those needing help. Isaiah's words to his community hint that there might be those in our immediate communities, such as in churches, schools, and workplaces, who might need a bit of aid or support.

Also important to note is that Isaiah 63 emphasizes God's reaffirmation of Israel as his people. What is stressed therefore is the sense of belonging—of being recognized and acknowledged. So, preachers might use this passage as a springboard to discuss issues of connectedness and isolation. In what ways do we as individuals and as the church help people feel more connected, either to God or to their community? In what ways have we thwarted this sense of belonging? How can we help to restore or improve connectedness? This question is especially pertinent in an age of digital distraction.

Relatedly, there are many in our congregations and communities who may feel isolated and detached in a variety of ways. Feelings of isolation and loneliness, which can be a particular problem for the elderly, constitute an epidemic that can have dreadful mental and physical consequences.[1] Indeed, individual seclusion cannot and should not be detached from issues concerning reclusiveness and segregation of larger groups of people, such as those who are incarcerated, undocumented, or disabled. This passage from Isaiah therefore lends itself to a sermon on isolation, barriers, and boundaries, whether individual, communal, or national, which thwart the expression of divine kinship and community.

Moreover, much of this passage from Isaiah entails thanking God. A sermon might reflect upon the ways in which we can acknowledge with gratitude God's mercies in our lives. How

---

1. Dhruv Khullar, "How Social Isolation Is Killing Us," https://www.nytimes.com/2016/12/22/upshot/how-social-isolation-is-killing-us.html.

do we behave as if we are thankful for "all that the LORD has done for us" and the "great favor" shown us? I am not advocating unfounded optimism or fake cheerfulness. "Reckless" optimism, especially the kind fueling belief in the American dream, has tremendous negative effects.[2] It can lead to unrealistic expectations as well as a decrease in mercy, grace, and connectedness, as blame for hardships and failures is placed on a person's attitude or lack of effort instead of on systemic hindrances. It can also heap shame upon those already suffering from depression or negative feelings.

Instead of unrealistic optimism, this passage gently reminds us of the importance of gratitude. While excessive positive thinking can be harmful, practicing gratitude can improve happiness and health.[3] Interestingly, one benefit of gratitude is more connectedness, more sense of belonging, as it opens doors to deeper relationships, enhanced empathy and self-esteem, and general psychological improvement. Gratitude, as the biblical writer clearly shows, is the natural aftereffect of understanding God's salvific activity.

If we are truly appreciative of God's mercies and actions in our lives, it is appropriate and indeed important to explore how we can, in gratitude, become better conduits of God's grace in this world. How do our behavior and attitude make it easier or harder for God's goodness to be manifest in our world? How do we thwart or hinder God's goodness and steadfast love from becoming evident in our own lives and in the lives of others? How should we act so that God's love is more fully manifest?

These questions are especially pertinent if we recall the context of the biblical writer. Though the excerpt selected for our lection seems joyful, 63:7 is actually the start of a communal lament (63:7–64:12). Indeed, the parts of Isaiah 63 excised from today's lection hint of darker realities. In the verses before and after 63:7–9, we find the prophet not only calling for vengeance but also pleading with God to remember Israel

and act. The author recounts God's past salvific deeds in 63:7–9, not because deliverance has occurred, but as a reminder and a plea to God to deliver Israel. In short, the excerpt from Isaiah is the author's attempt to be grateful during times of suffering. It is through gratitude, by reminding God of past divine acts of grace, that the biblical writer attempts to encourage God to act similarly in the present.

The gratitude expressed in 63:7–9, then, is not about how to behave during happy times, when we have something to be joyful and thankful about, but the opposite. This passage is about how we should behave during times of difficulty. A sermon on how to be grateful during periods of adversity might seem a natural expression of this interpretation. Preachers should take care to acknowledge the reality of suffering; it would be neither pastorally sensitive nor homiletically appropriate to recommend simply that the faithful put on a happy face. What Isaiah 63 shows is that, as much as we may need a reminder of our many blessings, expressions of genuine frustration, dismay, or fear are not always unwarranted. Every believer will know seasons of rejoicing and seasons of lament. At times, lament is precisely what is called for, especially if it leads to divine or human action.

Isaiah 63 is shrewdly situated in the lectionary cycle on the First Sunday after Christmas, for it suggests how to live in this world after the glow of Christmas has worn off. How can we act as if our Savior has been born, not just at Christmas, when we celebrate the birth liturgically, but throughout the year, in times of joy and challenge alike? How should this affect how we behave and what we prioritize? This Sunday and this passage offer us a chance to reflect and reexamine, even on hard days, recalling the past salvific actions of God, filling ourselves with gratitude and a desire to love in kind, and thereby filling ourselves in hopeful anticipation of future divine mercies.

SONG-MI SUZIE PARK

2. Morgan Mitchell, "The 'Tyranny' of Positive Thinking Can Threaten Your Health and Happiness," : https://www.forbes.com/2010/01/05/positive-thinking-optimism-society-opinions-book-review-michael-fumento.html#3c8a74f39001; Sarah Elizabeth Adler, "The Power of Negative Thinking," https://www.theatlantic.com/magazine/archive/2018/01/the-power-of-negativity/546560/.

3. Amy Morin, "7 Scientifically Proven Benefits of Gratitude," https://www.psychologytoday.com/blog/what-mentally-strong-people-dont-do/201504/7–scientifically-proven-benefits-gratitude; Harvey B. Simon, "Giving Thanks Can Make You Healthier," https://www.health.harvard.edu/healthbeat/giving-thanks-can-make-you-happier.

Psalm 148

¹Praise the LORD!
Praise the LORD from the heavens;
　　praise him in the heights!
²Praise him, all his angels;
　　praise him, all his host!

³Praise him, sun and moon;
　　praise him, all you shining stars!
⁴Praise him, you highest heavens,
　　and you waters above the heavens!

⁵Let them praise the name of the LORD,
　　for he commanded and they were created.
⁶He established them forever and ever;
　　he fixed their bounds, which cannot be passed.

⁷Praise the LORD from the earth,
　　you sea monsters and all deeps,
⁸fire and hail, snow and frost,
　　stormy wind fulfilling his command!

⁹Mountains and all hills,
　　fruit trees and all cedars!
¹⁰Wild animals and all cattle,
　　creeping things and flying birds!

¹¹Kings of the earth and all peoples,
　　princes and all rulers of the earth!
¹²Young men and women alike,
　　old and young together!

¹³Let them praise the name of the LORD,
　　for his name alone is exalted;
　　his glory is above earth and heaven.
¹⁴He has raised up a horn for his people,
　　praise for all his faithful,
　　for the people of Israel who are close to him.
Praise the LORD!

Connecting the Psalm with Scripture and Worship

At this time when people over the whole wide earth celebrate the dawning of light and new birth, when Christians exuberate at the birth of the Messiah, Jesus, how fitting it is to join the heavens and the earth in singing God's praises. Psalm 148 begins and ends with the exhortation that all created beings are to praise (*halle*) YHWH. Hallelujah! This word of praise resounds again and again as the psalmist calls every thinkable aspect of creation to do that for which they were created, give glory to God. An ancient cosmological understanding of how the world is ordered underpins the tripartite framework of Psalm 148, shaping the way that the composer fashions this artistry.[1]

YHWH's graciousness is Israel's life source. What YHWH does is reason enough for praise. There is a deep connection with Israel, for YHWH has called Israel into being, out of an abundance of steadfast love and mercy. YHWH brings into existence (out of the chaos, as it were) a people gathered from the nations, to be peculiarly YHWH's own. So Israel is summoned to life—out of exile and, before, out of slavery. What happens on earth garners God's attention. What happens next results from YHWH's intervention (Isa. 63:7–9), and the psalmist exhorts every creature on earth and in the seas to praise God. The watery elements of primeval chaos, the waters above the cosmos, in the heavens, and the waters that cover the earth, as well as "fire and hail, snow and frost" unite in praising God.

This scene reminds us to attend: the heavens and the earth declare the wondrous presence of God in glory. When we fix our hearts and minds on the holy child and the Holy Family, we join the cosmos in bearing witness to what transpires in the watches of the night. Everything everywhere is called to give glory to God. Celestial voices unite with earthly choirs in singing, Praise YHWH!

There is, in the celebrations of these days and nights, mystery and innocence. There is also foreboding and suffering. Celebration is often grieved by storm. So we hear in the appointed Gospel for this day a warning given to Joseph in a dream: "Get up, take the child and his mother, and flee to Egypt, and remain there until I tell you" (Matt. 2:13b). Joseph pays attention to the dream, and he and Mary and the child flee. Herod is enraged, tricked by the wise men, and is so infuriated that he unleashes his hatred, calling for the death of all the children in and around Bethlehem, two years old or younger. YHWH once again hears, "Rachel, weeping for her children, she refused to be consoled, because they are no more" (Matt. 2:18).

This family on the run settles for a while in the very land where their ancestors once lived in captivity. Living under threat is not God's intention, and YHWH conspires with the heavenly host once again to bring salvation.

YHWH's compassionate intervention once again is highlighted, and we learn that this child will be instrumental. As God says through the prophet Hosea, "When Israel was a child, I loved him, and out of Egypt I called my son" (Hos. 11:1). Here we see what lies at the heart of our understanding of who Jesus the Messiah is. The Gospel narrative looks backward, referring to Israel's experience of exodus. It also looks forward, anticipating the unfolding of the *kairotic* event of Jesus.[2] During this time when we celebrate Christmas, our songs of praise and expressions of joy are pierced by the underpinnings of suffering. Not long after the wise men offer their gifts and their adoration, Herod unleashes violence, destruction, and woe.

What God unleashes in Jesus, however, brings hope and possibility for life, and the day's psalm helps us to give voice to our faith. Just as the Gospel reading looks both back to the past and forward to the future, so does the psalm. Looking back to creation, the psalmist marvels at how God's command brings even the most menacing phenomena to praise YHWH (Ps. 148:7–8). Looking to the future, the psalmist anticipates the praise of the entire created order. Life in its totality, represented by the pairing of "mountains and hills," "steep high masses and level, easy rises," "fruit trees and all cedars," "wild beasts and all cattle," "creeping things and winged things that fly," attends a cosmic celebration of communion.[3] The world is meant to be a "sounding" universe to praise YHWH.

JOSEPH A. DONNELLA II

1. Mitchell Dahood, *Psalms III, 101–150*, Anchor Bible (Garden City, NY: Doubleday & Co., 1984), 352.
2. Artur Weiser, *The Psalms: A Commentary*, trans. Herbert Hartwell (Philadelphia: Westminster Press, 1962), 838.
3. Weiser, *Psalms*, 837.

First Sunday after Christmas Day

Hebrews 2:10–18

¹⁰It was fitting that God, for whom and through whom all things exist, in bringing many children to glory, should make the pioneer of their salvation perfect through sufferings. ¹¹For the one who sanctifies and those who are sanctified all have one Father. For this reason Jesus is not ashamed to call them brothers and sisters, ¹²saying,

"I will proclaim your name to my brothers and sisters,
    in the midst of the congregation I will praise you."
¹³And again,
    "I will put my trust in him."
And again,
    "Here am I and the children whom God has given me."

¹⁴Since, therefore, the children share flesh and blood, he himself likewise shared the same things, so that through death he might destroy the one who has the power of death, that is, the devil, ¹⁵and free those who all their lives were held in slavery by the fear of death. ¹⁶For it is clear that he did not come to help angels, but the descendants of Abraham. ¹⁷Therefore he had to become like his brothers and sisters in every respect, so that he might be a merciful and faithful high priest in the service of God, to make a sacrifice of atonement for the sins of the people. ¹⁸Because he himself was tested by what he suffered, he is able to help those who are being tested.

Commentary 1: Connecting the Reading with Scripture

It is the Sunday after Christmas. Gifts have been opened, relatives returned home, leftovers are in the refrigerator. Some favorite carols are left to sing today, and greenery remains in the sanctuary. Things are starting to quiet down in anticipation of the new year. Still, the preacher has some gifts to open in the form of the appointed readings for the morning. Together they help shift our attention from the celebration at the birth of the Christ child to reflection on what the Christ has come in God's name to do among us.

Today's readings from the Hebrew Bible extend the joy of Christmas Day, but within them you can hear some dissonant notes. The birth of Jesus has taken place within the history of "the gracious deeds of the LORD" (Isa. 63:7). Significantly, such deeds are often performed in the face of human resistance or in the midst of scenes of suffering. They are a cause for celebration as well as a call for loyalty and faithfulness

among God's people. Isaiah's recall of God's goodness and promise of God's presence is accompanied by the joyful chorus in Psalm 148. Meanwhile, however, in the Gospel text Herod emerges from the shadows as the embodiment of resistance to God's intentions to bring about justice for God's people. Hebrews presents Jesus' faithfulness as counterpoint to Herod's murderous intentions—and this to a congregation likewise suffering beneath powerful oppressors. The preacher for the day meets a preacher in this text, one who rises to bear witness to Jesus' faithfulness as royal priest, fellow sufferer, and spiritual pioneer to a congregation whose zeal is fading and whose faithfulness is slipping in the face of persecution.

These congregants are certainly our ancestors in faith: they are believers (Heb. 2:3–4), they have been baptized (6:4–5; 10:22), they are familiar with teachings of the apostles (6:1–2), some have even become teachers (5:12). They have been known for their love for others and for their performance of good works (6:10). They have not yet completely faltered in practicing their faith (6:4–8), but afflictions are causing their hands to droop and their knees to weaken (12:12). We get from this sermon-as-letter a picture of collective weariness, a congregation too despondent to encourage each other or even "meet together" (10:25). This is a congregation that is not sure how it can sustain hope while in distress.

The preacher in Hebrews knows the extent of the crisis that afflicts the members of the congregation. Some have been imprisoned; others have had their property taken away (10:34). More persecution may be lurking around the corner. They have suffered the hostility of their contemporaries (12:3), and some have even experienced torture (13:3). Is it any wonder that a congregation in such dire straits might fall into deep discouragement? What word does the preacher who authors this text fashion to address this issue? The answer is a bold claim about the person and work of Jesus Christ.

The preacher in Hebrews is creating a profile of Christ similar to other profiles found in the New Testament. In Colossians, Christ is "the image of the invisible God, the firstborn of all creation," through whom "all things have been created" (Col. 1:15–16b). John's Gospel begins with the proclamation that Jesus was "in the beginning with God" and "all things came into being through him" (John 1:2–3). The sermon in Hebrews begins by amplifying the sound of Christ being exalted in the cosmos. The "Son" is the "heir of all things, through whom [God] . . . created the worlds" (Heb. 1:2–3). The theme of the preexistence of the "Son" that punctuates the New Testament in these places is an echo of Jewish Wisdom theology. As Cynthia Briggs Kittredge explains: "Early Christ-believers used the language of wisdom, particularly in the christological hymns, to interpret and understand Jesus Christ and his relationship with God."[1] The writer-preacher in Hebrews, for example, draws from the imagery found in a passage from

the Wisdom of Solomon to speak of Christ as a "reflection of God's glory" (v. 3): "For she [Wisdom] is a reflection of eternal light, a spotless mirror of the working of God, and an image of [God's] goodness" (Wis. 7:26). Christ, declares this preacher, is the "exact imprint of God's very being, and he sustains all things by his powerful word" (Heb. 1:3).

How does this proclamation about the relationship between God and Christ help encourage a spiritually exhausted, persecuted congregation? It might help those in the congregation who wonder why a Jewish peasant is confessed as Lord. If the sermon had stopped here, we might imagine weary listeners shrugging their shoulders and sighing, "How nice for Jesus. What difference does that make in my life?" How can such an exalted figure understand a listener's lived experiences in time?

To address that concern, the preacher starts bringing the sermon down to earth. It is similar to the proclamation expressed in Philippians 2:5–8, wherein Christ "empties himself" in order to "be found in human form." Using the words of a psalmist, the preacher in Hebrews starts moving the Son toward the congregation's need to know whether God has abandoned them. Christ comes to demonstrate God's "mindfulness" and "care" for mortals by becoming (like them) "a little lower than angels" but "crowned with glory and honor" (Heb. 2:6b–7). This Christ who comes from God, who was with God in the beginning, and who bears God's likeness, also comes from humankind. Clothed in humanity, the One who has come is "family," that is, he will suffer with those he calls "brothers and sisters" (vv. 11–12).

Discouragement tells those who suffer that their suffering has no meaning, no end except in the finality of death. To counter that attitude, the preacher declares that in Jesus they have a fellow sufferer. It is that experience of suffering as a human being that makes Jesus fully one with human beings. The idea that the preexistent Son was joined with human beings in the experience of suffering infuses the sufferer's plight with meaning. The sufferer has "help" in

---

1. Cynthia Briggs Kittredge, "Hebrews," in *Searching the Scriptures: A Feminist Commentary*, vol. 2, ed. Elisabeth Schüssler Fiorenza (New York: Crossroad, 1994), 428–52, 435.

the person of Jesus (2:18), who serves as "pioneer" and "priest" on their behalf—"priest" because through him they have access to God's abundant grace and are brought into God's presence; "pioneer" because he models trust in God, even as his faith in the goodness of God is being tested. It is a depth of trust that takes Jesus through the experience of death so that even the power of death (and the one who holds it, "the devil") is destroyed (v. 14). Salvation in this passage looks like liberation from the fear of death, and from all that was death-dealing in the experience of the Hebrews—from persecution, political oppression, loss of possessions, even loss of confidence in their faith tradition to deliver them.

Today's preacher would do well to follow the lead of the preacher in Hebrews and make a bold declaration of what Christ has come to do. Christ being among us is God's promise fulfilled. Jesus Christ is a royal priest who mediates God's presence, one who became "like his brothers and sisters in every respect," one who is with us in our suffering, a guide through the valley of the shadow of death.

RICHARD F. WARD

Commentary 2: Connecting the Reading with the World

We do not know who wrote the Letter to the Hebrews, where or when it was written, or to whom it was addressed. However, we do know it was written by an early Christian leader to believers who identified with Jesus and struggled to maintain their commitment in the face of persecution, and we know their lived faith entailed "a hard struggle with sufferings, sometimes being publicly exposed to abuse and persecution [including the confiscation of property], and sometimes being partners with those so treated" (Heb. 10:32–34).

We read this passage on the Sunday after Christmas. It may seem odd that the lectionary offers a passage addressing the suffering of Jesus so soon after we have prepared for his coming and celebrated his birth. The author wants to make clear to beleaguered followers that the "pioneer of their salvation" and ours, whose birth we have just celebrated, came to free us from the fear of death that enslaves us, to sanctify us, to embrace us as sisters and brothers, and to present us to the one "for whom and through whom all things exist" (2:10). The author also wants to make clear that our loving, courageous brother, Jesus, was made "perfect through sufferings." We, like the Hebrews, can take heart that his suffering gives meaning to and dignifies our own.

How did Jesus' suffering perfect him? How might it perfect us? Throughout the church's history, believers have sought to understand and explain what seems to be mystery at the heart of our faith: how exactly did Jesus pioneer our salvation? There has never been a dogmatic or conciliar statement about atonement, as there was for the christological and Trinitarian doctrines of Christ's two natures and God's three persons. There are, however, three predominant streams of thought about the way Jesus pioneered our salvation.

In the first, Jesus' unmerited death is thought to have paid the debt for our sins—death, incurred by humanity through the disobedience of Adam and Eve—thereby reconciling humanity to God. This theory of "satisfaction" solves the objective problem of reconciling God's justice and God's mercy. A second, subjective theory holds the problem is not "out there" in a resistance within God; the problem is within human beings, who have ceased to understand and trust the love of God. Jesus' death is a means by which God, through Jesus, shows humanity the depth of God's love: God would rather die than remain unreconciled to us. A third way of thinking about atonement, prevalent among Christians before Constantine's marriage of empire and church in the fourth century, affirms that Jesus Christ won a victory over the devil, and that has the potential to liberate believers from enslavement to him because of their fear of death.[2]

---

2. Gustaf Aulén, *Christus Victor: An Historical Study of the Three Main Types of the Idea of the Atonement* (New York: Macmillan, 1951).

Our text reflects this third approach: Jesus through his death destroys the devil, who has the power of death. One of the most compelling articulations of this view is that of the second-century bishop of Lyons, Irenaeus. Following Colossians 1:15, Irenaeus believed that Jesus was the image of God by which human beings were created. Like Jesus, they were to grow up into the full image of and communion with God. Irenaeus saw humanity as one body with many members, all of whom, taken together, supplied each other with the knowledge, nourishment, and fellowship needed to reach that image and communion. Growing into the image of God would take time, the help of others, and the slow development of human emotional, intellectual, and physical potential.

Irenaeus believed God's proscription of eating the fruit of the tree of the knowledge of good and evil was not permanent but temporary, necessary only until Adam and Eve reached sufficient maturity to understand and make good use of that knowledge. The devil opposed God's intentions for human community, growth, and flourishing, convinced the first couple (with Adam as the progenitor of humanity) to rush God's plan and skip steps necessary for mature development toward the image of God.

Adam and Eve and their progeny did not stop growing, but their development became stunted and distorted. Their relationships were ensnarled by dynamics that made them think they were enemies, so they withheld from each other gifts God had given them to share with their neighbors. They became isolated and lacked many things necessary for proper growth into the image of and communion with God.[3] Sin, from this perspective, is a turning away from or refusal to participate in the great interdependent body of humanity. That refusal renders our potential

Room in Our Hearts

It is no use to say that we are born two thousand years too late to give room to Christ. Nor will those who live at the end of the world have been born too late. Christ is always with us, always asking for room in our hearts.

But now it is with the voice of our contemporaries that he speaks, with the eyes of store clerks, factory workers and children that he gazes; with the hands of office workers, slum dwellers and suburban housewives that he gives. It is with the feet of soldiers and tramps that he walks, and with the heart of anyone in need that he longs for shelter. And giving shelter or food to anyone who asks for it, or needs it, is giving it to Christ.

Dorothy Day. "Room for Christ." *The Catholic Worker,* December 1945, 2. https://www.catholicworker.org/dorothyday/articles/416.html.

unfulfilled and our bodies, souls, minds, and hearts distorted and disfigured.

Though many of us might not speak of a supernatural, personal devil, we may acknowledge that the dynamics which isolate us, stunt our proper growth, and pit us against one another are more powerful, enduring, and destructive than we can manage to eliminate, try as we might. Today, we might name some of the dynamics that separate us and cut deep lacerations in the body of humanity as sexism, heterosexism, racism, classism, and ableism. Irenaeus believed sin was a socially transmitted disease—as, for example, sexist and racist attitudes and behaviors seem to be. Because they are transmitted through patterns of thought and the behavior of communities that overlap with and interpenetrate redeemed communities, they can be transformed by new patterns practiced by new kinds of communities. Irenaeus asserted that Jesus, by the outpouring of the Spirit in his death, was the progenitor of a new, reconciled humanity. His story of grace and self-sacrificial love, in other words, can become the foundation of our story as well. In his new body, as Paul proclaimed (likely using a baptismal formula): "There is no longer Jew or Greek, there is no longer slave or free, there is no longer male and female; for all of you are one in Christ Jesus" (Gal. 3:28).

When we are baptized into Christ's body, we may not face persecution from imperial forces

---

3. Justo L. González, *A History of Christian Thought: From the Beginnings to the Council of Chalcedon,* rev. ed. (Nashville: Abingdon, 1970), 1:157–70.

coercing our loyalty at sword point. Still, insofar as we become new creatures, we struggle to heal lacerations in the body of humanity. If we are men, we reach out and work with women and those of other gender identities to change stereotypes and end harassment and inequities. If we are middle-class or professional, we reach out to those who have not had like opportunities and work with them to open access to those opportunities. If there are cultural, ethnic, or religious differences between us, we reach across those boundaries to make common cause in loving networks of mutuality.

Insofar as we do such things effectively, we are likely to face opposition, resentment, hostility, even violence, from those who fearfully see only the way things are and not the way God wants them to be. When we face persecution from a broken world, our author assures us that God made Jesus, the "pioneer of our salvation," perfect in suffering, and as we share in like suffering for the realization of God's will on earth, we, like the Hebrews, can take heart that his suffering gives meaning to and dignifies our own.

STEPHEN B. BOYD

Matthew 2:13–23

¹³Now after they had left, an angel of the Lord appeared to Joseph in a dream and said, "Get up, take the child and his mother, and flee to Egypt, and remain there until I tell you; for Herod is about to search for the child, to destroy him." ¹⁴Then Joseph got up, took the child and his mother by night, and went to Egypt, ¹⁵and remained there until the death of Herod. This was to fulfill what had been spoken by the Lord through the prophet, "Out of Egypt I have called my son."

¹⁶When Herod saw that he had been tricked by the wise men, he was infuriated, and he sent and killed all the children in and around Bethlehem who were two years old or under, according to the time that he had learned from the wise men. ¹⁷Then was fulfilled what had been spoken through the prophet Jeremiah:

¹⁸"A voice was heard in Ramah,
   wailing and loud lamentation,
Rachel weeping for her children;
   she refused to be consoled, because they are no more."

¹⁹When Herod died, an angel of the Lord suddenly appeared in a dream to Joseph in Egypt and said, ²⁰"Get up, take the child and his mother, and go to the land of Israel, for those who were seeking the child's life are dead." ²¹Then Joseph got up, took the child and his mother, and went to the land of Israel. ²²But when he heard that Archelaus was ruling over Judea in place of his father Herod, he was afraid to go there. And after being warned in a dream, he went away to the district of Galilee. ²³There he made his home in a town called Nazareth, so that what had been spoken through the prophets might be fulfilled, "He will be called a Nazorean."

Commentary 1: Connecting the Reading with Scripture

On this First Sunday after Christmas the texts move us quickly from the stable in Bethlehem to the larger world of human suffering and pain. The Christ child is king, but he is not like Herod and other earthly kings. His power is shown not in might and domination but through a loving faithfulness that, in a world of injustice, results in his suffering and death.

God's covenantal faithfulness is present throughout the lectionary readings for this Sunday. Psalm 148, a psalm of praise, celebrates the Lord's faithfulness shown through creation. Isaiah 63 remembers God's acts of love and mercy toward Israel, and the ways God's presence has guided and saved God's people. Hebrews 2 recounts Jesus' redemptive acts and how he was made "perfect through sufferings" (Heb. 2:10).

Both the prophet Isaiah and Jesus in Hebrews testify to their trust in God, despite the suffering they have experienced and witnessed. Matthew 2 also shows the suffering of a community and the stubborn trust of Joseph, who obediently follows God in his effort to keep his family safe. Celebrating the incarnation during the Christmas season, these readings rejoice in the incredible reality that the transcendent God enters into and is revealed in human vulnerability.

God's faithfulness in Matthew 2 is seen through the journey one family undertakes, escaping death threats and a violent ruler's anxieties. The three distinct sections that make up this passage are held together by dreams, divine action, and geographical movement. The shepherds have left, the magi have begun their return home, and Mary, Joseph, and Jesus are seemingly on their own. This is a story about God's actions—guiding Joseph, protecting the infant—and it shows God's activity in Jesus' life from the very beginning.

Within this section of Matthew are three "fulfillment quotations." Matthew seeks throughout his Gospel to relate the story of Jesus to the story of God's faithfulness to Israel. He quotes the Hebrew Scriptures forty times. Steeped in Scripture, Matthew seeks to proclaim and confess that Jesus is Christ and that his coming fulfills Scripture as a whole.[1] The promises begun to Abraham and his descendants are realized in Jesus. Matthew begins with a genealogy placing Jesus within David's line, providing continuity with Israel's story. Chapter 2 then shows how God's faithfulness toward Israel extends to the magi, who are outsiders, and therefore satisfies the hopes of all humanity.

After the magi depart, Joseph receives instructions in a dream to flee, and he immediately obeys, leaving Bethlehem for Egypt (Matt. 2:13–15). Joseph's continual response to God's messages is obedience. "Out of Egypt I have called my son" (2:15), a citation from Hosea 11:1, was not originally thought of as a prophetic, messianic text, but Matthew uses it to link the story of Jesus with the story of Israel. The reader is to connect Herod with Pharaoh, and to notice how both Jesus' family and Jacob's family found safety in Egypt.

Herod's subsequent slaughter of the innocents (2:16–18) is not found in historical records, but it is in character for this ruthless king. It is ironic that such a powerful man could feel threatened enough by a child to kill all of the babies in Bethlehem. These verses lead to many theological questions about divine activity and theodicy. Why does God warn one family and not the many others who lost children that day? Why does God not prevent such atrocities? These questions cannot and should not be easily resolved. Matthew does not address them, for he is focused upon the ways God was active in protecting the infant Jesus from such worldly atrocities, thereby enabling his salvific mission, illustrating, perhaps, how it is possible to have

faith in the ultimate fidelity of God even as we face present tragedies.

The second fulfillment quotation is from Jeremiah 31:15. The prophet speaks of the matriarch Rachel weeping at Ramah for her children, the Israelites, as they are taken into captivity in Babylon. Ramah is the place where the exiles had been forcibly detained on their way to Babylon (Jer. 40:1). Jeremiah 31 expresses deep grief, but it is also a passage of hope, looking toward the day when the Israelites will return to the promised land. The loss expressed in this passage, the devastation of parents who have lost children, should not be treated lightly. Jeremiah and Matthew name the loss and trauma, and the preacher may choose to do this as well. Yet loss and darkness are not the final word; hope remains for the Israelites and for readers of Matthew's Gospel. Even amid the prospect of exile in a foreign land and the devastation of the slaughter of children, one can trust in the ultimate faithfulness of God.

The last section, 2:19–23, once again begins with a dream. Joseph is commanded to leave Egypt and go back to Israel; he complies and establishes a home in Nazareth. It is unclear exactly what is fulfilled in the Messiah being from Nazareth (2:23); this fulfillment notice is based on no passage from the Hebrew Scriptures. Perhaps sound-play was intended subtly to portray Jesus as a nazirite, one set apart for holy service (Num. 6; Judg. 13:5–7). Another possibility could relate to the fulfillment of Israel's hope for a Davidic king. The Hebrew word for "branch" sounds similar to the word "Nazareth," and so may evoke the "branch" that comes from the root of Jesse (Isa. 11:1). Joseph's move to Nazareth could also stress that Jesus hails from an insignificant place, marking God's continued preference for those on the outskirts of society. The contrast between Jesus as king and Herod as king is in this sense stark. One lives quietly in an insignificant town, offering a ministry of inclusion and restoration, and manifests power in love and humility. The other lives in a palace, surrounded by wealth, and manifests power in violence and killing.

This passage links the story of Jesus with the story of Israel. Both Jesus and the Israelites go to

---

1. See M. Eugene Boring, "Matthew," in *The New Interpreter's Bible*, vol. 8 (Nashville: Abingdon Press, 1995).

Egypt to seek safety and eventually come back. Water links them: Israel is guided to deliverance through the Red Sea and Jesus is declared God's Son in baptism. Both experience a period of testing in the wilderness. Israel is unable to uphold their end of the covenant with God. According to the prophets, they rebel, turn away, and experience exile.

Jesus redeems their story by retracing many of the same steps, but remaining faithful even unto death on a cross (Phil. 2:8), thereby offering a new way and new outcome. Jesus' story, the incarnation, redeems humanity's story, providing hope amid loss, and ultimately liberation. Whenever we meet refugee children, mothers who mourn, strangers in an unfamiliar land, we are to remember the incarnation, God's presence among us, power manifest in love and humility. In this way Jesus' story helps us rewrite our stories.

This is a story of hope and joy mingled with bitter loss. The shadow of the cross is already present as the Christ child threatens a powerful ruler and upends usual, hierarchical notions of authority. Recalling the story of God's faithfulness toward Israel as well as the salvation found in Christ, these readings can aid the listener to persist in trusting God despite disheartening circumstances. For even in the midst of suffering and death we can remember signs of God's faithfulness, love, and humility; we can remember that hope is found in a child, God incarnate, and in the divine promise of ultimate restoration—not just for Israel but for the whole world.

KRISTIN STROBLE

Commentary 2: Connecting the Reading with the World

Biblical narratives like today's reading lend themselves to the visual. Picture the scene. Who are you in the story? What do you hear? Smell? What feelings emerge as you listen? Such prompts open the possibility of encountering Scripture in new, visceral ways, and with regard to today's text—caution!—in a way that helps ensure we feel the brutality depicted. Matthew 2:13–23 could be approached from this angle, perhaps even utilizing a preacher/congregation dialogical style. A slow, dialogic reading of this heartrending story may bear fresh fruit. Hearing what those on the other side of the pulpit glean, and then discerning threads to knit together an impromptu proclamation, means trusting the Spirit to move within both the congregation and the preacher. This requires the preacher to relinquish control and to be attentive, open, quick thinking, and wise. Perhaps, imitating Joseph in this text, it will mean being willing to go where divine instruction dictates, on the fly, unsure of the outcome, certain only of the One giving the command.

Not all congregations are comfortable with sharing unscripted comments, however, and this story of the slaughter of the innocents challenges the understanding of the most learned biblical scholars. The preacher might name up front the utter horror of this story. Baby Jesus and the Holy Family survive, thanks to the intervention of angels and Joseph's obedience to their directions, but at what cost? All the children two years old and under in and around Bethlehem are murdered. The birth of the One who comes to save ushers in a wave of death at the hands of Herod.

This gives hard-won wisdom: worldly powers do not take threats to their authority lightly. Good does not go unchallenged by evil—neither yesterday nor today. Terror employed to subdue citizens has not ceased. Examples, sadly, are myriad. Global current events—and for that matter any era of history—will offer illustrations. We should acknowledge that Christians have participated in and instigated such savagery.

The preacher could use this sermon as an occasion for corporate confession and repentance. Sometimes we are solidly on the side of Herod, scrambling to maintain status and power, doing anything to crush perceived threats to our wealth, privilege, and control. The Crusades, ecclesial execution of heretics, the quietism of some German Christians during the Nazi period, slavery, colonialism, Jim Crow: Christians have been involved in so many oppressive chapters of history. Then there are the abolitionists, the suffragettes, the Martin Luther Kings and Óscar Romeros, and so many other Christians who have struggled and even been slaughtered in solidarity with innocents.

The First Sunday after Christmas on the cusp of a new calendar year affords the preacher the important opportunity to examine and confess our own complicity with Herod and then to exhort us to join forces with Jesus, the wise men, and other saints and martyrs of our faith, and to speak and act in solidarity with innocents who are currently suffering and threatened.

The sermon could move from confession and repentance to celebration and a call to action. Who today are the vulnerable under the boot of oppressors? Who are the Rachels grieving unspeakable loss (Jer. 31:15)? How are we responding to them? How do we stand with them and against those who would destroy them? North Carolina novelist David Joy wrote a powerful essay titled "Digging in the Trash." He writes about people dubbed "trailer trash" and others struggling mightily to survive. He says, "I recognized some folks had more than others, that I had a little more than them, and the rest of the world had a lot more than any of us. I recognized class. It's just that I don't remember ever equating class to a person's worth, and I count myself lucky for that."[2]

He then shares what one reviewer wrote about his novel *Where All Light Tends to Go*: "He wrote that I should 'leave the peeling trailers, come down out of the hollers, and try writing about *people* for a change.' He actually italicized that word, people, to be sure and say that what lives in those trailers, what finds itself in a world consumed by hopelessness, addiction, and violence, those aren't people at all."[3] David Joy believes otherwise. Those who follow the baby born in a manger to poor parents should too.

The preachers could proclaim the humanity and God-given worth of the innocents, those too often treated as disposable, expendable, and less than, whoever they might be in their congregations and in their communities. The list is long of those whose value on earth is not what it is in heaven: migrant workers exploited due to their political vulnerability or fear of deportation, the Rohingya in Myanmar, unarmed people of color shot and killed by authorities, children bullied in school, LGBTQ youth living on the streets, mentally ill people housed in prisons, the elderly facing food insecurity.

Jesus, the Word born in poverty in Bethlehem, was sent for the sake of all of them. This troubling text challenges preachers to see the outcasts and marginalized closest to their congregations, perhaps within their congregations, to remember them, to witness to their worth, and to challenge parishioners to treat them as the beloved children of God for whom Jesus, though innocent, will be killed.

Reaching for hope in a sermon on a text imbued with such horror calls upon the preacher to dig deep and lift up the larger narrative context. The infant whom God saves from Herod will eventually be the innocent who is slaughtered in order to redeem the world and overturn every earthly power. Consolation comes for Israel, for Rachel, for all creation, for every person labeled "other," "less than," or "trash." The preacher can also proclaim this wondrous truth.

The story of the angels, dreams, and Joseph also reveals hope. Preaching about the strange, unexpected, yet God-directed journey of the Holy Family reassures us God directs our paths and families too. Preachers could share their own experiences, speaking of less-than-ideal changes that turned out to be of God, reminding hearers that God speaks not only in dreams and through angels, but also through epiphanies, other people, and Scripture. Of course, sometimes God's purposes remain elusive; yet daily we must ask: Are we listening for God? Are we willing to act on divine dictates when we perceive them?

Given the horror so prevalent in the news, Scripture's unwillingness to shy away from terror also provides the preacher with an opportunity not only honestly to name suffering of today, but to place it within the arc of God's salvation story of Jesus' birth and the promise

---

2. David Joy, "Digging in the Trash," http://bittersoutherner.com/digging-in-the-trash-david-joy/.
3. Joy, "Digging in the Trash."

that comes as a result. Confession and repentance regarding complicity with the Herods who unleash violence in order to secure their own earthly positions of power enable a different kind of truth-telling that brings with it the assurance of forgiveness ushered in with the incarnation. Such repentance and assurance open avenues for action as they call Christians to stand with the vulnerable, with One born in a manager, and against those who would forget, cast aside, or even harm them.

The afflicted can remember that the God whose Son was crucified does not turn aside from the depth of their pain, but willingly entered into our world of suffering; resurrection and redemption have the last word. Proclaiming that even the most harrowing of journeys are not God-forsaken, and perhaps even serve God's purposes, provides hope, no matter if those listening are fleeing to Egypt, in the middle of the wilderness, or finally headed safely home.

JILL DUFFIELD

Second Sunday after Christmas Day

Jeremiah 31:7–14   Ephesians 1:3–14
Psalm 147:12–20   John 1:(1–9) 10–18

Jeremiah 31:7–14

7For thus says the LORD:
Sing aloud with gladness for Jacob,
    and raise shouts for the chief of the nations;
proclaim, give praise, and say,
    "Save, O LORD, your people,
    the remnant of Israel."
8See, I am going to bring them from the land of the north,
    and gather them from the farthest parts of the earth,
among them the blind and the lame,
    those with child and those in labor, together;
    a great company, they shall return here.
9With weeping they shall come,
    and with consolations I will lead them back,
I will let them walk by brooks of water,
    in a straight path in which they shall not stumble;
for I have become a father to Israel,
    and Ephraim is my firstborn.

10Hear the word of the LORD, O nations,
    and declare it in the coastlands far away;
say, "He who scattered Israel will gather him,
    and will keep him as a shepherd a flock."
11For the LORD has ransomed Jacob,
    and has redeemed him from hands too strong for him.
12They shall come and sing aloud on the height of Zion,
    and they shall be radiant over the goodness of the LORD,
over the grain, the wine, and the oil,
    and over the young of the flock and the herd;
their life shall become like a watered garden,
    and they shall never languish again.
13Then shall the young women rejoice in the dance,
    and the young men and the old shall be merry.
I will turn their mourning into joy,
    I will comfort them, and give them gladness for sorrow.
14I will give the priests their fill of fatness,
    and my people shall be satisfied with my bounty,
                                    says the LORD.

Commentary 1: Connecting the Reading with Scripture

It is the Second Sunday after Christmas, and the church is prepared to sing. On cue, Jeremiah 31:7–14 begins, "Sing aloud with gladness."

The glad tidings of the birth of Jesus constitute both fulfillment and promise. Emmanuel, God-with-us, is to become the Christ of the cross and resurrection, the One who saves. With the birth of Christ, a new age of grace begins.

Grace, as Dietrich Bonhoeffer reminds us, exacts a heavy cost. It is not earned, but neither is it extended on the cheap. As Norman Maclean beautifully expressed in reference to his father, a Presbyterian pastor and fly fisherman: "To him, all good things—trout as well as eternal salvation—came by grace; and grace comes by art, and art does not come easy."[1]

The other lectionary texts of the week bear this out. John's prologue proclaims that with Christ, the "true light, which enlightens everyone, was coming into the world" and with it "grace upon grace" (John 1:9, 16). One gets the distinct impression that the light is small and the darkness vast (v. 5). To make matters much worse, God's people preferred darkness to the light (vv. 10–11).

Ephesians ties grace to an atonement that is not without blood. "In [Christ] we have redemption through his blood . . . according to the riches of his grace" (Eph. 1:7). At Christmas, the church celebrates the coming of grace while also keeping in mind Maclean's caveat that "grace . . . does not come easy."

Jeremiah 31 places redemption—as covenant fulfillment—in the context of anguish. Rachel weeps and Ephraim pleads (Jer. 31:15, 18). It begins with the counterintuitive insight that redemption is "found . . . in the wilderness" (v. 2). It is in this crucible that YHWH establishes a new, more intimate relationship with God's people in which the covenant is written upon the heart (v. 33).

Verses 7–14 act as prelude to this new covenant. YHWH leads the people Judah and Israel home "with [divine] consolations" to accompany them (31:9). Upon arrival, their experience of grace is deeply personal. "Mourning" turns to "joy" and "sorrow" gives way to "gladness" (v. 13). The newly redeemed people sing songs of praise to the "goodness" of God (v. 12), yet there are still hues of gray. "With weeping they shall come," prophesies Jeremiah (v. 9).

Why weeping? One answer might be because this is a walk of repentance. In the emotionally tense language of the book of Jeremiah, we see that the "ransom of Jacob" did not come easy (v. 11).

YHWH's heart is broken by inexplicable infidelity. First, God's people turn away. Then their stubbornness metastasizes into open rebellion. "As a well keeps its water fresh, so she keeps fresh her wickedness" (Jer. 6:7a). The Lord has watched in disbelief as Judah and Israel "have turned aside and gone away" (5:23), and the heart of YHWH breaks. The protective hand of YHWH is removed.

In 597 BCE, leading Judeans are sent into exile. In 587, Jerusalem falls; many other Judeans are killed or deported. They are not just conquered. They are devoured. The Babylonians "eat up your harvest . . . eat up your sons and daughters . . . eat up your flocks and your herds . . . eat up your vines and fig trees" (5:17). The immediate reaction was anguish. Yet the situation was not without hope. Somehow even in exile, God would be present. Keeping this tension in mind, Jeremiah counsels God's people to build houses, plant gardens, marry, and bear children; they are to seek "the welfare of the city" even in Babylon (29:5–7).

How can this be? Because grace abounds even in the wilderness of sin. YHWH remains personally involved in the well-being of a stubborn, rebellious people. The heart of YHWH retains its supple softness, but repentance and amendment of life will be necessary. "Stand at the crossroads," God beckons, "and ask for the ancient paths, where the good way lies; and walk in it, and find rest for your souls" (6:16). "Amend your ways," God pleads, "and let me dwell with you" (7:3; 26:13).

Throughout the canon of the Holy Scriptures we find the tenacity of an intimate grace: "I will be your God, and you shall be my people" (Jer. 7:23; 11:4; 24:7; 30:22; 31:33; see also Exod. 6:7; Lev. 26:12; Ezek. 14:11; Zech. 8:8; 2 Cor. 6:16; Rev. 21:3). This leads us to surmise that what is gracious about God's covenant with us is the belonging. God chooses us. God, as Karl Barth said again and again, chooses to be the God who is for us.

We see this clearly in Jeremiah 31:9, which evokes the Twenty-Third Psalm: "I will let them

---

1. Norman Maclean, *A River Runs through It and Other Stories* (Chicago: University of Chicago Press, 2017), 8.

walk by brooks of water, in a straight path in which they shall not stumble; for I have become a father to Israel, and Ephraim is my firstborn." Grace emanates from the beating heart of divine love. This is the source of hope in Jeremiah. New life can be imagined by a community that must have wondered whether they had any future at all (29:11; 31:17). The prophet helps exiled refugees to see beyond the cruel power of Nebuchadnezzar to the ultimate mercies of God. Every time of suffering raises searching questions. Where do we turn when all hope seems lost? Where is our relief when we are under the thumb of cruelty? Where do we find rest when we fear we cannot go home again? For Jeremiah, the answer is always the same: God. God is our hope. God is our help. God is our home.

Sadly, the days after Christmas have been considered "between time." We are either winding down from the multitude of holiday parties or gearing up for New Year's festivities. Christmastide gets confused with cultural celebrations of success, leisure, and plenty. Jeremiah 31 provides a counterbalance. In the time immediately following Christmas, these evocative verses may remind us all that *Emmanuel*—"God is with us"—is a message of grace during times of personal failure, fatigue, and dearth. Even during these experiences, people of faith still manage to "sing aloud with gladness." Those who cannot sing may be assured that the Christian community sings for them, raising our voices on behalf of those who have grown hoarse from grief.

At Christmas, the church sings. It clears its throat and celebrates the fulfillment of divine grace in the life of Jesus, a grace that never excludes his agonizing, sacrificial death. This joins Jeremiah 31:7–14 to John's prologue and the message of the Gospel. "God spoke to our ancestors . . . by the prophets," says the author of Hebrews, "but in these last days he has spoken to us by a Son" (Heb. 1:1–2). The new covenant prophesied by Jeremiah becomes even more intimate, even more personal. It manifests in the sacrificial gift of God's own person, whose redeeming power is a choice not to make suffering obsolete but to suffer with us. As Jeremiah 31:7–14 makes evident, Jeremiah is more than a weeping prophet. He is more even than a prophet of hope in the midst of social collapse. He is a harbinger of Jesus Christ. His message summarizes the trajectory of the message from the prophets to the Son.

Norman Maclean was correct to follow Jeremiah's prophetic insight that "grace does not come easy." Perhaps after close attention to the weeping prophet, we are able to see that it was never meant to be so. Grace may never be easy, but the prophetic message endures: the love of God is relentlessly steadfast.

MARK RALLS

Commentary 2: Connecting the Reading with the World

Jeremiah's inspirited assurance that Israel will return to its land in Jeremiah 31:7–14, part of what is known as the Book of Consolation (Jer. 30–31), is made right before or during the exile of Judah. In the midst of ruin and dispersion, the prophet prophesies the opposite: healing, restoration, reestablishment. Indeed, Jeremiah promises not only that the exiles will return to Jerusalem, but that they will come back in such great numbers that Jerusalem's boundaries will be enlarged; moreover, the city will never again be overrun by enemies (31:38–40).

No doubt this prophecy sounded absurd to the worried population of Judah. Jeremiah's

speech may sound bombastic to the modern listener. Yet it is important to remember that Jeremiah is not talking about what is, but what is possible through God. He affirms something for which the Judeans yearn that has not yet occurred. Considering this hope emanates from God's prophet, we should assume these wishes parallel those of God. Stability, prosperity, and return: that is what God wants for this beloved covenant people.

Jeremiah's authenticity and authority as a true spokesperson for God is confirmed when the prophet's optimistic prophecy eventually comes true. Though it appeared impossible in the midst of Judah's destruction, the exiled Israelites were eventually allowed to return to their homeland, rebuild the temple, and reestablish their worship in the Persian period. We also have to remember that *part* of Jeremiah's prophecy still remains unfulfilled; God, through the prophet, promises the people of God that their city "shall never again be uprooted or overthrown" (31:40). As a quick perusal of today's headlines makes clear, however, the eternal rootedness promised by Jeremiah has not yet come to pass.

The ambivalence embodied by this prophecy—a prophecy that inhabits the space between partial fulfillment and full eschatological realization—is fitting in terms of the text's liturgical placement between Christmas and Epiphany, that is, after the birth of the promised Savior but right before Jesus' manifestation to the world. Indeed, Jesus' first manifestation or Epiphany looks forward to the final manifestation of Christ, who will return in glory.

The liturgical placement of this passage and the ambivalence it embodies offer a potential topic for a sermon: how do we, as the people of God, behave and believe authentically and faithfully in this space between partial fulfillment and full eschatological realization? A brave preacher might ponder the dissonance between our lives and the promises made in our tradition. Our lives daily seem to contradict the miraculous assurances made and depicted as occurring in our canonical text. What is the appropriate response when we are confronted with this contradiction? What do we do when it seems that life and belief, or life and canon, do not correspond?

The temptation when belief and reality come into conflict is to urge the people of God to ignore life, to simply maintain hope and faith in the midst of misery and hardship. Such urgings do little to ease the pain of those suffering. How can we both affirm the truthfulness of people's lived experiences—their sufferings, hardships, questions, and doubts—and also affirm the great promises pledged and professed by our church and our tradition?

The context of displacement and dislocation is also enduringly pertinent. Recent disasters such as hurricanes, storms, earthquakes, fires, and mudslides present modern-day examples of the horrors that cause dislocation and ruin. The displacement caused by natural disasters offers an important opportunity for preachers to speak about issues concerning the environment. Extreme weather is frequently exacerbated, and its effects worsened, because of environmental damage. The harm, suffering, and death caused by climate change are borne disproportionately by the most vulnerable and defenseless among us: the poor, the elderly, and children.[2] How can we, the people of God, side with the vulnerable and with those most affected by environmental damage? As Jeremiah reminds us, when we side with the most vulnerable, we ally ourselves with the redemptive purposes and hopes of God (31:8).

Environmental displacement, moreover, is entangled with issues concerning refugees, immigrants, and migrants. In 2015, nearly 60 million people from all over the world, many of whom were children, were displaced because of war, conflict, persecution, and poverty.[3] The displaced whom God addresses through Jeremiah—"the blind and the lame, those with child and those in labor" (31:8)—parallel similarly defenseless people in our world today. The image of a crowd of "those with child and those in labor" brings to mind pregnant women who have desperately fled their homelands and crossed forbidding barriers such as the Mediterranean Sea or American deserts, in hopes of finding safety for themselves and their families, only to be held in detention centers and forcibly sent back.

Difficult questions with no easy answers confront the prophetic preacher. How can the people of God help and stand with desperate people displaced today? How can we as the people of God help those who are victims of larger systems of oppression and injustice? How can we work to become part of God's promise to transform people's lives so that they become "like a watered garden" (v. 12)?

---

2. Suzanne Goldenberg, "Climate Change: The Poor Will Suffer Most," *The Guardian*, March 30, 2014, https://www.theguardian.com/environment/2014/mar/31/climate-change-poor-suffer-most-un-report.

3. Jake Silverstein, "The Displaced: Introduction," *New York Times Magazine*, November 5, 2015; Tatiana Sanchez, "Mothers Explain Why They Fled Honduras," https://www.usatoday.com/story/news/nation/2014/07/09/mothers-explain-fleeing-honduras-with-children/12423979.

Displacement and dislocation are euphemisms for homelessness. The prophet Jeremiah in this passage is speaking to a group of people who have been removed, or shortly will be removed, from their homes and homeland. Homelessness is a complex issue that raises many important topics and questions—for instance, concerns about gentrification, poverty, and access to affordable housing, which intersect with issues of racial and socioeconomic equality—that are vital for the people of God to reflect and act upon. Homelessness is also entangled with issues of mental and physical health, and affordable health care. Medical expenses, and the joblessness that can often result from illness or injury, often lead to homelessness. Homelessness in turn causes mental and physical damage; those without a home may die decades earlier than those with housing. In short, homelessness equals death—to use an analogy made by Jeremiah. In the verse immediately following today's lection (31:15), the prophet envisions the Israelite matriarch, Rachel, weeping for her exiled and displaced children, for they "are no more."

If we worship the God of love and life, then we, like Jeremiah, will be passionate about addressing causes of suffering and death, and we will be especially sensitive to those most vulnerable. These are not light topics. However, true prophets of Yahweh often challenged, spoke out, and confronted their communities to open their eyes to injustice and suffering. They reminded the people that God is always on the side of the persecuted, marginalized, poor, suffering, and, as in the case of Jeremiah 31, the exiled and homeless.

How do we treat prophets and other truth-tellers in our society, our churches, and our communities? Who are they, and what forces are attempting to drown out their voices? How might we, the people of God, be complicit in the silencing? Most important, how are we joining with and amplifying the voices of God's messengers, so that God's desire to turn mourning into joy and sorrow into gladness (31:13) might finally come to pass?

SONG-MI SUZIE PARK

Second Sunday after Christmas Day

Psalm 147:12–20

[12]Praise the LORD, O Jerusalem!
    Praise your God, O Zion!
[13]For he strengthens the bars of your gates;
    he blesses your children within you.
[14]He grants peace within your borders;
    he fills you with the finest of wheat.
[15]He sends out his command to the earth;
    his word runs swiftly.
[16]He gives snow like wool;
    he scatters frost like ashes.
[17]He hurls down hail like crumbs—
    who can stand before his cold?
[18]He sends out his word, and melts them;
    he makes his wind blow, and the waters flow.
[19]He declares his word to Jacob,
    his statutes and ordinances to Israel.
[20]He has not dealt thus with any other nation;
    they do not know his ordinances.
Praise the LORD!

Connecting the Psalm with Scripture and Worship

God saves the afflicted, gathering outcasts, to reconstitute the people that is Israel (Ps. 147:1–2). After a lengthy time of exile, God restores Israel, reestablishing Jerusalem, returning those who dwelt in misery as strangers and outsiders in circumstances and places where those in power neither knew Israel's heart, nor believed in Israel's God. Here the psalmist moves from the particular to the universal in describing how God chooses Israel.

Israel is God's beloved. God rescues this people from slavery in Egypt and releases them from exile. Israel's peculiar call, to not be like other nations, happens in, with, and through God's saving intervention. Seeing God in action, Israel now voices praise upon praise, for the God who rescues and restores is the very same God who administers creation: the world, the seasons, the cycles of fallowness and harvest. Praising YHWH is good, beautiful, and worthwhile; to praise YHWH is to participate in God's glorifying.

The psalmist names the reasons for praise: YHWH strengthens and blesses (v. 13), YHWH acts to assure peace, *shalom* (v. 14). YHWH fortifies the borders, protecting Israel from enemies, assuring that the city will be what it is meant to be, the home of a vital community where grace, mercy, and the power of God are evident.[1] In the psalm, we witness the assumed realization of YHWH's promise heard in Jeremiah 31:7–14.

Israel exists as a people, as the outward expression of a decision made by YHWH out of divine love. The love of God for Israel is an eternal love, unshakable in its will toward good. Therefore, the city of Jerusalem is a place of peace where there is security, contentment, and community. The prophet declares that the people's suffering and misery will be relieved

---

1. Artur Weiser, *The Psalms: A Commentary,* trans. Herbert Hartwell (Philadelphia: Westminster Press, 1962), 837.

by God and God's word, a creative word that brings into being what God desires.[2]

Festal celebration then is cause and effect of God's Word enacted. The remnant that YWHW gathers from "the farthest parts of the earth" will include "the blind and the lame," "those with child and those in labor," constituting together, "a great company," who shall return to the place where God is guardian and shepherd (31:8, 10). Restoration is the fulfillment of the divine will, wherein the life-giving power of God's Word is lifted up and compared to "rain and snow come down from heaven." These are a refreshment that lingers, never returning from whence they have come until they have accomplished their purpose.

The melting of snow, the "watering the earth," were rare occasions in the desert-like climate of Sinai's wilderness. When this happens, it makes an indelible impression on the minds and within the hearts of those who witness it. God's Word brings gentle power to bear, causing the earth to sprout and flourish, as the prophet Isaiah describes; the Word from heaven results in "giving seed to the sower and bread to the eater" (Isa. 55:10).[3]

On this Second Sunday after Christmas, we cannot help but think of the incarnation. God's loving self-disclosure, enfleshed in the Word incarnate, dwells among us anew as hope for the hopeless, as light in our darkness, as comfort and joy. Beyond anything we usually imagine, God crushes oppression—not by imperialistic behavior, terrorizing acts, arrogant displays of military prowess, or by the adulation born out of conspicuous consumption and coveting. God rebuilds trust with the remnant God restores, by becoming one with those who suffer, those who know little of life's wealth, who live with the misery born of poverty and want, as God's promises are denied them. The deep freeze of cruelty is thawed by the Word-made-flesh who breathes new life, melting the frozen tundra of hardened hearts and minds.

God dwells with us, as one of us, so that we might more fully live into God's grace and mercy and compassion. By raising Israel out of exile, out of slavery, out of being disappeared, God chooses to demonstrate God's will to bind up the brokenhearted, release the captives, cast down the wicked, and add to the number—a number too numerous to count—of God's holy people. To be in God's presence, to dwell with God, is to live in grace and truth, with fullness. So we see gladness, praise, and exultation once again. For those who return (Jer. 31:12, 13b–14) shall "sing aloud" and "be radiant over the goodness of the LORD," who provides "grain, and wine, and oil," flocks and herds for young and old. Those who return shall find that "their life shall become like a watered garden, and they shall never languish again." They will be always rejoicing, delighting in the comfort and satisfaction that comes out of living, knowing the Lord's bounty. For Christians celebrating the birth of Jesus, Psalm 147 is a vehicle to offer praise for God's saving ways, past, present, and future.

JOSEPH A. DONNELLA II

---

2. R. E. Clements, *Jeremiah*, Interpretation (Atlanta: John Knox Press, 1988), 186.

3. Weiser, *Psalms*, 836.

Ephesians 1:3–14

³Blessed be the God and Father of our Lord Jesus Christ, who has blessed us in Christ with every spiritual blessing in the heavenly places, ⁴just as he chose us in Christ before the foundation of the world to be holy and blameless before him in love. ⁵He destined us for adoption as his children through Jesus Christ, according to the good pleasure of his will, ⁶to the praise of his glorious grace that he freely bestowed on us in the Beloved. ⁷In him we have redemption through his blood, the forgiveness of our trespasses, according to the riches of his grace ⁸that he lavished on us. With all wisdom and insight ⁹he has made known to us the mystery of his will, according to his good pleasure that he set forth in Christ, ¹⁰as a plan for the fullness of time, to gather up all things in him, things in heaven and things on earth. ¹¹In Christ we have also obtained an inheritance, having been destined according to the purpose of him who accomplishes all things according to his counsel and will, ¹²so that we, who were the first to set our hope on Christ, might live for the praise of his glory. ¹³In him you also, when you had heard the word of truth, the gospel of your salvation, and had believed in him, were marked with the seal of the promised Holy Spirit; ¹⁴this is the pledge of our inheritance toward redemption as God's own people, to the praise of his glory.

Commentary 1: Connecting the Reading with Scripture

The lively word for this season is doxology, praising the God who has humbly come to us in Christ Jesus (John 1:14), but also praising the God who, ever since light first broke in creation, has been saving, rescuing, liberating, and preparing communities to bear witness to God's extravagant grace. Notes of doxology sound throughout the appointed readings.

Choosing selections from Sirach and the Wisdom of Solomon would introduce a feminine voice into today's repertoire of praise. In the first instance, Wisdom herself is speaking, "prais[ing] herself" and telling of her "taking root in an honored people," namely, "in Zion" (Sir. 24:1, 10, 12). In the Wisdom of Solomon, she speaks of delivering "a holy people and blameless race . . . from a nation of oppressors," and conducts the righteous in singing hymns to God's "holy name" (Wis. 10:15, 20). The prophet Jeremiah too urges his people to lift their voices in doxology, to "sing aloud with gladness for Jacob," who "has been ransomed, and redeemed from hands too strong for him" (Jer. 31:7, 11). The praise to God uttered

in Psalm 147 is built on strong action verbs that show how God has been active on behalf of God's people: God "strengthens," "grants peace," "gives," "sends out," and "declares." The structure of the psalm may suggest the structure of the sermon: it begins and ends with praise.

The theme of doxology is most fully developed today in the passage from Ephesians. As if following the lead of the psalmist, the writer lays out the gifts God has lavished on humankind, particularly through the agency of Christ Jesus. Through him, God has "blessed us with every spiritual blessing in the heavenly places" (Eph. 1:3b). Those blessings include adoption as God's children, forgiveness of sins and redemption, disclosure of what God wills for the human family, and the granting of an inheritance. A sermon might elaborate on one or more of these blessings. In the second half of the letter, the writer provides guidelines on how to live in the light of these blessings, but for now the emphasis is on thanks and praise for the blessings.

The "first cousin" of Ephesians in the Christian canon is Colossians. Neither Ephesians nor

Colossians is a letter in the strict sense of the term. They are more like theological treatises framed as letters, meant to circulate not just in Ephesus and Colossae but among faith communities throughout Asia Minor toward the end of the first century. The historical Paul is the author of neither letter. Both, however, bear the marks of Pauline preaching and teaching and faithfully develop Paul's understanding of "the mystery" that God has now made known to God's holy ones (Col. 1:26–27; Eph. 1:9). These texts emphasize one aspect of the mystery: that in Christ, God has accomplished a merger of two "ethnic groups" (Jew and Gentile) "under one economical salvific plan."[1] Christ is now "in [them]" and is "the hope of glory" (Col. 1:27). Furthermore, the divine plan ordains that "in the fullness of time" all things, "things in heaven and things on earth," will be gathered up in Christ (Eph. 1:10) in the manner that Jews and Gentiles gather in Christ when they meet to worship together. For this accomplishment, and for all that remains to be done in creation, God is worthy to be praised.

Since Ephesians begins on such a theologically effusive note, one wonders at the situation its author aims to address. It would seem from the text that a number of communities in its orbit are struggling to find their significance *as* communities of faith. Why else would the writer choose to emphasize the status of these communities in the eyes of God? They are "blessed in Christ" and have been "chosen" and "adopted as God's children."

Stress upon their status as adopted children counters the sense that they have been abandoned by God and left without a future. In fact, to be adopted by the Creator of the universe assures them that they have a destiny, a valuable place in the realm of God, a place intended for them from the beginning. Perhaps they are struggling with the significance of their mission. The Ephesians and faithful communities like them are attempting to do something wonderful, but also something quite strange in the spiritual ecosystem of their time: they are forging a new kind of alternative and inclusive community that resists cultural divisions based on gender, race, national origins, or tribe.

To be sure, the inscription of the household codes into the letter (5:15–6: 9) shows how difficult it is—even for this writer—to keep full inclusion in view. It demonstrates how deeply embedded are hierarchical ways of thinking, even within those communities that are "in Christ." One can easily become discouraged when "rulers . . . authorities . . . cosmic powers of darkness . . . and spiritual forces of evil in heavenly places" (Eph. 6:12b) work their harm. Communities doing the difficult work of resisting these powers and working for full inclusion in the name of Christ need the kind of encouragement this writer offers in 1:4, 8, 9. The effort to forge a new unity between separated ethnic groups, while respecting the particularities of each, is therefore linked to something that God has been doing in creation since the beginning, something that will in God's time be fully accomplished.

With that end in view, the author steps into the role of worship leader to call for praise from a congregation that may be losing its voice. In addition to outside pressures ("spiritual forces of evil in the heavenly places," 6:12), the writer seems to be aware of forces within the community muffling corporate praise. Take, for instance, the shift in pronouns between "we" and "you" in 1:12–13. "We" appears to refer to those the writer represents, namely those Jewish believers who were first to receive from God's hand the blessings of adoption, redemption, promise of an inheritance, and disclosure of the "mystery." They had been the first to "set [their] hope on Christ" (1:12). It is tempting, then, for the Jewish believers to claim special status in the community. To counter that impression, the writer makes a definitive turn toward the "you," toward those Gentiles who may be wondering how fully inclusive the community is. To them the writer offers assurance that they too are "marked with the seal of the promised Holy Spirit" (1:13) and therefore have an equal share in "redemption as God's own people."

Another inhibition to praising God is the embedded belief that all human life is

---

1. Mitzi J. Smith, "Ephesians," in Brian K. Blount, gen. ed.; Cain Hope Felder, Clarice J. Martin, and Emerson B. Powery, assoc. eds., *True to Our Native Land: An African American New Testament Commentary* (Minneapolis: Fortress Press, 2007), 348–62, 348.

entrapped by "fate" or subjected to the wills of capricious gods who compete with one another for the claim to human subservience. The writer breaks the power of that claim by linking the destiny of the community not to the "will of the gods," but to the plan of the one God disclosed in Jesus Christ. In that name, God has brought into being this new community, which lives under the lordship of the risen One. Today the preacher is invited to look around and see how God continues the work imagined by the writer of this text. Such a God is worthy of thanks and praise.

RICHARD F. WARD

Commentary 2: Connecting the Reading with the World

The writer of Ephesians expresses a compelling and comprehensive view of Christ's work and our role in it. That work is "to gather up all things in him, things in heaven and things on earth" (Eph. 1:10). Forgiven of our trespasses (1:7), "marked with the seal of the . . . Holy Spirit" (1:13), and "created in Christ Jesus for good works" (2:10), we participate in a "new humanity" (2:15), wherein everyone and everything in heaven and on earth is reconciled to God and one another.

God chose us from "before the foundation of the world" (1:4) for this work. It is the plan of God expressed by Isaiah: "I have given you as a covenant to the people, a light to the nations, to open the eyes that are blind, to bring out the prisoners from the dungeon, from the prison those who sit in darkness" (Isa. 42:6–7), and to "bring forth justice to the nations" (42:1). For Paul and the writer of this letter, that call has been extended beyond Israel; it includes all who respond. It is a universal call to anyone willing to be a light to everyone else. Why? We cannot reach our God-given potential without them, and they cannot reach theirs without us.

There are ecclesial, social-ethical, and personal connections that might be made to the affirmations in today's text.

Catherine of Siena, the great fourteenth-century mystic and teacher of the church, affirms God's will for human interdependence in creation. Speaking in God's voice, she says, "I could easily have created [humanity] possessed of all that they should need both for body and soul, but I wish that one should have need of the other, and that they should be my ministers to administer the graces and gifts that they have received from me. Whether [one] will or no, [one] cannot help making an act of love."[2] To fulfill God's intention for us, we must make an act of love toward others, for they have what we need—materially and spiritually—and we have what they need.

When we are born, we cannot survive without receiving comprehensive care from others such as mothers, fathers, siblings, and grandparents. As we mature, our brains cannot develop to their full intellectual potential without proper nutrition, sensory stimulation, and the tutelage of those around us. We cannot eat a bowl of cereal without a host of others, seen and unseen, having cooperated in growing grain, processing it, and bringing the cereal to our tables. All this care is theologically significant, for without the love of God embodied in our families, churches, or friends, we could not imagine the God of whom our author speaks. "We are," Dr. Martin Luther King Jr. said, "caught in an inescapable network of mutuality, tied in a single garment of destiny."[3]

There is, however, a problem: that single garment has giant tears in the fabric. We have been alienated from one another by "dividing walls" of hostility (Eph. 2:14). We belong to groups: men, women, or gender-nonconforming folks, black or white, Jew, Christian, or Muslim, straight or gay, professional or working class, with long histories of wounds, distrust, suspicion, and hatred

2. Catherine of Siena, "Treatise on Divine Providence," in Ray C. Petry, ed., *Late Medieval Mysticism*, Library of Christian Classics 13 (Philadelphia: Westminster Press, 1957), 270–84.

3. Martin Luther King Jr., "Letter from Birmingham Jail," in James Washington, ed., *A Testament of Hope: The Essential Writings and Speeches of Dr. Martin Luther King Jr.* (San Francisco: HarperSanFrancisco, 1991), 290.

between and among us. We struggle against "cosmic powers" and against "spiritual forces of evil" (6:12). Christ, however, has broken down the walls between us and made us "one new humanity" (2:15). He has made peace, reconciling "both groups to God in one body" (2:15–16).

The work of reconciliation is far from complete, even within and between our churches. The "cosmic powers" are still at work tearing at the fabric of God's creation; there are many who believe that others, different from themselves, are enemies. The work to which God calls us in Christ is not easy, and it can be frightening to reach across these rips in the fabric of creation toward others who may view us as enemies.

Unless we personally know people of other races, religious traditions, socioeconomic classes, or sexual orientations or identities, it is almost impossible to overcome the social chasms that separate us. We may simply hold on to stereotypes of members of other groups—stereotypes that would seem to justify our distance or even mistreatment of them—rather than develop relationships that might dispel inaccurate images. Only this kind of knowledge leads to the empathy necessary to love our neighbors as ourselves. If we do not know them, their contexts, their strengths, and the social and institutional constraints they face, we cannot hope to act in ways they would identify as loving.

According to a survey of white Americans, black Americans, and Hispanic Americans, our "core social networks tend to be dominated by people of the same race or ethnic background."[4] The members of whites' social networks are 91 percent white; members of blacks' social networks are 83 percent black; members of Hispanics' networks are 64 percent Hispanic. So many of us (statistically speaking, most especially whites) have a problem—isolation from others different from ourselves—that gets in the way of our participation in the new humanity headed by Christ, whereby everyone and everything in heaven and on earth is reconciled to God and one another.

Because the historical and contemporary force fields of ignorance, suspicion, fear, dislike, and even revulsion so easily drive us apart, reaching across these social divides requires courage, faith, hope, and discipline. To change the configuration of our core social networks requires intentional commitment and concrete steps that create new social patterns. A white American, for instance, who can often avoid social contexts dominated by members of another race, might seek out a predominantly black organization, such as the NAACP or an Urban League chapter, and begin, perhaps with a friend, to attend meetings.

On an institutional level, our churches remain some of the most racially segregated institutions in our society. If we dream of racially desegregated or even integrated congregations, having a dominant-culture congregation develop a partnership with a congregation made up primarily of worshipers of another race can be a good first step. The pastor and lay leadership might reach out to the corresponding leadership in the other congregation to see if there would be interest in pulpit exchanges, joint book discussions, partnership on a Habitat for Humanity build, or working together on a public issue (e.g., education) that affects both congregations. Such projects provide a new cultural space for meeting, exchange, and forming relationships. Even small steps can lead to transforming reconciliation.

In this ministry of reconciliation, Christ calls us to care not just for ourselves and our own; we are called to look across the gaps, to find folks of goodwill on the other side, and to take up our needles and thread and sew toward them. Christ calls us to mend the tears in the fabric of our communities, so as "to gather up all things in him, things in heaven and things on earth" (1:10).

STEPHEN B. BOYD

---

4. Daniel Cox, Juhem Navarro-Rivera, and Robert P. Jones, "Race, Religion, and Political Affiliation of Americans' Core Social Networks," from a 2013 study by the Public Religion Research Institute, https://www.prri.org/research/poll-race-religion-politics-americans-social-networks/.

John 1:(1–9) 10–18

¹In the beginning was the Word, and the Word was with God, and the Word was God. ²He was in the beginning with God. ³All things came into being through him, and without him not one thing came into being. What has come into being ⁴in him was life, and the life was the light of all people. ⁵The light shines in the darkness, and the darkness did not overcome it.

⁶There was a man sent from God, whose name was John. ⁷He came as a witness to testify to the light, so that all might believe through him. ⁸He himself was not the light, but he came to testify to the light. ⁹The true light, which enlightens everyone, was coming into the world.

¹⁰He was in the world, and the world came into being through him; yet the world did not know him. ¹¹He came to what was his own, and his own people did not accept him. ¹²But to all who received him, who believed in his name, he gave power to become children of God, ¹³who were born, not of blood or of the will of the flesh or of the will of man, but of God.

¹⁴And the Word became flesh and lived among us, and we have seen his glory, the glory as of a father's only son, full of grace and truth. ¹⁵(John testified to him and cried out, "This was he of whom I said, 'He who comes after me ranks ahead of me because he was before me.'") ¹⁶From his fullness we have all received, grace upon grace. ¹⁷The law indeed was given through Moses; grace and truth came through Jesus Christ. ¹⁸No one has ever seen God. It is God the only Son, who is close to the Father's heart, who has made him known.

Commentary 1: Connecting the Reading with Scripture

The prologue of the Gospel of John poetically celebrates the coming of Jesus into the world and introduces key theological themes developed throughout the Gospel. The opening recalls the ancient words of Genesis 1:1, "in the beginning," and announces oneness between the Word and God. Several verses later, John identifies Jesus with the Word, thereby declaring the beginning of this man to be ultimately beyond time and history. The allusion to Genesis connects Jesus, the Word made flesh, with God's acts and promises in the Old Testament. Through the Word creation was spoken into being, the law was revealed to Moses at Sinai, and truth was spoken through the prophets. Through the Word the heavens were made (Ps. 33:6). This is the same Word that Isaiah proclaims will never fade away (Isa. 40:6–8) and will bring true life (Isa. 55:10–11). These verses provide one of the central claims of John's Gospel: when one sees Jesus, one sees God.

Like Mark, this Gospel does not contain a birth story, but together with Matthew, Mark, and Luke, it does introduce us to the important figure who witnesses to the light, John. In this Gospel, John is never identified as "the Baptist," for here his one function is to bear witness to Jesus. His presence also moves the prologue from speech about the eternal Word to focus upon the concrete, historical Word made flesh. Indeed, the prologue dances back and forth as the eternal, cosmic Word of God interacts with the temporal world of John the Baptist and of Jesus, the incarnate Word.

Two key themes introduced here and developed throughout the Gospel are (1) Jesus' oneness with God (Jesus as Word) and (2) Jesus' oneness with humanity (Jesus as incarnate). "Jesus as Word" is proclaimed by John just after Jesus' baptism, in terms of Jesus being the Son of God (John 1:34) and is developed throughout

We Look to Christ

Here we have the supreme illustration of the truth which lies at the base of Christian doctrine, that in Jesus Christ we have true revealing of God. This does not mean something technical, as if in Christ we had received a formula concerning the divine nature. It means that Jesus and his life and work constitute a great expression of God and exhibition of his character. It is true, as the Fourth Gospel declares, that Jesus is not alone and does not speak from himself. His word is not his own word, but what he has seen with the Father he speaks to men, and the action of his life is not his own but God's (Jn. viii. 28; xiv. 10). Thus he represents the unseen Father, and sets forth to human knowledge the character of the eternal will. What he does God is doing, and such as he is God is. In him God does that most direct and simple work of revelation—he shows himself as he is. Christ we know as Savior, and God, we thereby know, is Savior also. Christ who has lived and died among men, and God whom no man hath seen, are called by this one name. Therefore, if we wish to understand God as Savior, we look at Christ. In his life and spirit is the authorized interpretation of the divine Saviorhood.

William Newton Clarke, *The Christian Doctrine of God* (New York: Charles Scribner's Sons, 1910), 215.

---

the Gospel. Soon thereafter, Nathanael, one of the first disciples, also says Jesus is the "Son of God" (1:49). Jesus' connection to God is revealed throughout the Gospel as he performs wondrous signs and engages in inspired conversations. Later, Nicodemus is told that Jesus is "the only Son of God" (3:18), and after that Martha tells him that she believes he is "the Son of God" (11:27). Indeed, near the end of the book John confesses to readers that his Gospel from beginning to end has been "written so that you may come to believe that Jesus is the Messiah, the Son of God, and that through believing you may have life in his name" (20:31).

A discordant shift occurs when the prologue cautions that while the world owes its existence to the Word, despite the testimony of John, the world "did not know him" (1:10) and "did not accept him" (v. 11). "World" in John can also refer specifically to humanity, instead of creation in general. Jesus enters the "world" or physical universe (v. 10), but the "world" does not recognize him; some do believe, but many do not accept him (vv. 11–12). Jesus has come to offer salvation, yet humans have the choice of whether to receive him. In the end, the world will crucify him.

The concepts of "knowing" and "seeing" are seen throughout the Gospel and influence whether people believe. John the Baptist does not recognize Jesus until he sees the Spirit descending as a dove and hears God's voice

(1:30–34). Jesus calls to Andrew and Simon Peter with the invitation "come and see" (1:39). The Samaritan woman who encounters Jesus at the well urges her neighbors to "come and see a man who told me everything I have ever done!" (4:29). The culmination of this theme occurs at the tomb when the beloved disciple "went in, and he saw and believed" (20:8). Jesus has been revealed as God's Son through signs, teachings, an empty tomb, and the witness of disciples, but the decision between acknowledging or rejecting him as Christ continues to face believers in every new generation, even today.

The climax of the prologue is at 1:14, "And the Word became flesh and lived among us." This is the story not just of the origins of Jesus, but of God and God's interaction with the world. In the incarnation, God's glory is revealed in human flesh. Already it has been stated that "the Word was God" and the "Word became flesh." These statements must be held together. This is the fulfillment of God's promise to be with God's people. Moses was taught how to make a tabernacle so that God may "dwell among them" (Exod. 25:8). The Greek verb for "lived among us" contains the same root as "tabernacle" or "tent," recalling the place where God spoke to Moses (33:9) and the place where God's glory was seen (40:34). Through the voices of the prophets, God covenants to dwell with them (Ezek. 37:27; Zech. 2:10–11).

The Word became flesh so that humans might see God's glory. This is another prominent theme in the Fourth Gospel. In the Old Testament, glory was thought of as the presence of God. Moses asked to see God by saying, "Show me your glory" (Exod. 33:18), and God responded, "No one shall see me and live" (33:20). God's glory or presence is now visible in Jesus Christ (2 Cor. 4:6). Jesus continues to reveal his glory in signs (John 2:11; 4:54; 6:14; 12:18), miracles, and ultimately in his death and resurrection. If one wants to know and see God, one must look to Jesus Christ.

John makes an appearance again in 1:15 as the first witness to Jesus. His testimony is given as evidence for what has been proclaimed in these verses. He speaks in the present tense, because his witness to Jesus continues for all who continue to read and hear. He also introduces human response into the story of the Word made flesh. Now that humans can see, hear, and know God, they must choose whether to participate in this new relationship or reject it and miss out on the life and light that are offered. The prologue concludes that Jesus has come to make God known (1:18), a claim that serves to introduce the rest of the narrative. John witnesses to Jesus' ministry and saving work as the one who makes God known (1:18–34).

The first twelve chapters of the Gospel present persons and events that testify to Jesus' identity as God's son. Preachers can illustrate how the chain of witnesses continues from the Old Testament prophets to John the Baptist to the disciples and eventually to those who witness today. The light of Christ is seen, heard, and known when disciples heal, teach, preach, and love in the name of Christ.

Connections can be made between the other lectionary readings for the day about God's gift of Jesus Christ and the human response of praise and gratitude. Jeremiah 31:7–14 is written to a people in exile who are experiencing despair and grief, offering the hope that God will gather them up and mourning will be replaced with joy. Jeremiah and John do not deny the darkness that is present, but affirm that light triumphs and God's new world is at hand. Paul, in Ephesians 1:3–14, summarizes the redemption that has been received through the incarnation. In Jesus Christ, God has been revealed and an inheritance given to God's people. The response to these gifts is to follow John the Baptist's example by pointing the way to Jesus, witnessing to his glory, and, like the psalmist, lifting our voices and hearts in praise and singing.

KRISTIN STROBLE

Commentary 2: Connecting the Reading with the World

What does a preacher do with poetry? Few things kill the impact of imagery like explanation, and yet the preacher is tasked with standing in the pulpit and interpreting John's stunning prologue. "The Word became flesh and lived among us." How can such beauty be improved upon or dissected? The mystery these verses invoke overwhelms, no matter how often they are read. Grace and true light shine in the darkness. What preacher would ever claim to understand the miracle of the incarnation and the glory such embodiment brings close to us?

Recognizing the awesome task set before the preacher this Second Sunday after Christmas instills humility in anyone who stands to proclaim this Word. Perhaps this stance of awe is

exactly the place to begin: invite hearers to marvel at the mystery of God's majesty and God's loving choice to send the Son to join wholly with humanity in all our vulnerability and suffering. Perhaps this could provide an avenue for worshipers to awaken to the amazing grace upon grace of the incarnation.

On August 21, 2017, a swath of the United States lay in the path of a total solar eclipse. The media hype was huge. Towns in the path of totality readied for an onslaught of people. Special solar glasses needed to view the cosmic occurrence sold out. Many traveled hundreds of miles to be in the path of totality and experience the 160.2 seconds when the moon completely covered the sun and the skies went dark. As the moon covered the sun, crowds of onlookers spontaneously cheered and even wept, overwhelmed by the beauty, the scale, the wonder of experiencing darkness in the middle of day.

This brief moment of shared awe created community, unity, a collective experience too big, too rare not to transform viewers' perception of their place in the universe and their relationship to one another. Those moments of being overcome and transformed in awe at the cosmic interplay of light and darkness may give us some sense of the awe the Johannine prologue is striving to awaken in us about the divine light that came into the world, a light that might be obscured, but never extinguished.

NASA invited witnesses to tell them what the eclipse meant to them in six words. Perhaps the preacher, in the run-up to this Second Sunday after Christmas, might ask the congregation to submit six words—"I know I am never alone," "In the darkest night, Christ shines," "I am a child of God," "Grace comes crashing in unexpected waves"—describing what the birth of Jesus, the Word made flesh, means to them. Incorporating these into the sermon or liturgy for the day, perhaps with visual supplements, could connect the majesty to the real lives of the congregation and concretely embody their awe over the incarnation. An "Incarnation in Six" project could prove to be fruitful ground for a sermon series based on this rich text, which foreshadows themes found throughout John's Gospel.

Another approach could be to focus upon the performative power of God's Word and upon the subsequent power of the words of witness of God's children. Given the timing of this text, a look back at various "words of the year"—contenders in 2017, for instance, were "complicit," "post-truth," "fake news," "resistance"—could provide a jumping-off point, allowing us to compare these words to the words of Scripture and to the Word made flesh. What might it mean that God's Son, full of grace and truth, enters a post-truth world? How is the good news heard (or not) amid claims of fake news?

Every year's "words of the year" highlight aspects of the current cultural context that should be compared to the light of Christ, the light that reveals truth and exposes falsehood, that draws some toward it and sends others scattering for cover. The preacher could use a sermon at the beginning of the calendar year to invite hearers to hit "reset" and not just make New Year's resolutions but to seek to align their words and actions with God's performative, good, creating Word. How is it that followers of Jesus Christ might witness, like John, to the true light, when darkness feels so pervasive?

In her commentary on John, Marianne Meye Thompson writes, "Three assertions characterize this Word: the Word was with God, became flesh, and is now ever with God. With these assertions, John further identifies the Word in relationship to God, the world, and humankind."[1] Preachers could explore the implication of these relationships or, more broadly, the significance of God's relational character. The world that does not recognize or accept their own Savior may be immune to the importance of relationship, refuse to be children of God and therefore siblings to one another, and choose instead to be rivals, competitors, or even enemies. Lifting up the Word's relationship to God, creation, and humankind allows preachers to emphasize the call of followers of Jesus Christ also to be in loving relationship to God, creation, and one another.

Thompson goes on to note, "There is no disembodied way to behold the glory of the Word, to receive God's life, or to experience God's love."[2] "Relationships Required" could be emblazoned on bulletin covers, church signs, and sanctuaries. This theme, unlike "No shirts, no shoes, no service," is not an ultimatum, but invites Christians into relationship with the One who later in John's Gospel will wash his disciples' feet. Relationships are involved, with Jesus, and also with those in the pews and those on the streets, with our social media followers and those absent from social media platforms, with the environment and all creatures great and small, the gift and joy of being in community.

While such relationships challenge and stretch us, God provides. A focus upon God's gratuitous abundance is yet another possible

1. Marianne Meye Thompson, *John: A Commentary*, New Testament Library (Louisville, KY: Westminster John Knox Press, 2015), 25.
2. Thompson, *John*, 26.

emphasis for this Sunday. Grace upon grace. Overflowing goodness. The Word made flesh, enabling those of us born in the flesh to be made holy and see God's glory: what wondrous love is this? Pouring forth praise for the light, the truth, and the grace of God, could provide a needed contrast to the parade of pain rarely interrupted by the goodness found within, around, and above it. Even as we struggle with current suffering, we are assured of God's presence and goodness. This is the season of good news of great joy for all people. Preachers would be remiss not to proclaim it, not as a means for hearers to bury their heads in the sand, but rather as a way to point others to the light that they, like John, have witnessed.

Brother David Steindl-Rast, writing about the connection between prayer and gratefulness, says this: "Our eyes are opened to that surprise character of the world around us the moment we wake up from taking things for granted. . . . Gratuitousness burst in on us, the gratuitousness of all there is."[3] Explicit recognition of God's goodness reorients our focus toward God and strengthens our ability to see God present and at work not just in hindsight but in the messiness of daily living. Preaching about waking up from taking the grace of God for granted could become a touchstone for the congregation's life together throughout the year.

JILL DUFFIELD

3. David Steindl-Rast, *Gratefulness, the Heart of Prayer: An Approach to Life in Fullness* (New York: Paulist Press, 1984), 9–10.

Epiphany of the Lord

Isaiah 60:1–6
Psalm 72:1–7, 10–14

Ephesians 3:1–12
Matthew 2:1–12

Isaiah 60:1–6

¹Arise, shine; for your light has come,
    and the glory of the LORD has risen upon you.
²For darkness shall cover the earth,
    and thick darkness the peoples;
but the LORD will arise upon you,
    and his glory will appear over you.
³Nations shall come to your light,
    and kings to the brightness of your dawn.

⁴Lift up your eyes and look around;
    they all gather together, they come to you;
your sons shall come from far away,
    and your daughters shall be carried on their nurses' arms.
⁵Then you shall see and be radiant;
    your heart shall thrill and rejoice,
because the abundance of the sea shall be brought to you,
    the wealth of the nations shall come to you.
⁶A multitude of camels shall cover you,
    the young camels of Midian and Ephah;
    all those from Sheba shall come.
They shall bring gold and frankincense,
    and shall proclaim the praise of the LORD.

Commentary 1: Connecting the Reading with Scripture

Our passage begins with a summons to set aside spiritual weariness. "Arise" (Isa. 60:1). The image recalls a passage from Second Isaiah where God's people are exhorted to "mount up with wings like eagles," to "run and not be weary" (40:31). This is fitting because the proclamation of Isaiah 60:1–6 is offered to those on the cusp of fulfillment of promises made throughout Second Isaiah (chaps. 40–55). The triumphant tone evokes other pivotal moments in Scripture such as Job 19:25: "For I know that my Redeemer lives, and that at the last he will stand upon the earth." Isaiah 60:1 is no less triumphant. God's people are encouraged not only to arise but to "lift up your eyes and look around" (60:4)—a powerful phrase found also in Isaiah 49:18.

The descendants of God's people in exile return home in glory, while the descendants of those who made them captive return in humble praise (v. 14). Each group is drawn to Zion's radiant light. Together, they will work to rehabilitate the temple and its worship. The result is a new era of moral righteousness and authentic worship. This passage is all about redemption.

Isaiah 60 continues the theme of promise that closes the previous chapter, "[God] will come to Zion as Redeemer" (59:20). In this chapter what is emphasized is the fact that redemption—the graciously intimate presence of God—is not far beyond the horizon. It is imminent. The first and final verses of the chapter frame this triumphant portrait: "Arise, shine; for your light has come" (60:1); "I am the LORD; . . . I will accomplish it quickly" (v. 22). This is the *present* reality of redemption, no longer restricted to the dim past (as originating covenant) or to the distant future (as longed-for fulfillment). Redemption is vitally present. "Light *has* come" (v. 1, emphasis added). How significant this message is in our lives! There are so many times—such as in the loss of a job or a spouse or a home—when salvation seems "a long way off." It is easy in such times to discount the present as an arena where God is present. Isaiah reminds us: because God is always with us, we live each day on the cusp of redemption.

Lest we be distracted by the potentially depersonalized metaphor (light), Isaiah is emphatic that this redemptive work is the Lord's doing: "The sun shall no longer be your light by day, nor . . . the moon . . . by night; but the LORD will be your everlasting light" (v. 19). This message too resonates with experience. So often—in times of success and failure—we lose sight of the fact that God is intimately engaged in our lives. God cherishes our victories (however small) and mourns our defeats (however large) with the rapt attention of a doting grandparent. Isaiah reminds us that God is not only with us, God is truly present.

A thematic cord emerges. Redemption is a present, personal reality. This cord runs throughout the canon of Scripture. First, redemption is present. "Today," Jesus says in the temple, "this scripture has been fulfilled in your hearing" (Luke 4:21). Second, redemption is personal. "I will write [my covenant] on their hearts," God proclaims (Jer. 31:33). A way of expressing this intimate encompassing is through the imagery of light. In the ancient world, light is unambiguously positive. It symbolizes redemption. At the beginning of the Bible, God creates with the pronouncement, "Let there be light" (Gen. 1:3). Near the end, James declares God "the Father of lights" (Jas. 1:17). In our passage, seeing the light of God results in human radiance (Isa. 60:5). The prophet has in mind the beaming face of one enraptured by God's saving presence.

Important in the larger literary context is the medium of prophecy itself. Prophets are intermediaries acting as God's mouthpiece. They do not just arrive upon the scene. They are sent.

"Go and say," hears Isaiah, in the moment of his calling (6:9). The book of Isaiah charts a broad sweep of at least a dozen generations. It stretches from King Uzziah's reign to the rule of the Persian emperor Cyrus, under whom the rebuilding of the temple was completed. What is commonly called First Isaiah (chaps. 1–39) is associated with the prophet himself, the son of Amoz. Second Isaiah (chaps. 40–55) could have been written by scribes who knew Isaiah personally and were directly influenced by his teachings. The prophecies known as Third Isaiah (chaps. 56–66) are the products of later generations, after the rebuilding of the temple. These last chapters span from the late sixth to the early fifth centuries BCE. The formation of the book of Isaiah is still debated, with some scholars now seeing a two-part book and others emphasizing literary connections across different parts. One thing is certain: the Isaiah traditions highlight the power of God to redeem.

Isaiah 60:1–6 lies at the heart of Third Isaiah. In these verses, the promise of redemption is unrestrained. Such is not always the case with Third Isaiah. The prophecy ends with an ominous counting of the dead "who have rebelled against me" and the harsh judgment that awaits, "for their worm shall not die, their fire shall not be quenched" (66:24). Even a less bleak passage such as 58:9–10 renders strict conditions: "If you remove the yoke from among you, the pointing of the finger, the speaking of evil, if you offer your food to the hungry and satisfy the needs of the afflicted, then your light shall rise in the darkness."

There are no conditions in our passage. Redemption is sheer gift and surprisingly inclusive. Pairing with evocative lines that introduce the book as a whole and Third Isaiah specifically, the resulting message is radically inclusive: "And all nations shall gaze on [Zion] with joy. And the many peoples shall go" (2:2–3 JPS). "My house," God proclaims, "shall be called a house of prayer for all peoples" (56:7).

Like the magi of Matthew 2:1–12, the nations come paying homage with gold and frankincense, along with exotic woods to adorn the temple. In these passages, movement takes priority: nations come (Isa. 60:3); kings bow down (Ps. 72:11); magi journey (Matt. 2:1).

God too is moved to act. "Grace," says the author of Ephesians, is "given" (Eph. 3:2, 7, 8). What is implied is that redemption may be a constant state, but it is not static. Our redemption is sealed by the Holy Spirit, but it is not cast in concrete; we are much more than mere statues of faith. Redemption is dynamic, moving in and among people fully alive in faith.

From homiletic reflection, a sermon might emerge that reflects upon redemption in counterintuitive ways. For instance, a congregation may be challenged to consider how a combined effort to revitalize a struggling neighborhood might be a redemptive process for all concerned. An opportunity for service might help a miserly person to acquire a generous outlook on life; this might be said to be redemptive. The preacher may describe two long-estranged friends who rediscover space in their hearts for one another; such reconciliation, too, might be redemptive. More than a future, otherworldly hope, redemption comes also to be seen as a present reality. Heaven "by and by" makes room for redemption here and now. Appeal could also be made to the insistence of Jesus that in him the kingdom of heaven has "come near" (Matt. 3:2).

Redemption is not just an eschatological hope but also a present, personal reality. This is reason enough to renew our souls, to arise in the light of the Lord.

MARK RALLS

Commentary 2: Connecting the Reading with the World

It is easy to see why Isaiah 60:1–6 was chosen as the Old Testament lesson for the celebration of Epiphany or the Feast of the Three Kings. The joyful announcement that finally the light and glory of God have appeared (Isa. 60:1–2), the mention of foreign kings and dignitaries flocking to this luminous vision (v. 3), the image of downtrodden yet hopeful people slowly gathering around the light (v. 4), and foreigners bringing gifts of gold and frankincense (v. 6), when read through the lens of the New Testament, cannot but evoke images of Jesus' birth—indeed, this passage was quite likely in the mind of the writer of Matthew as he shaped his birth narrative. Of particular importance is the mention of the visitation of foreigners and the bringing of gifts of frankincense and gold, which Matthew references when describing the visitation of the magi to the Christ child.

These verses from Isaiah exude the feeling and tone of this holiday. The writer uses a chain of verbs to urge and excite the reader to rejoice in the coming light. "Arise, shine," the writer commands in verse 1, asking Zion—Jerusalem personified—to imitate God, who will ascend over the people and act on their behalf. Zion is further encouraged to "lift up" her eyes, to "look around," and to "see and be radiant" (vv. 4–5). The emphasis on sight and vision hints that the role of Jerusalem and its people is not just to be present, but also to bear witness and testify to God's salvific acts. God has burst onto the scene, and we, like the magi, are commanded to arise and look and witness and rejoice.

The spirited tone of this passage brings to mind rays of bright morning sunlight piercing a dark, stuffy room, or audiences rising to their feet with excited applause when an athlete or artist has triumphed over a challenge. *Northam Castle, Sunrise*, a painting by J. M. W. Turner, known as the English "painter of light," perfectly captures the mood: piercing through dense mist on a quiet, still morning, a burst of sunlight illuminates two deer quenching their thirst in a gently flowing river. In tune with the soft glories illuminated in Turner's painting, the point of the ascendant light proclaimed in Isaiah 60 is to illumine and display God's mercies in the world, such as the giving of water to the thirsty—mercies that, despite being obscured by darkness and gloom, have never ceased. The light reveals God's gracious deeds in and for the world, be they mundane or miraculous.

As we reflect upon Isaiah 60 and the celebration of Epiphany, we might ask what divine actions in our lives we, as individuals and as the church, may have failed to recognize or see. What mercies of God have we allowed darkness and gloom—bad attitudes, fears and phobias, sheer busyness or distraction—to obscure and conceal? What exactly are these distractions, these dark clouds that hide the dealings of God in this world? How can we learn to be more aware of them so as to see beyond them? As the Isaianic writer urges, how can we too learn to "lift up" our eyes and "look around" so that we can see "the glory of the LORD" that has risen around us (60:1), so that we too can "see and be radiant"?

This concern over the darkness that eclipses the ascendant light and glory of God (v. 2) invites us to reflect critically about modern distractions that obscure the mercies of the light. One such distraction—a major issue in the United States—is addiction to technology. Continual interaction in and with technology has been linked to isolation, lack of focus, loss of sleep, mental-health issues, damage to cognitive ability, and even fatalities stemming from distracted driving and walking.[1] Equally distressing, the addictive aspect of this technology can be and already has been utilized to exploit public thoughts and political opinion.[2] The great irony here, of course, is that technologies we created to bridge the gaps between individuals and communities have instead, through our addictive behavior, pushed us apart and isolated us. It is not difficult to see technology addiction as a kind of darkness. We might gently remind ourselves and others that it is difficult to "look around" and see "the glory of the LORD"—indeed, to see anything—if our eyes are glued to our technological devices.

The question of how we might be present so we can witness the revelations of God in the world is intimately intertwined with how we, in turn, in our own living witness, reveal God to the world. This missionary aspect is central to the celebration of Epiphany, which commemorates the visitation of the magi and the theophany—that is, the manifestation of God—to these figures and, from there and through their living witness, to the rest of the world.

The idea of God's manifestation to the world raises important questions about our role as individuals and as the church in the ongoing theophany of the Lord. If Epiphany is about revelation, who or what in the world has revealed God to us, and how can we, in turn, unveil and show God back to the world? How do we as the people of God respectfully live into our missional call to act as witnesses and bearers of God's transformation? In what ways have we, individually and as the church, obscured the revelation of God? What can we do to incarnate the Gospel more fully in the future?

In thinking about those who help reveal God to others in the world, it is important to understand the context of Isaiah 60. Despite the triumphant tone of Isaiah 60, the chapters that immediately precede this one (chaps. 58–59) describe a trying time of suffering, injustice, and oppression. Indeed, the sudden burst of joy embodied by shouts of "arise, shine" cannot be fully understood apart from a remembering of the hardships described in the previous chapters. The sudden shifts in tone suggest that the writers were themselves likely those with little power, those on the margins, whose voices were not being heard. In Isaiah 60, we hear these writers, despite their suffering and marginality, remaining confident in a better future. The dawn described in Isaiah 60, they hoped in full faith, was just a matter of time.

There are modern equivalents of this burst of divine light described by Isaiah 60 that teach us to maintain hope just as those writers did: the marchers during the civil rights movement, the defiant laborers of the United Farm Workers movement led by Cesar Chavez, and student survivors from school shootings. "Darkness shall cover the earth, and thick darkness the peoples" (60:2); morning has not yet come, but as the Isaianic writer promises, God's glory will indeed appear.

SONG-MI SUZIE PARK

1. Kelly Wallace, "Half of Teens Think They're Addicted to Their Smartphones," https://www.cnn.com/2016/05/03/health/teens-cell-phone -addiction-parents/index.html; Jean M. Twenge, "Have Smartphones Destroyed a Generation?," https://www.theatlantic.com/magxazine/archive /2017/09/has-the-smartphone-destroyed-a-generation/534198/; Kyle Stock, Lance Lambert and David Ingold, "Smartphones Are Killing Americans But Nobody's Counting," https://www.bloomberg.com/news/articles/2017–10–17/smartphones-are-killing-americans-but-nobody-s -counting.

2. Paul Lewis, "'Our Minds Can Be Hijacked': The Tech Insiders Who Fear a Smartphone Dystopia," https://www.theguardian.com/technology /2017/oct/05/smartphone-addiction-silicon-valley-dystopia.

Psalm 72:1–7, 10–14

[1]Give the king your justice, O God,
    and your righteousness to a king's son.
[2]May he judge your people with righteousness,
    and your poor with justice.
[3]May the mountains yield prosperity for the people,
    and the hills, in righteousness.
[4]May he defend the cause of the poor of the people,
    give deliverance to the needy,
    and crush the oppressor.

[5]May he live while the sun endures,
    and as long as the moon, throughout all generations.
[6]May he be like rain that falls on the mown grass,
    like showers that water the earth.
[7]In his days may righteousness flourish
    and peace abound, until the moon is no more.
. . . .
[10]May the kings of Tarshish and of the isles
    render him tribute,
may the kings of Sheba and Seba
    bring gifts.
[11]May all kings fall down before him,
    all nations give him service.

[12]For he delivers the needy when they call,
    the poor and those who have no helper.
[13]He has pity on the weak and the needy,
    and saves the lives of the needy.
[14]From oppression and violence he redeems their life;
    and precious is their blood in his sight.

Connecting the Psalm with Scripture and Worship

A cry of hope directly voiced to God, the first verse of Psalm 72 petitions God to "give to the king, the justice that is derived from God; give to the king, God's own justice; and give to the king's son, God's own righteousness." This singular utterance, juxtaposed with the double exclamation of Isaiah 60:1, "Arise, shine," directs the people to dwell in hope, for YHWH's light has come. God's power is evident in the changing order. A downtrodden people, shackled with the weight of subordination, can be lifted up. They now see, despite the "darkness that covers the earth." These joint cries celebrate the beginning of something new: the inauguration of a royal leader who will bring about a new order in which the poor and the needy are neither forsaken nor forgotten.[1]

The psalmist then describes the cosmic and social manifestations of this reign. Blessings flow out of the created order, out of mountains and

---

1. Frank-Lothar Hossfeld and Erich Zenger, trans., *Psalms 2: A Commentary*, Hermeneia (Minneapolis, Fortress Press, 2011), 201.

hills (Ps. 72:3), blessings whose implications make clear that the new king and/or the new-born prince is fit to rule. What we do locally has global implications, for what is done now shall be indicative of what will be in the future. The king and the king's son receive from YHWH a transfer of justice *tsedeq/tsedeqa*); from the rulers. YHWH's justice and righteousness flow to the land, especially to those people who are poor.[2]

Here we see that the hoped-for blessings the people envision will come to them as a new royal leader is enthroned. As the king's son, the new crown prince is born in splendor (not the ignominious circumstances of the infant Jesus) and begins the establishment of a new rule, the shape and form of which are articulated in verses 2–7.

Psalm 72 is a royal enthronement psalm and has long been the appointed psalm for the Epiphany of the Lord. The psalm describes a reign of righteousness and justice where the earthly king's rule mirrors that of the divine king, God.[3] In this reign, justice, truth, and peace will prevail, especially for the poor, the orphan, and the widow. This new realm will be free from war and hostility and will last from now (this moment) until time is no more (eternity). With this new realm comes deliverance from every evil, harm, and danger.

That is what it means to govern rightly with justice. We do well to recall that in our world, the right to rule is seldom bestowed on the leaders of nations as a statutory privilege by birth. Even in established monarchies, the jurisdictional powers of oversight are held as instrumental services, as the responsibilities of office—given, we hope, along with divine providence for the well-being of people and nations.

On Epiphany, as we celebrate Christ's birth and messianic introduction to the nations, we imagine that in and through the holy rule of this newborn, the world will be set aright. So we see and place our hopes in the messianic hope of Israel, in this child, and we further see in this child, and in Israel's hope, an awakening occurring for and within the cosmos.

As the nations bring tribute, and caravans from across the globe intersect in honoring this newborn leader, we also exult, finding in this child blessings for all the world (vv. 11, 17). By placing our hopes and dreams in this child, we once again engage in creative and imaginative reframing, along with all those who long for a better life, in a better world, with better possibilities for the future. When the current generation finds little evidence or reason to believe positive change will occur, they often put their hopes in their children. They do not just stop; they go on, continuing to live, dream, and act with confidence and trust that God still governs the world and will bring light and justice to light.

We hear Psalm 72 along with the day's Gospel reading from Matthew, in which we hear of an imperial appointee, Herod, whose legitimacy was questionable. The way Herod governed (or did not) led to despicable life circumstances. Herod did not want his time of sovereignty to end. So, like many despots and tyrants, he sought to eliminate any future competition. Herod saw Jesus, the newborn messianic king, as a rival.

What Herod did not and could not understand was that legitimacy of rule comes not from imperial domination, or the exercise of abusive power. Legitimate authority is derived from good and right relationships with God and God's people. The cultivation of grace and gladness brings patterns of justice and mercy, defense of the oppressed and needy. Rulers who banish the cruelty that has given sway to evil create a realm of peace, righteousness, and justice. Such shalom is the opposite of Herod's rule.

On Epiphany, we celebrate this child who will make a difference. The very announcement of this child's birth ushers in a new way. Strangers journey from afar to meet this child. Despite foreboding corners of darkness, light glimmers as if to say, what God promised now will be.

JOSEPH A. DONNELLA II

---

2. Hossfeld and Zenger, *Psalms*, 201.

3. Artur Weiser, *The Psalms: A Commentary*, trans. Herbert Hartwell (Philadelphia: Westminster Press, 1962), 501–2.

Ephesians 3:1–12

¹This is the reason that I Paul am a prisoner for Christ Jesus for the sake of you Gentiles—²for surely you have already heard of the commission of God's grace that was given me for you, ³and how the mystery was made known to me by revelation, as I wrote above in a few words, ⁴a reading of which will enable you to perceive my understanding of the mystery of Christ. ⁵In former generations this mystery was not made known to humankind, as it has now been revealed to his holy apostles and prophets by the Spirit: ⁶that is, the Gentiles have become fellow heirs, members of the same body, and sharers in the promise in Christ Jesus through the gospel.

⁷Of this gospel I have become a servant according to the gift of God's grace that was given me by the working of his power. ⁸Although I am the very least of all the saints, this grace was given to me to bring to the Gentiles the news of the boundless riches of Christ, ⁹and to make everyone see what is the plan of the mystery hidden for ages in God who created all things; ¹⁰so that through the church the wisdom of God in its rich variety might now be made known to the rulers and authorities in the heavenly places. ¹¹This was in accordance with the eternal purpose that he has carried out in Christ Jesus our Lord, ¹²in whom we have access to God in boldness and confidence through faith in him.

Commentary 1: Connecting the Reading with Scripture

Our attention today is focused first upon Jesus' "beginnings," but quickly turns to the expanding significance of the Christ event through the ministry of Paul. Today's lectionary reading from Matthew's Gospel (Matt. 2:1–12) stresses the importance of the visit of the magi in the story of Jesus' birth. The text points to what was becoming apparent in the Matthean community: the sphere of Jesus' influence included Israel, but was expanding beyond Israel, as persons from "the East" pay Jesus homage. Mark's Gospel points to another "beginning" in Jesus' life. Mark 1 unfolds the scene of John baptizing Jesus in the Jordan River (Mark 1:9–11). It is the inaugural event in Jesus' ministry. In both cases, we hear the voice of the prophet Isaiah in the background: "Arise, shine; for your light has come" (Isa. 60:1–3). The season of Epiphany begins with these ancient words coming alive in our speech and hearing.

Epiphany marks an expansive pattern of God's self-disclosure, not only to God's people, but also "to the rulers and authorities in the heavenly places" (Eph. 3:10). In each incidence, the faithful depict it as the coming of light. According to the reading from Isaiah, the exiles released from the dark days of captivity are greeted by God's light upon their return home. This is a startling declaration to those returning from exile in Babylon. They left the darkness of captivity only to return to the darkness of chaos and destruction in their own homeland. When they "lift their eyes to look around" them (Isa. 60:4), they see anything but "the glory of the LORD" (v. 1). Jerusalem has become a city in shambles in their absence, due to years of misrule by those left to fend for themselves. The residents have created a culture of political and religious corruption and exist within a climate of devastation. The light of God's blessing shining on the exiles' homecoming not only greets them but illumines their mission—they are to rebuild, replant, and renew their faith. What the prophet offers as inspiration for the task is a vision of nations coming to the light (v. 3).

That the Mighty Not Be Lifted Up

Now, then, my dearly beloved sons and heirs of grace, look to your vocation and, since Christ has been revealed to both Jews and Gentiles as the cornerstone, cling together with most constant affection. For He was manifested in the very cradle of His infancy to those who were near and to those who were afar—to the Jews whose shepherds were nearby; to the Gentiles whose Magi were at a great distance. The former came to Him on the very day of His birth; the latter are believed to have come on this day. He was not revealed, therefore, to the shepherds because they were learned, nor to the Magi because they were righteous, for ignorance abounds in the rusticity of shepherds and impiety amid the sacrileges of the Magi. He, the cornerstone, joined both groups to Himself since He came to choose the foolish things of the world in order to put to shame the wise and "to call sinners, not the just," so that the mighty would not be lifted up nor the lowly be in despair.

Augustine. *Sermons on the Liturgical Seasons*, trans. Sister Mary Sarah Muldowney, RSM, The Fathers of the Church (Washington, DC: Catholic University of America Press, 1959), 66–67.

The passage from Ephesians marks another building project, namely the construction of a community in which Jews and Gentiles worship God together. The presence of the Gentiles represents many nations that have come to the light of Israel by means of Jesus Christ. Whereas Isaiah was looking into the future to inspire Israel's endeavors to rebuild, the writer to the Ephesians looks back to the "foundation of the world" (Eph. 1:4) when God's plan for the construction of an inclusive human community took shape. It would be a community that would be "holy and blameless before him in love" (v. 4). It is this divine project that Ephesians celebrates as the letter begins. As God's plan unfolds, the "mystery" (3:5) is disclosed that in "the fullness of time," God will "gather up all things in [Christ], things in heaven and things on earth" (1:10).

For the preacher, Isaiah's imagery can bring God's vision for humanity down to earth. To encourage the efforts of the exiles in their mission, he employs the familiar imagery of domestic life. The prophet declares that their "sons shall come from far away," their daughters being "carried on their nurses' arms" (Isa. 60:4). Ephesians echoes Isaiah with the language of adoption (Eph. 1:5). Those who "were far off have been brought near" (2:13), incorporated into the family of God through Christ who has "broken down the dividing wall" (2:14) between Jew and Gentile. The picture the writer draws is of an expanding household. Indeed, it is of a "whole structure . . . joined together . . . into a holy temple in the Lord" (2:19, 21).

The declaration that this new, divinely ordained community had become God's dwelling place was good news to Jewish believers within the Ephesian community. Once again, the temple in Jerusalem lay in ruins, the cult attending it dispersed, the dwelling place of God defiled. With the temple destroyed, the rites and rituals that offered "access to God" (3:12) were no longer available. The proclamation that God had chosen the body of Christ as a new dwelling place reassured them that in the aftermath of war and defeat, God had not abandoned them, and that through Christ's sacrificial death and resurrection God was offering new means of grace. Through the lordship of Christ, Gentile believers are released from obeisance to other gods residing in their own temples. The wisdom revealed to them—that they were coheirs with Israel of the "boundless riches of Christ" (3:8)—surpassed that offered by other gods and goddesses.

The writer, who is not Paul, shines the spotlight on Paul's role in this divine disclosure by speaking in the first person as if he were Paul. This practice of pseudonymous writing may seem strange to us, but he writes under the name of Paul not to deceive but in order to authenticate his own witness. Prior to reading the text aloud in worship, a lector or preacher can explain to the congregation that in the Hellenistic world of the first century it was acceptable, even honorable, to write in the name of a revered figure who has definitively inspired one's own writing. In so doing, a writer aimed to extend the influence of a thinker by interpreting his teaching for a new generation.

Since there does not seem to be evidence within the letter that the writer had knowledge of or personal connections within the community, writing under Paul's name lent the weight of apostolic authority to his words. Even though it was a familiar rhetorical device, it still may have been startling for the Ephesians to hear "Paul" speaking to them when the letter was read aloud. It was one way that the writer would have gotten their attention! The writer aims at strengthening the tie between the Ephesians' self-understanding and the "commission of God's grace" that was given to Paul (3:2).

Commitment to that commission was costly for Paul, and perhaps also to the writer. The writer writes as one imprisoned, perhaps drawing on his own experience or perhaps to express solidarity with Paul's suffering when Paul had been incarcerated. Paul was usually under attack because of his inclusive interpretation of the gospel. To defend himself and justify his efforts as an apostle to Gentiles, Paul points to his own suffering for their sake (2 Cor. 11:16–30).

Unlike Paul, the writer of Ephesians does not dwell on the details of Paul's suffering for the sake of the gospel. Instead he chooses to focus upon and develop Paul's gospel, tracing it back to its origins in the mind and heart of God.

Paul himself notes in his letter to the Galatians that the good news he proclaimed to Gentiles, that the Gentiles were equal to the Jews in God's household, was "not of human origin," for in fact, he received it "through a revelation of Jesus Christ" (Gal. 1:11–12). The writer is keen to show the Ephesians that the reality of this gospel, namely, that the "Gentiles have become fellow heirs, members of the same body, and sharers in the promise in Christ Jesus" (Eph. 3:6), has taken shape within their own community. It is a light shining in the darkness of a world divided by ethnicity, race, and class. The unity is visible not only to "flesh and blood" but also to the powers that control the world (3:10; 6:12). The light of Epiphany shines not only upon Jesus' "beginnings" but also upon vibrant communities that embody God's inclusive gospel of grace.

RICHARD F. WARD

Commentary 2: Connecting the Reading with the World

Liturgically, today's passage illuminates the church's celebration of the Epiphany, the manifestation of Christ to the Gentiles. The author confirms Paul's vocation to bring the gospel to non-Jews, affirms that the "Gentiles have become fellow heirs, members of the same body, and sharers in the promise in Christ Jesus through the gospel" (Eph. 3:6). Further, the author exults in the reality that "through the church the wisdom of God in its rich variety might now be made known to the rulers and authorities in the heavenly places" (v. 10).

One might connect this passage to the universalizing motifs of the Old Testament prophetic traditions and the Gospel traditions, unfolding what they may mean for the church's ministry today.

After a scorching critique of the wicked rulers and prophets of the kingdom of Judah,

who, through unjust economic and political policies, "tear the skin off [God's] people" (Mic. 3:2), Micah offers a universal vision of peace, with justice: "[God] shall arbitrate between strong nations far away; they shall beat their swords into plowshares, and their spears into pruning hooks; nation shall not lift up sword against nation, neither shall they learn war any more" (4:3–4). Similarly, Isaiah, speaking to people suffering through the Babylonian exile, offers the Lord's word of hope, "I am the LORD, I have called you in righteousness, I have taken you by the hand and kept you; I have given you as a covenant to the people, a light to the nations, to open the eyes that are blind" (Isa. 42:6). The author of Luke–Acts picks up this universalizing theme: "But you will receive power when the Holy Spirit has come upon you; and you will be my witnesses in Jerusalem, in all Judea and Samaria, and to the ends of the earth" (Acts 1:8).

What does it mean in our day for members of Christ's body, the *ekklēsia*, to experience the power of the Spirit and to "witness . . . to the ends of the earth"? Today, traditional mainline and evangelical denominations and congregations are experiencing acute shrinkage, and fully one-third of church plants never achieve financial self-sufficiency. To flourish, congregations may need to reverse the expectation of a centripetal dynamic, in which people are drawn from the outside into the church. Rather, Beth Ann Estock and Paul Nixon suggest that the contemporary world is disposed more readily to a centrifugal movement, which is in line with the suggestion of Luke–Acts. When Jesus sent out first the twelve (Luke 9:1–6) and then the seventy (10:1–20), they were called not to welcome the stranger, but, rather, "to *be* the stranger seeking welcome." Estock and Dixon believe we are now called to do the same—to move "from settled camp to shalom on the move."[1]

Among the examples Estock and Nixon lift up is Broadway Church in Indianapolis. Broadway shuttered their food pantry, clothing ministry, after-school program, and summer youth program. They hired a "roving listener" who asked not, "What can I do for you?" but "What three things do you do well enough that you could teach others how to do them? What three things would you like to learn? Who, besides God and me, is going with you along the way?" One result of this effort to connect people sharing common interests was a farmer's market of forty-five backyard gardeners that began to heal an urban food desert.

Our writer also avows that "through the church the wisdom of God in its rich variety might now be made known to the rulers and authorities in the heavenly places" (Eph. 3:10). How might we understand these rulers and authorities in the heavenly places? What might it mean for the wisdom of God to be made known to them?

Walter Wink offers helpful suggestions to the first question. He believes that New Testament authors, including the writer of Ephesians, when speaking of rulers and authorities in heavenly places, or powers, or demons, or Satan, were referring to experienced realities with destructive effects. They are "the actual spirituality of systems and structures that have betrayed their divine vocations."[2] Since the New Testament writers wrote during a period of Roman imperial domination, many of the economic, political, and cultic institutions evinced what Wink calls a Domination System, which established, though violence, hierarchies that pitted groups of people and individuals against one another, separated by what our author calls dividing walls of hostility. These rulers and authorities—these institutions and their cultures—though created good by God, have fallen and are in need of redemption.

Our author affirms that "[Christ] is our peace; in his flesh he has made both groups into one and has broken down the dividing wall, that is, the hostility between us" (Eph. 2:14). Now, through the church, the body of Christ, the wisdom of God in its rich variety is made known to them. These institutions, structures, and cultures are redeemed by the reconciliation of those formerly divided into hostile camps—women and men, Jew and Gentile, slave and free (Gal. 3:28). It is the rich diversity of God's unified creation through which the powers are redeemed.

Do our churches embody the reconciliation and unity of often hostile groups—Caucasian and African American, Christian and Muslim, heterosexually identified and LGBTQ persons, the one percent and the working poor? Do they manifest the wisdom of God in its rich variety? Not enough of our congregations do, but there are some that are experiencing rich and deep reconciliation among their members. Mary McClintock Fulkerson describes Good Samaritan Church in Durham, North Carolina, which intentionally cultivates practices of worship, Bible study, and communal meals

---

1. Beth Ann Estock and Paul Nixon, *Weird Church: Welcome to the Twenty-First Century* (Cleveland: Pilgrim Press, 2016), vi–vii, 18, and chap. 2.
2. Walter Wink, *Engaging the Powers: Discernment and Resistance in a World of Domination* (Minneapolis: Augsburg Fortress, 1992), 8–9.

that both accommodate and express the cultures and styles of a rich variety of people who traditionally have not been members of the same congregation: African Americans, Africans, Caucasians, Koreans, and differently abled.[3]

During the week, Good Samaritan conducts three different worship services with three different styles. One service includes an extemporaneous sermon, with call and response between the preacher and congregants. Another, led by a Bahamian minister, includes more formal liturgies and a sermon from a manuscript. The third kind, designated a "special needs" service, occurs once a month and includes a variety of communications to which participants are accustomed. Members routinely attend one or more of these different services. In addition to frequent potlucks, there are regular international dinners at which one chooses from African American, southern, and African dishes. Several forms of Bible study are offered. In one study, the passages to be studied are published in the Sunday bulletin; then on Wednesday evening, a diverse group gathers and, after a brief introduction to the text, the room is open to anyone who wants to share how a particular story or part of a story speaks to them.

To transform the alienating and destructive aspects of our economic, political, and religious institutions by making known the wisdom of God, we must intentionally make places that welcome the rich diversity of God's creation. Creative practices that invite a variety of people to eat together, interpret the Scriptures together, and worship together might just do that work.

STEPHEN B. BOYD

---

3. See Mary McClintock Fulkerson, *Places of Redemption: Theology for a Worldly Church* (New York: Oxford University Press, 2010).

Matthew 2:1–12

¹In the time of King Herod, after Jesus was born in Bethlehem of Judea, wise men from the East came to Jerusalem, ²asking, "Where is the child who has been born king of the Jews? For we observed his star at its rising, and have come to pay him homage." ³When King Herod heard this, he was frightened, and all Jerusalem with him; ⁴and calling together all the chief priests and scribes of the people, he inquired of them where the Messiah was to be born. ⁵They told him, "In Bethlehem of Judea; for so it has been written by the prophet:

⁶'And you, Bethlehem, in the land of Judah,
    are by no means least among the rulers of Judah;
for from you shall come a ruler
    who is to shepherd my people Israel.'"

⁷Then Herod secretly called for the wise men and learned from them the exact time when the star had appeared. ⁸Then he sent them to Bethlehem, saying, "Go and search diligently for the child; and when you have found him, bring me word so that I may also go and pay him homage." ⁹When they had heard the king, they set out; and there, ahead of them, went the star that they had seen at its rising, until it stopped over the place where the child was. ¹⁰When they saw that the star had stopped, they were overwhelmed with joy. ¹¹On entering the house, they saw the child with Mary his mother; and they knelt down and paid him homage. Then, opening their treasure chests, they offered him gifts of gold, frankincense, and myrrh. ¹²And having been warned in a dream not to return to Herod, they left for their own country by another road.

Commentary 1: Connecting the Reading with Scripture

Light, power, and kingship are themes found in the passages for the celebration of the Epiphany of our Lord. In Matthew 2, the magi follow a star to find God revealed in Jesus Christ, the light of the world. The prophet Isaiah provides encouragement to the people, saying, "Arise, shine; for your light has come, and the glory of the LORD has risen upon you" (Isa. 60:1). Judean exiles have returned from Babylon to a land filled with decay and corruption. To them is given a glorious vision of God's light shining in their present darkness. Not only will this glory be for Israel, but strangers from near and far will be drawn to this light. God's presence made manifest in the light of Isaiah and in the Christ child in Matthew is for all people, Jews and Gentiles.

Ephesians 3 also emphasizes the inclusion of Gentiles in God's promises. In Christ, people from all nations are included as heirs to Israel's promises. As heirs, they also join in the responsibility of preaching the gospel and proclaiming God's reign of peace and justice. Psalm 72, a royal psalm, is a prayer for the reign of God to be realized in the human king who rules over Israel. The people long for a king who rules with justice, protects his people, defends the poor, and liberates the oppressed. In Matthew, this psalm's image of kingship is juxtaposed against the rule of King Herod, allowing the reader to explore power, leadership, and authority. All the readings emphasize Matthew's claim that the only true king, for both Jews and Gentiles, is the one who was born in a manger, not a palace, and who shows God's power by hanging on a cross: Jesus the Christ.

Matthew's account of the birth of Jesus differs significantly from Luke's. Threats abound from the beginning, as Joseph decides whether to leave the pregnant Mary and as Herod finds out about this child who is being called a king. Matthew's characters include royalty, chief priests, and wealthy foreigners, which alerts readers to the threats Jesus will continue to face as well as the promise that God's salvation is for all people.

Chapter 1 of Matthew, the genealogy of Jesus, relates the story of the Messiah to the ongoing story of God and God's people. Jesus is the long-awaited and promised Messiah for the Jews. Very quickly, however, chapter 2 expands the promise to all people. Like the movement of a sermon, the first chapter provides continuity between the Old and New Testaments, while the second chapter tells of the present fulfillment of the promise. This is also the task of the preacher: to merge the biblical world with the world in which the listener lives.

Matthew 2:1 sets the stage for the story by focusing in on a specific time and place. Jesus is born in Bethlehem during the reign of King Herod. Herod the Great was a violent king who established himself through military conquest. Herod did great things, such as enlarge and renovate the temple in Jerusalem, but he was also brutal and ruthless. A vassal of the Roman Empire, he was held in contempt by many Jews. Already in Matthew 2, the conflict that will be seen between the kingdom of Rome and the kingdom of God is established. Herod and Jesus present two very different pictures of kingship. Throughout the Gospel, Jesus' ministry and very presence confront Roman power represented by Herod and Pilate, testifying to the fact that true greatness is found in service, humility, and love.

The first humans to speak in the Gospel are the magi, who ask Herod, "Where is the child who has been born king of the Jews?" (Matt. 2:2). It is worth noting that the first to speak, and the first to call Jesus "king," are outsiders,

foreigners, pagans. The next time he will be called "king of the Jews" is at the end of his life, by Pilate's soldiers, who do not understand the truth they speak (27:29). Their mockery ironically underscores the truth that Jesus' kingdom fulfills the hopes of Jews and Gentiles.

The magi search for the child because they have observed a star. The ones who first notice God's light get the first opportunity to worship the child. The star in the sky is notable for both Jews and Gentiles. For pagans, an astrological phenomenon was often associated with the birth of a new ruler. For Jews, the star fulfills the biblical promise voiced by a Mesopotamian seer, that "a star shall come out of Jacob" (Num. 24:17).[1]

Herod is not the only one frightened by the star's indication of the birth of a "king of the Jews"; "all Jerusalem" fears as well (Matt. 2:3). An astrological phenomenon draws attention and causes anxiety. If the very heavens can change, if a new king has been born, what is next? The collapse of power, privilege, the status quo? Herod calls together the chief priests and scribes to confront this threat and figure out where the child will be born. In one room are gathered those who will continue to oppose Jesus and eventually hand him over to Pilate for crucifixion (27:1–2).

The quotation about Bethlehem in 2:6 combines 2 Samuel 5:2 and Micah 5:2. Bethlehem is the place where David, once a shepherd, was anointed king. Jesus is an heir of David, fulfilling God's promises to Israel. While Bethlehem signifies the importance of the Messiah to the Jewish people, the presence of the magi serves to extend the promise to outsiders. The presence of these sages from afar signals that Gentiles are already included in God's promises.

The magi come to the place where the child is and, "overwhelmed with joy," they kneel and offer gifts of gold, frankincense, and myrrh (2:10–11). These gifts leave no doubt that they believe Jesus is king, for they are gifts fit for royalty. The gold and frankincense recall the offerings in Isaiah 60:6 given by the Gentile kings. Frankincense is a fragrant resin used for

---

1. M. Eugene Boring, "Matthew," in *The New Interpreter's Bible* (Nashville: Abingdon Press, 1995), 8:142.

sacrificial offerings presented to God (Exod. 30:34; Lev. 2:1; 24:7). Myrrh is a resin used for anointing (Exod. 30:23–32) and embalming (John 19:39).

After giving these gifts, the magi are warned in a dream not to return to Herod. The motif of divine guidance given through dreams is a trademark of Matthew seen six times (1:20; 2:12, 13, 19, 22; 27:19). It connects this story with the rest of the birth narrative. Joseph will soon follow divine revelation imparted in dreams to keep Mary and Jesus safe from harm. At first glance God does not seem to be present in this part of the story, but God's activity can be seen in a star in the sky, and in angelic voices in dreams, guiding God's people.

This story shows the reception given by the world to the Messiah. The inclusion of the magi in this story shows God is fulfilling not only God's promises to Israel, but the longing of all humans for salvation. Already in Jesus, God is breaking down established cultural and religious boundaries and hierarchies. Matthew's Gospel ends with the call to "go therefore and make disciples of all nations" (28:19), and that call is anticipated in this story. The true king, the one who will make manifest the image of a loving sovereignty, has been born, and all are invited to come and present whatever gifts they have, to be used in building God's beloved and love-filled kingdom.

KRISTIN STROBLE

Commentary 2: Connecting the Reading with the World

How often do you hear "homage"? No one says they are going to pay homage any more. Preachers must often translate biblical language and culture into contemporary context. Epiphany likewise calls the preacher to important translating because "epiphany," "magi," "chief priests," "King Herod," and maybe even "messiah" do not roll off the twenty-first-century tongue any more easily than "homage." Fortunately, the story of the visit of the magi to baby Jesus offers several on-ramps for modern hearers that allow for a variety of entrance points for the sermon.

Preachers could focus upon the importance of place. Matthew 2:1–12 talks of Bethlehem, Jerusalem, Judea, and the land of Judah. Jesus does not come to some generic location with no identifiable features. He is born in a particular sociocultural place, a place linked to prophecy (Mic. 5:2–5), and also a place with specific customs, unique history, and complicated people. The preacher might note the biblical significance of the places mentioned in Matthew. Bethlehem is the home of David, for example, and the Messiah comes from the house of David. We see here the fulfillment of prophecy, and we see God working through specific places and people. Bethlehem, despite

all evidence to the contrary, is "by no means least among the rulers of Judah" (Matt. 2:6). All this suggests we should attend to the specific places we inhabit, no matter how seemingly insignificant, and ask how God might be at work in these contexts. Preachers could mine the history of their churches and towns and seek to name times of epiphany, moments or even seasons when God's presence and power were especially palpable.

In Matthew, epiphanies require attentiveness. Preachers may also help congregations be attentive to signs of the Messiah's presence. Seeing the star means looking up and taking notice. The preacher could take Epiphany as an opportunity both to read the past and to scan the horizon for signs of God's presence. For example, one church, while preparing to celebrate a milestone anniversary, learned about its participation in the Underground Railroad, and as a result began to see dismantling racism as central to their ongoing mission. Epiphany happens in Bethlehem, in the land of Judah. Epiphanies can continue to happen in particular places all over creation. We must look and take notice of where God is calling for our attention and ministry. Preachers could ask where the holy is being birthed in their communities.

Another touchpoint is the repeated phrase "pay him homage." "Paying homage" means worshiping or offering signs of reverence. In Matthew's time, homage meant a recognition of dependence; words like "submission" and "deference" could be coupled with homage. Even prostrating oneself and falling on the floor accompanied homage. Detailing the ancient concept could invite hearers to consider how strange such an attitude and behaviors are in our time. At the same time, we understand such behavior. Our cultural context does not include falling at someone's feet so much as doing whatever it takes to get close to power, wealth, and status in order to secure favor and benefit from proximity.

King Herod *is* the earthly power, not likely to pay homage to anyone, let alone a baby born in a worldly outpost. Yet three non-Jewish wise men pay homage to an infant. These outsiders recognize that this infant is, in fact, the king of the Jews and worship him. Two preaching avenues could be mined here. First, do we recognize Jesus when he appears? Second, if we do recognize him, are we willing to submit to him totally? The preacher could offer a contrast between our tendency to revere the powerful and wealthy with the reality that the One to whom reverence is paid in this text is a seemingly powerless infant with no earthly possessions. The temptation to bow down to the Herods of the world, rather than the Messiah in the manger or on the cross, remains constant. The preacher, after naming that truth, might explore what homage, properly directed, looks like.

Of course, knowing the future of this babe, and of so many of the faithful, the preacher can also note the cost of fidelity, and the confusion of identifying fidelity and divine favor with worldly success. Karen Marsh tells the story of Sophie Scholl, a German university student whose Christian convictions led her, her brother, and several friends to form a secret group called the White Rose, which distributed flyers and painted walls resisting Hitler. Marsh writes of this small group of students, "From Protestant, Catholic, and Russian Orthodox backgrounds, they shared the convictions of the Christian faith in opposition to Hitler."[2] Their homage to Jesus Christ was total. Scholl's faithful resistance to Herod, to Hitler, never wavered, even unto her execution at the hands of the Nazis. The preacher could wrestle with to whom, and how, we and others are paying faithful homage, and at what cost.

Another avenue worthy of exploring is the question of how God speaks, directs, and guides us. The heavens are telling the glory of God and, in this text, pointing the way to the greatest manifestation of that glory, Jesus Christ. An increasingly popular way to mark Epiphany is with "star words" that are distributed on this Sunday, with the invitation to allow the word received to be a guiding star throughout the year. Words like "peace," "courage," "kindness," or "love" provide a focus for contemplation. Could one of those stars be a beacon that leads to the holy?

Divine guidance comes in many forms in this story: from stars to dreams to the words of Scripture and religious leaders. Invite hearers to be on the lookout for God's direction through both the cosmic and the pedestrian, through the stars above and the Bible or newspaper at our side. God still speaks in all the ways evident in this Matthew text. Sharing the ways God has guided you could open the door to others sharing their epiphanies. If your congregation has shared star words in previous years, collect stories from those who found the experience revelatory, demonstrating God's ongoing guidance, direction, and presence through stars, word, and worship.

Preachers might also look to the story of the three wise men as an opportunity to be joyful. When the wise men discovered the child, they were overwhelmed with joy. When was the last time an experience of Jesus overwhelmed you with joy? While pointing to the brokenness and suffering of our world comes easily to us, seeing the holy right in front of us and responding with joy often eludes us. If where the Holy Spirit is, there is joy, then surely our lives and our worship and our congregations should be, at least some of the time, overwhelmed with joy. If not, the preacher could raise the question,

---

2. Karen Wright Marsh, "To Knock a Chip Out of the Wall: Sophie Scholl," *Comment Magazine* 35 (Winter 2017): 13.

why not? In his book *The Joy of Ministry,* considering Barth's understanding of how God teaches us about beauty, Thomas Currie writes, "Knowledge of God that is joyless is not knowledge of the God to whom Scripture bears witness."[3] Marveling at the beauty revealed to us through Jesus Christ, the grace and mercy, the love come down to earth, would be a welcome contrast to the litany of suffering repeated in the 24/7 news cycle. Further, proclaiming the truth that the incarnation embraces that very suffering, and our own, might even overwhelm your hearers with joy.

JILL DUFFIELD

3. Thomas W. Currie III, *The Joy of Ministry* (Louisville. KY: Westminster John Knox Press, 2008), 44.

Baptism of the Lord

Isaiah 42:1–9   Acts 10:34–43
Psalm 29   Matthew 3:13–17

Isaiah 42:1–9

¹Here is my servant, whom I uphold,
    my chosen, in whom my soul delights;
I have put my spirit upon him;
    he will bring forth justice to the nations.
²He will not cry or lift up his voice,
    or make it heard in the street;
³a bruised reed he will not break,
    and a dimly burning wick he will not quench;
    he will faithfully bring forth justice.
⁴He will not grow faint or be crushed
    until he has established justice in the earth;
    and the coastlands wait for his teaching.

⁵Thus says God, the LORD,
    who created the heavens and stretched them out,
    who spread out the earth and what comes from it,
who gives breath to the people upon it
    and spirit to those who walk in it:
⁶I am the LORD, I have called you in righteousness,
    I have taken you by the hand and kept you;
I have given you as a covenant to the people,
    a light to the nations,
    ⁷to open the eyes that are blind,
to bring out the prisoners from the dungeon,
    from the prison those who sit in darkness.
⁸I am the LORD, that is my name;
    my glory I give to no other,
    nor my praise to idols.
⁹See, the former things have come to pass,
    and new things I now declare;
before they spring forth,
    I tell you of them.

Commentary 1: Connecting the Reading with Scripture

This passage of Scripture is part of a longer thematic narrative on the Servant. The Old Testament scholar Bernard Duhm is credited with identifying the four, or possibly five, songs in the Isaiah material that speak of a Servant of YHWH. Duhm argued in his 1892 *Commentary on Isaiah* that there were at least three different authorial hands that formed what we call the book of Isaiah and that it was more accurate to speak of Isaiah, Deutero-Isaiah, and Trito-Isaiah. He further argued that the narrative regarding the Servant was a fairly late addition.

While from a textual standpoint the Servant narrative might be a kind of addendum, from a theological standpoint this thematic strand might provide a path to tying the entire book together.

This passage can be divided into three distinct sections, each of which contributes to a theological progression culminating in an affirmation of the one and only true God. The first section introduces the Servant in the context of the elective prerogative of God and the emotive affirmation of God. That is, God has chosen this Servant, and God delights in him. The election of this Servant and the delight that it elicits represents the positive experience that the people of God celebrate in their cultic rituals. The fact that God has chosen them and delights in them is reason for rejoicing. But there is another side of the experience of the people of God—that of rejection and wrath. While not a part of this pericope, the book of Isaiah also speaks of the Servant who was despised and rejected, but for the moment it is the positive side of that cultic experience that is expressed in this song of the Servant. The reason for the divine election and delight is that the Servant is devoted to the realization of the aims and purposes of God. In fact, God's spirit will be upon the Servant and the evidence of the presence of that spirit is the unrelenting pursuit of justice.

Theologically, the text suggests that the spirit of God and the pursuit of justice cannot be separated. Further, this justice is not a narrow, nationalistic kind but a justice for the nations. This suggests that justice is relational. One cannot achieve justice for oneself and avoid seeking justice for others. The work of this Servant will be marked by humility. He will not draw attention to himself by shouting in the streets or raising his voice over those of others.

The work of this Servant will also be marked by compassion. This is suggested by the fact that he will not break a bruised reed or snuff out a smoldering wick. Those who are bruised and wounded in society will not be confronted by one who will break those who have already been bruised, nor will they have the tiny flames of life to which they have been clinging simply snuffed out. The work of this Servant will also be marked by persistence. The Servant will not falter or be discouraged until the goal of justice has been achieved. The text suggests an acknowledgment that the achievement of justice does not occur in a vacuum or simply by fiat. Justice is sought in the rough-and-tumble history of our comings and goings and against real adversarial powers.

In the second section of this text the narrative shifts from a consideration of the identity of the people of God as expressed in the figure of the Servant, toward an identity rooted in their transcendent purpose. It is here that the creation narrative is expressed in summary form. God is described as the Creator of the heavens, who stretches them out, who spreads out the earth with all that springs from it, who gives breath to its people and life to those who walk on it: this summary of the creation is almost immediately the theme of the covenant. Here the creation story is not a treatise on the origin of all things per se, but a fundamental claim about the relationship of everything to God. In this context the covenant emerges not just as a pretext to privilege but as a reminder of the mission to which God calls his people. It is a missional covenant because the partners in that covenant are to be a light unto the Gentiles.

An important but sometimes overlooked theological insight into this text is that these words are cited in the New Testament (Matt. 12:18–21) as referring to Jesus of Nazareth. Note here in Isaiah that it is the people, the community, who have the mission to open eyes that are blind, to free captives from prison, and to release from the dungeon those who sit in darkness. It may be possible that our traditional interpretation of the use of these words in Jesus' annunciation of his ministry are not to be understood as his personal mission but the mission of the community to whom he speaks.

This way of viewing the text draws upon the theme of corporate personality, where an individual can represent a group. However, it is also possible that the group might find its essential identity in an individual. This literary and theological tension might compel us to look beyond a strict individualism and a recalcitrant collectivism when thinking about identity. If one chooses to see the Servant as a figure of Christ, it is important to note that the identity of Christ is established within the spiritual and prophetic dimensions of the Judaism of his day as well as over against its political and cultic distortions. This is why Jesus affirms his mission as tearing down and building up simultaneously.

The final section of this text is brief but represents the achievement of a particular clarity and theological insight. The overall trajectory of this text is to ultimately behold the glory of God. "I am the LORD, that is my name; my glory I give to no other, nor my praise to idols" (Isa. 42:8). The ultimate aim of the formation of the national identity of the people of God is not hypernationalism or distorted patriotism, but to know the Lord and the Lord's name. The ultimate aim in the pursuit of justice for the nations is, likewise, to know the Lord and the Lord's name.

This concluding text also addresses the issue of idolatry. In addition to declaring the majesty of his name, the Lord stands over and against the temptation to idolatry. This admonition is not so much about a challenge to divine power from other deities as it is about the praise that belongs to God, which is being given to others. His text concludes with a divine proclamation that God continually introduces novelty into our experience. God is dynamic and has promised us a preliminary glimpse into God's future.

Here as in the creation narrative, divine proclamation precedes historical manifestation. God's word is always future oriented. The aim of this word is to announce for the purpose of actualization. We are left not only with a proclamation about the future in God but with a sense of anticipation as well. Because God announces the future even before its manifestation is visible to us, we are strengthened in our faith and commitment. It is fitting that this text provides an important entry into the fascinating world of the prophet Isaiah and confirms its relevance for the church today. As the first of four songs about the Servant, its stanzas provide structure and rhythmic foundation for those to follow.

JAMES H. EVANS JR.

Commentary 2: Connecting the Reading with the World

The context for this famous first Servant Song of Isaiah is crucial. It is written in the Babylonian exile of Israel, and probably late in that nearly sixty-year experience. Judah and Jerusalem had suffered two exilic shocks, in 597 BCE and 587 BCE. In the former, the Babylonian armies had not caused significant damage to the Holy City, but in the latter, the city was devastated, the king blinded, and he and his court herded off to Babylon. For the next two full generations, the political and religious leaders of the community lived in a suburb of one of the world's greatest cities and attempted to survive in any way they could. Some probably abandoned their faith in YHWH, some became deeply cynical in the face of all they had lost, some were simply confused about what had happened. Second Isaiah, that unnamed one who wrote Isaiah 40–55, offered to his community an enormous measure of hope by means of an ongoing vital mission from the God who had clearly not forgotten the chosen people.

His uplifting words of power, spoken in the midst of despair and confusion, still speak to us today. We too live in confusing and dispiriting times, where expectations have been dashed, hopes have been called into question, where a sense of purpose has been rendered illusive. We are in desperate need of a new infusion of optimism and intention, a clear idea that God still has a plan for us, a plan beyond mere local goals, but a plan that encompasses something far larger. In short, we need a reminder that God has not given up on us, but calls us to the larger purposes of God for the entire universe. As we have now celebrated the coming of Jesus into history, his appearance as a baby before simple shepherds and wise men, we now turn to ask what this child of God has come to do, and what he has come to call us to do.

Isaiah's portrait of the Servant of God, laid out in four unforgettable verbal canvases, begins in Isaiah 42. "Look at my servant! I cause him to stand up! My chosen one! I am delighted in him!" (Isa. 42:1a, my trans.). The identity of this Servant has been the subject of centuries-long debate. Various commentators have identified

The Claim That God Makes upon Us

Baptism is a sacrament of truth and holiness; and it is a sacrament, because it is the sign which directs us to God's revelation of eternal life and declares, not merely the Christian "myth," but—the Word of God. It does not merely signify eternal reality, but is eternal reality, because it points significantly beyond its own concreteness. Baptism mediates the new creation: it is not itself grace, but from first to last a means of grace. As the question which men put to God is always also His answer to it; as human faith is enclosed invisibly by the faithfulness of God; so also the human act of baptism is enclosed by that action of God on behalf of men which it declares. . . .

To those who are not ignorant the sign of baptism speaks of death. To be baptized means to be immersed, to be sunk in a foreign element, to be covered by a tide of purification. The man who emerges from the water is not the same man who entered it. One man dies and another is born. The baptized person is no longer to be identified with the man who died. Baptism bears witness to us of the death of Christ, where the radical and inexorable claim of God upon men triumphed. He that is baptized is drawn into the sphere of this event. Overwhelmed and hidden by the claim of God, he disappears and is lost in this death. The arrogant illusion of the likeness of men to God is loosened and stripped from him. In the light of the Cross, what indeed is left to him? He has forfeited his identity with the man who sins in will and act; he is free of the power of sin, free also of the status of sin. The man over whom sin has power and dominion has died (vi. 2, 7). The death of Christ dissolves the Fall by bringing into being the void in which the usurped independence of men can breathe no longer. It digs up the invisible roots of visible sin . . . . Beyond this death the man who asks that he may continue in sin (vi. 2) and be like God lives no longer. He is dissolved by the claim which God makes upon him.

Karl Barth, *The Epistle to the Romans,* trans. Edwyn C. Hoskyns (London: Oxford University Press, 1933), 192–93.

the Servant as Moses, one of the prophets, one of the kings, King Cyrus of the Persians, the nation Israel, even Second Isaiah himself. Of course, for early Christians, not surprisingly, the Servant was seen as Jesus of Nazareth.

Christian believers read the words of Isaiah and saw in them much of what they had witnessed and hoped for in the one they called Lord and Christ. Perhaps the exact identity of the Servant is less important than understanding what this Servant has been called by God to do, for the actions of the Servant are in some senses the summation of God's will and way for any who would call themselves children of God.

God's "delight" in the Servant leads God to "put my spirit upon him" such that "he will bring forth justice to the nations" (v. 1b). There is the basic task of the Servant of God; he will do the work of justice for all people. The Hebrew *mishpat,* a participial form of the verb "to judge," has a broad meaning in the Bible, but it may perhaps be summarized as follows: justice aims at making possible an egalitarian community where all people can maintain and live by their basic human rights (see Amos 5:14–21; Mic. 6:6–8; Ps. 113:5–9 for representative passages). Thus the central role of the Servant is to establish justice for all on earth.

Isaiah then turns to the particular ways in which the Servant will enact justice. "He will not cry out, nor raise his voice, forcing it to be heard in the streets. He will not break a bruised reed, nor extinguish a barely burning wick; he will faithfully bring justice" (Isa. 42:2–3, my trans.). The work of the Servant will be unobtrusive, quiet, barely noticeable, but the result nevertheless will be justice.

Will he ever become discouraged and defeated by the task of justice creation? "He will not faint or be crushed before he establishes justice on earth, until the coastlands yearn for his Torah [his teaching]" (v. 4, my trans.). Nothing will be able to impede the Servant's work for justice for all; he will not cease his work until justice reigns everywhere, even until the coastlands, the farthest reaches of the known world, thirst for the servant's Torah. Torah is the will and way of YHWH, and due to the work of the Servant, everyone, everywhere will desire that teaching.

After declaring who God is, "creator and stretcher out of the heavens, the one who spread out the earth, and all that comes from it, the one who gives breath to the people, and spirit to those who walk on it" (v. 5, my trans.), God returns to talk of the Servant. We should note that in verse 5 the same spirit (Heb. *ruach*) that God gave to the Servant God also gives to all the people who inhabit the earth. In other words, the work of the Servant is at the same time the work that is expected of the people of God. We are not asked merely to admire the wonderful Servant of God; we are called to join the Servant in that work. In the same way that early Christians were asked not only to wonder at the work of Jesus' life, death, and resurrection, but to join his work of reconciliation of the fractured world, so Isaiah bids his dispirited exiled community to witness to the work of the Servant by joining him in that work.

Isaiah now specifies the sort of work that justice requires. "I have given you as a covenant to the people, a light to the nations to open blind eyes, to bring out prisoners from the dungeon, from the prison those in darkness" (vv. 6–7, my trans.). These more specific demands are perhaps meant both literally and figuratively. Something

new from God is afoot; the work of the Servant may open the eyes of the blind (note the work of Jesus here), but blind eyes may also be those who have been blinded by sadness and despair in exilic hopelessness. The dark prisons may be actual jails as well as the darkness of exile itself. The Servant will announce the "new things that (God) will now declare" (v. 9), new things that will include light flowing into former places of darkness. Many today feel in exile—from their expectations for unity and wholeness among nations and peoples, from their hopes for a future of peace. Sixth-century Israel surely felt like this in their physical exile.

There is little wonder that early followers of Jesus read these passages as announcements of his coming. For them, the one called Servant could only be the one they called Christ. It is fair to conclude that Isaiah was not thinking of Jesus of Nazareth when he spoke and wrote these words, but whoever he may have had in mind, that one was chosen by God to announce the new hope and promise of God to the whole world. This promise is the very essence of the understanding of the babe of Bethlehem, and as we celebrate this day of his baptism, we at the same time celebrate the new thing of God, the hope and promise of justice for all, inaugurated by Jesus and worked for by all who would follow him.

JOHN C. HOLBERT

Psalm 29

¹Ascribe to the LORD, O heavenly beings,
  ascribe to the LORD glory and strength.
²Ascribe to the LORD the glory of his name;
  worship the LORD in holy splendor.

³The voice of the LORD is over the waters;
  the God of glory thunders,
  the LORD, over mighty waters.
⁴The voice of the LORD is powerful;
  the voice of the LORD is full of majesty.

⁵The voice of the LORD breaks the cedars;
  the LORD breaks the cedars of Lebanon.
⁶He makes Lebanon skip like a calf,
  and Sirion like a young wild ox.

⁷The voice of the LORD flashes forth flames of fire.
⁸The voice of the LORD shakes the wilderness;
  the LORD shakes the wilderness of Kadesh.

⁹The voice of the LORD causes the oaks to whirl,
  and strips the forest bare;
  and in his temple all say, "Glory!"

¹⁰The LORD sits enthroned over the flood;
  the LORD sits enthroned as king forever.
¹¹May the LORD give strength to his people!
  May the LORD bless his people with peace!

Connecting the Psalm with Scripture and Worship

Possibly the oldest psalm in our Bible, Psalm 29 reflects the timeless human impulse to offer divine praise within the context of God's power in and over the natural world. It is likely that Psalm 29 is an adaptation of a Canaanite hymn to Baal, and borrows from that hymn the pattern of repetition used throughout the psalm, seen most notably in "the voice of the LORD," which is repeated seven times (vv. 3, 4, 5, 7, 8, 9).

Traditionally categorized as an enthronement psalm, Psalm 29 is unique in that its invitation to praise is directed toward those in the heavens rather than those on earth, with human beings mentioned only in the last verse. Even there, the movement of the psalm remains consistent in its direction, in that the action being taken is that of God toward God's people, not the other way around. This is a psalm entirely about God, and though God never speaks directly, the voice of God is heard in the response of everything and everyone else.

Psalm 29 offers multiple liturgical possibilities. Spoken or sung as a call to worship, it sets the stage for a robust opening round of praise. It works well in a call-and-response format, but the verses could also be voiced from different sections within the sanctuary (e.g., left side, right side, transepts, balcony, and choir) or by various groups of people within the congregation (e.g., high voices and low voices, or adults, youth, and children). The rising and falling of voices throughout the sanctuary echoes the all-encompassing nature of this psalm. Psalm 29 could also form the basis of a prayer of confession, expressing the ways we forget to praise God's glory and strength and fail to respect God's sovereignty. For a children's sermon it could be wonderful to act out the multitude of ways in which God's voice makes itself known. In contexts where liturgical dance is used, the stunning visuals of Psalm 29 provide rich images for creative expression.

The connection in Psalm 29 between God's voice and the actions that result can be heard in the other lectionary readings for this day. In the passage from Isaiah, the prophet speaks for God, offering the first of the Servant Songs. There God's voice, which contains the power to shake the wilderness (Ps. 29:8), commissions a Servant who will not break "a bruised reed" or quench "a dimly burning wick" (Isa. 42:3). There is a gentleness in God's voice that is heard again in Matthew, when Jesus emerges from the waters of the Jordan to the voice of God naming him as "Beloved." In the text from Acts, the voice of God is heard in the message that spread throughout Judea. Read in connection with Psalm 29, one can envision that message spreading out among people much as the voice of God is broadcast over the waters. When God speaks, there is always a response, a movement, be it in the world around us or in the hearts of humankind.

The shift from outright examples of power found in Psalm 29 to the more subtle forms of power found in Matthew and Acts finds a natural bridge in the passage from Isaiah. The temptation is to see this bridge in Isaiah as representing a shift in God's persona; rather, what we find in Isaiah is a shift in God's tone of voice. A preacher might explore the use of God's voice in these passages as God's self-disclosure to us. In the complexity of expressions within God's voice we find a God that will not conform to any expectations we may have about who God is or should be.

Another avenue for the preacher to explore might be the connection between the words and actions of faith. Isaiah's text raises the question of the identity of the Servant. Some, like John Calvin, suggest that the Servant is Jesus Christ. Others suggest that the Servant may not be a person but a people; Israel may be the Servant. Still others maintain that who the Servant is, is less important than what the Servant does. Our God is the God of the Word, but not a God of just words. Whenever God speaks, creation responds.

On this Sunday celebrating the baptism of Jesus, the preacher might consider how the promises we make in baptism—be they the ones made by an individual, parents, or the congregation—are made known (or not) in the actions that result. Some congregations have the practice of rising to their feet during a baptism as a way of indicating their promise to stand with the child and their family. Such an action echoes the action of whirling oaks (Ps. 29:9) that respond to the voice of God.

The connection between God's voice and our actions is made most explicit in Isaiah's vision of the world that will be created in response to what God has spoken. It is a world of justice, freedom, and peace. Some preachers hesitate to speak for God in response to the harm done by others who claim to be God's mouthpiece. Our preaching and worship might reclaim God's voice in light of world events as a way to bear witness to the sovereignty of God expressed in the texts for today.

ERIN KEYS

Acts 10:34–43

³⁴Then Peter began to speak to them: "I truly understand that God shows no partiality, ³⁵but in every nation anyone who fears him and does what is right is acceptable to him. ³⁶You know the message he sent to the people of Israel, preaching peace by Jesus Christ—he is Lord of all. ³⁷That message spread throughout Judea, beginning in Galilee after the baptism that John announced: ³⁸how God anointed Jesus of Nazareth with the Holy Spirit and with power; how he went about doing good and healing all who were oppressed by the devil, for God was with him. ³⁹We are witnesses to all that he did both in Judea and in Jerusalem. They put him to death by hanging him on a tree; ⁴⁰but God raised him on the third day and allowed him to appear, ⁴¹not to all the people but to us who were chosen by God as witnesses, and who ate and drank with him after he rose from the dead. ⁴²He commanded us to preach to the people and to testify that he is the one ordained by God as judge of the living and the dead. ⁴³All the prophets testify about him that everyone who believes in him receives forgiveness of sins through his name."

Commentary 1: Connecting the Reading with Scripture

The Acts of the Apostles can be understood as a book of transitions with respect to both its position in the canon and its content. In its position, it is a transition between Gospels and Epistles. In its content, it is a transition between the ministry of Jesus and the mission of the Holy Spirit through the church. Our text is a part of a central transition within the mission of the Holy Spirit. This transition is found in the story of Peter and the Roman centurion Cornelius, the beginning of the outreach to the Gentiles. Our passage forms the very center of that story.

A more theological word for transition is *conversion*. Some Christian traditions will find stories of individual conversion congenial, while they may seem more foreign for others. Preachers from those traditions may have difficulty with the word or its connotations. "Conversion" has the advantage, however, of describing a complete change or revolution in the person. This story describes just that kind of change in two persons, Cornelius and Peter. It is "a tale of two conversions."

Both Peter and Cornelius are unlikely converts: Peter because he is a faithful Jew and therefore apparently in no need of conversion,

and Cornelius because, as a Roman centurion, he is a quintessential Gentile. The conversion of Peter may be the more difficult. Perhaps it is always harder for those within the church to be converted than those who come to the gospel for the first time. That may be a connection worth exploring.

A third conversion, of Paul, is found in the immediate literary and theological vicinity of our passage. Though it is not mentioned in our passage, that third conversion should be kept in mind by the preacher. These conversion stories are so important in Acts that they are repeated, so that readers will get the point the second time if they missed it the first time. (The conversion of Paul is described three times: Acts 9:1–19; 22:6–16; 26:12–18!) The three conversions together lead to yet another conversion, the most important and difficult conversion of all, the conversion of the church to a new sense of mission.

Conversion may also represent the chief connection to our present situation. The centrality of stories of conversion in Acts invites the preacher of any tradition to consider the nature of conversion in the contemporary church. Perhaps the Holy Spirit is also at work in our circumstances, converting both individuals and, indeed, the church of our day, to a new sense of mission. The conversion of the church is still in our day more difficult than the conversion of an individual. It is harder for a church to "get saved" than a person. Perhaps that remains the chief need in the church today, however. The preacher might explore what a church that experienced conversion would look like.

In our passage, the conversion of Peter is actually taking place. The translation of the beginning of Peter's speech, "I truly understand," is correct, but a little abstract and cerebral. It might better be translated as a reality that is happening at the present time, as Peter is speaking. "I am grasping" would be a literal translation. A livelier rendering might be "I am catching on." Perhaps that leads to a good nontechnical definition of conversion: conversion is catching on to what God is doing around us and in us. What is true of an individual is also true for the church. Not only is conversion a matter of catching on to what God is doing. It may also be catching up to what God is doing. That may be one of the major preaching connections of our passage.

While the story of the conversion of Peter and of Cornelius must be described as the background of our text, our passage may not be the best one on which to base a sermon on the conversion itself. It may, however, be the text that leads to a consideration of what the conversion of the church is *for*. The surprising thing is that Peter does in this completely new situation what he has spent most of the book of Acts doing. There are echoes here of the encounter with the beggar in the temple in Acts 3: "I have no silver or gold, but what I have I give you" (Acts 3:6). What Peter has to give in this case is not healing, but the good news about Jesus. So, faced with something entirely new in his life, as new as filling himself with "unclean" foods, Peter does what he has so often done. He preaches a sermon, telling his listeners about the love of Jesus.

For listeners who find stories of individual conversion uncongenial and who have never considered the possibility that fundamental change in the church can be described as conversion, this may be of some comfort. What can the church do in the new situation? It can preach the gospel of Jesus Christ. Like Peter it can tell people about Jesus. It is all that we really have to offer in the church. In our passage, Cornelius is willing to listen, a willingness that is a necessary part of the story and of Cornelius's own conversion. It may be that, like Cornelius, the people we encounter will listen.

The content of the sermon is a repetition or summary of Luke's Gospel as a whole. It is not dumbed down or even particularly adapted for Gentile ears. For example, the emphasis on "hanging him on a tree" (10:39) is an obscure reference to the First Testament, which Gentiles might find difficult. Nevertheless, the Holy Spirit breaks in, as we hear in the verses immediately following our passage. So may it be with our preaching.

There is a danger that in preaching this passage we may inadvertently reinforce the anti-Judaism that lies just below the surface in many Christians. The people of Israel may be pictured primarily as Christ killers, but the message of peace is sent to Israel and some receive it gladly in Acts, beginning with three thousand on the day of Pentecost. Perhaps even more dangerously, it may seem from this story that Judaism is an exclusive religion that divides itself strictly from the rest of humanity, an attitude from which Peter is freed in his conversion. It would be wise to emphasize that Peter, in this case, does not represent Judaism but rather the early church as being in need of conversion. It would also be gracious to acknowledge that the insight that God shows no partiality is not far from the teaching of the school of Hillel in rabbinic Judaism. That school of thought maintained a gracious attitude to righteous Gentiles, of whom Cornelius would certainly be one.

The big-picture good news in the story for the anxious church of the early twenty-first century may be simply that with God's help the early church got through its first great crisis. Acts shows us that the conversion of the church to a new sense of itself and a new sense of mission was not easy. It was not easy to reach out to Gentiles. They were different, after all, and it is always difficult to reach out to those who are different. The tensions of transition are manifest, even at the distance of two millennia. They did get through their crisis and perhaps, with God's good aid, so will we.

STEPHEN FARRIS

Commentary 2: Connecting the Reading with the World

When believers gather to commemorate Jesus Christ's baptism, the purpose has to go beyond acknowledging that Jesus himself was baptized and remembering that our own baptisms bear witness to our union with him. The much more vital liturgical and theological topics to ponder this day revolve around what God declares about Godself through the baptism of Jesus. This short excerpt from a pivotal passage in Acts helps preachers and teachers make those connections, for the brief sermon Peter delivers in Cornelius's home can prompt them to consider that this same God remains present now, still committed to healing and claiming the world.

Jesus' Ministry as an Epiphany. Peter's capsule summary of the plot of Luke's Gospel mentions John's baptismal ministry and refers to Jesus as one who was anointed "with the Holy Spirit and with power" (Acts 10:38). In doing so, Peter's sermon declares that Jesus' baptism and the events that immediately followed initiated a public ministry in which God was active. Peter's repeated use of "God" as the subject of active verbs creates a refrain to assert that all of Jesus' life and activity was an *epiphany*—an embodied manifestation of God's presence, compassion, fidelity, and power. God empowered Jesus to perform the good news of God's salvation. In Jesus' baptism, the arrival of the Holy Spirit, and all the healing, liberation, and forgiveness of Jesus' ministry, we come to understand anew who God is, what God values, and what it means to be called into the people of God.

Because Peter refers to Jesus' death and resurrection, the witnesses who observed those events, and the proclamation Jesus' followers made in response, the lectionary assigns these verses from Acts to Easter Sunday every year. Peter's sermon has a much wider field of vision than the resurrection alone, making it a meaningful contributor to Epiphany reflections also. As this new season in the church year kicks into gear, the passage draws attention to another fundamental Christian conviction: in Jesus we see God. That claim constitutes more than theological nostalgia about the historical Jesus of Nazareth; it describes the activity of the Christ as the emergence of an altogether new reality. As Willie James Jennings notes, in Peter's sermon

> the Jesus of recent history becomes the defining moment of all history. Here is the deliverance of the world and its restoration toward health and life. Luke presses the cosmic through the words of Peter, pulling back the curtain to reveal the hand of God in Jesus. . . . The content of the gospel comes home in this sermon to its sharpest truth. This is God.[1]

To see God's priorities in action, look to the activity of Jesus.

No Partiality. Preachers and teachers should remember that Peter's sermon serves as the theological climax to a much larger story in which God leads the apostle and the Gentile centurion Cornelius to discover that "God shows no partiality" (v. 34). The sermon plays a part in a drama about two very different men, along with their associated communities, as they begin to build a relationship of hospitality under the same roof. Peter's words express the new reality he has recently discerned: the family of God recognizes no ethnicity-based restrictions or privileges among its members, since anyone who "fears" God and "does what is right" can enjoy God's welcome (v. 35).

This divine impartiality deserves the church's attention in any age, but especially so during times when congregations find themselves in settings full of strife and anxiety. A God who "shows no partiality" is not politically neutral or aloof; the expression in this context indicates God's active concern for *all* humanity. Peter would have already known this from Jewish scriptural traditions, but he sees it coming to pass now in an unexpected way, with old boundaries passing away and new solidarity and fellowship springing into being, sealed by the

---

1. Willie James Jennings, *Acts*, Belief: A Theological Commentary on the Bible (Louisville, KY: Westminster John Knox Press, 2017), 112.

Holy Spirit. If God shows this kind of impartiality, so should God's people.

Acts describes Peter, Cornelius, and others (see 11:1–18) gradually but definitively living into their new understanding. None of them saw it coming at the beginning of Acts 10. They learned it through openness, obedience, risk, and vision. At one level, their story is about how ancient Christ-followers came to understand the theological imperative behind Gentiles' admission into the church—an actual historical development in the early church that had tremendous and permanent consequences for how Christianity eventually would conceive of itself.

This is also a story about the unity that the Holy Spirit continually creates among all believers, no matter what dividing lines or value judgments we may be tempted to import into the church's ethos and ministry. Divine impartiality is good news but also, of course, perennially challenging news. Peter characterizes Jesus as one who freed people from the devil's oppression. It is therefore tragic—even diabolical—when churches reinforce oppressive prejudices and systems. Congregations defy their Christ when they put criteria and fundamentals in place to measure true believers. When Christians propose theological justifications for making such distinctions, they discredit Jesus himself and throw a shroud over the bright epiphany of God's activity through Christ.

Expanding Horizons. Living in the still-emerging light of Epiphany requires believers to consider that the energy of the Christian gospel radiates outward. Peter senses that dynamic in his sermon's reference to Christ as "Lord of all" (v. 36). Jesus is a Lord who establishes peace and heals "all" (v. 38; cf. v. 35); he has assumed the prerogative to judge all people, whether living or dead. Nothing and no one resides beyond the reach of Jesus Christ and his gospel. In the immediate narrative context, the emphasis on the universal scope of God's deliverance and Jesus' authority tells Cornelius and the audience of Acts that, indeed, truly *anyone* "who calls on the name of the Lord shall be saved" (2:21; cf. Luke 2:29–32; 3:6). There are no barriers.

In a broader context, Peter's claims also assert Christ's superiority. Christ resides at the pinnacle of Peter's perceptions of what power is and how it works, whether in a cosmic or sociopolitical sense. If Christ is Lord of all, then any thought that the Roman emperor deserves that title must be abandoned. That assertion might catch the attention of a centurion of the Italian Cohort (Acts 10:1), of all people.[2] It should surely inform how modern Christians sort out their own allegiances and their ways of evaluating people and movements that amass significant influence in political and cultural arenas.

Peter's rhetoric about Christ's universal lordship holds open a door for Cornelius and continues to inform the personal faith of countless believers, connecting an individual's devotion to the God whose care and authority encompass all that exist. Living in fellowship with the "Lord of all" has the potential to endow a person's or a community's existence with deep meaning and purpose. At the same time, similar rhetoric easily finds itself pressed into service as a weapon for those who advocate a kind of Christian supremacy or exceptionalism. Even though the book of Acts shows little eagerness to build bridges for what we might call multifaith understanding or interfaith cooperation, it is worth noting that Peter in this passage shows no interest in bullying or humiliating Cornelius and his associates. Rather, his efforts concentrate on welcome and embrace. In this, he imitates the ministry and message of the Lord of all himself.

MATTHEW L. SKINNER

---

2. Beverly Roberts Gaventa, *Acts*, Abingdon New Testament Commentaries (Nashville: Abingdon Press, 2003), 171. Gaventa also notes that Epictetus refers to the emperor with this title (*Discourses* 4.1.12).

Baptism of the Lord

Matthew 3:13–17

¹³Then Jesus came from Galilee to John at the Jordan, to be baptized by him. ¹⁴John would have prevented him, saying, "I need to be baptized by you, and do you come to me?" ¹⁵But Jesus answered him, "Let it be so now; for it is proper for us in this way to fulfill all righteousness." Then he consented. ¹⁶And when Jesus had been baptized, just as he came up from the water, suddenly the heavens were opened to him and he saw the Spirit of God descending like a dove and alighting on him. ¹⁷And a voice from heaven said, "This is my Son, the Beloved, with whom I am well pleased."

Commentary 1: Connecting the Reading with Scripture

The story of Jesus' baptism is drenched in scriptural citations and allusions that highlight central claims and themes of the whole Gospel. At this early stage in the Gospel, these claims serve to raise questions that can be answered only as the narrative continues: How does Jesus' submission to John for baptism align with John's call to repentance? How does his baptism fulfill all righteousness? What is meant by the claim that Jesus is God's Son? How is his identity as God's Son related to his role as servant? Finally, ancient readers would have heard in this story and in the heavenly voice (Matt. 3:17) not only direct citations of Psalm 2:7 and Isaiah 42:1 but numerous allusions to the creation story. In what sense does the baptism and subsequent ministry of Jesus signal the fulfillment of God's intentions not just for humankind but for the whole creation?

Because John associates his baptism with repentance and confession of sin (3:1–2, 5–6), readers have naturally wondered whether Jesus, like "Jerusalem and all Judea," also sees himself as sinful and in need of repentance. Does his baptism by John suggest that Jesus too is a sinner? None of the Gospels, however, say anything about sin in relation to Jesus' motivations for baptism. Jesus' baptism more likely signals his identification with God's kingdom, which John announces and anticipates and which Jesus himself will soon proclaim and inaugurate (4:17).

Here repentance is not only preparation for, but the right response to, God's presence and power among us. In addition, Jesus' baptism signals (1) his humility in submitting to God's call through John, (2) his full identification with all those who are coming to John seeking deliverance, and possibly (3) his preparation for the suffering to come for God's chosen servant (16:21; 17:22–23; 20:17–19; 20:20–23). John's activities at the Jordan also imply a vote of no-confidence in the Jerusalem authorities and in the temple as the exclusive locus of God's redemptive activity. In light of this, Jesus' baptism by John also anticipates Jesus' own eventual denunciation of the temple authorities and his crucifixion at their hands.

Christian baptism today is typically associated with belonging to the church community, as well as cleansing from sin. It is less clearly connected in popular imagination with the reality of God's reign in our midst. Baptism may still signal for us a turn from the power of sin and death, but it is often less clear what false gods in our lives we are turning from and what new ways we are turning toward. Jesus' baptism signals his denial of the power of sin over him generally, and a refusal to bow before any power but God, including the powers of empire that dominate Jerusalem. Our baptisms signify our commitments to his story, his ways, and his fate as our own. What does it mean, however, when so many baptized Christians continue to be committed to the false forms of redemption offered through modern political and economic systems, or to consumerism, racism, sexism, or tribalism? What ongoing practices does baptism entail, especially with regard to the value systems and practices of the American way of life?

John expresses aloud his reluctance to baptize Jesus (3:14), but Jesus overrules his protest, asserting that in this way they will "fulfill all righteousness" (v. 15). This assertion, the first words Jesus speaks in Matthew, includes two words that are programmatic in this Gospel. Matthew uses some form of "fulfill" sixteen times, mostly in reference to Old Testament prophecy, which suggests that here too we should look for the "prophecies" that are highlighted in the immediate context. In 3:17, the heavenly voice announces that Jesus is "my Son, the Beloved, with whom I am well pleased," which draws upon both Psalm 2:7 and Isaiah 42:1 (the first verse of the OT lesson for this Sunday). Psalm 2 is a Davidic coronation song, celebrating God's victory over the rulers and nations that conspire against God's son and king. Isaiah 42:1 is the beginning of the first of Isaiah's Servant Songs (see also Matt. 12:18–21), addressed originally to God's servant Israel, which is to bring justice, light, sight, and liberation not only for Israel itself, but to the nations and the earth (Isa. 42:4–7).

To "fulfill all righteousness" means nothing less than the realization of this vision. Whereas modern audiences may think of righteousness primarily in terms of individual moral conduct, in Matthew, righteousness is focused on restoration and relationships made whole. To be sure, fulfilling the commandments is part of this righteousness (Matt. 5:17–20), but they too are aimed ultimately at the realization of God's intentions for the redemption and reconciliation of the whole creation. How does the church today keep its sights on this same goal? Can we too be a part of the fulfillment of all righteousness, not only at the level of personal morality, but especially within our communities, nations, and world? Will we not need our enemies as well as our neighbors in order to fulfill this vision (5:43–48)? How might we realize our own vocation, with Israel and Jesus, to be a living covenant and light for the all nations (Isa. 42:6)?

On the surface level, the story presents Jesus as God's beloved Son and servant, using these terms to define one another. This claim also aligns his vocation with that of Israel, which in many Old Testament passages is identified as God's chosen son and servant. Just as Israel was borne from the waters while fleeing the Egyptians and was tested in the wilderness, so Jesus is borne as God's Son from the waters of baptism and will be tested in the wilderness (Matt. 4:1–11). Jesus' baptism thus also signifies a new exodus and a new beginning for God's people. His story is the continuation of Israel's story and fulfills her vocation.

Finally, Jesus' baptism bears striking parallels with the creation stories of Genesis 1–3, enough to suggest that the baptism is, in a sense, a creation story: the created world itself comes from watery chaos (Gen. 1:3, 6–8; cf. Isa. 43:2, 16–21 regarding Israel's creation); God's Spirit or breath sweeps over the waters (Gen. 1:2); and God repeatedly distinguishes and declares new elements of creation and expresses pleasure. The open heaven (Matt. 3:16) suggests that a cosmic shift is taking place, in which the boundaries that have divided heaven and earth are now being breached.

Matthew, moreover, begins this Gospel with the words "the book of the genesis or genealogy," which echo Genesis 2:4 and 5:1 and may be meant to serve as a title for the whole Gospel. If the Gospel is the book of the Genesis of Jesus the Christ, then the baptism scene marks formally a new stage in God's actions as Creator. A new creation is being brought forth, the realization of God's intentions not only for humankind, but for the whole of heaven and earth (cf. Matt. 6:10), whose unity, disrupted by human disobedience, is now being restored by the obedience of God's Son and servant. Matthew's story of Jesus is not merely about the salvation of humans, nor about our transport from earth to heaven, but about the reconciliation of the whole of heaven and earth. This is what new creation means, and why the baptism of Jesus is not only a singular event for him, but the beginning of the fulfillment of God's purposes for the whole of heaven and earth. How do our baptisms prepare us to participate in the work of bringing forth this new creation?

STANLEY P. SAUNDERS

Commentary 2: Connecting the Reading with the World

Social and Ethical Context: Doing Flows from Being. Jesus' baptism leads us to reflect on our own identity, each one unique, a woven tapestry of multicolored threads. Where are you from? Who are your parents? What language do you speak? What are your gender, ethnicity, race, and religion? All of these threads and many more make up our identity. Leaving the original context that shaped our identity feels threatening at first.

This is particularly true for those who came to consciousness in a relatively homogeneous place where most people are very similar. In a new context, one does not fit in and often feels judged. This change of context and familiar identity markers challenges us to adapt to the new situation. It may entail learning a new language and culture altogether. Persons immigrating to the United States often sense a shift in their identity as they adjust to their new home. Those who adapt most successfully are those who have a solid sense of who they are within themselves. They can take on new customs and adjust to new environments without feeling fundamentally threatened by the changes. Their core sense of personhood has not changed—only the external contexts.

The descent of the Spirit and the voice from heaven in Jesus' baptism give testimony to and affirm Jesus' core identity. Jesus goes on to challenge fundamental identity markers of his society, and the strength and self-confidence that he manifests may be traced to this identity-affirming event. His core relationship with God the Father grounds his identity and character, as well as guiding and empowering his ministry.

Ecclesial Context: Rites of Passage. Matthew's depiction of Jesus' baptism also reminds us of rites of passage. Various rites of passage mark our journey through life, such as those at the end of a formative process, like graduation. Whether it is from kindergarten, high school, university, or graduate school, graduations tell the world that we are equipped to advance to a new dimension in our lives.

Other rites of passage, such as a presidential inauguration, come at the beginning. This is not so much a completion as a launch. The inauguration marks the transfer of responsibility and a commissioning for the task. The launch-style rite of passage tends to have specific purpose and direction. While the person may exercise considerable freedom, the authorizing power behind the inauguration provides the framework for their actions.

In some ways ordination combines both types of rites of passage. Ordination recognizes a prior path of study and formation, but it is also a launching for mission. The community represented by the denomination provides both the guidelines for the mission and the sustaining source of support and authority.

Baptism as a rite of passage needs to be considered from both directions. It gives public witness to God's saving grace, one's new birth in Christ, and incorporation into Christ's body. At the same time it is a commissioning for God's mission that we share with Christ. Baptism is a rite of passage that signifies what has come prior: the ongoing story of God's redemption of God's people, and a marker of our being sent into the world to make disciples.

Cultural Context: Symbols Matter. Each social group marks out its sense of identity, either consciously or unconsciously, through the cultural symbols it adopts. One of the latest fad symbols is the tattoo. When I was growing up, tattoos were associated with sailors, prisoners, and circus workers. Those who had tattoos had an exotic air about them, a sense of danger or mystery. Now tattoos are almost ubiquitous, on people of all ages and social positions. Major sports figures, celebrities, news anchors, and even preachers have tattoos. Tattoos have moved from representing the margins of society to becoming mainstream.

In our highly polarized society, we make judgments by observing the cultural symbols and behavior patterns others adopt. People dress not only according to their socioeconomic status but also in line with the groups they identify with. If you go to the mall, you can identify discrete groups by their style: speech patterns, clothing, piercings, tattoos, flags, and other symbols. Tell me what news sources you consult and what social media pages you frequent, and I can probably figure out your political and social views.

When Jesus accepted John's baptism, he was making a big statement symbolically. He was identifying with a renewal movement within Israel. John dressed and ate like a desert prophet. Water, a heavenly voice, and a descending dove connected with biblical symbols that communicated not only Jesus' identity but also the beginning of a new phase of God's activity in the world. When we accept baptism, we also connect with powerful symbols that are loaded with meaning.

Liturgical Context: Coming to Consciousness. Raising a child is an experience of coming to consciousness, for both the parent and the child. Even before the child is born, the parents are thinking about names. Some of the names connect to special people in their lives, and others are just names that sound nice to them. When the parents see the first ultrasound images of the baby squirming around in the womb, they begin connecting with who this person will be.

As the child grows, certain events, decisions, or actions stick out because they seem to vividly illustrate who this person really is—their character, ambition, and potential. It could be joining a sports team, playing music, or displaying a particular attraction to and tenderness with animals. So both for the observing parents and for the child, certain events are markers along the road of coming to consciousness about who this person is and where she or he is headed.

Epiphany is about coming to consciousness, both for Jesus and for those around him. For Jesus' parents the angelic visitation to Mary gave her and Joseph a strong sense of the uniqueness of their child. The shepherds, the magi's visit,

and Herod's threat confirmed this sense. We can see from Jesus' actions in the temple as a young boy that his developing self-consciousness follows the trajectory his parent discerned. When Jesus asks to be baptized by John, he is openly identifying with a new move of God. With the gift of the Spirit, God confirms Jesus' identity and expands his consciousness by commissioning him to messianic ministry. Epiphany is all about coming to consciousness.

Personal Context: Will Things Be Different? Before we baptize a young person or adult, we usually put them through a process of study. A very natural question may arise from the baptismal candidate: "Will things be different for me after baptism?" Of course, the best response is with another question. "What would you expect to be different, and why?"

Pentecostals may respond differently from those in other Christian traditions. A visible manifestation of the Spirit, such as speaking in tongues, may accompany the water sign. Others may sense an inner confirmation of the Spirit's presence without an outward display. Persons from the Reformed tradition may consider baptism an outward sign of an invisible grace when they witness the baptism of infants.

However, long-term change, in whatever Christian tradition one worships, will likely depend on reinforcing two fundamental elements of baptism: one's sense of identity and one's mission. In baptism we are affirmed and confirmed as children of God. Our union with God in Christ expressed in baptism anchors our identity in God's character and mission, particularly as these are revealed in Jesus Christ. By adopting spiritual practices that support and nurture our baptismal identity, we can be confirmed in and transformed by our Christ-identity.

MARK ABBOTT

Second Sunday after the Epiphany

Isaiah 49:1–7
Psalm 40:1–11

1 Corinthians 1:1–9
John 1:29–42

Isaiah 49:1–7

¹Listen to me, O coastlands,
    pay attention, you peoples from far away!
The LORD called me before I was born,
    while I was in my mother's womb he named me.
²He made my mouth like a sharp sword,
    in the shadow of his hand he hid me;
he made me a polished arrow,
    in his quiver he hid me away.
³And he said to me, "You are my servant,
    Israel, in whom I will be glorified."
⁴But I said, "I have labored in vain,
    I have spent my strength for nothing and vanity;
yet surely my cause is with the LORD,
    and my reward with my God."

⁵And now the LORD says,
    who formed me in the womb to be his servant,
to bring Jacob back to him,
    and that Israel might be gathered to him,
for I am honored in the sight of the LORD,
    and my God has become my strength—
⁶he says,
"It is too light a thing that you should be my servant
    to raise up the tribes of Jacob
    and to restore the survivors of Israel;
I will give you as a light to the nations,
    that my salvation may reach to the end of the earth."

⁷Thus says the LORD,
    the Redeemer of Israel and his Holy One,
to one deeply despised, abhorred by the nations,
    the slave of rulers,
"Kings shall see and stand up,
    princes, and they shall prostrate themselves,
because of the LORD, who is faithful,
    the Holy One of Israel, who has chosen you."

Commentary 1: Connecting the Reading with Scripture

The passage of Scripture continues the unfolding narrative of the prophet Isaiah. It contains themes that are common to but not exclusive to this particular prophet. These themes form a theological continuum that reveals but also often transcends the personality of the prophet proper. This passage is rather neatly divided into five distinct sections. Verses 1–3 describe the call of the prophet; verses 4–5 present the backdrop of futile pursuits of the prophet; verse 6a introduces the theme of the restoration of Israel; verse 6b points to the expansion of the divine covenant; and the final verse promises the glorification of the prophet because of his faithfulness to the assigned task.

The call section of this text affirms themes common to other call stories in the Old Testament. The prophet claims a prenatal summons to service, and this summons is unmistakable, because the prophet is given a name within the context of this call. This cements the identity of the prophet as inseparable from his commission. The prophet is also prepared because his mouth has been prepared for the task of uttering the Word of the Lord. The prophet is also preserved or hidden by God until the commencement of his prophetic ministry. The final section of the call narrative describes the prophet as a weapon, fashioned for combat against apostasy and infidelity.

The similarity between call narratives in the book of Isaiah and within the prophetic literature in general suggests that these narratives are more than the individual testimonies of a personal call to prophetic service. These narratives may reveal more about the communities out of which they emerged than about the individual to whom they are traditionally attributed. That is, their essential meaning may be more theological than historical. The similarities among these narratives might suggest that they are a communal theological confession rather than an individual testimony. This possibility suggests that the prophetic call is more than an individual vocation; rather, it is part of the theological affirmation of the community of God's election of leadership. This observation provides a corrective to hyperindividualistic and historically isolated views of the prophetic call, without removing the personal dimension and without neglecting the fact that the call is situated within the divine unfolding of history.

The second section situates the prophetic call within the context of the futile pursuits of the prophet. The prophet confesses to failure and frustration with the work. This is the richly textured work of the prophet. The word that goes forth from the prophet's lips is tempered and tested by rejection, refusal, and ridicule. This context of frustration is not to be dismissed as just an obstacle that the prophet must overcome; rather, it says something about the nature of prophecy itself.

The prophetic word, like the creative word, accomplishes its task not primarily in the absence of something, but in the presence of that which resists the word. The word creative or prophetic is not actualized ex nihilo in the sense that this nothingness is passive and lacking true substance. This nothingness is actually something that the prophetic word is cast against and finally overcomes. Prophetic utterance can be understood not primarily as the triumphant victory of the spoken word over the material conditions of the world, but as the word at work against evil and injustice in the world; uncovering and unveiling the presence of God in the world. This prophetic work occurs within the certain promise of God, or as the prophet states, "Yet surely my cause is with the Lord, and my reward is with my God" (v. 4b).

The third section of this text focuses on the theme of restoration. Here the aim of prophecy is the restoration of Israel. This theme, which appears throughout the prophetic corpus, has often been associated with the return of Israel to their native faith and land. It has been argued that the scattering of Israel stands as a stark reminder of the failure of the covenant. In addition, it is possible that the restoration of Israel is not primarily about the redemption of Israel, but serves as a concrete historical expression of who God is—the internal drive toward the restoration of Israel is, in this instance, confirmation that God cannot be truly God while alienated from those whom he loves.

This theme of the restoration of Israel is quickly followed by the divine declaration to extend salvation to the ends of the earth as a fourth theme. The juxtaposition of the restoration of the prototypical community of Israel as a people with the whole earth as a perfected community continues to shape prophetic utterance in both the Old and New Testaments. Any temptation to understand the prophetic word as a call to a protonationalism is countered by the call to take this promise of God to all. Here, the expansion of the divine mandate is symbolized by the inclusion of the Gentiles (*goyim*). It might be helpful for the interpreter here to note that the NSRV names "the end of the earth" (v. 6b) as the extent of God's restoring activity, while other translations specifically mention the "Gentiles" as included.

Perhaps this points to the deep-seated ambivalence with which the people of God struggle as they hear the promise of God extended not only to them, but to those who are not them. It is important to note that over time the term "Gentile" has come to refer not to a specific people but to any people who are not Jewish. Perhaps the radicality of their inclusion in God's restoring work is that God is doing for the Gentiles what God has already done for Israel, that is, declare, "I will take you as my people, and I will be your God" (Exod. 6:7). The call to take the prophetic word to both the original recipients of the covenant and the subsequent recipients of the promise is the dynamic and creative vortex in which the prophet works. It is in this creative space that the one who is called is empowered to employ what Walter Brueggemann calls "the prophetic imagination," where unforeseen possibilities for human flourishing now come into view.[1]

This brings us to the fifth theme in this passage: glorification. The work of the prophet is construed here as focused not on the condemnation of a headstrong and resistant people, but ultimately on the glorification of God. This insight suggests that prophetic speech is to be understood as a kind of worshipful speech. In our contemporary setting, prophetic speech is too often characterized as a kind of political speech concerned with power and the material conditions of life. Here the text states that the result of the work of the prophet is the glorification of God (Isa. 49:7).

Here God is glorified as the prophet witnesses and embodies the power of the word. It is within the context of glorification that the structures of power are confronted, that kings will stand and princes will bow down, because the prophet has been chosen by God. One of the critical insights of the African American understanding of this prophetic tradition is that praise and protest cannot be ultimately separated, and that the exaltation of the One who sends includes the elevation of the one who is sent. Theologically, this passage deepens our understanding of the prophetic task and provides clues to appropriating the task in our own time and place.

JAMES H. EVANS JR.

Commentary 2: Connecting the Reading with the World

On this second Sunday after the public appearance of Jesus in Bethlehem, we again explore the religious ramifications of being a follower of the one who has come to us. Just as the earliest followers read and reflected on the rich Servant Songs of Second Isaiah to sharpen and deepen their understanding of the one they named Lord, so we can still learn much from the poet of the exile of Israel. We remember that his words were spoken and written during the latter part of the sixth-century-BCE exile of the leaders of Judah/Jerusalem in one of the world's greatest cities, Babylon. Most of his hearers knew nothing else but life in that city, having never seen Jerusalem.

Isaiah, with his wide-canvased view of God's ongoing plan and purpose for the chosen people, admonished the exiles to hear and experience YHWH's new word for them in the midst of their exile, an exile that many imagined would never end. The defeated Judeans in Babylon had perhaps given up hope of return to their land and had assumed that Babylon was their home forever. Isaiah challenged them to envision a very different future. In the cauldron of our modern exiles, where our own expectations have been dashed, our dreams made small, our hopes pummeled by harsh realities, the old prophet's words, made fresh for us, may be just what we need.

---

1. See Walter Brueggemann, *The Prophetic Imagination*, 2nd ed. (Minneapolis: Fortress Press, 2001).

This second song of the Servant of YHWH begins with the claim that what is to follow is for all the world's peoples: "Listen to me, coastlands; pay attention, far away peoples! YHWH called me from the belly; from my mother's womb God remembered my name" (Isa. 49:1, my trans.). The NRSV's translation, "he named me," is the general intent of the words, but the more literal "remembered my name" captures an important nuance of the poet. The exiles have been forgotten, as far as they can see, but the remembered Servant suggests that YHWH has not in fact forgotten them. The anguished cry of the poet of Psalm 137 about the absolute necessity of remembering Zion, since he/she feels that YHWH's song cannot be sung in a foreign land, is called directly into question by the prophet. YHWH has not forgotten the chosen ones, and the Servant's remembrance makes that fact certain.

Unlike the quiet and unobtrusive Servant portrait of Isaiah 42, the Servant here is given a mouth like a "sharp sword," like a "polished arrow," albeit hidden in YHWH's hand, secreted away in YHWH's quiver (49:2). These images suggest a Servant who will be active and powerful in the work of God. "And God said to me, 'You are my servant, Israel, in whom I will be made splendid'" (v. 3, my trans.). There has been much argument about the identification here of the Servant as Israel; some Hebrew manuscripts lack the word, but it makes excellent sense in this context. The next verse offers an anguished rejection of YHWH's call by the Servant, indicating an exiled people who cannot join Isaiah in his brightly optimistic announcement of a new and fresh hope and promise for an Israel far from their native land.

A bitter Servant Israel says, in reply to YHWH's remembrance of them, "I have worked in vain; I have squandered my strength for empty nothings, though (supposedly) my justice is with YHWH and my reward with my God" (v. 4, my trans.). My translation is quite different from NRSV; I have connected the bitterness of the first part of verse 4 to the second part, indicating that the exilic people's expectations for YHWH have been shattered; they expected justice and reward from their God, but have received only the pain and suffering

of exile. YHWH answers that bitterness with a larger vision of God's plans for them.

The God who formed them in the womb to be God's Servant, primarily to "bring Jacob back to God," for which task I am to be honored in YHWH's sight, and for which God has become their strength (v. 5), has now a huge surprise in store for these restive and bitter exiles. Apparently, the exiles imagined that what YHWH wanted from them is to restore Jacob, that is, the people and custom of Israel, perhaps to return to Judah and reconstitute the Holy City as YHWH's sacred place once again. It could be that that vision might drag them out of their despair and gain for them the honor and strength of God.

YHWH, through Isaiah, is having none of that! "It is too tiny a thing (merely) to be my servant to raise up the tribes of Jacob, to restore the remnant of Israel. I make you a light to the nations so that my salvation may reach to the ends of the earth" (v. 6, my trans.). Like a thunderclap, YHWH shakes the despondent exiles out of their lethargy by giving to them the largest task they could ever conceive, nothing less than divine responsibility for the entire world. Centuries after YHWH called Abram from Haran to "become a great nation" and to live as one whose life and descendants "will be a blessing to the nations" (Gen. 12:3), now in exile YHWH calls the chosen ones to act in precisely the same way.

Little wonder that the early Christians heard in these literally cosmic words echoes of what Jesus admonished his disciples to do on the mountain of Samaria at the end of the Gospel of Matthew: "Go therefore and make disciples of all nations, . . . teaching them to obey everything that I have commanded you. And remember, I am with you always, to the end of the age" (Matt. 28:19–20). Jesus on the mountain calls his followers to act as Isaiah called his people in exile to act and as YHWH called Abram to act at the very start of the theological history of Israel. This repeated call is one of the golden cords that bind the testaments together in the ongoing work of God with God's people.

Isaiah's song concludes with stirring words about the certain success of this vast work of being a light to the nations. YHWH, "the redeemer and Holy One of Israel" now speaks to the Servant, Israel, "one whose life is despised, abhorred by the nations, a slave of rulers," and says, "Kings will see (the work of becoming a light to the nations) and will stand (in honor); princes will fall on their faces, because of YHWH, the faithful one, the Holy One of Israel, who has chosen you'" (v. 7, my trans.). Just as the Servant Israel has been chosen for this great work, so we, heirs of God's chosen ones, are also chosen to be nothing less than a light for all the world. In our time, it is crucial that we feel our work for Jesus is a part, however small, of that light for the world.

Matthew 25 reminds us that any work for the marginalized is a work for the Christ, a work of the light.

This astonishing passage is perhaps the clearest place one could find in the Bible to suggest that Judaism and Christianity are not about individual salvation. It is about God's call to be a light to the nations, in order that the will and way of God may reach to the whole earth. For those who choose to follow this God into service, the promise of success is offered; nations and their leaders will honor those who act as lights to the nations.

JOHN C. HOLBERT

Second Sunday after the Epiphany

Psalm 40:1–11

¹I waited patiently for the LORD;
    he inclined to me and heard my cry.
²He drew me up from the desolate pit,
    out of the miry bog,
and set my feet upon a rock,
    making my steps secure.
³He put a new song in my mouth,
    a song of praise to our God.
Many will see and fear,
    and put their trust in the LORD.

⁴Happy are those who make
    the LORD their trust,
who do not turn to the proud,
    to those who go astray after false gods.
⁵You have multiplied, O LORD my God,
    your wondrous deeds and your thoughts toward us;
    none can compare with you.
Were I to proclaim and tell of them,
    they would be more than can be counted.

⁶Sacrifice and offering you do not desire,
    but you have given me an open ear.
Burnt offering and sin offering
    you have not required.
⁷Then I said, "Here I am;
    in the scroll of the book it is written of me.
⁸I delight to do your will, O my God;
    your law is within my heart."

⁹I have told the glad news of deliverance
    in the great congregation;
see, I have not restrained my lips,
    as you know, O LORD.
¹⁰I have not hidden your saving help within my heart,
    I have spoken of your faithfulness and your salvation;
I have not concealed your steadfast love and your faithfulness
    from the great congregation.

¹¹Do not, O LORD, withhold
    your mercy from me;
let your steadfast love and your faithfulness
    keep me safe forever.

Connecting the Psalm with Scripture and Worship

Psalm 40 appears to have once been two separate psalms. Verses 1–10 are a psalm of thanksgiving for healing and deliverance from sickness that could have led to death. Verses 12–17 are a psalm of lament and a plea for rescue, with verse 11 acting as a transition that may have been added by an editor. The psalm's final form presents a unified theme, however; the psalmist remembers past deliverance with gratitude, and petitions God to help again. Neither the remembering nor the asking is passive, for the psalmist responds to God's salvific work by saying, "Here I am." Salvation from illness inspires the psalmist to declare her faithfulness to God not only with words (Ps. 40:9–10) but also with deeds. Her very life is now dedicated to doing God's will (v. 8).

In this way, verses 12–17 follow as a natural continuation of the psalmist's dedication to God. Having been saved before, the psalmist anticipates God's saving work again. One interpretation is to read this is as reflective of humanity's ongoing need for salvation. Another is to consider that once one has truly given oneself to God, there is no turning back. Utter dependence on God becomes the way of life.

Psalm 40 is heard in Northern Hemisphere churches during a time that for many can be "the bleak midwinter." Christmas is over, and Easter is months away. Even though the psalm is not one of outright praise and joy, it does offer the potential for both by encouraging reflection on the times in one's own life (or in the life of a congregation) when God provided deliverance. In response to Psalm 40, worshipers might share their own stories of times when God saved them. This could take the form of a liturgy of remembrance that mirrors the psalm, allowing worshipers to give thanks and offer petitions, individually and corporately. This could be a powerful witness in a culture where there are so many other gods claiming to do the same.

Psalm 40 is a fitting response to the day's text from Isaiah 49. The entirety of chapter 49 has been divided into distinct units representing particular genres of literary style. The verses for this Sunday, however, pose the greatest challenge in genre assignment, because of the multitude of themes represented. Scholars agree that verses 1–7 constitute a Servant Song similar to what is heard in Isaiah 42, but within this song we find what resembles a hymn of thanksgiving (Isa. 49:1–3), followed by a note of despair (v. 4), followed by a renewed commitment and commissioning (vv. 5–7).

While not a mirror of Psalm 40, Isaiah 49:1–7 is another take on the same ideas the psalm raises. In some ways it is like two painters offering their own version and unique take on the same scene—the hills and valleys that represent the life of the one who says to God, "Here I am." Isaiah speaks these same words in his call story (Isa. 6:8). Both the prophet and the psalmist find that although the life of faith includes suffering, fear, failure, and sorrow, they can rely on God's promise for help because God has been faithful in the past.

Isaiah 49:1–7 in conversation with Psalm 40, then, offers a number of avenues for preaching. One is to take a wide-angle view of human history and note the ways in which times of darkness and despair are not the last word in the story of human life. As Barack Obama said in his farewell address, "Yes, our progress has been uneven. . . . For every two steps forward, it often feels we take one step back. But the long sweep of America has been defined by forward motion."[1] His words echo those of the Reverend Dr. Martin Luther King Jr., who said, "The arc of the moral universe is long, but it bends toward justice." A sermon taking this approach might lead to a time of commissioning, drawing on Psalm 40:5–8. How can we respond to the challenges of today's world? What are our prayers for deliverance, and how are we called to serve, even in spite of our past failings? For some, present struggles overshadow memories of the good that God has done for us. How can we, in the midst of life's challenges, believe the promises of God? When seen through the long view of all God has done before, how do we find courage to persevere in the present?

ERIN KEYS

---

1. Barack Obama, "President Obama's Farewell Address," January 10, 2017, https://obamawhitehouse.archives.gov/farewell.

1 Corinthians 1:1–9

¹Paul, called to be an apostle of Christ Jesus by the will of God, and our brother Sosthenes,

²To the church of God that is in Corinth, to those who are sanctified in Christ Jesus, called to be saints, together with all those who in every place call on the name of our Lord Jesus Christ, both their Lord and ours:

³Grace to you and peace from God our Father and the Lord Jesus Christ.

⁴I give thanks to my God always for you because of the grace of God that has been given you in Christ Jesus, ⁵for in every way you have been enriched in him, in speech and knowledge of every kind—⁶just as the testimony of Christ has been strengthened among you—⁷so that you are not lacking in any spiritual gift as you wait for the revealing of our Lord Jesus Christ. ⁸He will also strengthen you to the end, so that you may be blameless on the day of our Lord Jesus Christ. ⁹God is faithful; by him you were called into the fellowship of his Son, Jesus Christ our Lord.

Commentary 1: Connecting the Reading with Scripture

This reading introduces us to the troubled church in Corinth. The troubles themselves are not named directly in these verses. It may be, however, that the most obvious connection to the contemporary church of this or any text in 1 Corinthians lies in those troubles. It is unlikely that listeners will grasp how surprising the material is in our reading, if they know nothing of those troubles. We might think that our reading—the address and salutation to the Corinthians, together with an introductory thanksgiving, all of which is standard in Paul's epistles—is merely formulaic. It contains surprisingly rich preaching material, however, with many connections to the contemporary church.

Most of the troubles and conflicts in Corinth can be paralleled in our churches, from disputes over doctrine to lawsuits to wildly inappropriate sexual behavior. Even with troubles in Corinth that are not exactly paralleled today, as for example, drunkenness at the Lord's Table, a little thought will show that there are present difficulties that are similar in some essential characteristic to a conflict in Corinth. We may not see drunkenness at communion but we cannot claim that there is not addiction to alcohol

in our churches! It may not be inaccurate to see in Corinth a church of drunks, sex fiends, and argumentative troublemakers. There is likewise no shortage of such folk in the contemporary church. Should the church be defined by its troubles or by something else?

It would be difficult to know how many contemporary churches experience conflict, partly because it is difficult to draw the line between normal friction and those more painful troubles that can be defined as conflict. Instinctively, however, we know there is a great deal of conflict in our churches. If, by the mercy of God, the particular congregation in which we preach does not experience Corinth-style troubles, we do not have to look very far into the wider church to see them. Few preachers will have difficulty finding illustrative material here.

At some point, preachers must name those troubles. The homiletical challenge lies in deciding how extensively they should be described. There is, however, a surprising reason for not accentuating the negative overmuch. Paul does not begin his letter with the troubles in the church. Rather, he greets the church in astoundingly positive terms and then, in the major part of our reading, gives thanks for the church in Corinth. Naming the troubles may be necessary in order to help listeners grasp how surprising the otherwise ordinary material in our reading actually is.

The content of that material tells us that trouble should not be the key word of the sermon. This observation may give the contemporary preacher not just the content of the sermon but the strategy for it. Paul seems to think that the Corinthians needed not to be "told off" but rather "told who." That is, they must be reminded *who they are* and *whose they are*. Perhaps that is also the case with the churches to whom we preach. Our churches too may have a theological identity problem, and it may be the preacher's task to remind us who we are.

The epistle begins, then, with identity language; the senders, Paul, together with Sosthenes, and receivers are named in the address of the letter. As is characteristic of Paul, these statements are lengthy and theologically weighty. Paul is "called to be an apostle by the will of God." The call that gives his identity comes from God and because of that call Paul is an apostle already (cf. Galatians). Then the receivers are named. They are not in the first place drunks, sex fiends, and argumentative troublemakers but, in the NRSV, "saints." Different words appear in other translations, but all affirm the holiness of the Christians in Corinth. The most important thing in Corinth is not the conflict but the call. The language of call is emphasized here in the initial words of the epistle and again in verse 9 at the climax of our reading.

It is vital to note that just as Paul is already an apostle, the Corinthians are saints now, not in some future where they will be better Christians than they are in the present . . . if they pay attention to what they are told to do. The structure of what is said about the saints is identical to what Paul says about his own apostleship. Moreover, the holiness of the saints is a gift of God, as is the call to apostleship.

If you are developing this theme in the sermon, it will be necessary to be clear that Paul does not use the word "saint" the way it is used in our society. To us a saint is a spiritual superstar, one who has achieved great things for God.

Manifestly, the Corinthians are scrubs, not superstars—if they are defined by their own achievement. They are, however, saints because God has called them and sanctified them. The achievement belongs to God, not to them, and it is from God's call that their identity is derived.

The identity language of the epistle extends beyond Corinth, however. The Corinthians are saints together with all those who call on God in every place and, one might add, at all times. Perhaps this would be a useful reminder when preaching in one of our many small and declining congregations. Our fellowship is not limited to the handful scattered about the empty pews of a local sanctuary.

The key connection in our reading is one of a continued identity. When God looks at our church, as is the case with Corinth, God does not see failures and troublemakers, but saints.

Paul then greets the church with two more weighty theological terms, common in his letters, "grace" and "peace." It is easy to pass over greetings. Who thinks about common niceties of our day like saying, "Good morning" and "Good-bye"? Yet these formalities are profoundly meaningful if we pause to consider them. Certainly "grace" and "peace" are even more profound greetings. What do grace and peace look like in the life of a church afflicted with many troubles and yet filled with called saints?

The remainder of our reading consists of a thanksgiving for the Corinthians: "I give thanks to my God always for you" (1 Cor. 1:4)—more precisely, for the grace that God has given them. In the contemporary church we spend much energy naming our problems. What would church life be like if we began, as Paul does, by naming not our troubles, but the ways we have been blessed? One of the blessings may be of particular interest. Paul gives thanks that the Corinthians "are not lacking in any spiritual gift" (v. 7). Later in the epistle we learn that quarrels over spiritual gifts are a major problem of the church. It might be interesting to reflect on the idea that the reality behind some of our problems in the church might actually be blessings, if used rightly. That too is a connection that might be preached.

Many of us feel a sense of disappointment about our Christian life. We know that our troubles and conflicts do not reflect well on the Savior. When God looks at us, God sees not failures, but saints. Who are we to disagree with God?

The Corinthians are saints, not because of their own efforts, but because God has chosen them, has reached out and called them and made them his own. Who was Paul to disagree with God?

STEPHEN FARRIS

Commentary 2: Connecting the Reading with the World

The community of Christ-followers in Corinth may have been "Paul's problem child," as Michael J. Gorman puts it, but no one would guess that from the way 1 Corinthians opens.[1] Paul and his coauthor Sosthenes affirm the audience's identity as saints and offer gratitude to God for the grace and blessings that were manifest in Corinth. Later, the letter will repeatedly rebuke the Corinthians for the factionalism, competition, and spiritual smugness that Paul believes were poisoning their community, but the opening verses make it clear that the looming criticisms do not invalidate the Corinthians' basic standing as people whom God has declared holy. Apparently, churches can grow unsteadily into their identity, manage disagreements, receive correction, and learn together what it means to live the Christian life in particular contexts without anyone having to call into doubt either the authenticity of someone else's commitment or the effectiveness of God's grace.

Attending to the opening chapters of 1 Corinthians during the season after the Epiphany offers congregations opportunities to reflect on what it means for them to manifest God's grace in a world that often struggles to detect it. Paul might approve of this seasonal strategy, since he devoted much of his own pastoral energy toward helping churches live in accordance with God's gracious work in Christ. Taken as a whole, 1 Corinthians urges its original audience to consider themselves as people who stand at the threshold of the conclusion of an old age and the dawning of a new age (10:11; cf. 2 Cor. 5:17).

Because of Christ, everything has changed. Old conventions and values give way to new wisdom God has revealed. Believers live in the light of new realities God has instituted through the execution and resurrection of Jesus. God brings Christ-followers into a new way of being as they await another kind of epiphany—a final one, in which "the revealing [*apokalypsis*] of our Lord Jesus Christ" (1 Cor. 1:7) will occur. In the meantime, believers learn how to express the peculiar and at times countercultural good news in their collective existence. Paul recognizes that for the church in Corinth to learn this, they will need help. He wastes no time offering it.

The Communion of Saints—with Gifts. The help comes at the letter's beginning, as Paul reminds the Corinthians who they are. He instructs them about basic aspects of Christian identity. As a result, several vital ecclesial connections can be derived from the opening verses, as Paul subtly informs the Corinthians of what it means to be the church of Christ. For one thing, there are no individual saints, only a "communion of saints," as the Apostles' Creed puts it, for all whom God has made holy participate in God's sanctifying "together with all those who in every place call on the name of our Lord Jesus Christ" (1:2). Likewise, Paul notes his teamwork with Sosthenes in the opening verse and later refers to his partnership with Timothy (4:17).

Later in the letter Paul will insist that unity is an essential mark of the church, not because he sees unity as an expression of positive collegiality or good manners, but because unity declares a key and organic aspect of Christian identity. Believers belong to Christ (3:23; 6:15; 15:23); therefore they belong to one another (8:6; 12:12), together forming the body of Christ (12:27). It is difficult for preachers and teachers

---

1. Michael J. Gorman, *Apostle of the Crucified Lord: A Theological Introduction to Paul and His Letters* (Grand Rapids: Eerdmans, 2004), 227.

to overstate the importance of this theological insight in a culture that too often sacrifices unity in its eagerness to shame difference, victimize the vulnerable, idolize majority rule, and identify scapegoats.

In addition, the church is an arena—though certainly not the sole arena—for a range of spiritual gifts that God bestows. Paul writes that God does not leave the church to its own devices but richly equips it through spiritual speech, knowledge, and gifts. In later chapters Paul will discuss spiritual gifts at length, but here he signals that gifts belong to and benefit the whole community and its ministry. As is usually the case in all of Paul's letters, every instance of "you" in these opening verses is plural in Greek. The letter speaks to the church as a corporate entity. Taken together, the members of the church possess every spiritual gift the church might possibly need.

The solutions to the problems Paul will identify in Corinth, like the solutions many churches seek today, do not require a commanding hero to rise up and take charge; nor will any heavy-handed guidance and scolding from Paul do the trick. He will not impart techniques for effective leadership, other than to urge the Corinthians to look to one another for the gifts and grace that God has bestowed on them so they can thrive. His idea of thriving, however, will probably not correspond to familiar standards of strength and success. Paul will make that clear later, beginning in next Sunday's lection, when he discusses "the message about the cross" and its apparent foolishness (1:18).

Discovering Our True Selves in Christ. We misunderstand Paul and what he says it means to exist "in Christ Jesus" if we portray him as someone trying to build up Christian communities through ethical exhortations or organizational efficiencies. Paul's passion is theological encounter; he urges churches to inhabit a gospel that involves actual participation with God in Christ. Susan Grove Eastman shines light on Paul's perspective and illuminates why the unity of the saints matters so much in Paul's *theological*—or *christological*—imagination: "the change that takes place as persons are reconstituted in Christ is not discovered through an inward look for the Spirit within some core self, but rather in the interactions that take place between believers."[2] In other words, God brings people into a new identity, one established solely on God's gracious terms, as we encounter Christ in one another on an ongoing basis. To know who we are in Christ, we need one another.

As a result, there is a sacramental character to Christian community, which might sound astounding to the multitudes in the general population who have been burned by congregations and the sheer meanness of some communities. Nevertheless, each of us lives into the new self that God has freed us to be, not by retreating into ourselves, but by embracing our connections to others. There is no purely individualistic spirituality in this vision of Christian existence. Perhaps ideals of the self-sufficient maverick and the isolated "spiritual" sojourner would compel Paul today to dash off more letters if he could.

The biblical notion of believers *together* undergoing transformation as an act of God among them is not necessarily unique or even so peculiar. Philosopher Timothy Chappell expresses a similar outlook when he describes communion with others as hardly a burdensome intrusion but a gift: "Each of us becomes a mind, and a person, only by being 'always already' in relation with other persons, both human and divine, as a precondition of her own mindedness. Personhood, in short, is not something I achieve on my own; it is a gift, the gift of me to others."[3] The journey of Christian sainthood follows a similar trail—and it is wide.

MATTHEW L. SKINNER

2. Susan Grove Eastman, *Paul and the Person: Reframing Paul's Anthropology* (Grand Rapids: Eerdmans, 2017), 170. Eastman's focus in this quotation is on the theological imagination expressed in Galatians 2, but the point also applies well to the issues in 1 Corinthians.

3. Timothy Chappell, "Knowledge of Persons," *European Journal for Philosophy of Religion* 5, no. 4 (2013): 18; quoted in Eastman, *Paul and the Person*, 171.

John 1:29–42

²⁹The next day he saw Jesus coming toward him and declared, "Here is the Lamb of God who takes away the sin of the world! ³⁰This is he of whom I said, 'After me comes a man who ranks ahead of me because he was before me.' ³¹I myself did not know him; but I came baptizing with water for this reason, that he might be revealed to Israel." ³²And John testified, "I saw the Spirit descending from heaven like a dove, and it remained on him. ³³I myself did not know him, but the one who sent me to baptize with water said to me, 'He on whom you see the Spirit descend and remain is the one who baptizes with the Holy Spirit.' ³⁴And I myself have seen and have testified that this is the Son of God."

³⁵The next day John again was standing with two of his disciples, ³⁶and as he watched Jesus walk by, he exclaimed, "Look, here is the Lamb of God!" ³⁷The two disciples heard him say this, and they followed Jesus. ³⁸When Jesus turned and saw them following, he said to them, "What are you looking for?" They said to him, "Rabbi" (which translated means Teacher), "where are you staying?" ³⁹He said to them, "Come and see." They came and saw where he was staying, and they remained with him that day. It was about four o'clock in the afternoon. ⁴⁰One of the two who heard John speak and followed him was Andrew, Simon Peter's brother. ⁴¹He first found his brother Simon and said to him, "We have found the Messiah" (which is translated Anointed). ⁴²He brought Simon to Jesus, who looked at him and said, "You are Simon son of John. You are to be called Cephas" (which is translated Peter).

Commentary 1: Connecting the Reading with Scripture

John's prologue (John 1:1–18), where both Jesus and John are first introduced, winds together the foundational claims of this Gospel: Jesus is the Word in the flesh, through whom all things came into being, as well as light and life for all people (vv. 1–5). He embodies God's glory and makes God known (v. 18). John, on the other hand, is a man, sent from God to testify to the light, so that all might come to believe (vv. 6–8) and become children of God (v. 12). The two characters first introduced in the prologue, Jesus and John, continue to be the focus of attention in John 1:19–42, where John's witness comes to fruition and Jesus begins gathering disciples.

When John is challenged by priests and Levites from Jerusalem to account for his ministry, he persistently refuses the boxes—wondrous though they are—into which the people from Jerusalem seek to locate and define him: he is not the Messiah, nor Elijah (contrary to

his depiction in the Synoptics), nor the prophet. He is simply "the voice of one crying out in the wilderness," who is to "make straight the way of the Lord" (citing Isa. 40:3). The two sections that comprise John 1:29–42 focus first on the continuation of John's story (John 1:29–34), then on the gathering of Jesus' first disciples (vv. 35–42). Along the way, the evangelist continues to develop characterizations, themes, and motifs that were first set forth in the prologue and that will be further developed throughout the Gospel, including Jesus' identity as "coming one," "Lamb of God," and "the one who baptizes with the Holy Spirit," as well as the themes of knowing, seeing, seeking, following, and abiding.

John has a singular view of his call, which comes straight from God. John 1:29–34 is built upon the literary conventions of an initiatory prophetic vision followed by the seer's denials of his adequacy or worthiness. John persistently

Beholding, We Become like Christ

There is but one requirement in the text, and that declares the grand spiritual requirement of the soul. "Behold the Lamb of God which taketh away the sin of the world." Yes, plain, simple, trivial as it seems, yet all man has to do is to look and to see. Surely, you can understand this. Is it not clear and certain that the Divine Father would have us look no longer anywhere else in the universe save to His blessed Son? And is it not true that the eye of man's soul does wander, the world over, for safety, save to the Son of Man?

But now the invitation comes to every soul, "Behold the Lamb of God." Summon all the scattered, wasted powers of your heart, and fasten them upon the Christ. He is able and willing to save every man from himself and from his sins, in time and for eternity.

You ask, perchance, have we nothing to do but to look? And what is there in looking that can serve to change the heart or save the mind?

Why, don't you see that if you sit and gaze upon the Lamb of God, look with all your heart, and mind, and soul, look with all your sorrow and desires, look with all your tears and all your longings upon your Saviour, that this is believing in Him and accepting Him as your Master and your all?

Salvation comes by looking. Sight is the most vivid and most transforming of all of our senses, the soul's mightiest organ for apprehension. . . . So the Bible teaches us that by beholding a thing we become like unto it. Thus, beholding the Lamb of God saves men. If you want salvation, look to Jesus.

Alexander Crummell, "The Lamb of God," in *The Greatness of Christ, and Other Sermons; by Alex. Crummell* (New York: T. Whittaker, 1882), 68–69.

---

denies that his witness has anything to do with his own special insight or character. Twice he says he did not know Jesus (vv. 31, 33). Instead, his witness concerning Jesus comes from God-given vision. The Fourth Gospel, in fact, reports its version of the baptism of Jesus not directly, but as a vision experienced by John, focusing exclusively on the Spirit descending on Jesus (vv. 32–33). John says that the sole purpose of his ministry is to reveal to Israel the Lamb of God/Son of God, who baptizes with the Spirit (vv. 29–34).

The vision of the descent of the Spirit on Jesus is the foundation upon which everything else John sees and knows is based. This rendering effectively removes John's witness from the realm of human actions, intellect, observations, and categories. With this we learn the first of many lessons tucked into this passage: the single focus of John's witness, and that of the church, is Jesus. The evangelist resists any inclination to define either Jesus or John with reference to any scheme or typology (even biblical), any human leader or hero, any party or ideology. How often are we held captive by our own idealistic and often idolatrous models in rendering him

today? How does the church continue to bear witness solely to this Jesus, who cannot be contained within human ideals and categories?

God uses us as witnesses not because we fit the right profile or have the right skill set. Seeing and naming what God is doing is about *God*, not about us, just as John's witness is not about himself, but about *Jesus*. The other passages assigned for this Sunday (Isa. 49:1–7; Ps. 40:1–11; and 1 Cor. 1:1–9) all provide models of witness and testimony. In Isaiah 49, in particular, the same Israel that has "labored in vain" and squandered its strength in emptiness (Isa. 49:4) now speaks of its own calling of restoration, not only for its own sake, but to be a light to the nations, so that God's salvation might reach the ends of the earth. In Psalm 40 also, God's actions are the source of the singer's vision, and in 1 Corinthians 1, God's grace leads to the recipients' enrichment in speech and knowledge, not for their own sake, but for the "testimony of Christ" (1 Cor. 1:3–6). Together these readings invite us to explore the nature of call and witness, but especially the need to learn to trust God as the source, sustainer, and focus of our witness.

The content of John's vision is, of course, also crucial. John focuses on the descent of the Spirit onto Jesus. When he then sees Jesus, however, he identifies him as "the Lamb of God" (John 1:29, 36) who removes the world's burden of sin. Whatever else "take away the sin of the world" might mean, it is surely a promise of liberation for the whole of the cosmos. "Sin of the world" (not "sins") refers less to personal choices and wrongs than to the condition in which humanity exists when idolatry, alienation, and violence become normative factors in our lives. The Jesus with whom the Spirit abides comes to bring an end to those forces. The divine revelation of the Lamb of God/Son of God is a cosmic event. The evangelist does not see this liberation as something we still await, but as already underway, albeit visible at this point in the Gospel story only to the Baptizer.

Finally, the evangelist's language in this passage invites us to slow down and reflect on the verbs around which the narrative is ordered, which together invite us to grapple with the deep yet ineffable sense of presence that pervades the whole passage. John sees Jesus "coming toward him" and names him as "the one coming after me" (1:29–30; cf. 1:15; 1:27). This echoes and expands upon the earlier designation of the Word as "the true light, coming into the world" (1:9). The "one coming" then turns toward (in 20:14–15 a move toward intimacy) two of John's disciples who have begun to follow him to "come and see" where he abides. The evangelist here evokes the image of God coming to dwell with God's people (e.g., Lev. 26:11–12; Ezek. 37:27; Rev. 21:3).

English translations typically render the Greek verb *menō* ("to remain, rest, stay, or abide"; used five times in 1:29–42) in two ways, thereby obscuring the connections between the two portions of this passage. In verses 32–33, John twice says that the Spirit of God descended and "remained" on Jesus, whereas in verses 38–39, the two disciples ask Jesus where he is "staying" and then "stay" with him that day. If, however, we translate *menō* consistently, then the Spirit "abides" or "dwells" with Jesus, and the disciples ask him not merely where he is staying but where he "abides." They, in turn, "abide" with him that day. This may also help us make sense of Jesus' initial question to the would-be disciples, his first words in this Gospel: "What are you seeking?" (v. 38). They reply, "Where do you dwell/abide?" Later they claim that they have "found" the "Messiah" (v. 41).

The one with whom the Spirit dwells has become the focal point of all the movement in the passage, the locus of abiding, rest, and remaining. This is, then, not only a story of calling and witness, but of seeking and abiding. It recalls in very broad strokes the goal of the Sabbath, rest and abiding in God's presence, and the realization of God's presence with the whole of creation. What are we looking for? Human success? Peace on the world's terms? A dwelling place with God who has come to us?

STANLEY P. SAUNDERS

Commentary 2: Connecting the Reading with the World

Social and Ethical Context: The Lamb of God. When John declares, "Here is the Lamb of God who takes away the sin of the world!" (John 1:29), John is evoking an image of sacrifice. Such sacrificial language and imagery continues elsewhere in the NT narrative. One way to connect this imagery to listeners today is to discuss the role of sacrifice in working for justice. Although Jesus Christ is the Lamb of God, that role did not end with him. Christ's followers continue suffering with and on behalf of others, so that they might be forgiven, liberated, and empowered for new life. The apostle Paul said: "I am completing what is lacking in Christ's afflictions for the sake of his body" (Col. 1:24).

One of the ways Christ's followers do this is through advocacy. People who stand up against socially accepted norms or practices that violate human dignity and perpetuate injustice suffer, so that these "sins" may be taken away. Martin Luther King Jr. led a nonviolent revolution against racial injustice and inequality. He was ultimately killed in the process. Was he not a lamb of God? Nelson Mandela spent twenty-five years in prison and contributed to the downfall of apartheid in South Africa. Mother Teresa of Calcutta treated those tossed out as useless refuse as though they were Jesus himself and offered an alternative vision for humanity. Persons well-known, as well as Christians whose names we may not recognize, are continually working on behalf of others who have been impacted by the sin of the world.

John the Baptist and the apostle Paul are right. Jesus is the Lamb of God who takes away the sin of the world, and that work continues through Jesus' followers.

Ecclesial Context: Revelation Is Missional, Not Egocentric.

John the Baptist said: "I myself did not know him; but I came baptizing with water for this reason, that he might be revealed" (v. 31). John probably baptized lots of people, but he was looking for that one special person. In the church we baptize lots of people. We are not looking for just one special person, or trying to create celebrity, but we are looking for signs of God's special calling on people. Then, once they are identified, we can mentor them to fulfill God's special mission for their lives.

Epiphany is about God's self-revelation in the incarnation. John the Baptist says, "I came baptizing with water for this reason, that he might be revealed" (v. 31). Often, once the secret is revealed, we disconnect and lose interest. As soon as we know Jesus is the Lamb of God who takes away the sin of the world, or that he is the only begotten Son of God, the revelation becomes old news, just another data point.

I suspect this disconnect is due in part to our culture's individualistic, egocentric approach to identity. We think of identity as coming to self-consciousness, and life is about self-actualization and self-fulfillment. Although this happens in the context of broader society, the individual remains at the heart of what life is all about.

This is not the case with the revelation of Jesus as the Lamb of God. John the Baptist had a mission greater than himself. He came to prepare the way for another. His life was not just about John. Jesus as the Lamb of God obviously

has a world-encompassing purpose. It was certainly not all about him!

Andrew and Simon were followers of John the Baptist, and when they heard him say that Jesus is the Lamb of God, they followed Jesus and asked him, "Where are you staying?" They progressed from being fishermen, to being followers of John, to becoming disciples of Jesus. For both of them life was about more than the self.

John, Jesus, Andrew, and Simon all go through a process of discovering their respective identities. For each of them their individual sense of identity and meaning was inextricably tied to a purpose, a calling, a mission. Each of them was part of something much bigger than themselves, because they were connected to Someone much bigger.

When Jesus realized that Andrew and Simon were tagging along, he turned and asked them: "What are you looking for?" This is precisely the question each of us must answer for ourselves. What are you looking for out of life? When you come to church, or when you pray, what are you looking for? Often we need revelation to come to a true answer.

Epiphany is about God's self-revelation in the incarnation. In this story we see that the *who* and the *why* of life are connected. Jesus' missional purpose as the Lamb of God is connected to who he is as Son of God, and vice versa. We come to understand that identity is not primarily an egocentric discovery but a missional revelation. We are connected to Someone much bigger than us, and our lives take on meaning as we engage in God's mission. We find our true epiphany when we find our place in God's world.

Personal Context: Symbols.

God told John the Baptist: "He on whom you see the Spirit descend and remain is the one who baptizes with the Holy Spirit" (1:33). It so happens that the Spirit descended like a dove. "I saw the Spirit descending from heaven like a dove, and it remained on him" (v. 32).

The dove is one of the most recognizable symbols of the Holy Spirit, even to this day. Almost all churches have it enshrined in their art. God told John to watch for the Spirit's descent on someone, but God did not tell John in what way the Spirit's descent would be visible. It must have been a great Aha! moment when John saw the dove light on Jesus.

Recently I was in a conversation about the sacrament of Holy Communion, and someone said, "It's only a symbol." I replied, "Oh, but symbols are necessary!" I believe my conversation partner was reducing symbol to its external representation. Symbols combine a physical or artistic representation with a deeper meaning. My wedding ring is just a circle of metal, but its shape and content (a precious metal) point to both a life reality and an aspiration and commitment. The symbol represents and reminds me of the depth of meaning.

Rituals are acted-out symbols. They not only remind us of the realities but also can help us connect to the deeper dimension that they represent. Kneeling in prayer often helps people connect with God in a special way, for example. The external posture helps orient the internal one.

The lectionary reading contains another important symbol, the renaming of Simon. "'You are to be called Cephas' (which is translated Peter)" (v. 42). In New Testament times one's name communicated many things. In an honor and shame society, one's reputation became associated with one's name. In this way, one's name could be associated with one's character.

In today's society, identifying oneself as a Christian communicates a myriad of possible meanings, not all of them positive. It is vital that by our actions we provide the content for the name. Our actions are visible symbols of the deeper meaning of the name. So we should live in such a way that when we call ourselves Christian, people associate the proper meaning to the name. In this way, we can recover the power of the name and the symbol.

MARK ABBOTT

Third Sunday after the Epiphany

Isaiah 9:1–4
Psalm 27:1, 4–9

1 Corinthians 1:10–18
Matthew 4:12–23

Isaiah 9:1–4

¹But there will be no gloom for those who were in anguish. In the former time he brought into contempt the land of Zebulun and the land of Naphtali, but in the latter time he will make glorious the way of the sea, the land beyond the Jordan, Galilee of the nations.

²The people who walked in darkness
   have seen a great light;
those who lived in a land of deep darkness—
   on them light has shined.
³You have multiplied the nation,
   you have increased its joy;
they rejoice before you
   as with joy at the harvest,
   as people exult when dividing plunder.
⁴For the yoke of their burden,
   and the bar across their shoulders,
   the rod of their oppressor,
   you have broken as on the day of Midian.

Commentary 1: Connecting the Reading with Scripture

This text draws the reader into the prophetic announcement that, in spite of the sufferings and apparent abandonment by God, divine mercy has triumphed and will continue to triumph over earthly misery. The announcement is made against the backdrop of the plight of the humbled lands of Zebulun and Naphtali.

These two biblical territories and their tribal origins provide a historical context for the writer as well as a theological point of reference. Historically, Zebulun was the tribe of Israel given a specific territory in the book of Joshua. This territory was located at the southern end of Galilee and bordered the Sea of Galilee. It represented a kind of outpost at the edge of the land of the Gentiles. Theologically important is that the name Zebulun means "dwelling; habitation, or home." It suggests that from the outset of its existence as a newly liberated nation, Israel would have to find its home on the boundary with other nations.

Naphtali was borne by Rachel's servant, Bilhah, to Jacob. In Genesis 30:8 NIV, Naphtali's birth led Rachel to exclaim, "I have had a great struggle with my sister, and I have won." Thus "Naphtali" means "my struggle." Naphtali has a longer and more checkered biblical history than Zebulun. There are moments of greatness and episodes of shame. This tribe showed extraordinary bravery under Gideon and in support of King David. There were other moments marked by apostasy and disobedience. However, the theological significance of Naphtali is its association with Galilee, which was despised, and with Nazareth, from which nothing good could come (John 7:40–42; 1:46). (Interestingly, neither the text nor the supporting literature mentions the geographical location of Naphtali. Perhaps its spiritual and social location is more important to the writer and thus the readers of this.)

This text suggests that God can and does exalt the humble and employs that which is despised to fulfill divine purposes. It sets the stage for the appearance of one who is acclaimed as the Messiah from the most unexpected circumstances, one who has a home among the Gentiles and is truly "humble in heart" (Matt. 11:29).

In the Gospel of Matthew, this text is used to announce the beginning of the ministry of Jesus: Here the preacher should recall verses of the fourth chapter, in which Jesus travels "by the lake in the area of Zebulun and Naphtali—to fulfill what was said through the prophet Isaiah: 'Land of Zebulun and land of Naphtali . . . the people living in darkness have seen a great light'" (Matt. 4:13–16 NIV). It is not accidental that for the writer of the Gospel of Matthew the history of these two tribes and territories might be the setting for the inauguration of Jesus' ministry. Speaking to a Jewish audience primarily, the writer sets the inauguration of Jesus' ministry in the volatile and perilous context of communities that are marginalized, under siege, and oppressed.

It is interesting to note that the Lukan version of the inauguration of Jesus' ministry is framed by another passage from Isaiah: "The spirit of the Lord GOD is upon me, because the LORD has anointed me; he has sent me to bring good news to the oppressed, to bind up the brokenhearted, to proclaim liberty to the captives, and release to the prisoners" (Isa. 61:1). While the Lukan annunciation carries powerful themes of liberation and release, the Matthean annunciation picks up the themes of sorrow and grief following the imprisonment and impending execution of John the Baptist. John's apocalyptic message of righteousness and the approaching kingdom of heaven provided a distinct texture to the identity and mission of Jesus.

The historical tropes of Zebulun and Naphtali, with their theological and cultic significations of both "home" and "struggle," established a bridge from the prophetic promise of God to the appearance of the fulfillment of that promise. Zebulun and Naphtali were among the first tribes from the northern kingdom of Israel carried away into captivity by the Assyrians. This event, happening some seven hundred years before the Gospel of Matthew was written, was so traumatic that Zebulun and Naphtali as names for these tribes and territories receded from the conscious memory of the people. At the time of Jesus' ministerial annunciation, these territories had ceased to be called by these names. By recalling these names, the Gospel writer draws into conscious memory experiences in which the preaching of Jesus finds fertile soil.

These names may also be potent symbolic summaries of the two Scripture passages that precede them in the Matthean narrative. Jesus' baptism by John and the divine confirmation of Jesus that follows establish Jesus' place within the story of Israel. This baptism provides a textual resting place that Jesus can claim as "home." The next passage, Jesus' temptation in the wilderness, introduces the idea of "struggle" and testing as inescapable, even for the one who has found a home in the divine will.

These themes, home and struggle, symbolized by Zebulun and Naphtali, suggest a fresh theological insight, namely, that we do not simply struggle to find home, but that once home is found, struggle ensues. It is possible that apocalyptic struggle and eschatological striving are not aimed at some final consummation and beatific realization of home, but that it is the very grasping of home as where we reside that inaugurates the struggle to confirm what has already been established.

It was perhaps this notion that C. H. Dodd was attempting to express in his articulation of "realized eschatology." Charles Harold Dodd (1884–1973) was an influential Welsh New Testament scholar and theologian who proposed that many of the New Testament verses that appear to point to a future eschatological event actually posit a "realized eschatology" by which believers are challenged to live as if the kingdom of God were already present. The messianic hopes of the Israelites, for many, prefigured in the writings of the prophet Isaiah and confirmed in the appearance of Jesus of Nazareth, were often couched in terms of the appearance of some future kingdom. This is one way to understand the kingdom of heaven language of Matthew and the kingdom of God language in the other Gospels. However, it is possible that the kingdom here sought might be found among the suppressed and dismissed memories of the people.

Recalling the names of Zebulun and Naphtali could be a call to the hearers to look within their experiences and not just beyond them to find evidence that God is keeping God's divine promises. This lectionary passage concludes by exhorting the hearers to remember God's actions "in the day of Midian's defeat" (v. 4 NIV). Midian's defeat was led by an insignificant and humble, if not reluctant, leader, Gideon. It reminds them that God's promises are already being fulfilled and that struggle is simply confirmation of such. Read in tandem with its Lukan counterpart, where Jesus' identity as liberator of the poor and oppressed is emphasized, the Matthean passage places the theological focus on Jesus Christ as reconciler.

Here, reconciliation is not primarily concerned with resolving the theological conundrums that have occupied Christian thinkers for centuries, but with reuniting a people with their past. A people whose alienation is symbolized by significant names long forgotten are now called upon to remember who God is. Thus recovering this passage of prophetic Scripture from Isaiah and employing it to frame the beginning rather than the conclusion of Jesus' ministry allowed the Gospel writer to powerfully connect the past of the Israelites with their hopes for the future in Jesus Christ.

JAMES H. EVANS JR.

Commentary 2: Connecting the Reading with the World

"The people walking in darkness have seen a great light" (Isa. 9:1, my trans. In many English translations, this verse appears at 9:2, but the Hebrew 8:23 is prose, while 9:1 in the Hebrew is poetry, suggesting a change in context). These famous words begin the familiar oracle from the prophet Isaiah that includes the announcement of the birth of "a son given for us" (v. 6), language that the earliest Christians seized as a harbinger of the coming of the Christ at Bethlehem. Though the focus has often been on the reference to the son and his identity as "Wonderful Counselor, Mighty God, Everlasting Father, Prince of Peace" (v. 6), the first four verses of the text contain crucial information about precisely what this son will bring with his coming. On this Third Sunday after Epiphany, we pursue further the full meaning of the coming of the Christ into the world and how Isaiah's proclamation has enriched both Jewish and Christian understandings of the continually surprising work of God.

YHWH has from the foundations of the nation searched for ways to implement righteousness and justice in the land, and thereby to "bring salvation (wholeness) to the ends of the earth" (49:6, my trans.). Much of the prophecy of Isaiah, both in his eighth-century-BCE person and his sixth-century-BCE successor, looks forward to a time when darkness will give way to light. For the former, that darkness took the historical form of the Assyrian destruction of northern Israel and the subsequent threat to Judah and Jerusalem; for the latter, the exile to Babylon was the great darkness to be overcome. In addition, especially for First Isaiah, the refusal of the people to follow the ways of YHWH, their continual oppression of the poor in their midst, their denial of the cause of the widow, orphan, and immigrant among them, were further signs of darkness in the nation (1:4; 3:13–15; 5:1–7, among many other texts). Of course idolatry, the source of this evil, was ever a sore reality among the people of God, an idolatry that did not end with the exile (44:9–20). Yet Isaiah foresees light breaking in on a darkened land.

I have translated the opening phrase, "the people walking in darkness," rather than the more traditional "the people who walked" (NRSV). The literal grammar is a participle, suggesting ongoing behavior, not past behavior. Those to whom Isaiah speaks are those who are now walking in darkness, and who need an infusion of light. Isaiah announces that that light has come: "on them light has shined"; the verb is clearly a past tense. For those who wish to see the light, that light has come. The implication may be, however, that not all those in darkness can see the light.

One of the difficult concerns about this oracle is the occasion of its composition. Much scholarly argument has ensued about the possible historical context, but no resolution has yet been found. Nevertheless, the history of Israel included numerous times of darkness, punctuated again and again by prophetic hopes and assurances of light. YHWH, all the prophets say, is always in the business of offering light to those whose eyes are open wide enough to take it in, to see the dispelling of whatever darkness there may be. The fact is, says Isaiah, that "you [YHWH] have multiplied [or "magnified"] the nation, you have increased its joy; they rejoice before you as with joy at the harvest, as people exult when dividing plunder" (v. 3).

Despite the rather grim metaphor of joy that concludes verse 3, the point is that YHWH is in the business of magnifying the glory of the chosen ones and increasing their joy in the light YHWH provides. Again, no exact historical occasion is in evidence, but that is perhaps a better reality for those of us in our own time. We, like our forebears, are asked to dwell in the light of God, even when the darkness threatens to overwhelm us.

Better days are surely ahead for those who see God's light. "For the yoke of their burden, and the bar across their shoulders, the rod of their oppressor, you have broken as on the day of Midian" (v. 4). This reference to Midian is almost certainly to the glorious defeat of the Midianite warriors by Gideon and his ragtag band of heroes (Judg. 6–8). Armed only with torches, trumpets, and clay jars, three hundred Israelite fighters defeat a vast horde of Midianites, with the help of YHWH. The enormous victory is apparently long remembered, and serves Isaiah as a model for the ways in which God will always struggle on behalf of the chosen people.

Yet the next verse offers us a great surprise. After exulting in the joyous military victory over the forces of Midian, a victory that YHWH will repeat in the future, Isaiah suggests that the means of that war will finally be destroyed. "Surely, all the boots of the marching soldiers, and all the garments soiled with blood, shall be burned, consumed in the fire" (v. 5, my trans.).

Isaiah here mirrors his earlier, very famous conviction that in the day of YHWH's light, all who participate in the Torah of God "shall beat their swords into plowshares, and their spears into pruning hooks; nation shall not lift up sword against nation, neither shall they learn war any more" (Isa. 2:4, echoed in Mic. 4:3). It appears that for Isaiah the light of God will not be evidenced in joy at plunder or military victory over enemy forces, but in the miraculous work of a son, a new Davidic king, whose power is not found in great force, but in the ways of righteousness and peace.

"His authority shall grow continually, and there shall be endless peace for the throne of David and his realm. He will establish and uphold it with justice and with righteousness from this time onward and forevermore" (Isa. 9:7 alt.). It is this picture of the "Prince of Peace" that has been paramount in Christian hopes for the coming of Jesus of Nazareth. God, said the early Christians, was still offering the world light in darkness, this time in the star of Bethlehem, lighting the way for the wise men to come from afar and honor the son, the Prince of Peace.

Unfortunately, the promise of that birth and the appearance of that light have not brought the promised righteous peace to our troubled earth. It is all too easy to become cynical in the face of the centuries of wars, unrest, and suffering occurring in the name of the one who is supposedly the Prince of Peace. However, Christians who look always for the light of God in the darkness can never become cynical, because we trust in the God who always is bringing light. However dim that light appears to be at times, we are convinced that that light can never be overcome by darkness. John's unforgettable Gospel says that with beauty and clarity: "The light shines in the darkness, and the darkness did not overcome it" (John 1:5). Despite the horrors of the crucifixion, the ultimate scene of darkness, the promise of the resurrection is the light of God that can never be overcome. The light of God again and again breaks into whatever darkness we create, or is created by others, or appears naturally in our world. That is the central and basic power of the gospel. Isaiah knew that power in his time, and we must grasp that power in ours.

JOHN C. HOLBERT

Third Sunday after the Epiphany

Psalm 27:1, 4–9

¹The LORD is my light and my salvation;
   whom shall I fear?
The LORD is the stronghold of my life;
   of whom shall I be afraid?
. . . .
⁴One thing I asked of the LORD,
   that will I seek after:
to live in the house of the LORD
   all the days of my life,
to behold the beauty of the LORD,
   and to inquire in his temple.

⁵For he will hide me in his shelter
   in the day of trouble;
he will conceal me under the cover of his tent;
   he will set me high on a rock.

⁶Now my head is lifted up
   above my enemies all around me,
and I will offer in his tent
   sacrifices with shouts of joy;
I will sing and make melody to the LORD.

⁷Hear, O LORD, when I cry aloud,
   be gracious to me and answer me!
⁸"Come," my heart says, "seek his face!"
   Your face, LORD, do I seek.
   ⁹Do not hide your face from me.

Do not turn your servant away in anger,
   you who have been my help.
Do not cast me off, do not forsake me,
   O God of my salvation!

Connecting the Psalm with Scripture and Worship

On this Third Sunday after the Epiphany, the first reading and the psalm return to the themes of the day of Epiphany: the light that shines in the darkness and the promise of God's coming reign of justice. Psalm 27 demonstrates a profound confidence in God as the psalmist proclaims that faith triumphs over fear, even in the face of enemies and evildoers. To live in the house of the Lord (Ps. 27:4) is to be protected, set apart, and lifted up (v. 5) from all that might otherwise overwhelm and overtake a person's life. The lectionary does not include verses 2–3 and 10–14 of the psalm, which name the types of fears one might encounter, which weakens its overall effect.

Part of what makes the Psalms such a rich representation and expression of the human soul is that they do not shy away from naming before

197

The High-Water Mark of Prophetic Religion

Fear is one of the persistent hounds of hell that dog the footsteps of the poor, the dispossessed, the disinherited. There is nothing new or recent about fear—it is doubtless as old as the life of man on the planet. Fears are of many kinds—fear of objects, fear of people, fear of the future, fear of nature, fear of the unknown, fear of old age, fear of disease, and fear of life itself. Then there is fear which has to do with aspects of experience and detailed states of mind. Our homes, institutions, prisons, churches, are crowded with people who are hounded by day and harrowed by night because of some fear that lurks ready to spring into action as soon as one is alone, or as soon as the lights go out, or as soon as one's social defenses are temporarily removed. . . .

Nothing less than a great daring in the face of overwhelming odds can achieve the inner security in which fear cannot possibly survive. It is true that a man cannot be serene unless he possesses something about which to be serene. Here we reach the high-water mark of prophetic religion, and it is of the essence of the religion of Jesus of Nazareth. Of course God cares for the grass of the field, which lives a day and is no more, or the sparrow that falls unnoticed by the wayside. He also holds the stars in their appointed places, leaves his mark in every living thing. And he cares for me! To be assured of this becomes the answer to the threat of violence—yea, to violence itself. To the degree to which a man knows this, he is unconquerable from within and without.

Howard Thurman, *Jesus and the Disinherited* (Nashville: Abingdon-Cokesbury Press, 1949), 36, 56.

God all that encompasses the human experience. Within the Psalms we find the full range of emotions laid bare before God as expressions of faith within their own right. Indeed, the emotions of despair, rage, and particularly fear, are often presented as intrinsically bound to the life of faith. In this way the either-or tension between faith and fear does not find validation in the Psalms. The psalmist does not tell us to choose faith over fear; rather, we hear that we can, in fact, have both faith and fear at the same time. They are not mutually exclusive.

A powerful liturgical use of this psalm, then, might be to use it as a way to support a congregation in the naming of their fears—not to dwell on that which frightens us, but to call the darkness of our world out into the light. If the psalmist can put forth every fear before God, why should we, in our worship, not do the same? In this sense, especially if Psalm 27 is used in its entirety, a congregation might be invited into a liturgy where they name all those things in our world that frighten them. Gun violence, nuclear war, economic disarray—unfortunately, there is no shortage when it comes to the issues that might cause us to fear. What would happen if we named them and in the process named our faith, in light of and in spite of our fear?

The specificity of such liturgy could provide a profound opportunity for a congregation to experience what the psalmist describes in verse 6, "Now my head is lifted up above my enemies all around me."

Such interaction with Psalm 27 could prove a powerful response to the reading from Isaiah. Isaiah speaks at a time when the Israelites are in the grip of great fear after the invasion of the Assyrians upon the northern kingdom. He does not shy away from naming the fears of the people, but uses highly charged images of the Israelites' experiences at the hands of their captors, describing the "yoke of their burden and the bar across their shoulders, the rod of their oppressor" (Isa. 9:4). Yet Isaiah declares that the people have seen a "great light" (v. 2) and announces the birth of the Prince of Peace (v. 6). This announcement, however, is spoken not to the people but to God. Like the psalmist, Isaiah professes confidence in God's promise to protect and deliver God's people, even in the midst of the fear that surrounds. Furthermore, in the Gospel reading for the day, we hear Jesus quoting Isaiah's proclamation.

This Sunday's texts offer the preacher an opportunity to explore the interconnection of fear and faith. Yes, within the Bible there are nearly three hundred admonitions of "do not be afraid," but are we to take that phrase literally as many often do? It is possible that to "do not be afraid" is not to eradicate the emotion of fear, but rather to echo the psalmist and Isaiah, expressing our faith in the midst of our fear, thus demonstrating a greater confidence than one born of no fear at all. Pastorally, these texts invite preachers to encounter their own fears, as well, because any avoidance or discomfort with the topic will likely be readily recognized by the congregation. When preachers name their own fears in relationship to their faith, adding their voices to those of the psalmist and Isaiah, they create an opening for others to do the same. For while there are those who may be uncomfortable with direct confrontation of fear, the tension raised by Psalm 27 and Isaiah 9 asks, Which is a more powerful declaration of faith: to say one has no fear, or to say one has fear but believes anyway?

ERIN KEYS

1 Corinthians 1:10–18

¹⁰Now I appeal to you, brothers and sisters, by the name of our Lord Jesus Christ, that all of you be in agreement and that there be no divisions among you, but that you be united in the same mind and the same purpose. ¹¹For it has been reported to me by Chloe's people that there are quarrels among you, my brothers and sisters. ¹²What I mean is that each of you says, "I belong to Paul," or "I belong to Apollos," or "I belong to Cephas," or "I belong to Christ." ¹³Has Christ been divided? Was Paul crucified for you? Or were you baptized in the name of Paul? ¹⁴I thank God that I baptized none of you except Crispus and Gaius, ¹⁵so that no one can say that you were baptized in my name. ¹⁶(I did baptize also the household of Stephanas; beyond that, I do not know whether I baptized anyone else.) ¹⁷For Christ did not send me to baptize but to proclaim the gospel, and not with eloquent wisdom, so that the cross of Christ might not be emptied of its power.

¹⁸For the message about the cross is foolishness to those who are perishing, but to us who are being saved it is the power of God.

Commentary 1: Connecting the Reading with Scripture

The most obvious connection between almost any passage in 1 and 2 Corinthians and our world will likely be that the troubles of First Christian Church in Corinth are similar to troubles in the contemporary church. First Church, Corinth was a church divided, like many of our parishes, congregations, or denominations. Judging by the part of the correspondence between Paul and Corinth that survives in our canonical epistles, the church fought about most things one could imagine. The first issue Paul discusses, however, has to do with disputes over clergy, to describe the problem anachronistically. Many readers will have direct experience of churches in which there are similar disputes over clergy or, since eloquent speaking is so prominent a feature of the first chapters of 1 Corinthians, preachers.

The fact that this issue is discussed first may or may not indicate that it is of primary importance in Corinth. It may indicate, however, that Paul needs to deal with the issue, lest it complicate other matters that he will address later in the epistle, if it is left unresolved. Paul will be exercising an implicit authority in writing these

epistles, part of being an apostle. He does not shy away from the authority of an apostle, but he must clarify the nature of that authority, lest the primacy of the gospel of Christ crucified be obscured by his own person. If the Corinthians do what Paul tells them to do because they draw their primary identity from their relationship with Paul, there is a wrongness at the heart of their faith. It remains vital not "to do the right deed for the wrong reason" (from the final and climactic temptation of Archbishop Thomas Becket in T. S. Eliot, *Murder in the Cathedral*).[1]

It is still the case that the preacher can get in the way of Jesus. While the traditional authority of the preacher and of the clergy in general has certainly waned in Western culture, there is always an implicit authority claim in the act of preaching itself. That authority must serve the proclamation of the gospel, not obscure it or divert attention from it. This may particularly be a problem for effective preachers. We do not want—or perhaps more honestly, we ought not want—people to admire our skills rather than to love Jesus. As Paul will say at the conclusion of our reading, "For Christ [sent me] to proclaim

1. T. S. Eliot, *Murder in the Cathedral* (New York: Harcourt Press, 1935), 44.

the gospel, and not with eloquent wisdom, so that the cross of Christ might not be emptied of its power" (1 Cor. 1:17). This may not need to be spoken about from the pulpit, but it should be thought about in the study, well before we stand up to preach. It is always the case that a text must speak to the preacher before it can speak to the congregation, but this is more clearly the case with this passage than many others. It demands a great deal of "pre-preaching" thought from us. That kind of reflection may not show up in the words we preach but it may correct the way we preach.

To return to our passage, we see that the church is divided into a series of groups that seem to draw their identity from their adherence to particular leaders or preachers. It is likely that there will always be identifiable groups in a church. Ironically, the news about this problem in Corinth comes from such a group, "Chloe's people." The real problem comes when a group appears to draw its primary identity from something other than the gospel. This may be why Paul uses so much identity language in the introduction to the epistle, found in verses 1–9. Those who do not follow the lectionary religiously might consider combining this passage with that reading. The contrast between the two passages is homiletically striking.

It is not clear whether there are three groups or four in the church. One possibility is that there are three. These would be the people who say, "I belong to Paul," and those who say the same about Apollos or about Cephas respectively. All these allegiances are understandable: Paul had founded the church and remained a figure of such authority that at least some Corinthians still consulted him about church problems. Apollos was a notably eloquent preacher and Cephas, Peter in Aramaic, was the figure in the early church closest to the earthly Jesus. Paul corrects these people by saying, "I belong to Christ." Our identity is not drawn from a relationship with any preacher or authority figure, no matter how admirable, but rather from Christ. This reading is grammatically possible and spiritually useful in a similar situation of church conflict today. The preaching connection would be to emphasize the centrality of our relationship with Christ.

It may be possible, however, that there are four groups in Corinth, the three previously named groups and also a fourth party whose watchword is "I belong to Christ." This reading, also grammatically possible, appears to be the one preferred by the NRSV, and is perhaps more homiletically interesting. The point that it is theologically superior to say, "I belong to Christ," rather than to some earthly leader, is, after all, a rather obvious one. It is hard to imagine that some spiritually sensitive people had not thought it up for themselves already . . . and formed a group of like-minded spiritually sensitive, indeed spiritually superior, people in Corinth. These people would, of course, be "right," but being right can still be a problem.

The emotional connection of many readers of this resource, and also the members of too many churches, is that they have experienced conflicts similar to the one in Corinth. We have seen and been bruised by life in churches where one group loves the minister and another group wants her or him gone. Perhaps it is a church where some admire the lead minister and others, the minister of pastoral care or the church musician. Perhaps our readers have served on committees or commissions sent by church judicatories to help resolve this kind of problem. All the parties in the church assure the visiting committee that their side is right.

That may well be true, but it is still a problem. People are as likely to be wounded by the group that is right as by the one that is wrong. In a situation of church conflict, being right is never good enough, if there is no love. Paul will return to that point in chapter 13, which has little to do with weddings, and a great deal more to do with church fights. Paul will also raise again and more directly, in connection with eating meat offered to idols, the point that being right is not enough (1 Cor. 8).

There is another connection here, however, that may belong in the study rather than the pulpit. Paul uses the people who admire him as the negative example. He says, "Was Paul crucified for you?" not Apollos or Cephas. He does not say, "Were you baptized in the name of Apollos or Cephas?" To be more contemporary, he does not say, "The real Christians in this church are behind me. The ones who want me out are fringe people." (This is not an invented quotation.) Amid church conflicts, the people who are behind us are also part of the problem if they are following us rather than Christ. That, too, may never get beyond the study but, if taken to heart, may aid our preaching.

STEPHEN FARRIS

Commentary 2: Connecting the Reading with the World

Most commentators recognize that the appeal for unity in 1 Corinthians 1:10 is the place where Paul expresses one of the letter's primary concerns and purposes. His stated desire for "agreement," "no divisions," and a "united . . . mind and . . . purpose" among the Corinthian believers needs to be viewed within the letter's wider context, however, if one is to understand it and discern its true relevance for Christian living. Interpreters also do well to consider the ecclesial, ethical, and theological implications of the communal realities Paul prizes so greatly; otherwise, discussions of unity risk devolving into platitudes.

In particular, no one should identify Paul's references to "agreement" and "no divisions" as a plea for "no differences" or "no variety" in the church. Also, the unity Paul longs to foster among the Corinthians does not represent a strategy for building a more illustrious community. Rather, Paul encourages the Corinthians because he wants them to be more like the Christ in whom they dwell—committed to new values that align with a new Christ-defined identity, and unwilling to regard dominance as the means toward securing greatness.

Unity, Not Uniformity. Paul's claims about baptism and churches' traditional language around the sacrament emphasize initiation, incorporation, and unity. Those themes direct attention to a person's unity with Christ; because of that foundational unity, baptism also signifies a kinship shared with everyone else who resides in Christ. However, this interpersonal unity does not erase all the qualities that make a person distinctive from others. In fact, those whose view of the church imagines it as a melting pot, in which everyone takes on a singular and seemingly generic Christian identity, are at risk of turning congregations and denominations into places where the members with the most cultural or political capital get to define and impose on others the specific details of a uniform Christian belief, worship, leadership, and outreach.

Brad Braxton grasps the significance of differences for individuals and their communities and describes the nuance well: "When one enters the Christian community through belief in Christ and baptism one does not necessarily lose the ethnic, social, or gender distinctions that have characterized one's existence. Even 'in Christ' there is still human difference. The dominance of one over the other based on these differences is the reality that is abolished!"[2] A unity that celebrates otherness and repents of past domineering and oppression requires intentional activity; it cannot come from promises and slogans. The sinister habits we have grown used to perpetuating and suffering are persistent. They make it difficult for communities to progress beyond anemic truces based on mutual tolerance, which masquerades as unity. As the social damages of racial tension, economic disparity, political polarization, misogyny, homophobia, and shoddy hospitality continue to show their corrosive effects, distinctively Christian values and practices concerning authentic unity become all the more vital for congregations' self-understanding and patterns of behavior.

Paradoxical Power. It is no accident that Paul's appeal for unity appears in the same paragraph as the letter's first mentions of Jesus' crucifixion. When Paul assails the existence of factions and interest groups in Corinth, he does so not because he cherishes effective cooperation or comfortable coexistence but because he understands Christian living as an experience of

---

2. Brad Braxton, *No Longer Slaves: Galatians and the African American Experience* (Collegeville, MN: Liturgical Press, 2002), 94. Braxton's focus in this quotation is on the claims Paul makes in Gal. 3:26–29, but his points also apply to how one interprets Paul's notions of unity more broadly.

conforming to Christ. That conformity entails unity with an executed Savior, the only one who was "crucified for you" (1 Cor. 1:13). Therefore baptism occurs in the name of Christ, making it an expression of participation in his death and new life. As a result, the unity for which Paul advocates has a distinctively theological— and christological—basis. It indicates a way in which the church lives into and lives out the gospel, manifesting to the world what God accomplishes through Christ.

Precisely because Jesus was *crucified*, Christian faith should mirror what God revealed through the cross: power in the guise of foolishness. Paul's statement about the cross of Christ being "the power of God" (v. 18)—a statement that opens up a larger discussion extending until the end of chapter 2—affords teachers and preachers an opportunity to explore the inverted accounting criteria that course through Paul's understanding of Christian existence. For Paul, Jesus' crucifixion prompts a thorough reassessment of everything—every assumption, every virtue, every agenda.

To comprehend the ramifications of Paul's perspective, it is imperative to weigh the social implications and psychological torment of crucifixion in the Roman Empire. The spectacle of this type of public execution branded its victims with ignominy in manifold ways. As Fleming Rutledge summarizes,

> Crucifixion as a means of execution in the Roman Empire had *as its express purpose* the elimination of victims from consideration as members of the human race. . . . It was meant to indicate to all who might be toying with subversive ideas that crucified persons were *not of the same species* as either the executioners or the spectators and were therefore not only expendable but also deserving of ritualized extermination.[3]

With good reason, James H. Cone compellingly likens Roman crucifixions to American lynchings.[4]

Because of the degradation and desecration that characterized Roman crucifixions, any suggestion that a crucified man might somehow possess a connection to the presence or power of a deity would have struck most of Paul's contemporaries as laughable. In the eyes of both Jews and Gentiles, death on a cross would appear to rule out the possibility that a victim could be furthering the work and priorities of any god or somehow contributing to the good order of the universe at large. Paul perceives things differently. He detects divine power there.

Paul thus depicts Christian faith as operating with a strange and nonintuitive value system, one normed by Jesus' death on a cross. At work in his idea of Christian faith is more than an appeal to humility or a delight in ironic ingenuity. At its core, Christian faith rejects common assumptions about the power of coercion, dominance, shame, and brute force. Those things may be effective tools for elevating oneself and bringing others in line, but they are not God's tools—at least not as far as Jesus' crucifixion and Christian baptism are concerned.

There are consequences for a Christian community's perspective and conduct. People who perceive divine power where others see only foolishness will spot God's presence in other unexpected places too. People who know that transformative holiness exists where others presume there is nothing but depravity or debris will find significance—and may encounter God—in acts of service and compassion.

No wonder Paul is so critical of the factionalism for which he indicts the Corinthian church. The letter's argument reaches beyond them to correct other audiences too. No people of faith who define themselves or decorate their building with a cross can aspire to subjugate other groups or trumpet their own power and cleverness. A church cannot vainly revel in its own causes, accomplishments, insights, or canons of law and morality if it is going to proclaim a salvation revealed in a crucifixion. Conventional metrics of success and progress do not apply. The new age that Christ has initiated demands altogether different systems of measurement and meaning, based on a cross-shaped understanding of God's ways of being in—and transforming—the world.

MATTHEW L. SKINNER

---

3. Fleming Rutledge, *The Crucifixion: Understanding the Death of Jesus Christ* (Grand Rapids: Eerdmans, 2015), 92.
4. James H. Cone, *The Cross and the Lynching Tree* (Maryknoll, NY: Orbis, 2011).

Matthew 4:12–23

¹²Now when Jesus heard that John had been arrested, he withdrew to Galilee. ¹³He left Nazareth and made his home in Capernaum by the sea, in the territory of Zebulun and Naphtali, ¹⁴so that what had been spoken through the prophet Isaiah might be fulfilled:

> ¹⁵"Land of Zebulun, land of Naphtali,
>   on the road by the sea, across the Jordan, Galilee of the Gentiles—
> ¹⁶the people who sat in darkness
>   have seen a great light,
> and for those who sat in the region and shadow of death
>   light has dawned."

¹⁷From that time Jesus began to proclaim, "Repent, for the kingdom of heaven has come near."

¹⁸As he walked by the Sea of Galilee, he saw two brothers, Simon, who is called Peter, and Andrew his brother, casting a net into the sea—for they were fishermen. ¹⁹And he said to them, "Follow me, and I will make you fish for people." ²⁰Immediately they left their nets and followed him. ²¹As he went from there, he saw two other brothers, James son of Zebedee and his brother John, in the boat with their father Zebedee, mending their nets, and he called them. ²²Immediately they left the boat and their father, and followed him.

²³Jesus went throughout Galilee, teaching in their synagogues and proclaiming the good news of the kingdom and curing every disease and every sickness among the people.

Commentary 1: Connecting the Reading with Scripture

Because this passage is sandwiched between attention-grabbing materials—the baptism and temptations, on the one hand, and Sermon on the Mount, on the other—it is easy to overlook its importance. Here, however, we find the first and foundational acts of Jesus' ministry, in which he inaugurates his mission and calls his first disciples, setting in place the paradigm for all that follows. He begins the work of gathering and restoring the people of Israel, first through the Twelve, not merely for the sake of Israel alone, however, but for all peoples, for whom Israel was called to be a witness and light. Gathering and restoration are the basic practices of resistance in a fragmented, disintegrating world. They are also deeply rooted in the biblical images of who God is. As Jesus begins to pursue this ministry, he also enacts and embodies

other practices that attend the coming of God's rule: calling, healing, and liberating. Everything else Jesus accomplishes in the Gospel should be understood in light of these basic goals and practices, which are still the first concerns of the mission of the church today.

The passage begins on a note of danger. In response to news of John's arrest, Jesus withdraws to Galilee, but not to hide. Matthew treats the shift in location as a sign of the fulfillment of prophecy, but not merely in order to proof-text. Matthew's citation of Isaiah 9:1–2, the first part of the Old Testament lesson for this day, signals that things are not what they seem. Zebulun, where Nazareth is located, and Naphtali, where Capernaum is found, were according to Jewish Christian traditions the first of the twelve tribes to go into exile under Assyria (2 Kgs. 15:29) and thus the first who might expect to be restored. Isaiah 9:1 describes the "contempt" suffered by Zebulun and Naphtali prior to their restoration, but goes on to affirm that, with the appearance of the heir of the Davidic throne, light will dawn on those who walked in darkness (Isa. 9:2) and peace and justice will be restored (v. 7). In short, these place names are not incidental, but signify the beginnings of the reversals that attend the coming of the son (v. 6). Both Matthew 4 and Isaiah 9 affirm that God brings about justice not through the powerful, but for and by means of the lowliest (cf. Matt. 18:1–14).

The more general place name, Galilee, coupled with "of the Gentiles/nations," is notable in both Isaiah 9 and Matthew 4. In Isaiah, it suggests that the Israelites that lived in these portions of Galilee had fallen under the influence—the darkness—of the nations, which in Isaiah 7–9 refers to the Assyrian Empire. In Matthew, they are the Romans who occupy both Judea and Galilee. In both Isaiah and Matthew, the redemption of the people in darkness entails liberation *from* the nations, but in Matthew, who carefully affirms that Jesus' mission was directed first to the people of Israel (10:5–6; 15:24), the mission *to* the nations, with which the Gospel will culminate (28:16–20), is also ever on the horizon. The redemption that Jesus here announces and inaugurates is not just for Judeans or Galilean Jews, nor even just for the twelve restored tribes of Israel, for whom the twelve disciples will serve as symbols, but also ultimately for those who held them captive. Here is a reminder that the church's mission is not just for people like us, but for all, even for our enemies (5:43–48). The tribalistic triumphalism of much modern Christendom is a betrayal of this gospel.

"Repent, for the kingdom of heaven has come near" perfectly duplicates the heart of John the Baptizer's proclamation (3:2). For Matthew, this signals the essential continuity and consistency of the ministries of John and Jesus. Yet there is a significant difference, indicated not by the language, but by the context: when John says the kingdom is near, by implication he means "near, but not here yet." When Jesus says it, however, he means "near, here at hand." John is setting expectations, Jesus is calling to participation. Jesus' ministry of gathering

and healing both works toward and embodies the realization of God's empire.

Ideally, the church lives still more fully, not less, in the reality of God's rule. Modern exegetes have often driven a wedge between the "kingdom of heaven," which they associate with the ministry of Jesus, and the "last days" still to come, when God's rule will finally be realized. This distinction is not clear in the pages of the New Testament. The early Christians saw themselves living already in the realization of God's promises, even if plenty of the fallen world was still visible.

The mission of the church, which continues that of Jesus and his disciples, runs on this same realization. The church still bears witness to the reality of God's rule first in repentance, turning away from the world's ways toward God. The repentance to which Jesus calls, in other words, happens as much in response to the nature of God's presence and power as it does in anticipation of God's coming. How do we train congregations to live more fully in this world in realization of the promise and reality of God's rule, especially in dark times, rather than in anticipation of another world still to come?

Immediately after the proclamation that God's rule has drawn near, Matthew tells the story of Jesus' call to two sets of brothers, all fishermen, set forth in two parallel panels. These bear the imprint of classic call stories, especially the template of Elijah's call of Elisha in 1 Kings 19:19–21. The prophet is traveling, discovers/sees others working, and calls them from their work; the one called then follows/comes after. Ancient readers would thus have recognized these as prophetic call stories (see Matt. 9:9 for another example). Jesus initiates each of these calls: he first sees, then calls those who are chosen, who apparently have no choice in the matter. In 1 Kings 19, Elijah grants permission to Elisha to turn back to say good-bye to his parents, and Elisha then also sacrifices the oxen with which he was plowing, as a sign of the break from his past. The brothers Jesus here calls simply leave their vocations and families behind. Elsewhere Jesus does not permit would-be disciples even to bury the dead (Matt. 8:21–22).

The call to discipleship is thus presented not as something chosen by the disciples, but as the decisive, commanding act of Jesus. Because the kingdom of heaven has come near, there are no compromises to be made with the world as it is. This is unlike our modern notion of discipleship, in which "disciples" typically weigh, choose, and pursue their "calling" largely on their own terms. How do we encourage Christians both to listen to God's call more carefully and to respond on God's terms, rather than our own? In a world fraught with catastrophic risks, recovering this sense of call may be important.

Jesus calls these first disciples to "fish for people," an identification that has few precedents. In Jeremiah 16:16, God sends for both fishermen and hunters, in order to gather human prey—the people of Judah—for judgment. This scene culminates in Jeremiah, however, in the "conversion of the nations" (Jer. 16:19–21). Jesus' call may thus already anticipate a similar eschatological harvest (see Matt 9:36–38), entailing gathering for both judgment and redemption, which were in the prophetic tradition two sides of one coin. Ministry in the twenty-first century surely again requires coming to grips with this dual reality, for the sake of both the church and the world.

STANLEY P. SAUNDERS

Commentary 2: Connecting the Reading with the World

"People who sat in darkness have seen a great light" (Matt. 4:16). Isaiah the prophet and the evangelist Matthew are both able to speak a word of hope to people "sitting" in darkness. The Babylonian exile for one and the Roman occupation for the other represent darkness at various levels. Whether it be the deprivation of freedom, imperial taxes, injustice, and inequality, or the imposition of alien gods, darkness hovered like a thick fog. The voices of Isaiah the prophet, John the Baptist, and Jesus penetrate the fog with a hopeful ray of light. "The kingdom of heaven has come near!" (v. 17).

During this third week of Epiphany, we celebrate the revelation of God in the person of Jesus. His coming heralds the inbreaking of God's kingdom, the penetration of the darkness by the incarnate light. We must recognize that just as the darkness has personal, structural, and creational dimensions, so too does the light penetrate and transform each of those dimensions.

On a personal level some people are ignorant of the light, and they need to be informed. Others deliberately ignore the light until the darkness gets too suffocating and they turn toward light. Christ's followers keep the light shining, waiting with open arms.

Just as darkness has many levels, hope comes in many forms. It may be the granting of refugee status to one fleeing a war-torn homeland. The arrival of an ambulance signals that help is here. A food bank supports a family living on the brink of starvation. Disaster assistance after a storm, or a job for the unemployed, make all the difference. The light of hope penetrates the darkness of despair. While hope comes in many forms, during Epiphany we celebrate the source of light and hope incarnate in Jesus.

Repent. Why does Jesus' message about God's kingdom begin with a call to repent? This is terrible sales strategy. You do not make a demand on a customer before you sell them the benefits. I suppose that it worked for Jesus because the listeners already had a solid vision of the benefit: "the kingdom of heaven has come near." We all see advertisements with before and after pictures. People apparently go through dramatic transformations in their appearance; the before and after pictures are astounding. However, what we do not see behind the scenes are the costly, painful procedures, along with lifestyle changes necessary to produce results.

Very often the church has called people to repentance without making clear the vision of the kingdom of God. The kingdom has been presented as an equivalent to going to heaven after one dies, rather than what it is, the active presence and rule of God in one's life, in the world, and in all creation.

The church as Christ's body is to model the kingdom, to give people a clear vision of what life with God is like. The values, vision, and passion of God's kingdom are to take life in the local church so that people see the benefits. This vision, concretely lived out by the church, provides the motivation to fulfill the call to repent.

The life change that repentance entails actually makes sense when one considers the benefits of life with God. These benefits are not only personal but also societal and creational, as the kingdom of God. The life of the church is to put the benefits on display. Just as in the before and after pictures in the advertisements, when people see the results, the sacrifices are all worth it.

"The kingdom of heaven has come near" (v. 17).

In the *Lord of the Rings* we find a curious parallel to Jesus' message that "the kingdom of heaven has come near."[1] Frodo's main helper and protector is Strider, chieftain of the rangers of the North. We soon learn that his true identity is Aragorn, son of Arathorn. He is the heir to the throne of Gondor.

However, a steward, Denethor, rules Gondor. His stewardship is to last only until the heir to the throne appears. When Aragorn shows up in Gondor and reveals his identity as the rightful ruler, Denethor refuses to hand over the kingdom. We see here an example of right versus might. Denethor has all the trappings and power of the throne, but Aragorn has the moral and legal right to it.

The ruler of the "kingdom of heaven" is God, and God has full moral and legal rights over creation. According to the biblical story, these rights have been usurped by both spiritual powers and humanity. The coming of God's kingdom in some ways is reclamation of divine right and the fulfillment of the divine creative purpose. The incarnation is the culmination of God's plan to fulfill the divine creative purpose through redemption rather than through destructive judgment. Jesus' calling disciples to follow him shows that God's plan continues to work itself out in human history.

"Follow me" (v. 19).

Activists are people who champion causes for political or social change. For example, Susan B. Anthony was an activist for women's rights in general and for women's suffrage in particular. Martin Luther King promoted civil rights and social equality of the races in America.

Are Jesus and the apostles activists? Jesus had one theme: the kingdom of God. He proclaimed the inbreaking of this kingdom and recruited people to help him spread the word.

Activists should not be confused with supporters. Supporters are on the team and help in many different ways, but they are not focused in the same way as the activists. When Jesus calls two sets of brothers to follow him and become fishers for people, he is calling them to a level of activity different from the regular disciple. Most of Jesus' disciples did not accompany him on the road, for example.

Those disciples who are supporters and not activists are still not off the hook. Every local church is to be an activist for the kingdom of God in the name of Jesus. The local church bears witness to Jesus and exemplifies life in the kingdom of God. When churches band together, such as in a denomination, they can leverage this impact on a much larger scale. Jesus' activism for God's kingdom continues through the church.

"Immediately they left their nets and followed him" (v. 20).

Charles Duhigg in his popular book *The Power of Habit* talks about keystone habits.[2] Some habits are more strategic than others because they connect with and lead to other habits. For example, if you develop the habit of going to the gym four times a week, it will have all kinds of beneficial effects in your life. So we can be very strategic about choosing to develop certain keystone habits and focus on those.

When the two sets of brothers, Peter and Andrew, James and John, responded to Jesus' call to follow him, they made a keystone decision. This one decision automatically made

---

1. J. R. R. Tolkien, *Lord of the Rings* (London: Allen & Unwin, 1954).

2. Charles Duhigg, *The Power of Habit: Why Do We Do What We Do in Life and Business* (New York: Random House, 2012).

other decisions very easy to make. Are you going to keep your job as a fisherman? No. Is financial security your main priority? No. Some things that may have been difficult to decide prior to the keystone decision became easy or decided themselves because of the one key decision.

Responding to Jesus' message of the kingdom of God is a keystone decision. This is one reason that repentance has to accompany it. The decision is life changing and requires deliberate life changes.

MARK ABBOTT

Fourth Sunday after the Epiphany

Micah 6:1–8
Psalm 15

1 Corinthians 1:18–31
Matthew 5:1–12

Micah 6:1–8

¹Hear what the LORD says:
Rise, plead your case before the mountains,
and let the hills hear your voice.
²Hear, you mountains, the controversy of the LORD,
and you enduring foundations of the earth;
for the LORD has a controversy with his people,
and he will contend with Israel.

³"O my people, what have I done to you?
In what have I wearied you? Answer me!
⁴For I brought you up from the land of Egypt,
and redeemed you from the house of slavery;
and I sent before you Moses,
Aaron, and Miriam.
⁵O my people, remember now what King Balak of Moab devised,
what Balaam son of Beor answered him,
and what happened from Shittim to Gilgal,
that you may know the saving acts of the LORD."

⁶"With what shall I come before the LORD,
and bow myself before God on high?
Shall I come before him with burnt offerings,
with calves a year old?
⁷Will the LORD be pleased with thousands of rams,
with ten thousands of rivers of oil?
Shall I give my firstborn for my transgression,
the fruit of my body for the sin of my soul?"
⁸He has told you, O mortal, what is good;
and what does the LORD require of you
but to do justice, and to love kindness,
and to walk humbly with your God?

Commentary 1: Connecting the Reading with Scripture

Everyone loves Micah 6:8, a verse that scholar Jim Nogalski has called "biblical ethics in a nutshell."[1] The verse supplies inspiration for songs, projects, foundations, scholarships, newsletters, T-shirts, visor clips, key rings, bracelets, travel mugs, and plaques of all sorts and sizes available on Etsy. Appropriating this nugget of wisdom—not as an inspiring quip, but as a way of life—necessitates reading it carefully in context. Micah 6:8 concludes a dialogue the prophet

---

1. James Nogalski, *The Book of the Twelve: Micah–Malachi*, Smyth & Helwys Bible Commentary (Macon, GA: Smyth & Helwys, 2011), 573.

imagines between God and a human defendant, a dialogue correcting a perennial misapprehension of divine judgment and mercy.

Micah was an eighth-century contemporary of the prophets Hosea and Isaiah. He lived west of Jerusalem in an area hit hard by King Hezekiah's economic and military policies. Scholars agree that Micah's own words are found only in chapters 1–3, which condemn Jerusalem to destruction for violent economic injustice. When we remember that Hezekiah's defiance against the Assyrian Empire led to King Sennacherib's campaign to obliterate nearly all of Judah's cities and towns (2 Kgs. 18:13)—though Jerusalem itself was spared—we can understand the prophet's enraged prediction that Jerusalem would itself become a heap of ruins (Mic. 3:12).

Chapters 4–5, which may be among the book of Micah's latest portions, are far more hopeful in tone and message. Chapter 6 returns us to judgment speeches reminiscent of the prophet's own words in earlier chapters. While Micah 6:1–8 is clearly a coherent unit, the speech that follows in 6:9–7:7, with its discussion of bribes, dishonest weights, violence, and other perversions of morality, clarifies what it means to do justice, love kindness, and walk humbly before God.

The vignette in 6:1–8 unfolds as a controversy in a courtroom setting. God opens in verses 1 and 2 by calling witnesses—not human ones, but mountains and hills and even the earth's foundations, similar to Isaiah's invocation of heaven and earth as witnesses of God's frustration with the people of Judah (Isa. 1:2). This is more than hyperbole; as both prophets demonstrate, and as we see today, ecological violence accompanies social violence. Even the landscape has a stake in human behavior.

God's controversy, or lawsuit, begins with exasperated reminders of past saving deeds: freeing the Israelites' ancestors from slavery, delivering them from enemies, and welcoming them hospitably to a new land. Everything Micah and other prophets demand from Israelites is premised on divine grace seen in Israel's story. But three specifics here are striking. After a reminder of rescue from Egypt, God claims to have "sent before you Moses, Aaron, and Miriam" (Mic. 6:4). Listing the three siblings

as coleaders suggests more prominent roles for Aaron and especially for Miriam than the pentateuchal narratives portray, raising questions about other ways they may have been remembered than Exodus and Numbers describe.

God moves on to recall King Balak of Moab, whose repeated attempts to curse the Israelites were confounded in Numbers 22–24. Even though Balak's story is quite lengthy and suspenseful, Micah is the only prophet to mention it—and only in passing. Following these two unusual forays into the wilderness tradition, a cryptic reference is made to "what happened from Shittim to Gilgal" (Mic. 6:5), two encampments on the way to Jericho. At Shittim, on the east side of the Jordan River, the Israelites incurred divine vengeance for sexual indiscretions (Num. 25:1–15). In contrast, at Gilgal, west of the river, the Israelites' first stopping place in the promised land, a stone monument was raised, the men were circumcised, the Passover kept, and the manna ceased, signaling the end of their journey (Josh. 4:19–5:12). Specific reference by God to all these persons and places is striking. The stories recall God's provision of leadership, favor, and clemency in Israel's very early days.

The human's response, beginning in verse 6, might sound at first like the polite question people may ask when invited to dinner: "How lovely! What can we bring?" In the context of God's very specific reminders, and as the questions escalate, the defensiveness is clear. The response begins with the empty placeholder "what" and progresses quickly from the reasonable to the extreme. Burnt offerings were standard fare, even if calves would have been a step beyond the more usual lambs. Sacrifices by the thousands were the responsibility of kings (1 Kgs. 3:4). Ten thousand oily rivers belong to the realm of fantasy—or archsarcasm. The biblical tradition never approved human sacrifice. It is as if the human defendant were asking, "Is there anything we can do to appease you, or will you always be holding that exodus thing over our heads? Sacrifices? Multiple sacrifices? Ultimate sacrifices? Because if you are going to play the guilt card, nothing can suffice."

It is not as if the Israelites had asked to be delivered from Egypt, or had invited themselves to the promised land. God had summoned

Unity of the Spirit in the Bond of Peace

Now the onely way to avoyde this shipwracke, and to provide for our posterity, is to followe the counsell of Micah, *to doe justly, to love mercy, to walk humbly with our God.* For this end, wee must be knitt together, in this worke, as one man. Wee must entertaine each other in brotherly affection. Wee must be willing to abridge ourselves of our superfluities, for the supply of other's necessities. Wee must uphold a familiar commerce together in all meekeness, gentlenes, patience and liberality. Wee must delight in eache other; make other's conditions our oune; rejoice together, mourne together, labour and suffer together, allwayes haueving before our eyes our commission and community in the worke, as members of the same body. Soe shall wee *keepe the unitie of the spirit in the bond of peace.* The Lord will be our God, and delight to dwell among us, as his oune people, and will command a blessing upon us in all our wayes. Soe that wee shall see much more of his wisdome, power, goodness and truthe, than formerly wee haue been acquainted with. Wee shall finde that the God of Israell is among us, when ten of us shall be able to resist a thousand of our enemies; when hee shall make us a prayse and glory that men shall say of succeeding plantations, "the Lord make it likely that of *New England.*" For wee must consider that wee shall be as a citty upon a hill. The eies of all people are uppon us. Soe that if wee shall deale falsely with our God in this worke wee haue undertaken, and soe cause him to withdrawe his present help from us, wee shall be made a story and a by-word through the world. Wee shall open the mouthes of enemies to speake evill of the wayes of God, and all professors for God's sake. Wee shall shame the faces of many of God's worthy servants, and cause theire prayers to be turned into curses upon us till wee be consumed out of the good land whither wee are a goeing.

John Winthrop, "A Modell of Christian Charity," in *Collections of the Massachusetts Historical Society*, vol. 7 of the Third Series (Boston: Charles C. Little & James Brown, 1838), 46–47.

them, singling them out as recipients of divine hospitality, not because they had done anything to deserve it, but because God chose them for God's own reasons. They were never allowed to forget this. Bitter sarcasm erupts in the human's frustrated recognition of the human condition. Everything we return to God came first as a gift to us. The clothes on our backs, the food on our tables, the very children in our arms—all proceed from divine generosity. So what is the point of a thank offering that cannot lift the burden of beholdenness?

At that moment of standoff between God's viewpoint and the human's, help comes, as it so often does, from changing the subject. The question "With what shall I come?" is ignored completely. The issue is not what humans bring, but what we care about. The three virtues named in Micah 6:8 are hardly controversial. Justice is good. Who would ever despise kindness? Who would argue with humility? Who would call themselves "arrogant, and proud of it"? The Etsy plaques and mugs testify that everyone likes Micah 6:8 as a saying.

The trick is in the living. Unlike offerings, lifelong habits of kindness, justice, and humility are not transactions to dispense and check off, duty done. Rather, they characterize a stance of leaning toward others: extending grace reflexively, without measure, as God has done, not because others deserve it but because they need it; promoting fairness, especially toward those at risk; and certainly not trying to appease and be done with God, but instead humbly keeping hearts open and pliant. What God sought from the Israelites, what faith says God still seeks from us, is to cultivate capabilities we have seen in our Maker, capabilities we who are made in God's image already possess: a warm heart for all, a passion for fairness, and the flexibility to learn as we go in this complex matter of seeking grace alongside justice.

Being a guest in God's world, living at the mercy of God's hospitality, means vulnerability that no good deed can erase. When we empty ourselves to humility, when we long for kindness whether we see it or not, when we do justice whether we benefit or not, we are not consoled with the confidence that we have repaid God's gifts to us. However, we can rest assured, knowing we have brought the most fragrant offering humans can bring.

PATRICIA K. TULL

Commentary 2: Connecting the Reading with the World

Liturgically, this reading falls in the season of Epiphany, which presents an interesting connection. Micah 6:1–5 opens with a courtroom scene in which God argues the divine case against Israel. God calls several witnesses to the stand, including Moses, a woman, and, strikingly, a Gentile magician. Micah takes us back to Numbers 22, where King Balak, frightened of Israel's presence, hires Balaam to curse the unwelcome invaders. Balaam and his famous talking donkey encounter God's angel along the way, leading Balaam to repent and to speak the word of the Lord to Balak instead. In the story of Epiphany, we remember the journey of the magi, and through the lens of Micah we can see how it bears a striking resemblance to what God did through Balaam. In both stories, evil rulers seek to use foreign magi against the people of God. Herod hopes the magi will reveal the location of the child born to usurp him. Balak is hoping Balaam will remove Israel's threat with a curse. In both stories the outsiders play the unlikely role of hero, with Matthew's magi going home by another road, and Balaam sparing the people. Lifting up this connection, the preacher could wonder, through what unlikely, outsider allies might God be working today?

This passage offers a strong word to the church. While the early church denounced Marcion's heretical contrast between a violent Old Testament demiurge and a New Testament God of grace, sadly many contemporary Christians continue this unfortunate and inaccurate stereotype. Too many Christians continue to ask how they can reconcile the God of the Old Testament, the God of judgment, with the loving New Testament God of Jesus—and it is not just congregants. In her excellent book *Jesus the Misunderstood Jew,* A.-J. Levine criticizes otherwise progressive leaders for depicting the Pharisees as misogynistic and overly legalistic in order to show how supposedly different and loving Jesus is in contrast.[2]

Preachers might take on this challenge, highlighting these words of Micah. Indeed, in this passage Micah, in the voice of Israel, even suggests an ever-increasing level of sacrifice to appease God. What is required? Only justice, kindness, and love are necessary—precisely the opposite of what one would expect from an overly legalistic faith. In an era when white supremacists have openly chanted anti-Semitic slogans like "blood and soil," it is more important than ever that the church honor our Jewish roots, rather than define ourselves against synagogue stereotypes.

The courtroom setting is worth giving extra attention to in light of environmental ethics and what social scientists understand about perception and cognitive bias. In terms of ethics, the preacher will want to focus on who is participating in the drama. God appears to be playing the role of the plaintiff bringing a complaint against Israel, acting the role of the defendant. Acting as judge are the mountains, hills, and foundations of the earth. Perhaps the mountains and hills serve as judge because they have been there long enough to watch how God has acted in Israel's life over the eons.

How evocative, to imagine humanity arguing our case for justice before the environment itself! The mountains and hills are especially significant in light of how mountaintop removal mining has literally reshaped the geography of Appalachia, poisoning water supplies and impacting not only the earth but some of the poorest of the poor. Preachers could take what is a very familiar text in a new direction here, pairing Micah 6:8 with creation care and justice for the marginalized.

---

2. Amy-Jill Levine, *The Misunderstood Jew: The Church and the Scandal of the Jewish Jesus* (New York: Harper Collins, 2006), 167.

Social science provides another fascinating avenue of exploration here. Especially in legal settings, we expect and hope that those sitting in judgment make decisions with impartiality. Unfortunately, the reality often falls short of the mark. In one study of over 1,100 decisions made by an Israeli parole board, *when* cases were heard proved more significant than the actual details of the cases themselves. Documenting what social scientists refer to as decision fatigue, prisoners appearing before the court in the morning were granted clemency 65 percent of the time; fewer than 10 percent of those unlucky enough to come before the court late in the day were given parole.[3] As members of the parole board made more and more decisions, they became unconsciously less willing to render clemency judgments, regardless of the details before them. This is not because they are unjust judges or unusually flawed in some way; this happened because they are fully human and limited in their abilities.

In the context of Micah, we know that the people themselves are not particularly just. In the rest of chapter 6 we hear the common prophetic lament about unfair scales, dishonest weights, and the rich using violence to get their way. This could provide an easy out for church members who rightly do not see themselves perverting justice in such obvious ways. What the parole board study shows, along with so many others like it, is that even when people are doing their best, because of cognitive bias and physical limitations, we still fall into error. Given this study is the tip of a large iceberg of research, preachers could leverage the work of social scientists to show how, in line with Paul, *all* of us fall short.

The response of the people in Micah is our response as well. Faced with such entrenched, intransigent brokenness, what are we to do? Here Micah anticipates the future in ways that might have surprised even himself. While behavioralists agree that we cannot completely mitigate the impact of cognitive bias and effects like decision fatigue, there are ways to adjust for these predictable blind spots. Social scientists have demonstrated that awareness of our bias and mindfulness practices can significantly improve behavior toward the poor and other marginalized groups.[4] When Micah suggests that the Lord is not interested in ritual sacrifice but in doing justice, loving kindness, and walking humbly, Micah is pointing out specific practices likely to truly change our behavior.

Finally, this text is inherently personal. In 6:8, Micah is not addressing Israel or people in general, but the reader. Those of us living in postmodern industrial economies know what it is to be trapped in an inherently unjust system. The privileged few command and consume vast amounts of resources, while the many toil away in multiple jobs, one emergency away from economic disaster. What is any single individual to do? Micah's words offer a warning and promise. The warning is that simply acknowledging inequity and having the appearance of socially just opinions are not enough. Like empty sacrificial rituals, just thinking the right thoughts or feeling guilty over privilege does not square us with the Holy One of Israel. Seeking ways to do justice, no matter how small; loving kindness, not just to those who will benefit us but to the least of these; and walking in humility: this may not change the world overnight, but cultivating these practices surely will help change the small corners of it in which we live.

KEN EVERS-HOOD

---

3. Roy F. Baumeister, *Willpower: Rediscovering the Greatest Human Strength* (Penguin Publishing Group. Kindle Edition), 97.

4. Stefania Parks, Michelle Birtel, and Richard J. Crisp, "Evidence That a Brief Meditation Exercise Can Reduce Prejudice Towards Homeless People," *Social Psychology* 45, no. 6 (2014): 458–65.

Psalm 15

[1]O LORD, who may abide in your tent?
 Who may dwell on your holy hill?

[2]Those who walk blamelessly, and do what is right,
 and speak the truth from their heart;
[3]who do not slander with their tongue,
 and do no evil to their friends,
 nor take up a reproach against their neighbors;
[4]in whose eyes the wicked are despised,
 but who honor those who fear the LORD;
who stand by their oath even to their hurt;
[5]who do not lend money at interest,
 and do not take a bribe against the innocent.

Those who do these things shall never be moved.

Connecting the Psalm with Scripture and Worship

Psalm 15 is classified as one of the entrance psalms, which may have been used as part of the liturgy upon entering the temple for worship. Psalm 15 begins with two questions to God that essentially address the same topic: Who may abide in your tent? Who may dwell on your holy hill? "Tent" and "holy hill" signify the very presence of God. Praise and prayer take place in the presence of God, yet no one has the right to be in the presence of the Holy One. Even so, the worshiper asks the questions directly to God: "Who may abide in *your* tent . . . who may dwell on *your* holy hill?" The psalm begins with questions, the verses that follow give the answer.

While Psalm 15 is classified as an entrance psalm, "abiding" and "dwelling" seem to be about more than just entering a building. Abide (*yagur*, v. 1) and dwell (*yiskom*, v. 1) are verbs used to describe a longer stay. "Sojourn" is often used in English translations, indicating that the tent of the Holy One, while it is not home to the people, is a place where they are invited to stay for a while.

Although the psalmist asks a specific question of *who* may abide or dwell with God, no one is named as qualified to enter the tent of the

Holy One. Who may abide, who may dwell? The answer rests in the verbs. The ones who may abide are described by their actions, or in some cases, their nonactions. Those who do not slander. Those who do no evil. Those who fear the Lord. Those who stand by their word. Those who do not lend money with interest. Those who do not accept bribes. In brief, those who follow the commandments, or those who live out what it means to be a person of God, are the ones who may dwell with God.

Actions and even nonactions are important in the relation between God and the people who follow in the way of the Lord. The psalmist declares that "those who walk blamelessly, and do what is right" (v. 2) may abide with God, echoing the prophet's exhortation to "walk humbly with your God" (Mic. 6:8). In the sixth chapter of Micah, the people of Israel are on trial as they plead their case. In this passage, Yahweh asks the questions: What have I done to you? In what way have I wearied you? Then the people ask, With what shall I come before the Lord? In other words, what do you want from us . . . thousands of sacrificed animals or gallons of expensive oil? Do you want our firstborn?

They hear a huge no in response. The Lord has told you what is required, says the prophet; do justice, love kindness, walk humbly with God. Once again, verbs are important. The God of Israel is pleased with those who do, who love, who walk with God.

Once, while driving down a country road, I saw a sign in a front yard: "It's hard to walk humbly with God when you're still running with the Devil." Whether one believes in a personification of evil complete with red tights, horns, and pitchfork is not important. What is important is that following the way of God means living in a different way than you did before, a constant turning from evil and a continuous turning to following the way of the Lord. Those who walk humbly with God live a different life that can be seen in the actions of doing, loving, and walking.

The list of "dos" and "don'ts" in Psalm 15 is quite extensive: the psalmist mentions those who walk blamelessly, those who do right, those who do not slander, and those who do no evil, to name just a few. If we are honest, we must confess that we do not make the cut; though we may try, we fail time and time again in living

a blameless life. Certainly, it is only by God's mercy that we are welcomed in the tent or invited to ascend the holy hill where we may join with others in praise of our God.

Psalm 15 could serve as the basis for a prayer of confession:

> O Lord, we want to dwell in your presence,
> but we have failed to walk blamelessly
> and to do what is right.
> We do not always speak the truth;
> we even speak ill of our neighbors.
> We confess that our words and our actions
> hurt others and you.
> Forgive us, O God,
> that we might dwell in your presence
> not only in this life, but in the life to come.

Following a prayer of confession based on Psalm 15, an announcement of God's extravagant love and mercy, proclaimed with passion, could indeed convince the worshiper of the good news that we are in the very presence of the Holy One. Psalm 15 concludes with a promise that those who "do these things" shall never be moved. This is, indeed, good news.

ERIC TODD MYERS

1 Corinthians 1:18–31

[18]For the message about the cross is foolishness to those who are perishing, but to us who are being saved it is the power of God. [19]For it is written,

"I will destroy the wisdom of the wise,
    and the discernment of the discerning I will thwart."

[20]Where is the one who is wise? Where is the scribe? Where is the debater of this age? Has not God made foolish the wisdom of the world? [21]For since, in the wisdom of God, the world did not know God through wisdom, God decided, through the foolishness of our proclamation, to save those who believe. [22]For Jews demand signs and Greeks desire wisdom, [23]but we proclaim Christ crucified, a stumbling block to Jews and foolishness to Gentiles, [24]but to those who are the called, both Jews and Greeks, Christ the power of God and the wisdom of God. [25]For God's foolishness is wiser than human wisdom, and God's weakness is stronger than human strength.

[26]Consider your own call, brothers and sisters: not many of you were wise by human standards, not many were powerful, not many were of noble birth. [27]But God chose what is foolish in the world to shame the wise; God chose what is weak in the world to shame the strong; [28]God chose what is low and despised in the world, things that are not, to reduce to nothing things that are, [29]so that no one might boast in the presence of God. [30]He is the source of your life in Christ Jesus, who became for us wisdom from God, and righteousness and sanctification and redemption, [31]in order that, as it is written, "Let the one who boasts, boast in the Lord."

Commentary 1: Connecting the Reading with Scripture

Paul writes passionately to the Corinthians, seeking to help them heal from multiple conflicts and spiritual shortcomings. Within this passage, Paul sets up a contrast between the wisdom of the world and God's "foolishness." God acts foolishly in at least two ways: using the cross for salvation and entrusting the message about the cross to the imperfect church. The cross seems foolish both to Judaism (because of the shame associated with crucifixion) and to Greco-Roman culture (because crucifixion typically was used as an act of power against insurgents). The main idea of the passage comes in verse 21, which recognizes that wisdom itself does not lead one to understand the cross. Because only revelation interprets the cross, God chooses to work through the church's proclamation to spread the word about the salvation enacted in the cross.

Paul uses the situation of his readers to illustrate his point. Although the church's problems with the sacrament indicate that some of the members of the Corinthian church were rich or upper class, the majority of the church was of humble origin, but became part of God's plan to proclaim the gospel.

Paul quotes two verses of Scripture as part of his argument, beginning in verse 19, where he quotes Isaiah 29:14. Paul quotes from the Septuagint (a Greek translation of the Hebrew), so that the grammar of the quote differs from the text of Isaiah in the NRSV. In the NRSV, wisdom "shall perish," whereas in Paul's quote, God will actively "destroy" wisdom. Isaiah makes the point that the "wisdom" of building military alliances will do them no good. Paul uses the quote to support his understanding that only proclamation will reveal God's plan of salvation. The second quotation comes in verse 31, where he likely alludes to Jeremiah 9:23–24. Paul's words sound similar also to 1 Samuel 2:3, which condemns proud and arrogant talk.

At this point in the letter, Paul wants to undermine the competitiveness that has led to the divisions in the church. He reminds the Corinthians of their humble origins, seeks to deflate their self-aggrandizement, and reminds them of their important mission.

Paul's words in this section of the letter come after his passionate plea that the Corinthians put aside their divisions. He uses a phrase just before this that he uses in other letters, that the church be "united in the same mind" (1 Cor. 1:10, see also Phil. 4:2). The divisions hurt the church's "purpose." Paul apparently experiences distress that the church has divided over allegiance to former leaders. The phrase "I belong to Christ" (v. 12) strikes the reader as curious. Does this represent Paul's answer to the three groups (that they should belong to Christ instead of the three leaders), or does a fourth group even use "belonging" to Christ as a source of pride and superiority? Verse 17 serves as a transition from the discussion about baptism to the words about wisdom and foolishness. In chapter 2, Paul continues the discussion about wisdom, reminding the church that he did not proclaim the gospel to them in human wisdom, but in weakness and humility.

The competitiveness displayed in the loyalty to former leaders manifests itself later in the letter as well. The Corinthians seem to take any blessing from God and turn it into a source of rivalry. They use baptism to delineate factions. They make class distinctions at the Lord's Supper (chap. 11). They boast about spiritual gifts (chap. 12). Paul seeks to subvert their understanding by describing the foolishness of God to act through the cross. Paul also famously exhorts them to a deeper understanding of Christian love (chaps. 8 and 13) and community.

Paul's teaching about resurrection in chapter 15 continues his ideas about God's reversal of expectations. The Greek-thinking Corinthians believed either in no life after death or in the inherent "immortality" of the soul. Paul proclaims resurrection of the body. Human

wisdom will not reveal the resurrection because it is a "mystery" (15:51).

The theme of the limitations of wisdom occurs even within the Wisdom literature of the Old Testament. Wisdom literature operates from an affirmation that wisdom served as an agent of creation itself (Prov. 8:22), so that one can discover some of the ways of God by observation and thoughtfulness. Nevertheless, the Wisdom literature recognizes that wisdom cannot explain everything (see Eccl. 9:11–12).

Different NT authors interpret the cross in a variety of ways. Some of those ways bear similarity to Paul's emphasis on the cross as weakness and foolishness. In the Gospel of Mark, Jesus' crucifixion appears more desolate than in the other accounts. Jesus' followers desert him, and Jesus feels abandoned by God (Mark 14:50; 15:34). One could draw some interesting reflections comparing Paul's teaching on God's use of the cross here and Jesus' statement in John, "And I, when I am lifted up from the earth, will draw all people to myself" (John 12:32).

The theme of humility connects this passage to the reading from Micah for the day. The Corinthians have set up a competition over loyalty to former leaders. Paul exhorts them to humility based on the foolishness of the cross and God's choice of them for the mission of the church. In Micah 6:8, humility forms one part of the "sentence" in the trial scene for the prophet. The Beatitudes from Matthew share the theme of God's reversal of expectations. Just as worldly wisdom would not expect salvation through a cross, so worldly wisdom would not expect the poor in spirit, those who mourn, or any of the other groups named to be blessed. These groups will experience blessing in the kingdom of heaven. Just as one cannot access the foolishness of God's plan of salvation through the cross, so one cannot discern the blessing of the poor in spirit by human wisdom. God reveals this blessing.

Within the larger biblical canon, Isaiah 50:4–9 and 53:1–9, two of the Suffering Servant Songs, explore vicarious suffering. The Servant in Isaiah 50 chooses to endure suffering, not out of self-debasement, but out of obedience. Surely, worldly wisdom would consider such a choice "foolish." The injuries of the Servant in

Isaiah 53 have vicarious benefits. The Servant suffers on behalf of others. His suffering brings healing. The exact process of how the suffering of the Servant brings healing does not appear in the text. This absence supports Paul's point that human wisdom cannot explain the foolishness of God, who acted in the cross for salvation.

This passage offers much potential for reflecting on how to address divisions within the church, either at the local level or in a wider context. In what ways does a competitive spirit make disagreements about doctrine and ethics more difficult to resolve? Can an acknowledgment of limitations serve as a starting point for dialogue? If God can work through the cross and through the ragtag Corinthians, can God not work through a church that cannot come to agreement on social and theological issues? If a church in disagreement seems weaker than one with doctrinal harmony, cannot Paul's conviction encourage the church to continue despite its weakness? Even if a church disagrees about doctrine and ethics, God can work through that church to show the world that the church loves each other.

Paul's specific analysis of the Corinthian church as beginning in social and economic lowliness might resonate better in some congregations than others. Nevertheless, no congregation or denomination has the resources to "save the world." The church always relies on the foolishness of God to act through the cross. Salvation does not lie in the hands of the church.

CHARLES L. AARON JR.

Commentary 2: Connecting the Reading with the World

Those who preach this text ought to do so with weak knees. Those in positions of power—which structurally corresponds with anyone standing behind a pulpit with the Word of God open and challenged to say something divine to God's people—are put on notice when the message is about the "cross" and Christ crucified (1 Cor. 1:18, 23), when the question interrogates anyone who thinks they might be among the "wise" (1:20), when the gospel itself is equated with "foolishness" (1:21), and when the strength of the message is "weakness" (1:25). The sophistication of sermon preparation with its yearning for articulation for a congregation is contradicted by God's choice of the "foolish" (1:27). No, the preacher's only strength is that he or she is preaching the crucified Christ as God's wisdom (1:30–31). A sense of irony must displace our certainty. We gain power only when we know we lack it; we preach Christ only when we are no longer on display for our giftedness.

The Unlikely becoming Somebody, the invisible becoming visible, and the lowly becoming exalted and God's free choice over against human selection runs right through our texts. What God honors is not what we honor. God honors those who "do justice" and "love kindness" and who "walk humbly" (Mic. 6:8). Those invited into God's presence at the Eucharist table are those who have learned a gracious tongue (Ps. 15:3), who devalue evil (Ps. 15:4), who value others who seek God (Ps. 15:4), and whose value is not money (Ps. 15:5). When Jesus stood on the (so-called) mount on the north shore of the Sea of Galilee, his manifesto was to announce that kingdom people were not conventional, high-status Galileans but those whom conventions would choose last for God's work (Matt. 5:3–12). The Beatitudes then are not a list of would-be virtues for high-status people but a countercultural list of people least likely to be valued for God's ultimate kingdom mission. These, Jesus announces for all to hear, are kingdom people. The most common reaction to Jesus' list had to be, "What about me? Why didn't you mention me?" Exactly.

Our text offers the uncommon commonness of a biblical trajectory that values all, great or small. This devaluing of what we value highlights the Bible's incongruity of grace and radical democratization of a status rooted in a different kind of spirituality. Perhaps we need to ponder how in our churches, which are to be our community's best signposts of the kingdom of God on earth, we have created structures of exclusion: Are all invited? Are our activities—unintentionally we would hope—economically or educationally forms of exclusion? Are our illustrations understandable to those of a different political party or a different heritage? Does our church embody the foolishness of the cross as the wisdom of God? Do we prefer to offer positions of decision to those who will make decisions we like, or are we silencing voices who might offer an alternative view? This text points us at Ralph Ellison's *The Invisible Man,* Marilynne Robinson's old pastor marrying the marginalized Lila (*Gilead, Home, Lila*), and Anthony Trollope's clamoring for wealth and status in *The Warden.*

Paul's sharp countercultural terms confronted the esteem-driven and status-conscious Roman world, especially the social-ladder climbers in Corinth, a city famous for wannabes. The path into social status was called the *cursus honorum,* the course toward social honor. The highly regarded city of Rhodes had more than three thousand monuments honoring its honorable. Who were they? Those noble of birth, benevolent with their wealth, capacious in their public speaking, courageous in battle, and virtuous in behaviors. Status drove the Roman Empire, and competition for honor became the game. Paul points a long finger at the game, and one scholar has called his approach the *cursus pudorum,* the path of dishonor, while another speaks of the problem of "Corinthianization" of leadership in Corinth.[1] Which is to say, they desired Paul to play the game of the *cursus honorum,* and he intentionally countered it with the *cursus pudorum.*[2]

The way of Rome is typified in Caesar Augustus's famous *Res Gestae Divi Augusti,* in which he narrates his own accomplishments, many of them surely exaggerated. Boasting was the way of Rome, and it was deeply ingrained on monuments and behaviors in Corinth. Being connected was called patronage, and it

ran deep at Corinth, for in 1 Corinthians 1:12 Paul excoriates the Corinthian way of patronage centers (and surely embodied in separate house churches in Corinth) with "I belong to Paul" and the list goes on (Apollos, Cephas, Christ).

So, when Paul is verbally crucified (in 2 Cor. 10–13 we see the accusations laid at his door by the honor-conscious Corinthians), what's his cruciform response? We preach a crucified Christ, and we will join him in the crucifixion! He says, "We are fools for the sake of Christ" (1 Cor. 4:10), and "We have become like the rubbish of the world" (4:13). Everything about a status-driven culture is turned inside out by Paul, because God turned everything upside down in Christ (1:18–31). If eloquence was valued, Paul bragged about his inability (though his letters disprove him; see 1 Cor. 2:1–5). If they valued leisure for study and the pursuit of the good life, Paul boasted about working manually (cf. Cicero, *On Duties* 1.150–151: "for no workshop can have anything liberal about it," with Paul at 1 Cor. 4:12; 9:6; 2 Cor. 12:14). If they valued titles and labels all framed into a hierarchy of status, Paul values Spirit-giftedness for all (1 Cor. 12). The Roman way was to boast in one's accomplishments; Paul covered that boasting by bragging about persecutions (1 Cor. 1:28; 2:3; 2 Cor. 11:16–33).

Elitism and populism, whose accusations are the backbone of 1 Corinthians 1:18–31, now shape every newscast, and far too many blogs and websites are little more than soapboxes for political opinion. We are a country divided, bragging about "We, the people," a nation known less for its Micah 6–like graces than its Joshua-like guns, and a church seen less for its love than for its strident partisanship. Populists may well label their opponents as elites, but even a cloudy mirror will reveal the opposite case as well. Paul's message of the crucified Christ haunts the church first, and points its long finger at the church, urging it to clean up its own act first. The elite is the person who uses power

1. David I. Starling, *UnCorinthian Leadership: Thematic Reflections on 1 Corinthians* (Eugene, OR: Cascade Books, 2014).

2. Joseph H. Hellerman, *Reconstructing Honor in Roman Philippi: Carmen Christi as* Cursus Pudorum, Society for New Testament Studies Monograph Series 132 (Cambridge: Cambridge University Press, 2005).

to one's own advantage rather than empowering others, and the populist is the one who uses a voice for accusation rather than consolation.

How so? It begins when we come to terms with what God values: a heart turned toward God, and therefore toward all God's people. How so? When the sophisticated articulate a message that the populist is as welcome to the Eucharist table as the elite, because the Eucharist preaches a message that there is no populism or elitism, because there is only "one in Christ." Those who see God most in the crucified Christ dare not become crucifiers of others. When Christ is wisdom, what we value is radically reshaped into the new family of God.

SCOT MCKNIGHT

Matthew 5:1–12

¹When Jesus saw the crowds, he went up the mountain; and after he sat down, his disciples came to him. ²Then he began to speak, and taught them, saying:

³"Blessed are the poor in spirit, for theirs is the kingdom of heaven.

⁴"Blessed are those who mourn, for they will be comforted.

⁵"Blessed are the meek, for they will inherit the earth.

⁶"Blessed are those who hunger and thirst for righteousness, for they will be filled.

⁷"Blessed are the merciful, for they will receive mercy.

⁸"Blessed are the pure in heart, for they will see God.

⁹"Blessed are the peacemakers, for they will be called children of God.

¹⁰"Blessed are those who are persecuted for righteousness' sake, for theirs is the kingdom of heaven.

¹¹"Blessed are you when people revile you and persecute you and utter all kinds of evil against you falsely on my account. ¹²Rejoice and be glad, for your reward is great in heaven, for in the same way they persecuted the prophets who were before you."

Commentary 1: Connecting the Reading with Scripture

Matthew 5:1–2 marks the transition to the first of Matthew's five discourses, the famous Sermon on the Mount. Matthew 5 begins by focusing on Jesus and his response to the crowds. The preceding passage (Matt. 4:18–23) describes the start of Jesus' public ministry of "proclaiming the good news of the kingdom" and "curing every disease and every sickness among the people" (4:23). By the end of chapter 4, news of Jesus has spread and "great crowds" from Galilee and beyond follow him (4:25). Upon seeing these crowds, Jesus ascends the mountain, sits down, and begins to teach his disciples (5:1–2) whom he has just called (4:18–23).

Jesus' mountaintop teaching is pregnant with meaning, both within the narrative of Matthew and that of the Old Testament. In Matthew, Jesus' presence on a mountain signals momentous occasions. It was on a "very high mountain" (4:8) that Satan promised to give Jesus the kingdoms of the world, if Jesus would worship him. His presence on the mountain in 5:1–2 anticipates his withdrawal from the crowds to pray by himself (14:23), his powerful transfiguration (17:1, 9), and his final solemn

hours on the Mount of Olives before his crucifixion (26:30). Jesus' final discourse, the so-called eschatological discourse (chaps. 24–25), occurs on the mountain, with Jesus once again seated and addressing his disciples (24:3). After his resurrection, Jesus meets his eleven disciples once again on a mountain (28:16), where they worship him and receive their commissioning (28:19). In Matthew, the mountain is a set-apart place where the disciples receive instruction and catch glimpses of Jesus' identity.

The motif of the mountain in Matthew also recalls important themes from the Old Testament. Most obvious is the connection between Jesus and Moses, who ascended Mount Sinai after Israel's redemption from Israel (Exod. 19), and who saw the promised land from atop Mount Nebo before his death (Deut. 34:1–4). As in one of the other lectionary readings for this week (Ps. 15:1), the Psalms contain frequent references to the mountain as the dwelling place of God (Ps. 3:4) and as the site of God's king (Ps. 2:6). According to Ezekiel, God's glory that left the temple (Ezek. 10:18) comes to dwell on the mountain (Ezek. 11:23). Zechariah 14, moreover, anticipates God becoming king over all the earth and reigning from the Mount of Olives (Zech. 14:9). These references from the Old Testament color Jesus' presence on the mountain, not only as a new Moses or as Israel's long-awaited Messiah, but also as the manifestation of God's kingly rule as "God with us" (Matt. 1:23).

Starting with Matthew 5:3, Jesus pronounces a series of nine blessings, commonly known as the Beatitudes. While the Beatitudes resist simple subdivision or grouping, there is some correspondence between the first three blessings (5:3–5), the middle four (vv. 6–9), and the final two (vv. 10–12). All but the final blessing in verses 11–12 follow a common structure: Jesus identifies certain conditions or behaviors as blessed and then provides an explanation (*hoti*) for that blessing. The Greek adjective *makarios* (NRSV "blessed") has a fairly wide range of meaning. It can refer to the state of being fortunate, happy, or privileged. It often denotes humans who are the privileged recipients of divine favor.

The repetition of the phrase "the kingdom of heaven" in verse 3 and verse 10 provides an important context for understanding Jesus' Beatitudes. Proclaiming the advent of the "kingdom of heaven" links the preaching of John the Baptist (3:2), Jesus (4:17), and the disciples (10:7). Elsewhere, certain behaviors or actions are required for "entering" the kingdom (5:20; 7:21; 18:3; 19:23). Matthew's parables of the kingdom express the kingdom's surprising growth (13:24, 31, 33, 52), its great value (13:44, 45), and its unexpected makeup (18:23; 20:1; 22:2; 25:1). The "kingdom of heaven" is more than simply a synonym for heaven. To ancient readers, the announcement of a different *basileia* ("kingdom") would have been heard as an alternative to that of Rome. The kingdom of heaven denotes a whole new order of things brought about by the dawning reign of God.

The first three blessings (5:3–5) name those who are paradoxically the special recipients of God's favor. It is not those in positions of power or prestige who are identified as blessed but those on the margins. It is the poor in spirit, the mourners, and the meek who are the objects of God's special favor and concern (see also 25:40, 45). Jesus' pronouncement of God's favor on those who exist precariously on the underbelly of social, religious, and economic power structures connects with Paul's statement about the wisdom of the cross in 1 Corinthians 1:18–31, which also rests in God's choice of those whom the world viewed as foolish, weak, low, and despised (1 Cor. 1:27–28). Similarly, Psalm 34 affirms that God watches the righteous and responds to their cries (Ps. 34:15), that God hears and rescues them from their troubles (v. 17), and that God is near to the brokenhearted and saves the "crushed in spirit" (v. 18). Both Psalm 34 and Matthew 5 assure those who have been beaten down by the world and its systems of power that such experiences are not the end of the story, nor are they indicators of God's absence.

The middle four blessings (Matt. 5:6–9) describe practices that embody the hoped-for kingdom of heaven and the promise of eschatological reward. Longing for justice (v. 6), practicing mercy (v. 7), acting with authenticity and single-mindedness (v. 8), and making peace (v. 9) are kingdom-shaped and kingdom-making practices. They also relate to the Old Testament lectionary texts. These kingdom practices recall God's demand for doing justice, loving kindness, and walking humbly with the Lord in Micah 6:8, actions that are echoed and expanded in Psalm 15:2–5. Together, these three readings emphasize the centrality of what Matthew's Gospel names the "fruits of the kingdom" (Matt. 21:43), those practices, birthed by a vision of God's coming kingdom, that anticipate and activate the promised transformations and reversals that come with it.

The final two blessings (5:10–12) speak of the adverse consequences of adopting the practices demanded by verses 6–9. The second of these blessings (vv. 11–12) restates and expands the sense of the first (v. 10). The parallel between these two is lost slightly in the NRSV translation. The first notes persecution that comes "because of [*heneken*] righteousness"; the longer list of verbal and physical abuse in verse 11 comes "because of [*heneken*] me" (my trans.). The parallel implies that persecution arises from affiliation with Jesus and from the distinctive righteousness he demands (5:20). The two are parallel as well in terms of the eschatological reversal maintained in each ("for theirs is the kingdom of heaven" and "your reward is great in heaven"). Mention of the prophets in the final words of the passage links Jesus and his followers to the Hebrew prophets. They too delivered a "word of the Lord" to a people unwilling to hear the message and all too willing to go to great lengths to discredit or silence their message.

Hearing the Beatitudes in the twenty-first century demands that we hear them both as a consolatory word, blessing the "least of these," in verses 3–5, and as a hortatory word, blessing those who desperately work for justice, practice mercy, and make peace, in verses 6–12. It is not enough for the church to repeat God's blessing on the poor and marginalized; it must also commit to transformative actions, kingdom practices that work for their liberation.

CHRISTOPHER T. HOLMES

Commentary 2: Connecting the Reading with the World

For some, this reading may feel as if someone has thrown a bucket of ice water on an epic story about cosmic apparitions, a virgin birth, mysterious foreign astrologers, a murderous king, a fugitive night-flight into Egypt, a locust-eating baptizer dressed in camel's hair who yells stuff about the "kingdom of heaven" and repentance, while exposing hypocrites and announcing the coming of another One crazier (?!) than him who would baptize with the Holy Spirit and, yes, fire!

The anticipation grows as Jesus is led into the wilderness to be tempted by the enemy—the devil himself. Jesus' kick-derrière responses and victory over the devil rival Luke Skywalker's fight against Darth Vader's invitation to "give himself to the Dark Side" in *Star Wars' Return of the Jedi*;[1] they rival any contemporary meme! Scene after scene keeps us on the edge of our seats while our senses are imbued with all sorts of fascinating impressions. We *like* this hero-like Jesus! Then the action stops, and Jesus sits down and gives the so-called Sermon on the Mount (chaps. 5–7)—a didactic and seemingly long list of dos and don'ts that is as astounding as it is challenging.

This sudden transition in the story's movement is important, and we do well to consider the impact it may have on the listener. Why might this reading not elicit the same excitement as the first four chapters? How might we be different from the disciples who, when Jesus finished, "were astounded" and continued following him (7:28; 8:1)? Given our earthly possessions and comforts, are we even desirous of the rewards? Do we not already live "for God and country"? Why another kingdom? What is the purpose of his teaching? Given Jesus' demands, *who* can do any of this? *Who* would want to and, why? *What* is at stake?

Matthew 5:1–12 continues focusing on Jesus' proclamation and expression of the good news of the kingdom of heaven (Matt. 4:17, 23; 5:3, 10, 12; note that the Beatitudes begin and end with the kingdom as reward). Nine beatitudes describe the nature and character of true disciples. Their demands are radical and thoroughly contrary to the values that seem to galvanize our imaginations and, often, our lives.

Worldly values about who is in or out and what it takes to "make it" have not changed much since the first century. Then and now, those who stand out as heroes of their own destiny take the bull by the horns and let nothing and no one stand in their way. The world describes them as aggressive; they show their power by edging out the inconvenient or the weak; they know how to toot their own horn, they keep a "stiff upper lip," and they "never let you see them sweat!" The goal—not those charged to carry it out—is often what is most dear; a good leader stays focused, whatever the cost. Who you are as a person really does not matter, as long as you get the job done. Unless, you are one of Jesus' disciples. This is where the rubber meets the radical kingdom road.

In Jesus' discourse, the blessed ones—often translated as "happy" but really beyond this passing sentiment to a quality of life that characterizes the person's existence—are the poor in spirit,

---

1. *Star Wars: Episode VI—Return of the Jedi* was released in 1983.

those who mourn, the meek, those who hunger and thirst for righteousness, the merciful, the pure in heart, peacemakers and those persecuted for Christ. For those of us who call ourselves followers of this Christ, these Beatitudes are difficult to hear. If we are a little uncomfortable, it is because we have stopped being passive spectators of Jesus' ministry and have now become the target and reason for his discourse. The Beatitudes become a gauge for character that elicits kingdom-like fruit, and, well, many of us might just be missing the mark (compare the Beatitudes to the "woes" in Matt. 23).

While the preacher may not have time to explain each of the Beatitudes, it may be helpful to show first that the actions (merciful, peacemaking) of those called "blessed" spring from, and are congruent with, the essence of the person. Jesus encapsulates this later in Matthew 12:35, when he says, "The good person brings good things out of a good treasure, and the evil person brings evil things out of an evil treasure" (also Luke 6:45). The blessed are not merciful because it is advantageous for them or because they want to impress. Peacemakers are called children of God because they imitate the Prince of Peace.

Second, given cultural sexualization of terms (insinuating gender), a brief explanation of the term "meek" seems in order. Too often, the term "meek" (Gk. *praus*) has been sexualized to refer to women and is, therefore, considered a less than desirable trait for men (1 Pet. 3:4, women's spirit ought to be "meek and quiet"). However, we find that Christ himself is described as "meek" (Matt. 11:29; 21:5)! A meek spirit is "very precious" in "God's sight" (1 Pet. 3:4) and, Jesus says that the meek will "inherit the earth" (Matt. 5:5; also Ps. 37:11 et al.). So what does this mean?

Briefly, "meek" does not mean shy, weak, or powerless. Rather, the biblical contexts imply the power of self-control against oppressors and antagonists. The meek live in the power of God to do God's will; they feed off the Spirit and

wisdom of God rather than any anger or feeling of reprisal.

Followers show their inner Christ through their everyday behavior and attitudes. The amazing story of forgiveness by the Amish community of the man who shot ten young school girls, killing five, and their outreach to his widow and children, even while they themselves mourned, seems foolish and weak to the world but speaks volumes about the love of God.[2]

On the other hand, meekness does not mean cowardliness. Women, like men, are not called to be victims of abuse. Too often, this text has been used to keep people "in their place" so that others could do with them as they please. Meekness and the promise that such will inherit the earth do not equal, for instance, a kind of "manifest destiny" that justifies enslavement and the displacement of people groups. It does not assume or appropriate its reward. The Gandhis, Martin Luther King Jrs., Cesar Chavezes, the Malala Yousafzais, and Tegla Loroupes know this all too well. In short, meekness does not preclude the courage to be peacemakers, justice seekers, or prophets (Matt. 5:12); it is a prerequisite for it.

Third, Christ often referred to himself and the kingdom of God interchangeably. If Christ and the kingdom of God (and the gospel) are synonymous (Matt. 19:29; Luke 18:29, 30; Mark 10:29, 30), and if the character traits in the Beatitudes reflect who Christ is and, thus, who we are to imitate, then those traits also describe the character of the kingdom over which Christ reigns. The one flows from the other. This may be a good time to evaluate how personal and communal New Year resolutions or mission statements align with kingdom values.

God is not looking for heroes but for followers—even "foolish" ones—to shame the wise and the strong (1 Cor. 1:27). Who can do this? Although not all in the lectionary readings, a cliffhanger pointing to God's power in Matthew 11:28–30; 1 John 2:1; 1 Corinthians 1:31, and other places, would be welcome.

ZAIDA MALDONADO PÉREZ

---

2. Joseph Shapiro, "Amish Forgive School Shooter, Struggle with Grief," *NPR, Religion,* https://www.npr.org/templates/story/story.php?storyId=14900930.

Fifth Sunday after the Epiphany

Isaiah 58:1–9a (9b–12) 1 Corinthians 2:1–12 (13–16)
Psalm 112:1–9 (10) Matthew 5:13–20

Isaiah 58:1–9a (9b–12)

¹Shout out, do not hold back!
  Lift up your voice like a trumpet!
Announce to my people their rebellion,
  to the house of Jacob their sins.
²Yet day after day they seek me
  and delight to know my ways,
as if they were a nation that practiced righteousness
  and did not forsake the ordinance of their God;
they ask of me righteous judgments,
  they delight to draw near to God.
³"Why do we fast, but you do not see?
  Why humble ourselves, but you do not notice?"
Look, you serve your own interest on your fast day,
  and oppress all your workers.
⁴Look, you fast only to quarrel and to fight
  and to strike with a wicked fist.
Such fasting as you do today
  will not make your voice heard on high.
⁵Is such the fast that I choose,
  a day to humble oneself?
Is it to bow down the head like a bulrush,
  and to lie in sackcloth and ashes?
Will you call this a fast,
  a day acceptable to the LORD?

⁶Is not this the fast that I choose:
  to loose the bonds of injustice,
  to undo the thongs of the yoke,
to let the oppressed go free,
  and to break every yoke?
⁷Is it not to share your bread with the hungry,
  and bring the homeless poor into your house;
when you see the naked, to cover them,
  and not to hide yourself from your own kin?
⁸Then your light shall break forth like the dawn,
  and your healing shall spring up quickly;
your vindicator shall go before you,
  the glory of the LORD shall be your rear guard.
⁹Then you shall call, and the LORD will answer;
  you shall cry for help, and he will say, Here I am.

If you remove the yoke from among you,
  the pointing of the finger, the speaking of evil,

¹⁰if you offer your food to the hungry
>   and satisfy the needs of the afflicted,
> then your light shall rise in the darkness
>   and your gloom be like the noonday.
> ¹¹The LORD will guide you continually,
>   and satisfy your needs in parched places,
>   and make your bones strong;
> and you shall be like a watered garden,
>   like a spring of water,
>   whose waters never fail.
> ¹²Your ancient ruins shall be rebuilt;
>   you shall raise up the foundations of many generations;
> you shall be called the repairer of the breach,
>   the restorer of streets to live in.

Commentary 1: Connecting the Reading with Scripture

In Isaiah 58, a prophet calls hearers to ponder what sincere prayer and worship look like. The audience has apparently complained of divine unresponsiveness, saying, "Why do we fast, but you do not see? Why humble ourselves, but you do not notice?" (Isa. 58:3). They seem truly baffled. We are not told what leads them to accuse God of inattention. Perhaps they long for a change in their fortunes that they do not see coming.

This chapter returns to themes from the prophet Isaiah's own days at least two hundred years before. The book's prologue in Isaiah 1 had characterized the bringing of offerings and calling of festivals—long-accustomed acts of devotion—as trampling God's courts. The prophet had claimed that God would cease listening to the people's prayers until they began defending the interests of widows and orphans, those most vulnerable in Israelite society. Various wrongdoings were spelled out in chapters that followed: taking of bribes (1:23; 5:23) robbing the poor (3:15; 5:8; 10:2), and even rewriting, in their own favor, the laws themselves (10:1)—in brief, calling evil good and good evil (5:20). Like his contemporary Micah, Isaiah had warned that such practices would lead to Jerusalem's destruction. This outcome did not emerge immediately, but when it did, more than a century later, the urgency of the prophetic ethic became unforgettable.

Babylonian-era prophets like Jeremiah, Ezekiel, and the poet of Isaiah 40–55 had likewise pointed out the shameful social ethics of Jerusalem's wealthy citizens. Nevertheless each prophet expressed hope that eventual restoration would build a chastened society, ready to cooperate with God's plans. Second Isaiah especially envisioned a reconciliation that would result in righteousness and prosperity for all.

The books of Ezra and Nehemiah testify that Jerusalem's rebuilding came gradually, in fits and starts over the course of several generations. Isaiah's final eleven chapters likewise attest to continued hope, accompanied by disappointment and setback. Humans being human, it is not surprising that injustices lamented by the prophet Isaiah at least two centuries before reappeared, as Isaiah 58 reveals, despite the "furnace of adversity" (48:10) through which the society had come.

Responding to the questions, "Why do we fast, but you do not see? Why humble ourselves, but you do not notice?" (58:3), the prophet accuses worshipers of insincerity. People who mean their prayers change their behavior, not just their clothing, he says. In verses 5 and 6, he spells out a distinct contrast: it is not enough to go about looking gloomy in mourning clothes while continuing to oppress workers and even quarrel and fight. Rather, worshipers must "loose the bonds of injustice" (v. 6).

The reason for this goes back to Egypt. The God to whom the people pray is the God who once sent Moses to the king of Egypt with a divine directive to abandon his slave economy, to "let my people go" (Exod. 5:1). Forty years later, before the former slaves entered the promised land, Moses told them to provide for one another's needs, remembering their own days of suffering: "You shall not deprive a resident alien or an orphan of justice; you shall not take a widow's garment in pledge. Remember that you were a slave in Egypt and the LORD your God redeemed you from there" (Deut. 24:17–18). An economy in which employees are ill-treated, in which some go hungry or homeless or ill clothed, is not one in which freedom is being gratefully remembered.

So now, after centuries of drama, as his hearers complain that God is ignoring their prayers, the prophet essentially replies, "You are ignoring God's prayers to you." At the end of a list of generous blessings that would follow human observance of the Torah, Leviticus 26:13 had said: "I am the LORD your God who brought you out of the land of Egypt, to be their slaves no more; I have broken the bars of your yoke and made you walk erect." What followed this was a prospectus of the terrors Judah would endure, and did endure: war, exile, scattering—a fate, Leviticus maintained, that repentance could change at any time. Here in Isaiah the prophet, by way of reminder, echoes the same imagery, repeating "yoke" twice in verse 6 and once more in verse 9. True responsiveness means, he says, "to loose the bonds of injustice, to undo the thongs of the yoke, to let the oppressed go free, and to break every yoke . . . to share your bread with the hungry, and bring the homeless poor into your house; when you see the naked, to cover them, and not to hide yourself from your own kin" (Isa. 58:6–7).

True repentance is indeed a journey inward for self-examination, as the worshipers in Isaiah 58 seem to intend. It is also a journey outward, adopting practices that mend the world, just as God had done on their ancestors' behalf. Worship alone, unaccompanied by righteous habits, cannot bring reconciliation with God.

Knowing that criticism can only discourage if it lacks a vision of alternatives, the poet then presents what he imagines could be. A just society is a healed one. Reconciliation with neighbors brings holiness. Using imagery that echoes Isaiah 52:12, which was itself drawn from the wilderness wandering stories, the poet pictures God both leading them to a new spiritual place and protecting them from behind as they go: "your vindicator shall go before you, the glory of the LORD shall be your rear guard" (58:8). When that reconciliation comes about, worshipers' wishes will be fulfilled. When they pray, God will answer.

The poet then reiterates the lesson in "if/then" language: if they remove the yoke of bondage they have placed on others, if they cease from blame and accusation, and instead practice generosity, then their darkness will turn into light—an apt image for the season of Epiphany when this passage appears. They will become, in the words of the week's Gospel passage, a city built on a hill that cannot be hidden (Matt. 5:14). The future they long for will be realized: they themselves will be healed and whole, flourishing like a watered garden, and the city will be rebuilt. In fact, the very people being addressed by the prophet will be credited with its restoration. The chapter's final two verses, which stand outside the lectionary reading, further reinforce this hope, saying that such honoring of the Sabbath will result in their riding "upon the heights of the earth" (Isa. 58:14).

The social evils that the prophet Isaiah criticized in the eighth century continued to appear not only after the exile, but throughout history until today. Appropriately, Isaiah 58 is read not only during Epiphany, but also every year on Ash Wednesday, where it reminds Christians, at a moment of deepest repentance and devotion, not only of Jesus' forty days in the wilderness, and not only of their own vulnerability and mortality, but also of the inseparability of devotion from social action. On such days, when Christians turn inward, we hear the prophet's message that our prayers are only as meaningful as our actions toward those who daily depend upon us. If people of faith, hearing this word, renew the world with justice toward the vulnerable, we will rightly be identified as "the repairer of the breach, the restorer of streets to live in" (Isa. 58:12).

PATRICIA K. TULL

Commentary 2: Connecting the Reading with the World

While Christmas garners most of the attention during the winter holiday season, Epiphany, the liturgical setting of this pericope, deserves better, and Isaiah's image of the light rising in the darkness can help. Church historians tell us Epiphany not only predates Christmas, but Epiphany captures a more robust sense of the incarnation as well.[1] Along with Christ's birth, Epiphany celebrates the magi following the star's light, becoming the first to honor Christ's divinity, and extends to the beginning of Jesus' baptism and the beginning of his ministry. More than just a history lesson, however, Epiphany brims with possibilities for the present.

Preachers might take this opportunity, for example, to educate their congregations on the potential cultural alternative Epiphany provides. Rather than simply complain about the commercialization of Christmas, some choose to place more emphasis on the season of Epiphany. Reminiscent of the magi following the star and the light of God reflected in the Christ child, Isaiah lifts up the light of the people of God: "If you remove the yoke from among you, the pointing of the finger, the speaking of evil, if you offer your food to the hungry and satisfy the needs of the afflicted, then your light shall rise in the darkness and your gloom be like the noonday" (Isa. 58:9b–10). In what is still a dark time of the year both physically and emotionally, this emphasis on light is a needed gift. Instead of a season predicated on the economics of gift giving, Isaiah offers a welcome moral grounding. Instead of discussing who received what, this focus on the light might prod us to wonder how we cared for one another with our language, fed the hungry, and cared for the poor.

Building on this theme of action, Isaiah's text challenges the church during what is traditionally a season heavily focused on worship. Especially during a time of year when preachers are spending extra time on sermons, and choirs devote more energy to preparing beautiful music, Isaiah's words remind us if the light of the Christ child illuminates only our worship,

we are missing both the point of Epiphany and Christ's prophetic message. The community Isaiah addresses seems to be hoping that worship might be a sufficient condition for God's blessing rather than being merely a necessary or desired practice. Instead, the prophet sears those with ears to listen, reminding us that God is interested in religious formalities only after the demands for basic social justice are met.

For preachers seeking to put flesh on this aspect of Isaiah's text, the organization Repairers of the Breach led by the Rev. Dr. William Barber III provides a living illustration of how people of faith might go about this. Lifting their name from verse 12 in this passage, Repairers of the Breach, according to their website, "is a non-partisan, not-for-profit organization that seeks to build a moral agenda rooted in a framework that uplifts our deepest moral and constitutional values to redeem the heart and soul of our country."[2] A modern-day prophet, Barber seeks to bridge historic divides of race, gender, and sexual orientation to focus on the marginalized. Powerful and influential, he created grassroots gatherings like his "Moral Day of Action" on September 12, 2016, the largest coordinated action on state capitals ever. At a time when preachers are tempted to moderate our messages, it is worth lifting up the work of Barber, who creates unity across historic divides by speaking clearly and boldly.

Another angle preachers might consider is the ethical implication, given Isaiah's likely exilic context. It is fascinating that Isaiah directs his sermon on social justice at his own people, rather than the easier target of their Babylonian captors. While I would understand a preacher not wanting to kick his people when they were down, Isaiah saves his withering critique for Israel. In verse 3, captive Israel wonders why they fast and God does not seem to care, or why they humble themselves and God does not seem to notice. Isaiah tells them it is because even though Israel is captive, they oppress those working for them and ignore the cries of the

---

1. James F. White, *Introduction to Christian Worship*, rev. ed. (Nashville: Abingdon Press, 1980), 66.
2. https://www.breachrepairers.org/.

hungry and homeless. Why is God not paying attention to their pious devotion? Because they are neglecting justice!

Preachers could take this opportunity to introduce the powerful language of intersectionality to their congregations. Pioneered by theorists like Kimberlé Crenshaw, intersectional theory instructs us that categories like race and gender can merge, or intersect, to form even more powerful forms of discrimination. It is one thing to experience discrimination in the workplace as a white woman, and entirely another thing to face this as an African American woman. In the case of Isaiah's community, wealthy Israelites might have experienced discrimination in Babylonian society, but poor Israelites expressed a kind of double discrimination, being disadvantaged by their captors as well as by their own people. Congregations, even those who consider themselves sensitive to those on the margins, might benefit from the opportunity to reflect on this intersectionality, and ask themselves how they are seeing and caring for members of groups historically overlooked.

The practical implications of Isaiah's critique, especially Isaiah's emphasis on economic justice, provide yet another avenue to explore. Isaiah targets the selfishness of the Israelites. Yes, the Israelites fast, but in Isaiah's eyes their fast benefits themselves at the expense of their workers. Isaiah's solution of sharing is simple, but economics is often more complicated than we expect. Many in our congregations have been taught to believe that in the "real world" Isaiah's words sound nice, but they are not really practical—that people are basically selfish. Perhaps they agree with Isaiah's words in theory, but when it comes to practical living, Isaiah is naive. Rather than complain about such difficult people in our pews, preachers might take this opportunity to engage this conversation and construct a thoughtful response based not only on biblical interpretation but on sound social science too. Preachers may find behavioral economists, for instance, to be helpful and underutilized conversation partners.

In *Predictably Irrational: The Hidden Forces That Shape Our Decisions,* Dan Ariely questions how innately selfish people really are. Ariely cites examples like an Israeli day care that was experiencing a challenge with parents coming in late to pick up their children.[3] While the problem was not serious, the owners of the day care decided that if they instituted a financial penalty for tardy parents, surely they would eradicate the problem. Indeed, if parents are purely self-interested, rational actors, then the penalty should have put an end to the late pickups. What happened, however, was just the opposite. After the day care instituted the penalty, more and more parents started picking their children up late.

People are not as selfish in the "real world" as some would have it. Interpreting this situation, Ariely notes how there are at least two kinds of economies: family economies and business economies. Family economies run on trust, goodwill, and warm feelings, rather than on financial incentives and punishments. By establishing a financial penalty, the day care eroded the family feeling they were not aware was benefiting everyone. Treating one another like family, and exercising forgiveness, tolerance, and sharing, was not just nice; it was also good business.

KEN EVERS-HOOD

---

3. Dan Ariely, *Predictably Irrational, Revised and Expanded Edition: The Hidden Forces That Shape Our Decisions* (New York: Harper Perennial, 2008), Kindle ed. p. 84.

Fifth Sunday after the Epiphany

Psalm 112:1–9 (10)

[1]Praise the LORD!
    Happy are those who fear the LORD,
    who greatly delight in his commandments.
[2]Their descendants will be mighty in the land;
    the generation of the upright will be blessed.
[3]Wealth and riches are in their houses,
    and their righteousness endures forever.
[4]They rise in the darkness as a light for the upright;
    they are gracious, merciful, and righteous.
[5]It is well with those who deal generously and lend,
    who conduct their affairs with justice.
[6]For the righteous will never be moved;
    they will be remembered forever.
[7]They are not afraid of evil tidings;
    their hearts are firm, secure in the LORD.
[8]Their hearts are steady, they will not be afraid;
    in the end they will look in triumph on their foes.
[9]They have distributed freely, they have given to the poor;
    their righteousness endures forever;
    their horn is exalted in honor.
[10]The wicked see it and are angry;
    they gnash their teeth and melt away;
    the desire of the wicked comes to nothing.

Connecting the Psalm with Scripture and Worship

Psalm 112 opens with a shout, "Praise the LORD!" The psalm is one of the Wisdom psalms that typically call attention to those who follow God (the righteous) and those who do not (the wicked). Bernard Anderson characterizes Wisdom psalms as "meditations on the good life."[1] Psalm 112 is crafted as an acrostic poem, that is, each line begins with one of the twenty-two letters of the Hebrew alphabet in sequential order. Many believe the alphabetical schema was an aid to memorization. The mechanism is lost in most English translations.

After the initial exclamation, the psalmist states, "Happy are those who fear the LORD" (Ps. 112:1). For the English reader, the word "fear" gives reason to pause. What does it mean to fear the Lord? Fear (*yare*) can mean to be scared or terrified, such as the feeling one might get while walking alone down a dark alley or watching a horror movie. Fear (*yare*) can also mean to revere, to stand in awe, to honor or respect someone. This is the better interpretation in Psalm 112.

I once led a midweek Bible study on this question of what it means to fear the Lord. I asked the group what came to mind when they heard the phrase "fear the Lord." "Do you get an image of driving through the mountains and you come around a tight turn and there on your right is the most amazing mountain vista ever to be seen— undulating summits, low-lying clouds, incredible sunset? Do you instead get a mental picture of a mail carrier opening the gate of the yard of a

---

1. Bernard W. Anderson, *Out of the Depths: The Psalms Speak for Us Today* (Philadelphia: Westminster Press, 1983), 218.

The Great Deed That God Has Ordained

And so in these same five words that were said before: "I may make all things well," etc., I understand a great comfort in all the works of our Lord God that are yet to come. There is a deed which the blessed Trinity shall do on the last day, as I see it, and when that deed shall be and how it shall be done is not known to any creatures that are beneath Christ; and so it shall be until it is done. And why he wants us to know this is that he wishes that we be more at ease in our soul and at peace in his love, disregarding all tempests that might keep us from truth but only enjoying in him.

This is the great deed that God has ordained from without beginning, treasured and hidden in his blissful breast, known only to himself, the deed by which he will make all things well. For just as the blessed Trinity made all things from nothing, even so the same blessed Trinity shall make well all that is not well. And in this sight I marveled greatly and beheld our faith and I began to think as follows: our faith is grounded in God's word, and it belongs to our faith that we believe that God's word shall be kept in all things. Now one point of our faith is that many shall be damned—such as the angels that fell from heaven on account of their pride and are now fiends; or again a person here on earth who dies without the faith of the holy Church, that is to say those heathen people and also anyone that, having been a Christian, lives an unchristian life and comes to die out of charity—all these shall be condemned to hell without end, for so holy Church teaches me to believe. And thinking about all this, I thought it was impossible that all manner of things should be well as our Lord showed me at this time. And as for the difficulty contained in this showing, I had no answer from our Lord but this: "What is impossible to you, is not impossible to me. I shall keep my word in all things, and I shall make all things well."

Julian of Norwich, *Revelation of Love* 27, trans. John Skinner (New York: Image/Doubleday, 1997), 63.

home, only to be met by a vicious, teeth-showing guard dog on point?" Juanita said, "God is like the vicious dog and we should be very afraid."

Psalm 112 declares, however, that those who fear God are happy, because they delight in the commandments of God. Those who follow God are blessed (*asre*) by God. In other words, the one who reveres God is blessed already. This is more than a transient mood. Rather, those who revere the Lord, those who follow the commandments of God, live in God's goodness because of God's steadfast love.

Through God's love, they are a light for others. They are generous and upright in business affairs. They live a life that gives freely to those in need. They do not earn the blessings of the Creator because of the good they do, but because of the goodness of the Creator.

Most of Psalm 112 focuses on the life of the righteous. The psalm's concluding verse addresses the status of "the wicked," those who do not revere the Lord. Who are the wicked? They are the ones who do not trust in God and who do not live out their lives following God's commandments. We are not told that they are punished for not following the commandments. They see the life of the happy ones and are angry. Instead of fearing the Lord, the wicked ones are full of rage. They gnash their teeth. Their lives are miserable at best. The psalm ends with their miserable lives amounting to nothing.

Psalm 112 is an interesting reading to be paired with the lectionary text from Isaiah 58. The prophet is called to announce rebellion to the house of Jacob. It seems the people believe they are doing what they are called to do. They fast but still quarrel and take advantage of workers. Isaiah calls them to practice a fast of justice, to let the oppressed go free, to share bread with the hungry, to give housing to the homeless. Then they shall shine like a light in the darkness. Then they will know the presence of the Lord in their lives and in the world.

The Gospel reading from Matthew for this Sunday continues from the previous Sunday's reading, which includes the Beatitudes from Jesus' sermon on the mountainside. Here Jesus declares that those who follow his teachings will be salt and light. The theme of being a light in darkness echoes the language of both the prophet and the psalmist. Jesus calls for his disciples to shine with good deeds, which is how followers live out the commandments even today.

There are a number of ways Psalm 112 could give rise to words for worship. Verse 1, "Praise the Lord! Happy are those who fear the Lord, who greatly delight in his commandments" could be spoken as a refrain in a responsorial call to worship. A simple sung refrain using the words of the psalm's first verse could be used as a people's refrain when the psalm is sung as a response to the first reading. The receiving of the offering might be introduced using verse 9, "They have distributed freely, they have given to the poor; their righteousness endures forever."

ERIC TODD MYERS

1 Corinthians 2:1–12 (13–16)

[1]When I came to you, brothers and sisters, I did not come proclaiming the mystery of God to you in lofty words or wisdom. [2]For I decided to know nothing among you except Jesus Christ, and him crucified. [3]And I came to you in weakness and in fear and in much trembling. [4]My speech and my proclamation were not with plausible words of wisdom, but with a demonstration of the Spirit and of power, [5]so that your faith might rest not on human wisdom but on the power of God.

[6]Yet among the mature we do speak wisdom, though it is not a wisdom of this age or of the rulers of this age, who are doomed to perish. [7]But we speak God's wisdom, secret and hidden, which God decreed before the ages for our glory. [8]None of the rulers of this age understood this; for if they had, they would not have crucified the Lord of glory. [9]But, as it is written,

"What no eye has seen, nor ear heard,
     nor the human heart conceived,
what God has prepared for those who love him"—

[10]these things God has revealed to us through the Spirit; for the Spirit searches everything, even the depths of God. [11]For what human being knows what is truly human except the human spirit that is within? So also no one comprehends what is truly God's except the Spirit of God. [12]Now we have received not the spirit of the world, but the Spirit that is from God, so that we may understand the gifts bestowed on us by God. [13]And we speak of these things in words not taught by human wisdom but taught by the Spirit, interpreting spiritual things to those who are spiritual.

[14]Those who are unspiritual do not receive the gifts of God's Spirit, for they are foolishness to them, and they are unable to understand them because they are spiritually discerned. [15]Those who are spiritual discern all things, and they are themselves subject to no one else's scrutiny.

[16]"For who has known the mind of the Lord
     so as to instruct him?"

But we have the mind of Christ.

Commentary 1: Connecting the Reading with Scripture

This passage falls clearly into two parts: 2:1–5, and 2:6–16. In 2:1–5, Paul continues his thought from 1:17, where he reminds the church that he did not preach with eloquent wisdom. In this first part, Paul talks about both the content of his preaching and his own internal response to approaching the Corinthians. He chose to "know" nothing among the Corinthians except the crucified Christ. Paul does not explain that sentence, but one might assume he contrasts himself with the Greek philosophers who parade their erudition. He seems to say that he did not try to impress them with his scholarship, but to focus on the cross. Rather than feeling an abundance of confidence, he experienced fear in the initial stages of his ministry. In a sense, Paul embraces the very accusations against him. When the Corinthians and his opponents at that church accuse him of lacking rhetorical skill (see below), he claims that accusation as a qualifying credential. His message consisted only of the crucifixion. His personal fear only highlighted the power of God.

In the second part of this passage, Paul seems to shift gears. He does claim a kind of wisdom, but a hidden, mysterious wisdom. The reader must take Paul's words here in context. He has claimed to this point that the cross represents God's "foolishness," but here he speaks of a hidden wisdom that only the Spirit can reveal. One gains this wisdom, not by erudition, but by revelation of the Spirit. Perhaps Paul would call the reader to approach the revelation of the Spirit with the same humility that he has encouraged thus far in the letter, as well as the fear and trembling that he himself experienced. That humility would enable one to appreciate that God has revealed something of the divine self through the Spirit.

The CEB offers as translation of verse 11 an alternative to the NRSV. Using plural pronouns as a means of inclusion, the CEB translates, "Who knows a person's depths except their own spirit that lives in them?" Both translations seek to render Paul's Greek phrase, which literally means "the things of a human being/person." The CEB may have drawn a parallel between God's depths and human depths. God has revealed some of what only God can know. Just as people know things about themselves that remain hidden to others, so only God knows the deepest things about the divine self.

Just before this passage, Paul reminded the people of their own humble beginnings (1:26). In a sense, Paul establishes solidarity with them by disclosing his trepidation. Neither Paul nor the Corinthians can claim privilege or superiority from a traditional human perspective. They both rely on the power of God. Moving on in his teaching in chapter 3, Paul exhorts the Corinthians to recognize that their quarreling, divisions, and competition indicate that they are not ready for the revelation of God's mysterious wisdom.

Throughout both of the letters to the Corinthians, Paul spends much effort defending himself against the accusations of his opponents. Second Corinthians 11:5 mentions "super-apostles," who seem more impressive to the church. Compared to them, Paul does not speak as well, nor seem as wise. In 2 Corinthians 10:10 we gain some insight into the accusations against Paul. Paul defends himself by describing the hardships and indignities he has endured. His willingness to persevere in spite of these painful events should give him credibility to the Corinthians. Enduring these things demonstrates both physical and spiritual stamina. Nevertheless, he will boast only in his weakness.

In chapter 12, he relates in a humble way an experience he had. Whether he had a mystical or near-death experience or something else (2 Cor. 12:2–5) does not come through clearly in the account. He then describes a "thorn" that has afflicted him (v. 7). The exact nature of the thorn has generated much debate, but God's grace has enabled Paul to continue. This revelation of God has come despite Paul's weakness. Paul argued in the passage for today that one can know the mystery of God's ways in the cross and for creation only by the revelation of the Spirit. In chapter 12, that revelation comes to one who experiences hardship and weakness as manifested in the "thorn."

In 1 Corinthians 2:1, Paul refers to the "mystery" of God (NRSV). The word in Greek is usually translated as "witness" or "testimony" (see the NRSV footnote). In 15:51, the NRSV contains the English word "mystery," but the Greek is the usual word for mystery (*mystērion*). In any case, both texts refer to God's ways that lie beyond human comprehension. In chapter 2 the mystery is God's ways in the cross of Christ. In chapter 15, the mystery is the transformation that occurs in resurrection.

The reader might note some of the irony of Paul claiming that he does not speak with gifts of rhetoric. Paul's defense is actually quite eloquent and profound. Even his self-effacing comments show disarming skill. First Corinthians 13 displays poetic and literary genius. While Paul often writes (or dictates) in a somewhat disorganized manner, jumping from topic to topic, nevertheless he writes well, using arresting images and metaphors. Acts 17 portrays Paul as one who can stand up among the philosophers and make a powerful speech, an orator who can hold his own in the Areopagus. Though scholars doubt the historical value of Luke's presentation of Paul in Acts 17, the reader might safely assume from all of the evidence that Paul was a compelling figure. He founded churches, and attracted even Gentiles to the church.

The preacher can make some interesting links between the lectionary readings. Matthew 5:13–16 identifies the church as the salt and light of the world. Paul calls the church to spiritual discernment and maturity. Those qualities enable the church to live into its identity. The text from Isaiah 58 speaks of the human search for God. Paul proclaims that God's Spirit reveals what is hidden about God. The humility and maturity to which Paul calls the church enables the church to receive the revelation from the Spirit. Just as Christians seek God, so God seeks to bridge the gap, revealing through the Spirit the divine nature.

One can find the theme of mystery and deep secrets of God in various places in Scripture. In Daniel 2, Nebuchadnezzar wants to know the meaning of his dream. In a blessing, Daniel speaks of God's revelation of "deep and hidden things" (Dan. 2:22) and tells the king that God "reveals mysteries" (v. 28). Part of that revelation

is the establishment of an enduring "kingdom" (v. 44). In Ephesians, part of the deutero-Pauline material, God's plan for the reconciliation of all things is a "mystery" (Eph. 1:9–10).

Using Paul's understanding of the church in 1 Corinthians, the preacher can inspire the church to seek greater unity on the basis of humility and spiritual maturity. Reflection on Paul's message that God has revealed mysteries and part of God's very self can produce an experience of awe and wonder. The highest learning and the deepest thinking, although helpful to the church, cannot plumb the depths of the mysteries of God. If God has chosen to reveal such mysteries, can the church not work together despite its differences to appreciate the gift God has bequeathed to it?

Preachers can enable the church to move beyond a self-help mentality about its ministry. God has revealed the mysteries of the creation. The church seeks a deeper understanding of God and the mind of Christ. The church offers more than just advice for daily living. It offers a sense of awe at God's revelation.

CHARLES L. AARON JR.

Commentary 2: Connecting the Reading with the World

At times it is the irrelevancy of Christ crucified that is most relevant. Nowhere is Christ less relevant than with our communication styles, but it is precisely here that Christ is now most relevant. Relevancy is then a two-edged sword: it cuts into culture with the gospel and it cuts into the gospel with culture. Relevancy heals, and relevancy poisons. When it heals, it does so because it cuts into a space we call our own, but that space is the world, and the world is in need of redemption.

There is a theory in the social sciences called encapsulation.[1] In the church, it may go like this: an advocate for the Christian faith (evangelist) initiates and exposes a potential convert to something that borders on a self-contained world where the advocate's faith (Christianity)

surrounds the potential convert in order to facilitate conversion. Some parents shield their children from outside influences, and most parents do this to one degree or another. Some pastors attempt to shield parishioners from alternative beliefs and communities. Some youth pastors create encapsulating experiences for their youth group by taking them on retreat, both by shielding them from outside voices (like the internet and a cell phone and ideologies they want to mute) and exposing them to the preferred voice (theirs, their church's, their theology's). Such encapsulating experiences can be physical (a retreat house), social (removing the potential convert from social peers whom the parents or youth pastor deems negative), and ideological (silencing one ideology so that another can be

1. Scot McKnight, *Turning to Jesus: The Sociology of Conversion in the Gospels* (Louisville, KY: Westminster John Knox Press, 2002), 92–98.

heard more clearly). New relationships can be formed, alternative rituals embodied, and a new rhetoric can be heard.

Why does this sound like manipulation? Is it? Is this the way of revivalism, of Sunday morning sermons, of adult Bible study groups in homes, of conferences for church folks, and of education itself? Yes and no. In some ways, but not in other ways. Paul's words in 1 Corinthians 2:1–12 address our communication techniques directly. The church needs to become a place where a cruciform model of communication permeates all its words. When this happens, communication is not coercive encapsulation, but redemptive. Redemptive communication shaped by the way of Christ is known for the freedom it permits and by the freedom it creates.

Paul learned this the hard way. His communications were a constant source of antagonism with the Corinthians who had embraced the Roman way of status and honor, eloquence and coercion. As Kathy Ehrensperger has demonstrated,[2] Paul's theology of Christ crucified and his ethic of cruciformity (or Christoformity) were not abstractions of the mind but instead an embodied way of life. Aggression, competition, and domination were the ways of Roman communication—seen in nearly every street in Corinth, engraved on every monument, highlighted in every act of benevolence, heard in every public speech (and there were many)—but Paul believed everything was to be conformed to Christ in his life, death, burial, resurrection, and ascension. This includes how to communicate. Hence, "I did not come proclaiming the mystery of God to you in lofty words or wisdom" (1 Cor. 2:1). Instead, his words were "not with plausible words of wisdom, but with a demonstration of the Spirit and of power, so that your faith might rest not on human wisdom but on the power of God" (2:4–5). Whether Paul lived up to this is another issue (see Gal. 2:11–14).

Paul did know the freedom of Christian communication. Paul surrendered his words about Christ to the Spirit (1 Cor. 2:4, 10–13). A church's language and the pastor's pulpit are easily turned into bully pulpits or partisan posturing. Coercion and manipulation are consequences of words not surrendered to the freedom of the Spirit. Words surrendered to the Spirit are gone; their consequences are not measured, their effectiveness not calculated. Words surrendered to the Spirit are in a sacred trust with God the Spirit, so the Spirit can do what the Spirit does. We speak the redemptive word of Christ, and the Spirit does the redemption. We seek to create space for the word of Christ to be heard. We lose control; we cease coercion; we surrender to what God wills to do with the message of redemption. When we become strident in our words or when we bully those who do not conform to our ideas, we cease Christian community and fall for the way of empire. When we speak the words of Christ to others and give those words to the Spirit, we create Christian communication.

Surrendering words to the Spirit is what it means to be the church: to be a place where our words about the Word (living and written and preached) are given to the Spirit to become inscribed in the heart of the auditor. Dietrich Bonhoeffer said that sanctification through the Spirit becomes a struggle: "It is the struggle that seeks to prevent the world from wanting to be church, and the church from wanting to be world."[3] Which is precisely what Paul was attempting to embody for the Corinthians: he wanted the church to be the church in its wordiness by letting the Word be nurtured by the Spirit instead of by our manipulation, calculation, and measurement. He struggled with the Corinthians over letting Spirit-born words not become the wisdom of this world, the wisdom of an empire known for force.

Wisdom, then, for Paul is not about knowledge, study, expertise, technology, and mastery. Wisdom is Christ, and if Christ is Christ crucified, then wisdom is redefined into Christoformity or cruciformity. Wisdom is to live in God's world in God's way, and God's way is Christ, and Christ's way is the cross. Wisdom is cruciformity. Cruciform wisdom is not the world

---

2. Kathy Ehrensperger, *Paul and the Dynamics of Power: Communication and Interaction in the Early Christ-Movement*, Library of New Testament Studies 325 (London: T. & T. Clark, 2007), 115.

3. Dietrich Bonhoeffer, *Discipleship*, Dietrich Bonhoeffer Works 4 (Minneapolis: Fortress Press, 2001), 262.

(1 Cor. 2:6) and is comprehended only through the Spirit (2:10–13).

The lectionary readings for this Sunday are exhibitions of cruciform wisdom and communication. Fasting (Isa. 58) unfortunately has become today, as it was then, as manipulative as our communication styles. We think that, if in a difficult situation, we fast and pray, then we will get what we want. This turns fasting into an instrument we use to our own benefit and pleasure. Fasting in the Bible, however, is not instrumental but is responsive. That is, in a grievous situation we fast *in response* to the grievous situation, and sometimes the situation is resolved. This means that fasting identifies with God's own grief over a situation.

Cruciform wisdom reveals that fasting is the act of identifying with pain, as Christ identified with us in his death. Hence the psalmist extols the obedient, but he defines the obedient as "those who deal generously and lend, who conduct their affairs with justice" and "have given to the poor" (Ps. 112:5, 9). It is an act of cruciform sacrifice for others to surrender what we have for the good of others. This is what it means to be "salt" and "light" (Matt. 5:13–16). Jesus, in other words, is the embodiment of God's will because he is the one who "fulfills" the "law and the prophets" (v. 17). How does he embody the will of God? He gave himself for the redemption of others.

SCOT MCKNIGHT

Fifth Sunday after the Epiphany

Matthew 5:13–20

¹³"You are the salt of the earth; but if salt has lost its taste, how can its saltiness be restored? It is no longer good for anything, but is thrown out and trampled under foot.

¹⁴"You are the light of the world. A city built on a hill cannot be hid. ¹⁵No one after lighting a lamp puts it under the bushel basket, but on the lampstand, and it gives light to all in the house. ¹⁶In the same way, let your light shine before others, so that they may see your good works and give glory to your Father in heaven.

¹⁷"Do not think that I have come to abolish the law or the prophets; I have come not to abolish but to fulfill. ¹⁸For truly I tell you, until heaven and earth pass away, not one letter, not one stroke of a letter, will pass from the law until all is accomplished. ¹⁹Therefore, whoever breaks one of the least of these commandments, and teaches others to do the same, will be called least in the kingdom of heaven; but whoever does them and teaches them will be called great in the kingdom of heaven. ²⁰For I tell you, unless your righteousness exceeds that of the scribes and Pharisees, you will never enter the kingdom of heaven."

Commentary 1: Connecting the Reading with Scripture

In Matthew 5:13–20, Jesus continues to instruct his disciples from the mountain. This passage focuses on the identity of the disciples (Matt. 5:13–16) and the relationship between the teaching of Jesus and that of the law and the prophets (vv. 17–20).

Two images characterize the identity of the disciples: salt and light. In verse 13, Jesus identifies his disciples as "the salt of the earth." In the Old Testament, salt occurs in the context of Israelite worship (Lev. 2:13; Ezek. 43:24), including the mention of a "covenant of salt" (Num. 28:19; 2 Chr. 13:5). The Old Testament also attests to the more common idea of salt as a seasoning intended to add flavor to food (Job 6:6). In 2 Kings 2:20–21, Elisha performs one of his first miracles by using salt to make a spring wholesome again, suggesting a purifying or life-giving quality of salt. It is likely that early readers of Matthew would have recognized salt as an agent of enriching, preserving, and transforming. What would it mean, then, for salt to become tasteless? Although pure salt cannot actually lose its flavor, the salt used in antiquity was rarely pure. Because of its mixed quality, the sodium chloride that gave salt its flavor could dissipate in humid weather.[1] Salt becomes tasteless when it is not used or when it is used sparingly.

Light is the controlling image in verses 14–16. Reference to the disciples' light (vv. 14, 16) frames the identification of the disciples as a city on a hill and as a light set on a stand. The metaphor of the disciples as a city on a hill highlights the visible, conspicuous nature of their existence. Their distinctiveness cannot or should not be hidden. This sense is all the more clear in Jesus' saying about the lamp in verse 15. A lit lamp illuminates dark places, a function that would be limited, if not eliminated, by putting it under a basket. Applied to the disciples, the lit lamp signifies their utility, distinctiveness, and conspicuousness. In this way, the metaphor of light aligns with the metaphor of salt. Like light, the image of salt pertains not only to the particularity of the disciples but also to their usefulness.

---

1. See "hals, halos" (5.25) in Johannes P. Louw and Eugene A. Nida, *Greek-English Lexicon of the New Testament Based on Semantic Domains*, 2 vols., 2nd ed. (New York: United Bible Societies, 1989).

Just as salt left in a container becomes ineffective, so too a basket renders a lit lamp inept.

The reference to "earth" and "world" in verses 13–14 add a sense of comprehensiveness to the other features of the disciples' identity. While Jesus' mission discourse suggests some reserve in moving beyond the house of Israel (see Matt. 13), his commissioning the disciples in Matthew 28 aligns with this expansive scope. Such a scope may evoke the vision of Isaiah 2:2–4 of all the nations streaming to the mountain of the Lord.

The image of light figures prominently in two of the other lectionary texts for this week. The passage from Isaiah 58, like Matthew, speaks metaphorically of a people's light. In Isaiah, it is the light of the people of Israel, but Isaiah speaks of their light, not as a present reality, but as a condition that will come about in the future (Isa. 58:8, 10). It is significant that the light of Israel will shine when they practice righteousness. Specifically, light arises when the people free the oppressed (v. 6); care for the hungry, the poor, and the naked (v. 7); and provide for the hungry and the afflicted (v. 10). Isaiah 58 connects thematically as well when the text indicates that one consequence of Israel practicing righteousness—one consequence of their light rising—is the restoration or rebuilding of a city (v. 12).

The passage from Psalm 112 pronounces blessing on those who fear the Lord and who delight in God's commandments (Ps. 112:1). These people "rise in the darkness as a light for the upright" (v. 4). Once again, the metaphor of human light connects with human behavior. Light is connected with those whose "righteousness endures forever" (vv. 3, 9), those who are gracious, merciful, and righteous (v. 4), those who conduct their affairs with justice (v. 5), and those who give freely to the poor (v. 9).

These qualities related to the metaphors of salt and light connect to Jesus' declaration of God's favor on those who experience persecution. Those who practice the righteousness that Jesus demands, and who do so boldly or without fear, will experience the sort of hardships described in Matthew 5:11 and elsewhere in Matthew's Gospel (see Matt. 10:17, 19; 24:9). In contrast to this, another consequence of the disciples' distinctive identity is that others will see their good works and give glory to God (5:16). The idea of other people glorifying God on account of human actions occurs only two other times in Matthew's Gospel. Both times it describes the response of the crowds in reference to Jesus' healing (9:8; 15:31). The idea of God receiving glory because of the "light" of the disciples' actions and lifestyle stands in contrast to the hypocrites mentioned later in the sermon who perform religious rites for the praise of human audiences (6:2, 5, 16).

The remainder of the text (5:17–20) is held together by reference to the teachings that Israel received in the past (the law and the prophets) and the teaching that Jesus offers. The basic sense is clear: Jesus' teaching is not opposed to the law and the prophets, nor is it meant to undermine or eliminate them (v. 17). Rather, Jesus' teaching is said to fulfill (v. 17) and enact (v. 18) the law in its entirety. In this way, these final verses anticipate the antitheses found in the following passage (5:21–48). These verses also highlight the distinctive righteousness demanded of the disciples of Jesus, a righteousness that "exceeds that of the scribes and Pharisees" (v. 20).

Given the negative view of the scribes and the Pharisees elsewhere in Matthew (see esp. chap. 23), their mention here presents certain problems for contemporary interpreters. How are we to understand this need for exceeding righteousness in a way that does not vilify ancient and modern Judaism? Attention to historical context is an important first step. We misunderstand these words about the scribes and the Pharisees if we interpret them as a contrast between Christianity and Judaism, since Jesus and his earliest followers were Jewish.

These words are better understood as indicators of a conflict within Judaism, a contest over identity, practice, and sacred traditions among rival groups of Jews. In this regard, the strong words of Jesus can be understood as analogous to ideas found in some of the Dead Sea Scrolls, which preserve some sharp words of another group of Jews who were critical of and disaffected from the Jerusalem establishment.

Finally, the focus on teaching is important. Matthew's depiction of Jesus, and the righteousness that he teaches, is presented in contrast to the teaching of Matthew's adversaries. As we know from similar in-fighting among the popular philosophers at the time, polemic among rival teachers is rarely fair or unbiased. Rather, the rhetorical purpose of such polemic is to uplift one's own perspective while using shame and slander to discredit the views of others. While these details provide some context for Jesus' words about the scribes and the Pharisees, they do not resolve fully the problems they present, especially given their use in the history of interpretation as tools for prejudice and even violence against the Jewish people.

CHRISTOPHER T. HOLMES

Commentary 2: Connecting the Reading with the World

This reading continues the so-called Sermon on the Mount, which ends in 7:29. Rather than the essence of rewards for expressing kingdom values that define the "blessed" in God's eyes, Jesus focuses on the nature of their mission to the world. This mission is as much a reflection of *who* they are (followers) as *what* they are, or should be, in Christ (salt and light). These very earthy metaphors, "salt" and "light," are more than pedagogical props with spiritual admonitions. If by "kingdom" Christ means a new, love-imbued "order" or "kin-dom"[2] (kind-om?!), where we live in ways that gratify the just and merciful God and "king," then being light and salt has all sorts of sociopolitical and economic implications for life and ministry.

Unless previously addressed, a brief pause may help clarify misinterpretations creating two kingdoms: "of God" and "of heaven." Bifurcation of creation into spirit and matter by some has engendered creative exegetical gymnastics arguing for a supposed qualitative and historical difference between the "kingdom of God," gained through the righteousness of Christ, and the "kingdom of heaven," to be gained through good works in a period called by dispensationalists the tribulation. Because some listeners may have been exposed to such views, or simply wonder why Mathew uses "kingdom of heaven" while Luke uses "kingdom of God," you may allay confusion by explaining that Matthew's preference for "heaven" as an analogy for the Lord's name is in line with his Jewish audience and their fear of using God's name in vain.

Although light and salt are precious commodities even today, most Western, twenty-first-century listeners will not understand the weight of Jesus' metaphors without some context. It may be more suitable to find equivalent objects without which our lives would be impacted in many ways. It might be Wi-Fi, Google, mobile phones, electrical outlets (for all of the above), coffee (?!), and/or clean water and air. Inviting the audience to hold their breath for a few seconds beyond what they are accustomed to, or imagining themselves with no recourse to light in a very dark alley, may be one way of making the weight of the metaphors more lucid.

On the other hand, it may be as fun as it is insightful, to talk about the role of salt as "manure" or fertilizer. Luke 14:35 helps us make this connection; without its "saltiness," Jesus says, "it is fit neither for the soil nor for the manure pile, they throw it away." Humbling? Only if we lose our saltiness and are good merely to be trampled on! In any case, this seemingly indecorous metaphor for followers reminds us again of the earthy nature of the gospel. As salt, followers are to enrich the "earth" in ways that prepare it (creation and people) for the good news.

Israel was well aware of the use of light or fire in Gentile cult initiations (e.g., Mazda was the god of light in Zoroastrianism) and of the many "sun" deities called upon to shoo away demons that lurked in the dark. During Israel's exodus from Egypt, God was present as a pillar of light by night leading them to the promised land. Theologically, then, references to being "light" would have made sense to Jews recalling God's admonition to be light in darkness. In Psalm

2. Ada María Isasi-Díaz, "Kin-dom of God: A Mujerista Proposal," in Benjamín Valentín, ed., *In Our Own Voices: Latino/a Renditions of Theology* (Maryknoll, NY: Orbis Books, 2010), 171–90.

112 to be "light" is to be gracious, merciful, and righteous. Those who "rise in the darkness" (Isa. 58:10) are generous; they give to the poor and are just.

For later followers, reference to light would be reminiscent also of Jesus' "I Am" sayings recorded in John (John 8:12). Because ancient hierarchical divisions between deities (e.g., Greek gods) and their worshipers were normative, Jesus' identification of his followers as light is radical. His light analogy challenges qualitative divisions between God's followers and the common practice of heightening a deity by denigrating the worth of followers. To denigrate creation is to denigrate its Creator.

Finally, light is no respecter of persons. Its rays reach unlikely places and welcome *all* to its benefits. This too is a reflection of God's reign. Like a city built on a hill, the light of followers *around the world* and throughout history is to shine for all to see. It (i.e., their good works) is to be a natural and grateful expression of the light of God in them.

As *God's people*, Jesus reminds them of their mission; *as the Son of God*, Jesus reminds them whose Spirit they are reflecting and to whom all glory belongs (1 Cor. 2:12; Matt. 5:20b). This brings us to our present Western-nation context.

While it is critical to consider the implications of our call for daily life and ministry, it is just as critical to reconsider the audience Jesus is addressing. The "you" (*hymeis*, second person plural) in the discourse are the "meek," the "poor in spirit," "peacemakers," those who "mourn," those who are "merciful" and "hunger and thirst for righteousness" (Matt. 5:3–9). People used to being singled out (or singling themselves out) as the center and paragon of all that is good and right in the world often, and all too easily, equate such passages with themselves and with their nation.

We should be especially careful not to associate the "city on a hill" (v. 14), for instance, with an ideology called American exceptionalism. In his 1630 sermon "A Model of Christian Charity," John Winthrop associated a "city upon a hill" with the colonizing project in hopes that others would say of succeeding plantations, "may the Lord make it like that of New England."[3] While well intended, various US presidents have since used the analogy to refer to the United States and a "manifest destiny." Nations, however, are not the kingdom of God or its equivalent. The kingdom of heaven is a way of *being* that proclaims the dawning of a new hope, a new way—the "here not yet" that God will establish but we are to live out, even now. It is the loosing of the bonds of injustice, sharing our bread, bringing the homeless poor into our house, and clothing the naked (Isa. 58:6–10; Matt. 25).

Jesus also indirectly addresses another group: the Pharisees and scribes, whose righteousness we are to surpass, should we want to enter God's reign. Pharisees and scribes thought themselves examples of righteous living, yet it is clear here that, in God's eyes, the opposite is true. Breaking the commandments, they teach others to do the same. Jesus, however, comes to fulfill the commandments and not to "abolish the law or the prophets" (his "do not think" seems to indicate some believed this was the case). Jesus summarizes these commandments as "'You shall love the Lord your God with all your heart, and with all your soul, and with all your mind,'" and "'You shall love your neighbor as yourself.' On these two commandments," says Jesus, "hang all the law and the prophets" (Matt. 22:36, 39, 40.)

Having said all this, sometimes a story may be all that is needed to guide understanding and evoke the passion that instruction may subdue. Leo Tolstoy's simple yet powerful story *Where Love Is, There God Is Also* gets at the heart of what it means to live out the kin-dom of God. One might consider using it as an example, with several persons reading it to the congregation or using all or part of the free LibriVox recording.[4]

ZAIDA MALDONADO PÉREZ

---

3. John Winthrop, "A Model of Christian Charity," https://www.losal.org/cms/lib/CA01000497/Centricity/Domain/340/City_upon_a_Hill_document.pdf. Portions of this are found on p. 211 in this volume.

4. Leo Tolstoy, *Where Love Is, There God Is Also*; see #20 at https://librivox.org/short-story-collection-vol-051-by-various/.

Sixth Sunday after the Epiphany

Deuteronomy 30:15–20   1 Corinthians 3:1–9
Psalm 119:1–8   Matthew 5:21–37

Deuteronomy 30:15–20

[15]See, I have set before you today life and prosperity, death and adversity. [16]If you obey the commandments of the LORD your God that I am commanding you today, by loving the LORD your God, walking in his ways, and observing his commandments, decrees, and ordinances, then you shall live and become numerous, and the LORD your God will bless you in the land that you are entering to possess. [17]But if your heart turns away and you do not hear, but are led astray to bow down to other gods and serve them, [18]I declare to you today that you shall perish; you shall not live long in the land that you are crossing the Jordan to enter and possess. [19]I call heaven and earth to witness against you today that I have set before you life and death, blessings and curses. Choose life so that you and your descendants may live, [20]loving the LORD your God, obeying him, and holding fast to him; for that means life to you and length of days, so that you may live in the land that the LORD swore to give to your ancestors, to Abraham, to Isaac, and to Jacob.

Commentary 1: Connecting the Reading with Scripture

Congregants representing diverse ages and interests may recollect a variety of less-than-helpful associations when they hear Moses' key phrase, "Choose life," in Deuteronomy 30:15–20.

"Choose life," riffed Edinburgh youth Mark "Rent Boy" Renton in the opening lines of the 1996 film *Trainspotting*. What he calls "life" in that scene could hardly contrast more with that envisioned by Moses. "Choose a job," he continues. "Choose a career. Choose a family. Choose a f***ing big television, choose washing machines, cars, compact disc players, and electrical tin openers," he begins. His speech continues to devolve into cheerless portrayals of mind-numbing consumerism as the only alternative he perceives to what he himself is choosing, which is heroin addiction.

Renton returns twenty-one years later in *Trainspotting 2* with a new version of his infamous, oft-quoted monologue. To a woman who has heard the phrase used by one of their friends, Renton explains, "'Choose life' was a well-meaning slogan from a 1980s antidrug campaign, and we used to add things to it,"

demonstrating with a new riff, not this time on materialism but, among other aspects of the contemporary world, social media obsession.

Though many movie fans believe the phrase "Choose life" to have originated with *Trainspotting*, Renton's explanation is accurate, if incomplete. The words had been printed in block letters on T-shirts in 1983 by fashion designer Katharine Hamnett to preach against suicide as well as drugs. She, in turn, had been inspired by Buddhist thinking, exemplified by nuclear disarmament advocate Daisaku Ikeda in his "choose life" dialogues with British historian Arnold Toynbee in the 1970s. Many music fans first saw Hamnett's T-shirts being worn in the performing group Wham!'s joyous video "Wake Me Up Before You Go-Go." To complicate associations further, the same year *Trainspotting* appeared, the slogan was also adopted by pro-life groups raising money for antiabortion campaigns through specialty license plates.

In short, whether sincerely or ironically, each of those late-twentieth-century manifestations envisions what it means to choose life in differing, usually narrower, ways than Moses does in Deuteronomy. Preachers should be aware of the various voices of peace advocates, T-shirt makers, musicians, activists, and movie characters that may compete with Moses when congregants hear these words.

This passage is part of the conclusion to Moses' lengthy hortatory speeches on the plains of Moab, just before his own death and the entrance of the wandering tribes into the promised land. The verses ring with calls to decision making based on all that Moses has already explained. Throughout his speeches, Moses has assured the Israelites repeatedly that, out of all the earth's tribes, God has chosen them (Deut. 7:6; 14:2). This choice came not because they were the greatest nation in numbers (7:7) or even in goodness (9:5), but because God loved their ancestors (4:37; 10:15), God has chosen to make a "treasured possession" (7:6; 14:2) out of this mass of people that is not yet a nation.

The word "choose" is used frequently in Deuteronomy to describe God's choices. Here it offers an invitation to hearers themselves. It conveys that things can certainly go another way. God could have chosen others, but chose the Israelites, running the risk of not being chosen in return. Divine choice means nothing unless those chosen return the favor.

The passage maintains throughout that it is life itself that is at stake. The noun "life" recurs four times, contrasted almost always with death, and the verb "live" appears an additional four times, as the qualities of living before God are described. Moses spells out the choices: obedience to God's commandments will lead to long life and prosperity, while opting to follow other gods will lead to destruction. When obedience is equated to life itself, the choice appears straightforward.

The passage may strike us several ways. It may strike some as simplistic. Who would not choose life over death, if we could see clearly where diverging paths led, and if we could overcome our own resistance to sensible choices? Whether as youths deciding how far to take risks, middle-aged adults reconsidering unhealthy habits, or elders finding our way to gratitude over bitterness, we would be helped by recognizing how these choices improve or even

save our lives. If choosing life is so rational, one might ask, why do we often choose badly? Is the mantra "Choose life" a sufficient guide? Can we win the will to choose life only through encountering the alternatives?

Readers may also be put off by the portrayal in Deuteronomy of God as the author of the many forms of death that human disobedience triggers. Preceding chapters, especially Moses' recital of blessings for obedience and curses for disobedience in chapter 28, present God as the immediate agent of reward and punishment, opening the storehouses of rain and blessing to those who keep the commandments, and for the disobedient, sending pestilence, disease, blight and mildew, "madness, blindness, and confusion" (28:28), and, ultimately, a foreign nation to besiege and destroy. This is an off-putting portrayal that for many contemporary people inspires ethical difficulties with the God of Deuteronomy.

Another stream of biblical witness to either-or choices offers the same message in language that better suits contemporary sensibility. The book of Proverbs is built from two-line sayings that present the alternatives between which a person may wisely choose, not as paths to divine favor or wrath, but as prudence that intrinsically invites better outcomes than folly does. In Proverbs, as in Deuteronomy, humans are understood as having and exercising choices, but the rewards and punishments are built into the universe's structures, rather than arising case-by-case from personalized divine reactions. According to Proverbs 8:22–31, in fact, wisdom precedes God's creation of the earth.

In the end, though, what Proverbs and Deuteronomy teach—as well as the prophets and the rest of the Hebrew Scriptures—is that choices are indeed available. These choices offer far more attractive outcomes than the unsavory alternatives of death by heroin versus death by ennui portrayed in *Trainspotting*. They may include, but also transcend, the particular life-seeking choices represented in modern echoes of the phrase: sobriety, demilitarization, antimaterialism, defense of the unborn. They embrace, for example, keeping the Sabbath, and allowing the whole household and even the animals to do so. They involve seeking the welfare of widows, orphans, and strangers. They encompass remembering gratefully, and passing on to children, all that one has learned from God. In short, they include choosing a wide range of decisions that support life for self, family, neighbors, strangers, and even, according to Deuteronomy 20:19, for fruit trees.

Despite their abuse and diminishment, the words "Choose life" offer inspiration and hope. They imply that, though buffeted about by so much lying beyond our control—in the chance circumstances of the universe, in the decisions of powerful governments and corporations— we humans do actually have a say in things that matter to us. We can change our future—if not

the details of that future, at least its fundamental tone and direction. No matter what else is going on around us, no matter how narrow the straits, this passage implies, at every moment we still have two roads diverging before us, if we can but perceive them. As we choose our own actions and allegiances, these decisions over a lifetime define the distinctiveness of our path. The encouragement to choose life reminds us that we do have options. In fact, we doubtless possess more control of our own and our society's outcomes than we might perceive.

PATRICIA K. TULL

Commentary 2: Connecting the Reading with the World

Many attribute Oliver Wendell Holmes with the saying: "For the simplicity that lies this side of complexity, I would not give a fig, but for the simplicity that lies on the other side of complexity, I would give my life."[1] In Moses' farewell address, the great prophet offers a simple message: choose life and not death, but its simplicity was born through the complexities and adversities of forty years in the wilderness. Here, simple does not mean easy.

Preachers taking the liturgical season into consideration encounter this text in Epiphany, which offers another story fraught with consequence. The magi come from the East, searching after the child born to be king. Anxious Herod, feigning legitimate interest, sends them to discover the child's whereabouts. Upon discovering the child and his family, the magi face a choice: return to Herod and report what they have learned, or leave for home by another way. Quite literally here, the magi face a choice between life and death. Reporting Jesus' location to Herod would mean the death of the child while they lived. Withholding this information, while safeguarding the child, could very well have meant their own demise. Through the lens of Epiphany preachers might highlight how the choice Moses presents to the Israelites is simple but far from easy. Indeed, sometimes

choosing life entails a subversive act requiring courage and sacrifice.

Ecclesially, many congregations and denominations face this choice on a daily basis. Aging churches experiencing numerical decline face painful decisions: stay the course and continue their current practices and traditions, or innovate and play with new possibilities. From the outside it can seem obvious that declining congregations choosing to maintain the status quo are opting for death. For the faithful living within these systems, these choices can be excruciatingly difficult. For one thing, neither path provides a guarantee. It is always possible a church in decline could hold fast and experience a surprising revitalization. A congregation that tries every innovative trick up a church consultant's sleeve can still wind up moribund.

More challenging than the uncertain outcome lies the fear of change itself and the loss it inevitably entails. Stepping into change means venturing into the unknown. Courageous preachers might preach these words from Deuteronomy in light of the changes facing their own congregation. Rather than answering the question herself, the preacher might consider allowing the question to do the work.

Ethically, the conditional, polar nature of Moses' language presents interesting and

---

1. John Paul Lederach, *The Moral Imagination: The Art and Soul of Building Peace* (New York: Oxford University Press, 2005), Kindle Locations 700–701.

troubling possibilities. On the one hand preachers might celebrate the uncompromising tone of Moses' words here. Moses is not pandering to the masses, just telling the people what they want to hear. Individuals and states constantly desire gods who support and defend our ways. Moses reminds the people that God is free, and God's covenant with us is conditional.

Preachers might lean on Brueggemann's work, particularly in *The Prophetic Imagination,* where he cautions against the state's constant attempt to co-opt religion for its own purposes. Brueggemann contrasts the royal consciousness of Pharaoh and its religion of static triumphalism, with the prophetic insistence on God's freedom seen most sharply in the conditional nature of Moses' language.[2] While it can feel comforting to talk about God's unconditional grace and love, when this unconditionality begins to imply God is on our side no matter what, power easily eclipses justice, and the church can lose its ability to remind the state that God is God and we are not. Religion is always in danger of being used by the powers that be for political ends. Here, preachers have an opportunity to point out that God will not be mocked, our choices are real, and our choices matter.

On the other hand, Moses' rhetorical strategy—and indeed the rhetorical structure of the entire Deuteronomistic history—presents a danger preachers may want to confront. A staple of political rhetoric is the use of the false dilemma: creating an either-or choice for the purposes of persuasion when the reality is more complicated. Although logically fallacious, leaders across the spectrum create false dilemmas because they are so effective. President Obama successfully argued that Congress should either support the agreement with Iran regarding nuclear ambitions or choose war, while voices like Robert Kagan pointed out the reality was more complicated. Perhaps as no other American president in modern history, Donald Trump argued he alone offered strength and protection while his opponents created and sustained what he called "this American carnage." Preachers may want to question this kind of dangerous

rhetoric both in Moses and in others. Preachers wanting to complicate the Mosaic binary might look to the Wisdom literature. In Ecclesiastes 9:2, Qoheleth points out that the same fate comes to the righteous and the wicked, which is echoed in Matthew 5:45, where Jesus says the rain falls on the just and unjust alike.

To return to a more positive view of the conditional nature of the Mosaic covenant, social science offers a fascinating angle for the insightful preacher. Psychologists observe people playing social dilemma games to gain a better understanding of cooperation and selfishness. One of the most commonly studied games is known as the prisoner's dilemma. A prisoner's dilemma involves two players, each having a choice whether or not to cooperate with the other. While it would be best for both players if each cooperated, there is a significant temptation to act selfishly.

In his groundbreaking work *The Evolution of Cooperation,* Robert Axelrod studied thousands of interactions to determine the strongest patterns of behavior.[3] Axelrod assumed the most powerful pattern would be selfish, manipulative, and sneaky. Surprisingly, the most robust pattern, known as Tit for Tat, proved to be cooperative, forgiving, but tough in a fair and predictable way. Tit for Tat always sought to cooperate with others, but, when another player acted selfishly, Tit for Tat pushed back by not cooperating for a round. Then, modeling forgiveness, Tit for Tat then returned to being cooperative again. This pattern proved the strongest not only for the first tournament but for a second as well.

Conflict impacts every organization and every individual. Preachers could focus on conflicts within their own denominations or congregations. Moses highlights God's desire for community but does not shy away from a divine willingness to punish. In the same way, game theorists like Axelrod point out that in conflicted situations behavior patterns that hold together the desire to cooperate with the willingness to push back on antisocial behavior create the conditions for community to flourish.

---

2. Walter Brueggemann, *The Prophetic Imagination,* rev. ed. (Minneapolis: Fortress Press, 2001), Kindle ed., p. 7.
3. Robert Axelrod, *The Evolution of Cooperation* (New York: Basic Books, 2006), 30.

Individuals and groups tend to execute only one or two of these behaviors well.

Many congregations, wanting to seem "nice," struggle with maintaining boundaries and effectively punishing individuals harming the social fabric. Other congregations, however, more than willing to be punitive, can create unwelcoming systems finding it hard to trust newcomers.

Fusing these insights, preachers might consider posing this work as a question. When experiencing conflict, what kind of behavior comes easily to a listener? What kinds of behavior might they need to practice and strengthen? These questions might draw hearers into deeper reflection about the conflicts they are personally experiencing.

KEN EVERS-HOOD

Sixth Sunday after the Epiphany

Psalm 119:1–8

¹Happy are those whose way is blameless,
    who walk in the law of the LORD.
²Happy are those who keep his decrees,
    who seek him with their whole heart,
³who also do no wrong,
    but walk in his ways.
⁴You have commanded your precepts
    to be kept diligently.
⁵O that my ways may be steadfast
    in keeping your statutes!
⁶Then I shall not be put to shame,
    having my eyes fixed on all your commandments.
⁷I will praise you with an upright heart,
    when I learn your righteous ordinances.
⁸I will observe your statutes;
    do not utterly forsake me.

Connecting the Psalm with Scripture and Worship

The short selection from Psalm 119 appointed for this day is but a portion of the longest psalm and the longest chapter in all of Scripture. Psalm 119 is one of a small group of psalms classified as Torah psalms. Torah psalms "extol the *torah* of Yahweh as the medium through which the will of God is known and hence the basis for true wisdom and happiness."[1] It is important to note that *torah* is often translated as "law," which leads us to think in terms of legalism—a list of rules. *Torah* is best translated as "instruction" or "teaching." For Walter Brueggemann, *torah* is related to creation. He writes, "The good order of *creation* is concretely experienced in Israel as the *torah*. The torah is understood not simply as Israelite moral values, but as God's will and purpose, ordained in the very structure of life."[2] God's good creation is God's gift; living a life which follows the commandments of the Torah is the grateful response of the people of God.

This acrostic psalm, 176 verses in length, is divided into twenty-two sections. Each line of each section begins with the same letter of the Hebrew alphabet, with the letters of the alphabet appearing in sequential order. The creative skill of the psalmist is lost in translation. The selection for the Sixth Sunday after Epiphany in Year A includes the first eight verses.

Nearly all of the 176 verses of Psalm 119 include some synonym or allusion to the Torah. Torah is definitely the focus of the psalm! Each of the eight verses of today's reading includes some reference to the torah: law (v. 1), decrees (v. 2), walking in God's ways (v. 3), precepts (v. 4), statutes (v. 5), commandments (v. 6), ordinances (v. 7), and again, statutes (v. 8). The torah is not merely a list of rules directing behavior, but rather a way for God to be present with the people of Israel. The first eight verses of the psalm explore what a life of torah might look like.

An interesting shift occurs within these eight verses. Verse 1 begins with a seemingly simple statement: "Happy are those who live the life of torah" (my trans.). The psalm then shifts to

---

1. Bernard W. Anderson, *Out of the Depths: The Psalms Speak for Us Today* (Philadelphia: Westminster Press, 1983), 218.
2. Walter Brueggemann, *The Message of the Psalms* (Minneapolis: Augsburg Publishing House, 1984), 38.

Adorned with the Brightness of Virtue

But I say to you: If God is good, why do you put such little value on knowing His goodness, which gave His Son over to deliver you by sorrows and labors from death? When you say that you cannot do good works, you speak in unjust wickedness. For you have eyes to see with, ears to hear with, a heart to think with, hands to work with and feet to walk with, so that with your body you can stand up and lie down, sleep and wake, eat and fast. Thus God created you. Therefore, resist the desires of your flesh, and God will help you. For when you set your-self against the Devil like a strong warrior against his enemy, God delights in your struggle, wanting you to invoke Him in every hour, in all your troubles, constantly. But when you do not try to subdue your flesh, you make it feast with vice and sin, for you free it from the bridle of the fear of the Lord, with which you should be curbing it lest it go to perdition. . . .

But God knows what good you are capable of . . . [for] God wishes from the beginning to the end of the world to take pleasure in His elect, that they may be faithfully crowned, adorned with the brightness of virtue.

Hildegard of Bingen, *Scivas*, trans. Mother Columba Hart and Jane Bishop, Classics of Western Spirituality (New York: Paulist Press, 1990), 126.

a tone of supplication, as the psalmist declares a desire to remain steadfast in keeping the law. The psalmist understands the covenant and promises to follow torah earnestly, but prays to God for help in doing so.

Psalm 119:1–8 is a worthy response to the first reading from Deuteronomy, part of Moses' farewell speech to the people of Israel. Moses' speech uses an "if . . . then" method of argument: "If you do such and such, then such and such will happen." Here Moses outlines the covenant to the people: live according to God's commandments, and the Lord will bless you. The Torah serves as instruction on how to live out God's desire for God's people. In this way, the Torah is not a heavy burden but rather direction as to how to live in joy following God's way.

The reading from Matthew appointed for this day includes explanation of several of the laws of the Torah and how they have been misinterpreted. "You have heard it said . . . ," proclaims Jesus, "but I say to you . . ." In so doing, Jesus clarifies the intention of the covenant agreement. Just prior to this pericope, Jesus makes it clear that he did not come to do away with the law but to fulfill it. "Therefore, whoever breaks one of the least of these commandments, and teaches others to do the same, will be called least in the kingdom of heaven; but whoever does them and teaches them will be called great in the kingdom of heaven" (Matt. 5:19). In a way that echoes the "if . . . then" statements of Deuteronomy, Jesus instructs his listeners concerning how to live. Keeping the commandments is more than what is seen on the outside of a person. Keeping the commandments involves a change of heart, an inward change.

Because we are in relationship with God, we seek to follow the commandments. Because we are people of the covenant, we strive to keep torah. Following God's way guides how we parent, how we vote, the manner in which we conduct business, how the church is the church, and even how we pastor and preach.

As noted above, Psalm 119:1–8 serves well as a response to the reading from Deuteronomy. A simple refrain based on verse 1 could be spoken or sung, interspersed with the verses of the psalm. The image of walking in God's way is an important image in the psalm verses for today and is akin to following torah. The refrain from Doris Akers's African American gospel hymn, "Lead Me, Guide Me," could also serve well as a refrain while the verses are read.[3]

ERIC TODD MYERS

3. See Doris Akers, "Lead Me, Guide Me," *Glory to God* (Louisville, KY: Westminster John Knox Press, 2013), no. 740.

1 Corinthians 3:1–9

[1]And so, brothers and sisters, I could not speak to you as spiritual people, but rather as people of the flesh, as infants in Christ. [2]I fed you with milk, not solid food, for you were not ready for solid food. Even now you are still not ready, [3]for you are still of the flesh. For as long as there is jealousy and quarreling among you, are you not of the flesh, and behaving according to human inclinations? [4]For when one says, "I belong to Paul," and another, "I belong to Apollos," are you not merely human?

[5]What then is Apollos? What is Paul? Servants through whom you came to believe, as the Lord assigned to each. [6]I planted, Apollos watered, but God gave the growth. [7]So neither the one who plants nor the one who waters is anything, but only God who gives the growth. [8]The one who plants and the one who waters have a common purpose, and each will receive wages according to the labor of each. [9]For we are God's servants, working together; you are God's field, God's building.

Commentary 1: Connecting the Reading with Scripture

Perhaps we should consider ourselves lucky that the letters of Paul survived at all. One might expect that the whole letter of 1 Corinthians would have ended up in the first-century version of a shredder, perhaps especially because of this passage. Paul bluntly tells the church that they are spiritually immature, "infants in Christ" (1 Cor. 3:1). Paul uses important theological language and creative metaphors to make his point. He contrasts "spiritual" with "fleshly" to describe their immaturity. Although some strands of Greek philosophy sharply contrasted spirit/soul with flesh/body, Paul does not write as though the body itself is inherently evil. For Paul, "flesh" refers to human weakness and sinfulness. "Fleshy" connotes the natural state of a person who has not experienced the influence of the Holy Spirit. Accusing the Corinthians of "fleshiness" confronts them with the underlying condition that has led to their divisions.

Paul uses the creative metaphor of a mother deciding when she can wean her baby off of milk and begin to offer solid food. Paul has reluctantly decided that the Corinthians remain suckling children, not ready to grow up. Despite the tenderness of the metaphor, Paul's words sound devastatingly severe. In rebutting the tendency to align with former leaders, Paul uses an agricultural metaphor of planting and watering. Neither planting nor watering alone would suffice. Even with the work that Paul and Apollos did, only God gave the growth. Paul presents two metaphors of growth: a baby weaning from nursing and a plant growing from a seed. Paul wants the church to grow out of its immaturity. The metaphor of planting and watering also downplays the role of the two former church leaders. They merely served the role God assigned them, exactly what Paul wants the church to do.

Paul's words here follow directly what he said at the end of the previous chapter. He described how the Spirit enables access to God's secret wisdom and even to the very nature of God. Those who are "unspiritual" cannot access what the Spirit reveals. By calling the Corinthians "fleshy," Paul comes close to saying that they more resemble people outside the church than those inside the church. They have become part of the church but have not grown in their discipleship. Their fleshiness not only creates division; it blocks their access to the deep mysteries that the Spirit reveals to those who seek the gifts of the Spirit.

Paul follows up his admonitions from chapter 1 about those who identify with one of the former leaders of the church. He explains that each former leader played an important role in their growth. The leaders do not seek their own recognition, and neither should the church members.

Verse 10 begins a section in which Paul follows up with his metaphor of the church as God's building. Having compared himself to a nursing mother and a farmer in the earlier verses, he now compares himself to an expert builder. Later in the chapter (vv. 16–17), he reveals that the building is a temple. Those who tear down the church are like one who destroys a beautiful temple containing costly materials. The spiritual immaturity of the church leads to several consequences: lack of growth, inability to access the Spirit with God's mysteries, and destruction of something carefully constructed. Paul may lay it on thick, but the accumulation of accusations might just grab the church's attention.

Within the whole letter, the irony exists that the church argues about whose spiritual gifts should take precedence (12:4–11). Even though they possess spiritual gifts such as tongues and prophecy, they do not really understand the Holy Spirit. For that argument, Paul teaches that the spiritual gifts have the purpose of building up the church. The fact that they argue over spiritual gifts indicates how unspiritual, how fleshy, how immature they really are.

Scripture contains much material about people who consider themselves in relationship to God, but who lack spiritual maturity. In Matthew 26:41, Jesus exhorts the disciples against lethargy and temptation with the words, "the spirit indeed is willing, but the flesh is weak." In Psalm 51:10, the poet wants to grow, but realizes that only God working within him can help him over his hurdles to that growth.

Romans 8:1–17 contains an extended discussion of flesh and spirit. Paul here uses "flesh" to mean more than simple weakness. Flesh is a power, strong enough even to cripple the good law, which was given by God. People can come under the influence of the flesh by walking according to the flesh, living according to it, or setting the mind on it. Each of these metaphors suggests thinking and behaving in ways that succumb to human weakness and the genuine power of the flesh, perhaps another way of saying evil. One can choose instead to live by the Spirit, the life-giving power that leads to relationship with God.

The Gospel reading from Matthew contains the teaching from Jesus about interpreting and living out the Torah given by Moses. Jesus calls the church to live more deeply than controlling actions, so that the Torah becomes part of the church's very being. The ethic of the Sermon on the Mount leads to the teaching that good trees bear good fruit (Matt. 7:17). Paul's teaching about becoming spiritual people supports Jesus' teaching about living out the Torah with all of our being.

The maternal image that Paul uses appears within the larger canon of Scripture. Paul compares himself to a mother deciding when a child should stop nursing. Despite the uncompromising language that Paul uses in confronting the church, the image of a mother conveys Paul's deep care and concern for them. The prophet Isaiah describes both Jerusalem and God using the same image of a nursing mother. In Isaiah 66:10–13, the prophet promises the postexilic community that they will find comfort in both Jerusalem and in God. The home from which they have been estranged will become a source of consolation and delight. God also will act as a nursing mother to them.

The agricultural image of a field also appears often in Scripture: Isaiah 5:1–7; John 15:1–11. One finds the construction metaphor in Colossians 2:7.

Preachers should remember that this particular passage contains mostly words of judgment. Paul confronts the church, accusing it of spiritual immaturity. Any similar word should come from the contemporary preacher with wisdom, care, and genuine pastoral love. The preacher can walk the fine line between speaking the truth and moralism. Preachers can speak with honesty without scolding. Given these cautions, the preacher can find in this passage a warning that spiritual immaturity has a pervasive effect. Paul uses as his example of spiritual immaturity the divisions within the body, suggesting that the immaturity was a communal problem. The spiritual problems of a church can affect the individuals within the church. The spiritual immaturity of individual members can permeate the whole community. Congregations and denominations face similar divisions and competition.

The word of grace and hope in the passage comes in Paul's promise to the people that they are God's field, God's building. God continues to work within the fractured community. The preacher can explore Paul's diagnosis that divisions and competition derive from a lack of attention to the leading of the Spirit. The preacher can exhort the church to seek spiritual depth, trusting that the Spirit can lead the church to new life, new purpose, and new mission.

CHARLES L. AARON JR.

Commentary 2: Connecting the Reading with the World

There was a war in Corinth between various house churches. Paul says, "For when one says, 'I belong to Paul,' and another, 'I belong to Apollos,' are you not merely human?" (1 Cor. 3:4; cf. 1:12). Some have conjectured the battle in these house churches in Corinth was over theology, but it is more likely that the battle was over personality cults. One can argue that personalities are prior to theological splits. Patronage has always been a big issue, even bigger in the days of the Roman Empire. The Corinthians struggled to embrace a kingdom reality and preferred instead an empire reality, and the empire was held together economically, socially, and politically by allegiances to patrons—the wealthier and higher the status, the better. One gave allegiance and in return received benefits. Such patronage was the way of Rome. Unfortunately, such patronage continues today.

Think of how churches today are known: Are they known for their people? For their denominational name? For their pastor? Do we say, "That's where Janet goes to church" or "That's the Lutheran church"? Or do we say, "So and so is the pastor at that church"? When congregations are known for the preacher/pastor, there is an inevitable slide into a personality-shaped understanding of the church and how that church operates. Personality shaping quickly leads to competition among personalities, and the next thing we know, we are back in Corinth, once again in need of hearing the words of the apostle Paul. There is a moral problem at work in personality-cult churches (and it is not wise to think that every "successful" pastor is a personality-cult leader, but pastors with capacious gifts for preaching know this temptation).

In the pages of the Bible there is a rich variety of approaches to human flourishing and morality. In the books of Moses we encounter a covenant-formed set of laws (Torah) that are designed for Israel's life in the land. This is both externalized in embodied form and internalized in intention, heart, and will throughout the Old Testament, but especially in the prophets. Today's reading in Deuteronomy 30:15–20 has plenty of clarity about the "heart," and the psalm lesson does too: "who seek him with their whole heart" (Ps. 119:2). When a scribe approached Jesus about the most important commandment (Mark 12:28–34), Jesus interpreted the entirety of the Torah as contained in two commands: love God, love others. Paul picks this up. Love is the whole law in one word. Love, defined, is a rugged and affective commitment to another in presence, in advocacy, and in mutual growth into Christoformity.

The opposite of love in Christian morality and social ethics is *flesh*. The word "flesh" in Paul's writing means unredeemed embodied existence, which includes the systemic nonredemptive realities brought about by "Flesh." Flesh is self-centered egoism and power mongering, fighting off compassion for others, resisting justice and sustaining injustice, and finding ways to divide one person from another because Flesh hates peace. Flesh wants power in the way of the empire. Flesh coerces, teams up against others, brags about its accomplishments, and touts only its own line. Love empowers others in the way of Christ; love knows freedom to trust God and others. Flesh, Paul says, looks like this: "For as long as there is jealousy and quarreling among you, are you not of the flesh, and behaving according to human inclinations?" (1 Cor. 3:3; cf. Gal. 5:19–21). Throughout Christian history, splits and factions have demonstrated the way of the Flesh, resisting Paul's words that "There is one body and one Spirit . . . one Lord, one faith, one baptism, one God and Father of all" (Eph. 4:4–6).

Paul's message to the Corinthians resonates with the work of pastors in Christian churches today. The Christian ethic Paul speaks about here summons each of us to perceive churches not as led by personalities that form into divisive personality cultures, but as a church formed by God and nurtured by God with leaders as nothing more than "servants."

Pastors are called not to the limelight but to be culture makers. The kind of cultures pastors are called to make includes God-oriented, Christ-based, and Spirit-intoxicated cultures that embody the breadth of God's kingdom, that value each person as a specific gift to the church, and that form leaders who serve the people, who in turn serve one another. "What then is Apollos?" Paul asks. "What is Paul?" he queries (1 Cor. 3:5). The answer is that leaders in the church are "servants" who lead to Christ only by what God has gifted them to do. They are not the story; they tell the story of a God "who gives the growth" (v. 7).

A pastor who creates a God-oriented, Christ-based, and Spirit-intoxicated culture is "working together" (v. 9) with others called to minister the gospel to the church, which is "God's field, God's building" (v. 9). The personality-cult syndrome of modern Christianity is hardly new, but it seems to be new every morning. Pastors who work with other pastors create churches that work with other churches, and when pastors and churches work together in a given community, the church becomes a witness against the divisiveness of the empire, the power mongering of the personality cults, and the evil one's operation in the Flesh that wants more than anything to keep us apart.

In the United States, the history of racism represents the Flesh that stands for systemic unredeemed embodied existence. In the personifying force called Flesh, we discover what sociologist Korie Edwards describes as the invisibility of white privilege and white power.[1] Whiteness is about power in the deepest structures of American society, and it is sadly mirrored in white American churches. Whiteness can be unmasked by the gospel, but it is patched together by the Flesh. The invisibility of whiteness is also inscribed into our churches by the kind of Flesh that propagates personality cults that lead us to believe their way is the way of Christ.

Resistance to the Flesh of racism is the way of Christ. We can turn to Harper Lee's stunning *To Kill a Mockingbird*; to Clarence Jordan's interracial working culture called Koinonia Farm in Americus, Georgia; to M. L. King Jr.'s activism in Sweet Auburn neighborhood in Atlanta; to Orlando Patterson's *The Culture Matrix*, which puts into bold relief what racism and slavery have done to America's African Americans and inner cities; to Vashti McKenzie's *Not without a Struggle*, which documents female leadership in African American communities; or to the piercing vision of racism in the movie *Hidden Figures*. Each unmasks the Flesh called racism.

In a glorious way, Toni Morrison subverts systemic Flesh by turning human embodied flesh into a positive against the systemic Flesh. In her novel *Beloved*, the character Baby Suggs calls on the community of freed slaves to love their flesh, since the outside world would not love it: "In this here place, we flesh; flesh that weeps, laughs; flesh that dances on bare feet in grass. Love it. Love it hard. Yonder they do not love your flesh. They despise it. . . . You got to love it. This is flesh I'm talking about here. Flesh that needs to be loved."[2]

SCOT MCKNIGHT

1. Korie L. Edwards, *The Elusive Dream: The Power of Race in Interracial Churches* (New York: Oxford University Press, 2008).
2. Toni Morrison, *Beloved* (New York: Random House, 1987), 102.

Matthew 5:21–37

21"You have heard that it was said to those of ancient times, 'You shall not murder'; and 'whoever murders shall be liable to judgment.' 22But I say to you that if you are angry with a brother or sister, you will be liable to judgment; and if you insult a brother or sister, you will be liable to the council; and if you say, 'You fool,' you will be liable to the hell of fire. 23So when you are offering your gift at the altar, if you remember that your brother or sister has something against you, 24leave your gift there before the altar and go; first be reconciled to your brother or sister, and then come and offer your gift. 25Come to terms quickly with your accuser while you are on the way to court with him, or your accuser may hand you over to the judge, and the judge to the guard, and you will be thrown into prison. 26Truly I tell you, you will never get out until you have paid the last penny.

27"You have heard that it was said, 'You shall not commit adultery.' 28But I say to you that everyone who looks at a woman with lust has already committed adultery with her in his heart. 29If your right eye causes you to sin, tear it out and throw it away; it is better for you to lose one of your members than for your whole body to be thrown into hell. 30And if your right hand causes you to sin, cut it off and throw it away; it is better for you to lose one of your members than for your whole body to go into hell.

31"It was also said, 'Whoever divorces his wife, let him give her a certificate of divorce.' 32But I say to you that anyone who divorces his wife, except on the ground of unchastity, causes her to commit adultery; and whoever marries a divorced woman commits adultery.

33"Again, you have heard that it was said to those of ancient times, 'You shall not swear falsely, but carry out the vows you have made to the Lord.' 34But I say to you, Do not swear at all, either by heaven, for it is the throne of God, 35or by the earth, for it is his footstool, or by Jerusalem, for it is the city of the great King. 36And do not swear by your head, for you cannot make one hair white or black. 37Let your word be 'Yes, Yes' or 'No, No'; anything more than this comes from the evil one."

Commentary 1: Connecting the Reading with Scripture

Matthew 5:21–37 outlines the "exceeding" righteousness (5:20) that Jesus demands from his followers through a series of statements that compare something that "was said" (*errethē*) in the past with Jesus' teaching in the present. There are six of these statements or antitheses in chapter 5; four of them are included in this week's lectionary reading.

Before considering them in depth, a few general words about the antitheses are necessary. First, while some place stipulations from the Decalogue (Exod. 20:1–17; Deut. 5:1–21)

in contrast with Jesus' teaching, Jesus' words are not meant to contradict or invalidate the Decalogue. On the contrary, Jesus' words fulfill the law (Matt. 5:17). They "fill out" the Decalogue by extending, intensifying, and even deepening the original teaching. Second, the antitheses call attention to human intention and thought. They illustrate the behaviors of those who "hunger and thirst for righteousness" (v. 6), the "pure in heart" (v. 8), and the "peacemakers" (v. 9) upon whom Jesus pronounces God's favor earlier in this same chapter. The broader literary context implies that "exceeding righteousness" demands a whole new way of life, a radical commitment that moves beyond checking the boxes of various behavioral requirements. Finally, these sayings emphasize Jesus' authority. His emphatic "But I say to you" (vv. 22, 28, 32, 34, 39, 44) likens him to Moses, the one through whom God spoke to the people of Israel.

The first antithesis (vv. 21–26) takes up the prohibition of murder, the sixth of the Ten Commandments (Exod. 20:13; Deut. 5:17). Jesus extends the prohibition to include both anger toward a brother and the speaking of unkind words against a brother (Matt. 5:23). While the reference to brother (*adelphos*, translated "brother or sister" in the NRSV) can be understood as a reference to anyone in the church (see Matt. 18:15–20), the enmity experienced between brothers may also allude to the story of Cain and Abel (Gen. 4). Drawing heavily from that story, 1 John 3:15 equates hatred with murder, a conclusion resembling Jesus' teaching in Matthew 5:22. James 1:19–20 makes a similar connection between anger and speech, insisting that anger does not produce God's righteousness. Following the antitheses, Jesus provides two concrete illustrations of his teaching (vv. 23–24 and vv. 25–26) that stress the need for reconciliation. Both place the impetus on the offender to make amends with the offended, and they align with the perspective elsewhere in Matthew that the community should embody practices of regular and repeated forgiveness (Matt. 6:12; 18:21–22).

The second antithesis (vv. 27–30) extends the prohibition of adultery in the Decalogue (Exod. 20:14; Deut. 5:18). As the NRSV translation indicates ("everyone who looks at a woman with lust," 5:28), Jesus' words are often understood as a prohibition of thoughts that are sexual in nature. This tendency, however, downplays an important connection with the Decalogue, namely, the prohibition of coveting (Exod. 20:17; Deut. 5:21). The word for coveting in the Greek translation of the Old Testament (*epithymeō*) is the same as the verb used in Matthew 5:28. This verb denotes strong desire, which is not always sinful in nature (see Matt. 13:17; Luke 17:22; 1 Tim. 3:1; 1 Pet. 1:12), nor does it always carry a sexual connotation (see 1 Cor. 10:6, Jas. 4:2). Coveting is an eager desire to acquire something that belongs to another. If Matthew 5:28 is connected with the prohibition of coveting, Jesus' teaching takes on a different emphasis. The man who covets the wife of another commits adultery with her in his heart, since he desires to possess a woman who belongs (through marriage) to another.

This connection highlights just how different first-century understandings of marriage and gender are from our own. Viewing a woman as just another object in a man's possession should cause us to bristle. We can affirm that the desire prohibited by Jesus, whether understood in a possessive or sexual way, is wrong because it objectifies another person. It refuses to recognize others as God's image-bearers and turns them into commodities to be used or controlled. Preachers can apply Jesus' emphatic words in verse 30: anything that causes us to objectify or commodify others must be cut away and discarded.

The third antithesis (vv. 31–32) relates to the Old Testament's regulations on divorce in Deuteronomy 24:1–4, which permits a man to divorce his wife if he finds something objectionable about her. Jesus' teaching assumes a man's right to initiate divorce, but he limits this practice, allowing divorce only on the "ground of unchastity" (Matt. 5:32; cf. Matt. 19:3–9; Mark 10:2–9). While there is some debate about the meaning of *porneia* (translated "unchastity" above), it implies any sort of sexual activity outside of and in violation of a marriage covenant (see also Matt. 19:9). Since this saying does not have the full introductory phrase of the other antitheses, it can be understood as an extension of the second antithesis, since both pertain to adultery.

Unlike the prohibition against desire in verses 27–30, a man's divorcing his wife does not cause him to commit adultery. Rather, it causes his former wife to commit adultery, since she would be forced to remarry, and it causes the man she marries to commit adultery, since she remains the wife of another. This view of marriage as a sacred and permanent covenant between two people resembles the view expressed elsewhere in the Gospels (Matt. 19:6; Mark 10:9) and in the New Testament (Eph. 5:31).

The fourth antithesis (vv. 33–37) concerns oaths. While the Torah forbids making a false oath in the name of the Lord (Lev. 19:12), Jesus prohibits oath taking altogether (Matt. 5:34). In verses 34–35, those things that might serve as the basis of an oath (heaven, earth, and Jerusalem) are all related to God, indicating that oaths taken by these are ultimately oaths taken in the name of the Lord. Though less obvious, the reference to swearing by "your head" (v. 36) is also prohibited because it also belongs to the Lord. The basic sense of Jesus' teaching is made clear in verse 37: a person's "yes" or "no" should suffice. There is no need to make a vow or swear by anything to corroborate one's statement because of her integrity and honesty in speech. The interpersonal dimension is evident once again: there is no need for oaths within a community of honesty and truthfulness.

As a whole, the antitheses of Jesus focus on interpersonal relationships. Each can be understood as an elaboration of the love command. Like Paul (Rom. 13:9) and James (Jas. 2:9, 11), many of Jesus' statements stem from the command to love your neighbor as yourself. Jesus' teachings do not only elaborate or expand the love command; they also radicalize and internalize it. Elsewhere, Jesus indicates that sinful behaviors like murder, adultery, fornication, theft, false witness, and slander originate in the heart (Matt. 15:19; Mark 7:21). Much in the antitheses recalls the practical teaching of James, especially his demand for a purified heart (Jas. 4:8) and single-minded obedience (Jas. 1:8; 4:8).

The antitheses connect in important ways with the Old Testament readings for this week as well; they, too, identify the heart as the control center for right action (Deut. 30:17; Ps. 119:2, 4, 7). The Old Testament readings also indicate that observing God's commandments leads to life and prosperity (Deut. 30:15–16; Ps. 119:1–2; Sir. 15:17). The intensified commands of Jesus have tangible consequences. The dispositions and practices demanded by Jesus bear fruit in the form of communities of justice, peacemaking, and reconciliation.

CHRISTOPHER T. HOLMES

Commentary 2: Connecting the Reading with the World

In Spanish there is a tongue-in-cheek expression about gossip, "*el bochinche no me gusta pero me entretiene*" (I do not like gossip but I find it entertains me). It is usually said right after someone says something like, "Did you hear about . . . ?" or "Can you believe what so and so . . . ?" Its intention is to motivate the person about to share the so-called information. It is possible to picture the people listening to Jesus' long and challenging discourse, especially leaning in when he began the next words with, "You have heard that it was said . . ." Could some juicy "information" follow this familiar opening? Surely *any* would be welcome right about now in his long and challenging discourse! Jesus' words may have gotten the crowd oohing and aahing but not for the reasons they may have thought. Any expression of shock and awe would have stemmed, not from the "You have heard it said to those of ancient times," but from the preface to his next sentences, "But I say to you"—the heart of the *bochinche*!

Then, as now, Jesus' so-called antithetical statements called into question the matter of authority. Through them, Jesus affirmed his divine rule; he is the new Moses differentiating "ancient times" (law of Moses) from the new law of Christ—a fuller expression of true servanthood. Hence, as he exclaims in 5:17, 18, Jesus is not abolishing Torah. He is getting at the heart of its purpose: calling followers to obey God, not out of duty (to the Law-Giver), but from a desire that stems from the very core of their being, their love.

Jesus' discourse is a summons to radical love, countercultural in all it feels, thinks, and does. Hence, it will not be enough for followers not to commit murder. Non-followers are able to do this as well! Rather, a true follower also will not harbor anger, or insult a sister or brother. Should any have something against us, it is *we* who are admonished to be reconciled before offering our gift to God! No longer is adultery an outward act, but everyone who looks at a woman *with lust* has already committed adultery with her in his heart! God judges our actions by the heart that engenders them.

The double reference to men's actions against women in Jesus' statements is telling. Men's view of women as objects of their pleasure has led to many unconscionable acts against them throughout history (rape, female genital mutilation, child marriage, infanticide, sex trafficking, etc.). Men are not to treat women and girls as objects of lust; neither are they to lure them into such relationships. Coercion, victimization, and disdain (v. 28, 32) of any kind are as evil as murder! Before God, men have no recourse to blaming women for their lust. Women (or any other human beings) are not the root of the problem. The onus is on men, as the ones historically wielding social and religious institutional power.

Emotional and physical violence against girls and women (or men and boys!) desecrates their body and psyche, damaging their perspective about relationships, the world, themselves, and even God, who too often is reified as male. "What kind of a God would allow this?!" For many, the conclusion is that a male God, with little understanding and apparently little love for women, allowed it. This view calls for diligent and continual introspection of how our churches are enabling a condescending view of women—and therefore also of their God. One would be alarmed to find out how many persons in our churches may have been abused and how we may have been complicit.

Jesus underscores the place of women and girls in the heart of God to the point of admonishing men to "tear out" or "cut off" eye or hand (see Col. 3:5) rather than for "the whole body to be thrown into hell" (Matt. 5:29, 30). Such is the gravity of the command and the depth of God's love. Women and men need to hear this for the sake of the church—which, unfortunately, limits women's voice—and for a more

pristine witness to God's countercultural kindom, where all are called to "work together," to be "God's field" and "God's building" (1 Cor. 3:9). In such a building, all blocks are indispensable. There is no hierarchy to God's love.

To bring the subject home for the preacher and/or listeners, a short clip that highlights the leadership role of men, women, and institutions in ameliorating the culture may be insightful.[1]

The invectives in verses 29 and 30 also underscore the divine pathos behind them. Indeed, to know God is to experience God's pathos; you cannot know God's pathos and not be moved. God is not an "unfeeling," impassible, "anesthetized" God who literally cannot be bothered. Would that we could pin our own callousness to imitating an apathetic God that can be loved but just cannot love back! As followers, we must face the joy and challenge of consistently asking God to help us to love—and thus also to suffer hurt, as God does for others and for creation.

There is an analogy to be made here. Often we talk about humanity searching for truth and love but ignore the fact that God too seeks truth and love—not because God has a deficiency in God's understanding or knowledge of persons and things, or because there is any lack of love among the persons of the Trinity, but because God has opted to be in relationship, and true relationship is built on trust, faithfulness, and love (Deut. 30:17; Ps. 119:7; John 4:23). The epitome of this search for true love reverberates through God's own questions, "Will you be my people?" and through Christ's, "Who am I to you?" "Do you love me?" and his, "But I say . . ."

Finally, reference to "ancient times" and Jesus' insinuation about its new direction bring us to the role of history. Whatever we think of it—a sorry result of the fall, or a part of God's plan for creation—it is the canvas or stage for God's epiphanies throughout time; a vessel, sanctified and made worthy of bearing holy displays of grace, love, justice, and mercy. We are called to be agents in this holy history-making drama of salvation, not merely to await the

---

1. Tony Porter, "A Call to Men," at TEDWo,men 2010, https://www.ted.com/talks/tony_porter_a_call_to_men, (11.13 minutes). Jackson Katz, "Violence against Women—It's a Men's Issue," at TEDxFiDiWomen, https://www.ted.com/talks/jackson_katz_violence_against_women_it_s_a_men_s_issue/transcript (17.40 minutes).

kingdom. We cannot do this without the power of the Spirit of God daring us to "make history" our aim (Matt. 5:13, 14).

God calls for nothing less than the heart, an innermost desire for God that seeks to express itself by doing God's will. This means not only that we are to live out and grow our relationship, but that God will honor God's promises in that relationship (Deut. 30:20; Ps. 119:1, 2). Is it possible to love God in such a way that,

kingdom or no kingdom, all that matters is the grace that, despite our failures, embraces and shows us new and higher (divine) dimensions of purpose, joy, and true humanity? The anonymous author of a sixteenth-century Spanish sonnet beautifully expresses this challenge: "My God, I love Thee, . . . Not for the hope of winning heav'n or . . . escaping hell. . . . Not seeking a reward; But as Thyself hast loved me."[2]

ZAIDA MALDONADO PÉREZ

---

2. Sometimes titled, "To Christ Crucified." See *An Introduction to Christian Theology* by Justo L. González and Zaida Maldonado Pérez (Nashville: Abingdon Press, 2002), 158. Other translations are in http://users.ipfw.edu/jehle/poesia/acristen.htm.

Seventh Sunday after the Epiphany

Leviticus 19:1–2, 9–18
Psalm 119:33–40

1 Corinthians 3:10–11, 16–23
Matthew 5:38–48

Leviticus 19:1–2, 9–18

¹The LORD spoke to Moses, saying:
  ²Speak to all the congregation of the people of Israel and say to them: You shall be holy, for I the LORD your God am holy. . . .
  ⁹When you reap the harvest of your land, you shall not reap to the very edges of your field, or gather the gleanings of your harvest. ¹⁰You shall not strip your vineyard bare, or gather the fallen grapes of your vineyard; you shall leave them for the poor and the alien: I am the LORD your God.
  ¹¹You shall not steal; you shall not deal falsely; and you shall not lie to one another. ¹²And you shall not swear falsely by my name, profaning the name of your God: I am the LORD.
  ¹³You shall not defraud your neighbor; you shall not steal; and you shall not keep for yourself the wages of a laborer until morning. ¹⁴You shall not revile the deaf or put a stumbling block before the blind; you shall fear your God: I am the LORD.
  ¹⁵You shall not render an unjust judgment; you shall not be partial to the poor or defer to the great: with justice you shall judge your neighbor. ¹⁶You shall not go around as a slanderer among your people, and you shall not profit by the blood of your neighbor: I am the LORD.
  ¹⁷You shall not hate in your heart anyone of your kin; you shall reprove your neighbor, or you will incur guilt yourself. ¹⁸You shall not take vengeance or bear a grudge against any of your people, but you shall love your neighbor as yourself: I am the LORD.

Commentary 1: Connecting the Reading with Scripture

Holiness in Leviticus 19 is not a measure of how often one says grace over a meal, but how often one acts graciously toward others. It is not a measure of how many times one sits in the synagogue on Shabbat or in church on Sunday, but how one stands for those who need the faithful to raise their voices on their behalf. Holiness does mean "to be set apart *from*" petty pursuits that distract us from living into God's grand vision. It also means "to be set apart *for*" a life lived on behalf of others. Because our God is "holy," we also are to be holy, every day, every hour.

Leviticus 19 provides a provocative picture of the holiness of God. Holiness (*qadash*) in this text is not something that occasionally we "take time to be," per the old revival hymn "Take

Time to Be Holy." Holiness is what those created in the image of God *do*, every hour, every day. Why? Leviticus answers that question definitively and with precise clarity sixteen times in this one chapter. We live holy lives because "the LORD your God is holy."

When many people consider the concept of holiness, they picture saints like Mother Teresa tending to the needs of the poor in Calcutta and Archbishop Desmond Tutu speaking words of opposition to the practice of apartheid in South Africa. Many people conclude that a holy person is an exceptional religious leader who exhibits its an extraordinary spiritual grace. A far less inspiring concept of holiness derives from the "holier than thou" crowd who always pretend to be more spiritually enlightened than others. In either use, "holy" is a word that is laden with meaning in its English usage not consistent with its usage in Leviticus 19.

"Holy" in Leviticus 19:1–2, 9–18 is a description of the nature of God and how followers of God are to live in response. Walter Kaiser offers this concrete insight into "holy" and "holiness": "To be holy is to roll up one's sleeves and to join in with whatever God is doing in the world."[1] To be holy in response to God's holiness is not a matter simply for the spiritually elite or an occasion for some believers to separate themselves from the common rabble. To be holy in response to God's holiness has concrete consequences.

The most immediate consequence of a holy life is a life lived attentive to and in support of the needs of neighbors. Kaiser goes on to say: "In Leviticus, if you want to be holy, don't pass out a tract; love your neighbor."[2] In Leviticus 19 those who would be holy as the "LORD your God is holy" will hold a broad and generous notion of the neighbor. One responds to God's holiness with holy lives when the neighbor is more than the person living next door or the friend at school. In this text, the neighbor includes the poor, immigrants, refugees, laborers, the deaf, the blind, and the good earth itself.

By modern inference from this next, neighbors are also those being sent to substandard schools, living in substandard housing, or having no housing at all. Neighbors are teens being sold into sexual slavery on the street corners of Atlanta and DC, Chicago and LA; neighbors are also the sea and sky being polluted by waste and wasteful ways. Being "holy" as the Lord God is "holy" will not condone silence by believers when hateful speech against neighbors becomes the standard speech on the right and on the left.

Leviticus insists that God's people not only pray for neighbors, but provide for the most basic needs of neighbors. A fundamental generosity toward neighbors is outlined in Leviticus 19:9–10: "When you reap the harvest of your land, you shall not reap to the very edges of your field, or gather the gleanings of your harvest. You shall not strip your vineyard bare, or gather the fallen grapes of your vineyard; you shall leave them for the poor and the alien: I am the LORD your God." A holy life, therefore, has concrete economic consequence and is always lived with a view toward the most vulnerable neighbor.

Too often, the Bible is taught as a "spiritual" book uninterested in mundane earthly affairs like economics—like picking melons and leaving some in the field (vv. 9–10); like fair labor practices (v. 13); like avoiding slander and libel (v. 16); like cheating or stealing from your neighbor (v. 11, 35–36); and like attending to the needs of the alien in the land (vv. 33–34). Leviticus 19 knows that believers will never get their economics and public policy right until they get their theology right. As people of the covenant (see Exod. 20), our ethical life follows from understanding God's grace and mercy, as well as God's claim on our lives.

A holy life, lived in response to the holiness of God, is not a life lived to one's own advantage, but a life lived in compassion for those not of similar advantage. A holy life per Leviticus 19 is not about wearing haloes but wearing the scars that may result from living faithfully in response to the holiness of God. Anyone who travels the road from Epiphany to Good Friday will witness what God's holiness looks like in human flesh.

The theme of God's holiness and living holy lives is woven throughout the course of the biblical witness. The companion biblical texts for this Sunday speak to different dimensions of God's holiness and the call to live holy lives. Psalm 119:33–40 is a prayer from the psalmist for God to instill God's holiness in the person praying, a holiness that will result in a faithful life, lived for others (Ps. 119:35–36). The Matthean text, 5:38–48, is one in which Jesus expands both the scope of God's holiness and the Levitical notion of neighbor, even to include love of the enemy (Matt. 5:44). The advice from Paul in 1 Corinthians 3 is for believers to have a clear assessment of themselves and to recognize that they can live holy lives, only because

1. Walter Kaiser, "Leviticus 19:1–37, Holiness in Social Ethics," in *The New Interpreter's Bible* (Nashville: Abingdon Press, 1994), 1:1132.
2. Kaiser, 1132.

Surrendering Ourselves to God's Direction

He again presents the same prayer which he has already frequently done in this psalm, it being of the last importance for us to know that the main thing in our life consists in having God for our governor. The majority of mankind think of anything rather than this. . . . The Holy Spirit, therefore, often inculcates this desire, and we ought always to keep it in mind, that not only the inexperienced and unlearned, but those who have made great progress, may not cease to aspire after farther advancement. . . .

The world esteems as wise those only who look well to their own interests, are acute and politic in temporal matters, and who even excel in the art of beguiling the simple. In opposition to such a sentiment, the prophet pronounces men to be void of true understanding as long as the fear of God does not predominate among them. For himself he asks no other prudence than the surrendering of himself entirely to God's direction. . . .

Seeing that the end of man's existence ought to consist in profiting in God's school, we nevertheless perceive how the world distracts him by its allurements, and how he also forms for himself a thousand avocations calculated to withdraw his thoughts from the main business of his life. . . .

He confesses the human heart to be so far from yielding to the justice of God, that it is more inclined to follow an opposite course. Were we naturally and spontaneously inclined to the righteousness of the law, there would be no occasion for the petition of the Psalmist. . . .

He informed us of the reigning of that depravity in the hearts of men, which he now says reaches also to the outward senses. . . . If our eyes must be turned away from vanity by the special grace of God, it follows, that, as soon as they are opened, they are eagerly set on the impostures of Satan, by which they are beset on all sides. . . .

For we perceive the prophet allows not himself to petition or wish any thing but what God hath condescended to promise. And certainly their presumption is great, who rush into the presence of God without any call from his word; as if they would make him subservient to their humor and caprice. . . .

Above all, it becomes holy men to dread the reproach of being suffused with shame at God's judgment-seat.

This is a repetition of what he declared a little before, with regard to his pious affection, and his love of righteousness; and that nothing was wanting but God to complete the work which he had commenced. . . . But as the word righteousness is ambiguous, my readers may, if they choose, understand it thus: Restore, defend, and maintain me for the sake of thy goodness, which thou art wont to show to all thy people.

John Calvin, "Psalm 119," in *Commentary on the Book of Psalms,* vol. 4, trans. James Anderson (Grand Rapids: Eerdmans, 1949), 375–79.

---

they are following a holy God, who took human form in the person of Jesus (1 Cor. 3:21).

Leviticus is a book filled with many obscure and arcane texts, some even in chapter 19 (see, e.g., vv. 20–22). The verses under consideration today are neither obscure nor arcane, but point with clarity and passion to a holy God who calls forth holy lives. The concept of holiness is an infrequent visitor to Christian pulpits. Even when this text is considered on a Sunday morning, it is often dismissed as being a part of the archaic Old Testament. Too many Christians believe with the heretic Marcion of the second century that Jesus arrived to delete the first half of what we know as the Bible, especially to delete such tedious and often arcane books as Leviticus. The problem with that hermeneutic of Scripture is that Leviticus 19 was one of the favorite chapters of Jesus. Perhaps on this Seventh Sunday after the Epiphany, it would be a fine occasion to follow the lead of Jesus and reclaim the vision of covenant and holy life articulated in Leviticus 19.

GARY W. CHARLES

Commentary 2: Connecting the Reading with the World

The preacher who preaches from this text has to make a choice, deciding from among several different directions. On the one hand, the preacher could focus on a personal call to be holy, which is elaborated in detail through several moral injunctions in the selected verses that echo the Ten Commandments. On the other hand, the preacher could focus on the social implications for holy living, showing how these verses highlight current injustices in how marginalized members of our society are treated. Indeed, several different social justice issues arise, each of which could constitute a whole sermon. A middle way of addressing both the implications for personal holiness and the issues relating to society at large would be to focus on the call for holy communities or holy congregations—how this text offers signs for what holy living looks like in community.

For the personal call to holiness, the text seems to lend itself to direct and individual application. Not stealing, not lying, not hating others, not taking vengeance or holding a grudge, loving your neighbor as yourself; these are all personal ways that individuals can connect these verses into their lives today. Many of these commands echo the Ten Commandments, including the prohibition against swearing in the Lord's name or profaning God's name. Preachers could study this passage in relationship to the Ten Commandments in Exodus, pointing out the similarities and differences and how such commandments relate to Christian living in the present.

The preacher could also point to the connection between the command in verse 18 to "love your neighbor as yourself" and the "new" commandment that Jesus gives in the Gospels. Drawing attention to the labeling of this commandment in John's Gospel as "new," listeners can consider ways that Christians have talked about Judaism in a supersessionist way, assuming Christ's "new" law is distinctively different, when his teachings tended to flow from a life lived as a faithful Jew. By emphasizing Jesus' knowledge of the law of Moses, the preacher can avoid some of the anti-Jewish sentiment that Christian preaching has portrayed in the past.

Other possible applications include addressing habits in the workplace. The listener who operates a small business will hear in these verses the call to deal justly with one's employees, not taking all of the profits for oneself, and making sure there are sufficient benefits for all those who labor, as well as providing for the poor and unemployed. The verses about stealing and dealing falsely with others can also be applied to business models that are deceitful and unfair. Companies that offer payday loan services can often be exploitive of the poor, charging exorbitant rates that reinforce a cycle of debt and poverty. Verse 16 talks about being "a slanderer among your people" and could be linked to the emotional toll that toxic work environments can create, when workers gossip and talk about each other behind their back.

Preachers could also link the text "you shall not profit by the blood of your neighbor" (Lev. 19:16) to the historical legacy of slavery, since many institutions that still stand can point to their origins as stemming from slave labor. Colleges and universities that have acknowledged the role of the slave trade in their history have done so in order to repent from the profits they gained by the blood of enslaved Africans. Still, the prison industry profits from mass incarceration, which disproportionately impacts communities of color. The Thirteenth Amendment to the US Constitution allows for persons to work as slaves still today as a punishment for crime, which means that in prison inmates are still working fields and doing labor that benefits someone else, with no ability to build up wealth or pass on income to their families.

Several opportunities to criticize current social systems exist in these verses. Returning to the verses regarding the edges of the harvest, it is important for preachers to emphasize a less cutthroat economic model for society. Rather than fighting for every last achievement and working for perpetual growth in industry, some economists have argued for a more just way of understanding the role of society in ensuring the well-being of all. The concept of "neoliberal" economic policies includes the rampant unbridled growth mind-set, and several scholars have pointed out the pitfalls in this economic policy.[3]

This text can also highlight issues of accessibility and accommodation for persons who are differently abled. "You shall not revile the deaf or put a stumbling block before the blind" calls attention to how society treats individuals and groups with loss of hearing or sight. Within congregations, persons may be aware of members with these disabilities, while other disabilities remain hidden. Some may have various forms of learning disabilities, mental illness, or chronic disease that make it more difficult to do some activities. It is important for preachers to lift up the call to care for all members of society, including those who need accommodations based on their particular needs.

This also means being intentional for how we shape worship spaces. Is the church building compliant with the Americans with Disabilities Act (ADA)? Can the congregation make the church more accessible for people in wheelchairs or who have mobility challenges? Who is represented by the persons who help lead in worship? Preachers can draw from this text questions that congregations should consider as they seek to not "revile" anyone who is differently abled or put a stumbling block in front of someone who needs us to help make the way clear.

Another social issue that this text addresses is the criminal justice system. Studies have shown that persons of color are more likely to receive harsher sentences than white persons convicted of a crime. Preachers could focus on verse 15 and call their congregations to consider where persons are receiving an "unjust judgment." The second half of the verse, "you shall not be partial to the poor or defer to the great," presents a challenge for a society where persons who are wealthy or have a lot of prestige are more likely to avoid punishment for crimes.

Finally, weaving the personal with the social considerations this text offers, preachers can lift up specific ways listeners can engage in their communities in order to raise awareness about issues of injustice and try to make a difference where they can. Several verses in this selection mention "neighbor." Using the idea of one's own neighborhood as a locus of attention, preachers can call on their congregations to consider where in their own neighborhoods people are being defrauded, or where grudges or biases are being held against certain groups. When verse 17 tells the reader to "reprove" our neighbor, the preacher can offer concrete steps for conflict mediation and how best to raise issues with members of the community. If injustice is taking place in the midst of one's neighborhood, it is helpful to have a set of guidelines for how to go about addressing this issue in a way that brings the community together.

The preacher has to discern between a multitude of directions this text can take a sermon. Choosing to take on too many of these issues may overwhelm the listener. At the same time, the call to be holy, as the Lord is holy, is itself an overwhelming task. Perhaps remembering the final verse of this text, loving your neighbor as you love yourself, can remind us to take time to care for ourselves in the midst of pursuing personal and social holiness.

CAROLYN BROWNING HELSEL

---

3. For example, see Rosemarie Hinkle-Rieger and Joerg Rieger, *Unified We Are a Force: How Faith and Labor Can Overcome America's Inequalities* (St. Louis: Chalice Press, 2016).

Psalm 119:33–40

[33]Teach me, O LORD, the way of your statutes,
  and I will observe it to the end.
[34]Give me understanding, that I may keep your law
  and observe it with my whole heart.
[35]Lead me in the path of your commandments,
  for I delight in it.
[36]Turn my heart to your decrees,
  and not to selfish gain.
[37]Turn my eyes from looking at vanities;
  give me life in your ways.
[38]Confirm to your servant your promise,
  which is for those who fear you.
[39]Turn away the disgrace that I dread,
  for your ordinances are good.
[40]See, I have longed for your precepts;
  in your righteousness give me life.

Connecting the Psalm with Scripture and Worship

Matthew's Sermon on the Mount includes an expansion and an interiorization of the Ten Commandments. Yet such an elaboration on the law is found also elsewhere in the Scriptures, one place being this day's first reading, from Leviticus 19. Like the Ten Commandments, this passage condemns stealing and false witness among those who are bound to God and to one another through the covenant, but this passage from the Holiness Code (Lev. 17–26) adds regulations concerning a social security system for the poor, legal justice for all classes of society, and even an interior attitude free from any hatred.

Psalm 119:33–40 is a most appropriate communal response to our proclamation of Leviticus 19. The longest psalm in the psalter, Psalm 119 is a doubly alphabetical acrostic. For each of the twenty-two letters of the Hebrew alphabet, there is a stanza of eight lines, each line of which begins with that letter: thus, a a a a a a a a, b b b b b b b b, and so on. (Can we inspire a scholar to prepare just such a translation for liturgical use?!) Seven of the twenty-two stanzas are appointed in the Revised Common Lectionary. The psalm is probably a composition of the late seventh century before Christ, a period marked by Deuteronomic reforms.

The structure of such Hebrew acrostic poems suggests that herein is recorded all knowledge. A Jewish legend tells of a poor peasant who got stuck in the fields at sundown on Friday and thus could not walk the distance back to the synagogue for Sabbath prayers. The next week the rabbi asked him how he had kept the Sabbath apart from the community, and he replied that although as an ignorant man he did not know the correct prayers, he recited the alphabet, and the angels rearranged the letters. Another Jewish legend says that when God formed the earth, the first thing to be created were the letters of the alphabet, from which came everything else. Most impressive is the alphabetical confession of sins prayed on Yom Kippur: "We abuse, we betray, we are cruel. We destroy, we embitter, we falsify," and through until "We yield to evil, we are zealots for bad causes."[1] This tradition

---

1. *Mahzor for Rosh Hashanah and Yom Kippur*, ed. Rabbi Jules Harlow (New York: The Rabbinical Assembly, 1972), 379–81.

of reverence for the alphabet as a symbol of all knowledge governs also Psalm 119. The alphabet means to celebrate the whole law of God, and through the law comes life from God.

Much of our culture finds quite alien the notion of delighting in law. Thus our first task as interpreters of this word may be to suggest examples of gratitude for law. The premier ballerina Margot Fonteyn was once asked whether she was weary of rising every morning and going to the barre for her exercises, and she responded with her pleasure for a life in which she knew, every single day, what she was to do: go to the barre and exercise. The discipline was a gift, and following the discipline offered great reward. Christians who are formed by Paul's criticism of Torah and Americans who define freedom as the absence of laws are ill prepared to understand how the psalmist rejoices in God's commandments.

For this psalmist, God's law is the gift that brings order and beauty to the chaos and selfishness of normal human life. The ordinances of God are good, and only by living in such righteousness can there be wholesome life. The psalmists are unremitting realists: life can be, and often is, terrible, but living in covenant with the community under God offers some relief. Psalm 119 presents no charming fantasy about how lovely life is and how kind people are. Rather, only by adherence to the law can life be worth living. Indeed, the law is not dull or tedious: the author's use of synonyms for "law"—in the NRSV "statutes, commandments, decrees, promise, ordinances, and precepts"—means to inspire our thinking with various ways of envisioning the commandments. The stanza concludes with almost lovers' speech: we long for life in God.

Verses 33–40 present clear parallels to the Leviticus reading. The several metaphors of walking—the way of your statutes, the path of your commandments—recall the rules in Leviticus about the owner surveying the fields and the poor gleaning in the aftermath of the harvest. According to the psalm, I will observe the law "with my whole heart"; that is, the law directs my interior orientation, as well as my daily walk through the fields. Just as the Leviticus passage situates the likelihood of immorality between owners and workers, the rich and the poor, the able-bodied and the handicapped, even those who have been harmed in the past and thus bear a grudge, the psalmist acknowledges that humans are always on the brink of selfishness. It seems as if the Holiness Code lets none of us off the hook.

We join with the ancient Israelites to affirm that, as in Leviticus 19:18, we are to love our neighbors as ourselves. Yet we join in this psalm as Christians, who, following New Testament tradition, do not closely observe the regulations of Leviticus. For us, the Alpha and the Omega of all is Christ, whom we hear about in the second reading of the day. The people of the resurrection are the temple. Our foundation is no longer the Holiness Code, but now Jesus Christ, whom we encounter in our needy neighbor.

GAIL RAMSHAW

1 Corinthians 3:10–11, 16–23

[10]According to the grace of God given to me, like a skilled master builder I laid a foundation, and someone else is building on it. Each builder must choose with care how to build on it. [11]For no one can lay any foundation other than the one that has been laid; that foundation is Jesus Christ. . . .

[16]Do you not know that you are God's temple and that God's Spirit dwells in you? [17]If anyone destroys God's temple, God will destroy that person. For God's temple is holy, and you are that temple.

[18]Do not deceive yourselves. If you think that you are wise in this age, you should become fools so that you may become wise. [19]For the wisdom of this world is foolishness with God. For it is written,

"He catches the wise in their craftiness,"

[20]and again,

"The Lord knows the thoughts of the wise,
    that they are futile."

[21]So let no one boast about human leaders. For all things are yours, [22]whether Paul or Apollos or Cephas or the world or life or death or the present or the future—all belong to you, [23]and you belong to Christ, and Christ belongs to God.

Commentary 1: Connecting the Reading with Scripture

The apostle Paul continues his warning against the Corinthians' immature wrangling over their favorite pastoral leaders and his teaching them, instead, proper God-honoring ways to interpret the ministerial role. In this passage, he moves abruptly—indeed, midsentence!—from the imagery of field and farmer to that of building and builder. "You are God's field, God's building" (1 Cor. 3:9).

Additionally, his chiding of Corinthian immaturity (vv. 1–4) seems now to shift dramatically to a warning issued to teachers who have come, or would in the future come, to the Corinthian church (vv. 11–15). Earlier in the letter, Paul had barely gotten his greeting completed before plunging into this problem of "divisions" and "quarrels among you" (1:10, 11). The fault seems to be placed directly upon the Corinthian congregation (1:12–13). In the present passage, though, Paul directs his attention to other ministerial servants: "Each builder must choose with care how to build on [the foundation]" (3:10).

In this imagery, Paul is the "skilled master builder" who laid the building's foundation, and others (e.g., Apollos, Cephas [1:12]) are building on the foundation, identified as none other than Jesus Christ (3:11). It is noteworthy that Paul boldly claims that he laid that foundation for the Corinthian church, which certainly is empirically true; however, he hastens to add that neither he nor anyone else can lay a foundation "other than the one that has been laid," the passive verb likely denoting divine activity. Paul is God's human instrument, but ultimately it is God who has laid the church's one foundation.

At least in some traditions of interpretation, Paul's description of building upon this foundation laid by God has been misunderstood or misappropriated. The passage is not about how an individual "builds" his or her life upon the foundation of Christ. The warning of verses 11–15 is intended for the teachers or ministers who followed Paul's founding ministry in Corinth. It is their grave responsibility to build the church faithfully, in accordance with God's foundation.

Paul's ecclesiological metaphor shifts suddenly again in 3:16 from "God's building" to "God's temple." This of course ups the ante considerably. If the Corinthian church[1] is a divine temple in which God's Spirit dwells, then the congregation's divisiveness verges on blasphemy. Whom is Paul warning in verse 17? Is it a teacher who is visiting, or has visited, Corinth? Is it even perhaps Apollos? Does he have in mind certain congregants who are sowing the seeds of division? Of course, those possibilities are not mutually exclusive. In any case, the warning here is probably the sternest in all of his extant letters: "If anyone destroys God's temple, God will destroy that person" (3:17).

The destructive potential of divisiveness in the church is a dominant and recurring theme in this letter. Other than in the opening chapter, the concern resurfaces most dramatically in chapter 11, when Paul once again demonstrates considerable displeasure in the Corinthians: "when you come together it is not for the better but for the worse," because "there are divisions among you" (11:17, 18). These divisions are playing a destructive role in their practice of the Lord's Supper. Indeed, it becomes clear now that their differences are not simply rooted in pastoral preferences but also include socioeconomic factors (11:20–22). They are failing in their calling to become, collectively, the temple of God's Spirit or, in another of Paul's images, Christ's body (11:29; 12:12–27). Such failure is a betrayal of God's desire for a holy people to represent God and embody God's purposes in the world.

The connections between the Pauline text and the other lectionary readings are obvious and rich. God's calling upon the people of Israel to be holy is predicated precisely on God's own self-description, "I the LORD your God am holy" (Lev. 19:2). God's vocation for this people is to be a community whose life together is an embodied, social testimony to God's character, as well as an approximation of God's vision for human existence. Accordingly, much of the instruction in Leviticus 19 regarding Israel's calling is framed in terms of interpersonal relations, coming to a rather fine point (certainly from the perspective of the New Testament!)

with the command to "love your neighbor as yourself" (19:18). In essence, through Jesus Christ as the foundation, God has extended this calling to the non-Jewish people and peoples of the world. Paul's frustrations with the Corinthians lay in their immature, even pagan, refusals to become such a people who together embody divine holiness through love for one another (cf. Rom. 13:8–10; Gal. 5:13–15).

Similarly, in Jesus' Sermon on the Mount, another of our lectionary texts, we encounter his description of a renewed Israel (his twelve apostles) and God's calling upon them, through Jesus, to be "the light of the world" and a "city built on a hill" (Matt. 5:14). The social nature of these images ought not to be overlooked. As denizens of this renewed divine community ("the reign of God"), they and we are called by God through Christ to "love [our] enemies and pray for those who persecute [us]" (5:44). Jesus extends this sociality even to the seemingly mundane act of greeting a stranger: "And if you greet only your brothers and sisters, what more are you doing than others?" (5:47). He then summarizes this calling in a recalling of Leviticus 19:2: "Be perfect, therefore, as your heavenly Father is perfect" (5:48).[2] It is significant that this "perfection" or maturity is framed explicitly in terms of love not simply for one's neighbors, but for evildoers (specifically in the NT era, the Roman military!) and the needy, along with those we identify as our "enemies."

This calling to be a holy people, whose life together is, in Paul's imagery, a temple or dwelling place of God's own Spirit in the world, resonates throughout Scripture as a fundamental theme. God, Creator of all things and all peoples, seeks to call forth a particular or distinctive people to be a collective representation of the divine character and purposes in the world. This has its deepest roots in Genesis 1, where *adam* (humanity) as a collective is created by God for the purpose of imaging or representing the Creator within creation (1:26–28; cf. Ps. 8). With humanity's collective failure through disobedience, God rebooted humanity's calling through the calling of Israel, and then through Israel's faithful Son, this calling is extended again to the

---

1. It is theologically important to note, as the NRSV does, that the second person "you" in vv. 16 and 17 is plural.
2. The term translated "perfect" is *teleios* (from the noun *telos*) and implies maturity or the fulfilling of one's purpose.

church. This vocation is issued always with the implication that Israel and the church are called upon by God to be God's people(s) for the sake of all peoples and all creation.

Thus, Paul's description of the Corinthian church as the temple of God's Spirit implies that this congregation, and by implication every Christian congregation since, is—or, more precisely, ought to be—a microcosm of what God desires for creation. In the words of Nazarene theologian Eric M. Vail, "God's purpose for creation is that all creation might come to an abundance and wholeness of life in community to such a degree that God's self-giving love might shine through every relationship in the community. . . . Creation comes to its fulfillment as God's temple, or dwelling place."[3]

MICHAEL LODAHL

Commentary 2: Connecting the Reading with the World

"Humblebrag" is a term coined by Harris Wittels, referring to statements that cover boasting under a thin veneer of self-deprecating humor or complaint.[4] "I feel so lazy today. I only did weights at the gym—no cardio at all!" "Embarrassing! I'm wearing an old T-shirt in the newspaper photograph with my son winning the state spelling bee. I had to run straight from my daughter's All-Star game, and I did not expect she would win!"

While a humblebrag is a form of boasting that pretends to be humble, Paul is teaching the Christians at Corinth about boasting that really is humble. It is a delicate balance that Paul models in the first two lines of this reading. Paul takes credit for laying the theological foundation upon which the Corinthian church is built, likening himself to a master builder. At the same time, Paul is not the foundation; the foundation is Jesus Christ alone.

The image of Jesus as the foundation of the church is familiar. We hear it in traditional hymns, such as "The Church's One Foundation" by Samuel J. Stone, written in the 1800s. It begins, "The church's one foundation is Jesus Christ her Lord." Another hymn, "How Firm a Foundation," emphasizes the sturdiness of faith based on Christ. It begins, "How firm a foundation, ye saints of the Lord, is laid for your faith in his excellent Word!" Both of these hymns assure us that, regardless of external dangers or internal strife, the church ultimately rests on the stable ground of Jesus Christ.

Our reading continues with a further architectural image. Paul declares that the Corinthian Christians are God's temple. This statement has become so commonplace that it is easy to overlook its radical edge. The idea that we are temples is something used by health-food stores and fitness gurus to convince us to eat right and exercise. In this colloquial use, calling us temples is a compliment that also encourages a shame-inducing guilt trip. Paul's use of the term has none of that. It is a bold declaration of the extraordinary value—the holiness—of each person.

Instead of warning the Corinthians that their status as God's temple means they need to treat themselves in a certain way, Paul announces that God will destroy anyone who destroys God's temple. The Corinthians' status—and ours, as well—as the temple of God means that God is invested in our well-being. God will never be neutral toward any person or power that brings us destruction. This radical affirmation of value falls on our neighbors as well as ourselves. Because the Corinthians are God's temple— both individually and collectively—each one is to treat the others as holy and valued by God.

The Gospels image Jesus as the temple. In Matthew and Mark, false witnesses reported to the chief priests that Jesus said he would destroy the temple and rebuild it in three days (Matt. 26:61; Mark 14:58). Those who passed by repeat the same rumor (Matt. 27:40; Mark 15:29). The Gospel of John attributes the saying to Jesus directly. When asked for a sign, Jesus responds, "Destroy this temple, and in three days I will raise it up" (John 2:19).

---

3. Eric M. Vail, *Atonement and Salvation: The Extravagance of God's Love* (Kansas City: Beacon Hill Press, 2016), 42, 43.
4. Harris Wittels, *Humblebrag: The Art of False Modesty* (New York: Grand Central Publishing, 2012), xi.

Paul identifies the church—both the particular church at Corinth and the church universal—as the temple raised in the resurrection of Jesus Christ. We are God's temple because God's Spirit dwells within us, the Spirit of Jesus. This requires a kind of exercise in attending to Jesus' Spirit in our midst, embodying Jesus' Spirit in our congregation, and living Jesus' Spirit in the world.

Lest the Corinthians might get too haughty about such honorific status, Paul follows quickly with an admonition: "Do not deceive yourselves" (1 Cor. 3:18). What passes for wisdom in Corinth, and in any human society, is foolishness. In order to become truly wise, the Corinthians must become fools.

There are at least two aspects of this. The first is about scale. Scientists and scholars recognize that every discovery leads to new questions. Intellectual exploration does not simply fill in the map of known territory; rather, it takes us to new expanses of uncharted lands. Inventing a more powerful telescope reveals mind-boggling multiple galaxies. Increased knowledge leads to recognition of how little we know. If this is true with subjects like geography and astronomy, is it not so much more so with God? Surely the more we know of the God of mystery, the more we understand the limitations of our knowledge.

The second aspect of Paul's counsel that those who consider themselves wise must become fools is made explicit in verse 19: "For the wisdom of this world is foolishness with God." This aspect is about values. What human cultures value as wisdom and what God values as wisdom do not often align. What does our contemporary culture see as wisdom? Perhaps business acumen, financial success, professional accomplishment, or high esteem in a community. Perhaps sophisticated tastes, expertise in a particular field, advanced education, or a position of religious leadership. There is reason to believe that Paul would see all of this as "foolishness" in God's accounting.

Paul surrendered many of his own worldly claims to wisdom after his conversion. Once an upstanding member of his community and a staunch defender of the faith of his ancestors, Paul became an itinerant evangelist, telling fantastic tales of the dead returning, barely scraping by financially, and unable to stay out of prison! God's wisdom is a holy infant, Divinity in diapers. God's wisdom is lived outside the margins of polite company, offering nourishment, healing, transformation, and eternal life. Central for Paul, God's wisdom dies on a cross in an act of love for the world and then, incomprehensibly, rises again from the grave. The wisdom to which Paul testifies throughout his writings is, when judged by worldly standards, ridiculous folly.

In both scale and values, acknowledged folly is the better part of wisdom. In the more eloquent words of William Shakespeare, "The fool doth think he is wise; but the wise man knows himself to be a fool."[5]

Paul tells the Corinthians not to boast about which person had the better teacher. These teachers simply laid the foundation of Jesus Christ, whose Spirit dwells in the temple that is the church community. Our text ends with a master lesson in the art of the theologically sound humblebrag. "For all things are yours," Paul writes, including the world, life, death, the present, and the future. All these things and more belong to the Christians Paul addresses. "And," he continues, "you belong to Christ, and Christ belongs to God" (vv. 21–23).

The task for the Corinthians is to see themselves rightly in relation to the world, to one another, and to God. Paul rhetorically sets them in an elevated place of honor: "all belongs to you." Yet this honor is not due to the Corinthians' own qualities; it is not about which teacher they follow or how much wisdom they have. Instead, it is about their relationship with Jesus Christ, the foundation of their faith, to whom they "belong." All things belong to the Corinthians only in so far as they belong to Christ, who belongs to God. Paul portrays a nesting doll of belonging, with the Corinthians rightly placed in the middle—encompassing the world and life and the future, embraced by Jesus Christ and the God of all creation.

SHANNON CRAIGO-SNELL

---

5. William Shakespeare, *As You Like It*, in *The Riverside Shakespeare*, ed. G. Blackmore Evans (Boston: Houghton Mifflin Co., 1974), 395.

Matthew 5:38–48

38"You have heard that it was said, 'An eye for an eye and a tooth for a tooth.' 39But I say to you, Do not resist an evildoer. But if anyone strikes you on the right cheek, turn the other also; 40and if anyone wants to sue you and take your coat, give your cloak as well; 41and if anyone forces you to go one mile, go also the second mile. 42Give to everyone who begs from you, and do not refuse anyone who wants to borrow from you.

43"You have heard that it was said, 'You shall love your neighbor and hate your enemy.' 44But I say to you, Love your enemies and pray for those who persecute you, 45so that you may be children of your Father in heaven; for he makes his sun rise on the evil and on the good, and sends rain on the righteous and on the unrighteous. 46For if you love those who love you, what reward do you have? Do not even the tax collectors do the same? 47And if you greet only your brothers and sisters, what more are you doing than others? Do not even the Gentiles do the same? 48Be perfect, therefore, as your heavenly Father is perfect."

Commentary 1: Connecting the Reading with Scripture

In these two paragraphs of his inaugural discourse, Jesus speaks against two ways the law of Moses has been taught in Israel ("you have heard it said") and gives alternative commands ("but I say to you") by which the law and the prophets are to be fulfilled in the dawn of the kingdom from heaven. Each paragraph, 5:38–42 and 5:43–48, follows the pattern of the larger section of Matthew 5:21–48. Jesus highlights commands of the law whose force is being minimized or sidestepped under current teachers in Israel, and then teaches how that force must instead be repentantly maximized in the life of his listeners.

The command of the law, "Eye for an eye, tooth for a tooth" (5:38; Exod. 21:24; Lev. 24:20; Deut. 19:21), aims to prevent impunity for violence and to limit retribution. Its concern, as the companion lectionary passage of Leviticus 19:1–2, 9–18 attests, is not to authorize revenge but to protect people, especially the vulnerable, from bodily harm in their contact with one another and thus to nurture the fabric that unites them as neighbors in their shared place. However, the force of this command has been minimized in Israel so that it encourages retaliation against evildoers, resulting in a

tattered fabric of relations. As Jesus' teaching goes on to imply, it reduces justice to retribution and turns victims into rivals of their aggressors, robbing them of the power to promote neighborliness. Jesus says that the meaning of the law's command must instead be maximized, "Do not resist an evildoer," so as to encourage subversive self-giving, which he specifies with his own commands in three summary scenarios (5:39–41).

When someone shames you by striking you on the side of the face, show him the other cheek instead of retaliating (v. 39). If he exploits legal structures to the extreme of suing for your primary garment, give him your outer coat, too, although that is your one blanket by right (v. 40; cf. Exod. 22:26–27; Deut. 24:12–13). If he forces you to go with him one mile, here an occupying Roman authority who oppresses you directly by making you carry his equipment that distance, offer him a second (Matt. 5:41).

At first blush, Jesus' directives seem a recipe for the impunity the cited command of Moses aims to curb, but the self-giving he teaches is not passive acquiescence to various forms of abuse. It is the subversion of the rules of power assumed and exploited by an evildoer, who would seduce others into a game of rivalry and impugn "resistance" with his pretense of restraint (e.g., the "restraint" of striking only the cheek, leaving the accused with his outer coat, demanding only one mile when he could impose more).

Jesus thus teaches his people to refuse to play rival to evildoers and so reinforce with their "resistance" the façade of evildoers' "restraint." This subversive nonresistance exposes the limits of evildoers' power to control the oppressed, who show that they cannot be forced to fight on their oppressors' terms. When they endure even Roman oppression with grace, they strip Rome of moral authority, weakening its hold on Israel, not least on their own hearts. They lay bare the injustice of evildoers and embody the transformative way to the justice of heaven's kingdom.

Jesus extends the direction of his three commands with his last one of the paragraph (v. 42), which concerns the response not to an evildoer but to someone in need. He addresses his listeners now as holding some power over others. We who have enough are tempted to settle for our current security, refusing the risk of lending to the needy in a kind of preemptive retaliation: we deprive the needy when they "threaten" to deprive us, thus investing in nothing but a deteriorating status quo. By lending to those who beg to borrow from us, however, knowing that we may not recover what we lend, we refuse to submit our relationships and our future to a rule of rivalry and scarcity. By risking loss, we insist that our life together be fed by something more than transactions of quid pro quo. We invest in a life of fullness fed by practically loving God and one another, one the psalmist seeks to learn along the path of God's commandments according to the lectionary psalm (Ps. 119:33–40).

Jesus introduces the second paragraph, 5:43–48, with a central command of the law of Moses, "You shall love your neighbor" (cf. 22:39), followed by a way it has been taught under current teachers in Israel, "and hate your enemy." Enemy neighbors have not only been excluded from the purview of the law's love command; by its prevailing force Jesus' people have found themselves ordered to do something the law nowhere commands, to hate their enemies, as if loving their other neighbors required

this. This justice, Jesus says, is not enough to enter the kingdom coming to earth from heaven (cf. 5:20).

In the light of that kingdom, *to love your neighbor means to love your enemies.* It means to pray for the very people who persecute you (v. 44), especially those of the current Gentile power occupying the land and their accomplices from Jesus' own people and place. To love so indiscriminately is to love as God our Father in heaven does, and therefore to inherit as God's human heirs (i.e., "children") the kingdom coming from heaven (v. 45). Thus, being children of God as Father is to live and to love a certain way. It is not a status or a sentiment but an activity, a behavior. It is to be perfect as our heavenly Father is perfect (v. 48), that is, perfectly promiscuous in the love of neighbors, transgressing parochial security by extending love generously, even to enemies. The Father of Israel in heaven does not withhold sunshine from evil people or rain from the unrighteous. This God pours out mercy upon all, and so God's heirs are to be promiscuous in our love in like manner.

If we treat with love only those who love us, how can we claim to be heirs of this Father of Israel? What reward is there for that? In what future does that stingy "love" invest? Do not even tax collectors, who trample God's law and exploit their sisters and brothers for their own shortsighted gain, do that (v. 46)? Do not even such haters of neighbors love those who love them? To be salty and bright, by contrast (5:13–16), is to love not only those who love you, but also those who hate you. If you greet only your Israelite family and neglect to extend the grace and hospitality of a greeting to foreigners in Israel, how are you being any different from the Gentiles, who do not know the creator as Father and are thus apt to treat those foreign to them as intruders? Instead, Jesus urges, be promiscuous in your love, as the Father of Israel is promiscuous in the Father's love. Be perfect, as your heavenly Father is perfect.

While the demands of Jesus' Sermon on the Mount have led many Christian teachers to minimize and restrict its force to "personal" rather than political matters, its place in Matthew and the canon make that impossible. Matthew has presented Jesus, like John before him, as a figure of political significance and influence, who eventually threatens the established regime in the land enough for it to execute him as "King of the Jews." Like the law of Moses that Jesus is interpreting in this discourse, his commands express not a merely personal ethic but directives for a fabric of community life, where the kingdom of heaven is taking place.

TOMMY GIVENS

Commentary 2: Connecting the Reading with the World

In this season of Epiphany, Jesus continues to shed light on God's desires for our relationships. Throughout the Sermon on the Mount, Jesus leads us toward wisdom, making his argument in classic rabbinic fashion—point, counterpoint—against the claims of other voices: "You have heard it said . . . But I say to you" (Matt. 5:21, 27, 31, 33, 38). He delves deeply into some of the most difficult aspects of personal life. He warns us that while it is obvious that we should not murder, it is just as crucial that we acknowledge the damage our anger and insults can do (vv. 21–26). While it is obvious that we should not commit adultery, Jesus warns us that lust itself holds destructive power (vv. 27–30). While it is obvious that we should fulfill our vows and speak truth while under oath, Jesus calls us to account for every word we say (vv. 33–37). Now Jesus turns to the toughest relational issue of all: how to deal with those who hurt us.

The Judaic law is resoundingly clear: "An eye for an eye" is just and fair. In three different contexts, we are told:

- "When people who are fighting injure a pregnant woman so that there is a miscarriage . . . if any harm follows, then you shall give life for life, eye for eye, tooth for tooth, hand for hand, foot for foot, burn for burn, wound for wound, stripe for stripe" (Exod. 21:22–25).
- "Anyone who maims another shall suffer the same injury in return: fracture for fracture, eye for eye, tooth for tooth; the injury inflicted is the injury to be suffered" (Lev. 24:19–20).

- "Show no pity: life for life, eye for eye, tooth for tooth, hand for hand, foot for foot" (Deut. 19:21).

Our modern justice system is built on the premise that those who cause pain deserve punishment commensurate with the damage they inflict. We cannot know what Jesus is suggesting for political structures, but his instructions for those who want to live according to God's reign could not be clearer. Our highest aspiration is nothing short of seeking to return to our identity in the image of God: to be perfect, that is, complete (*telos*), even as God is perfect/complete (Matt. 5:48). Jesus himself models this for us in his choice not to destroy his enemies, but to love them, even by laying down his life for them.

Is generosity toward those who harm us, or love for our enemies, easy? Hardly. A 2017 study shows that "we feel measurably happier after taking action against others who have harmed us." David Chester and C. Nathan DeWall discovered that "people do not just feel good undertaking vengeful acts, but that they actually seek out these opportunities to make themselves feel better."[1]

Revenge is a natural reaction to harm. Jesus reminds us that it is not our only option. We can instead choose love. When Judas betrayed him with a kiss, Jesus called him "friend." When another disciple reacted by attacking the slave of the high priest, Jesus stopped him and healed the injured man (Luke 22:51). Even on the cross, Jesus' last words included a blessing for those who had him killed: "Father, forgive them; for they do not know what they are doing" (Luke 23:34).

---

1. Stacy Liberatore, "Revenge Really IS Sweet," *The Daily Mail*, January 10, 2017, http://www.dailymail.co.uk/sciencetech/article-4103314/Revenge-really-sweet-Study-finds-feel-measurably-happier-taking-action-against-did-wrong.html.

In our political climate, which celebrates disdain and disparagement, what if we practiced the "still more excellent way" of love (1 Cor. 12:31)? In our culture, which rewards vitriol on social media and sports events, what if we chose to "speak the truth in love" (Eph. 4:15)? Imagine the shocking surprise of kindness. Revenge is sweet; but sweeter still is the reign of God.

Fred Rogers, the Presbyterian minister who created *Mister Rogers' Neighborhood*, recalled the impact of Pittsburgh Seminary professor Bill Orr: "He was a great influence—not just because he was brilliant. He was the kind of person who would go out on a winter's day for lunch and come back without his overcoat." One Sunday while visiting Dr. Orr at the nursing home, after singing the hymn "A Mighty Fortress Is Our God," Fred asked about the phrase "the prince of darkness grim." "What," Fred asked, "is that one thing that would wipe out evil?" Dr. Orr said, "When you look with accusing eyes at your neighbor, that is what evil would want; . . . the more [Satan] can spread the accusing spirit, the greater evil spreads. On the other hand, if you can look with the eyes of the Advocate on your neighbor, those are the eyes of Jesus."[2]

What might it look like to aspire to be more like God in our relationships with others? What would it mean to love our enemies? What difference would it make? In 2012, a single photo took social media by storm: a picture of a young woman in a turban sporting a beard and sideburns. The post on the "funny" thread on Reddit generated numerous disparaging comments. The disdain and mockery would be crushing for any of us. Instead of retaliating and raging in defense, the woman in the photo, a sophomore at Ohio State University, responded with dignity and grace. She said that she discovered the post through one of her friends on Facebook and offered that she would be willing to smile for a photo any time. She also explained that she is not embarrassed or humiliated, that, although she looks very different than other women because of her facial hair, as a Sikh woman she is not humiliated at all.

Instead, she explained, the Sikh believe that the body is sacred, a gift of the "Divine Being" not to be rejected. More importantly, setting down society's view of beauty and embracing the transience of the body is freeing. Her body, she said, will return to ash after this life is over; there is no need to fuss over that which is transient. Rather, it is her attitude, thoughts, and actions that will have more value, because they will have lasting impact: "When I die, no one is going to remember what I looked like; heck, my kids will forget my voice. However, my legacy will remain: and, by not focusing on physical beauty, I have time to cultivate those inner virtues and hopefully, focus my life on creating progress for this world in any way I can."[3] This, she says, is what is important: not her face, but the happiness that lies beneath the surface.

What impact did her actions have? First, her choice to love her enemy softened the heart of the one who had originally mocked her. The Reddit user who posted the photo apologized and reached out to Kaur personally. He said, "She was glad . . . I posted it so more people could see, and so much positivity came out of what started as a negative thing. [Talking to Kaur] completely opened my eyes." But her reaction reverberated far beyond her original attacker as the beauty of her inner qualities and attitudes were demonstrated and were seen by others. Surely Balpreet Kaur is not far from the kingdom.

CHRISTINE CHAKOIAN

---

2. Wendy Murray Zoba, "Won't You Be My Neighbor?" *Christianity Today*, March 6, 2000, https://www.christianitytoday.com/ct/2000/march6/1.38.html.
3. Lindy West, "Reddit Users Attempt to Shame Sikh Woman, Get Righteously Schooled," September 26, 2012, https://jezebel.com/5946643/reddit-users-attempt-to-shame-sikh-woman-get-righteously-schooled.

Eighth Sunday after the Epiphany

Isaiah 49:8–16a

Psalm 131

1 Corinthians 4:1–5

Matthew 6:24–34

Isaiah 49:8–16a

⁸Thus says the LORD:
In a time of favor I have answered you,
    on a day of salvation I have helped you;
I have kept you and given you
    as a covenant to the people,
to establish the land,
    to apportion the desolate heritages;
⁹saying to the prisoners, "Come out,"
    to those who are in darkness, "Show yourselves."
They shall feed along the ways,
    on all the bare heights shall be their pasture;
¹⁰they shall not hunger or thirst,
    neither scorching wind nor sun shall strike them down,
for he who has pity on them will lead them,
    and by springs of water will guide them.
¹¹And I will turn all my mountains into a road,
    and my highways shall be raised up.
¹²Lo, these shall come from far away,
    and lo, these from the north and from the west,
    and these from the land of Syene.

¹³Sing for joy, O heavens, and exult, O earth;
    break forth, O mountains, into singing!
For the LORD has comforted his people,
    and will have compassion on his suffering ones.

¹⁴But Zion said, "The LORD has forsaken me,
    my Lord has forgotten me."
¹⁵Can a woman forget her nursing child,
    or show no compassion for the child of her womb?
Even these may forget,
    yet I will not forget you.
¹⁶See, I have inscribed you on the palms of my hands.

Commentary 1: Connecting the Reading with Scripture

There are clear divisions in Isaiah 49, each with specific emphases. The lection for the Eighth Sunday after the Epiphany focuses on one of the units within this chapter, verses 8–16a. Before focusing too closely on these specific verses, preachers would be wise to explore the witness of chapter 49 in its entirety and in its setting within chapters 49–53. To do otherwise is to risk missing the dramatic theological flow of these chapters and of chapter 49 in particular.

Chapter 49 opens with the second of three Servant Songs in Deutero-Isaiah. In verse 6, the Servant is identified as the one who will not only restore the broken "tribes of Jacob" and "survivors of Israel," but will fulfill the call first made to Abraham (Gen. 12:3). God declares: "I will give you as a light to the nations, that my salvation may reach to the end of the earth" (Isa. 49:6). As Walter Brueggemann wisely cautions: "These verses constitute an enormous problem in Isaiah studies because they celebrate 'the servant of the Lord,' whose identity is unfathomable."[1] The Servant's identity may be "unfathomable," but that has not stopped much of Jewish interpretation seeing the Servant as the community of Israel and much of Christian interpretation positing the Servant as Jesus or a forerunner of Jesus.

The unit to be considered on this Sunday is a part of the second Servant Song. Christopher Seitz posits a key question of the vexing beginning to verses 8–16a. "The central question in part is, Who is being answered (v. 8): Israel or the servant of vv. 1–6?" He goes on to conclude, "The elaboration of 49:8–12 cannot be his [the servant's] own word to himself or his own word to an Israel who will apportion the land and free the prisoners. Rather, it is an elaboration made by the servants [i.e., the followers of the first servant], promising that God's intention with the servant will finally prevail."[2]

In some of the most powerful and evocative poetry in the Hebrew canon, these verses testify to prior promises made to God's people and evince a proleptic vision of God's promises yet to be fulfilled. It is not the last time that Deutero-Isaiah will refer to the Servant as being "despised and abhorred" (v. 7). This description of the Servant will be expanded with poetic brilliance in chapter 53. Despite the circumstances facing the Servant—"despised, abhorred by the nations"—God's purpose will prevail through this Servant chosen by God. The Hebrew canon is replete with stories of servants chosen by God, often reluctant servants, who accomplish the purpose of God, from Noah to Sarai and

Abram to Esther to Jeremiah to Ruth to Job. To be called as a servant of God is to engage in the transformative promises of God, even in dire circumstances and often against formidable resistance.

When the Servant is chosen by God, this call is not for privilege but in order to exercise a vocation. The Servant is chosen by God "as a covenant." In this Servant, people will witness the promises of God take on flesh. The Servant is to tell prisoners to "come out" (v. 9). "The verb 'come out' is an exodus verb, asking the Babylonian exiles to leave the thralldom of Babylon as their ancestors left the certitudes of Egypt (see 52:11)."[3] The Servant is called by God to revitalize the imagination of God's people, to dare them to dream again after living a nightmare, to call them out of the confines of a circumscribed life lived in Babylon. It is a dangerous thing to call people, especially people accustomed to living under oppressive regimes, to dream. God's Servant is given a task that can be carried out only by trusting in the author of the task.

The promises—"they shall not hunger or thirst" (v. 10)—hearken back to wilderness wanderings when manna met them in the morning (Exod. 16:35) and water burst forth from a rock (Exod. 17:6). For Christians, the promises spoken by the Servant also anticipate the final vision of the Apocalypse (Rev. 21:6). The grand promises of the psalmist in Psalm 23 also echo through these verses, especially when the Servant assures listeners that God "by springs of water will guide them" (see Ps. 23:2).

An earlier promise in Deutero-Isaiah resurfaces when the Servant is called to announce in verse 11, "I will turn all my mountains into a road, and my highways shall be raised up" (see Isa. 40:4). Though the road from exile to freedom may seem daunting, if not impossible, the Servant is to remind the people, as Jesus will later remind the people, that with God all things are possible (see Matt. 19:26).

The Servant is called not only to challenge the people to trust in God's faithfulness, but also to gather people who have been exiled from

1. Walter Brueggemann, *Isaiah 40–66*, Westminster Bible Companion (Louisville, KY: Westminster John Knox Press, 1998), 109.
2. Christopher Seitz, "Isaiah 40–66," *New Interpreter's Bible* (Nashville: Abingdon Press, 2001), 6:430.
3. Seitz, 114.

their country, and in many cases from each other. Just as the shepherd is to gather the sheep and guarantee their safety from predators, so God through the Servant promises compassion on formerly displaced people (see v. 13).

Some promises are hard to hear and even harder to trust. The people to whom the Servant preaches are stuck in the narrative that "God has forgotten us, God has forsaken us" (v. 14). The Servant rejects their lament and confronts them with a truth that the faithful should have always known about God: "Can a woman forget her nursing child, or show no compassion for the child of her womb? Even these may forget, yet I will not forget you" (v. 15). This theme will resound not only throughout Isaiah and the Psalms, but will be the fundamental theological promise spoken by the apostle Paul to the church in Rome (see Rom. 8:38–39).

The Servant dares people who are returning from exile or have recently returned to a devastated Jerusalem to trust that God will be with them in their rebuilding and that their time of desolation is over (v. 16). God holds the future of God's people in the palm of God's hand; their future is no longer in doubt. This could well be the most outrageous promise for the people to claim, given their years in captivity

and the destruction they are about to or are now witnessing. Even so, the Servant insists laying hold of this promise from God will be cause for them to sing (v. 13). They will no longer sing dirges and lamentations. The people of God will sing of a God who honors promises and restores to wholeness even those who have broken covenant.

The texts that accompany Isaiah 49:8–16a on the Eighth Sunday after the Epiphany share some similar themes. Just as Deutero-Isaiah seeks to restore the hope of disconsolate exiles or despondent returned exiles, the psalmist declares, "O Israel, hope in the LORD from this time on and forevermore" (Ps. 131:3). The apostle Paul returns to Deutero-Isaiah's plea to trust in the promises of God when he invites the Corinthians to trust that the Lord "will bring to light the things now hidden in darkness" (1 Cor. 4:5). Even as Deutero-Isaiah addresses an anxious community of current or recent exiles, so Jesus addresses an anxious people under Roman rule, urging them to trust in God's promise, especially when worries threaten to jeopardize such trust (Matt. 6:24–34). Call, promise, faith: a plethora of theological themes, each of them clear and urgent, is offered by these texts.

GARY W. CHARLES

Commentary 2: Connecting the Reading with the World

In this passage from Isaiah 49, the writer declares that God is speaking to postexilic Israel, specifically to the "servant" named in verse 3, through whom God is proclaiming the good news of restoration and healing for God's people. These verses present an image of God's redemption of the world, a redemption that is both present now and still to come. The preacher can point to this reality by making connections between sections of this text and the larger world today.

Some of the possible connections the preacher could choose from include the image of freeing the prisoners, ending hunger, comforting people after disasters, and the love God has for God's people that surpasses even the love of a mother for her nursing child. The text can serve as a prophetic call to action in one's

community, as well as a pastoral message of consolation and comfort. With the announcement that the receiver of this message is to be given as a "covenant to the people" (Isa. 49:8), the preacher can highlight the role of the church today as ministers of God's covenant to the world. Part of that covenant means calling out injustice and righting wrongs. Another part of that covenant includes tending lovingly to those who suffer, offering them the consolation of the Lord who loves them more fiercely than a nursing mother.

In the image of freeing the prisoners (v. 9), the text points to God's care for all people, and God's desire that all should be free. In considering the larger scope of God's redemption for the world, this verse brings to mind the brokenness of our current prison system. Several theologians have reflected on the problem of the prison industrial complex today, and how for-profit prisons thwart the flourishing of persons and communities. Perhaps the preacher knows of persons in the congregation directly impacted by the prison system. If there is a prison in close proximity to the church, perhaps this is an opportunity to discuss prison ministry and the possibilities of making care for prisoners a part of the church's mission. For example, a group of seminaries in the Atlanta area came together to offer theological education to inmates of a local prison. There may be other examples closer to your own congregation.

Preachers may find it helpful to turn to outside resources for framing the larger problem of mass incarceration. One such resource is James Logan's book *Good Punishment? Christian Moral Practice and U.S. Imprisonment.*[4] In today's context, the prison system in the United States is an industry that profits from the poor and people of color, incentivized to increase the number of inmates in order to increase financial profit of the corporations that oversee and benefit from prison labor.

Another connection the preacher can make is to a theology of food and the importance of ending hunger. Verses 9–10, "They shall feed along the ways, on all the bare heights shall be their pasture; they shall not hunger or thirst," remind the reader that God's redemption includes enough food for all people. The pasture imagery also evokes the shepherd and sheep relationship that occurs several times in the Bible (Ps. 23; Isa. 53:6; Luke 15:3–7; John 10:11), comparing God's love and care to that of a shepherd meeting the needs of the sheep. Such needs include feeding. In Isaiah's image of God's redemption, the people's hunger is met at last.

David Beckmann, president of Bread for the World, author of *Exodus from Hunger: We Are Called to Change the Politics of Hunger,* argues for the role of Christians and all people to work together to end world hunger, something that

is within our capacity to do.[5] Within Isaiah's vision for God's redemption, the expectation is that God is both currently redeeming God's people as well as promising future redemption. Ending hunger is something that God may be doing with our help and in our lifetime.

The verses that declare "neither scorching wind nor sun shall strike them down" also call to mind the consolation needed by persons who have experienced natural disasters. In Isaiah's context, the people had lost their land in their captivity. Today, as natural disasters occur around the world, people continue to lose their land and their sense of safety within their homes. Whether it be earthquakes, wildfires, hurricanes, or flooding, natural disasters "strike them down," and the residents of such communities are left to literally pick up the pieces.

Persons in such communities may have difficulty trusting again in the ability of the earth to proclaim God's glory. It may be hard for them to hear the words of Isaiah in verse 13: "Sing for joy, O heavens, and exult, O earth; break forth, O mountains, into singing!" When earth has been broken by destructive forces, it can be a challenge to believe that the earth can still "sing for joy." The preacher may want to reflect on how caring for creation, whether after a natural disaster or in light of the onslaught of worldwide natural disasters, is part of our vocation as part of God's creation. Calling forth joyful singing from the earth may be possible only when we make the effort to care for this earth.

Old Testament scholars have identified verse 13 as a hymnic affirmation, showing the traditional form of a summons to praise followed by a reason for praise.[6] This verse can lead to musical selections of hymns in worship that focus on creation's acts of praising God. Traditional hymns such as "How Great Thou Art," "For the Beauty of the Earth," and even the Doxology, with its line "Praise God, all creatures here below," are just a few examples of resources for worship that can tie into this text and offer an example of earth and the heavens singing for joy.

---

4. James Logan, *Good Punishment? Christian Moral Practice and U.S. Imprisonment* (Grand Rapids: Eerdmans, 2008). See also Michelle Alexander, *The New Jim Crow: Mass Incarceration in the Age of Colorblindness* (New York: The New Press, 2010).

5. David Beckmann, *Exodus from Hunger: We are Called to Change the Politics of Hunger* (Louisville, KY: Westminster John Knox Press, 2010).

6. Walter Brueggemann, *Isaiah 40–66* (Louisville, KY: Westminster John Knox Press, 1998), 115.

Verse 14 offers an interruption from the praises sung by creation, asking if God has truly remembered Zion, when the experience of exile is painfully still in memory. This interspersion of doubt is a helpful voice, acknowledging how our faith is rocked when we go through tumult and tragedy. Listeners who are hearing from this text the promises of God's redemption both now and in the future may still feel dubious, wondering if God continues to redeem broken situations. Emphasizing this strain of doubt is also a pastoral response, allowing persons in your congregation to feel accepted in their moments of doubt.

The image of the nursing mother forgetting her child highlights the maternal love God has for God's people, reminding the people that God wants to care for and nurture us. As highly unlikely as it would be for a nursing mother to forget her child, the text suggests that even if they did forget, God would not forget, since God's love is even more intense than that of a mother for her child. The final verse in this selection reiterates this tender love, describing God as having inscribed Israel's name on God's hands, like a tattoo, permanently demonstrating God's care for the people. Though the people have been in exile and feel forgotten by God, these words proclaim that God could never forget those whom God loves so dearly.

CAROLYN BROWNING HELSEL

Psalm 131

¹O LORD, my heart is not lifted up,
   my eyes are not raised too high;
I do not occupy myself with things
   too great and too marvelous for me.
²But I have calmed and quieted my soul,
   like a weaned child with its mother;
   my soul is like the weaned child that is with me.

³O Israel, hope in the LORD
   from this time on and forevermore.

Connecting the Psalm with Scripture and Worship

The first reading from Isaiah 49 is one of the few Old Testament passages in which God is compared to a nursing mother. Despite the fact that the people of Israel were still in exile (see the second Servant Song of Isa. 49:1–6), despite the people's near despair—"my LORD has forgotten me"—the prophet attests that God is still in a loving covenant relationship with the people of Israel, still speaking comfort into their distress, never forgetting them in their neediness (Isa. 49:8–15). Although the people may feel themselves to be prisoners locked apart from God's pleasure, the prophet urges the community to sing of its confidence in God's care.

So we join with the exiled Israelites to sing such confidence. Our response to the Isaiah reading is Psalm 131, a brief psalm that, uncharacteristically for the Psalter, places its poetic focus on the interior psychological state of a single psalmist. The authoritative voice we usually encounter in the psalms—the speaker as a monarch, a warrior, a priest, a shepherd responsible for a large flock, a knowledgeable historian—is absent here. Rather, the speaker is small, lowly, without a significant role to play in the community, and is accepting of this status. It does not matter whether the community's situation is filled with misery, as was described in the Isaiah reading. Although I am merely like a child cared for by my mother, I take comfort that I am fed by her very body, sitting in peace

on her lap. That mother is God, the Lord of life and the hope of all the people.

In the Middle Ages, it was commonly thought that a nursing mother does not menstruate because her monthly fluid more or less backed up and was reconstituted as milk for the infant. Thus, blood and milk merged into one. This understanding of the human body meant that both male and female Christian mystics spoke of the wine of Holy Communion not only as the blood of Christ, but also as Christ's milk, as if at the Table of the Lord we are nursed by our divine mother. Do you think that perhaps in our time we are brave enough to resurrect this imagery? The psalm speaks of my soul, that is, my deepest personal self, the core of my being; remember that the psalmist would not have imagined that humans have some immortal "soul." My soul is like a contented infant in my body, and this can be because I am like a contented infant on the lap of God the Mother.

We can rest peacefully in the arms of God our Mother, ready to hear the Gospel reading from Matthew 6, in which we are invited to trust in God our Father.

When as Christians we hear the closing line of the first reading—"See, I have inscribed you on the palms of my hands"—we inevitably picture the crucifixion. The divine compassion of Christ our mother is seen in the wounds of Jesus

The Greatness of God's Providential Care

Hereby He teaches us not only to take no thought, but not even to be dazzled at the costliness of men's apparel. Why, such comeliness is of grass, such beauty of the green herb: or rather, the grass is even more precious than such apparelling. Why then pride thyself on things, whereof the prize rests with the mere plant, with a great balance in its favor? . . . when He had said, "Consider the lilies of the field," He added, "they toil not:" so that in desire to set us free from toils, did He give these commands. In fact, the labor lies, not in taking no thought, but in taking thought for these things. And as in saying, "they sow not," it was not the sowing that He did away with, but the anxious thought; so in saying, "they toil not, neither do they spin," He put an end not to the work, but to the care. . . .

Now when, as you see, He had demonstrated the greatness of God's providential care, and they were in what follows to be rebuked also, even in this He was sparing, laying to their charge not want, but poverty, of faith. Thus, "if God," saith He, "so clothe the grass of the field, much more you, O ye of little faith."

Which also itself again is an instance of providential care: that even when He sees us unworthy to receive good, He withholds His benefits, lest He render us careless. But if we change a little, even but so much as to know that we have sinned, He gushes out beyond the fountains, He is poured forth beyond the ocean; and the more thou receivest, so much the more doth He rejoice; and in this way is stirred up again to give us more. For indeed He accounts it as His own wealth, that we should be saved, and that He should give largely to them that ask. And this, it may seem, Paul was declaring when He said, that He is "rich unto all and over all that call upon Him." Because when we pray not, then He is wroth; when we pray not, then doth He turn away from us. For this cause "He became poor, that He might make us rich;" for this cause He underwent all those sufferings, that He might incite us to ask.

Let us not therefore despair, but having so many motives and good hopes, though we sin every day, let us approach Him, entreating, beseeching, asking the forgiveness of our sins. For thus we shall be more backward to sin for the time to come; thus shall we drive away the devil, and shall call forth the lovingkindness of God, and attain unto the good things to come, by the grace and love towards man of our Lord Jesus Christ, to whom be glory and might forever and ever. Amen.

John Chrysostom, "Homily XXII: Matt. VI. 28, 29," in *Chrysostom: Homilies on the Gospel of Saint Matthew,* trans. George Prevost, *Nicene and Post-Nicene Fathers,* Series 1, ed. Philip Schaff (Edinburgh: T. & T. Clark, 1888), 10:148–49.

on the cross. In these wounds, we place our hope. On her crowded lap, we sing our praise. In the final verse of the psalm, we borrow our forebears' language and call ourselves "Israel" (v. 3), the people chosen by God to live in covenant. Together we calm ourselves, accepting the embrace of God's benevolent care. Christians have come to believe that our gathering weekly with one another strengthens our capacity to trust, our reliance on a loving God, our nourishment through the body of Christ.

GAIL RAMSHAW

1 Corinthians 4:1–5

¹Think of us in this way, as servants of Christ and stewards of God's mysteries. ²Moreover, it is required of stewards that they be found trustworthy. ³But with me it is a very small thing that I should be judged by you or by any human court. I do not even judge myself. ⁴I am not aware of anything against myself, but I am not thereby acquitted. It is the Lord who judges me. ⁵Therefore do not pronounce judgment before the time, before the Lord comes, who will bring to light the things now hidden in darkness and will disclose the purposes of the heart. Then each one will receive commendation from God.

Commentary 1: Connecting the Reading with Scripture

In this passage, Paul continues his instruction to the Corinthian church regarding proper estimation of ministers as "servants of Christ and stewards of God's mysteries" (1 Cor. 4:1). The steward is one to whom God entrusts teaching about God's mysterious ways in the world, who serves as a safeguard for the good news in Jesus Christ. Paul adds that the role of stewards is to "be found trustworthy" (v. 2), a theme that nicely binds this week's lectionary texts. While hardly a comprehensive clue, this criterion of trustworthiness may shed light on Paul's earlier description of the purging judgment that awaits these stewards; he anticipates "the Day" that will disclose "the work of each builder" regarding their faithfulness to the foundation he has laid (3:10–13). That foundation is Jesus Christ, and building true to this foundation includes being a person worthy of trust.

Paul has grown impatient with the Corinthians' penchant for offering their own judgments regarding the worthiness of various ministers of the gospel (1 Cor. 1:10–12). Only God can rightly judge. While Paul is "not aware of anything against" himself (4:4), he also knows he cannot judge himself; he acknowledges it is God alone who judges the secret motives and motions of the heart (Rom. 2:16). All those who serve as builders of congregations upon the foundation of Jesus Christ will be judged; on this great Day of reckoning "each one will receive [the appropriate] commendation from

God" (4:5), even if the work of some is "burned up" and the builder suffers loss, saved "only as through fire" (3:15).

If there is at least a veiled warning in 3:10–15 against those "servants" who have followed his foundational labors in Corinth, Paul now returns to confronting the Corinthian congregation itself, "so that none of you will be puffed up in favor of one against another" (4:6). He prefers to speak softly rather than to carry a big stick, but will do the latter if the Corinthian situation demands it (4:21). It is clear from the tone of the letter as a whole that Paul fears that this indeed might be the case. He barely got beyond his standard salutation before launching into a heated reproof of the quarrels within the congregation reported "by Chloe's people" (1:11). He uses words of ultimate divine threat: "if anyone destroys God's temple [through quarreling and divisions], God will destroy that person" (3:17). He scolds the Corinthians during his instructions regarding Holy Communion, insisting even that "when you come together, it is not really to eat the Lord's supper" (11:20), because their divisions are only being reinforced by their practice of the meal (11:17–34). Their lack of faithfulness to one another betrays the faithful character of the One who called them (cf. 1 Thess. 5:12–13, 24).

The lectionary psalm (Ps. 131) is a beautiful complement to Paul's acknowledgment that the judging of ministers—even of himself!—is a task given neither to him nor to the Corinthians but to God alone. "O LORD, my heart is not lifted up, my eyes are not raised too high; I do not occupy myself with things too great and too marvelous for me" (v. 1). The vocation of the minister is to be a trustworthy steward of divine mysteries, not the master of those mysteries. There is far too much we do not know about the lives and deep histories of those we too often presume to judge. It is the Lord, Paul insists, who "will bring to light the things now hidden in darkness and will disclose the purposes of the heart" (1 Cor. 4:5).

Similarly, the lectionary reading from Isaiah promises "a day of salvation" when the Lord shall say to the prisoners, "Come out!" and "to those who are in darkness, 'Show yourselves'" (Isa. 49:8, 9). This "day of salvation" is surely also a day of *judgment*; but that judgment, like the biblical doctrine of judgment generally, is a day of *justice* and *compassion* (vv. 9–13). Even if the people of Israel feel themselves abandoned, forsaken by their divine Mother in judgment, God's word through the prophet promises otherwise (vv. 14–15). Even if a nursing mother could somehow forget her child, "yet I will not forget you" (v. 15).

The God of Israel is faithful and therefore trustworthy, this One whose faithful character is the plumb line and criterion for the trustworthiness of the Pauline "steward" of God's mysteries. Indeed, it is Jesus Christ who is the foundation in whom God's trustworthiness is unveiled (again, see 2 Cor. 1:18–22). It is difficult for Christians to read Isaiah 49:16 and *not* be moved to think of the Crucified One: "See, I have inscribed you on the palms of my hands."

It is this same Jesus, faithful even unto the cross, who assures his disciples that God is indeed trustworthy. Further, it is Jesus' resurrection from the dead that seals the promise of divine faithfulness (see Rom. 4:16–25). Our temptations to worry and tendencies to fret are brought under the judgment of Jesus' Sermon on the Mount, particularly in this Sunday's lectionary reading. If our heavenly Father feeds the birds of the air and clothes the grass of the field, then God can be trusted to provide for our essential needs (Matt. 6:26, 30–31). Just as the stewards of God's mysteries, according to

Paul, are called by God to be trustworthy, so Jesus' disciples are to rely on the trustworthiness of God and seek only God's reign and justice (6:33). It is not difficult to make a connection between the divine character of faithfulness and the divine expectation that God's people, including but not limited to God's stewards of the word, are to be faithful as God is faithful.

The calling upon the people of God to become a faithful people, even as God is faithful, provides the pretext for a doctrine of divine judgment. Paul's conviction that there will be a day—"the Day," he calls it (1 Cor. 3:13)—of judgment for God's stewards, and indeed for all people, is an enduring theme throughout the Scriptures. It is likely Paul understood "the Day" to be the OT's "Day of the LORD" (Isa. 2:12; Joel 2:28–32; Amos 5:18–20), "the day when," in Paul's words, "God, through Jesus Christ, will judge the secret thoughts of all" (Rom. 2:16).

It is not a judgment simply of thoughts. Paul elsewhere insists that "all of us must appear before the judgment seat of Christ, so that each may receive recompense for what has been done in the body, whether good or evil" (2 Cor. 5:10). It is significant that Paul specifically mentions our *bodily actions* as subject to divine judgment. We are reminded that we are bodies living in concert with other bodies (human and otherwise) in a material world, and that what we do as bodies, in every moment given us, really does matter. It matters because God is the Creator of all things, and "the LORD's compassion is over all that [God] has made" (Ps. 145:9). Because God has created and called us to become creatures of trustworthiness, of faithfulness, we are called to give an account to the One before whom "no creature is hidden," this One who is "a consuming fire" (Heb. 4:13; 12:29).

Such sobering considerations should be taken seriously but should also should be seasoned with the gracious description of our divine judge as the God of deep compassion, in the palms of whose hands our lives are inscribed (Isa. 49:16). In the words of Charles Wesley's classic hymn "Arise, My Soul Arise," "Five bleeding wounds he bears, received on Calvary; they pour effectual prayers; they strongly plead for me!"

MICHAEL LODAHL

Commentary 2: Connecting the Reading with the World

In this passage, Paul is giving a job description for himself and his colleagues. He starts with lines of accountability, identifying himself as a "servant of Christ" (1 Cor. 4:1). Paul works for Jesus. He is not, first and foremost, a servant of any particular congregation or even of the church universal. He is a servant of Jesus Christ. As such, Paul is one of the "stewards of God's mysteries." The term "steward" refers to a servant entrusted to manage the affairs of a household. Although clearly a servant, a steward still has a good deal of responsibility, as well as a good deal of authority among the servants. Paul has a strong sense of his own dignity, but it depends entirely on the dignity of the one he serves.

Paul and his colleagues are entrusted specifically with the stewardship of God's mysteries. What is meant by mysteries? At the very least, this term indicates truth that cannot be arrived at by human effort alone. God's mysteries cannot be discovered by humanity; they must be revealed by God. Paul and his colleagues are thereby stewarding God's mysteries when they preserve and pass on the good news of Jesus' birth, life, death, and resurrection.

Centuries later, we too are charged with preserving and passing on these same mysteries. Presbyterian theologian Letty Russell notes that the word "tradition" literally means "handing over."[1] As Christians, we have been handed the good news. This means more than simply being given a copy of the Bible. The "handing over" of the gospel of Jesus Christ is often far more "hands-on" than that. At some point in our lives, some person or group of people gave to us the good news that we are beloved children of God, redeemed by the grace of Jesus Christ, held in the Holy Spirit.

Perhaps it was immediate family, who held hands to say grace at supper and lived out a life of grace day to day. Perhaps it was a friend who offered welcome when family would not. Perhaps it was neighbors in church, who shook hands to pass the peace and showed up with casseroles after a loved one's death. Somehow,

somehow, someone handed Jesus to us. This process of traditioning has been going on for nearly two thousand years, and we are called, like Paul, to be faithful stewards of our Christian traditions.

One aspect of this is pedagogy, or the theory and practice of teaching. To be trustworthy stewards, we must learn well the mysteries of the faith, the inherited wisdom of Christian traditions. The disciplined study of the Bible, theology, and church history is our responsibility; we must know it well so we can hand it over well. We must teach it carefully, mindful of the details, that nothing be lost.

Another aspect of this is mystagogy, leading students to mystery. In some church traditions, mystagogy refers specifically to the final stages of catechesis before baptism. For Karl Rahner, a twentieth-century Roman Catholic theologian, mystagogy has a broader sense. Handing on faith includes bringing someone to recognize the mystery of God and to interpret their own life in relation to that mystery.[2]

In Rahner's theology, mysteries are more than truths that have been revealed by God. No matter how well we know the Bible and theology, there is still more to God. Even when God reveals God's self to us, we cannot fully comprehend God. In part, this is because our minds are too small and our concepts too weak. More importantly, this is because God is incomprehensible! The character of God is such that if any person is certain they know exactly who God is, they are wrong. What they imagine to be God is an idol or an illusion. God cannot be fully known in certainty like a script or a diagram. God is simply beyond that. God is mysterious; God is mystery. Christian faith involves learning all we possibly can about God, and realizing that God is more than that. It involves handing ourselves over to that which is beyond our comprehension, trusting in the God of Jesus Christ.

This is the distinction between a magician and a preacher. A magician uses camouflage and distraction to keep the mechanics of the trick

---

1. Letty Russell, *Human Liberation in a Feminist Perspective: A Theology* (Philadelphia: Westminster Press, 1974), 74, 76–77.
2. Karl Rahner, "The Theology of the Future," *Theological Investigations*, trans. David Bourke (New York: Crossroad, 1983), 13:40–41, 46.

from being revealed. The magic relies on what the audience does not know. In stark contrast, a preacher rolls up her sleeves, shows all her cards, and reveals every technique. She brings the audience to recognize the mystery that remains when knowledge is complete. The magician's task is to conceal the magic; the preacher's task is to reveal the mystery. This is the focus of the season of Epiphany, the context for our lectionary text. When the wise men arrive to see God, they find a vulnerable newborn. This is not the revelation of certain and precise data, but the revelation of God's unfathomable love for humanity, that God would become flesh.

Paul's job description, "stewards of the mysteries of God," beautifully holds together pedagogy and mystagogy. He is a steward of mystery, chief servant to an inscrutable reality. We will fail to follow his example if we neglect to learn, preserve, and teach what God has revealed to us. We will also fail to follow his example if we forget that God is far more than we can know or comprehend, if we do not lead others to God's mystery.

Whether or not Paul is a trustworthy steward is left for God alone to judge. Paul is unconcerned about any judgment that might be rendered by the Corinthians. Indeed, if they are busy evaluating Paul and their other teachers, including Apollos, they have misunderstood the job description. Paul and Apollos are servants of Christ, and God gives the only performance evaluation that matters.

Paul does not consider himself able to adequately judge his own stewardship. He writes,

"I am not aware of anything against myself, but I am not thereby acquitted" (v. 4). There are at least three reasons why Paul cannot confidently declare himself trustworthy. The first is sin. This is the communal brokenness of humanity that we live out in our individual turning from God. Sin clouds our senses, muddles our thinking, and easily turns toward self-flattery.

The second is situation. Many of the greatest figures from history have huge, gaping blind spots clearly visible from the vantage point of the twenty-first century. Thomas Jefferson was profoundly racist. Martin Luther was anti-Semitic. Many of the icons of the early years of the women's movement were clueless on issues of race and class; many of the famed leaders of the civil rights movement participated in discrimination based on gender. Looking back, we see the smartest and saintliest among us were dismally ignorant and small-minded in ways typical of their situations. While they were ahead of the game in some areas, in others they were terribly in step with their times. It would be foolish to imagine that we are not equally blinded by our own situations. Surely, our descendants will see our own blind spots and small-mindedness in ways that we cannot yet see.

The third impediment to Paul's reliable self-evaluation is precisely the mysteries he is entrusted to steward. If the task is basic math facts, we can check our work and be certain we have the correct answers. When it comes to talking about God, being certain we are correct is always an error.

SHANNON CRAIGO-SNELL

Matthew 6:24–34

24"No one can serve two masters; for a slave will either hate the one and love the other, or be devoted to the one and despise the other. You cannot serve God and wealth.

25"Therefore I tell you, do not worry about your life, what you will eat or what you will drink, or about your body, what you will wear. Is not life more than food, and the body more than clothing? 26Look at the birds of the air; they neither sow nor reap nor gather into barns, and yet your heavenly Father feeds them. Are you not of more value than they? 27And can any of you by worrying add a single hour to your span of life? 28And why do you worry about clothing? Consider the lilies of the field, how they grow; they neither toil nor spin, 29yet I tell you, even Solomon in all his glory was not clothed like one of these. 30But if God so clothes the grass of the field, which is alive today and tomorrow is thrown into the oven, will he not much more clothe you—you of little faith? 31Therefore do not worry, saying, 'What will we eat?' or 'What will we drink?' or 'What will we wear?' 32For it is the Gentiles who strive for all these things; and indeed your heavenly Father knows that you need all these things. 33But strive first for the kingdom of God and his righteousness, and all these things will be given to you as well.

34"So do not worry about tomorrow, for tomorrow will bring worries of its own. Today's trouble is enough for today."

Commentary 1: Connecting the Reading with Scripture

The driving concern of Matthew 6:24–34 is freedom from economic anxiety and freedom for an economic life that hastens God's kingdom and justice. In the footsteps of John the Baptist in Matthew's narrative, Jesus has been calling his people to a life of repentance in view of the kingdom coming from heaven. Now in his inaugural discourse in Matthew, Jesus is teaching his first disciples, in the hearing of the crowds (Matt. 5:1; 7:28–29), how to live repentantly together so as to enjoy and spread the gifts of that kingdom on the earth; and in 6:19–7:12, he presents what might be called a political economic vision of the heavenly kingdom he has been proclaiming.

Today's readers are apt to interpret the economic anxiety addressed in 6:24–34 as a matter of individual psychological states. However, the closing words of the passage (6:33–34), along with the themes of the whole discourse (Matt. 5–7), clarify that Jesus is teaching about God's justice and therefore about economic anxiety as

also a social problem. The lectionary passage of Isaiah 49:8–16a reinforces this concern with the shared life and influence of the people of God; it prophesies the material uplift of the needy and the consolation of the whole community. Likewise in Psalm 131, the hope of the psalmist is inextricable from that of his people Israel.

Just as the eye cannot at once fill the body with darkness and with light (6:22–23), so we cannot serve two masters, God and mammon (v. 24). Our eye fixes upon one and is thus diverted from the other. We will serve one and despise the other. Our shared and embodied life will be directed by the illuminating vision of God, or by the opaque guide of corruptible goods, which fills us with anxiety and acquisitiveness rather than hope and hospitality. Our eye, and therefore our body and its appetites, is always being formed by one over the other; so let us train our eye to see the light of the kingdom coming from heaven, Jesus urges, and in this way serve God rather than mammon.

Serving the God of heaven, whom we can trust to care for us, frees us from predatory anxiety (v. 25). We need not obsess over the food and drink needed to nourish our life, or the clothing required to shelter our bodies, to say nothing of our addiction to a fossil-fuel industrial economy and metals mined destructively for our electronic technology. Such myopic obsessions sacrifice people and places to the assurance of ephemeral material plenty for ourselves. They sacrifice justice to mammon.

Notice that Jesus does not instruct his people to be unconcerned about their lives or their bodies. Rather, he says there is more to sustaining life than food and more to sheltering the body than clothing. As Jesus has already declared to the devil about the way he will rule (i.e., as Son or Heir of God), human beings do not live by bread alone (4:4). While we cannot live without basic provisions for embodied life, we do not in fact enjoy these by anxiously securing them at any price to our neighbors and others, or to our place and other places. We do not enjoy them by serving mammon. As Jesus illustrates with the examples of birds and lilies (6:26–29) and as the institution of the Sabbath was to reveal in Israel's life, we live by the gifts of God, which teach us to share rather than hoard. We do not live because we have bread and clothing, but because God has provided for a shared life of which these are but one important manifestation. The fullness of embodied life is not less than bread or clothing then, but it is certainly more. If we anxiously serve mammon, we will find that in the deteriorating life with others that results, even our bread and clothing grow insecure.

As the birds and the lilies show us, God feeds and clothes life that is not troubled with guaranteeing its own sources of food and clothing, and God is even more committed to providing for human life (vv. 26–30). If such forms of animal and plant life do not provide for themselves by even the most humble forms of work—farming or weaving—why do we live anxiously as if we secured our life by such work, to say nothing of the anxiety animating more "sophisticated" labor or even the rapacious destruction of others and their places in pursuit of our own provisions and comforts? God feeds the birds, which neither sow nor reap and are free from anxiety over food and shelter (v. 26). Yet as human beings we can trust God to show even greater concern for our life.

In fact, God nurtures the life of God's people as a mother does the child at her breast, a reminder from our companion text in Isaiah 49:15. What is more, anxiety about our life adds nothing to our life; it only blinds us to God's provision (Matt. 6:27). God clothes lilies more abundantly than God arrayed the most gloriously powerful and industrious king of Israel's past, King Solomon (vv. 28–29). Yet such plant life, for which God has provided so abundantly, is lush with vitality one day and destroyed the next by fire for warmth or cooking (v. 30), quite unlike the greater duration and worth of human life. How much more then can we trust God to provide for our lives, in which God is invested not only as creator but also as our Father?

In 6:31, Jesus repeats the command of 6:25, that we not be anxious about the basic material needs of our life, making explicit the rhetorical force of his intervening words about birds and lilies. We must envision our life together without being controlled by anxious questions about how to guarantee the future of our embodied life, about where the supposedly scarce provisions for that life will come from (v. 31). Living by such faithless questions drives us to serve not God but mammon, the god of apparent security, prosperity, and unassailable stability. This anxious drive starves our trustful bonds of sharing and healthy interdependence, fraying the fabric of our life together and the life of each one of us. It blinds us to the light of God's justice, and living by such worry fills our bodies with the darkness of greed, suspicion, and rivalry. In the lectionary passage of 1 Corinthians 4:1–5, the apostle Paul diagnoses an analogous obsession with impressive appearances as the judgmentalism dividing the Corinthian church into rivals of one another.

Anxious questions about material security may drive the economy of Gentile peoples who do not know God as Father (v. 32), an economy captive to a life of striving for their embodied future as predators. Competing for scarce goods whose source cannot be trusted, the Gentiles court the injustice and hostility that are the price of serving mammon. In contrast, God has revealed God's self to Israel so as to empower us to live in trust that our heavenly Father knows all of our needs.

We must remember by practice, then, that our heavenly Father knows our needs and can be trusted to provide them. We must seek first the now-dawning kingdom and justice of that God, knowing that the basic needs of our embodied life will hardly be lacking where our Father's kingdom and justice are found (v. 33). Let us not bring our life to ruin by a distrustful fixation on tomorrow. Our heavenly Father can be trusted with tomorrow, which will pose plenty of worrying challenges to a life of loving one another when it comes, as we already find today (v. 34).

TOMMY GIVENS

Commentary 2: Connecting the Reading with the World

The Gospel text for the Eighth Sunday after the Epiphany is a marvelous treat for the preacher and a rich text for any season! As we continue in texts from the Sermon on the Mount, these wisdom teachings of Jesus provide a fitting preparation for the introspective work of Lent (soon to arrive in the church calendar). Indeed, they are a primer for discipleship, both for individuals and for our life together as we aspire to be Christ's church. He begins with the Beatitudes—what it means to be blessed in the kingdom, in contrast to worldly aspirations. He then instructs us about relationships to one another: regarding anger, lust, oaths, retaliation, and love for enemies, in contrast to the world's encouragement for self-absorption and revenge (5:21–48). Next he turns to our relationships with God, expressed in almsgiving, prayer, and fasting, in contrast to the world's worship of material treasure. Like much Wisdom literature (e.g., in Proverbs), Jesus lays out two alternative aspirations for life throughout the Sermon on the Mount. The function of Wisdom literature is, after all, to invite intentionality about things we take for granted and the values that guide our decisions.

In this text, Jesus raises this question, Whom will we serve, God or wealth? These two are not the only aspirations the world provides. Our Western culture lays out a plethora of choices for us. Money is not the only idol that the world encourages us to worship. Among many options, we are encouraged to pursue happiness, fame, pleasure, achievement, power, and, especially for women, beauty. In verses just prior to this passage (6:19–21), Jesus intimates that there are numerous "treasures" we are prone to seek. The problem is that *wherever* our treasure is, Jesus warns us, there our heart will be also (v. 21)—*either* in heaven *or* on earth, but not both.

The first question this passage confronts us with is this: Which "master" will we serve? Which "treasure" will we seek? Wisdom begins with awareness that we have a choice. Discipleship propels us to choose to serve God—God's reign and God's righteousness—instead of choosing the lesser aspirations of the world.

It is not just individuals who face the temptation of worshiping other "gods" and being enslaved to other "masters." Congregations and denominations are prone to the same problem. Our institutions are prone to measuring our success not in terms of fidelity to the reign of God, but instead by counting the number of members on the rolls, people in the pews, and money in the plate. Survival needs trump everything else.

Of all the masters the world has to offer, Jesus warns us that money may well be the most seductive, particularly due to its promise of security. On an individual level, the basic needs of food and clothing that Jesus identifies (v. 25) are central to our survival and safety. These were affirmed in Abraham Maslow's 1943 paper *A Theory of Human Motivation* and form the base of the pyramid in the human hierarchy of needs. Those basic needs must be met before higher aspirations can even come into focus. Whenever humans feel that these concerns are vulnerable, our anxiety spikes.[1]

---

1. Neel Burton, "Our Hierarchy of Needs: True Freedom Is a Luxury of the Mind," *Psychology Today*, posted May 23, 2012, updated September 17, 2017, https://www.psychologytoday.com/blog/hide-and-seek/201205/our-hierarchy-needs.

This makes sense to us, especially if we have ever personally experienced the realities of deprivation. Yet is anxiety our only option?

Almost two millennia before Maslow's theory was published, Jesus spoke directly to this question. His answer? "Do not worry about your life, what you will eat or what you will drink, or about your body, what you will wear" (v. 25). Notice that Jesus is not dismissing our needs. He acknowledges that life requires food and drink and clothing; God knows we need such things (v. 32). Instead, Jesus suggests that we miss the point of life if we are focused *only* on these basic bodily needs (v. 25). Physical survival is necessary but insufficient as a purpose for living. To reduce our human aspiration to survival is to miss our true nature and our higher calling. Jesus presents a radical alternative: "Strive *first* for the kingdom of God, for God's righteousness" (v. 33).

What does it look like to strive first for God's reign and righteousness? It begins with our flipping over the pyramid of need, to lift our eyes from our lowest level of need, to focus instead on our highest aspirations. When we do, we remember that we are more than our physical bodies. We are, in fact, children of God, made in the image and likeness of God. We are part of something much larger than ourselves: a world of beauty and glory, in which the birds of the air and the lilies of the field testify to the abundant goodness of God.

Jesus' radical revisioning does more than flip over Maslow's pyramid. Jesus changes the framework of our highest aspirations altogether. Maslow would suggest that our aspirations rise from physical and safety needs to matters of social belonging and self-esteem, rising to the peak Maslow calls "self-actualization." Jesus revolutionizes this model. Instead of striving according to the human pyramid of aspiration, from survival to self-actualization—which the Gentiles (aka nations/cultures) do—Jesus offers a radically different ultimate purpose for life. Our highest calling is not *self*-actualization or *self*-fulfillment but, instead, the freedom of losing ourselves in *the reign and righteousness of God.* Not once but twice in Matthew's Gospel, Jesus invites us: "Those who want to save their life will lose it, and those who lose their life for my sake will find it" (10:39; 16:25).

David Brooks makes something similar to this argument when he posits two models of human development. He calls the first "The Four Kinds of Happiness." The lowest level is material pleasures like food and clothing; the next is achievement, for example, the pleasure we get from success; the next is generativity, the pleasure of giving back to others; and the highest, he says, is moral joy, the glowing satisfaction we get when we have surrendered ourselves to some noble cause or unconditional love.

Brooks contrasts this to Maslow's hierarchy of needs, which starts by seeking to fulfill our physical needs, moving up to safety needs like economic security, then up to belonging and love, to self-esteem, and only then to the ultimate goal of self-actualization—autonomy and the expression of our most authentic self. Brooks writes:

> The big difference between these two schemes is that The Four Kinds of Happiness moves from the self-transcendence individual to the relational and finally to the transcendent and collective. Maslow's hierarchy of needs, on the other hand, moves from the collective to the relational and, at its peak, to the individual. In one the pinnacle of human existence is in quieting and transcending the self; in the other it is liberating and actualizing the self.[2]

Which is more satisfying? The aspiration of self-fulfillment, or the goal of surrendering to a "noble cause" or "unconditional love"? The aspiration of self-actualization, or the joy of transcendence and freedom? This is Jesus' invitation: surrender to the reign of God, aspire to the righteousness of God, and you will find life and find it abundantly. We cannot choose two masters. Which master we choose makes all the difference in the world.

CHRISTINE CHAKOIAN

2. David Brooks, "When Life Asks for Everything," *New York Times,* Opinion, September 19, 2017, https://www.nytimes.com/2017/09/19/opinion/when-life-asks-for-everything.html.

Ninth Sunday after the Epiphany

Deuteronomy 11:18–21, 26–28   Romans 1:16–17; 3:22b–28 (29–31)
Psalm 31:1–5, 19–24   Matthew 7:21–29

Deuteronomy 11:18–21, 26–28

¹⁸You shall put these words of mine in your heart and soul, and you shall bind them as a sign on your hand, and fix them as an emblem on your forehead. ¹⁹Teach them to your children, talking about them when you are at home and when you are away, when you lie down and when you rise. ²⁰Write them on the doorposts of your house and on your gates, ²¹so that your days and the days of your children may be multiplied in the land that the LORD swore to your ancestors to give them, as long as the heavens are above the earth. . . .

²⁶See, I am setting before you today a blessing and a curse: ²⁷the blessing, if you obey the commandments of the LORD your God that I am commanding you today; ²⁸and the curse, if you do not obey the commandments of the LORD your God, but turn from the way that I am commanding you today, to follow other gods that you have not known.

Commentary 1: Connecting the Reading with Scripture

The opening instructions to readers in the text from Deuteronomy necessitate that teachers/preachers expand the lectionary limits of this text. Our text starts, "You shall put these words of mine in your heart and soul, and you shall bind them as a sign on your hand, and fix them as an emblem on your forehead" (Deut. 11:18). Without a full reading of the entire pivotal eleventh chapter of Deuteronomy, "these words" in verse 18 lack context. What are "these words"? Why are they of such importance that we are to bind them physically to ourselves? Why must we wear them like an obvious tattoo?

Before focusing on the specific Deuteronomic text for the Ninth Sunday after the Epiphany, it would be wise to examine the context in which these verses sit. Chapters 10 and 11 include the final words from Moses' sermon on the commandments (5:6–21) and the Shema (6:4–5). The first eleven chapters of Deuteronomy establish the theological groundwork upon which the Deuteronomic law code (chaps. 12–26) is based. As Moses closes his sermon in chapters 10–11, the people are called to "wear" on their bodies reminders that they did not deliver themselves from Egypt and that they will not deliver themselves into the promised land. These visual reminders will serve as prompts to a fickle, and often faithless, people that the choice to live in obedience to God's law is not a one-time choice, but must be made with each new day and by each new generation.

As this text opens, the Israelites are instructed to "put these words of mine" in the forefront of their existence. These words take us back to the commandments in chapter 5, to the Shema in chapter 6, and to the recurring promise of a new land for those who attend to these words from God. Religious faith in God has no room for casual or occasional observance. Thomas Mann wisely notes,

> Deuteronomy 10:12–11:32 is both retrospective and prospective in that it reiterates various motivations for obedience already cited and concludes with an explicit reference to blessing and curse. . . . It is primarily out of thankfulness for grace unearned, for redemption without precondition, for forgiveness undeserved, and for a land given without merit that Israel is called

to "diligently observe all the statutes and ordinances that I am setting before you today" (11:32).[1]

The God we meet in Deuteronomy calls us to observe all the statutes and ordinances not just today, but to choose to obey them again tomorrow.

These words are not simply for individual religious observance but are also the words that are to bind the "heart and soul" of children and future generations (11:18–19). Such ongoing, faithful obedience to God and God's commandments is the condition upon which the promise of the land is based. Circumcision, an outward form of obedience to God for males, is to be coupled with "circumcision of the heart" (10:16) which shall require that believers not only observe the commandments but embody them in their daily living and teach them to their young.

Deuteronomy 11:18–21, 26–28 is not the first time that the author recalls the commandments and the Shema, and it will not be the last to emphasize the blessing of following God and God's law faithfully and the curse of failing to do so in pursuit of other gods. Repetition of the call to choose God's blessing and to make choices that avoid God's curse is a theological thread that weaves its way through Deuteronomy. Verse 16 opens with the harsh recognition that often the people have demonstrated themselves to be capable of making choices that are not life-giving. Reading the Torah up until this point only confirms the necessity for the Deuteronomic author(s) to remind the people of their history. They have not always excelled in keeping the commandments of God. In fact, Israel has repeatedly made unfaithful decisions. Verses 26–28 articulate the consequence of living within the realm of God's blessing or dying under the certain consequence of God's curse, of entering a land of plenty or being cast out of the land.

Verses 26–28 are a powerful call to decision by the people of God. God does not seek out the occasional attention of God's people. To the extent that religious faith becomes a haphazard or perfunctory pursuit, Deuteronomy rails against such a diminishment and decentralization of the faith. "A choice has to be made," writes Patrick Miller. "Blessing and curse, the possibilities for life and death, are out there before Israel; it is up to the people now to choose. . . . God's people will shape their future as they decide between obedience and disobedience."[2] The public worship service at Shechem recounted in Joshua 24 will again warn the Israelites against straying toward foreign gods and insist that they "choose this day" (Josh. 24:15) to live in a land given by God, not one to which they are otherwise entitled.

Preaching the theology of the Deuteronomic writer(s) offers rich homiletical possibilities, but also carries with it significant landmines to be navigated with care. The "blessing-curse" motif—obey God and blessing follows, or disobey and curse ensues—that is a hallmark of the Deuteronomic theologian and will continue into 1 and 2 Samuel and 1 and 2 Kings does not always track with human experience and religious observance (see Job). At times, the people of God are faithful, and despite their faithfulness, life is accursed. At the same time, sometimes the people of God live under the curse of chasing other gods, and yet they prosper. Surely Jesus was faithful to God and yet suffered the curse of the cross. Preaching from this text is to emphasize the importance of choosing a life of faithfulness, while also recognizing that God's grace is not a reward for our faithfulness, but what inspires it in us.

For preachers engaged in interfaith conversations, the concept of a "promised land" can be extremely problematic. Does the land being promised "belong" to Israel, or is it contingent upon the faithfulness of Israel? Were the Assyrian and then Babylonian exiles a direct result of the people assuming ownership of the land and neglecting faithfulness to the divine covenant? How is the covenant of the land conceived and/ or reconceived in the person of Jesus? How are Jews, Christians, and Muslims to achieve a theological rapprochement with respect to land in the twenty-first century? The questions go on and preachers would benefit from taking

---

1. Thomas Mann, *Deuteronomy,* Westminster Bible Companion (Louisville, KY: Westminster John Knox Press, 1995), 105.
2. Patrick D. Miller. *Deuteronomy,* Interpretation (Louisville, KY: Westminster/John Knox Press, 1990), 128.

great care as they weave their homiletical way through this text.

In the psalm for this Sunday, a similar Deuteronomic theological chord is struck. "The LORD preserves the faithful, but abundantly repays the one who acts haughtily" (Ps. 31:23). Preachers would be wise to couple the texts from Deuteronomy and the Psalms with the theological argument about the relationship between faith and righteousness that Paul develops in the epistle lesson for the day (see Rom.

1:16–17; 3:22b–28). Paul introduces a level of theological nuance into the conversation that pushes the sometimes oversimplistic theology of the Deuteronomist. In Matthew 7:21–29, Jesus tells a miniparable to stress that faith in God requires living in righteousness. In many ways, it resonates with text from Deuteronomy, as Jesus insists that we build our lives on the solid rock of righteousness.

GARY W. CHARLES

Commentary 2: Connecting the Reading with the World

When preaching on this text, it is important for the preacher to be aware of what is omitted from this selection of verses and why. As they stand, these seven verses are clear and direct instructions for living faithfully. Preachers can make present-day connections with the challenges of parenting or sharing our faith in every area of our lives, or the notion of blessings and curses and how we understand God's action in the world. However, within the context of chapter 11, these verses are also removed from their imperialistic message of conquest (Deut. 11:22–25, 29–32). It is important for the preacher to keep in mind that our daily living is also related to larger national and social movements, and that our commitment to living faithfully should also consider our impact on the politics of the day.

In considering these verses as religious instruction, it is important to hold in tension the private and public nature of religious faith. The message in Deuteronomy is to the people about to enter the promised land, and the passage calls on them to remember the God who redeemed their ancestors from slavery in Egypt and to live in obedience to God. These words should be both privately absorbed, "in your heart and soul," as well as publicly attested, "as a sign on your hand . . . an emblem on your forehead . . . on the doorposts of your house and on your gates" (vv. 18, 20). Living into faith requires that persons make a commitment to the words passed on from generation to generation, words that should make a difference in individuals' lives both privately and publicly.

At the same time, our public expressions of faith must also discern the difference between our religious devotion to God and our political inclinations as citizens.

The verses that come between this selection and following, verses 22–25 and 29–32, speak of a particular kind of public faith that identifies religiosity with a certain nationalism. The verses describe God promising to drive out other nations, dispossessing them of land so the Israelites may settle there. These verses promise that by following God, the people will be granted ownership over the land they are invading.

Historically, US Christians have adopted this mentality by associating the success of their country in world affairs as a sign of God's favor and blessing. It is crucial that Christians disentangle their citizenship within their national politics from their citizenship in God's kin-dom, which knows no geopolitical boundaries. While this lectionary passage does not contain the verses that describe God's promises of national victory and imperial conquest, the preacher should not shy away from addressing the inadvertent harm our public expressions of faith can have in fusing our devotion to God with patriotism. It is important that our faith impact how we live our lives in public, but it is also important that we not confuse our obedience to God with our duty as citizens.

Focusing on the second verse within this passage, the text challenges listeners to teach God's words to our children, "talking about them when you are at home and when you are away" (v. 19). This command to teach children the faith is a common reminder at baptisms, when the congregation is invited to commit to telling children about God as they grow in faith. The offering of Sunday school to children is a way churches try to fulfill this commitment, but parents often feel the greatest amount of responsibility for passing on the faith to their children. Parents can take their children to church, make them go to Sunday school even when children do not want to go, and yet they cannot make their children have faith.

Verse 19 makes it seem so direct: "teach them to your children." While parents can pass on knowledge, they cannot teach children how to have faith in God for themselves. A primary way of living into this call is through embodied practice, letting children watch and hear how faith impacts their parents' own daily lives and decisions. Parents should be able to talk about faith at home, as well as how their faith forms how they behave at work and in their communities.

Another direction the preacher may choose to take is the question of blessings and curses. Within verses 26–28, the promise of blessing as a result of obedience and a curse for disobedience can set up a problematic theological claim for listeners. While Israel's history includes an interpretation of events as part of God's punishment, viewing God's activity in the world within this framework today leads to blaming victims of tragedies for the suffering they experienced. Still in recent memory, some Christians have claimed that hurricanes and violent crime are God's punishment for sin—a blasphemous claim that heaps insult onto injury. Forms of preaching described as promoting a "prosperity gospel" tell listeners that they will be blessed if they believe God's claim on their lives.

Homiletician Debra Mumford, in her book *Exploring Prosperity Preaching: Biblical Health, Wealth, and Wisdom,* has discussed some of the ways prosperity preaching appeals to listeners, suggesting that these preachers have something to teach the rest of us, while at the same time acknowledging the harms that can occur when this message is used abusively.[3] For instance,

shaming listeners into giving financially to the church as a way of ensuring God's blessing on their lives is an unjust manipulation. Most churches go through some kind of stewardship season, but when persons are guilted or coaxed into giving *in exchange for* some financial blessing from God, then preachers are perpetuating a false system of spiritual economy.

To avoid the more destructive message of manipulating God's favor through faithful obedience, it is important for readers of Deuteronomy to understand this text in its larger narrative context. The people of Israel have fled Egypt, freed by God, but repeatedly turned their back on God and the commandments given to them through Moses. They have experienced hardship and wandered the wilderness for forty years. Now, as they near the promised land, they are told to remember the lessons learned through their wanderings, and to hold tight to the promises of God even when they enter the land God is giving them.

A helpful way of framing this for listeners today is to invite reflection on the ways that following God has brought a sense of flourishing to persons, and then asking at what point did they see experiences as "curses" that came from living life apart from faith. Bringing the connection back to the larger social arena, where have we as a society been "cursed" because of the ways we have failed to support one another, or when we have oppressed the vulnerable? For instance, how does our country still suffer the curse it brought upon itself through the institution of slavery? How are the continuation of broken relationships, a segregated society, and a deep mistrust between communities forms of curses that we have brought upon ourselves as a society? How is the unrest and resentment of workers, fueled by the erosion of a social safety net and the growing wealth gap, another expression of the curse of unbridled capitalism? Asking these kinds of questions can help listeners move beyond a simplistic perception of God's blessings and curses, and can instead envision more broadly the complex ways human freedom and sin contribute to the blessing or cursing of one another.

CAROLYN BROWNING HELSEL

---

3. Debra Mumford, *Exploring Prosperity Preaching: Biblical Health, Wealth, and Wisdom* (Valley Forge, PA: Judson Press, 2012).

Ninth Sunday after the Epiphany

Psalm 31:1–5, 19–24

[1]In you, O LORD, I seek refuge;
   do not let me ever be put to shame;
   in your righteousness deliver me.
[2]Incline your ear to me;
   rescue me speedily.
Be a rock of refuge for me,
   a strong fortress to save me.

[3]You are indeed my rock and my fortress;
   for your name's sake lead me and guide me,
[4]take me out of the net that is hidden for me,
   for you are my refuge.
[5]Into your hand I commit my spirit;
   you have redeemed me, O LORD, faithful God.
. . . .
[19]O how abundant is your goodness
   that you have laid up for those who fear you,
and accomplished for those who take refuge in you,
   in the sight of everyone!
[20]In the shelter of your presence you hide them
   from human plots;
you hold them safe under your shelter
   from contentious tongues.

[21]Blessed be the LORD,
   for he has wondrously shown his steadfast love to me
   when I was beset as a city under siege.
[22]I had said in my alarm,
   "I am driven far from your sight."
But you heard my supplications
   when I cried out to you for help.

[23]Love the LORD, all you his saints.
   The LORD preserves the faithful,
   but abundantly repays the one who acts haughtily.
[24]Be strong, and let your heart take courage,
   all you who wait for the LORD.

Connecting the Psalm with Scripture and Worship

Depending on the dating of Easter, the readings for this Sunday (the Ninth after the Epiphany, Proper 4) may be situated either before or after Lent and the Easter season. In either case, the readings establish the assembly on the rock who is Christ, reiterate the commitment that is established in the covenant, and preach baptismal faith. We are not to trust in our own adherence to Torah, but rather in the sacrifice of the Crucified.

The first reading's contribution to this three-way proclamation is familiar Deuteronomic theology: if you live according to the covenant, God will bless you, but if you do not, you will be cursed. Not only Deuteronomy, but much of human religion and of personal spirituality, both historic and contemporary, relies on this dictum: classically stated, *do ut des*—I give to God, so that God will give to me. I obey, and therefore I will be blessed by God. When I am in deep trouble, I bargain with God, promising to be good from now on. In the day's second reading, our lectionary follows this proposal with a strikingly different belief, for Paul testifies that in truth God does not reward our goodness; rather, we live by faith in God's goodness. Between these two readings, we join in the opening and closing stanzas of Psalm 31.

Psalm 31 has been identified both as a personal lament and as thanksgiving for deliverance, for the psalm traverses the whole of an individual's spiritual journey. In the opening stanza, verses 1–5, the psalmist, crying out in pain, utilizes familiar metaphors of sorrow: my situation has shamed me; I need a rock of refuge; my enemies have laid a net to capture me; I look to God for rescue. Some interpreters have seen this psalm as inspired by the prophet Jeremiah, who described both personal and communal suffering in such graphic language. Because the Lukan passion narrative has Jesus on the cross praying verse 5, "Into your hand I commit my spirit," some Christians have described this entire psalm as the prayer of Jesus, which now we as the body of Christ are invited to pray. We present our misery to the Almighty, admitting our situation, standing with Christ, and pleading for all those who suffer.

As a response to the Deuteronomy reading, this psalm stanza acknowledges that we have indeed not made the right choices; we have not lived faithfully in accord with the covenant. In the words of the psalm we admit our shame. We cannot trust to ourselves for any standing before God. Rather, we require a rock that is greater than any we can construct on our own.

Our response then skips to verses 19–24, the third stanza of the psalm, which is exuberant praise to the God who has indeed saved us. It is Sunday, the day of the resurrection, and we gather not because of our own status and accomplishments, but in faith in God's miraculous power in the face of suffering and death. In the words of verse 20, "in the shelter of your presence," we might think about Christians huddling together at the foot of the cross, protected by God's Spirit. By ourselves, we were merely "a city under siege," but thanks to the goodness of God, we are safe. In the Hebrew the verb tenses of this psalm move back and forth through time, and in the last verse we are still to "wait for the LORD." Our salvation is already now, but not yet fully, for tomorrow we will still be in need of God's steadfast love.

It is as if in this stanza the Christian community praises God for being even more abundant in goodness than the ancient Israelites knew, more than the prophet Jeremiah imagined. We had thought that God's blessing depended on our obedience to the law, but through the incarnation, we have come to believe that despite our usual practice of choosing the wrong path, God still enters our lives with divine might and saves us. At the close of the psalm we address one another: "Love the LORD," we say to each other, whom we recognize as saints of God, no matter which way they trod over the last week. We cannot trust in our own lives of obedience, but we encourage one another to trust in God's faithfulness.

What would it mean for us to see Christ as our rock of refuge? What are examples of how God's faithfulness will uphold us? Addressing this inquiry, we might search not only personally, God, my private rock, during the struggles of my individual life; but also ecclesially, God as refuge for all the baptized; and culturally, God as the fortress for my community of choice; and politically, God as the courthouse of a just society. "Be strong," calls out verse 24. If you are close to despair, hang on, and receive the comfort proclaimed in today's Gospel: it is Christ who is our strong rock, the fortress that keeps us safe, the foundation of our house.

GAIL RAMSHAW

Romans 1:16–17; 3:22b–28 (29–31)

¹:¹⁶For I am not ashamed of the gospel; it is the power of God for salvation to everyone who has faith, to the Jew first and also to the Greek. ¹⁷For in it the righteousness of God is revealed through faith for faith; as it is written, "The one who is righteous will live by faith." . . .

³:²²For there is no distinction, ²³since all have sinned and fall short of the glory of God; ²⁴they are now justified by his grace as a gift, through the redemption that is in Christ Jesus, ²⁵whom God put forward as a sacrifice of atonement by his blood, effective through faith. He did this to show his righteousness, because in his divine forbearance he had passed over the sins previously committed; ²⁶it was to prove at the present time that he himself is righteous and that he justifies the one who has faith in Jesus.

²⁷Then what becomes of boasting? It is excluded. By what law? By that of works? No, but by the law of faith. ²⁸For we hold that a person is justified by faith apart from works prescribed by the law. ²⁹Or is God the God of Jews only? Is he not the God of Gentiles also? Yes, of Gentiles also, ³⁰since God is one; and he will justify the circumcised on the ground of faith and the uncircumcised through that same faith. ³¹Do we then overthrow the law by this faith? By no means! On the contrary, we uphold the law.

Commentary 1: Connecting the Reading with Scripture

In Romans 1:16–17, we find themes dear to the hearts of great Reformers like Luther, Calvin, Knox, and Wesley: salvation by divine grace "to everyone who has faith" (Rom. 1:16) in Jesus Christ, the Son of God. It should be added immediately that this faith is not simply intellectual assent to certain theological propositions (nor did the Reformers think so). Indeed, recent scholarship tends to place far greater accent upon the theme of faithfulness—first and most fundamentally God's faithfulness, revealed in the faithful obedience of Jesus.[1] That divine faithfulness always and inevitably calls for a human response of faithfulness to God.

We can illustrate the difference this shift in emphasis can make. In the immediate context of our lectionary reading, Paul writes in 3:22a about "the righteousness of God through faith in Jesus Christ for all who believe." As the NRSV notes indicate, the phrase *pistis Christou* could

also be translated "the faith of Jesus Christ" or, preferably, "the faithfulness of Jesus Christ." First, this avoids what seems to be a redundancy in Paul's sentence, "*faith in* Jesus Christ for all those who *believe*." More importantly, it places greater emphasis upon the central role of Jesus' faithfulness to God, even to death on a cross, in our salvation (cf. Phil. 2:5–8), rather than upon individual human subjectivity (i.e., "having faith").

Similarly, the NRSV translators' note on verse 26 suggests a possible alternative to the one "who has faith in Jesus": the possibly surprising phrase "who has the faith of Jesus." Again, probably the more faithful interpretation would be *the faithfulness of Jesus* to God as the great revelation of God's own faithfulness "to the Jew first and also to the Greek" (Rom. 1:16; cf. 2:9–11). In this reading, "faith in Jesus" is entrusting oneself to Jesus, whose faithfulness both reveals

1. For a compelling, insightful description of these scholarly trends and their critical importance, see Douglas Harink, *Paul among the Postliberals: Pauline Theology beyond Christendom and Modernity* (Grand Rapids: Brazos Press, 2003), esp. 26–28.

our faithful God and calls forth a corresponding faithfulness to God in our everyday lives.

To Protestant ears, this may begin to smack of salvation by works. It is likely that such concerns are misplaced. Paul's writings consistently emphasize the believer's active participation in Jesus' life of faithful obedience to God (Rom. 6:1–11). After his lengthy and tangled struggle in Romans 9–11 to understand Jewish resistance to the gospel of Christ alongside Gentile belief ("provided you continue in God's kindness," 11:22), Paul issues this call to his Gentile readers: "by the mercies of God, . . . present your bodies [plural] as a living sacrifice [singular], holy and acceptable to God" (12:1).

This language is obviously drawn from Israel's sacrificial system, what Paul in 9:4 summarizes as "the worship" given to the Israelites by God. Paul, now having turned his attention to these Gentile believers in the Messiah and his faithfulness, describes *their* "spiritual worship" (12:1). The Greek term *logikēn,* note the NRSV translators, may also be rendered "reasonable." Perhaps a term like "appropriate" might also fit, such that God has graciously given to Gentile believers a kind of sacrificial worship that is appropriate to their corporate location in history and the divine purpose. This "reasonable" form of worship involves, even demands, their bodies together in everyday obedience to God as members of Christ's own body (12:3–21). This is not a passive or interior faith, but an active, bodily, social *faithfulness.*

Accordingly, near the letter's conclusion Paul describes himself as a priest whose offering to God is "the Gentiles . . . sanctified by the Holy Spirit" (15:16) and whose calling is "to win obedience from the Gentiles, by word and deed" (15:18). Such obedience, again, corresponds to the faithfulness of God unveiled in the faithful obedience of Jesus Christ, God's Son.

It is arguable that the biblical proclamation generally upholds this far more active rendering of "faith." The lectionary readings that accompany the Romans text certainly support this reading. For example, the Deuteronomy passage insists that the Israelites were not simply to teach the Torah to their children (Deut. 11:19–21), but to "diligently observe this entire commandment that I am commanding you"

(v. 22). The Torah is a gift of life (vv. 26–28), not a burdensome set of impossible obligations intended to drive people to despair.

Reading Romans alongside Deuteronomy should help us to understand Paul's gospel: this divine gift of life, as well as the calling to join with the people of God, has been opened up now also to the non-Jewish peoples of the world through the faithfulness of Jesus. "See, I am setting before you today" (v. 26) is addressed not only to Israel, but now also to the Gentiles—for God is the God of the Gentiles and is faithful to the Gentiles as well as to the Jews (Rom. 3:29–30).

The lectionary psalm is a prayer of trust, of seeking refuge in God. God is faithful (Ps. 31:21) and also "preserves the faithful" (v. 23), a promise that the church testifies has been most profoundly fulfilled in Jesus Christ, the one who from the cross uttered the prayer of faithful trust, "Into your hand I commit my spirit" (Ps. 31:5; cf. Luke 23:46). Indeed, Psalm 31:5 continues to sound a note of trust, "You have redeemed me, O Lord, faithful God," that resounds majestically in God's raising of Jesus from the dead (cf. Rom. 4:21–25).

The Gospel reading could not coincide more perfectly. Jesus concludes his Sermon on the Mount with a warning against those who might think it sufficient for salvation simply to call upon him—"Lord, Lord"—when in fact it is only those "who do the will of my Father in heaven" that "will enter the kingdom of heaven" (Matt. 7:21). It seems unavoidable that the will of Jesus' Father essentially is what this sermon as a whole (Matt. 5–7) is describing. Like Moses among the people of Israel, Jesus sets before his disciples (and "the crowds," 7:28) "a blessing and a curse" (Deut. 11:26). Salvation by grace through faith*fulness* indeed!

This message is reiterated in the parable of the houses built on the sand and on the rock with which this week's Gospel reading (and the Sermon on the Mount itself) concludes. It is altogether too often overlooked that the distinction Jesus creates in this parable is between "everyone who hears these words of mine and acts on them" and "everyone who hears these words of mine and does not act on them" (Matt. 7:24, 26). Those who do not hear, let alone believe, Jesus' words do not even enter

Give Us Yourself

OH! for a seraph's voice to aid my strains!
    A seraph's hand, to guide the tuneful lyre,
A seraph's wing, to reach the heavenly
        plains
    And catch a ray of light—a spark of fire—
An emanation from the eternal Sire—
    Fresh ardours to enkindle in my song!
Oh! could my numbers equal my desire,
    How would I pour Jehovah's praise along,
And slumb'ring echoes wake, the rocks and
        woods among!

. . . .

Long time, deep hidden in the womb of
        earth
    Grovelling I lay—self buried like the mole!
Clung to the dust—refused the second
        birth—
    Call'd light false meteors—liberty
        controul—
Saw no disease—no need to be made
        whole—
    No prize worth fighting for—no crown to
        win;
The gloom of midnight hover'd o'er my
        soul—
    Darkness without—gross darkness all
        within—
The life one scene of wrong—the heart the
        seat of sin.

. . . .

Wrapp'd in a patch-work cov'ring of my own,
    Flimsy and torn, I met the morning air—
'Twas snatch'd in haste, and o'er my shoul-
        ders thrown,
    Yet neither large, nor warm, nor fine, nor
        fair—
But scanty—cold—its texture thin and bare
    It fann'd the breeze, and flutter'd in the
        wind—
Shiv'ring, I look'd around—put up a prayer—
    And whilst an unseen Power inspired my
        mind
I rent the cobweb robe, and cast the shreds
        behind!

Naked, ashamed, I knew not where to turn—
    I loathed myself—abhorr'd my former
        place—
Fear'd to advance, lest yonder Sun should
        burn—
    For red as crimson seem'd his glowing
        face.
Ah! little did I think 'twas sign of grace
    Or recollect that Sun in Blood was dyed
But choice was gone—I saw my desperate
        case—
    Forward I rush'd—I felt a beam applied—
Clapp'd my glad hands with joy, and "Abba
        Father" cried.

Where then were apprehensions? fled
        away—
    My soul exulted in the Heaven possess'd;
Where'er I went, the prospect seem'd as
        gay,
    And Adam's Eden flourish'd in my breast!
No storms arose—no tempests dared
        molest—
    The cheering sunshine gilded every
        hour—
I thought, I'd still be happy, then so blest,
    That every step should tread upon a
        flower,
And peace enrich the gale, and joy entwine
        the bower.

. . . .

E'er since that time has fight succeeded
        fight—
    Small intermission in assaults like these!
The war's protracted—victory's still in sight—
    Pain heightens pleasure—labour sweet-
        ens ease—
No way to conquer but upon our knees;
    No means to gain the crown, but
        persevere—
No shore to touch on, if we cross no seas—
    No bliss hereafter, if no trials here—
And not a transport thrills, but cost our Lord
        a tear!

Being of beings! my Reward above
    My only Source of happiness below!

Confirm the work of faith—encrease my
    love—
  Bid deep humility take root and grow—
Give me Thyself—and—nothing else to
    know;

'Tis Thou must satisfy my soul's desire—
'Tis Thou must comfort wheresoe'er I go—
  Possessing Thee—I'll joyfully expire—
And shout—triumphant shout—when earth's
    consumed by fire!

Anne Lutton, "Love," in *Poems on Moral and Religious Subjects* (New York: G. Lane and P. P. Sandford for the Methodist Episcopal Church Conference Office, 1842), 7–12.

into consideration in this passage! If we are to read the Romans passage coherently with these other lectionary readings, it likely requires far greater emphasis upon the idea that our salvation depends upon divine faithfulness, to be sure—but not a faithfulness that replaces or cancels the necessity of human responsibility. Rather, the faithfulness of God, manifest to us decisively in the faithfulness of Jesus to the Father's will, calls for and even demands a corresponding faithfulness from us.

Within the context of the entire biblical canon, we can safely assert that the Scriptures consistently avoid even a hint of what Dietrich Bonhoeffer famously called "cheap grace."[2] It is true that Jesus Christ is our Redeemer, but it is equally important that redemption is always for, or toward, the divine purpose of creating and sustaining a faithful people who will not only proclaim, but also embody, God's own faithfulness toward creation.

MICHAEL LODAHL

Commentary 2: Connecting the Reading with the World

"For I am not ashamed of the gospel." Paul's opening remark seems to rely on the idea that those he addresses might expect him to be ashamed. Indeed, there were several reasons in Paul's day why being a Christian might have been embarrassing. Mere decades after the resurrection, the fledgling movement becoming Christianity was neither well understood nor well respected. The central elements of Christian theology were not easy to wrap one's mind around, so it is not hard to imagine the questions that might have been posed to Paul and his friends. The one and only God, creator of the universe, became a finite, vulnerable human? This Son of God was executed as a criminal? Then he came out of the tomb? The doctrine of the Trinity had not yet been articulated in Paul's day, but even without the mind-blowing concept of three-as-one, Christianity was still hard to comprehend. Even if someone got the gist, it still seems as if Jesus is kind of a mediocre deity. Undignified, weak, and defeated. It might have been a little embarrassing for those

early followers to face their communities and confess their faith in Jesus Christ.

It might be a little embarrassing today. Two thousand years of study and scholarship have not made the central tenets of Christianity clear and easy to grasp. Incarnation and resurrection are no less mysterious, only more familiar. For some of us, the theological mysteries of incarnation and resurrection are like pieces of furniture that have been in the family for generations. We have lived with them so long we do not see their strangeness anymore. Outside of Christian communities, with friends from work or school or book club, it is not any easier to explain how the God of infinity takes on finite flesh than it was in Paul's era. For the many Christians who value education and honor scientific knowledge, it can be a bit tricky to acknowledge that this is an area of our lives that we cannot explain with precision or "prove" in some universally accepted way. It can feel awkward, and decidedly unsophisticated, to own up to Christian identity in certain circumstances.

2. See the classic Dietrich Bonhoeffer, *The Cost of Discipleship* (Touchstone Press; prev. pub. New York: Macmillan, 1959), 43–45.

Another reason we might feel embarrassed to claim our faith is the pesky matter of other Christians. Jesus is fabulous, but other Christians can be appalling. Christians who use the Bible as a blunt instrument to bludgeon other people for their religion, or sexual orientation, or gender identity. Christians who see faith and science as diametrically opposed. Christians who are certain they know exactly what God wants in every situation. It is embarrassing to be associated with them.

The unrespectable characters of the Gospel narratives have also, like the mysteries of our faith, become familiar. The tax collectors and Pharisees, the lepers and the prostitutes—of course we would have embraced them with compassion and solidarity, just as Jesus did! Christians in our own time who hold different views? It is easier to imagine that Jesus is not really in their midst.

The next part of Paul's sentence recalibrates the conversation. Any sense of shame at worshiping an incomprehensible Savior who associates with unsavory company pales in comparison with the power of God. This is not about how other people assess our intelligence or sophistication; this is about God's salvific power!

Paul emphasizes God's righteousness in verse 17. Scholar Luke Timothy Johnson explains that this refers to justice both as a characteristic of who God is and as a characterization of what God is up to in the world. God treats all others fairly, and God is "intervening actively in human affairs to establish right relationships where they do not yet exist because of human sin or folly."[3] Notice that righteousness is an inherently relational category, rather than the condition of an isolated individual. It is in this context of God's power and righteousness that Paul addresses the congregation in Rome. Salvation is not attained, he argues, through human perfection, but rather through God's righteousness, which we accept and respond to in faith. Righteousness comes in relation.

Like righteousness, sinfulness is also a relational category. It pertains to our relationships with God and one another, and it is characteristic of all humanity. In Romans 3:23, Paul

offers a description of the universal fallenness of humankind, our sinfulness, which continues to shape Christian theology and liturgy: "all have sinned and fall short of the glory of God." Paul's statement is not a derogatory assessment of humanity as "not good enough." It is, instead, a truthful recognition that our world is marked by unrighteousness, broken relationships, and systemic injustice. As individuals and as communities, we are so deeply formed by our broken world that we cannot imagine or enact an entirely new way of being that does not repeat fractured patterns. We cannot enact our own salvation. We cannot put our relationships to God and one another right on our own steam.

The good news is that God, out of God's own righteousness, offers us grace as a gift. This grace justifies us, putting us right with God, and calls us to participate in God's establishment of right relationships on Earth. It does not immediately eliminate injustice in human societies, but it is the basis out of which we can participate with God in that work. There is no Christian righteousness that does not involve being part of what God is up to in the world, creating relationships marked by the justice called for by the prophets, the compassion embodied by Jesus Christ, and the peaceful abundance promised in the new creation.

The concept of "gift" again implies relationship (v. 24). All the concepts Paul is using in this passage are relational: righteousness, sinfulness, and grace. Using these ideas in individualistic ways strays from Paul's meaning and from biblical usage more generally.

Because grace is a gift, we cannot earn it, deserve it, or somehow manipulate God into handing it over. Paul has again reframed the conversation so it is not about us—our embarrassments, inadequacies, or accomplishments—but about God's power.

Giving is very important to Christians. Acts 20:35 states, "It is more blessed to give than to receive." Indeed, giving can be one way in which we participate in God's work of righteousness in our world, using our assets and abilities to counter injustice and establish right relations. However, it is problematic when we

---

3. Luke Timothy Johnson. *Reading Romans: A Literary and Theological Commentary* (Macon, GA: Smyth & Helwys Publishing, 2001), 28.

think of ourselves as primarily givers. Theologian Howard Thurman identifies that the "lurking danger" of focusing on giving as central to Christianity is the subtle elevation of ourselves—the givers and helpers—over those to whom we render assistance.[4] This is a distortion of our relationships that actually furthers social injustices such as classism and racism. It also can be an obstacle to those in difficult circumstances if Christianity is presented as a religion for givers, rather than for people who stand, in Thurman's words, "with their backs against the wall."[5] Finally, it is a distortion of the gospel of Jesus Christ, which identifies all of us as, first and foremost, those who receive the unearned gift of God's grace.

This passage begins with Paul saying he is not ashamed of the gospel. It ends with an admonition that no one should boast of their justification. The more valuable a gift is, the more humbling it is to receive.

SHANNON CRAIGO-SNELL

---

4. Howard Thurman, *Jesus and the Disinherited* (Boston: Beacon Press, 1976), 12.
5. Thurman, 11.

Matthew 7:21–29

21"Not everyone who says to me, 'Lord, Lord,' will enter the kingdom of heaven, but only the one who does the will of my Father in heaven. 22On that day many will say to me, 'Lord, Lord, did we not prophesy in your name, and cast out demons in your name, and do many deeds of power in your name?' 23Then I will declare to them, 'I never knew you; go away from me, you evildoers.'

24"Everyone then who hears these words of mine and acts on them will be like a wise man who built his house on rock. 25The rain fell, the floods came, and the winds blew and beat on that house, but it did not fall, because it had been founded on rock. 26And everyone who hears these words of mine and does not act on them will be like a foolish man who built his house on sand. 27The rain fell, and the floods came, and the winds blew and beat against that house, and it fell—and great was its fall!"

28Now when Jesus had finished saying these things, the crowds were astounded at his teaching, 29for he taught them as one having authority, and not as their scribes.

Commentary 1: Connecting the Reading with Scripture

Jesus closes his inaugural discourse in Matthew in the dawn of the kingdom of heaven much as Moses concluded the commands of the law on the edge of the promised land, by laying two ways before his people: the foolish, fruitless way through the wide gate, and the wise, fruitful way through the narrow gate (Matt. 7:13–27). According to the lectionary passage of Deuteronomy 11:26–28, Moses laid before Israel the way of blessing and the way of curse. If they obeyed God's commandments in their life together in the land, they would find themselves on the way of blessing, the way of thriving. If they did not obey the commandments, they would find themselves on the way of a curse, the way of judgment. Elsewhere Moses describes these as the way of life and the way of death (Deut. 30:19) and specifies with long lists of blessings and curses how life and death name patterns of flourishing or decay in the fabric of Israelite relationships uniting human bodies, animals, and land (e.g., Deut. 27:11–28:68).

Jesus has come to fulfill these words of the law (Matt. 5:17–20); in doing so, he echoes Moses—with one important difference. Before the crowds of his people who are gathered in

Galilee, he does not lay one way of judgment and another of blessing, as Moses had, but two ways of judgment. The image with which he concludes the discourse, the building of a house in the shadow of an approaching storm, implies that both ways lying before his people lead to that same storm of judgment, the same tempest of hardships brought by generations of injustice and oppression, the culmination of the way of death foretold by Moses (7:24–27).

All people hearing Jesus' words, especially his disciples and other teachers, find themselves building the houses of Israel's life in response to what Jesus has taught to this point. They may build foolishly or wisely, but Jesus does not say that the storm is coming only for the foolish one who hears his words and does not do them. The difference between the wise and the foolish is not that one undergoes judgment and the other does not. They both undergo judgment. The difference between them is not that one hears Jesus' words and the other does not. They both hear Jesus' words. The difference is that one hears Jesus' words, obeys them, and so builds a house that weathers the coming storm, while the other hears Jesus' words, does not do them, and so builds a house that is swept away by the same storm.

What is this coming storm of judgment? For some, this language evokes an end-of-time "judgment" of humanity that divides it into the saved and the damned. However, that scenario does not fit the arc of Matthew's narrative or the Old Testament prophetic theme of judgment informing the present passage, both of which concern not the end of time but large-scale upheaval that drastically reorders the life of Israel and other peoples forever. Judgment as the consequence of deeply rooted injustice has been accumulating since long before Jesus' day, and it will gather on the horizon across Matthew. What it entails will become clear in Jesus' horrifying announcement in his final discourse (Matt. 24–25) and then his own passion. Within the generation of those to whom he is now speaking, the temple and Jerusalem will follow the course of his body, which will be destroyed by the civil strife of his people and Gentile power and then be raised from the dead transformed on the third day.

Through this storm, Jesus will give his own life in judgment and so, by the end of his generation, become the one house for all the people of God. Walking ahead of his people, Jesus will open for them not a way around judgment but through it; not blessing instead of curse but blessing that absorbs and depletes the curse; not life rather than death but life through death. The apostle Paul describes this culmination of Jesus' life as God's transformative gift in the lectionary passage of Romans 3:22b–31, urging us later in the same letter to be conformed in our bodily life together to this self-giving pattern of Jesus, and thus to offer "living sacrifice" (Rom. 12:1–2).

Against the horizon of this approaching storm for which Israelite teachers and their people are building houses to shelter them, Jesus foreshadows a most disturbing upheaval. There will be a violent scramble for control, for spoils, and, in the case of many, for survival. The way to which Jesus calls his people in the promised land will not be the obvious or easy road that avoids painful pressures. That foolish way leads to destruction. Jesus' way for Israel, which he has taught in terms of the fullness of justice

signaled by the law and prophets (5:21–48)—faithful patterns of almsgiving, prayer, and fasting (6:1–18), and a political economic vision of God's kingdom (6:19–7:12)—will be a hard road leading through a narrow gate. This wise way, by which the poor in spirit rather than the high and mighty are blessed, weathers the coming storm. It is the way of building one's house on the rock, reminiscent of the fortress of refuge the psalmist praises in the lectionary Psalm 31.

As with past times of turmoil and scrambling for power in a nearing shadow of regime change in Israel's history (e.g., Jer. 23), and with similar political economic upheaval throughout the world ever since, false prophets arise to tempt the people of God from the way of Jesus (Matt. 7:15–16). They beckon the people down the easy road to the wide gate of destruction. Their fruits reveal them to be not the trustworthy, considerate rulers who live alongside the other sheep, as they appear and claim to be, but ravenous wolves who exploit the people for their own, shortsighted gain (vv. 17–20).

Even if such authorities or the masses who follow them invoke Jesus as Lord, they will not avoid being carried away by the gathering storm (vv. 21–22). Having heard Jesus' words but not done the will of his Father in heaven by obeying them, they will not be held fast by the powerful name of Jesus but exposed as evildoers not known by him (v. 23). Entering the kingdom of heaven of the coming age, which will open with the passing of the storm and constitute regime change for Israel, is not a matter of acting impressively in Jesus' name. It is a matter of doing what he says. It is a matter of embodying the justice that is the will of Jesus' Father in heaven, who, as will be revealed, is giving the rule of Israel and the rest of the peoples to Jesus as heir and Son.

Thus the coming judgment will disclose and empower Israelite ways that have obeyed the law and the prophets as taught by Jesus. Meanwhile, it will wipe out Israelite ways that have despised the justice of the law and the prophets and led the people astray (e.g., the Sadducean way). Such authorities will leave behind a memory of shame and the whisper of warning that their ways not be repeated (vv. 24–27).

When Jesus finishes the sermon, the crowds are astounded at the power of his teaching. It is unlike that of the current teachers in the land, the scribes, who teach without the power of the kingdom coming from heaven (vv. 28–29). For congregations today, Jesus describes a judgment his generation endured, one that continues to ripple through the Christian community and beyond in our places today, guiding us to learn the way of the now risen Jesus.

TOMMY GIVENS

Commentary 2: Connecting the Reading with the World

It is appropriate that on this last Sunday after the Epiphany we come to the end of Jesus' Sermon on the Mount. His teachings have led his listeners through the way of discipleship, traversing the landscape of life. He has warned against idolatry and false piety, empty legalism, and self-congratulatory sacrifice. He has invited his hearers to embrace humility and compassion and, above all, the deep desire to please God alone. He has shed light on what really matters, and what does not, often to his listeners' surprise. He has reminded us that, in all things, we have a choice to make, both in our attitudes and in our actions.

It is as if, in our approach to the transfiguration and the season of Lent, Jesus invites us to carry his words with us as a field guide. In the verses just prior to this passage, we are cautioned to discern between similar-looking plants those that bear good fruit and those whose taste is poisonous, and between innocuous sheep and wolves masquerading in innocent disguise (Matt. 7:15–20). Now, in these final verses, Jesus warns of what is at stake in our decision, to heed his advice or to turn to our own way.

What does his teaching say to us today? First, he warns that we are fooling ourselves if we think that *claiming* to be Christian is the same as *being* Christian, if we act as if *wearing* the name of Christ is the same as *growing* to be more Christlike. One gets the sense that on the day of judgment, Jesus will be harsher on all of us who went through the motions than he will be toward those who never pretended to be his disciples. Lip service—saying, "Lord, Lord"— will not qualify one for entry into the kingdom of heaven. Only one "who does the will of my Father in heaven" will enter, Jesus says (v. 21).

Second, Jesus warns that even *actions* that we consider faithful may not matter to God. Doing "the will of my Father" is likely not the same as doing the things that *we* consider to be religious. Ironically, the examples Jesus offers are clearly behaviors associated with faithfulness: prophesying, casting out demons, doing deeds of power (v. 22); Jesus claims that these actions alone are not true measures of a person's heart. Even those who come back claiming these fruits of their labor may be rejected as people utterly unknown to him—or worse yet, as evildoers.

If such a warning was applicable to Jesus' first listeners, we ought to shudder when considering how much our generation may have utterly misread what faithfulness means. We have spent endless time in committees and board meetings, diligently seeking ways for our churches to thrive, or worship to be effective. We have given enormous effort to stewardship campaigns and building projects, meticulously working to keep the lights on or to pay the staff decent wages. We have shed copious amounts of blood, sweat, and tears trying to keep our church buildings open and our pews full. This passage makes us wonder, How do we know if any of it matters to Jesus? What, exactly, *does* Jesus want from us?

No one text can adequately summarize Jesus' entire teaching, but in these concluding verses of the Sermon on the Mount, perhaps we come near to the heart of it: "Everyone who hears these words of mine and acts on them" (v. 24). Amid the din of competing religious voices and the sirens of secular culture, Jesus wants us to *hear* his teaching—not just the parts we like on any given day, but all of it—as he shares his vision of what the reign of God looks like. The urgency of the Sermon on the Mount is captured in his plea to us to *listen . . .* and then to *act* on what we have heard (v. 24).

Listen to and act on the Beatitudes, in which the meek are strong and the merciful are blessed, and those persecuted for the sake of righteousness will inherit no less than the kingdom of heaven (5:1–12). Hear and honor our true identity, our calling to be salt of the earth and light for the world, so that all might stand in awe of the glory of God (5:13–16). Discern the consequence of our human relations—anger and adultery, divorce and oaths, injustice and retaliation—so that our behavior may surpass legalism and self-preservation, to the point where we might love even our enemies, as we aspire to reflect the very image of God (5:21–48). In addition, pay attention the import of our relationship to God—almsgiving and prayer, fasting and stewardship of our possessions and our bodies—to the point where our very survival is of less consequence than our joy and delight in the purposes of God (6:1–34).

Delight that our ultimate accountability is to God alone, freeing us to set down our judgment of others, inviting us to set all that we have and all that we are before God, liberating us from seeking the riches of the world or the approval of others, inviting us to treat all others as we desire to be treated (7:1–12). This is the summary of the "law and the prophets" (7:12); this is the "narrow gate" that opens to the only road "that leads to life" (7:13–14).

Why does Jesus press us again and again to listen to him, and to seek the will of God alone? Because we will always be vulnerable to the siren call of other voices. Though they change shape and form, they will never go away.

The Gentiles (or nations) of whom Jesus warns us? Though there were many then who lived good and decent lives of which Jesus would approve, the voices of the culture also took the form of hedonists who advocated for bodily pleasures; Stoics who promoted the independent, self-made person; and political leaders who surrounded themselves with cronies or delighted in their sycophants. These voices are still with us today.

The scribes and Pharisees? Their voices are still with us too. Though there were no doubt those who were deeply faithful and earned Jesus' respect, there were also many whose teaching we might recognize: scribes who would pick apart each letter of the law of Scripture, wielding their authority as a moral cudgel or contest of piety; Pharisees who wrestled with each other over the meaning of each verse and saw their success in terms of who could win the argument; priests who were so intent on protecting the purity of the temple that those who needed it most were locked out of its doors.

Today, as in Jesus' time, we are surrounded by voices that compete for our attention and loyalty. The question is, Whose voice will we choose to follow? To put it differently—to use the closing image Jesus offers us—we are given many options for the foundation on which we build our lives. We can foolishly choose to put our security in money or earthly treasure, in antinomian hedonism or vengeance, or even in religious fundamentalism or pietistic behavior. In the end, none of those will hold us fast. The only sure foundation is built on Jesus' wise, enduring words, which point us, only and always, to the living God.

CHRISTINE CHAKOIAN

Transfiguration Sunday

Exodus 24:12–18

Psalm 2 and Psalm 99

2 Peter 1:16–21

Matthew 17:1–9

Exodus 24:12–18

¹²The LORD said to Moses, "Come up to me on the mountain, and wait there; and I will give you the tablets of stone, with the law and the commandment, which I have written for their instruction." ¹³So Moses set out with his assistant Joshua, and Moses went up into the mountain of God. ¹⁴To the elders he had said, "Wait here for us, until we come to you again; for Aaron and Hur are with you; whoever has a dispute may go to them."

¹⁵Then Moses went up on the mountain, and the cloud covered the mountain. ¹⁶The glory of the LORD settled on Mount Sinai, and the cloud covered it for six days; on the seventh day he called to Moses out of the cloud. ¹⁷Now the appearance of the glory of the LORD was like a devouring fire on the top of the mountain in the sight of the people of Israel. ¹⁸Moses entered the cloud, and went up on the mountain. Moses was on the mountain for forty days and forty nights.

Commentary 1: Connecting the Reading with Scripture

This lectionary reading comes at the end of Epiphany, a liturgical season that attests consistently to God's revelation of God's purpose and self to the world. The whole of Exodus 24 describes an epiphany experienced by Moses and then shared with God's people, an epiphany that has shaped Israel and also Christianity. While 24:12–18 forms a valid unit of the chapter to consider, it omits a critical first half of the story, and preachers should consider this passage in the context of the entire epiphany of Exodus 24. If preachers choose to focus only on verses 12–18, they will still need to set this unit in its literary and theological context by providing the back story of the covenant ceremony (Exod. 24:1–11) that reaches its culmination in verses 12–18.

In Exodus 24:1–11, Moses, Aaron, Nadab, Abihu, and seventy elders worship God; afterwards, Moses and a silent Joshua move closer to God. Moses communicates with the people what God wants them to do, and the people agree to every word (v. 3). In response, Moses builds an altar, sacrifices burnt offerings, and scatters blood from oxen on the altar in a covenant confirming ceremony. In this ceremony, Moses reads the book of the covenant to the people and again they insist, "All that the LORD has spoken we will do, and we will be obedient" (v. 7).

Moses confirms the covenant promises the people have made. He dashes blood on the people, announcing a covenant is hereby established between God and the people. This covenant is not a contract between equal partners. This is a promise of God's gracious presence to the people of Israel, coupled with expectations of their conduct as God's people.

In an incredible scene that is in conflict with the clear divine pronouncement in Exodus 33:20 ("No one shall see my face and live"), not only Moses but his three companions and seventy elders see the God of Israel and live (v. 9). They even have a meal with God (v. 11). For Christian readers of this text, this scene flashes forward to breakfast on the beach with the risen Jesus and his disciples (John 21:12).

The author of Exodus sets the scene for verses 12–18, when Moses is once again summoned up the mountain by God to receive the stone tablets of the commandments. While on the mountain for "forty days and forty nights," Moses is first instructed about the construction and dedication of the tabernacle and then about the consecration of priests and their vestments (chaps. 25–28).

Moses ascends the mountain to encounter the living presence of God. In the Gospel text for this day (Matt. 17:1–9), Jesus will also go up a mountain, not to receive stone tablets from God, but to be transfigured by God in the presence of a small company of his disciples and then to be joined by Moses and the prophet Elijah, an occasion celebrating the fulfillment of the law and the prophets in God's Son, Jesus. The theophanies of Exodus 24:12–18 and Matthew 17:1–9 remind readers that these are holy moments of revelation from God and about God. They are *kairos* moments that demand careful attention.

The entire chapter of Exodus 24, especially verses 12–18, traverses the arena of awe. Using the language of theophany—mountain, cloud, devouring fire—readers travel with Moses to the place of awe, the place where the glory of God abides (Luke 9:32, 34). "At the center of the Sinai tradition," writes Walter Brueggemann, "is an act of contemplation, an awed, silent, respectful look at God."[1] In our modern era, which elevates frenzy to the level of an idol, these awe-filled verses in Exodus 24 invite readers to do nothing but sit quietly in the awesome presence of God.

On the Mount of Transfiguration, Peter wants to "do something." Standing in the presence of the transformed Jesus, Moses, and Elijah, Peter cannot be still. He offers to build booths for the guests (Matt. 17:4). Whereas Peter cannot be still in the midst of God's glory, the text from Exodus pictures Moses in quiet awe before the living God. In the Gospel text for the day, Moses appears atop a mountain silently, not to speak to the disciples or a crowd, but to witness the glory of God; he arrives not to speak but to listen, the same emphasis made in Exodus 24 when Moses is summoned up the mountain by God.

A preaching window into this text is through the avenue of awe. In a brilliant, yet brief sentence, Karl Barth articulates the conundrum anyone faces who dares to speak about the glory and majesty of God. "As ministers we ought to speak of God. We are human, however, and so we cannot speak of God."[2] What would it mean for preachers to speak less and call congregations to speak less, even in worship? What would it mean for church leaders to build time into the church calendar for awe and contemplation alongside stewardship season and Advent cantatas? What would it mean for churches to resist Peter's urge to "build booths" and to learn the wisdom of Moses, and in the words of the psalmist, to "Be still, and know that I am God" (Ps. 46:10)? What would it mean for preachers to model the behavior about which they preach, to declare daily occasions for disciplined meditation and prayer, to sit quietly in the divine presence on a regular basis, and to be known as those who listen first and only then speak?

Psalm 99 accompanies Exodus 24 on this Sunday. The psalmist also calls for a renewed sense of awe before the living God, writing:

> Let them praise your great and awesome
> name.
> Holy is he!
> Mighty King, lover of justice,
> you have established equity;
> you have executed justice
> and righteousness in Jacob.
> Ps. 99:3–5

The psalmist anticipates the consequence of the stone tablets that Moses receives from God. To embrace the divine law is not to receive personal privilege but to assume social responsibility to live just and merciful lives. To know that God is "great and awesome" is also to know that God is a "lover of justice." This explains much of the rage that Moses demonstrates when he returns to his people from the epiphany on Mount Sinai (see Exod. 32).

In 2 Peter 1:16–21, our lectionary text from the New Testament, the author recalls

1. Walter Brueggemann, "Exodus," in *The New Interpreter's Bible* (Nashville: Abingdon Press, 1994), 1:882.
2. Karl Barth, *The Word of God and the Word of Man* (New York: Harper & Bros., 1957), 186.

the transfiguration of Jesus, speaking specifically of the "Majestic Glory" of God (2 Pet. 1:17). This text is in conversation with Exodus 24, reminding all who will hear that the glory of God appeared both to Moses and to Jesus. It did more than "appear" to Jesus. Jesus did not receive a new set of commandments on the mountain of transfiguration. He became the new commandment of God, glorified and transfigured in the presence of Peter, James, and John. Like Moses, Jesus would descend the mountain of metamorphosis to encounter a faithless community below.

As referenced earlier, the Gospel reading from Matthew 17:1–9 is in constant conversation with Exodus 24. The divine pronouncement, "This is my Son, the Beloved; with him I am well pleased; listen to him!" (Matt. 17:5), calls the reader back into divine awe. Jesus will not descend the mountain with new commandments. He is the new commandment, God's love in human flesh.

GARY W. CHARLES

Commentary 2: Connecting the Reading with the World

Terence Fretheim, in his commentary on Exodus, points out that the law is centered in story; all the long passages of God telling Moses what to instruct the people come before and after narrative segments.[3] The law does not appear on its own, but comes from God only within the longer narrative of God's relationship with the people of Israel. This suggests that the law can be understood only in light of God's wider relationship with God's people. Obedience, therefore, is not to a disembodied set of rules or laws in and of themselves, but to God, based on a shared history of God's providential care for God's people. Preachers can remind listeners of the ways God's call to obedience reaches each person within our individual narratives, helping us to recall how we have experienced God in our lives.

These verses (Exod. 24:12–18) appear within a narrative context that is important to understand. This passage comes just after Moses has received from God the Ten Commandments and laws concerning the altar, slaves, violence, property, restitution, justice, Sabbath, and the promise of the conquest of Canaan (chaps. 20–23). The narrative section here in chapter 24 seems to be a repeated trip of Moses climbing up the mountain. He climbed it earlier (19:20), followed by a return trip down (19:25), immediately before God gives to Moses the Ten Commandments in chapter 20, requiring Moses to be on top of the mountain again. Fretheim comments that this "lack of smoothness no doubt reflects different traditions."[4] When telling our own stories, it may be common that we go back in time, returning to an earlier part in the story to make sense of what is still to come.

These verses come just before additional instructions given by God concerning the tabernacle, ark of the covenant, furniture within the tabernacle, the altar, lamps, vestments for the priests, ordination, offerings, incense, anointing oil, and the Sabbath (chaps. 25–31). At the end of these instructions, Moses returns to find that the people have built a golden calf and have taken up idolatry (chap. 32). However, it is earlier, here in chapter 24, that we learn Moses was up "on the mountain for forty days and forty nights" (24:18). This long period of time may help listeners have sympathy for the Israelites who asked Aaron for new gods. Their leader, who had brought them out of Egypt, seemed to have been swallowed up by a "devouring fire on the top of the mountain in the sight of the people of Israel" (v. 17). The people had no way of knowing that Moses was safe. How could they trust a God who had consumed their leader?

Empathizing with the Israelites in this narrative can help foster conversations among your congregation around trying to understand persons different from themselves. On first glance, and within the narrative presented in Exodus, the Israelites are justifiably judged harshly. Persons

---

3. Terence E. Fretheim, *Exodus*, Interpretation (Louisville, KY: John Knox Press, 1991), 201.

4. Fretheim, 255.

today judge one another harshly for different reasons, one of them being political affiliations or policy positions. Whether most of the members of your church lean to the left or right politically, it is important to stress greater understanding. Having a broader narrative framework for understanding why people make the decisions they do or vote the way they do, can help bring persons together to work for common values.

Perhaps the preacher could ask questions of the congregation such as: From this story, whom do we view as the Israelites in our own lives? Whom do we judge as having made their own "golden calves"? Where do we tend to put ourselves in the position of Moses, thinking of ourselves as having heard the truth directly from God's lips, so everyone else must be wrong? Letting the congregation enter into this narrative as an analogy for group conflicts can help foster willingness to see others' perspectives more hospitably.

Another image for the congregation to consider from this text is the cloud surrounding God on the mountaintop. Moses had to enter the cloud to be with God. For six days before God called for Moses to enter, Moses had to wait outside the cloud. The image of the cloud is repeated elsewhere in Scripture as a symbol of God's presence. God appears as a cloud or pillar of cloud multiple times throughout Exodus (13:21; 16:10; 19:9; 19:16; 20:21; 33:9–10; 34:5; 40:34–38), as well as in many other books in the Old Testament: Leviticus, Numbers, Deuteronomy, Judges, 2 Samuel, 1 Kings, 2 Chronicles, Nehemiah, Job, Psalms, Isaiah, Ezekiel, and Daniel. In the New Testament as well, God appears in a cloud at Jesus' baptism in Matthew 17:5; Mark 9:7; and Luke 9:34–35. Other New Testament texts refer to the cloud that surrounded God in the story of the Israelites in the wilderness, such as 1 Corinthians 10:1–2 and as a vision of God in Revelation 1:7.

Seeing clouds as an image for God makes a lot of intuitive sense: God is mysterious, beautiful, confounding, and reassuring. Clouds in the sky can be beautiful and awe inspiring. Dark clouds can elicit fear of bad weather or excitement for coming rain. Clouds on the ground create fog, making it hard for people to navigate their cars or see far ahead of them. When I was a child, growing up in Texas, the clouds that spanned the big endless sky always made me think of God. The display of colors on these clouds—so impossibly pink and deep blue, changing as the sun set—felt like a love letter to me, a reminder that God was in control and cared for me.

Preachers may want to reflect on their own experiences with clouds, and what associations arise for them or their congregants with the image of God in the clouds. One of the classics of the Christian mystical tradition is *The Cloud of Unknowing*, written anonymously in the fourteenth century, which advises Christians to seek God by *not* seeking God, knowing God by allowing oneself to begin *unknowing* God. For anyone who has experienced mental illness such as depression, trusting that God can be found, even in the unknowing and utter lack of feeling of God's presence, can be a source of comfort and consolation.

Fretheim points to the context of worship for this passage, seen in the preceding verses (24:1).[5] Before God invited Moses up the mountain in verse 12, God had called Moses and the elders to worship God from a distance in verse 1. It is during this time that Moses makes a sacrifice to collect basins of blood, half of which he dashes against the altar (v. 6), while the other half he dashes on the people (v. 8). The blood here represents the blood covenant between God and the people. Moses then waited for six days before God called him into the cloud. Six days was twice the amount of time specified for sanctification prior to going before God that priests were to observe (19:11).

This long purification time may be because of the blood spilled just prior to this narrative, giving Moses time to recover before going before God again. The task of ministry often feels like a nonstop commitment, with little time to recover. This text may be a good way to discuss with the congregation the importance of pastors taking sabbatical time away from their ministerial duties at the church, to refresh their strength and to renew their relationships with God.

CAROLYN BROWNING HELSEL

5. Fretheim, 260.

Psalm 2

¹Why do the nations conspire,
    and the peoples plot in vain?
²The kings of the earth set themselves,
    and the rulers take counsel together,
    against the LORD and his anointed, saying,
³"Let us burst their bonds asunder,
    and cast their cords from us."

⁴He who sits in the heavens laughs;
    the LORD has them in derision.
⁵Then he will speak to them in his wrath,
    and terrify them in his fury, saying,
⁶"I have set my king on Zion, my holy hill."

⁷I will tell of the decree of the LORD:
He said to me, "You are my son;
    today I have begotten you.
⁸Ask of me, and I will make the nations your heritage,
    and the ends of the earth your possession.
⁹You shall break them with a rod of iron,
    and dash them in pieces like a potter's vessel."

¹⁰Now therefore, O kings, be wise;
    be warned, O rulers of the earth.
¹¹Serve the LORD with fear,
    with trembling ¹²kiss his feet,
or he will be angry, and you will perish in the way;
    for his wrath is quickly kindled.

Happy are all who take refuge in him.

Psalm 99

¹The LORD is king; let the peoples tremble!
    He sits enthroned upon the cherubim; let the earth quake!
²The LORD is great in Zion;
    he is exalted over all the peoples.
³Let them praise your great and awesome name.
    Holy is he!
⁴Mighty King, lover of justice,
    you have established equity;
you have executed justice
    and righteousness in Jacob.
⁵Extol the LORD our God;
    worship at his footstool.
    Holy is he!

⁶Moses and Aaron were among his priests,
　　Samuel also was among those who called on his name.
　　They cried to the LORD, and he answered them.
⁷He spoke to them in the pillar of cloud;
　　they kept his decrees,
　　and the statutes that he gave them.

⁸O LORD our God, you answered them;
　　you were a forgiving God to them,
　　but an avenger of their wrongdoings.
⁹Extol the LORD our God,
　　and worship at his holy mountain;
　　for the LORD our God is holy.

Connecting the Psalm with Scripture and Worship

Of the two choices for the psalm on the Last Sunday after the Epiphany, which is the Sunday before the beginning of Lent, Psalm 2 is the preferred. Scholars judge the psalm to be an ancient composition, from perhaps the tenth century before Christ, written to celebrate the accession of an Israelite king. The king is not merely some tribal functionary, but is honored as the designate of the Lord of all. The monarch is to be received as God's representative on earth, the one established by God to bear royal authority and to enact divine justice. Verses 1–3 cite opposition to the reign of the new king; verses 4–9 record God's disdain for this rebellious attitude; and verses 10–12 urge all the nations to obey God by accepting the authority of this new king.

This psalm is most appropriate to complement Transfiguration Sunday and may even have been the background behind the creation of the Christian narrative of Jesus' transfiguration. This is not to say, as past interpreters have done, that the psalmist mystically foretold events in the life of Jesus. Rather, the evangelists relied on this and other psalms to supply details for the narratives that showed forth the meaning of Jesus Christ. The evangelists were not present at whatever mysterious event is described in the transfiguration narrative, yet Psalm 2 assists them in their Christian proclamation of the once and future resurrection.

Thus, in this Sunday's Gospel, Jesus is manifest on a mountaintop, and God speaks the very words of Psalm 2: "You, Israelite king, you, Jesus of Nazareth, are my Son." When we Christians speak of Christ the king, of Jesus as "king of kings," we have borrowed this royal imagery from ancient Israelite poetry, using its language to articulate our belief in the lordship of Jesus Christ. Just as in the ancient Near East a king was lauded as a son of the god, so Christians praise Jesus as the Son of God. Thus the assembly, in joining together with Psalm 2, is prepared to hear the details of the upcoming transfiguration narrative.

However, Psalm 2 not only propels us toward the Gospel reading with its repetition of royal imagery. As the assembly's response to the first reading, from Exodus 24, it presents yet another preeminent parallel between the Hebrew literary tradition and the Christian Gospels: Moses receives and bears the word of God, and Jesus is himself that Word. In Exodus 24, God sets the prophet Moses high on a hill; a cloud—commonly in the Hebrew Scriptures a manifestation of God's presence—covers the mountain; the six days of creation are recalled; on the seventh day God speaks; the fire of Mount Sinai flames forth once again; Moses enters the cloud, that is, is taken into the presence of God; and we listen to this story of the word of God spoken now to the people.

In Psalm 2, then, God has set the king—and Jesus Christ—on a holy hill. Jerusalem, the hill of Zion, is both the city of the Israelite king and the place of Jesus' crucifixion. In verse 7, God claims the king as son, and Christians hear those words spoken of Jesus at his transfiguration. In verse 8, God gives power to the king, and Christians believe that all authority has been given to Christ. "With trembling kiss his feet" (Ps. 2:11–12): we are to "bow in worship," reads a common liturgical translation of this verse, as Christians give to Jesus Christ the obeisance that ancient peoples were to grant their monarch. This week we will enter into Lent, serving our Lord, happy to take refuge in Christ, the Word of God.

An alternate psalm is Psalm 99, in which the royal imagery is tied especially to God, rather than to the earthly king. It is God who reigns from the hill of Zion; it is God's name that is awesome; it is God who will execute justice. In verse 6, the psalm lists Moses as one who models obeisance to God, and verse 7 recalls God's meeting with Moses in Exodus 24. Verses 8–9 stress both God's justice and God's mercy, as the community is called to offer praise to a God of power who yet forgives. "Holy" in verse 9 is not—as is common in English usage—about sinlessness, but about almighty presence, otherness from what is common, beyond what we know. It reiterates the otherness described in the Exodus 24 narrative of the cloud and fire of "the glory of the LORD." The triple repetition of "holy" (vv. 3, 5, 9) can prepare Christians for the "Holy, holy, holy" chant commonly sung throughout the centuries as believers gather at the Lord's Table.

To help you decide which psalm to choose: Psalm 2 closely reflects the Exodus narrative and anticipates the Gospel readings, while Psalm 99 focuses more on God as the one who meets with Moses—and with us—on the mountain. Both psalms provide imagery and vocabulary used by Christians as we worship Jesus as the Word of God and the monarch of all things.

GAIL RAMSHAW

2 Peter 1:16–21

[16]For we did not follow cleverly devised myths when we made known to you the power and coming of our Lord Jesus Christ, but we had been eyewitnesses of his majesty. [17]For he received honor and glory from God the Father when that voice was conveyed to him by the Majestic Glory, saying, "This is my Son, my Beloved, with whom I am well pleased." [18]We ourselves heard this voice come from heaven, while we were with him on the holy mountain.

[19]So we have the prophetic message more fully confirmed. You will do well to be attentive to this as to a lamp shining in a dark place, until the day dawns and the morning star rises in your hearts. [20]First of all you must understand this, that no prophecy of scripture is a matter of one's own interpretation, [21]because no prophecy ever came by human will, but men and women moved by the Holy Spirit spoke from God.

Commentary 1: Connecting the Reading with Scripture

This passage evokes recollection of the story of Jesus' transfiguration found in the Synoptic Gospels (2 Pet. 1:16–18). The author of this epistle identifies himself as "Simeon Peter, a servant and apostle of Jesus Christ" (v. 1). This authority is crucial to the letter's opposition to false teachers (2:1–3, 15–19; 3:15–17). Either these false teachers "follow cleverly devised myths" (1:16) or they accuse Peter and fellow apostles of doing so. In either case, Peter stands firmly upon the Mount of Transfiguration as the divinely bestowed ground for his teaching authority. The heavenly voice he and others ("we ourselves," 1:18) heard thoroughly trumps all claims of the false teachers.

The appeal to "the holy mountain" of trans-figuration is significant (v. 18). These "eyewitnesses of [Christ's] majesty" can testify that Jesus "received honor and glory from God the Father" who is further described as "the Majestic Glory" (v. 17). God who is Majestic Glory lavishes majesty and glory upon the Son (vv. 16–17)! This is a recurring theme through the NT corpus, highlighting the nature of God as generous, generative, outpouring love. Throughout the NT, "the glory ultimately accorded to God the Father [cf. Phil. 2:11] is a glory that the Father

did not grasp, exploit or hoard. Rather, it is a glory God outpoured upon Jesus. It is the glory of 'the name that is above every name,' a glory freely shared with the humble, crucified Son."[1]

The overflow of God's glory not only comes to the Son, but flows through Jesus to us. God's "divine power has given us everything needed for life and godliness, through the knowledge of him who called us by his own glory and goodness" (v. 3). God's intention and desire is to share the divine glory with finite, frail human creatures, that we through Christ might "become participants of the divine nature" (v. 4). It is clear, though, that this participation (from the same Greek root as *koinōnia*) in the very nature of God is not magic, nor does it occur automatically.

Rather, readers are to "make every effort to support your faith" through practicing a set of virtues (vv. 5–7). Not surprisingly, this list culminates in love (v. 7). The Majestic Glory, utterly transcendent to our creaturely realm, in abundantly overflowing love shares itself, through the glorified Son, with us. In the words of Maximus the Confessor, "Love, the divine gift, perfects human nature until it makes it appear in unity and identity with the divine

---

1. Michael Lodahl, *Claiming Abraham: Reading the Bible and the Qur'an Side by Side* (Grand Rapids: Brazos Press, 2011), xxx.

nature."[2] The glory of transfiguration is a glory happily shared by our Creator with us creatures.

To be sure, the lectionary Gospel reading discourages a facile appropriation of divine glory: God is God; humans are not. When the divine cloud of Majestic Glory overshadowed Peter, James, and John, and they heard the heavenly voice testify regarding Jesus, "they fell to the ground and were overcome by fear" (Matt. 17:6). This is no easy or natural interchange. All the more critical, then, that "Jesus came and touched them, saying, 'Get up and do not be afraid'" (v. 7). Jesus is the mediator of glory freely shared. No wonder that "when they looked up, they saw no one except Jesus himself alone" (v. 8). Even Moses is gone.

Nonetheless, Moses' appearance (along with that of Elijah of fiery chariot fame) on the Mount of Transfiguration provides an obvious connection to the lectionary reading from Exodus. In Exodus 24:12–18, the Majestic Glory calls to Moses from out of the cloud overshadowing Mount Sinai, and "Moses entered the cloud, and went up on the mountain" (Exod. 24:18). Moses' ascent into the cloud overshadowing Sinai was for the purpose of receiving the gift of the Torah (v. 12), the conditions of God's covenant with the people Israel. Similarly, on the Mount of Transfiguration the divine voice directs the attention of Peter, James, and John (and us) to Jesus, the condition of God's new covenant for the renewal of God's people: "This is my Son, the Beloved; with him I am well pleased; listen to him!" (Matt. 17:5).

This divine instruction, "Listen to him!" encourages us to circle back to the reading in 2 Peter when the author encourages his readers "to be attentive to this," since "we have the prophetic message more fully confirmed" (2 Pet. 1:19). Peter can encourage us to be attentive precisely because he has learned, against his own impetuous nature (Matt. 17:4; cf. Mark 9:5–6), to "listen to him" who is God's ultimate and decisive Word.

Psalm 2, another of our lectionary texts, is a coronation hymn for Israel's king-messiah, and its connections to our NT texts are immediate.

God speaks against all royal opposition ("the kings of the earth," Ps. 2:2) by proclaiming, "I have set my king on Zion, my holy hill" (v. 6). In reply, God's anointed king testifies, "[The LORD] said to me, 'You are my son; today I have begotten you'" (v. 7). The glorified Messiah on the holy mountain (cf. 2 Pet. 1:18) who receives the divine word of validation and approval, "You are my Son," provides the perfect backdrop for interpreting the story of Jesus' transfiguration. Further, for our reading from 2 Peter, the divine derision against those who say, "Let us burst their bonds asunder, and cast their cords from us" (Ps. 2:3) provides textual richness for Peter's opposition to the "false teachers among you, who . . . will even deny the Master who bought them—bringing swift destruction on themselves" (2 Pet. 2:1, 2).

Our second lectionary psalm (Ps. 99) proclaims the royal rule of the God of Israel. In addition to Moses, Aaron and Samuel are mentioned as "those who called on his name" (v. 6); significantly, the psalm proclaims that the Holy One "answered them," speaking to them "in the pillar of cloud" (v. 7). The people of God who read or hear this psalm are enjoined to "worship at his holy mountain" (v. 9; again, cf. 2 Pet. 1:18). The OT saints "kept his decrees, and the statutes that he gave them" (Ps. 99:7)—just as our reading from 2 Peter warns his audience to do (1:8–12, 19; 3:2, 11).

Within the biblical canon, we find repeatedly the teaching that the glory of God is manifest to the people of God that they might, indeed, share in that glory. Whether or not we find the idea of *theosis* or deification convincing or compelling, the idea that God bestows divine glory upon human creatures is richly sprinkled throughout Scripture. Moses may be the most obvious OT figure to shine with the glory of God (Exod. 34:29–35), but of course Paul boldly transmutes this theme into a Christian privilege (2 Cor. 3:7–18; 4:6).

Psalm 8 makes the more starkly and surprisingly universal claim that all humanity (Heb. *adam*, Ps. 8:4) is crowned by God "with glory and honor"; indeed, *adam* has been made "a

---

2. Cited in William Placher, *A History of Christian Theology: An Introduction*, 2nd ed. (Louisville, KY: Westminster John Knox Press, 2013), 80. Placher offers a brief but insightful introduction to *theosis*, or participation in the divine nature, on pp. 80–82.

little lower than God" (Heb. *elohim*, v. 5). In the Gospel of John, Jesus answers charges of blasphemy by quoting Psalm 82:6—"I said, 'You are gods'"—and interprets this surprising designation as applying to "those to whom the word of God came" (John 10:35). The Majestic Glory on the holy mountain is gloriously shared with us through the Word of God who has come to us in the flesh.

MICHAEL LODAHL

Commentary 2: Connecting the Reading with the World

The author of 2 Peter is the best adult Sunday school teacher the church has ever had. Addressing people who come to church each week and who are deeply familiar with Scripture, the author instructs them by reminding them of what they already know. The author takes for granted that the readers have "knowledge of our Lord Jesus Christ," but encourages them to make that knowledge more fruitful and effective by supporting it with self-control, endurance, godliness, mutual affection, and love (2 Pet. 1:6–7). The setup of this letter, which immediately precedes our passage, states, "Therefore I intend to keep on reminding you of these things, though you know them already and are established in the truth that has come to you" (1:12).

With verse 16 the focus shifts from *that* we know to *how* we know. The truth of Jesus Christ is not an intricate theory or a useful moral narrative. The author writes, "We had been eyewitnesses of his majesty" (v. 16). This refers to the transfiguration, which is recounted in Matthew 17:1–13, Mark 9:2–8, and Luke 9:28–36. In these accounts, Peter, John, and James accompany Jesus on a mountain, where Jesus' appearance is changed into dazzling glory, and Moses and Elijah appear with him. The apostles hear the voice of God declaring, "This is my Son, my Beloved, with whom I am well pleased" (2 Pet. 1:17). While the transfiguration is richly meaningful in different ways in each Gospel, here it is used as a stamp of authority on a particular kind of knowledge the author is claiming: eyewitness experience of the glory of God. This is different than book learning, no matter how sacred the book. It is a different way of knowing to experience something firsthand.

In 1982, author Annie Dillard published an essay titled simply "Total Eclipse" that narrates her experience of a total eclipse in Washington State. This brilliant essay includes this passage:

> What you see in an eclipse is entirely different from what you know. It is especially different for those of us whose grasp of astronomy is so frail that, given a flashlight, a grapefruit, two oranges, and 15 years, we still could not figure out which way to set the clocks for daylight savings time. Usually it is a bit of a trick to keep your mind from blinding you. But during an eclipse it is easy. What you see is much more convincing than any wild-eyed theory you may know.[3]

For Dillard, the experience of the total eclipse imparts a different kind of knowledge altogether than the elementary-school science experiments intended to convey a working understanding of the relative position and movements of the sun, moon, and Earth.

Likewise, in the Gospel transfiguration stories, the apostles understand in a new way what they have been seeing all along in Jesus' ministry. Peter, James, and John have heard Jesus' teaching, spent time in his presence, and watched him perform miracles. They knew, well before the transfiguration, that Jesus embodied the promises of God in a unique way. Of course, they were also clueless and bumbling (especially in Mark), but they knew enough to drop everything and follow Jesus every day. Yet the Synoptic Gospels present the transfiguration as a vital, experiential, and authoritative confirmation of all they knew before. To see the dazzling visage

---

3. Annie Dillard, "Total Eclipse," *The Atlantic*, https://www.theatlantic.com/science/archive/2017/08/annie-dillards-total-eclipse/536148/eclipse/536148/.

of Jesus, to hear the voice of God, to be in the presence of Elijah and Moses is, in Dillard's words "much more convincing than any wild-eyed theory you may know."

The trouble, of course, is that we were not there. Christians from the twenty-first century were not present on the mountain with Peter, James, and John, and therefore do not have the kind of knowledge that comes from firsthand experience. We are, to continue the Dillard metaphor, still fumbling around with citrus fruit and a flashlight—or are we?

New Testament scholars do not know precisely who wrote 2 Peter, but it is fairly obvious it was not the apostle present at the transfiguration. The author of 2 Peter is writing under the apostle Peter's name and authority, not as a means of deception, but rather as a common practice that would have been familiar to the readers of the letter. With this in mind, the author's statement, "We ourselves heard this voice come from heaven, while we were with him on the holy mountain" (2 Pet. 1:18) has a different ring. It can be understood less as a personal reflection and more as a communal memory. The author has stated the intention to remind the recipients of the letter of what they already know. Here, the author reminds them—and us—of the confirming revelation that has been given to our community.

In Jewish traditions, people retell the acts of God on behalf of the ancient Israelites during Passover Seder. By recounting the communal narrative, Jews take up their own place within the story, claiming the history of God's love for the Jewish people as their own. The Haggadah states, "In every generation a person is obligated to regard himself [*sic*] as if he [*sic*] had come out of Egypt."[4] In similar fashion, Christians remember the revelation of God as a revelation to the disciples that is also our own.

There are different kinds of experiential learning. In church, we repeat creeds and sing hymns that tell the stories of our faith, spur emotions of gratitude and wonder, and instill responses of humility and compassion. We, in some sense, experience that Jesus loves us in the act of singing that Jesus loves us.

Of course we long for more. We long for the undeniable confirmation of hearing God's voice from heaven and seeing a familiar face limned with glory. Karl Rahner, a twentieth-century Roman Catholic theologian, argued that in modern times, being a Christian could not be a matter of merely accepting a particular theory of how the world works or even a narrative of particular events. It is not enough to believe the teacher that Jesus exists, or even that he rose from the tomb. We must, in some way, have experiential knowledge.

This does not mean that only those select few who have visions or extraordinary experiences that we often equate with mysticism will be the only Christians left. Rather, it means that Christian faith—perhaps now more than ever—relies on an everyday mysticism, in which we who have been formed by the stories and rituals of the church are able to see the holy light of God in the world around us.

In the novel *Death Comes to the Archbishop*, Willa Cather writes, "The Miracles of the Church seem to me to rest not so much upon faces or voices or healing power coming suddenly near to us from afar off, but upon our perceptions being made finer, so that for a moment our eyes can see and our ears can hear what is there about us always."[5]

SHANNON CRAIGO-SNELL

4. *English Haggadah Text with Instructions*, Chabad.Org, http://www.chabad.org/holidays/passover/pesach_cdo/aid/661624/jewish/English-Haggadah.htm.

5. Willa Cather, *Death Comes to the Archbishop* (New York: Vintage Books, 1990), 50.

Matthew 17:1–9

¹Six days later, Jesus took with him Peter and James and his brother John and led them up a high mountain, by themselves. ²And he was transfigured before them, and his face shone like the sun, and his clothes became dazzling white. ³Suddenly there appeared to them Moses and Elijah, talking with him. ⁴Then Peter said to Jesus, "Lord, it is good for us to be here; if you wish, I will make three dwellings here, one for you, one for Moses, and one for Elijah." ⁵While he was still speaking, suddenly a bright cloud overshadowed them, and from the cloud a voice said, "This is my Son, the Beloved; with him I am well pleased; listen to him!" ⁶When the disciples heard this, they fell to the ground and were overcome by fear. ⁷But Jesus came and touched them, saying, "Get up and do not be afraid." ⁸And when they looked up, they saw no one except Jesus himself alone.

⁹As they were coming down the mountain, Jesus ordered them, "Tell no one about the vision until after the Son of Man has been raised from the dead."

Commentary 1: Connecting the Reading with Scripture

"After six days," the passage begins, placing its account of the mountaintop revelation of Jesus in the frame of the revelation of Israel's God on Mount Sinai that we see in the companion lectionary passage of Exodus 24:12–18. There the glory of the Lord settled on the mountain as a cloud for six days (v. 16) before the voice of the Lord called to Moses, as the same voice now calls from a cloud of light to Peter, James, and John. Jesus has led them, and only them, to this moment and this place, where they see his face shine with the very glory of Israel's God, his garments white with its light. They are seeing Jesus as no one else has seen him, which is to see him with Moses, the giver of God's law, and Elijah, the prophetic voice of Israel's promised future. Jesus thus embodies before their eyes the coming fullness of God's law for Israel and the eschatological fulfillment of their people's long and desperate hope.

Previous to this point in Matthew, Jesus has steadily, if also disturbingly, revealed who he is, and for the first time Peter openly has confessed him Israel's final king, the Messiah (Matt. 16:16). No easy criteria establish who Jesus is, however, so that Peter's confession was an expression of faith and commitment to a future not entirely known. Now, with his fellow disciples James and John, seeing Jesus in thus-far invisible heavenly light, flanked by Moses and Elijah, Peter is again moved to speak (17:4). Hospitality for heavenly visitors has a long history in his people. He infers that he and his fellow disciples have been invited to this revelation as servants, like Moses' successor Joshua (Exod. 24:13). So, speaking to Jesus, he offers to generously house him, Moses, and Elijah, each with his own tabernacle.

Israel's God interrupts him: "While he was still speaking" (Matt. 17:5), a cloud of intense light overshadows Peter, James, and John, as it had covered Mount Sinai, and a voice from the cloud speaks to them. The words of the voice, even in Greek, are identical to those spoken at Jesus' baptism (3:17), now with the added command to Jesus' three closest disciples: "Listen to him." Peter's calling, then, one he shares with the brothers James and John, is not to do anything he imagines as serving Jesus, Moses, and Elijah. It is to listen to Jesus, now disclosed by the drapery of heavenly light and the two key figures of Israel's epic past and hope.

The echo of the Father's words at Jesus' baptism, themselves an echo of the lectionary Psalm 2, declare that Jesus is the ultimate human heir of the ruling power of Israel's God. As the final

The Ardor of Light

We perceive, they say, that Jesus Christ was transfigured on Mount Tabor, where there were only three of his disciples. He told them that they must neither speak about it nor say anything about it until His resurrection. . . .

Now I tell you that, when Jesus Christ was transfigured before three of His disciples, He did it so that you might know that few folk will see the brightness of His transfiguration, and that He shows this only to His special friends, and for this reason there were only three. And still this happens in this world when God gives Himself through the ardor of light into the heart of a creature. Now you know why there were three.

Now I will tell you why this was on the mountain. This was in demonstrating and in signifying that no one can see the divine things as long as he mixes himself or mingles with temporal things, that is, with anything less than God. Now I will tell you why God told them that they were to say nothing until His resurrection. This was to demonstrate that you cannot say a word about the divine secrets lest you take vainglory from them. As far as this is concerned one must not speak of it to anyone. For thus I swear to you, says this Soul, that whoever has something to conceal or hide, he has something to show; but whoever has nothing to show, he has nothing to hide.

Marguerite Porete, *The Mirror of Simple Souls*, chap. 75, in *The Mirror of Simple Souls*, trans. Ellen L. Babinsky, Classics of Western Spirituality (New York: Paulist Press, 1993), 149–50.

king of Israel, he is the inheritor of the government of all the peoples of the world, whom he will subdue by his rule, which will extend to the ends of the earth (Ps. 2:8–9). This is what it means for Jesus to be "Son of God" or "Heir of God." It is not exactly news to Peter, since he himself just confessed Jesus "Son of the Living God" for the first time in the previous scene of the narrative (Matt. 16:16).

This exchange indicates why Peter must listen to Jesus as the one God confesses as God's Son. For when Jesus, after directing the disciples to tell no one he is the Messiah, reveals to Peter that being the Messiah means dying a shameful death at the hands of their corrupt rulers in Jerusalem, Peter recoils. He finds it within himself, as we still do today, to tell Jesus he is wrong and that messianic power must mean a satisfying triumph rather than such an unthinkable defeat (16:20–23). In this, Jesus says, Peter is playing the Satan to Jesus, tempting him away from the self-giving path of messianic rule. As if that were not deflating enough, Jesus then tells Peter and the other disciples that to follow him is not only to rebel against the established power in the land, which they knew, but to be tortured to death for it on crosses (16:24–28). Now Israel's God himself is telling Peter, James, and John that Jesus is indeed the king of their faith but

that they must listen to Jesus to learn what it means for him to be the ruling Son of God.

The three disciples do not find the voice of their God reassuring. Much like their and our ancestors at Sinai under the thunder of God, they "were terrified" (NRSV "were overcome by fear," a better translation than the RSV "filled with awe" (17:6). Jesus not only comes near to them; he "touched them," the text tells us (v. 7), saying, "Rise, and have no fear" (RSV). Israel's God is due fear, but it is fear answered by the loving touch and fear-dispelling words of his Son Jesus. It is in Jesus that the pleasure of this God is (v. 5).

The three disciples need the voice of their God and Jesus' word of assurance because a most fearful path stretches before them to Jerusalem, the road to the cross for both Jesus and them. They have just seen and heard the culmination of God's law and promise for Israel, its guiding force for us today: "Listen to Jesus." Neither they nor we can rely on our intuitions or well-established sense of what it means for Jesus to be Messiah, the final king of Israel who is bringing all the peoples of the world under his rule. Disciples must allow Jesus to teach them who Jesus is and what is involved in following him together. This path of disturbing formation, so that we learn to see by the light of Jesus as we have not yet seen, is thematic to the Gospel of Matthew.

It is also the consistent message of the law and the prophets: the saving revelation of God hides mistakably in what appears to human beings, especially to God's people, instead of conforming to the appearances we apprehend (e.g., Deut. 7:7–8; Isa. 45:15). This requires that we draw near enough to God, one another, and to the earth itself, to see how we are wrong and to see more truly as we are transformed. The lectionary passage in 2 Peter 1, which invokes the transfiguration of Jesus, also delivers this message, that the faith that leads to virtue and finally the practice of loving one another does not arise from the impulses of human beings but is the remembrance of eye-opening prophetic words. Remembering such words so as to embody them is the task of a lifetime of discipleship.

On the way down the mountain, Jesus directs his three disciples not to tell anyone about the vision they have seen, until after the Son of Man has been raised from the dead. As in 16:21, they do not know what this means. Resurrection names a vast transformation, and the raising of Jesus as the singular ruling figure of the Son of Man from Daniel 7 hardly fits prophetic expectation neatly. In light of 16:21, however, Jesus apparently tells them that the ruling glory they have seen on the mountain must not be presented through any light that is not his shameful death in Jerusalem. It is only his resurrection from that death that will enable all the peoples to see him for who he is, power that is not another human empire seeking its own life at the expense of its enemies, but the rule of the King of Kings who gives his life in the most shocking way imaginable and thus inherits all the peoples.

TOMMY GIVENS

Commentary 2: Connecting the Reading with the World

The holy day of transfiguration culminates the entire season of Epiphany. Epiphany begins with the visit of the magi or, in the Eastern Orthodox Church, the baptism of Jesus. In either case, Christians understand Epiphany to be among the first moments of revelation of who Jesus really is: not only the child of Mary and Joseph, but the Messiah, the Son of God.

"Epiphany," according to Merriam-Webster, means "an appearance or manifestation especially of a divine being," which is what the magi witnessed (Matt. 2:1–12), and what was revealed at Jesus' baptism (3:13–17). Yet in ordinary life, "epiphany" also means "a usually sudden manifestation or perception of the essential nature or meaning of something; an intuitive grasp of reality through something (such as an event) usually simple and striking; an illuminating discovery, realization, or disclosure; a revealing scene or moment."[1]

This is the bracket of this season: the revelation of the essential nature of Jesus, and its meaning for our lives. As the magi paid their visit, those who had been with the baby Jesus perceived his essential nature. As Jesus was baptized in the river Jordan, Jesus himself was visited with the reality of who he was and what he was called to do.

Now, with the transfiguration, the season of Epiphany closes with another revelation. There comes another manifestation of Jesus' essential nature, and another revealing scene of God's magnificent and intimate glory. It is, if you will, a second Epiphany, this time not to mark the beginning of Jesus' life and ministry, but his journey to the end.

The transfiguration poses a question for us: What are we able to see of God's revelation, and what are we unable (or unwilling) to grasp? Immediately prior to this passage, Jesus has asked his disciples who they believe he is. Simon Peter alone sees that Jesus is the Messiah, Son of the living God. Jesus affirms this as a revelation not of human flesh, but of God (Matt.

---

1. *Merriam-Webster Dictionary*, https://www.merriam-webster.com/dictionary/epiphany.

16:13–19). Then Jesus reveals more: that he will undergo suffering and death, and on the third day be raised. But *this* revelation is one his disciples cannot see.

Now, in our text, Matthew 17:1–9, Jesus takes Peter, James, and John up a high mountain. Immediately, they see Jesus transfigured—transformed in appearance and filled with light. Soon Moses and Elijah appear, and their presence confirms Jesus' messianic identity (cf. Mal. 4:4–5). Peter, knowing this significance, responds with deep joy. On this sacred territory, Peter desires to build three tabernacles, holding places for the holy.

When a cloud overshadows them (like the cloud that covered Moses on Mount Sinai), God confirms the meaning of this revelation: "This is my Son, my Beloved; with him I am well pleased. Listen to him!" (v. 5; see also Jesus' baptism, Matt. 3:17). The disciples react with fear; but Jesus, in one more revelation, commands them: "Get up, and do not be afraid." Then he leads them down the mountain—back to their calling to follow him.

What does this mean for us? First, like Peter, we are often unaware of which visions we are able to see. Scientists point out that our physical vision is limited, not just by farsightedness or nearsightedness, but by our brain's selective interpretation of what we perceive. For example, we can miss the repetition of a word in a sentence; we can see only a few dots on a chart at a time, even if there are many; we mistake changing colors depending on their surroundings. Worse, our social biases play tricks on us. Indeed, research has shown, "A black driver is about 31 percent more likely to be pulled over than a white driver, or about 23 percent more likely than a Hispanic driver. 'Driving while black' is, indeed, a measurable phenomenon."[2]

So also our spiritual vision can be unreliable, as Peter's was. His embrace of the transfiguration is surrounded by multiple equivocations. He declares Jesus the Messiah, then rebukes Jesus for naming the suffering ahead. Later he will proclaim his unending loyalty to Jesus, and then deny that he ever knew him. We are prone to this as well. We welcome accolades and resist painful chiding, spinning into cognitive dissonance to avoid it. We thrill at victories and glory, and then avoid the necessary challenges that face us along the way. Selective sight is not new. How much we will miss if we close our eyes to revelation, both of welcomed blessings and needed correction!

Second, the transfiguration reminds us that when God comes near to us, it changes everything. Suddenly, the disciples saw Jesus not only as a wise teacher or courageous leader, but as the fulfillment of God's messianic promise. Now they saw Jesus not only as a courageous truth-teller to the powerful, but as the one who carried the same divine Word spoken to Moses and Elijah. Now they saw Jesus not only as one who walked the road of life with them, but as the one who stood, like Moses and Elijah, on the mountaintop, in that sacred thin place where the veil is lifted between heaven and earth. The transfiguration changed not only their view of Jesus; it transformed them. So it is with us.

On April 3, 1968, the great twentieth-century prophet Martin Luther King Jr. stood at the Mason King Church of God in Christ headquarters in Memphis, Tennessee. King was in Memphis to plead for peace during a violent sanitation workers strike. He had not planned to speak; he did not come prepared with notes. Nevertheless, he addressed a crowd weary of the challenges they were facing: endemic racism, a costly war, and unjust labor and housing practices. He closed with these memorable words:

> Well, I don't know what will happen now. We've got some difficult days ahead. But it really doesn't matter with me now, because I've been to the mountaintop. And I don't mind. Like anybody, I would like to live—a long life; longevity has its place. But I'm not concerned about that now. I just want to do God's will. And He's allowed me to go up to the mountain. And I've

2. Christopher Ingraham, "You Really Can Get Pulled Over for Driving While Black, Federal Statistics Show," September 9, 2014, https://www.washingtonpost.com/news/wonk/wp/2014/09/09/you-really-can-get-pulled-over-for-driving-while-black-federal-statistics-show/.

looked over. And I've seen the Promised Land. I may not get there with you. But I want you to know tonight, that we, as a people, will get to the Promised Land. So I'm happy, tonight. I'm not worried about anything. I'm not fearing any man. *Mine eyes have seen the glory of the coming of the Lord.*[3]

King had no way of knowing that his life would end the next day. But thank God for the courage and faith of his mountaintop revelation that allowed Dr. King to keep going back down the mountain into the trenches of political, racial, and economic danger.

Who knows what we might be called to do at any time? Who knows what courage we might need to face injustices, speak encouragement, accompany the vulnerable, or challenge corrupt powers? May we be blessed with epiphanies that open our eyes to God's presence with us still— and may we be transformed by what we see.

CHRISTINE CHAKOIAN

---

3. Martin Luther King Jr., "I've Been to the Mountaintop." Memphis, Tennessee, April 3, 1968, in *Say It Plain. A Century of Great African American Speeches*, by American RadioWorks.

Contributors

CHARLES L. AARON JR., Co-Director of the Intern Program, Perkins School of Theology, Dallas, TX

MARK ABBOTT, Director of Hispanic Distributed Learning, Asbury Theological Seminary-Florida Dunnam Campus, Orlando, FL

STEPHEN B. BOYD, J. Allen Easley Professor of Religion, Wake Forest University, Department of Religion, Winston-Salem, NC

JOHN M. BUCHANAN, Pastor Emeritus, Fourth Presbyterian Church, Chicago, and Retired Editor/Publisher, *The Christian Century*, Chicago, IL

PATRICIA J. CALAHAN, Pastor, Cornwall Presbyterian Church, Cornwall-on-Hudson, NY

CHRISTINE CHAKOIAN, Vice President for Seminary Advancement, Pittsburgh Theological Seminary, Pittsburgh, PA

GARY W. CHARLES, Pastor, Cove Presbyterian Church, Covesville, VA

JIN YOUNG CHOI, Associate Professor of New Testament and Christian Origins, Colgate Rochester Crozer Divinity School, Rochester, NY

SHANNON CRAIGO-SNELL, Professor of Theology, Louisville Presbyterian Theological Seminary, Louisville, KY

DAVID A. DAVIS, Pastor, Nassau Presbyterian Church, Princeton, NJ

JOSEPH A. DONNELLA II, Pastor, St. Mark's Lutheran, Baltimore, MD

SHARYN DOWD, Baptist Pastor, Decatur, GA

JILL DUFFIELD, Editor, *The Presbyterian Outlook*, Richmond, VA

JAMES H. EVANS JR., Robert K. Davies Professor Emeritus of Systematic Theology and President Emeritus, Colgate Rochester Crozer Divinity School, Rochester, NY

KEN EVERS-HOOD, Pastor, Tualatin Presbyterian Church, Tualatin, OR

STEPHEN FARRIS, Professor Emeritus of Preaching and Dean Emeritus, Vancouver School of Theology and St. Andrew's Hall, Vancouver, British Columbia

JAMES D. FREEMAN, Pastor, Broadmoor Presbyterian Church, Shreveport, LA

TOMMY GIVENS, Professor of New Testament Studies, Fuller Theological Seminary, Pasadena, CA

MARCI AULD GLASS, Pastor, Southminster Presbyterian Church, Boise, ID

DEIRDRE J. GOOD, Faculty of the Stevenson School for Ministry (Diocese of Central PA), Harrisburg, PA

CAROLYN BROWNING HELSEL, Assistant Professor of Homiletics, Austin Presbyterian Theological Seminary, Austin, TX

JOHN C. HOLBERT, Lois Craddock Perkins Professor Emeritus of Homiletics, Perkins School of Theology, Southern Methodist University, Dallas, TX

CHRISTOPHER T. HOLMES, Director of Curriculum Development, Johnson C. Smith Theological Seminary, Atlanta, GA

SALLY SMITH HOLT, Professor of Religion, Belmont University College of Theology and Christian Ministry, Nashville, TN

CHRISTINE J. HONG, Assistant Professor of Educational Ministry, Columbia Theological Seminary, Decatur, GA

PAUL K. HOOKER, Associate Dean for Ministerial Formation and Advanced Studies, Austin Presbyterian Theological Seminary, Austin, TX

TODD B. JONES, Pastor, First Presbyterian Church, Nashville, TN

ERIN KEYS, Minister, Capitol Hill Presbyterian Church, Washington, DC

ERICA KNISELY, Director of Programs for Education Beyond the Walls, Austin Presbyterian Theological Seminary, Austin, TX

MICHAEL LODAHL, Professor of Theology and World Religions, Point Loma Nazarene University, San Diego, CA

SCOT MCKNIGHT, Professor of New Testament, Northern Seminary, Lombard, IL

ERIC TODD MYERS, Pastor, Frederick Presbyterian Church, Frederick, MD

RAJ NADELLA, Assistant Professor of New Testament, Columbia Theological Seminary, Decatur, GA

ANNA OLSON, Rector, St. Mary's Episcopal Church, Los Angeles, CA

SONG-MI SUZIE PARK, Associate Professor of Old Testament, Austin Presbyterian Theological Seminary, Austin, TX

ZAIDA MALDONADO PÉREZ, Professor Emerita of Church History and Theology, Asbury Theological Seminary, Clermont, FL

SANDRA HACK POLASKI, New Testament scholar, Richmond, VA

EMERSON B. POWERY, Professor of Biblical Studies, Messiah College, Department of Biblical and Religious Studies, Mechanicsburg, PA

MARK RALLS, Senior Pastor, First United Methodist Church, Hendersonville, NC

GAIL RAMSHAW, Professor Emerita of Religion, La Salle University, Philadelphia, PA

STANLEY P. SAUNDERS, Associate Professor of New Testament, Columbia Theological Seminary, Decatur, GA

MATTHEW L. SKINNER, Professor of New Testament, Luther Seminary, St. Paul, MN

DANIEL L. SMITH-CHRISTOPHER, Professor of Old Testament, Loyola Marymount University, Los Angeles, CA

KRISTIN STROBLE, Pastor, Eastminster Presbyterian Church, East Lansing, MI

PATRICIA K. TULL, A. B. Rhodes Professor Emerita of Old Testament, Louisville Theological Seminary, Louisville, KY

LEANNE VAN DYK, President and Professor of Theology, Columbia Theological Seminary, Decatur, GA

ROBERT W. WALL, Paul T. Walls Professor of Scripture and Wesleyan Studies, Seattle Pacific University and Seminary, School of Theology, Seattle, WA

RICHARD F. WARD, Fred B. Craddock Professor of Homiletics and Worship, Phillips Theological Seminary, Tulsa, OK

LAUREN F. WINNER, Associate Professor of Christian Spirituality, Duke Divinity School, Durham, NC

Author Index

Abbreviations

C1	Commentary 1		NT	New Testament
C2	Commentary 2		OT	Old Testament
E	Epistle		PS	Psalm
G	Gospel			

Numerals indicate numbered Sundays of a season; for example, "Advent 1" represents the first Sunday of Advent, and "Christmas 1" the first Sunday after Christmas.

Contributors and entries

Charles L. Aaron Jr.	Epiphany 4 E C1, Epiphany 5 E C1, Epiphany 6 E C1
Mark Abbott	Baptism of the Lord G C2, Epiphany 2 G C2, Epiphany 3 G C2
Stephen B. Boyd	Christmas 1 E C2, Christmas 2 E C2, Epiphany E C2
John M. Buchanan	Advent 1 E C2, Advent 2 E C2, Advent 3 E C2
Patricia J. Calahan	Christmas Day II E C1, Christmas Day III E C1
Christine Chakoian	Epiphany 7 G C2, Epiphany 8 G C2, Epiphany 9 G C2, Transfiguration G C2
Gary W. Charles	Epiphany 7 OT C1, Epiphany 8 OT C1, Epiphany 9 OT C1, Transfiguration OT C1
Jin Young Choi	Advent 1 E C1, Advent 2 E C1, Advent 3 E C1
Shannon Craigo-Snell	Epiphany 7 E C2, Epiphany 8 E C2, Epiphany 9 E C2, Transfiguration E C2
David A. Davis	Advent 1 OT C2, Advent 2 OT C2, Advent 3 OT C2
Joseph A. Donnella II	Christmas 1 PS, Christmas 2 PS, Epiphany PS
Sharyn Dowd	Advent 4 OT C1, Advent 4 G C1, Christmas Eve OT C1
Jill Duffield	Christmas 1 G C2, Christmas 2 G C2, Epiphany G C2
James H. Evans Jr.	Baptism of the Lord OT C1, Epiphany 2 OT C1, Epiphany 3 OT C1
Ken Evers-Hood	Epiphany 4 OT C2, Epiphany 5 OT C2, Epiphany 6 OT C2
Stephen Farris	Baptism of the Lord NT C1, Epiphany 2 E C1, Epiphany 3 E C1
James D. Freeman	Advent 4 OT C2, Christmas Eve OT C2
Tommy Givens	Epiphany 7 G C1, Epiphany 8 G C1, Epiphany 9 G C1, Transfiguration G C1
Marci Auld Glass	Advent 1 PS, Advent 2 PS, Advent 3 PS, Advent 4 PS
Deirdre J. Good	Christmas Eve G C1
Carolyn Browning Helsel	Epiphany 7 OT C2, Epiphany 8 OT C2, Epiphany 9 OT C2, Transfiguration OT C2

Scripture Index

Scripture citations that appear in boldface represent the assigned readings from the Revised Common Lectionary.